Solutions Manual

Auditing and Assurance Services

Fourteenth Edition

Alvin A. Arens
Randal J. Elder
Mark S. Beasley

Prentice Hall

Boston Columbus Indianapolis New York San Francisco Upper Saddle River

Amsterdam Cape Town Dubai London Madrid Milan Munich Paris Montreal Toronto

Delhi Mexico City Sao Paulo Sydney Hong Kong Seoul Singapore Taipei Tokyo

VP, Editorial Director: Sally Yagan
Executive Editor: Stephanie Wall
Editorial Project Manager: Christina Rumbaugh
Production Project Manager: Carol O'Rourke
Senior Operations Specialist: Diane Peirano
Printer/Binder: Offset Paperback Manufacturers

Prentice Hall
is an imprint of

www.pearsonhighered.com

10 9 8 7 6 5 4 3 2 1

ISBN-13: 978-0-13-257607-9
ISBN-10:   0-13-257607-4

CONTENTS

Chapter 1

The Demand for Audit and Other Assurance Services

■ **Review Questions**

1-1   The relationship among audit services, attestation services, and assurance services is reflected in Figure 1-3 on page 12 of the text. An assurance service is an independent professional service to improve the quality of information for decision makers. An attestation service is a form of assurance service in which the CPA firm issues a report about the reliability of an assertion that is the responsibility of another party. Audit services are a form of attestation service in which the auditor expresses a written conclusion about the degree of correspondence between information and established criteria.

The most common form of audit service is an audit of historical financial statements, in which the auditor expresses a conclusion as to whether the financial statements are presented in accordance with an applicable financial reporting framework such as U.S. GAAP or IFRS. An example of an attestation service is a report on the effectiveness of an entity's internal control over financial reporting. There are many possible forms of assurance services, including services related to business performance measurement, health care performance, and information system reliability.

1-2   An independent audit is a means of satisfying the need for reliable information on the part of decision makers. Factors of a complex society which contribute to this need are:

1. Remoteness of information
   a. Owners (stockholders) divorced from management
   b. Directors not involved in day-to-day operations or decisions
   c. Dispersion of the business among numerous geographic locations and complex corporate structures
2. Biases and motives of provider
   a. Information will be biased in favor of the provider when his or her goals are inconsistent with the decision maker's goals.
3. Voluminous data
   a. Possibly millions of transactions processed daily via sophisticated computerized systems
   b. Multiple product lines
   c. Multiple transaction locations
4. Complex exchange transactions
   a. New and changing business relationships lead to innovative accounting and reporting problems
   b. Potential impact of transactions not quantifiable, leading to increased disclosures

1-3 1. *Risk-free interest rate* This is approximately the rate the bank could earn by investing in U.S. treasury notes for the same length of time as the business loan.

2. *Business risk for the customer* This risk reflects the possibility that the business will not be able to repay its loan because of economic or business conditions such as a recession, poor management decisions, or unexpected competition in the industry.

3. *Information risk* This risk reflects the possibility that the information upon which the business risk decision was made was inaccurate. A likely cause of the information risk is the possibility of inaccurate financial statements.

Auditing has no effect on either the risk-free interest rate or business risk. However, auditing can significantly reduce information risk.

1-4 The four primary causes of information risk are remoteness of information, biases and motives of the provider, voluminous data, and the existence of complex exchange transactions.

The three main ways to reduce information risk are:

1. User verifies the information.
2. User shares the information risk with management.
3. Audited financial statements are provided.

The advantages and disadvantages of each are as follows:

	ADVANTAGES	**DISADVANTAGES**
USER VERIFIES INFORMATION	1. User obtains information desired. 2. User can be more confident of the qualifications and activities of the person getting the information.	1. High cost of obtaining information. 2. Inconvenience to the person providing the information because large number of users would be on premises.
USER SHARES INFORMATION RISK WITH MANAGEMENT	1. No audit costs incurred.	1. User may not be able to collect on losses.
AUDITED FINANCIAL STATEMENTS ARE PROVIDED	1. Multiple users obtain the information. 2. Information risk can usually be reduced sufficiently to satisfy users at reasonable cost. 3. Minimal inconvenience to management by having only one auditor.	1. May not meet needs of certain users. 2. Cost may be higher than the benefits in some situations, such as for a small company.

1-5   To do an audit, there must be information in a *verifiable form* and some standards (*criteria*) by which the auditor can evaluate the information. Examples of established criteria include generally accepted accounting principles and the Internal Revenue Code. Determining the degree of correspondence between information and established criteria is determining whether a given set of information is in accordance with the established criteria. The information for Jones Company's tax return is the federal tax returns filed by the company. The established criteria are found in the Internal Revenue Code and all interpretations. For the audit of Jones Company's financial statements the information is the financial statements being audited and the established criteria are generally accepted accounting principles.

1-6   The primary evidence the internal revenue agent will use in the audit of the Jones Company's tax return include all available documentation and other information available in Jones' office or from other sources. For example, when the internal revenue agent audits taxable income, a major source of information will be bank statements, the cash receipts journal and deposit slips. The internal revenue agent is likely to emphasize unrecorded receipts and revenues. For expenses, major sources of evidence are likely to be cancelled checks and electronic funds transfers, vendors' invoices, and other supporting documentation.

1-7   This apparent paradox arises from the distinction between the function of auditing and the function of accounting. The accounting function is the recording, classifying and summarizing of economic events to provide relevant information to decision makers. The rules of accounting are the criteria used by the auditor for evaluating the presentation of economic events for financial statements and he or she must therefore have an understanding of accounting standards, as well as auditing standards. The accountant need not, and frequently does not, understand what auditors do, unless he or she is involved in doing audits, or has been trained as an auditor.

	OPERATIONAL AUDITS	COMPLIANCE AUDITS	AUDITS OF FINANCIAL STATEMENTS
PURPOSE	To evaluate whether operating procedures are efficient and effective	To determine whether the client is following specific procedures set by higher authority	To determine whether the overall financial statements are presented in accordance with specified criteria (usually GAAP)
USERS OF AUDIT REPORT	Management of organization	Authority setting down procedures, internal or external	Different groups for different purposes — many outside entities
NATURE	Highly nonstandard; often subjective	Not standardized, but specific and usually objective	Highly standardized
PERFORMED BY: **CPAs**	Frequently	Occasionally	Almost universally
GAO AUDITORS	Frequently	Frequently	Occasionally
IRS AUDITORS	Never	Universally	Never
INTERNAL AUDITORS	Frequently	Frequently	Frequently

1-9 Five examples of specific operational audits that could be conducted by an internal auditor in a manufacturing company are:

1. Examine employee time records and personnel records to determine if sufficient information is available to maximize the effective use of personnel.
2. Review the processing of sales invoices to determine if it could be done more efficiently.
3. Review the acquisitions of goods, including costs, to determine if they are being purchased at the lowest possible cost considering the quality needed.

1-9 (continued)

    4.   Review and evaluate the efficiency of the manufacturing process.

    5.   Review the processing of cash receipts to determine if they are deposited as quickly as possible.

1-10 When auditing historical financial statements, an auditor must have a thorough understanding of the client and its environment. This knowledge should include the client's regulatory and operating environment, business strategies and processes, and measurement indicators. This strategic understanding is also useful in other assurance or consulting engagements. For example, an auditor who is performing an assurance service on information technology would need to understand the client's business strategies and processes related to information technology, including such things as purchases and sales via the Internet. Similarly, a practitioner performing a consulting engagement to evaluate the efficiency and effectiveness of a client's manufacturing process would likely start with an analysis of various measurement indicators, including ratio analysis and benchmarking against key competitors.

1-11 The major differences in the scope of audit responsibilities are:

    1.   CPAs perform audits in accordance with auditing standards of published financial statements prepared in accordance with U.S. GAAP or IFRS.

    2.   GAO auditors perform compliance or operational audits in order to assure the Congress of the expenditure of public funds in accordance with its directives and the law.

    3.   IRS agents perform compliance audits to enforce the federal tax laws as defined by Congress, interpreted by the courts, and regulated by the IRS.

    4.   Internal auditors perform compliance or operational audits in order to assure management or the board of directors that controls and policies are properly and consistently developed, applied and evaluated.

1-12 The four parts of the Uniform CPA Examination are: Auditing and Attestation, Financial Accounting and Reporting, Regulation, and Business Environment and Concepts.

1-13 It is important for CPAs to be knowledgeable about information technology, including e-commerce, because many of their clients rely extensively on these technologies. Examples of commonly used e-commerce technologies include purchases and sales of goods through the Internet, automatic inventory reordering via direct connection to inventory suppliers, and online banking. CPAs who perform audits or provide other assurance services about information generated with these technologies need a basic knowledge and understanding of information technology and e-commerce in order to identify and respond to risks in the financial and other information generated by these technologies.

■ Multiple Choice Questions From CPA Examinations

1-14 a. (3)   b. (2)   c. (2)   d. (3)

1-15 a. (2)   b. (3)   c. (4)   d. (3)

■ Discussion Questions And Problems

1-16 a. The relationship among audit services, attestation services and assurance services is reflected in Figure 1-3 on page 12 of the text. Audit services are a form of attestation service, and attestation services are a form of assurance service. In a diagram, audit services are located within the attestation service area, and attestation services are located within the assurance service area.

   b.
1.	(2)	An attestation service other than an audit service
2.	(1)	An audit of historical financial statements
3.	(2)	An attestation service other than an audit service
4.	(2)	An attestation service other than an audit service; or
	(3)	An assurance service that is not an attestation service (*WebTrust* developed from the AICPA Special Committee on Assurance Services, but the service meets the criteria for an attestation service.)
5.	(2)	An attestation service other than an audit service
6.	(2)	An attestation service other than an audit service
7.	(2)	An attestation service that is not an audit service (Review services are a form of attestation, but are performed according to Statements on Standards for Accounting and Review Services.)
8.	(2)	An attestation service other than an audit service
9.	(2)	An attestation service other than an audit service
10.	(3)	An assurance service that is not an attestation service

1-17 a. The interest rate for the loan that requires a review report is lower than the loan that did not require a review because of lower information risk. A review report provides moderate assurance to financial statement users, which lowers information risk. An audit report provides further assurance and lower information risk. As a result of reduced information risk, the interest rate is lowest for the loan with the audit report.

   b. Given these circumstances, Busch should select the loan from First City Bank that requires an annual audit. In this situation, the additional cost of the audit is less than the reduction in interest due to lower information risk. The following is the calculation of total costs for each loan:

1-17 (continued)

LENDER	CPA SERVICE	COST OF CPA SERVICES	ANNUAL INTEREST	ANNUAL LOAN COST
Existing loan	None	0	$ 247,500	$ 247,500
United National Bank	Review	$ 20,000	$ 202,500	$ 222,500
First City Bank	Audit	$ 45,000	$ 157,500	$ 202,500

c.   Busch should select the loan from United National Bank due to the higher cost of the audit and the reduced interest rate for the loan from United National Bank. The following is the calculation of total costs for each loan:

LENDER	CPA SERVICE	COST OF CPA SERVICES	ANNUAL INTEREST	ANNUAL LOAN COST
Existing loan	None	0	$ 247,500	$ 247,500
United National Bank	Review	$ 20,000	$ 180,000	$ 200,000
First City Bank	Audit	$ 55,000	$ 157,500	$ 212,500

d.   Busch may desire to have an audit because of the many other benefits that an audit provides. The audit will provide Busch's management with assurance about annual financial information used for decision-making purposes. The audit may detect errors or fraud, and provide management with information about the effectiveness of controls. In addition, the audit may result in recommendations to management that will improve efficiency or effectiveness.

e.   The auditor must have a thorough understanding of the client and its environment, including the client's e-commerce technologies, industry, regulatory and operating environment, suppliers, customers, creditors, and business strategies and processes. This thorough analysis helps the auditor identify risks associated with the client's strategies that may affect whether the financial statements are fairly stated. This strategic knowledge of the client's business often helps the auditor identify ways to help the client improve business operations, thereby providing added value to the audit function.

1-18   a.   The services provided by Consumers Union are very similar to assurance services provided by CPA firms. The services provided by Consumers Union and assurance services provided by CPA firms are designed to improve the quality of information for decision makers. CPAs are valued for their independence, and the reports provided by Consumers Union are valued because Consumers Union is independent of the products tested.

b. The concepts of information risk for the buyer of an automobile and for the user of financial statements are essentially the same. They are both concerned with the problem of unreliable information being provided. In the case of the auditor, the user is concerned about unreliable information being provided in the financial statements. The buyer of an automobile is likely to be concerned about the manufacturer or dealer providing unreliable information.

c. The four causes of information risk are essentially the same for a buyer of an automobile and a user of financial statements:
   (1) *Remoteness of information* It is difficult for a user to obtain much information about either an automobile manufacturer or the automobile itself without incurring considerable cost. The automobile buyer does have the advantage of possibly knowing other users who are satisfied or dissatisfied with a similar automobile.
   (2) *Biases and motives of provider* There is a conflict between the automobile buyer and the manufacturer. The buyer wants to buy a high quality product at minimum cost whereas the seller wants to maximize the selling price and quantity sold.
   (3) *Voluminous data* There is a large amount of available information about automobiles that users might like to have in order to evaluate an automobile. Either that information is not available or too costly to obtain.
   (4) *Complex exchange transactions* The acquisition of an automobile is expensive and certainly a complex decision because of all the components that go into making a good automobile and choosing between a large number of alternatives.

d. The three ways users of financial statements and buyers of automobiles reduce information risk are also similar:
   (1) *User verifies information him or herself* That can be obtained by driving different automobiles, examining the specifications of the automobiles, talking to other users and doing research in various magazines.
   (2) *User shares information risk with management* The manufacturer of a product has a responsibility to meet its warranties and to provide a reasonable product. The buyer of an automobile can return the automobile for correction of defects. In some cases a refund may be obtained.
   (3) *Examine the information prepared by Consumer Reports* This is similar to an audit in the sense that independent information is provided by an independent party. The information provided by *Consumer Reports* is comparable to that provided by a CPA firm that audited financial statements.

1-19 a.   The following parts of the definition of auditing are related to the narrative:

        (1)   Altman is being asked to issue a report about qualitative and quantitative information for trucks. The trucks are therefore the *information* with which the auditor is concerned.

        (2)   There are four *established criteria* which must be evaluated and reported by Altman: existence of the trucks on the night of June 30, 2011, ownership of each truck by Regional Delivery Service, physical condition of each truck and fair market value of each truck.

        (3)   Samantha Altman will *accumulate* and *evaluate* four types of *evidence*:

            (a)   Count the trucks to determine their existence.

            (b)   Use registrations documents held by Burrow for comparison to the serial number on each truck to determine ownership.

            (c)   Examine the trucks to determine each truck's physical condition.

            (d)   Examine the blue book to determine the fair market value of each truck.

        (4)   Samantha Altman, CPA, appears qualified, as a *competent, independent person*. She is a CPA, and she spends most of her time auditing used automobile and truck dealerships and has extensive specialized knowledge about used trucks that is consistent with the nature of the engagement.

        (5)   The *report results* are to include:

            (a)   which of the 25 trucks are parked in Regional's parking lot the night of June 30.

            (b)   whether all of the trucks are owned by Regional Delivery Service.

            (c)   the condition of each truck, using established guidelines.

            (d)   fair market value of each truck using the current blue book for trucks.

      b.   The only parts of the audit that will be difficult for Altman are:

        (1)   Evaluating the condition, using the guidelines of poor, good, and excellent. It is highly subjective to do so. If she uses a different criterion than the "blue book," the fair market value will not be meaningful. Her experience will be essential in using this guideline.

        (2)   Determining the fair market value, unless it is clearly defined in the blue book for each condition.

1-20 a. The major advantages and disadvantages of a career as an IRS agent, CPA, GAO auditor, or an internal auditor are:

EMPLOYMENT	ADVANTAGES	DISADVANTAGES
INTERNAL REVENUE AGENT	1. Extensive training in individual, corporate, gift, trust and other taxes is available with concentration in area chosen. 2. Hands-on experience with sophisticated selection techniques.	1. Experience limited to taxes. 2. No experience with operational or financial statement auditing. 3. Training is not extensive with any business enterprise.
CPA	1. Extensive training in audit of financial statements, compliance auditing and operational auditing. 2. Opportunity for experience in auditing, tax consulting, and management consulting practices. 3. Experience in a diversity of enterprises and industries with the opportunity to specialize in a specific industry.	1. Exposure to taxes and to the business enterprise may not be as in-depth as the internal revenue agent or the internal auditor. 2. Likely to be less exposed to operational auditing than is likely for internal auditors.
GAO AUDITOR	1. Increasing opportunity for experience in operational auditing. 2. Exposure to highly sophisticated statistical sampling and computer auditing techniques.	1. Little exposure to diversity of enterprises and industries. 2. Bureaucracy of federal government.
INTERNAL AUDITOR	1. Extensive exposure to all segments of the enterprise with which employed. 2. Constant exposure to one industry presenting opportunity for expertise in that industry. 3. Likely to have exposure to compliance, financial and operational auditing.	1. Little exposure to taxation and the audit of taxes. 2. Experience is limited to one enterprise, usually within one or a limited number of industries.

(b) Other auditing careers that are available are:
- Auditors within many of the branches of the federal government (e.g., Atomic Energy Commission)
- Auditors for many state and local government units (e.g., state insurance or bank auditors)

1-21 The most likely type of auditor and the type of audit for each of the examples are:

EXAMPLE	TYPE OF AUDITOR	TYPE OF AUDIT
1.	IRS	Compliance
2.	GAO	Operational
3.	Internal auditor or CPA	Operational
4.	CPA or Internal auditor	Financial statements
5.	GAO	Operational
6.	CPA	Financial statements
7.	GAO	Financial statements
8.	IRS	Compliance
9.	CPA	Financial statements
10.	Internal auditor or CPA	Compliance
11.	Internal auditor or CPA	Financial statements or operational
12.	GAO	Compliance

1-22 a. Financial statement audits reduce information risk, which lowers borrowing costs. An audit also provides assurances to management about information used for decision-making purposes, and may also provide recommendations to improve efficiency or effectiveness of operations.

b. Hogan and Czarnecki likely provide tax services, accounting services, and management advisory services. They may also provide additional assurance and attestation services other than audits of financial statements.

c. Student answers will vary. They may identify new types of information that require assurance, such as environmental or corporate responsibility reporting. Students may also identify opportunities for consulting or management advisory services, such as assistance with the adoption of international financial reporting standards.

■ **Internet Problem Solution: CPA Requirements**

Internet Problem 1-1

a. Answers will vary by state. Most states require 150 hours of education, with specific requirements for number of accounting hours and credit hours in other subject areas.

b. Most states have frequently addressed questions. Many of these address education requirements, as well as information on how to prepare for the exam, as well as information on applying for licensure.

Internet Problem 1-1 (continued)

    c.   The Elijah Watt Sells award program was established in 1923 by the American Institute of Certified Public Accountants (AICPA) to recognize outstanding performance on the Uniform CPA Examination. The Sells award is presented annually to ten candidates with the highest cumulative scores who completed testing during the previous calendar year and passed all four sections of the Uniform CPA Examination on their first attempt.

    d.   Passing information is available on the CPA Examination portion of the AICPA web site. Recent passing rates have been approximately 45% for each section.

(**Note**: Internet problems address current issues using Internet sources. Because Internet sites are subject to change, Internet problems and solutions may change. Current information on Internet problems is available at www.pearsonhighered.com/arens.)

Chapter 2

The CPA Profession

■ **Review Questions**

2-1 The four major services that CPAs provide are:

1. *Audit and assurance services* Assurance services are independent professional services that improve the quality of information for decision makers. Assurance services include attestation services, which are any services in which the CPA firm issues a report that expresses a conclusion about the reliability of an assertion that is the responsibility of another party. The four categories of attestation services are audits of historical financial statements, attestation on the effectiveness of internal control over financial reporting, reviews of historical financial statements, and other attestation services.
2. *Accounting and bookkeeping services* Accounting services involve preparing the client's financial statements from the client's records. Bookkeeping services include the preparation of the client's journals and ledgers as well as financial statements.
3. *Tax services* Tax services include preparation of corporate, individual, and estate returns as well as tax planning assistance.
4. *Management consulting services* These services range from suggestions to improve the client's accounting system to computer installations.

2-2 The major characteristics of CPA firms that permit them to fulfill their social function competently and independently are:

1. *Organizational form* A CPA firm exists as a separate entity to avoid an employer-employee relationship with its clients. The CPA firm employs a professional staff of sufficient size to prevent one client from constituting a significant portion of total income and thereby endangering the firm's independence.
2. *Conduct* A CPA firm employs a professional staff of sufficient size to provide a broad range of expertise, continuing education, and promotion of a professional independent attitude and competence.
3. *Peer review* This practice evaluates the performance of CPA firms in an attempt to keep competence high.

2-3 The Public Company Accounting Oversight Board provides oversight for auditors of public companies, including establishing auditing and quality control standards for public company audits, and performing inspections of the quality controls at audit firms performing those audits.

2-4   The purpose of the Securities and Exchange Commission is to assist in providing investors with reliable information upon which to make investment decisions. Since most reasonably large CPA firms have clients that must file reports with the SEC each year (all companies filing registration statements under the securities acts of 1933 and 1934 must file audited financial statements and other reports with the SEC at least once each year), the profession is highly involved with the SEC requirements.

The SEC has considerable influence in setting generally accepted accounting principles and disclosure requirements for financial statements because of its authority for specifying reporting requirements considered necessary for fair disclosure to investors. In addition, the SEC has power to establish rules for any CPA associated with audited financial statements submitted to the Commission.

2-5   The AICPA is the organization that sets professional requirements for CPAs. The AICPA also conducts research and publishes materials on many different subjects related to accounting, auditing, management advisory services, and taxes. The organization also prepares and grades the CPA examinations, provides continuing education to its members, and develops specialty designations to help market and assure the quality of services in specialized practice areas.

2-6   *Statements on Standards for Attestation Engagements* provide a framework for attest engagements, including detailed standards for specific types of attestation engagements.

2-7   The PCAOB has responsibility for establishing auditing standards for U.S. public companies, while the Auditing Standards Board (ASB) of the AICPA establishes auditing standards for U.S. private companies. Prior to the creation of the PCAOB, the ASB had responsibility for establishing auditing standards for both public and private companies. Because existing auditing standards were adopted by the PCAOB as interim auditing standards for public company audits, there is considerable overlap in the two sets of auditing standards.

2-8   *Generally accepted auditing standards* are ten general guidelines to aid auditors in fulfilling their professional responsibilities. These guidelines include three general standards concerned with competence, independence, and due professional care; three standards of field work including planning and supervision, understanding the entity and its environment, including its internal control, and the gathering of sufficient appropriate evidence; and four standards of reporting, which require a statement as to presentation in accordance with generally accepted accounting principles, inconsistency observed in the current period in relation to the preceding period, adequate disclosure, and the expression of an opinion as to the fairness of the presentation of the financial statements.

Generally accepted accounting principles are specific rules for accounting for transactions occurring in a business enterprise. Examples may be any of the opinions of the FASB, such as accounting for leases, pensions, or fair value assets.

2-9 Auditors can obtain adequate technical training and proficiency through formal education in auditing and accounting, adequate practical experience, and continuing professional education. Auditors can demonstrate their proficiency by becoming licensed to practice as CPAs, which requires successful completion of the Uniform CPA Examination. The specific requirements for licensure vary from state to state.

2-10 For the most part, generally accepted auditing standards are general rather than specific. Many practitioners along with critics of the profession believe the standards should provide more clearly defined guidelines as an aid in determining the extent of evidence to be accumulated. This would eliminate some of the difficult audit decisions and provide a source of defense if the CPA is charged with conducting an inadequate audit. On the other hand, highly specific requirements could turn auditing into mechanical evidence gathering, void of professional judgment. From the point of view of both the profession and the users of auditing services, there is probably a greater harm from defining authoritative guidelines too specifically than too broadly.

2-11 International Standards on Auditing (ISAs) are issued by the International Auditing and Assurance Standards Board (IAASB) of the International Federation of Accountants (IFAC) and are designed to improve the uniformity of auditing practices and related services throughout the world. The IAASB issues pronouncements on a variety of audit and attest functions and promotes their acceptance worldwide. As a results of efforts by the Auditing Standards Board to converge U.S. GAAS with international standards, U.S. GAAS and International Standards on Auditing are similar in most respects.

2-12 Quality controls are the procedures used by a CPA firm that help it meet its professional responsibilities to clients. Quality controls are therefore established for the entire CPA firm as opposed to individual engagements.

2-13 The element of quality control is personnel management. The purpose of the requirement is to help assure CPA firms that all new personnel are qualified to perform their work competently. A CPA firm must have competent employees conducting the audits if quality audits are to occur.

2-14 A peer review is a review, by CPAs, of a CPA firm's compliance with its quality control system. A mandatory peer review means that such a review is required periodically. AICPA member firms are required to have a peer review every three years. Registered firms with the PCAOB are subject to quality inspections. These are different than peer reviews because they are performed by independent inspection teams rather than another CPA firm.

Peer reviews can be beneficial to the profession and to individual firms. By helping firms meet quality control standards, the profession gains if reviews result in practitioners doing higher quality audits. A firm having a peer review can also gain if it improves the firm's practices and thereby enhances its reputation and effectiveness, and reduces the likelihood of lawsuits. Of course peer reviews are costly. There is always a trade-off between cost and benefits.

2-15 Firms may belong to Center for Audit Quality and the Private Companies Practice Section (PCPS) Firm Practice Center. The Center for Audit Quality is dedicated to enhancing investor confidence and public trust in global capital markets, including fostering high quality performance by public company auditors and promoting policies and standards that promote public company auditors' objectivity, effectiveness and responsiveness to dynamic market conditions. The PCPS Firm Practice Center provides practice management resources for firms of all sizes.

In addition to these resource centers, the AICPA also provides the Governmental Audit Quality Center and Employee Benefit Plan Audit Quality Center to provide resources for performing quality audits in these unique and complex audit areas.

■ Multiple Choice Questions From CPA Examinations

2-16   a.   (2)   b.   (2)   c.   (3)   d.   (3)

2-17   a.   (2)   b.   (1)   c.   (2)   d.   (3)

■ Discussion Questions And Problems

2-18   a.   The comments summarize the beliefs of many practitioners about the Sarbanes–Oxley Act and the PCAOB. The arguments against the Act can be summarized as four arguments:

1. Costs of complying with the Act are excessively high, especially the requirement to report on internal control over financial reporting, and will discourage companies from becoming public companies.
2. Relative cost for local audit firms is excessively high.
3. Additional oversight is not needed because sufficient quality controls have already been implemented by most audit firms.
4. Three other things already provide assurance of adequate quality: a competitive economic environment, legal liability, and auditing standards.

To support these comments, it can be argued that the profession has generally functioned well with relatively little controversy and criticism.

The arguments against these comments are primarily as follows:

1. Reporting on the effectiveness of internal control over financial reporting will provide benefits in improved controls, resulting in higher quality financial reporting and reduced losses from fraud.

2-18 (continued)

2. Increased confidence in financial reporting will increase access to capital and lower the cost of capital by reducing information risk.
3. Changes in the scope of CPA practices and other threats to audit quality required government regulation.
4. Regulation of public company audits will not affect most audit firms that do not have public company audit clients.

b. There is no correct answer to this question. Different people reach different conclusions, depending on the weights put on the various arguments. Time is needed to effectively assess both the costs and benefits of the Act.

2-19 a. Engagement performance
    b. Monitoring
    c. Acceptance and continuation of clients and engagements
    d. Engagement performance
    e. Engagement performance
    f. Engagement performance
    g. Relevant ethical requirement
    h. Human resources
    i. Human resources
    j. Leadership responsibilities

2-20 a. Olson and Riley should first evaluate whether they have the professional competence to perform all of the audit work for filing with the SEC, and whether they wish to accept the risk associated with such an engagement. In addition, if Olson and Riley have performed bookkeeping services or certain consulting services for Howard Mobile Home, they will not be independent under PCAOB and SEC independence requirements. The firm must also be a registered firm with the PCAOB.

    b. The filing with the SEC, in addition to normal audited financial statements, will require completion and registration with the SEC of Form S-1 which includes an audited summary of operations for the last five fiscal years as well as many additional schedules and descriptions of the business. Each quarter subsequent to the filing, Form 10-Q must be filed; and within 90 days of the end of each fiscal year Form 10-K must be filed with the SEC.

        In addition, Form 8-K must be filed whenever significant events have occurred which are of interest to public investors. These forms must be filed in conformity with Regulation S-X, which requires considerable disclosures in addition to those normally required in audited financial statements.

BRIEF DESCRIPTION OF GAAS	HOLMES' ACTIONS RESULTING IN FAILURE TO COMPLY WITH GAAS
GENERAL STANDARDS	
1. The auditor must have adequate technical training and proficiency to perform the audit.	1. It was inappropriate for Holmes to hire the two students to conduct the audit. The audit must be conducted by persons with proper education and experience in the field of auditing. Although a junior assistant has not completed his formal education, he may help in the conduct of the audit as long as there is proper supervision and review.
2. The auditor must maintain independence in mental attitude in all matters relating to the audit.	2. To satisfy the second general standard, Holmes must be without bias with respect to the client under audit. Holmes has an obligation for fairness to the owners, management, and creditors who may rely on the report. Because of the financial interest in whether the bank loan is granted to Ray, Holmes is independent in neither fact nor appearance with respect to the assignment undertaken.
3. The auditor must exercise due professional care in the performance of the audit and the preparation of the report.	3. This standard requires Holmes to perform the audit with due care, which imposes on Holmes and everyone in Holmes' organization a responsibility to observe the standards of field work and reporting. Exercise of due care requires critical review at every level of supervision of the work done and the judgments exercised by those assisting in the audit. Holmes did not review the work or the judgments of the assistants and clearly failed to adhere to this standard.

2-21 (continued)

BRIEF DESCRIPTION OF GAAS	HOLMES' ACTIONS RESULTING IN FAILURE TO COMPLY WITH GAAS
STANDARDS OF FIELD WORK	
1. The auditor must adequately plan the work and must properly supervise any assistants.	1. This standard recognizes that early appointment of the auditor has advantages for the auditor and the client. Holmes accepted the engagement without considering the availability of competent staff. In addition, Holmes failed to supervise the assistants. The work performed was not adequately planned.
2. The auditor must obtain a sufficient understanding of the entity and its environment, including its internal control, to assess the risk of material misstatement of the financial statements whether due to error or fraud, and to design the nature, timing, and extent of further audit procedures.	2. Holmes did not obtain an understanding of the entity or its internal control, nor did the assistants obtain such an understanding. There appears to have been no audit at all. The work performed was more an accounting service than it was an auditing service.
3. The auditor must obtain sufficient appropriate audit evidence by performing audit procedures to afford a reasonable basis for an opinion regarding the financial statements under audit.	3. Holmes acquired no evidence that would support the financial statements. Holmes merely checked the mathematical accuracy of the records and summarized the accounts. Standard audit procedures and techniques were not performed.
STANDARDS OF REPORTING	
1. The auditor must state in the auditor's report whether the financial statements are presented in accordance with generally accepted accounting principles (GAAP).	1. Holmes' report made no reference to generally accepted accounting principles. Because Holmes did not conduct a proper audit, the report should state that no opinion can be expressed as to the fair presentation of the financial statements in accordance with generally accepted accounting principles.

2-21 (continued)

BRIEF DESCRIPTION OF GAAS	HOLMES' ACTIONS RESULTING IN FAILURE TO COMPLY WITH GAAS
2. The auditor must identify in the auditor's report those circumstances in which such principles have not been consistently observed in the current period in relation to the preceding period.	2. Holmes' improper audit would not enable him to determine whether generally accepted accounting principles were consistently applied. Holmes' report should make no reference to the consistent application of accounting principles.
3. When the auditor determines that informative disclosures are not reasonably adequate, the auditor must so state in the auditor's report.	3. Management is primarily responsible for adequate disclosures in the financial statements, but when the statements do not contain adequate disclosures the auditor should make such disclosures in the auditor's report. In this case both the statements and the auditor's report lack adequate disclosures.
4. The auditor must either express an opinion regarding the financial statements, taken as a whole, or state that an opinion cannot be expressed, in the auditor's report. When the auditor cannot express an overall opinion, the auditor should state the reasons therefor in the auditor's report. In all cases where an auditor's name is associated with financial statements, the auditor should clearly indicate the character of the auditor's work, if any, and the degree of responsibility the auditor is taking, in the auditor's report.	4. Although the Holmes report contains an expression of opinion, such opinion is not based on the results of a proper audit. Holmes should disclaim an opinion because he failed to conduct an audit in accordance with generally accepted auditing standards.

2-22 a.	Generally accepted auditing standards.

b.	International auditing standards.

c.	PCAOB auditing standards.

d.	PCAOB auditing standards (reporting in the U.K. will be under international auditing standards).

e.	Generally accepted auditing standards.

f.	Generally accepted auditing standards.

g.	International auditing standards.

h.	PCAOB auditing standards (due to the publicly-traded debt).

■ **Internet Problem Solution: International Auditing and Assurance Standards Board**

Internet Problem 2-1

a.	The objective of the IAASB is to serve the public interest by setting high-quality auditing and assurance standards and by facilitating the convergence of international and national standards, thereby enhancing the quality and uniformity of practice throughout the world and strengthening public confidence in the global auditing and assurance profession. International Standards on Auditing (ISA) are used by auditors in countries that have adopted ISAs as their auditing standards.

b.	The IAASB follows a due process in setting standards.

•	The standards-setting Public Interest Activity Committees (PIAC) identify new projects based on review of international developments and consultation with the Public Interest Oversight Board.

•	The project may be assigned to a task force, which considers whether to hold a public forum or roundtable.

•	Draft pronouncements are exposed for a minimum of 90 days.

•	The task force considers all comments and whether re-exposure is needed.

•	The PIAC votes on the approval or withdrawal of the pronouncement. Affirmative vote of at least two-thirds of the members, but not less than 12, is required to approve an exposure draft.

c.	The IAASB is committed to transparency. Where practicable, meetings are broadcast over the Internet or recorded. Meeting agendas and minutes are published on the International Federation of Accountants (IFAC) website. All exposure drafts are subject to public exposure for a minimum of 90 days.

(**Note**: Internet problems address current issues using Internet sources. Because Internet sites are subject to change, Internet problems and solutions may change. Current information on Internet problems is available at www.pearsonhighered.com/arens).

Chapter 3

Audit Reports

■ Review Questions

3-1   Auditor's reports are important to users of financial statements because they inform users of the auditor's opinion as to whether or not the financial statements are fairly stated or whether no conclusion can be made with regard to the fairness of their presentation. Users especially look for any deviation from the wording of the standard unqualified report and the reasons and implications of such deviations. Having standard wording improves communications for the benefit of users of the auditor's report. When there are departures from the standard wording, users are more likely to recognize and consider situations requiring a modification or qualification to the auditor's report or opinion.

3-2   The unqualified audit report consists of:

1.   *Report title* Auditing standards require that the report be titled and that the title includes the word *independent*.
2.   *Audit report address* The report is usually addressed to the company, its stockholders, or the board of directors.
3.   *Introductory paragraph* The first paragraph of the report does three things: first, it makes the simple statement that the CPA firm has done an *audit*. Second, it lists the financial statements that were audited, including the balance sheet dates and the accounting periods for the income statement and statement of cash flows. Third, it states that the statements are the responsibility of management and that the auditor's responsibility is to express an opinion on the statements based on an audit.
4.   *Scope paragraph.* The scope paragraph is a factual statement about what the auditor did in the audit. The remainder briefly describes important aspects of an audit.
5.   *Opinion paragraph.* The final paragraph in the standard report states the auditor's conclusions based on the results of the audit.
6.   *Name of CPA firm.* The name identifies the CPA firm or practitioner who performed the audit.
7.   *Audit report date.* The appropriate date for the report is the end of fieldwork, when the auditor has gathered sufficient appropriate evidence to support the opinion.

The same seven parts are found in a qualified report as in an unqualified report. There are also often one or more additional paragraphs explaining reasons for the qualifications.

3-3   The purposes of the scope paragraph in the auditor's report are to inform the financial statement users that the audit was conducted in accordance with generally accepted auditing standards, in general terms what those standards mean, and whether the audit provides a reasonable basis for an opinion.
The information in the scope paragraph includes:

1.   The auditor followed generally accepted auditing standards.
2.   The audit is designed to obtain *reasonable assurance* about whether the statements are free of *material* misstatement.
3.   Discussion of the audit evidence accumulated.
4.   Statement that the auditor believes the evidence accumulated was appropriate for the circumstances to express the opinion presented.

3-4   The purpose of the opinion paragraph is to state the auditor's conclusions based upon the results of the audit evidence. The most important information in the opinion paragraph includes:

1.   The words "in our opinion" which indicate that the conclusions are based on professional judgment.
2.   A restatement of the financial statements that have been audited and the dates thereof or a reference to the introductory paragraph.
3.   A statement about whether the financial statements were presented fairly and in accordance with generally accepted accounting principles.

3-5   The auditor's report should be dated February 17, 2012, the date on which the auditor concluded that he or she had sufficient appropriate evidence to support the auditor's opinion.

3-6   An unqualified report may be issued under the following five circumstances:

1.   All statements—balance sheet, income statement, statement of retained earnings, and statement of cash flows—are included in the financial statements.
2.   The three general standards have been followed in all respects on the engagement.
3.   Sufficient appropriate evidence has been accumulated and the auditor has conducted the engagement in a manner that enables him or her to conclude that the three standards of field work have been met.
4.   The financial statements are presented in accordance with appropriate accounting standards such as generally accepted accounting principles or IFRS. This also means that adequate disclosures have been included in the footnotes and other parts of the financial statements.
5.   There are no circumstances requiring the addition of an explanatory paragraph or modification of the wording of the report.

3-7 The introductory, scope and opinion paragraphs are modified to include reference to management's report on internal control over financial reporting, and the scope of the auditor's work and opinion on internal control over financial reporting. The introductory and opinion paragraphs also refer to the framework used to evaluate internal control. Two additional paragraphs are added between the scope and opinion paragraphs that define internal control and describe the inherent limitations of internal control.

3-8 When adherence to generally accepted accounting principles would result in misleading financial statements there should be a complete explanation in a separate paragraph. The separate paragraph should fully explain the departure and the reason why generally accepted accounting principles would have resulted in misleading statements. The opinion should be unqualified, but it should refer to the separate paragraph during the portion of the opinion in which generally accepted accounting principles are mentioned.

3-9 An unqualified report with an explanatory paragraph or modified wording is the same as a standard unqualified report *except* that the auditor believes it is necessary to provide additional information about the audit or the financial statements. For a qualified report, either there is a scope limitation (condition 1) or a failure to follow generally accepted accounting principles (condition 2). Under either condition, the auditor concludes that the overall financial statements are fairly presented.

Two examples of an unqualified report with an explanatory paragraph or modified wording are:

   1.   The entity changed from one generally accepted accounting principle to another generally accepted accounting principle.
   2.   A shared report involving the use of other auditors.

3-10 When another CPA has performed part of the audit, the primary auditor issues one of the following types of reports based on the circumstances.

   1.   No reference is made to the other auditor. This will occur if the other auditor audited an immaterial portion of the statement, the other auditor is known or closely supervised, or if the principal auditor has thoroughly reviewed the other auditor's work.
   2.   Issue a shared opinion in which reference is made to the other auditor. This type of report is issued when it is impractical to review the work of the other auditor or when a portion of the financial statements audited by the other CPA is material in relation to the total.
   3.   The report may be qualified if the principal auditor is not willing to assume any responsibility for the work of the other auditor. A disclaimer may be issued if the segment audited by the other CPA is highly material.

3-11 Even though the prior year statements have been restated to enhance comparability, a separate explanatory paragraph is required to explain the change in generally accepted accounting principles in the first year in which the change took place.

3-12 Changes that affect the consistency of the financial statements may involve any of the following:

a.   Change in accounting principle
b.   Change in reporting entity
c.   Corrections of errors involving accounting principles.

An example of a change that affects consistency would be a change in the method of computing depreciation from straight line to an accelerated method. A separate explanatory paragraph is required if the amounts are material.

Comparability refers to items such as changes in estimates, presentation, and events rather than changes in accounting principles. For example, a change in the estimated life of a depreciable asset will affect the comparability of the statements. In that case, no explanatory paragraph for lack of consistency is needed because the same method of depreciation is used in both years, but the information may require disclosure in the statements.

3-13 The three conditions requiring a departure from an unqualified opinion are:

1.   *The scope of the audit has been restricted.* One example is when the client will not permit the auditor to confirm material receivables. Another example is when the engagement is not agreed upon until after the client's year-end when it may be impossible to physically observe inventories.
2.   *The financial statements have not been prepared in accordance with generally accepted accounting principles.* An example is when the client insists upon using replacement costs for fixed assets.
3.   *The auditor is not independent.* An example is when the auditor owns stock in the client's business.

3-14 A *qualified opinion* states that there has been either a limitation on the scope of the audit or a departure from GAAP in the financial statements, but that the auditor believes that the overall financial statements are fairly presented. This type of opinion may not be used if the auditor believes the exceptions being reported upon are extremely material, in which case a disclaimer or adverse opinion would be used.

An *adverse opinion* states that the auditor believes the overall financial statements are so materially misstated or misleading that they do not present fairly in accordance with GAAP the financial position, results of operations, or cash flows.

3-14 (continued)

A *disclaimer of opinion* states that the auditor has been unable to satisfy him or herself as to whether or not the overall financial statements are fairly presented because of a significant limitation of the scope of the audit, or a non-independent relationship under the *Code of Professional Conduct* between the auditor and the client.

Examples of situations that are appropriate for each type of opinion are as follows:

OPINION TYPE	EXAMPLE SITUATION
Disclaimer	Material physical inventories not observed and the inventory cannot be verified through other procedures. Lack of independence by the auditor.
Adverse	A highly material departure from GAAP.
Qualified	Inability to confirm the existence of an asset which is material but not extremely material in value.

3-15 The common definition of materiality as it applies to accounting and, therefore, to audit reporting is:

A misstatement in the financial statements can be considered material if knowledge of the misstatement would affect a decision of a reasonable user of the statements.

Conditions that affect the auditor's determination of materiality include:

■ Potential users of the financial statements
■ Dollar amounts of the following items: net income before taxes, total assets, current assets, current liabilities, and owners' equity
■ Nature of the potential misstatements—certain misstatements, such as fraud, are likely to be more important to users of the financial statements than other misstatements.

3-16 Materiality for lack of independence in audit reporting is easiest to define. If the auditor lacks independence as defined by the *Code of Professional Conduct*, it is always considered highly material and therefore a disclaimer of opinion is always necessary. That is, either the CPA is independent or not independent. For failure to follow GAAP, there are three levels of materiality: immaterial, material, and highly material.

3-17 The auditor's opinion may be qualified by scope limitations caused by client restrictions or by limitations resulting from conditions beyond the client's control. The former occurs when the client will not, for example, permit the auditor to confirm material receivables or physically observe inventories. The latter may occur when the engagement is not agreed upon until after the client's year-end when it may not be possible to physically observe inventories or confirm receivables.

A disclaimer of opinion is issued if the scope limitation is so material that the auditor cannot determine if the overall financial statements are fairly presented. If the scope limitation is caused by the client's restriction the auditor should be aware that the reason for the restriction might be to deceive the auditor. For this reason, a disclaimer is more likely for client restrictions than for conditions beyond anyone's control.

When there is a scope restriction that results in the failure to verify material, but not pervasive accounts, a qualified opinion may be issued. This is more likely when the scope limitation is for conditions beyond the client's control than for restrictions by the client.

3-18 A report with a scope and an opinion qualification is issued when the auditor can neither perform procedures that he or she considers necessary nor satisfy him or herself by using alternative procedures, usually due to the existence of conditions beyond the client's or the auditor's control, but the amount involved in the financial statements is not highly material. An important part of a scope and opinion qualification is that it results from not accumulating sufficient appropriate audit evidence, either because of the client's request or because of circumstances beyond anyone's control.

A report qualified as to opinion only results when the auditor has accumulated sufficient appropriate evidence but has concluded that the financial statements are not correctly stated. The only circumstance in which an opinion only qualification is appropriate is for material, but not highly material, departures from GAAP.

3-19 The three alternative opinions that may be appropriate when the client's financial statements are not in accordance with GAAP are an unqualified opinion, qualified as to opinion only and adverse opinion. Determining which is appropriate depends entirely upon materiality. An unqualified opinion is appropriate if the GAAP departure is immaterial (standard unqualified) or if the auditor agrees with the client's departure from GAAP (unqualified with explanatory paragraph). A qualified opinion is appropriate when the deviation from GAAP is material but not highly material; the adverse opinion is appropriate when the deviation is highly material.

3-20 When the auditor discovers more than one condition that requires a departure from or a modification of a standard unqualified report, the report should be modified for each condition. An exception is when one condition neutralizes the other condition. An example would be when the auditor is not independent and there is also a scope limitation. In this situation the lack of independence overshadows the scope limitation. Accordingly, the scope limitation should not be mentioned.

3-21 The standard wording required by U.S. auditing standards has the advantage of being consistent in how auditors communicate information about the fair presentation of financial statements to users of financial statements. Thus, any departures from the standard wording are more easily recognized. Furthermore, some users may question whether the auditor's conclusion about the financial statements differ when using "present fairly" rather than when using "true and fair view." Proponents of the alternative choices offered by ISAs may believe the choices allow the auditor to customize their report wording based on the auditor's preference of how to communicate to users. Others may also argue for U.S. adoption of similar alternatives so that U.S. audit reports conform to auditor reports based on ISAs. That consistency at a global level may help reduce misunderstandings between auditors and users of financial statements.

3-22 Given the global nature of the financial markets, investors, both in the U.S. and abroad, are frequently making investments in companies that are located all over the world. While many companies located outside the U. S. already prepare financial statements in accordance with International Financial Reporting Standards (IFRS), financial statements of U.S.-based entities are based on U.S. generally accepted accounting principles, differences in the basis of presentation makes the analysis of U.S. and non-U.S.-based company financial statements difficult. Similarly, differences exist in auditing standards issued across the globe, so the adoption of International Statements on Auditing (ISAs) would mean auditors from around the globe are conducting their audits using the same set of standards. The embrace of IFRS and ISAs will help investors in their analysis of audited financial statements prepared across the globe.

■ **Multiple Choice Questions From CPA Examinations**

3-23 a. (2) b. (3) c. (3)

3-24 a. (3) b. (4) c. (1)

3-25 a. (3) b. (2) c. (3)

■ **Discussion Questions and Problems**

3-26 a. "Correctly stated" implies absolute accuracy, whereas the alternative report states that no material misstatements exist.

b. The reference to generally accepted accounting principles specifies rules that were followed in accounting for the transactions to date; whereas "the true economic conditions" does not identify the specific accounting procedures applied.

c. The opinion paragraph is not intended to be a certification or a guarantee of the accuracy and correctness of the financial statements, but rather it is intended to be an expression of professional judgment based upon a reasonable audit of the statements and underlying records.

d. The name of the CPA firm rather than that of the individual practitioner should appear on the accountant's report because it is the entire firm that accepts responsibility for the report issued.

e. "Our audit was performed to detect material misstatements in the financial statements" is flawed because the purpose of the audit is to determine whether financial statements are fairly stated, not to specifically search for material errors and fraud. It also fails to recognize the audit standards followed by the auditor.

"We conducted our audit in accordance with auditing standards generally accepted in the United States of America" identifies the auditor's responsibilities for the conduct of the audit, accumulation of evidence, and reporting requirements. It is a much broader statement than the alternative clause. It also implies that if the auditor has conducted the audit in accordance with generally accepted auditing standards but does not uncover certain material errors or fraud, the auditor is unlikely to have responsibility for failing to do so.

3-27 a. Items that need not be included in the auditor's report are:

1. That Bellamy is presenting comparative financial statements. (Both years' statements will be referred to in the audit report.)

2. Specific description of the change in method of accounting for long-term construction contracts need not be included in the report since it is discussed in the footnotes. But, the auditor's report must state that there is a change in accounting principles and refer to the footnote.

3. The fact that normal receivable confirmation procedures were not used should not be disclosed since the auditor was able to satisfy him or herself through alternative audit procedures.

4. The lawsuit need not be discussed in the report since it has been included in a footnote.

3-27 (continued)

    b.   The following deficiencies are in Patel's report:

        1.   The audit report is neither addressed nor dated and it does not contain a title. The audit report date should be the last day of field work.

        2.   The balance sheet is as of a specific date, whereas the income statement and the statement of retained earnings are for a period of time. The scope paragraph should identify the period of time (usually one year).

        3.   There are comparative statements, but the audit report identifies and deals with only the current year's financial statements. An opinion must also be included for the prior period financial statements.

        4.   There is no separate introductory paragraph that states the financial statements audited, dates, and the responsibilities of management and the auditor.

        5.   There is no separate scope paragraph that describes what an audit is. Two required sentences are completely omitted: "An audit includes examining, on a test basis, evidence supporting the amounts and disclosures in the financial statements. An audit also includes assessing the accounting principles used and significant estimates made by management, as well as evaluating the overall financial statement presentation."

        6.   The audit was made in accordance with *auditing standards generally accepted in the United States of America* rather than *generally accepted accounting standards*.

        7.   The word *material* is excluded from the scope paragraph (free of material misstatement).

        8.   An additional paragraph should be included which describes the dividend restrictions and the refusal of the client to present a statement of cash flows.

        9.   The opinion paragraph states that accounting principles were consistent with those used in the prior year. The opinion paragraph should make no reference to consistency.

      10.   The opinion paragraph excludes the required phrase, "in all material respects."

      11.   The opinion paragraph includes the words "generally accepted auditing standards" rather than the phrase "accounting principles generally accepted in the United States of America."

      12.   A separate paragraph should be included stating that generally accepted accounting principles were not consistently applied.

      13.   The opinion should be qualified rather than being unqualified. Qualifications are caused by the:
            (a)   failure to present a statement of cash flows.
            (b)   failure to disclose the dividend restrictions.

(a) CONDITION	(b) MATERIALITY LEVEL	(c) TYPE OF REPORT	COMMENTS
1. Scope of the audit has been restricted	Highly material	Disclaimer	Because the client refuses to allow the auditor to expand the scope of his audit, a disclaimer of opinion is appropriate rather than a qualified as to scope and opinion.
2. Lack of independence	Not applicable	Disclaimer	Lack of independence by audit personnel on the engagement mandates a disclaimer for lack of independence.
3. None	Not applicable	Unqualified	The company has made a business decision to follow a different financing method for to have use of delivery trucks, which is adequately disclosed. There is no change of accounting principle.
4. Substantial doubt about going concern	Material	Unqualified—explanatory paragraph	Because the auditor has substantial doubt about the client's ability to continue as a going concern, the auditor should include add an explanatory paragraph to the unqualified opinion.
5. None	Material	Unqualified	While the auditor engaged a business valuation specialist to gather evidence about the fair value of the investment, the auditor would issue an unqualified opinion given he or she was able to conclude that the valuation specialist's work provides sufficient appropriate evidence.

3-28 (continued)

(a) CONDITION	(b) MATERIALITY LEVEL	(c) TYPE OF REPORT	COMMENTS
6. Failure to follow GAAP	Highly material or material. We need additional information regarding the auditor's preliminary judgment about materiality	Adverse (if highly material) or Qualified (if material)	The materiality of twenty percent of net earnings before taxes would be sufficient for many auditors to require an adverse opinion. That materiality question is a matter of auditor judgment.

3-29

(a) CONDITION	(b) MATERIALITY LEVEL	(c) TYPE OF REPORT	(d) MODIFIED WORDING / ADDITIONAL PARAGRAPHS (& OTHER COMMENTS)
1. None	Not applicable	(1) Unqualified—standard wording	There is no indication questioning the ability of the business to continue operations. The auditor does not automatically add an explanatory paragraph simply because there is a risky business.
2. None	Immaterial	(1) Unqualified—standard wording	The amount is immaterial. The facts are adequately disclosed in the footnote.
3. Failure to follow GAAP	Material	(4) Qualified opinion only—except for	The standards require the use of a qualified opinion for the failure to include a statement of cash flows. Third paragraph must be added stating the omission.

3-29 (continued)

(a) CONDITION	(b) MATERIALITY LEVEL	(c) TYPE OF REPORT	(d) MODIFIED WORDING / ADDITIONAL PARAGRAPHS (& OTHER COMMENTS)
4. None	Not applicable	(2) Unqualified—modified wording	U.S. auditing standards now allow an auditor to perform an audit in accordance with both U.S. GAAS and ISAs. The auditor's scope paragraph is modified to indicate that audit was conducted in accordance with both standards.
5. Scope of the audit has been restricted	Highly material	(6) Disclaimer	The client has restricted the scope of the audit and the auditor was not able to satisfy him or herself by alternative procedures. Because it was a client restriction rather than a condition beyond the client's control causing the limitation, and because the limitation is highly material, a disclaimer is appropriate. Introductory paragraph is modified, second paragraph is added describing the scope restriction, scope paragraph is omitted, and opinion paragraph is a disclaimer of opinion.
6. Report involving other auditors	Material	(3) Unqualified—modified wording	This is a shared audit report in which the auditor will identify the portion of work done by the other auditor in the introductory paragraph and still issue an unqualified opinion. The absolute dollar amounts of assets and revenues or percentages must be stated in the introductory paragraph. Introductory paragraph, scope paragraph, and opinion paragraph are all modified.

Type of Opinion	Description of Opinion	Comments
a.	7.	A change in consistency requires the addition of an explanatory paragraph that follows the opinion paragraph.
b.	4.	When the amounts are so material that a disclaimer of opinion is required, the auditor only uses three paragraphs. The scope paragraph found in a standard unqualified report is deleted to avoid stating anything that might lead readers to believe other parts of the financial statements were audited. The introductory and opinion paragraphs are modified and a new middle paragraph is added describing the scope limitation.
c.	8.	The auditor would add a new third paragraph preceding the opinion paragraph describing the GAAP departure resulting from inadequate disclosure. Another explanatory paragraph would follow the opinion paragraph describing the auditor's substantial doubt about going concern.
d.	3.	When the auditor references the work of other auditors, all three paragraphs are modified to reflect the involvement of other auditors.
e.	2.	The standard unqualified report contains three paragraphs with no modifications.
f.	5.	When a scope limitation is deemed to be material, but not highly material, the auditor's opinion is qualified to acknowledge "except for" the scope limitation. Also, a new third paragraph precedes the opinion paragraph to describe the scope limitation.
g.	6.	When the departure from accounting standards is deemed to be highly material, the auditor's opinion is modified to state that the financial statements do not present fairly. A new third paragraph precedes that opinion paragraph to describe the departure from accounting principles.
h.	1.	When the auditor is not independent, the auditor's report is limited to one paragraph that states that the auditor is not independent.
i.	9.	The change in consistency and the auditor's decision to add an emphasis of a matter paragraph both result in the addition of separate explanatory paragraphs that follow the opinion paragraph.

ITEM NO.	TYPE OF CHANGE	SHOULD AUDITOR'S REPORT BE MODIFIED?
1	An error correction not involving an accounting principle.	No
2	An accounting change involving both a change in accounting principle and a change in accounting estimate. Although the effect of the change in each may be inseparable and the accounting for such a change is the same as that for a change in estimate only, an accounting principle is involved.	Yes
3	An accounting change involving a change from one generally accepted accounting principle to another generally accepted accounting principle.	Yes
4	An accounting change involving a change in an accounting estimate.	No
5	Not an accounting change but rather a change in classification.	No
6	An accounting change involving a correction of an error in principle, which is accounted for as a correction of an error.	Yes
7	An accounting change involving a change in the reporting entity, which is a special type of change in accounting principles.	Yes
8	An accounting change from one generally accepted accounting principle to another generally accepted accounting principle.	Yes

3-32 Deficiencies in the staff accountant's tentative report include the following:

1. Report title must include the word "independent."
2. The report should generally be addressed to the board of directors or stockholders, not to the audit committee.
3. The introductory paragraph should state, "we have audited," not "we have examined."

4. When the principal auditor decides to make reference to the audit of another auditor, the report should indicate clearly in the introductory paragraph the division of responsibility regarding the portions of the financial statements audited by each. Also, the opinion paragraph should state that the opinion is based in part on the reports of other auditors. Neither of these was done.

5. When the principal auditor decides to make reference to the audit of the other auditor, the report should disclose the dollar amounts or percentages of the portion of the financial statements audited by the other auditor. This was not done.

6. The second paragraph is an inappropriately worded scope paragraph. It should be stated as follows:

> We conducted our audits in accordance with auditing standards generally accepted in the United States of America. Those standards require that we plan and perform the audit to obtain reasonable assurance about whether the financial statements are free of material misstatement. An audit includes examining, on a test basis, evidence supporting the amounts and disclosures in the financial statements. An audit also includes assessing the accounting principles used and significant estimates made by management, as well as evaluating the overall financial statement presentation. We believe that our audits and the report of other auditors provide a reasonable basis for our opinion.

7. Although the introductory paragraph referred to an audit of the financial statements for the years ended December 31, 2011 and 2010, an opinion was expressed only on the 2011 financial statements.

8. The statement of cash flows was not identified in the opinion paragraph, and financial statements were not referred to in the opinion paragraph as "consolidated."

9. The explanatory sentence for consistency should follow the opinion paragraph, not precede it. Also, the second sentence in the third paragraph should be omitted.

10. There is no inclusion of the phrase, "in all material respects" in the opinion paragraph.

3-33 The table presented below describes the seven distinct parts of the standard unqualified report and describes both similarities (part a.) and differences (part of b.) between the standard audit report and the audit report on the Les Meridian, Inc. financial statements.

Seven Distinct Parts of Standard Audit Report	a. Description of Similar Elements in the Les Meridian Auditor's Report	b. Different Elements in Les Meridian Auditor's Report
1. *Report title* Auditing standards require that the report be titled and that the title includes the word *independent*.	The report is titled "Independent Auditor's Report.	
2. *Audit report address* The report is usually addressed to the company, its stockholders, or the board of directors.	The report is addressed to the Shareholders of Les Meridian, Inc.	
3. *Introductory paragraph* The first paragraph of the report does three things: first, it makes the simple statement that the CPA firm has done an *audit*. Second, it lists the financial statements that were audited, including the statement of financial position dates and the accounting periods for the statement of comprehensive income and statement of cash flows. Third, it states that the statements are the responsibility of management and that the auditor's responsibility is to express an opinion on the statements based on an audit.	The report begins with the statement that the CPA firm has done an *audit*. The introductory paragraph lists the financial statements audited, including the time period of those statements. The second paragraph states that management is responsible for the preparation and fair presentation of the financial statements. The third paragraph describes the auditor's responsibility to express an opinion the financial statements.	The introductory paragraph also references the summary of significant accounting principles and other explanatory reports as being a part of the scope of the audit. A similar reference is not included in the U.S. standard audit report. The discussion of management's responsibility for the financial statements contained in the second paragraph is more extensive than the discussion in the standard audit report. It specifically notes that the financial statements are prepared in accordance with IFRS, and it describes management's responsibility for internal control.

Seven Distinct Parts of Standard Audit Report	a. Description of Similar Elements in the Les Meridian Auditor's Report	b. Different Elements in Les Meridian Auditor's Report
4. *Scope paragraph.* The scope paragraph is a factual statement about what the auditor did in the audit. The remainder briefly describes important aspects of an audit.	The third paragraph identifies the auditing standards used to conduct the audit, similar to the standard audit report. Like the standard audit report, the third paragraph notes that the auditor obtains reasonable assurance about whether the financial statements are free of material misstatements. The fourth paragraph also contains information related to other elements in the scope paragraph in the standard audit report. For example, the fourth paragraph describes the auditor's evaluation of accounting principles/ policies used, estimates made, and the overall presentation, similar to the scope paragraph in the standard audit report. The fifth paragraph acknowledges that the auditor believes the evidence obtained provides a sufficient basis for the opinion, similar to the last sentence of the scope paragraph of the standard audit report.	The third paragraph notes that the auditor conducted the audit in accordance with ISAs, rather than U.S. GAAS. The third paragraph notes that the auditor is required to comply with ethical requirements. The fourth paragraph contains more information than the standard audit report about the auditor's need to make judgments, the auditor's consideration of risks and internal control, and the fact that the risk and control assessments are not sufficient to express an opinion on internal control. The fourth paragraph also explicitly notes that risks of material misstatements due to error or fraud are considered.

3-33 (continued)

Seven Distinct Parts of Standard Audit Report	a. Description of Similar Elements in the Les Meridian Auditor's Report	b. Different Elements in Les Meridian Auditor's Report
5. *Opinion paragraph.* The final paragraph in the standard report states the auditor's conclusions based on the results of the audit.	The last paragraph includes the auditor's opinion about the financial statements and acknowledges the accounting principles used as the basis of presentation.	The wording associated with the opinion notes that the auditor's opinion is about the "true and fair view" of the financial statements, rather than the financial statements "present fairly" as stated in the standard audit report.
6. *Name of CPA firm.* The name identifies the CPA firm or practitioner who performed the audit.	The name of the CPA is included.	
7. *Audit report date.* The appropriate date for the report is the end of fieldwork, when the auditor has gathered sufficient appropriate evidence to support the opinion.	The date that the audit is completed is provided below the firm's signature.	

- **Internet Problem Solution: Research Annual Reports**

Internet Problem 3-1

   a.   ■   Form 8-K - This is the form that must be filed whenever a registrant encounters a significant event (e.g., a change in control of ownership, disposition or acquisition of a significant amount of assets, filing for bankruptcy, change in independent auditors).

   ■   Form 10-K - This is the annual report that most reporting companies file with the Commission. It provides a comprehensive overview of the registrant's business. The report must be filed within 60-90 days after the end of the company's fiscal year. This form is required by the Securities Exchange Act of 1934.

Internet Problem 3-1 (continued)

- Form 10-Q – This is the quarterly report that includes the quarterly financial statements filed with the SEC.
- DEF-14a – This filing includes the proxy statement sent to shareholders. The proxy statement includes information about the board of directors, including any requests for shareholder vote on the election of certain directors, and it includes information about executive compensation, auditor selection and related audit and other fees, and other information about board related activities and responsibilities.

b. 1. Ernst & Young LLP
   2. Separate reports were issued on the financial statements and on internal controls over financial reporting.
   3. Unqualified opinion on the financial statements
   4. Unqualified opinion on internal controls over financial reporting

c. 1. Unqualified opinions on both the financial statements and internal control over financial reporting are included in a single combined report.
   3. The combined report issued by PricewaterhouseCoopers does not follow the same standard wording format and paragraph order of a standard unqualified report on the financial statements or standard unqualified report on internal controls over financial reporting. However, all the required elements of both reports are present in the Yahoo auditor's report. While most audit firms use the standard unqualified report format as presented in Chapter 3, auditing standards only require that all required elements be included. Exact wording and paragraph format are not mandated by auditing standards. PricewaterhouseCoopers has chosen to present its standard audit reports using a different format.

(**Note**: Internet problems address current issues using Internet sources. Because Internet sites are subject to change, Internet problems and solutions may change. Current information on Internet problems is available at www.pearsonhighered.com/arens).

Chapter 4

Professional Ethics

■ **Review Questions**

4-1   The six core ethical values described by the Josephson Institute are:

1. Trustworthiness   4. Fairness
2. Respect   5. Caring
3. Responsibility   6. Citizenship

There are many other potential sources of ethical values, including laws and regulations, church doctrines, codes of professional ethics, and individual organizations' codes of conduct.

4-2   An ethical dilemma is a situation that a person faces in which a decision must be made about the appropriate behavior. There are many possible ethical dilemmas that one can face, such as finding a wallet containing money or dealing with a supervisor who asks you to work hours without recording them.

An ethical dilemma can be resolved using the six-step approach outlined on p. 80 of the text. The six steps are:

1.   Obtain the relevant facts.
2.   Identify the ethical issues from the facts.
3.   Determine who is affected by the outcome of the dilemma and how each person or group is affected.
4.   Identify the alternatives available to the person who must resolve the dilemma.
5.   Identify the likely consequence of each alternative.
6.   Decide the appropriate action.

4-3   There is a special need for ethical behavior by professionals to maintain public confidence in the profession, and in the services provided by members of that profession. The ethical requirements for CPAs are similar to the ethical requirements of other professions. All professionals are expected to be competent, perform services with due professional care, and recognize their responsibility to clients. The major difference between other professional groups and CPAs is independence. Because CPAs have a responsibility to financial statement users, it is essential that auditors be independent in fact and appearance. Most other professionals, such as attorneys, are expected to be an advocate for their clients.

PART	PURPOSE
1. Principles of Professional Conduct	1. Provide ideal standards of ethical conduct and help practitioners understand the ideal conduct of a CPA.
2. Rules of conduct	2. Provide minimum standards of ethical conduct stated as specific rules.
3. Interpretation of the rules of conduct	3. Provide formal interpretations of the rules of conduct to answer questions that frequently arise about the rules of conduct.
4. Ethical rulings	4. Provide more detailed guidance to practitioners about interpretation of the rules of conduct for less commonly raised questions.

4-5   At the international level, the International Ethics Standards Board for Accountants (IESBA) establishes ethical standards and guidance and fosters international debate on ethical issues faced by accountants through its *Code of Ethics for Professional Accountants.* This international ethics code contains five fundamental principles related to integrity, objectivity, professional competence and due care, confidentiality, and professional behavior.

4-6   *Independence of mind* exists when the auditor is actually able to maintain an unbiased attitude throughout the audit, whereas *independence in appearance* is dependent on others' interpretation of this independence and hence their faith in the auditor.

Activities which may not affect independence of mind, but which are likely to affect independence in appearance are: (Notice that the first two are violations of the *Code of Professional Conduct.*)

1.   Ownership of a financial interest in the audited client.
2.   Directorship or officer of an audit client.
3.   Performance of management advisory or bookkeeping or accounting services and audits for the same company.
4.   Dependence upon a client for a large percentage of audit fees.
5.   Engagement of the CPA and payment of audit fees by management.

4-7   Independence in auditing means taking an unbiased viewpoint. Users of financial statements would be unlikely to rely on the statements if they believed auditors were biased in issuing audit opinions.

4-8   Auditors of public companies are prohibited from performing the following nonaudit services:

1.   Bookkeeping and other accounting services
2.   Financial information systems design and implementation
3.   Appraisal or valuation services
4.   Actuarial services
5.   Internal audit outsourcing
6.   Management or human resource functions
7.   Broker or dealer or investment adviser, or investment banker services
8.   Legal and expert services unrelated to the audit
9.   Any other service that the PCAOB determines by regulation is impermissible

Nonaudit services that are not prohibited by the Sarbanes–Oxley Act and the SEC rules must be pre-approved by the company's audit committee. In addition, an accountant is not independent of an audit client if an audit partner received compensation based on selling engagements to that client for services other than audit, review and attest services.

Companies are required to disclose in their proxy statement or annual filings with the SEC the total amount of audit and nonaudit fees paid to the audit firm for the two most recent years. Four categories of fees are to be reported: (1) audit fees; (2) audit-related fees; (3) tax fees; and (4) all other fees. Companies are also required to provide further breakdown of the "other fees" category, and provide qualitative information on the nature of the services provided.

4-9   The rules concerning stock ownership by partners and professional staff:

A partner in the office of the partner responsible for an audit engagement cannot own stock in that audit client. A partner can own stock in an audit client, as long as (1) he or she cannot influence the audit engagement and (2) he or she is not in the same office as the partner responsible for the audit engagement.

A professional staff member cannot own stock in an audit client if he or she is assigned to the engagement or if he or she becomes a partner in the office of the partner responsible for the audit engagement. A professional staff member can own stock in a firm's audit client as long as he or she does not participate in the audit engagement.

Partner violation: A partner in the San Francisco office owns one share of stock of a client whose audit is conducted by a different partner in the San Francisco office.

Professional staff violation: An audit manager owns stock in a client whose audit is performed by the office where the audit manager works. The manager is promoted to partner mid-year. As soon as the manager becomes a partner, there is a violation of Rule 101.

4-10 Ways to reduce the appearance of the lack of independence are: the use of an audit committee to select auditors made up of directors who are not a part of management; a requirement that all changes of auditors and reasons therefore be reported to the SEC or other regulatory agency; and approval of the CPA firm by stockholders at the annual meeting. The Sarbanes–Oxley act requires that the audit committee of a public company consist only of independent members and be responsible for the appointment, termination, and compensation of the audit firm.

4-11 A CPA firm has several options when it decides it is not competent to perform an audit:

1. Withdraw from the engagement.
2. Obtain the expertise through continuing education and self-studies.
3. Hire someone who has the expertise.
4. Work on a consulting basis with another CPA firm.

4-12 A fee based upon the amount of time it takes to complete is *not* a violation of Rule 302. Rule 302 on contingent fees states that professional services for clients receiving assertion opinions shall not be offered or rendered under an agreement whereby no fee will be charged unless a specific finding or result is attained, or where the fee is otherwise contingent upon the findings or results of such services. The purpose of the rule is to prevent sacrificing the quality of audits because of the pressure felt by the auditor in producing the required audit outcome. An example would be the fee being dependent upon the issuance of an unqualified opinion or the obtaining of a loan by a client.

4-13 The following are exceptions to the confidentiality requirement for the CPA's audit files:

1. The confidentiality requirement cannot interfere with the member's obligation to follow auditing standards or generally accepted accounting principles.
2. A member must comply with a validly issued subpoena or summons enforceable by order of a court.
3. A review of a member's professional practice under AICPA or state CPA society or state Board of Accountancy authorization is permitted.
4. A member must respond to any inquiry made by the ethics division or trial board of the Institute or a duly constituted investigative or disciplinary body of a state CPA society or Board of Accountancy.

4-14 Audits should be maintained at a high level of quality even if solicitation, advertising, and competitive bidding are allowed for several reasons:

1. Professionals do high quality work because it is a characteristic of being a professional.

4-14 (continued)

2. A reputation of doing high quality work usually pays off in more clients and a more profitable practice.
3. Potential legal liability is also a deterrent to substandard work.
4. The *Code of Professional Conduct* requires a high quality of performance.

4-15 A member is permitted to advertise by Rule 502 except in a false, misleading, or deceptive manner. Interpretation 502-2 clarifies the meaning of false, misleading or deceptive acts, including activities that:

1. Create false or unjustified expectations of favorable results.
2. Imply the ability to influence any court, tribunal, regulatory agency or similar body or official.
3. Contain a representation that specific professional services will be performed for a stated fee, when it was likely at the time of the representation that such fees would be substantially increased and the prospective client was not informed of that likelihood.
4. Contain any other representations that would be likely to cause a reasonable person to misunderstand or be deceived.

When engagements are obtained through the efforts of third parties, Interpretation 502-5 indicates that the member has the responsibility to ascertain that all promotional efforts are within the bounds of the Rules of Conduct.

4-16 Prohibiting paying commissions to obtain clients who receive attestation services in Rule 503 is intended to discourage overly aggressive obtaining of clients by giving "finders' fees" to banks and others in a position to give business rather than on the basis of competitive and other qualifications. Prohibiting receiving commissions for referrals to other CPAs or other providers of services where attestation services are provided is intended to discourage referrals to others on the basis of a "sales commission" rather than the competition of those offering services. Commissions when attestation services are *not* provided are permitted to encourage competition for these types of services.

4-17 A CPA may practice in one of the following forms:

1. A proprietorship
2. A general partnership
3. A general corporation (if permitted by state law)
4. A professional corporation
5. Limited liability company (if permitted by state law)
6. Limited liability partnership (if permitted by state law)

■ Multiple Choice Questions From CPA Examinations

4-18   a.   (1)   b.   (3)   c.   (1)

4-19   a.   (1)   b.   (3)   c.   (3)

■ Discussion Questions And Problems

4-20

	Service	Violation?
a.	Providing bookkeeping services to a public company. The services were pre-approved by the audit committee of the company.	Yes
b.	Providing internal audit services to a public company that is not an audit client.	No
c.	Implementing a financial information system designed by management for a private company.	No
d.	Recommending a tax shelter to a client that is publicly held. The services were pre-approved by the audit committee.	No *
e.	Providing internal audit services to a public company client with the pre-approval of the audit committee.	Yes
f.	Providing bookkeeping services to an audit client that is a private company.	No

*   Recommending tax shelters is not prohibited as long as the service does not meet the characteristics of an abusive tax avoidance strategy and does not have the potential to impair independence.

4-21   a.   Rule 101 - Independence. No violation. If the services performed conform to the requirements of Interpretation 101-3, independence of Emrich would not be considered to be impaired. There would be a violation of SEC rules if the client were publicly held.

        b.   Rule 101 - Independence. No violation. Franz Marteens is not a partner nor is he assigned to the engagement team for the audit client.

        c.   Rule 201 - General Standards. Violation. Interpretation 201-1 states that a member who accepts a professional engagement implies that he or she has the necessary competence to complete the engagement according to professional standards. Wilkenson has violated the rule since he does not have the expertise to review the work of the consultant hired by Wilkenson. Wilkenson should have suggested that the company hire the consultant directly.

   d. Rule 102 - Integrity and Objectivity. Violation. This rule states that in tax practice, a member may resolve doubt in favor of his or her client as long as there is reasonable support for his or her position. In the example case, the client has provided no support for the unusual deductions. Sarah Milsaps has violated Rule 102 by not requiring reasonable support for the deductions.

   e. Rule 203 (Accounting Principles). Violation. This rule designates that the International Accounting Standards Board (IASB) is the established body for issuing international financial accounting standards. Roberta Hernandez's assertion that the financial statements are based on international financial accounting standards would be in violation of Rule 203 because she did not use standards issued by the IASB.

   f. Rules 101 (Independence) and 102 (Integrity and Objectivity). Violation. Appearance of independence has been impaired by Steve Custer's agency's financial dealing with his audit clients and participation in a business, which impairs his objectivity. It is also a conflict of duties to recommend his own firm to review the adequacy of the existing insurance coverage of existing clients

   g. Rule 301 - Confidential Client Information. Violation. The client should have been notified that the review was to take place, and an attempt should have been made to obtain the client's permission for such review because the review was not a part of an AICPA, state CPA society or Board of Accountancy review program. The firms violated Rule 301 by not obtaining consent from the client for the review.

   h. Rule 501 - Acts Discreditable. No violation. The rule is vague and the interpretation would be made by the state Board of Accountancy. In most states this will be a civil action and would not likely be a violation.

4-22 a. Violation of Rule 101 – When audit firms create a network with other firms to share certain characteristics, such as the sharing of audit methodologies and audit manuals, interpretations of Rule 101 require each network firm to be independent of audit and review clients of other network firms. The ownership by Miller and Yancy who are partners in one of the network firms in the stock of a client of another network firm would impair independence.

   b. Violation of Rule 501 – An interpretation of Rule 501 prohibits the inclusion of indemnification clauses and other limitations of liability provisions in engagement letters for audit and other attest services.

   c. No violation – While Jennifer's audit client has a material investment in Polex, her non-dependent parents' investment in Polex represents an indirect financial interest that is not material to her parents or Jennifer.

4-22 (continued)

    d.   No violation – Because Joe has no responsibilities for financial reporting in his new role and because the audit firm modified audit procedures to reduce the risk that Joe has knowledge of the audit plan, independence would not be impaired.

    e.   Violation of Rule 101 – Interpretations and rulings under Rule 101 note that independence is impaired if billed or unbilled fees remain unpaid for professional services provided more than one year before the date of the auditor's report. Because the report date for the 2011 financial statement audit would likely be in 2012, more than one year would have transpired.

    f.   Violation of Rule 101 – Only pre-existing mortgages provided by a new audit client that is a bank are permissible. No new mortgage loans are permitted, however.

    g.   No violation – Because Jessica promptly notified her office's managing partner of the offer and because she was removed from the audit engagement, no violation has occurred.

    h.   Violation of Rule 501 – Rule 501 prohibits the solicitation and disclosure of the Uniform CPA examination questions and answers without permission of the AICPA.

    i.   Violation of Rules 102 and 203 – Both Rules 102 and 203 would be violated by Audrey's actions whereby she knowingly included false and misleading transactions in the financial statements that were provided to the bank.

    j.   No violation – The prohibition of contingent fees does not extend to consulting services engagements as long as the CPA does not perform any other services for that client that might include audit, review, compilation, examinations of prospective financial information or certain tax return services.

4-23 a.   An audit committee is a special committee formed by the board of directors and made up of board members. The Sarbanes–Oxley Act requires that all the members of the audit committee be independent directors, and the committee should include at least one member who is a financial expert. The audit committee serves as a liaison between the independent auditor and the board of directors. The audit committee assists and advises the full board of directors, and, as such, aids the board in fulfilling its responsibility for public financial reporting.

    b.   The functions of an audit committee may include the following:

        1.   Select the independent auditor; discuss audit fee with the auditor; review auditor's engagement letter.

        2.   Review the independent auditor's overall audit plan (scope, purpose, and general audit procedures).

        3.   Review the annual financial statements before submission to the full board of directors for approval.

4. Review the results of the audit including experiences, restrictions, cooperation received, findings, and recommendations. Consider matters that the auditor believes should be brought to the attention of the directors or shareholders.

5. Review the independent auditor's evaluation of the company's internal controls.

6. Review the company's accounting, financial, and operating controls.

7. Review the reports of internal audit staff.

8. Review interim financial reports to shareholders before they are approved by the board of directors.

9. Review company policies concerning political contributions, conflicts of interest, and compliance with federal, state, and local laws and regulations, and investigate compliance with those policies.

10. Review financial statements that are part of prospectuses or offering circulars; review reports before they are submitted to regulatory agencies.

11. Review independent auditor's observations of financial and accounting personnel.

12. Participate in the selection and establishment of accounting policies; review the accounting for specific items or transactions as well as alternative treatments and their effects.

13. Review the impact of new or proposed pronouncements by the accounting profession or regulatory bodies.

14. Review the company's insurance program.

15. Review and discuss the independent auditor's management letter.

c. Management is frequently under considerable pressure from stockholders and the board of directors to maintain high earnings for the company. In some cases this may in turn motivate management to put pressure on auditors to permit a violation of accounting principles and therefore affect the reported earnings and disclosures in the financial statements. The board of directors has a greater responsibility to the stockholders for fairness in reported earnings. Directors, especially those who are outside directors, have less responsibility for high reported earnings.

Directors are therefore less likely to put pressure on auditors to deviate from high professional standards, and the audit committee can deal with the auditor in a less biased manner than can management. In addition, the board of directors has a legal responsibility to review the policies and actions of management.

4-23 (continued)

         Therefore, there is considerable incentive for them to work closely with the auditor. A small committee of outside directors from the audit committee is therefore equipped to help the auditor to maintain a more independent relationship with the client. If management exerts any pressure on the auditor, the auditor is likely to discuss that with the audit committee and thereby resolve the problem.

    d.   For public companies, the PCAOB's rules require a CPA firm, before its selection as the company's auditor, to describe in writing and discuss with the audit committee all relationships between the firm and the company, including executives in financial reporting positions, to determine whether there is any impairment of the CPA firm's independence. If the CPA firm is selected, these communications must occur annually.

    e.   The criticism of audit committees has been made by many smaller CPA firms. There may be some validity to the comment. At the same time, audit committees do have a responsibility to help a company control costs. Therefore if the cost of a smaller audit firm is significantly less than a large firm, assuming equal quality, the audit committee would be obligated to use the less expensive firm.

4-24 a.   Independence is essential for an auditor because users of financial statements expect an unbiased viewpoint in the CPA's attestation to the fairness of the financial statements. If users believe that auditors are not independent, the value of the audit function is eliminated.

    b.   Most other professions (attorneys, doctors, dentists, etc.) represent their clients and perform services intended primarily to assist their clients. For this reason no assumption of independence is required. The importance of independence for CPAs is similar to that for judges. For both, a nonadvocacy position is essential.

    c.   Independence in appearance is how independent the auditor appears to outsiders such as users of financial statements. Independence of mind refers to whether the auditor has maintained an attitude of independence throughout the engagement. For example, an auditor could possibly maintain an attitude of independence of mind (also described as independence in fact) even though he or she held shares of stock in a company and performed the audit (the auditor would have violated Rule 101). However, the auditor would not likely be independent in appearance in such a situation. Both independence in appearance and of mind are essential and the *Code of Professional Conduct* concerns both.

4-24 (continued)

 d. 1. He has violated the *Code of Professional Conduct*. Rule 101 prohibits any direct ownership by a partner or shareholder.

 2. Such a small ownership is unlikely to have any impact on a partner's objectivity in evaluating the financial statements. It is unlikely to affect the partner's independence of mind.

 3. Such ownership could affect the appearance of independence and therefore impact the reputation and credibility of auditors. Additionally these strict requirements eliminate any controversy as to the line between a material and immaterial ownership. It also shows outsiders the importance of independence to auditors and therefore hopefully improves the reputation of the profession.

 e.

INDEPENDENCE OF MIND	INDEPENDENCE IN APPEARANCE	SOCIAL CONSEQUENCES OF PROHIBITING
1. May cause the auditor to permit misstatements to enhance personal wealth.	Users may perceive that auditors would permit misstatements to enhance personal wealth.	Minor, if any.
2. Person doing this audit may not do the audit work carefully because he or she did the bookkeeping.	Users may perceive that the auditor may not independently audit his or her own work.	Some clients find it less expensive to have bookkeeping services performed by an outside service. It is often less expensive to have this done by the auditor because the auditor will already be knowledgeable about the business.
3. The audit team may become complacent due to familiarity and not carefully evaluate potential misstatements.	Users may perceive the possibility of complacency.	Knowledge gained by the audit team about a client's business is essential to evaluate when misstatements in the financial statements are likely and to plan the audit. It is costly for a new audit team to obtain that knowledge.

INDEPENDENCE OF MIND	INDEPENDENCE IN APPEARANCE	SOCIAL CONSEQUENCES OF PROHIBITING
4. The CPA firm may become complacent due to familiarity and not carefully evaluate potential misstatements.	Users may perceive the possibility of complacency.	The same conclusions reached in (3) about the audit team are applicable to CPA firms. The cost of a new CPA firm of obtaining the knowledge is even greater because of confidentiality requirements and communication difficulties between CPA firms.
5. The auditor may be unwilling to disagree with management for fear of being terminated.	Users may perceive that the auditor is unwilling to disagree with management.	Someone has to select the auditor. Management is usually in the best position to evaluate the effectiveness and cost of alternative auditors, especially for private companies.
6. There may be an absence of a careful independent check of the entries or preparation of the statements because they were originally prepared by the auditor.	Users may believe that the auditor may not independently audit his or her own work or that of a staff person from his or her firm.	Many clients lack technical expertise in accounting. Having services performed by the auditor is sometimes the least costly alternative.
7. The auditor may be reluctant to criticize or not rely on an accounting system that was originally recommended by the CPA firm. Additionally, if the CPA firm obtains considerable revenue from management advisory services, the CPA firm may fear the loss of the client and therefore be controlled by management.	Users may perceive either of the two concerns discussed under independence of mind.	A CPA firm gains considerable knowledge about a client and its business during the audit. Due to this knowledge, management services can often be provided by the same CPA firm at a lower cost than alternative sources such as other CPA firms or management consultants.

4-24 (continued)

INDEPENDENCE OF MIND	INDEPENDENCE IN APPEARANCE	SOCIAL CONSEQUENCES OF PROHIBITING
7. The auditor may be reluctant to criticize or not rely on an accounting system that was originally recommended by the CPA firm. Additionally, if the CPA firm obtains considerable revenue from management advisory services, the CPA firm may fear the loss of the client and therefore be controlled by management.	Users may perceive either of the two concerns discussed under independence of mind.	A CPA firm gains considerable knowledge about a client and its business during the audit. Due to this knowledge, management services can often be provided by the same CPA firm at a lower cost than alternative sources such as other CPA firms or management consultants.

f. The AICPA *Code of Professional Conduct* prohibits only e(1). The SEC prohibits e(1) if the person owning the stock is a member of the engagement team or is a partner in the office of the partner primarily responsible for the audit engagement. The SEC also prohibits e(2), and e(6) would also be considered a violation if the adjusting entries were so extensive that they are, in essence, bookkeeping services. The SEC also prohibits the management services in e(7) if they are one of the nine nonaudit services prohibited by the SEC. Because the Sarbanes–Oxley Act requires that the audit committee select the auditor, e(5) is now also a violation of SEC rules.

4-25 The *Code of Professional Conduct* and interpretations are not clear as to what constitutes a violation in these three situations. A central point is that Marie Janes must maintain independence of mind and in appearance because she is not an employee of the company and must not give the impression that she is one.

4-25 (continued)

(a) POTENTIAL THREATS TO INDEPENDENCE	(b) POSSIBLE SAFEGUARDS?	(c) RULES OF CONDUCT VIOLATED?	(d) APPROPRIATE ACTION?
1. The ability to purchase a car at a substantial discount due to Marie's long-standing audit service may cause Marie to be favorably disposed to the client when evaluating the client's financial statements. Also, if users of the financial statements heard of this arrangement, some might perceive that there is a lack of independence.	1. Marie Janes' firm could establish policies regarding services provided by attest clients that require the managing partner's approval prior to engaging in any transactions with the client. Some transactions could be explicitly prohibited by the policy, while other may require the managing partner's approval.	1. Marie Janes has likely not violated the rules; the discount is available to customers on a widespread basis. Presumably many of the employees of the CPA firm buy automobiles from the agency.	1. Marie Janes should discuss the discount with the firm's managing partner if she intends or wants to buy the automobile. She should certainly not feel compelled to buy the automobile but she should also not automatically turn it down. The situation would be entirely different if the sale were limited to employees. In such a case it would likely be a violation.
2. The ability to eat meals on an ongoing basis may cause Marie to be favorably disposed to the client when evaluating the client's financial statements. Also, if users of the financial statements heard of this arrangement, some might perceive that there is a lack of independence.	2. Marie Janes' firm could establish a policy regarding free services or gifts provided by clients. Perhaps the firm policy could establish a minimal dollar threshold of allowable free services or gifts. Those exceeding the threshold may either be prohibited by the policy or may require approvals by a more senior member of management of the audit firm.	2. If Marie Janes were to eat there on an ongoing basis that would likely be a violation of the rules of conduct. It would not likely be a violation if she occasionally eats with employees she is dealing with at the audit.	2. Marie Janes should eat elsewhere if it is practical to do so but if the only practical place for her to eat is the lunchroom, she should make arrangements with her firm to make certain that the company is reimbursed for the expenses.
3. Gifts from clients might be perceived as a subtle form of bribe, thus may create a lack of appearance of independence. Gifts may also cause Marie to be favorably disposed to the client when evaluating the client's financial statements. Also, if users of the financial statements heard of this arrangement, some might perceive that there is a lack of independence.	3. Marie Janes' firm could establish a policy regarding free services or gifts provided by clients. Perhaps the firm policy could establish a minimal dollar threshold of allowable free services or gifts. Those exceeding the threshold may either be prohibited by the policy or may require approvals by a more senior member of management of the audit firm.	3. Accepting such a gift is likely to be a violation of the rules of conduct. That gift is reasonably large and would be considered by many employees as equivalent to a bonus.	3. Ideally Janes should not accept the gift and state that since she is not an employee, she would prefer not to take it. If she believes that it would be embarrassing to the company, she should graciously accept it and return it with an explanation of her reasons as soon as practical.

4-26 1. No violation. Because JKB management selected the IT hardware and software and the external auditors merely installed it, the firm is not acting as a member of management and has no independence problem.

2. Violation. The Rules of Conduct state that a CPA cannot supervise client employees. The external auditors supervised employees in the daily operation of the IT system, which is a violation of Rule 101.

3. No violation. Because JKB management selected the specifications and options of the payroll software application, the CPA firm did not act as a member of management by customizing the package for the client's use.

4. No violation. The Rules of Conduct permit the external auditor to train client employees on the use of a newly installed information system.

5. Violation. By determining which of JKB's products would be offered on the company's Web site, the external auditors acted as part of JKB's management. Independence has presumably been impaired in this case.

6. Violation. Again, the external auditors are acting as members of management by operating the client's local area network. If JKB is an SEC client, this would also be a violation of SEC independence rules.

■ Cases

4-27 The answers to these questions are more judgmental than most others in the chapter. They may, in some cases, be a violation of the spirit of the *Code* if the CPA is acting in a certain manner, and they may not be a violation if the CPA is acting in a different manner. For example, in 2, if Davis is sending business executives in small companies to his small loan company, there's likely to be a violation of the rule of conduct. On the other hand if he recommends the small loan company along with several others, only for those clients who truly need the services of a small loan company, he is not likely to be in violation. (Changing the facts throughout the discussion may increase the value of the case.)

1. Rule 502 permits advertising as long as it is not false, misleading, or deceptive. The advertising expressly states two facts: 14 of 36 of the largest community banks are audited by their firm and second, the average audit fee, as a percentage of total assets, is lower than any of the other CPA firms in the city. Contel must be able to support those factual statements. Assuming he can, there is no violation. However, it may be difficult to support the comparison to the fees of other firms.

4-27 (continued)

2.	There is no violation because Rule 504--Incompatible Occupations no longer exists. There may have been a violation under old Rule 504 if Davis or his employees consistently sent clients of Davis to the small loan company and/or encouraged them to make loans from such company.

3.	There may be a material indirect interest in the audit client. Elbert owns a material amount of stock and if the mutual fund in turn invests a large portion of its money in an audit client of Elbert, Elbert in essence has a material investment in an audit client.

	Simply because the mutual fund's investment has increased dramatically in the audit client does not mean there is a material investment, however. For example, it may have increased from one percent to three percent of the total holdings of the mutual company. Nevertheless Elbert must evaluate whether the holding could be a material indirect investment under Rule 101.

4.	This would not be a violation of the rules of conduct or interpretations. It is common and acceptable for a CPA firm to inform a member of management of the availability of limited partnerships. Similarly it is common for management to inform the CPA firm of such investment opportunities. In many cases the limited partners do not know of the other investors in the limited partnership. If the CPA and owner of Marshall Marine Co. either earn or lose significant sums in the investment, it should have no effect on their relationship or on the audit of Marshall Marine Co.

5.	Contingent fee arrangements between the CPA and the client are a violation of the rules for clients receiving attestation services. However, Rule 302 specifically states that fees are not regarded as being contingent if fixed by courts or other public authorities or, *in tax matters, if determined based on the results of judicial proceedings and the findings of government agencies.* This situation involves tax matters the results of which are determined by judicial proceedings, therefore there is no violation.

6.	It is essential that Finigan retain both an attitude of independence in fact and in appearance. It is not possible to determine if Finigan is maintaining an attitude of independence in fact, given her involvement in the company, but it is certainly possible that she is. Finigan is not necessarily violating the *Code of Professional Conduct*. She does the audit, tax return, bookkeeping and management services work for the client, but that is not a violation if Gilligan is a private company.

	It is questionable whether Finigan is maintaining an attitude of independence in appearance, especially given the comments by Gilligan. It is essential that she maintain an attitude of independence throughout all her work. So she must be careful that she is not on the side of Gilligan without consideration of her professional responsibilities in conducting the audits and in all other aspects of her professional responsibilities.

4-28 a. It's an ethical dilemma for Barbara because she has a decision to make about what behavior is appropriate. If she throws the schedules away, as suggested by her supervisor, she may not be carrying out her professional responsibility to the public or the client. If she does not throw the schedules away, she will likely cause a confrontation between herself and her supervisor.

    b.   1.   Relevant facts: A number of misstatements were discovered. The aggregate amount of all discovered and undiscovered misstatements may be material. The audit supervisor wants Barbara to throw away some of her work.

            2.   Ethical issues: Is it ethical to throw away the schedules containing some small misstatements when her supervisor instructs her to do so?

            3.   Who is affected and how?

WHO IS AFFECTED?	HOW?
Barbara	1. Being asked to ignore misstatements is a possible violation of Rule 102. 2. Performance evaluation may be affected. 3. Future with firm may be affected.
Jack	1. Future with firm may be affected. 2. Performance evaluation may be affected.
Green, Thresher & Co., CPAs	1. If audit is completed late, they may lose the engagement. 2. May be sued if material misstatements are not detected. 3. Client may be unhappy with auditor if misstatements are subsequently discovered.
Delancey Fabrics	1. May not have opportunity to correct misstatements if they are not brought to light. 2. May be required to adjust financial statements if misstatements exist.

            4.   Alternatives
                (a)   Throw away schedules.
                (b)   Inform Jack that she will not throw schedules away.
                (c)   Talk to manager or partner about Jack's request.
                (d)   Refuse to work on the engagement.
                (e)   Quit the firm.
             5.   Consequences
                (a)   The misstatements may be discovered subsequently and the firm may lose the client, or be sued. Even if the misstatements are not material, the client may be justifiably upset because the problems giving rise to the misstatements may have been solved sooner.

4-28 (continued)

        (b)   Barbara informs Jack that she won't throw away schedules. This may result in a confrontation. She may get an unfavorable review.

        (c)   If she talks to the manager or partner, they may admire Barbara's attempt to be ethical, or they may think she is out of line for bypassing Jack's authority without discussing the matter with him in detail.

        (d)   If she refuses to continue on the engagement, it will not look good on Barbara's record. She may be labeled as "hard to get along with."

        (e)   If she quits, she will likely miss out on some potentially valuable experiences in public accounting.

6.   Appropriate Action

Only Barbara can decide. One reasonable approach is for Barbara to start by discussing the matter further with Jack. She should listen carefully to his reasoning and express her reservations about throwing the schedules away. She should not subordinate her judgment to Jack, as this would be a violation of Rule of Conduct 102. If Jack satisfies her that it is acceptable to throw the schedules away (this seems unlikely in the circumstances), then she may be justified in doing so. However, if she still has reservations, she should inform Jack that she intends to contact a manager or partner.

4-29   a.   Practitioners voluntarily agree to abide by the *Code* as they enter public practice. It is imperative that individuals at least comply with the minimum standards specified by the *Code of Professional Conduct*, despite pressures one may face. Concealing a known material misstatement in a client's financial statements is clearly a violation of a practitioner's responsibility to society.

      b.   Bob Smith in essence condoned Oake's behavior by doing nothing. His inaction is worthy of sanction by his firm, the AICPA, and the state Board of Accountancy.

      c.   At a minimum, practitioners must draw the line by complying with the Rules of Conduct specified in the *Code of Professional Conduct*. Violations of the *Code* are not acceptable. Hopefully, most practitioners strive to uphold the ethical principles specified in the *Code of Professional Conduct*.

4-30   1.   Relevant Facts

      a.   Frank believes the revenue recognition method is inappropriate.

      b.   The partner believes the revenue recognition method is appropriate.

4-30 (continued)

2.   Ethical issue: Is it ethical for Frank to conceal his disagreement with the partner by not writing a statement which follows the requirements of (AU 311)?

3.   Who is affected and how?

WHO IS AFFECTED?	HOW?
Frank	1. Promotion, future pay, and ability to meet personal financial obligations may be affected. 2. His relationship with partners and clients may also be affected.
Partner	1. Promotion, future pay, and ability to meet personal financial obligations may be affected. 2. Her relationship with partners and clients may also be affected.
The firm, Bright & Lorren	1. The firm faces potential liability if an improper decision is made regarding revenue recognition. 2. May lose the audit client.
The client, Machine International	1. Decision may affect the client's ability to obtain financing. 2. Decision may affect stockholder perceptions of management performance.
Users of Machine International's Financial Statements	1. Decision may affect individual decisions related to investments in Machine International.

4.   Alternatives
   a.   Write a statement and inform other partners if engagement partner refuses to include the statement in the audit files.
   b.   Agree with the partner.

5.   Consequences
   a.   If Frank agrees with the partner, a potentially inappropriate accounting method may lead to an unqualified opinion on materially misstated financial statements.
   b.   Other partners may be upset with Frank for failing to disclose his feelings on the matter.
   c.   The firm could be sued and suffer losses.
   d.   On the other hand, perhaps the partner is right and the revenue recognition method is appropriate.
   e.   If Frank writes the statement and expresses his disagreement, he may be labeled as "hard to get along with." However, most firms which do high-quality audit work encourage practitioners at all levels to express their views on matters which require professional judgment such as the appropriateness of a given accounting principle.

6. Appropriate action:

Frank should express his opinion, leaving room for the possibility that he may be wrong. He should be respectful of the position of all other partners in the firm. Most, if not all, of the other partners in the firm would probably appreciate Frank's willingness to express his opinion regarding the inappropriateness of the revenue recognition method used by the client.

■ **Internet Problem Solution: IESBA Code of Ethics**

Internet Problem 4-1

a. Students should have located the respective codes of conduct.
b. Refer to page 85 in Chapter 4 to see the descriptions of the six Principles in the AICPA *Code*. Below are the five principles of the IESBA *Code*. The table that follows that provides a comparison of the Princples in the two *Codes*:

Five Principles of the IESBA *Code*:

1. **Integrity** – to be straightforward and honest in all professional and business relationships.
2. **Objectivity** – to not allow bias, conflict of interest or undue influence of others to override professional or business judgments.
3. **Professional Competence and Due Care** – to maintain professional knowledge and skill at the level required to ensure that a client or employer receives competent professional services based on current developments in practice, legislation, and techniques and act diligently and in accordance with applicable technical and professional standards.
4. **Confidentiality** – to respect confidentiality of information acquired as a result of professional and business relationships and, therefore, not disclose any such information to third parties without proper and specific authority, unless there is a legal or professional right or duty to disclose nor use the information for the personal advantage of the professional accountant or third parties.
5. **Professional Behavior** – to comply with relevant laws and regulations and avoid any action that discredits the profession.

Internet Problem 4-1 (continued)

The following table compares the principles in each code of conduct

Principles in the AICPA *Code*	Comparison and Contrast to the five Principles in the IESBA *Code*
Responsibilities Public interest	***Professional Behavior*** – This Principle in the IESBA *Code* encompasses some of the elements in the Responsibilities and Public Interest Principles of the AICPA *Code*. The IESBA *Code* emphasizes the importance of complying with relevant laws and regulations and avoiding actions that discredit the profession. This is related to the AICPA's Principle that emphasizes serving the public interest and honoring the public trust. It also relates to the AICPA's Principle on Responsibilities that emphasizes carrying out professional responsibilities by exercising moral judgments.
Integrity	***Integrity*** – Like the AICPA *Code*, the IESBA *Code* contains a stand alone principle on Integrity. The AICPA *Code* emphasizes the end purpose of integrity - to maintain and broaden public confidence while the IESBA *Code* provides desired characteristics of integrity – straightforwardness and honesty.
Objectivity and Independence	***Objectivity*** – Like the AICPA *Code*, the IESBA Code has a specific principle on Objectivity. Both highlight the importance of removing conflicts of interest. The AICPA *Code* additionally emphasizes the importance of independence.
Due Care	***Professional Competence and Due Care*** – Both *Codes* emphasize the importance of observing technical standards and maintaining awareness of changes in the professional standards in order to maintain competency in services delivered.
Scope and Nature of Services	There is no companion Principle in the IESBA *Code*.
N/A	***Confidentiality*** – The IESBA *Code* has a specific Principle on respecting the confidentiality of information while the AICPA *Code* does not.

c. The IESBA addresses "public interest" indirectly through the Professional Behavior Principle that emphasizes the importance of complying with relevant laws and regulations and avoiding actions that discredit the profession. This is related to the AICPA's Principle that emphasizes honoring the public trust.

Internet Problem 4-1 (continued)

    d.   The organizational structure of both Codes starts with the overriding Principles. So, both are principles-based Codes. The remainder of both Codes is designed to provide more specific guidelines of how the Principles are to be applied. However, their organizational structures are different in how they do that. In addition to the Principles, the AICPA Code provides specific Rules that must be followed by CPAs and then there Interpretations of the Rules and Ethical Rulings that contain more specificity of application. In contrast, the IESBA follows the Princples in Part A, with more specific descriptions of how the framework applies in Parts B and C. Part B provides guidance for accountants in public practice while Part C provides guidance for accountants in business.

    e.   The IESBA *Code* addresses the importance of Independence in Section 290, which is a subset of Part B – Professional Accountants in Public Practice. It follows the discussion of Objectivity.

(**Note**: Internet problems address current issues using Internet sources. Because Internet sites are subject to change, Internet problems and solutions may change. Current information on Internet problems is available at www.pearsonhighered.com/arens).

Chapter 5

Legal Liability

■ **Review Questions**

5-1 Several factors that have affected the increased number of lawsuits against CPAs are:

1. The growing awareness of the responsibilities of public accountants on the part of users of financial statements.
2. An increased consciousness on the part of the SEC regarding its responsibility for protecting investors' interests.
3. The greater complexities of auditing and accounting due to the increasing size of businesses, the globalization of business, and the intricacies of business operations.
4. Society's increasing acceptance of lawsuits.
5. Large civil court judgments against CPA firms, which have encouraged attorneys to provide legal services on a contingent fee basis.
6. The willingness of many CPA firms to settle their legal problems out of court.
7. The difficulty courts have in understanding and interpreting technical accounting and auditing matters.

5-2 The most important positive effects are the increased quality control by CPA firms that is likely to result from actual and potential lawsuits and the ability of injured parties to receive remuneration for their damages. Negative effects are the energy required to defend groundless cases and the harmful impact on the public's image of the profession. Legal liability may also increase the cost of audits to society, by causing CPA firms to increase the evidence accumulated.

5-3 Business failure is the risk that a business will fail financially and, as a result, will be unable to pay its financial obligations. Audit risk is the risk that the auditor will conclude that the financial statements are fairly stated and an unqualified opinion can therefore be issued when, in fact, they are materially misstated.

When there has been a business failure, but not an audit failure, it is common for statement users to claim there was an audit failure, even if the most recently issued audited financial statements were fairly stated. Many auditors evaluate the potential for business failure in an engagement in determining the appropriate audit risk.

5-4 The prudent person concept states that a person is responsible for conducting a job in good faith and with integrity, but is not infallible. Therefore, the auditor is expected to conduct an audit using due care, but does not claim to be a guarantor or insurer of financial statements.

5-5   The difference between fraud and constructive fraud is that in fraud the wrongdoer intends to deceive another party whereas in constructive fraud there is a lack of intent to deceive or defraud. Constructive fraud is highly negligent performance.

5-6   Many CPA firms willingly settle lawsuits out of court in an attempt to minimize legal costs and avoid adverse publicity. This has a negative effect on the profession when a CPA firm agrees to settlements even though it believes that the firm is not liable to the plaintiffs. This encourages others to sue CPA firms where they probably would not to such an extent if the firms had the reputation of contesting the litigation. Therefore, out-of-court settlements encourage more lawsuits and, in essence, increase the auditor's liability because many firms will pay even though they do not believe they are liable.

5-7   An auditor's best defense for failure to detect a fraud is an audit properly conducted in accordance with auditing standards. SAS 99 (AU 316) states that the auditor should assess the risk of material misstatements of the financial statements due to fraud. Based on this assessment, the auditor should design the audit to provide *reasonable assurance* of detecting material misstatements due to fraud. SAS 99 also states that because of the nature of fraud (including defalcations), a properly designed and executed audit may not detect a material misstatement due to fraud.

5-8   Contributory negligence used in legal liability of auditors is a defense used by the auditor when he or she claims the client or user also had a responsibility in the legal case. An example is the claim by the auditor that management knew of the potential for fraud because of deficiencies in internal control, but refused to correct them. The auditor thereby claims that the client contributed to the fraud by not correcting material weaknesses in internal control.

5-9   An engagement letter from the auditor to the client specifies the responsibilities of both parties and states such matters as fee arrangements and deadlines for completion. The auditor may also use this as an opportunity to inform the client that the responsibility for the prevention of fraud is that of the client. A well-written engagement letter can be useful evidence in the case of a lawsuit, given that the letter spells out the terms of the engagement agreed to by both parties. Without an engagement letter, the terms of the engagement are easily disputed.

5-10   Liability to clients under common law has remained relatively unchanged for many years. If a CPA firm breaches an implied or expressed contract with a client, there is a legal responsibility to pay damages. Traditionally the distinction between privity of contract with clients and lack of privity of contract with third parties was essential in common law. The lack of privity of contract with third parties meant that third parties would have no rights with respect to auditors except in the case of gross negligence.

That precedent was established by the Ultramares case. In recent years some courts have interpreted Ultramares more broadly to allow recovery by third

5-10 (continued)

parties if those third parties were known and recognized to be relying upon the work of the professional at the time the professional performed the services (*foreseen users*). Still others have rejected the Ultramares doctrine entirely and have held the CPA liable to anyone who relies on the CPA's work, if that work is performed negligently. The liability to third parties under common law continues in a state of uncertainty. In some jurisdictions the precedence of Ultramares is still recognized whereas in others there is no significant distinction between liability to third parties and to clients for negligence.

5-11 In recent years the auditor's liability to a third party has become affected by whether the party is known or unknown. Now a known third party, under common law, usually has the same rights as the party that is privy to the contract. An unknown third party usually has fewer rights. The approach followed in most states is the *Restatement of Torts* approach to the foreseen users concept. Under the *Restatement of Torts* approach, foreseen users must be members of a reasonably limited and identifiable group of users that have relied on the CPA's work, even though those persons were not specifically known to the CPA at the time the work was done.

5-12 The differences between the auditor's liability under the securities acts of 1933 and 1934 are because the 1933 act imposes a heavier burden on the auditor. Third party rights as presented in the 1933 act are:

1. Any third party who purchases securities described in the registration statement may sue the auditor.
2. Third party users do not have the burden of proof that they relied on the financial statements or that the auditor was negligent or fraudulent in doing the audit. They must only prove that the financial statements were misleading or not fairly stated.

In conjunction with these third party rights, the auditor has a greater burden in that he or she must demonstrate that:

1. The statements were not materially misstated.
2. An adequate audit was conducted.
3. The user did not incur the loss because of misleading financial statements.

The liability of auditors under the 1934 act is not as harsh as under the 1933 act. In this instance, the burden of proof is on third parties to show that they relied on the statements and that the misleading statements were the cause of the loss.

The principal focus of accountants' liability under the 1934 act is on Rule 10b-5. Under Rule 10b-5, accountants *generally* can only be held liable if they intentionally or recklessly misrepresent information intended for third-party use. Many lawsuits involving accountants' liability under Rule 10b-5 have resulted in

5-12 (continued)

accountants being liable when they knew all of the relevant facts, but merely made poor judgments. In recent years, however, courts have decided that poor judgment doesn't necessarily prove fraud on the part of the accountant.

5-13 The auditor's *legal liability to the client* can result from the auditor's failure to properly fulfill his or her contract for services. The lawsuit can be for breach of contract, which is a claim that the contract was not performed in the manner agreed upon, or it can be a tort action for negligence. An example would be the client's detection of a misstatement in the financial statements, which would have been discovered if the auditor had performed all audit procedures required in the circumstances (e.g., misstatement of inventory resulting from an inaccurate physical inventory not properly observed by the auditor).

The auditor's *liability to third parties under common law* results from any loss incurred by the claimant due to reliance upon misleading financial statements. An example would be a bank that has loans outstanding to an audited company. If the audit report did not disclose that the company had contingent liabilities that subsequently became real liabilities and forced the company into bankruptcy, the bank could proceed with legal action against the auditors for the material omission.

Civil liability under the Securities Act of 1933 provides the right of third parties to sue the auditor for damages if a registration statement or a prospectus contains an untrue statement of a material fact or omits to state a material fact that results in misleading financial statements. The third party does not have to prove reliance upon the statements or even show his or her loss resulted from the misstatement. An example would be stock purchased by an investor in what appears, based upon audited financial statements, to be a sound company. If the financial statements are later found to be inaccurate or misleading, and the investment loses value as a result of a situation existing but not disclosed at the date of the financial statements, the investor could file legal proceedings against the auditor for negligence.

Civil liability under the Securities Act of 1934 relates to audited financial statements issued to the public in annual reports or 10-K reports. Rule 10b-5 of the Act prohibits fraudulent activity by direct sellers of securities. Several federal court decisions have extended the application of Rule 10b-5 to accountants, underwriters and others. An example would be an auditor knowingly permitting the issuance of fraudulent financial statements of a publicly held client.

Criminal liability of the auditor may result from federal or state laws if the auditor defrauds another person through knowingly being involved with false financial statements. An example of an act that could result in criminal liability would be an auditor's certifying financial statements that he or she knows overstate income for the year and the financial position of the company at the audit date.

5-14 The SEC can impose the following sanctions against a CPA firm:

    1.   Suspend the right to conduct audits of SEC clients.
    2.   Prohibit a firm from accepting any new clients for a period.
    3.   Require a review of the firm's practice by another CPA firm.
    4.   Require the firm to participate in continuing education programs.

5-15 Some of the ways in which the profession can positively respond and reduce liability in auditing are:

    1.   Continued research in auditing.
    2.   Standards and rules must be revised to meet the changing needs of auditing.
    3.   The AICPA can establish requirements that the better practitioners always follow in an effort to increase the overall quality of auditing.
    4.   Establish new peer review requirements.
    5.   CPA firms should oppose all unfounded lawsuits rather than settling out of court.
    6.   Users of financial statements need to be better educated regarding the attest function.
    7.   Improper conduct and performance by members must be sanctioned.
    8.   Lobby for changes in state and federal laws concerning accountants' liability.

■ **Multiple Choice Questions From CPA Examinations**

5-16 a. (2)   b. (1)   c. (2)

5-17 a. (3)   b. (4)   c. (1)   d. (2)

■ **Discussion Questions and Problems**

5-18 1.   d   (ordinary negligence)
             h   (privity of contract)
       2.   a   (due diligence)
       3.   e   (separate and proportionate)
       4.   i   (foreseen users)
       5.   g   (intent to deceive)
       6.   b   (reliance on the financial statements)
             k   (material error or omission)
       7.   f   (contributory negligence)
       8.   c   (fraud)
             i   (gross negligence)

5-19 a. Yost and Co. should use the defenses of meeting auditing standards and contributory negligence. The fraud perpetuated by Stuart Supply Company was a reasonably complex one and difficult to uncover except by the procedures suggested by Yost.

In most circumstances it would not be necessary to physically count all inventory at different locations on the same day. Furthermore the president of the company contributed to the failure of finding the fraud by refusing to follow Yost's suggestion. There is evidence of that through his signed statement.

b. There are two defenses Yost and Company should use in a suit by First City National Bank. First there is a lack of privity of contract. Even though the bank was a known third party, it does not necessarily mean that there is any duty to that party in this situation. That defense is unlikely to be successful in most jurisdictions today. The second defense which Yost is more likely to be successful with is that the firm followed auditing standards in the audit of inventory, including the employment of due care. Ordinarily it is unreasonable to expect a CPA firm to find such an unusual problem in the course of an ordinary audit. Because the CPA firm did not uncover the fraud does not mean it has responsibility for it.

c. She is likely to be successful in her defense against the client because of the contributory negligence. The company has responsibility for instituting adequate internal controls. The president's statement that it was impractical to count all inventory on the same day because of personnel shortages and customer preferences puts considerable burden on the company for its own loss.

It is also unlikely that First City National Bank will be successful in a suit. The court is likely to conclude that Yost followed due care in the performance of her work. The fact that there was not a count of all inventory on the same date is unlikely to be sufficient for a successful suit. The success of Yost's defenses is also heavily dependent upon the jurisdiction's attitude about privity of contract. In this case there is unlikely to be a claim of extreme negligence. Therefore it would be required for the court to both ignore the privity of contract precedence and find Yost negligent for the suit to be successful.

d. The issues and outcomes should be essentially the same under the suit brought under the Securities Exchange Act of 1934. If the suit were brought under Rule 10b-5, it is certainly unlikely that the plaintiff would be successful, inasmuch as there was no intent to deceive. The plaintiff would likely be unsuccessful in such a suit.

5-20   Yes. Normally a CPA firm will not be liable to third parties with whom it has neither dealt nor for whose benefit its work was performed. One notable exception to this rule is fraud. When the financial statements were fraudulently prepared, liability runs to all third parties who relied upon the false information contained in them. Fraud can be either actual or constructive. Here, there was no actual fraud on the part of Small or the firm in that there was no deliberate falsehood made with the requisite intent to deceive. However, it would appear that constructive fraud might be present. Constructive fraud is found where the auditor's performance is found to be grossly negligent. That is, the auditor really had either no basis or so flimsy a basis for his or her opinion that he or she has manifested a reckless disregard for the truth. Small's disregard for standard auditing procedures would seem to indicate such gross negligence and, therefore, the firm is liable to third parties who relied on the financial statements and suffered a loss as a result.

5-21   The answers provided in this section are based on the assumption that the traditional legal relationship exists between the CPA firm and the third party user. That is, there is no privity of contract, the known versus unknown third party user is not a significant issue, and high levels of negligence are required before there is liability.

> a. False.   There was no privity of contract between Thompson and Doyle and Jensen, therefore, ordinary negligence will usually not be sufficient for a recovery.
> b. True.   If gross negligence is proven, the CPA firm can and probably will be held liable for losses to third parties.
> c. True. See a.
> d. False.   Gross negligence (constructive fraud) is treated as actual fraud in determining who may recover from the CPA.
> e. False.   Thompson is an unknown third party and will probably be able to recover damages only in the case of gross negligence or fraud.

Assuming a liberal interpretation of the legal relationship between auditors and third parties, the answers to a. and e. would probably both be true. The other answers would remain the same.

5-22   a. Hanover will likely not be found liable to the purchasers of the common stock if the suit is brought under Rule 10b-5 of the Securities Exchange Act of 1934 because there was no knowledge or intent to deceive by the auditor. However, if the purchasers are original purchasers and are able to bring suit under the Securities Act of 1933, the plaintiffs will likely succeed because they must only prove the existence of a material error or omission.

> b. Hanover was aware that the financial statements were to be used to obtain financing from First National Bank. Hanover is likely to be held responsible for negligence to the bank as a known third party that relied on the financial statements.

5-23 a. The legal issues involved in this case revolve around the auditor's compliance with auditing standards and contributory negligence. Auditing standards require that accounts receivable be confirmed by the auditor in most circumstances. This procedure was employed in the case, and the legal issue is whether or not the auditor used due care in following up on the confirmation replies received.

  As a defense in the lawsuit, the auditor would claim to have followed auditing standards by properly confirming accounts receivable. In addition, the auditor may defend him or herself by testifying that the company controller was responsible for investigating the reason for the differences reported on the confirmation replies. The auditor may state that he or she had a right to conclude that the controller had reviewed the explanations provided by the bookkeeper, and concluded they were correct. The auditor might also use the defense that there was contributory negligence. The controller should not have delegated the work to the bookkeeper and should have recognized the potential for intentional wrongdoing by the bookkeeper.

  b. The CPA's deficiency in conducting the audit of accounts receivable was his or her failure to investigate and obtain evidence to substantiate the explanations provided by the bookkeeper. The auditor should have investigated each of the timing differences, through which he or she may have discovered that no sales allowance had been granted to the customer, but in fact, the customer had mailed payment for the merchandise which the bookkeeper had stolen.

5-24 a. Yes. Chen was a party to the issuance of false financial statements. The elements necessary to establish an action for common law fraud are present. There was a material misstatement of fact, knowledge of falsity (scienter), intent that the plaintiff bank rely on the false statement, actual reliance, and damage to the bank as a result thereof. If the action is based upon fraud there is no requirement that the bank establish privity of contract with the CPA. Moreover, if the action by the bank is based upon ordinary negligence, which does not require a showing of scienter, the bank may recover as a third-party beneficiary because it is a primary beneficiary. Thus, the bank will be able to recover its loss from Smith under either theory.

  b. No. The lessor was a party to the secret agreement. As such, the lessor cannot claim reliance on the financial statements and cannot recover uncollected rents. Even if the lessor was damaged indirectly, his or her own fraudulent actions led to the loss, and the equitable principle of "unclean hands" precludes the lessor from obtaining relief.

5-24 (continued)

      c.   Yes. Chen had knowledge that the financial statements did not follow generally accepted accounting principles and willingly prepared an unqualified opinion. That is a criminal act because there was an intent to deceive.

5-25

1.	c	Both. Material misstatements must be shown under both acts.
2.	c	Both. Monetary loss must be demonstrated under both acts.
3.	d	Neither. Plaintiff does not have to prove lack of diligence under the 1933 Act, but the accountant can use due diligence as a defense. Scienter must be demonstrated under the 1934 Act.
4.	d	Neither. Privity applies to common law and not the 1933 and 1934 acts.
5.	b	1934 Act only. Reliance is not required under the 1933 Act.
6.	b	Scienter is required under the 1934 Act, but not the 1933 Act.

5-26 a.   The case should be dismissed. A suit under Section 10(b) and Rule 10b-5 of the Securities Exchange Act of 1934 must establish fraud. Fraud is an intentional tort and as such requires more than a showing of negligent manner; the CPAs neither participated in the fraudulent scheme nor did they know of its existence. The element of scienter or guilty knowledge must be present in order to state a cause of action for fraud under Section 10(b) of the Securities Exchange Act of 1934.

      b.   The plaintiffs might have stated a common law action for negligence. However, they may not be able to prevail due to the privity requirement. There was no contractual relationship between the defrauded parties and the CPA firm. Although the exact status of the privity rule is unclear, it is doubtful that the simple negligence in this case would extend Gordon & Groton's liability to the customers who transacted business with the brokerage firm. However, the facts of the case as presented in court would determine this.

           Another possible theory which has been attempted recently in the courts is liability under Section 17 of the Securities Exchange Act of 1934, which requires registered brokers to submit audited financial statements to the SEC. In one such case, the plaintiff claimed that the accountant failed to perform a proper audit and thereby created liability to the customers of the brokerage firm who suffered losses as a result of the financial collapse of the brokerage firm.

5-27   The bank is likely to succeed. Robertson apparently knew that Majestic was "technically bankrupt" at December 31, 2010. Reporting standards require the auditor to add an explanatory paragraph to the audit report when there is substantial doubt about an entity's ability to continue as a going concern. She did not include such a paragraph. To make matters worse, it appears that Robertson was convinced not to issue the report with the going concern paragraph because of the negative impact on Majestic Co., not because of the solvency of the company. That may be interpreted as a lack of independence by Robertson and may indicate a fraudulent act, potentially a criminal charge that could result in a prison term.

Robertson's most likely defense is that after determining all of the facts, in part through discussion with management, she concluded that the Majestic Co. was not technically bankrupt and did not require an explanatory paragraph in the audit report. She might also argue that even if such a report was appropriate, her failure to do so was negligence or bad judgment, not with the intent to deceive the bank. Such a defense does not seem to be strong given the statement about her knowledge of Majestic's financial condition.

Robertson might also falsely testify that she did not believe that a going concern problem existed. Such statements would be perjury and are unprofessional and not worthy of a professional accountant. Perjury is also a criminal act and could result in further actions by the courts.

■ **Case**

5-28   PART 1

  a.   In order for Thaxton to hold Mitchell & Moss liable for his losses under the Securities Exchange Act of 1934, he must rely upon the antifraud provisions of Section 10(b) of the act. In order to prevail, Thaxton must establish that:

      1.   There was an omission or misstatement of a material fact in the financial statements used in connection with his purchase of the Whitlow & Company shares of stock.
      2.   He sustained a loss as a result of his purchase of the shares of stock.
      3.   His loss was caused by reliance on the misleading financial statements.
      4.   Mitchell & Moss acted with scienter (knowledge of the misstatement).

      Based on the stated facts, Thaxton can probably prove the first three requirements cited above. To prove the fourth requirement, Thaxton must show that Mitchell & Moss had knowledge of the fraud or recklessly disregarded the truth. The facts clearly indicate that Mitchell & Moss did not have knowledge of the fraud and did not recklessly disregard the truth.

5-28 PART 1 (continued)

b. The customers and shareholders of Whitlow & Company would attempt to recover on a negligence theory based on Mitchell & Moss' failure to comply with auditing standards. Even if Mitchell & Moss were negligent, Whitlow & Company's customers and shareholders must also establish either that:

1. They were third party beneficiaries of Mitchell & Moss' contract to audit Whitlow & Company, or
2. Mitchell & Moss owed the customers and shareholders a legal duty to act without negligence.

Although many cases have expanded a CPA's legal responsibilities to a third party for negligence, the facts of this case may fall within the traditional rationale limiting a CPA's liability for negligence; that is, the unfairness of imputing an indeterminate amount of liability to unknown or unforeseen parties as a result of mere negligence on the auditor's part. Accordingly, Whitlow & Company's customers and shareholders will prevail only if (1) the courts rule that they are either third-party beneficiaries or are owed a legal duty and (2) they establish that Mitchell & Moss was negligent in failing to comply with auditing standards.

5-28 PART 2

a. The basis of Jackson's claim will be that she sustained a loss based upon misleading financial statements. Specifically, she will rely upon section 11(a) of the Securities Act of 1933, which provides the following:

> In case any part of the registration statement, when such part became effective, contained an untrue statement of a material fact or omitted to state a material fact requirement to be stated therein or necessary to make the statements therein not misleading, any person acquiring such security (unless it is proved that at the time of such acquisition he knew of such untruth or omission) may, either at law or in equity, in any court of competent jurisdiction, sue every accountant who has with his consent been named as having prepared or certified any part of the registration statement.

To the extent that the relatively minor misstatements resulted in the certification of materially false or misleading financial statements, there is potential liability. Jackson's case is based on the assertion of such an untrue statement or omission coupled with an allegation of damages. Jackson does not have to prove reliance on the statements nor the company's or auditor's negligence in order to recover the damages. The burden is placed on the defendant to provide defenses that will enable it to avoid liability.

b. The first defense that could be asserted is that Jackson knew of the untruth or omission in audited financial statements included in the registration statement. The act provides that the plaintiff may not recover if it can be proved that at the time of such acquisition she knew of such "untruth or omission."

Since Jackson was a member of the private placement group and presumably privy to the type of information that would be contained in a registration statement, plus any other information requested by the group, she may have had sufficient knowledge of the facts claimed to be untrue or omitted. If this were the case, then she would not be relying on the certified financial statements but upon her own knowledge.

The next defense available would be that the untrue statement or omission was not material. The SEC has defined the term as meaning matters about which an average prudent investor ought to be reasonably informed before purchasing the registered security. For section 11 purposes, this has been construed as meaning a fact that, had it been correctly stated or disclosed, would have deterred or tended to deter the average prudent investor from purchasing the security in question.

Allen, Dunn, and Rose would also assert that the loss in question was not due to the false statement or omission; that is, that the false statement was not the cause of the price drop. It would appear that the general decline in the stock market would account for at least a part of the loss. Additionally, if the decline in earnings was not factually connected with the false statement or omission, the defendants have another basis for refuting the causal connection between their wrongdoing and the resultant drop in the stock's price.

Finally, the accountants will claim that their departure from auditing standards was too minor to be considered a violation of the standard of due diligence required by the act.

■ Internet Problem Solution: SEC Enforcement

Internet Problem 5-1

a.   The complaint alleges that between January 2006 and August 2007, Gagnon helped orchestrate a Ponzi scheme by Gregory McKight and Lexis Holdings, which raised approximately $72.6 million from over 3,000 investors. Gagnon also fraudulently offered and sold securities in a new company that purportedly developed resort properties, as well as fraudulent offering interests in a purported trading venture.

b.   Gagnon was charged with violating of Sections 5(a), 5(c), 17(a) and 17(b) of the Securities Act of 1933, and Section 10(b) and 15(a)(1) of the Securities Exchange Act of 1934 and Rule 10b-5.

(**Note**: Internet problems address current issues using Internet sources. Because Internet sites are subject to change, Internet problems and solutions may change. Current information on Internet problems is available at www.pearsonhighered.com/arens).

Chapter 6

Audit Responsibilities and Objectives

■ **Review Questions**

6-1   The objective of the audit of financial statements by the independent auditor is the expression of an opinion on the fairness with which the financial statements present financial position, results of operations, and cash flows in conformity with applicable accounting standards.

   The auditor meets that objective by accumulating sufficient appropriate evidence to determine whether management's assertions regarding the financial statements are fairly stated.

6-2   It is management's responsibility to adopt sound accounting policies, maintain adequate internal control and make fair representations in the financial statements. The auditor's responsibility is to conduct an audit of the financial statements in accordance with auditing standards and report the findings of the audit in the auditor's report.

6-3   An error is an unintentional misstatement of the financial statements. Fraud represents an intentional misstatement. The auditor is responsible for obtaining reasonable assurance that material misstatements in the financial statements are detected, whether those misstatements are due to errors or fraud.

   An audit must be designed to provide reasonable assurance of detecting material misstatements in the financial statements. Further, the audit must be planned and performed with an *attitude of professional skepticism* in all aspects of the engagement. Because there is an attempt at concealment of fraud, material misstatements due to fraud are usually more difficult to uncover than errors. The auditor's best defense when material misstatements (either errors or fraud) are not uncovered in the audit is that the audit was conducted in accordance with auditing standards.

6-4   Misappropriation of assets represents the theft of assets by employees. Fraudulent financial reporting is the intentional misstatement of financial information by management or a theft of assets by management, which is covered up by misstating financial statements.

   Misappropriation of assets ordinarily occurs either because of inadequate internal controls or a violation of existing controls. The best way to prevent theft of assets is through adequate internal controls that function effectively. Many times theft of assets is relatively small in dollar amounts and will have no effect on the fair presentation of financial statements, although there are some cases of material theft of assets. Fraudulent financial reporting is inherently difficult to uncover because it is possible for one or more members of management to override internal controls. In many cases the amounts are extremely large and may affect the fair presentation of financial statements.

6-5   True, the auditor must rely on management for certain information in the conduct of the audit. However, the auditor must not accept management's representations blindly. The auditor must, whenever possible, obtain appropriate evidence to support the representations of management. As an example, if management represents that certain inventory is not obsolete, the auditor should be able to examine purchase orders from customers that prove part of the inventory is being sold at a price that is higher than the company's cost plus selling expenses. If management represents an account receivable as being fully collectible, the auditor should be able to examine subsequent payments by the customer or correspondence from the customer that indicates a willingness and ability to pay.

6-6

CHARACTERISTIC	AUDIT STEPS
1. Management's characteristics and influence over the control environment.	■ Investigate the past history of the firm and its management. ■ Discuss the possibility of fraudulent financial reporting with previous auditor and company legal counsel after obtaining permission to do so from management.
2. Industry conditions.	■ Research current status of industry and compare industry financial ratios to the company's ratios. Investigate any unusual differences. ■ Read AICPA's *Industry Audit Risk Alert* for the company's industry, if available. Consider the impact of specific risks that are identified on the conduct of the audit.
3. Operating characteristics and financial stability.	■ Perform analytical procedures to evaluate the possibility of business failure. ■ Investigate whether material transactions occur close to year-end.

6-7   The cycle approach is a method of dividing the audit such that closely related types of transactions and account balances are included in the same cycle. For example, sales, sales returns, and cash receipts transactions and the accounts receivable balance are all a part of the sales and collection cycle. The advantages of dividing the audit into different cycles are to divide the audit into more manageable parts, to assign tasks to different members of the audit team, and to keep closely related parts of the audit together.

GENERAL LEDGER ACCOUNT	CYCLE
Sales	Sales & Collection
Accounts Payable	Acquisition & Payment
Retained Earnings	Capital Acquisition & Repayment
Accounts Receivable	Sales & Collection
Inventory	Inventory & Warehousing
Repairs & Maintenance	Acquisition & Payment

6-9 There is a close relationship between each of these accounts. Sales, sales returns and allowances, and cash discounts all affect accounts receivable. Allowance for uncollectible accounts is closely tied to accounts receivable and should not be separated. Bad debt expense is closely related to the allowance for uncollectible accounts. To separate these accounts from each other implies that they are not closely related. Including them in the same cycle helps the auditor keep their relationships in mind.

6-10 Management assertions are implied or expressed representations by management about classes of transactions and the related accounts and disclosures in the financial statements. These assertions are part of the criteria management uses to record and disclose accounting information in financial statements. AU 326 classifies assertions into three categories:

1. Assertions about classes of transactions and events for the period under audit
2. Assertions about account balances at period end
3. Assertions about presentation and disclosure

6-11 General audit objectives follow from and are closely related to management assertions. General audit objectives, however, are intended to provide a framework to help the auditor accumulate sufficient appropriate evidence required by the third standard of field work. Audit objectives are more useful to auditors than assertions because they are more detailed and more closely related to helping the auditor accumulate sufficient appropriate evidence.

6-12

RECORDING MISSTATEMENT	TRANSACTION-RELATED AUDIT OBJECTIVE VIOLATED
Fixed asset repair is recorded on the wrong date.	Timing
Repair is capitalized as a fixed asset instead of an expense.	Classification

6-13 The existence objective deals with whether amounts included in the financial statements should actually be included. Completeness is the opposite of existence. The completeness objective deals with whether all amounts that should be included have actually been included.

In the audit of accounts receivable, a nonexistent account receivable will lead to overstatement of the accounts receivable balance. Failure to include a customer's account receivable balance, which is a violation of completeness, will lead to understatement of the accounts receivable balance.

6-14 Specific audit objectives are the application of the general audit objectives to a given class of transactions, account balance, or presentation and disclosure. There must be at least one specific audit objective for each general audit objective and in many cases there should be more. Specific audit objectives for a class of transactions, account balance, or presentation and disclosure should be designed such that, once they have been satisfied, the related general audit objective should also have been satisfied for that class of transactions, account, or presentation and disclosure.

6-15 For the specific balance-related audit objective, all recorded fixed assets exist at the balance sheet date, the management assertion and the general balance-related audit objective are both "existence."

6-16 Management assertions and general balance-related audit objectives are consistent for all asset accounts for every audit. They were developed by the Auditing Standards Board, practitioners, and academics over a period of time. One or more specific balance-related audit objectives are developed for each general balance-related audit objective in an audit area such as accounts receivable. For any given account, a CPA firm may decide on a consistent set of specific balance-related audit objectives for accounts receivable, or it may decide to use different objectives for different audits.

6-17 For the specific presentation and disclosure-related audit objective, read the fixed asset footnote disclosure to determine that the types of fixed assets, depreciation methods and useful lives are clearly disclosed, the management assertion and the general presentation and disclosure-related audit objective are both "classification and understandability."

6-18 The four phases of the audit are:

1. Plan and design an audit approach.
2. Perform tests of controls and substantive tests of transactions.
3. Perform analytical procedures and tests of details of balances.
4. Complete the audit and issue an audit report.

The auditor uses these four phases to meet the overall objective of the audit, which is to express an opinion on the fairness with which the financial statements present fairly, in all material respects, the financial position, results of operations and cash flows in conformity with applicable accounting standards. By accumulating sufficient appropriate evidence for each audit objective throughout the four phases of the audit, the overall objective is met.

■ Multiple Choice Questions From CPA Examinations

6-19 a. (2)   b. (3)   c. (1)

6-20 a. (1)   b. (2)   c. (1)

6-21 a. (3)   b. (2)   c. (2)

■ Discussion Questions And Problems

6-22 a.   The purpose of the first part of the report of management is for management to state its responsibilities for internal control over financial reporting. The second part of the report states management's responsibility for the fair presentation of the financial statements.

   b.   The auditor's responsibility is to express an opinion on the fairness of the presentation of the financial statements and an opinion on the effectiveness of internal control over financial reporting.

6-23 a.   Auditing standards indicate that reasonable assurance is a high level of assurance. Accordingly, financial statement users should have a high degree of confidence in the financial statements. However, reasonable assurance is not an absolute level of assurance, and there is at least some risk that the audited financial statements may include material misstatements.

   b.   The responsibility of the independent auditor is to express an opinion on the financial statements he or she has audited. Inasmuch as the financial statements are the representation of management, responsibility rests with management for the proper recording of transactions in books of account, for the safeguarding of assets, and for the substantial accuracy and adequacy of the financial statements.

   In developing the basis for his or her opinion, the auditor is responsible for conducting an audit that conforms to auditing standards. These standards constitute the measure of the adequacy of the audit. Those standards require the auditor to obtain sufficient appropriate evidence about material management assertions in the financial statements.

   The informed judgment of a qualified professional accountant is required of an independent auditor. The auditor must exercise this judgment in selecting the procedures he or she uses in the audit and in arriving at an opinion.

   In presenting himself or herself to the public as an independent auditor, the auditor is responsible for having the abilities expected of a qualified person in that profession. Such qualifications do not include those of an appraiser, valuer, expert in materials, expert in styles, insurer, or lawyer. The auditor is entitled to rely upon the judgment of experts in these other areas of knowledge and skill.

6-23 (continued)

c. Auditors are responsible for obtaining reasonable assurance that material misstatements included in the financial statements are detected, whether those misstatements are due to error or fraud. Professional standards acknowledge that it is often more difficult to detect fraud than errors because management or employees perpetrating the fraud attempt to conceal the fraud. That difficulty, however, does not change the auditor's responsibility to properly plan and perform the audit. Auditors are required to specifically assess the risk of material misstatement due to fraud and should consider that assessment in designing the audit procedures to be performed.

There has been increased emphasis on auditors' responsibility to evaluate factors that may indicate an increased likelihood that fraud may be occurring. For example, assume that management is dominated by a president who makes most of the major operating and business decisions himself. He has a reputation in the business community for making optimistic projections about future earnings and then putting considerable pressure on operating and accounting staff to make sure those projections are met. He has also been associated with other companies in the past that have gone bankrupt. These factors, considered together, may cause the auditor to conclude that the likelihood of fraud is fairly high. In such a circumstance, the auditor should put increased emphasis on searching for material misstatements due to fraud.

The auditor may also uncover circumstances during the audit that may cause suspicions of fraudulent financial reporting. For example, the auditor may find that management has lied about the age of certain inventory items. When such circumstances are uncovered, the auditor must evaluate their implications and consider the need to modify audit evidence.

Adequate internal control should be the principal means of thwarting and detecting misappropriation of assets. To rely entirely on an independent audit for the detection of misappropriation of assets would require expanding the auditor's work to the extent that the cost might be prohibitive.

The auditor normally assesses the likelihood of material misappropriation of assets as a part of understanding the entity's internal control and assessing control risk. Audit evidence should be expanded when the auditor finds an absence of adequate controls or failure to follow prescribed procedures, if he or she believes a material fraud could result.

Because the auditor's responsibility is limited to material misstatements, we believe that the auditor's responsibility is appropriate. However, some students may take the position that the auditor's responsibility to detect fraud is too great because of the potential for collusion and deception by management.

The independent auditor is not an insurer or guarantor. The auditor's implicit obligation is that the audit be performed with due professional skill and care in accordance with auditing standards. A subsequent discovery of fraud, existent during the period covered by the independent audit, does not of itself indicate negligence on the auditor's part.

6-24   a.

CYCLE	BALANCE SHEET ACCOUNTS	INCOME STATEMENT ACCOUNTS
SALES AND COLLECTION	Accounts receivable Allowance for doubtful accounts Cash Notes receivable—trade	Bad debt expense Sales
ACQUISITION AND PAYMENT	Accounts payable Accumulated depreciation — furniture and equipment Cash Furniture and equipment Income tax payable Inventory Prepaid insurance Property tax payable	Advertising expense Depreciation expense— furniture and equipment Income tax expense Insurance expense Purchases Property tax expense Rent expense Telecommunications expense
PAYROLL AND PERSONNEL	Cash Accrued sales salaries	Sales salaries expense Salaries, office and general
INVENTORY AND WAREHOUSING	Inventory	Purchases
CAPITAL ACQUISITION AND REPAYMENT	Accrued interest expense Common stock Cash Loans payable Notes payable Retained earnings	Interest expense

6-24 (continued)

    b.   The general ledger accounts are not likely to differ much between a retail and a wholesale company unless there are departments for which there are various categories. There would be large differences for a hospital or governmental unit. A governmental unit would use the fund accounting system and would have entirely different titles. Hospitals are likely to have several different kinds of revenue accounts, rather than sales. They are also likely to have such things as drug expense, laboratory supplies, etc. At the same time, even a governmental unit or a hospital will have certain accounts such as cash, insurance expense, interest income, rent expense, and so forth.

6-25

    a.   Management assertions about transactions relate to transactions and other events that are reflected in the accounting records. In contrast, assertions about account balances relate to the ending account balances that are included in the financial statements, and assertions about presentation and disclosure relate to how those balances are reflected and disclosed in the financial statements.

    b., c.   (See following page)

6-25 (continued)

MANAGEMENT ASSERTION	b. CATEGORY OF MANAGEMENT ASSERTION	c. NAME OF ASSERTION
a. All sales transactions have been recorded.	Classes of transactions	Completeness
b. Receivables are appropriately classified as to trade and other receivables in the financial statements and are clearly described.	Presentation and disclosure	Classification and understandability
c. Accounts receivable are recorded at the correct amounts.	Account balances	Valuation and allocation
d. Sales transactions have been recorded in the proper period.	Classes of transactions	Cutoff
e. Sales transactions have been recorded in the appropriate accounts.	Classes of transactions	Classification
f. All required disclosures about sales and receivables have been made.	Presentation and disclosure	Completeness
g. All accounts receivable have been recorded.	Account balances	Completeness
h. There are no liens or other restrictions on accounts receivable.	Account balances	Rights and obligations
i. Disclosures related to accounts receivable are at the correct amounts.	Presentation and disclosure	Accuracy and valuation
j. Recorded sales transactions have occurred.	Classes of transactions	Occurrence
k. Recorded accounts receivable exist.	Account balances	Existence
l. Sales transactions have been recorded at the correct amounts.	Classes of transactions	Accuracy
m. Disclosures related to sales and receivables relate to the entity.	Presentation and disclosure	Occurrence and rights and obligations

6-26

SPECIFIC BALANCE-RELATED AUDIT OBJECTIVE	MANAGEMENT ASSERTION	COMMENTS
a. There are no unrecorded receivables.	2. Completeness	Unrecorded transactions or amounts deal with the completeness objective.
b. Receivables have not been sold or discounted.	4. Rights and obligations	Receivables not being sold or discounted concerns the rights and obligations objective and assertion.
c. Uncollectible accounts have been provided for.	3. Valuation or allocation	Providing for uncollectible accounts concerns whether the allowance for uncollectible accounts is adequate. It is part of the realizable value objective and the valuation or allocation assertion.
d. Receivables that have become uncollectible have been written off.	3. Valuation or allocation	This is part of the realizable value objective and the valuation or allocation assertion. There may also be some argument that this is part of the existence objective and assertion. Accounts that are uncollectible are no longer valid assets.
e. All accounts on the list are expected to be collected within one year.	3. Valuation or allocation	Accounts that are not expected to be collected within a year should be classified as long-term receivables. It is therefore included as part of the classification objective and consequently under the valuation or allocation assertion.
f. The total of the amounts on the accounts receivable listing agrees with the general ledger balance for accounts receivable.	3. Valuation or allocation	This is part of the detail tie-in objective and is part of the valuation or allocation assertion.

6-26 (continued)

	SPECIFIC BALANCE-RELATED AUDIT OBJECTIVE	MANAGEMENT ASSERTION	COMMENTS
g.	All accounts on the list arose from the normal course of business and are not due from related parties.	3. Valuation or allocation	Concerns the classification of accounts receivable and is therefore a part of the classification objective and the valuation or allocation assertion.
h.	Sales cutoff at year-end is proper.	3. Valuation or allocation	Cutoff is a part of the cutoff objective and therefore part of the valuation or allocation assertion.

6-27 a. Management assertions are implied or expressed representations by management about the classes of transactions and related accounts in the financial statements. AU 326 identifies five assertions about classes of transactions which are stated in the problem. These assertions are the same for every transaction cycle and account. General transaction-related audit objectives are essentially the same as management assertions, but they are expanded somewhat to help the auditor decide which audit evidence is necessary to satisfy the management assertions. Accuracy and posting and summarization are a subset of the accuracy assertion. Specific transaction-related audit objectives are determined by the auditor for each general transaction-related audit objective. These are done for each transaction cycle to help the auditor determine the specific amount of evidence needed for that cycle to satisfy the general transaction-related audit objectives.

    b.

and

    c. The easiest way to do this problem is to first identify the general transaction-related audit objectives for each specific transaction-related audit objective. It is then easy to determine the management assertion using Table 6-3 (p. 158 in text) as a guide.

6-27 (continued)

SPECIFIC TRANSACTION-RELATED AUDIT OBJECTIVE	b. MANAGEMENT ASSERTION	c. GENERAL TRANSACTION-RELATED AUDIT OBJECTIVE
a. Recorded cash disbursement transactions are for the amount of goods or services received and are correctly recorded.	3. Accuracy	8. Accuracy
b. Cash disbursement transactions are properly included in the accounts payable master file and are correctly summarized.	3. Accuracy	9. Posting and summarization
c. Recorded cash disbursements are for goods and services actually received.	1. Occurrence	6. Occurrence
d. Cash disbursement transactions are properly classified.	4. Classification	10. Classification
e. Existing cash disbursement transactions are recorded.	2. Completeness	7. Completeness
f. Cash disbursement transactions are recorded on the correct dates.	5. Cutoff	11. Timing

6-28

SPECIFIC PRESENTATION AND DISCLOSURE-RELATED AUDIT OBJECTIVE	MANAGEMENT ASSERTION
a. All required disclosures about fixed assets have been made.	2. Completeness
b. Footnote disclosures related to fixed assets are clear and understandable.	4. Classification and understandability
c. Methods and useful lives disclosed for each category of fixed assets are accurate.	3. Accuracy and valuation
d. Disclosed fixed asset dispositions have occurred.	4. Occurrence and rights and obligations

6-29 a. The first objective concerns amounts that should not be included on the list of accounts payable because there are no amounts due to such vendors. This objective concerns only the overstatement of accounts payable. The second objective concerns the possibility of accounts payable that should be included but that have not been included. This objective concerns only the possibility of understated accounts payable.

b. The first objective deals with existence and the second deals with completeness.

c. For accounts payable, the auditor is usually most concerned about understatements. An understatement of accounts payable is usually considered more important than overstatements because of potential legal liability. The completeness objective is therefore normally more important in the audit of accounts payable. The auditor is also concerned about overstatements of accounts payable. The existence objective is also therefore important in accounts payable, but usually less so than the completeness objective.

AUDIT PROCEDURE	BALANCE-RELATED AUDIT OBJECTIVE	TRANSACTION RELATED AUDIT OBJECTIVE	PRESENTATION AND DISCLOSURE AUDIT OBJECTIVE
a. Examine a sample of duplicate sales invoices to determine whether each one has a shipping document attached.		(9) Occurrence	
b. Add all customer balances in the accounts receivable trial balance and agree the amount to the general ledger.	(6) Detail Tie-In		
c. For a sample of sales transactions selected from the sales journal, verify that the amount of the transaction has been recorded in the correct customer account in the accounts receivable subledger.		(14) Posting and summarization	
d. Inquire of the client whether any accounts receivable balances have been pledged as collateral on long-term debt and determine whether all required information is included in the footnote description for long-term debt.			(15) Occurrence and rights
e. For a sample of shipping documents selected from shipping records, trace each shipping document to a transaction recorded in the sales journal.		(10) Completeness	
f. Discuss with credit department personnel the likelihood of collection of all accounts as of December 31, 2011 with a balance greater than $100,000 and greater than 90 days old as of year-end.	(7) Realizable value		
g. Examine sales invoices for the last five sales transactions recorded in the sales journal in 2011 and examine shipping documents to determine they are recorded in the correct period.	(5) Cutoff		

AUDIT PROCEDURE	BALANCE-RELATED AUDIT OBJECTIVE	TRANSACTION RELATED AUDIT OBJECTIVE	PRESENTATION AND DISCLOSURE AUDIT OBJECTIVE
h. For a sample of customer accounts receivable balances for December 31, 2011, examine subsequent cash receipts in January 2012 to determine whether the customer paid the balance due.	(1) Existence (7) Realizable value		
i. Determine whether all risks related to accounts receivable are adequately disclosed.			(16) Completeness
j. Foot the sales journal for the month of July and trace postings to the general ledger.		(14) Posting and summarization	
k. Send letters to a sample of accounts receivable customers to verify whether they have an outstanding balance at December 31, 2011.	(1) Existence		
l. Determine wither long-term receivables and related party receivables are reported separately in the financial statements.			(18) Classification and understandability

6-31

AUDIT ACTIVITIES	AUDIT PHASE
a. Examine invoices supporting fixed asset additions.	3. Perform analytical procedures and tests of details of balances (Phase III)
b. Review industry databases to assess the risk of material misstatements in the financial statements.	1. Plan and design an audit approach (Phase I)
c. Summarize misstatements identified during testing to assess whether the overall financial statements are fairly stated.	4. Complete the audit and issue an audit report (Phase IV)
d. Test computerized controls over credit approval for sales transactions.	2. Perform tests of controls and substantive tests of transactions (Phase II)
e. Send letters to customers confirming outstanding accounts receivable balances.	3. Perform analytical procedures and tests of details of balances (Phase III)
f. Perform analytical procedures comparing the client with similar companies in the industry to gain an understanding of the client's business and strategies.	1. Plan and design an audit approach (Phase I)
g. Compare information on purchase invoices recorded in the acquisitions journal with information on receiving reports.	2. Perform tests of controls and substantive tests of transactions (Phase II)

■ **Case**

6-32 a. A review provides limited assurance about the fair presentation of financial statements in accordance with accounting standards but far less assurance than an audit. Presumably, the bank decided that the assurances provided by a review were needed before a loan could be approved, but an audit was not necessary. A review includes a CPA firm performing analytical procedures, making inquiries about the fair presentation of the statements, and examining the information for reasonableness. Because of a CPA firm's expertise in accounting, the accountant from the CPA firm can often identify incorrect presentations in the financial statements that have been overlooked by the accountant for the company. Reviews are common for smaller privately-held companies with relatively small amounts of debt.

The bank probably did not require an audit because the additional cost of an audit was greater than the benefit the bank perceived. In many cases, the decision as to whether to have a review or an audit is negotiated between the company seeking a loan and the bank loan officer. Both the company and the bank have options in negotiating such things as the amount of the loan, the rate of interest, and whether to require an audit or a review. The bank can reject the loan request and the company can go to other banks that want to make loans.

Frequently, banks have a list of CPA firms in which they have considerable confidence due to their reputation in the community or past work they have done for other bank customers.

b.   Because the amount of the loans from the bank to Ritter increased, the bank probably wanted additional assurance about the reliability of the financial statements. It is also likely that Rene Ritter negotiated the one percent reduction of the interest rate by offering to have an audit instead of a review. A one percent reduction in the interest rate saves Ritter $40,000 annually compared to the $15,000 additional fee for an audit.

c.   Rene referred to the CPA firm as partners in a professional sense, not a business sense. The CPA firm had provided many consulting and tax services, as well as providing review and audit services over the entire business life of the company. Rene recognized that these professional services had contributed to the success of the business and she chose to acknowledge those contributions during her retirement comment. Assuming that the CPA firm retained an attitude of independence throughout all audits and reviews, no violation of professional independence standards occurred. Most well run CPA firms provide selected consulting, tax, and assurance service for their privately held clients without violating independence requirements.

d.   As the external auditor, the firm of Gonzalez & Fineberg provides the stockholders, creditors, and management an independent opinion as to the fair presentation of the financial statements. Given the potential biases present when management prepares the financial statements, the stockholders and creditors must consider the potential for information risk that might be present. The independent audit conducted by Gonzalez & Fineberg helps stockholders and creditors reduce their information risk. Management also benefits by having the external auditors independently assess the financial statements even though those statements are prepared by management. Due to the complexities involved in preparing financial statements, the potential for misstatement on the part of management increases the need for an objective examination of those financial statements by a qualified independent party.

6-32 (continued)

e. The auditor is responsible for obtaining reasonable assurance that material misstatements are detected, whether those misstatements are due to errors or fraud. To obtain reasonable assurance, the auditor is required to gather sufficient, appropriate evidence. Auditors' chief responsibility to stockholders, creditors, and management is to conduct the audit in accordance with auditing standards in order to fulfill their responsibilities of the engagement.

■ Internet Problem Solution: International and PCAOB Audit Objectives

Internet Problem 6-1

a. Paragraph .01 of AU 110 states that "[T]he objective of the ordinary audit of financial statements by the independent auditor is the expression of an opinion on the fairness with which they present, in all material respects, financial position, results of operations, and its cash flows in conformity with generally accepted accounting principles." U.S. GAAS require the auditor to express an opinion on whether the financial statements are presented in conformity with generally accepted accounting principles and to identify those circumstances in which such principles have not been consistently observed in the preparation of financial statements.

   Paragraph .11 of ISA 200 states that "In conducting an audit of financial statements, the overall objectives of the auditor are (a) to obtain reasonable assurance about whether the financial statements as a whole are free from material misstatement, whether due to fraud or error, thereby enabling the auditor to express an opinion on whether the financial statements are prepared, in all material respects, in accordance with an applicable financial reporting framework and (b) to report on the financial statements, and communicate as required by the ISAs, in accordance with the auditor's findings.

   While there are differences in the wording about the objective of an audit of financial statements, the overall objectives stated in U.S. GAAS and the ISAs are the same. Both U.S. GAAS and the ISAs note that the objective of the audit of financial statements is the expression of an opinion of whether the financial statements comply, in all material respects, with accounting standards.

b. Paragraph .03 of PCAOB Auditing Standard 5 states that "The auditor's objective in an audit of internal control over financial reporting is to express an opinion on the effectiveness of the company's internal control over financial reporting." That standard notes that to form a basis for an opinion, the auditor must plan and perform the audit to

Internet Problem 6-1 (continued)

        obtain competent evidence that is sufficient to obtain reasonable assurance about whether material weaknesses exist as of the date specified in management's assessment.

c.   Both U.S. GAAS and international auditing standards define financial statements as being fairly stated when they are free of material misstatements. PCAOB Auditing Standard 5 defines internal control as effective when no material weaknesses exist. These definitions are related. The presence of a material misstatement generally suggests the presence of a material weakness, since management's internal controls over financial reporting failed to detect the material misstatement. While the presence of a material weakness in internal control does not automatically mean the financial statements contain a material misstatement, there is a high likelihood that a material misstatement could occur.

(**Note**: Internet problems address current issues using Internet sources. Because Internet sites are subject to change, Internet problems and solutions may change. Current information on Internet problems is available at www.pearsonhighered.com/arens).

Chapter 7

Audit Evidence

■ **Review Questions**

7-1   In both a legal case and in an audit of financial statements, evidence is used by an unbiased person to draw conclusions. In addition, the consequences of an incorrect decision in both situations can be equally undesirable. For example, if a guilty person is set free, society may be in danger if the person repeats his or her illegal act. Similarly, if investors rely on materially misstated financial statements, they could lose significant amounts of money. Finally, the guilt of a defendant in a legal case must be proven beyond a reasonable doubt. This is similar to the concept of sufficient appropriate evidence in an audit situation. As with a judge or jury, an auditor cannot be completely convinced that his or her opinion is correct, but rather must obtain a high level of assurance.

The nature of evidence in a legal case and in an audit of financial statements differs because a legal case relies heavily on testimony by witnesses and other parties involved. While inquiry is a form of evidence used by auditors, other more reliable types of evidence such as confirmation with third parties, physical examination, and documentation are also used extensively. A legal case also differs from an audit because of the nature of the conclusions made. In a legal case, a judge or jury decides the guilt or innocence of the defendant. In an audit, the auditor issues one of several audit opinions after evaluating the evidence.

7-2   The four major audit evidence decisions that must be made on every audit are:

1. Which audit procedures to use.
2. What sample size to select for a given procedure.
3. Which items to select from the population.
4. When to perform the procedure.

7-3   An audit procedure is the detailed instruction for the collection of a type of audit evidence that is to be obtained. Because audit procedures are the instructions to be followed in accumulating evidence, they must be worded carefully to make sure the instructions are clear.

7-4   An audit program for accounts receivable is a list of audit procedures that will be used to audit accounts receivable for a given client. The audit procedures, sample size, items to select, and timing should be included in the audit program.

7-5   There are two primary reasons why the auditor can only be persuaded with a reasonable level of assurance, rather than be convinced that the financial statements are correct:

1.   The cost of accumulating evidence. It would be extremely costly for the auditor to gather enough evidence to be completely convinced.
2.   Evidence is normally not sufficiently reliable to enable the auditor to be completely convinced. For example, confirmations from customers may come back with erroneous information, which is the fault of the customer rather than the client.

7-6   The two determinants of the persuasiveness of evidence are appropriateness and sufficiency. Appropriateness refers to the relevance and reliability of evidence, or the degree to which evidence can be considered believable or worthy of trust. Appropriateness relates to the audit procedures selected, including the timing of when those procedures are performed. Sufficiency refers to the quantity of evidence and it is related to sample size and items to select.

7-7   Following are six characteristics that determine reliability and an example of each.

FACTOR DETERMINING RELIABILITY	EXAMPLE OF RELIABLE EVIDENCE
Independence of provider	Confirmation of a bank balance
Effectiveness of client's internal controls	Use of duplicate sales invoices for a large well-run company
Auditor's direct knowledge	Physical examination of inventory by the auditor
Qualifications of provider	Letter from an attorney dealing with the client's affairs
Degree of objectivity	Count of cash on hand by auditor
Timeliness	Observe inventory on the last day of the fiscal year

TYPES OF AUDIT EVIDENCE	EXAMPLES
1. Physical examination	■ Count petty cash on hand ■ Examine fixed asset additions
2. Confirmation	■ Confirm accounts receivable balances of a sample of client customers ■ Confirm client's cash balance with bank
3. Documentation	■ Examine copies of monthly bank statements ■ Examine vendors' invoices supporting a sample of cash disbursement transactions throughout the year
4. Analytical procedures	■ Evaluate reasonableness of receivables by calculating and comparing ratios ■ Compare expenses as a percentage of net sales with prior year's percentages
5. Inquiries of the client	■ Inquire of management whether there is obsolete inventory ■ Inquire of management regarding the collectibility of large accounts receivable balances
6. Recalculation	■ Recompute invoice total by multiplying item price times quantity sold ■ Foot the sales journal for a one-month period and compare all totals to the general ledger
7. Reperformance	■ Agree sales invoice price to approved price list ■ Match quantity on purchase invoice to receiving report
8. Observation	■ Observe client employees in the process of counting inventory ■ Observe whether employees are restricted from access to the check signing machine

7-9 The characteristics of a confirmation are:

1. Receipt
2. Written or electronic response
3. From independent third party
4. Requested by the auditor

A confirmation is prepared specifically for the auditor and comes from an external source. External documentation is in the hands of the client at the time of the audit and was prepared for the client's use in the day-to-day operation of the business.

7-10 *Internal documentation* is prepared and used within the client's organization without ever going to an outside party, such as a customer or vendor.

Examples:
- check request form
- receiving report
- payroll time card
- adjusting journal entry

External documentation either originated with an outside party or was an internal document that went to an outside party and is now either in the hands of the client or is readily accessible.

Examples:
- vendor's invoice
- cancelled check
- cancelled note
- validated deposit slip

7-11 Analytical procedures are useful for indicating account balances that may be distorted by unusual or significant transactions and that should be intensively investigated. They are also useful in reviewing accounts or transactions for reasonableness to corroborate tentative conclusions reached on the basis of other evidence.

7-12 The most important reasons for performing analytical procedures are the following:

1. Understanding the client's business and industry
2. Assessment of the entity's ability to continue as a going concern
3. Indication of the presence of possible misstatements in the financial statements
4. Reduction of detailed audit tests

7-13 The decrease of the current ratio indicates a liquidity problem for Harper Company since the ratio has dropped to a level close to the requirements of the bond indenture. Special care should be exercised by the auditor to determine that the 2.05 ratio is proper since management would be motivated to hide any lower ratio. The auditor should expand procedures to test all current assets for proper cutoff and possible overstatement and to test all current liabilities for proper cutoff and possible understatement.

7-14 Attention directing analytical procedures occur when significant, unexpected differences are found between current year's unaudited financial data and other data used in comparisons. If an unusual difference is large, the auditor must determine the reason for it, and satisfy himself or herself that the cause is a valid economic event and not an error or misstatement due to fraud.

7-14 (continued)

When an analytical procedure reveals no unusual fluctuations, the implication is minimized. In that case, the analytical procedure constitutes substantive evidence in support of the fair statement of the related account balances, and it is possible to perform fewer detailed substantive tests in connection with those accounts.

Frequently, the same analytical procedures can be used for attention directing and for reducing substantive tests, depending on the outcome of the tests. Simple procedures such as comparing the current year account balance to the prior year account balance is more attention directing (and provides less assurance) than more complex analytical procedures; i.e., those which rely on regression analysis or comparison to nonfinancial data. More sophisticated analytical procedures help the auditor examine relationships between several information variables simultaneously. The nature of these tests may provide greater assurance than simple procedures.

7-15 The purposes of audit documentation are as follows:

1. To provide a basis for planning the audit. The auditor may use reference information from the previous year in order to plan this year's audit, such as the evaluation of internal control, the time budget, etc.

2. To provide a record of the evidence accumulated and the results of the tests. This is the primary means of documenting that an adequate audit was performed.

3. To provide data for deciding the proper type of audit report. Data are used in determining the scope of the audit and the fairness with which the financial statements are stated.

4. To provide a basis for review by supervisors and partners. These individuals use the audit documentation to evaluate whether sufficient appropriate evidence was accumulated to justify the audit report.

Audit documentation is for several purposes, both during the audit and after the audit is completed. One of the uses is the review by more experienced personnel. A second is for planning the subsequent year audit. A third is to demonstrate that the auditor has accumulated sufficient appropriate evidence if there is a need to defend the audit at a later date. For these uses, it is important that the audit documentation provide sufficient information so that the person reviewing an audit schedule knows the name of the client, contents of the audit schedule, period covered, who prepared the audit schedule, when it was prepared, and how it ties into the rest of the audit files with an index code.

7-16 The Sarbanes-Oxley Act of 2002 requires auditors of public companies to prepare and maintain audit schedules and other information related to any audit report in sufficient detail to support the auditor's conclusions, for a period of not less than 7 years.

7-17 Audit schedules should include the following:

Name of the client Enables the auditor to identify the appropriate file to include the audit schedule in if it is removed from the files.

Period covered Enables the auditor to identify the appropriate year to which an audit schedule for a client belongs if it is removed from the files.

Description of the contents A list of the contents enables the reviewer to determine whether all important parts of the audit schedule have been included. The contents description is also used as a means of identifying audit files in the same manner that a table of contents is used.

Initials of the preparer Indicates who prepared the audit schedule in case there are questions by the reviewer or someone who wants information from the files at a later date. It also clearly identifies who is responsible for preparing the audit documentation if the audit must be defended.

Date of preparation Helps the reviewer to determine the sequence of the preparation of the audit schedules. It is also useful for the subsequent year in planning the sequence of preparing audit schedules.

Indexing Helps in organizing and filing audit schedules. Indexing also facilitates in searching between related portions of the audit documentation.

7-18 The permanent file contains data of an historical and continuing nature pertinent to the current audit. Examples of items included in the file are:

1. Articles of incorporation
2. Bylaws, bond indentures, and contracts
3. Analysis of accounts that have continuing importance to the auditor
4. Information related to the understanding of internal control:
    a. flowcharts
    b. internal control questionnaires
5. Results of previous years' analytical procedures, such as various ratios and percentages compiled by the auditors

By separating this information from the current year's audit files, it becomes easily accessible for the following year's auditors to obtain permanent file data.

7-19 The purpose of an *analysis* is to show the activity in a general ledger account during the entire period under audit, tying together the beginning and ending balances. The *trial balance* includes the detailed make-up of an ending balance. It differs from an analysis in that it includes only those items comprising the end of the period balance. A *test of reasonableness* schedule contains information that enables the auditor to evaluate whether a certain account balance appears to be misstated. One example of a test of reasonableness schedule is a schedule that compares current year expenses to prior years' amounts. This type of schedule is intended to show which accounts need investigation due to significant variances.

7-20 Unanswered questions and exceptions may indicate the potential for significant errors or fraud in the financial statements. These should be investigated and resolved to make sure that financial statements are fairly presented.

The audit files can also be subpoenaed by courts as legal evidence. Unanswered questions and exceptions may indicate lack of due care by the auditor.

7-21 Tick marks are symbols adjacent to information in audit schedules for the purpose of indicating the work performed by the auditor. An explanation of the tick mark must be included at the bottom of the audit schedule to indicate what was done and who did it.

7-22 Audit files are owned by the auditor. They can be used by the client if the auditor wants to release them after a careful consideration of whether there might be confidential information in them. The audit files can be subpoenaed by a court and thereby become the property of the court. They can be released to another CPA firm without the client's permission if they are being reviewed as a part of a voluntary peer review program under AICPA, state CPA society, or state Board of Accountancy authorization. The audit files can be sold or released to other users *if* the auditor obtains permission from the client.

7-23 When evidence can be examined only in machine-readable form, auditors use computers to read and examine evidence. There are commercial audit software programs designed specifically for use by auditors, such as ACL Software and Interactive Data Extraction and Analysis (IDEA). Spreadsheet software packages can also be used by auditors to perform audit tests on data that is available only in machine-readable form.

7-24 The purposes of audit documentation software are to convert traditional paper-based documentation into electronic files and to organize the audit documentation. The benefits of audit documentation software are as follows:

- The auditor can more efficiently prepare a trial balance, lead schedules, supporting audit documentation, financial statements, and ratio analysis using the computer rather than by hand.
- The effects of adjusting journal entries are automatically carried through to the trial balance and financial statements, making last-minute adjustments easier to make.
- Tick marks and review notes can be entered directly into computerized files.
- Data can be imported and exported to other applications. For example, a client's general ledger can be downloaded and tax information can be downloaded into a commercial tax preparation package after the audit is completed.

■ **Multiple Choice Questions From CPA Examinations**

7-25 a. (2) b. (2) c. (4) d. (4)

7-26 a. (3) b. (3) c. (4) d. (4)

■ Discussion Questions And Problems

7-27 a.

1. External	7. Internal	13. Internal
2. Internal	8. Internal	14. External
3. External	9. External	15. Internal
4. External	10. Internal*	16. External
5. Internal*	11. External	17. External
6. Internal	12. External**	18. External

    *   Even though these may be signed or initialed by employees, they are still internal documents.

    **   Bills of lading are ordinarily signed by the freight company. That signature will be included on the top of the bill of lading, therefore, it is an external document.

b. External evidence is considered more reliable than internal evidence because external evidence has been in the hands of both the client and another party, implying agreement about the information and the conditions stated on the document.

7-28

1.	(5)	inquiry of client
2.	(3)	documentation
3.	(6)	recalculation
4.	(1)	physical examination
5.	(2)	confirmation
6.	(6)	recalculation
7.	(2)	confirmation
8.	(3)	documentation
9.	(4)	analytical procedures
10.	(5)	inquiry of client
11.	(7)	reperformance
12.	(8)	observation
13.	(1)	physical examination
14.	(4)	analytical procedures
15.	(3)	documentation
16.	(5)	inquiry of client
17.	(4)	analytical procedures
18.	(2)	confirmation

7-29 Examples of audit evidence the auditor can use to support each of the functions are:

a. Examine invoice from vendor
    Direct confirmation with vendor
b. Physical examination
    Direct confirmation with custodian
c. Direct confirmation with customer
    Examine cash receipts journal and bank deposits for subsequent cash receipts
d. Examine title for ownership of asset
    Examine invoice from vendor
e. Direct confirmation with vendor
    Examine client's copy of vendor's statement
f. Physical examination
    Examine sales invoice of subsequent sale of goods showing marked down sale price
g. Count petty cash
    Direct confirmation with custodian

7-30 a. Confirmations are normally more reliable evidence than inquiries of the client because of the independence of the outside party confirming the information.
b. Confirmation of bank balances is considered highly reliable whereas confirmation of a department store charge account is often not considered reliable. Banks are accustomed to confirmations from auditors and normally maintain excellent accounting records, whereas most customers of department stores have neither characteristic.
c. If an auditor is not qualified to distinguish between valuable inventory (e.g., diamonds) and worthless inventory (e.g., glass), the physical examination of inventory would not be considered to be reliable evidence.
d. Recalculation tests are highly reliable because the auditor is able to gain 100% assurance of the accuracy, but the tests only verify whether the recorded amounts are accurately totaled. These tests do not uncover omissions or fictitious amounts.
e. Relatively reliable documentation examples include: vendor statements, bank statements, and signed lease agreements. Relatively unreliable documentation examples may be: copies of customer invoices, internal memoranda and other communications, and a listing of fixed asset additions.

     The difference between reliable and unreliable documentation examples above is whether they originate from outside or inside the client's organization. External information is considered more reliable than internal documentation.

7-30 (continued)

f. 1. Confirmation of accounts receivable - Corporation accustomed to confirmations compared to a member of the general public.
    2. Examination of the corporate minutes - Experienced partner compared to a new assistant.
    3. Physical observation of inventory - Auditor knowledgeable in the client's inventory compared to one who is not.
    4. Attorney's letter - General counsel compared to an attorney involved only with patents.

g. Analytical procedures are evidence of the likelihood of misstatements in the financial statements, but they are rarely sufficient by themselves to conclude that the statements are misstated. Other supportive evidence is needed to determine whether apparent misstatements are actually material.

7-31

ACCOUNT NAME	FROM WHOM CONFIRMED	INFORMATION TO BE CONFIRMED
CASH IN BANK	All banks in which Star had deposits during the year including those which may have had an account that was closed out during the year.	■ Name and address of the bank. ■ The amount on deposit for each account as of the balance sheet date plus the name of each account, the account number, whether or not the account is subject to withdrawal by check, and the interest rate if the account is interest bearing. ■ The amount for which Star was directly liable to the bank for loans as of the balance sheet date plus the date of the loan, the due date, the interest rate, the date to which interest is paid, and description of the liability and collateral. ■ If internal controls over cash are weak, the auditor may wish to request that the bank include a list of authorized signatures with the confirmation.

7-31 (continued)

ACCOUNT NAME	FROM WHOM CONFIRMED	INFORMATION TO BE CONFIRMED
TRADE ACCOUNTS RECEIVABLE	A representative sample of debtors at a selected confirmation date which may be either at the balance sheet or an interim date. Confirmations should also be requested for the following types of accounts: ■ Accounts with large balances; ■ Past-due accounts; ■ Accounts with zero or credit balances; ■ Accounts written off during the current period; ■ Accounts whose collection is considered questionable; ■ Other accounts of an unusual nature.	The confirmation can be either a positive or negative form of request. The positive form requests the debtor to directly notify the auditor whether the information is correct and if not correct, which items are considered incorrect. The negative form requests a reply only if the information is incorrect. In both cases the information should include: ■ Name and address of the debtor ■ Account number (if applicable) ■ The confirmation "as of" date ■ The aged account balance *or* individual invoices included in such balance (with invoice date).
NOTES RECEIVABLE	A selected sample of notes receivable outstanding at the balance sheet date. If a note receivable was written off during the year, the balance written off should be confirmed.	■ Name and address of the debtor. ■ Date of the note. ■ Due date. ■ Unpaid balance at balance sheet date. ■ Payment arrangements. ■ Interest rate. ■ Date of last interest payment. ■ Collateral, if any, to secure the note.
INVENTORIES	Public warehouses or other outside custodians (if any).	■ Name and address of public warehouse or other outside custodian. ■ The inventory date. ■ Detailed lists of inventory stored. Under auditing standards, direct confirmation is acceptable provided supplemental inquiries are made that the inventory is the property of the company, unless the amount is a significant percent of current or total assets.

7-31 (continued)

ACCOUNT NAME	FROM WHOM CONFIRMED	INFORMATION TO BE CONFIRMED
TRADE ACCOUNTS PAYABLE	Suppliers from whom substantial purchases have been made during the year, regardless of the balances of their accounts at the balance sheet date.	■ Name and address of the supplier. ■ The amount due and the amount of any purchase commitments as of the balance sheet date. When internal controls are considered effective, the confirmation can be at an interim date; however, a thorough review must then be made of changes in the major accounts during the intervening period between the confirmation date and year-end. It should also be noted that with interim confirmation, the auditor loses a desirable audit procedure for disclosing unrecorded and contingent liabilities at the balance sheet date. As an alternative to confirmation letters, it is a common practice to ask the vendor to send, directly to the independent auditor, a statement of the vendor's account with the client as of the balance sheet date rather than send an accounts payable confirmation.
MORTGAGES PAYABLE	Mortgagee for each mortgage that has a balance at the balance sheet date.	■ Name and address of mortgagee. ■ Original amount. ■ Date of note. ■ Maturity date. ■ Balance due at balance sheet date. ■ Payment arrangements. ■ Interest rate. ■ Interest payment dates. ■ Date of last interest payment. ■ Nature of defaults and if any events of default are known to mortgagee. ■ Location of mortgaged property.
CAPITAL STOCK	If Star uses an outside transfer agent and registrar, confirmations should be sent to both.	■ Name and address of transfer agent and registrar. ■ Number of shares of common stock authorized, issued, outstanding, and held as treasury shares for the company as of the balance sheet date.

7-31 (continued)

ACCOUNT NAME	FROM WHOM CONFIRMED	INFORMATION TO BE CONFIRMED
LEGAL FEES	All of Star's major attorneys. Letters should also be sent to attorneys that the independent auditor knows the client has used extensively in prior years.	The auditor should request a letter from each attorney as to litigation being handled as of and subsequent to the balance sheet date. For each case, the attorney should give a description, report on its status as of the balance sheet date and as of the date of the letter, and give his or her opinion as to the ultimate liability. The attorney should also state Star's indebtedness to him or her as of the balance sheet date.
SALES AND EXPENSE ACCOUNTS	Occasionally, confirmation may be requested from an outside party for individual transactions contributing to total expenses or sales. This may be true where a major item is based on a formal contract and the auditor wants independent confirmation of agreement on the significant term of the contract and that these terms have been satisfactorily completed.	■ Name and address of outside party. ■ Other specific information would depend on the nature of the item and the reason the auditor believes it is necessary to confirm the item.

AUDIT PROCEDURE	a. TYPE OF AUDIT EVIDENCE	b. TRANSACTION- RELATED AUDIT OBJECTIVE
1. Trace from receiving reports to vendors' invoices and entry in the acquisitions journal.	Documentation	Completeness
2. Add the sales journal for the month of July and trace amounts to the general ledger.	Recalculation	Posting and summarization
3. Examine expense voucher packages and related vendors' invoices for approval of expense account classification.	Documentation	Classification
4. Observe opening of cash receipts to determine that cash receipts are promptly deposited and recorded.	Observation	Timing
5. Ask the accounts payable clerk about procedures for verifying prices, quantities and extensions on vendors' invoices.	Inquiries of client	Accuracy
6. Vouch entries in sales journal to sales invoices and related shipping documents.	Documentation	Occurrence

AUDIT PROCEDURE	a. TYPE OF AUDIT EVIDENCE	b. BALANCE- RELATED AUDIT OBJECTIVE
1. Test extend unit prices times quantity on the inventory list, test foot the list and compare the total to the general ledger.	Recalculation	Detail tie-in
2. Trace selected quantities from the inventory list to the physical inventory to make sure that it exists and the quantities are the same.	Physical examination	Existence and Accuracy
3. Question operating personnel about the possibility of obsolete or slow-moving inventory.	Inquiry of the client	Realizable value
4. Select a sample of quantities of inventory in the factory warehouse and trace each item to the inventory count sheets to determine if it has been included and if the quantity and description are correct.	Physical examination	Completeness and Accuracy
5. Compare the quantities on hand and unit prices on this year's inventory count sheets with those in the preceding year as a test for large differences.	Analytical procedures	Accuracy
6. Examine sales invoices and contracts with customers to determine whether any goods are out on consignment with customers. Examine vendors' invoices and contracts with vendors to determine if any goods on the inventory listing are owned by vendors.	Documentation	Rights
7. Send letters directly to third parties who hold the client's inventory and request they respond directly to the auditor.	Confirmation	Existence, Completeness, and Accuracy

7-34 a. The six factors determining the reliability of evidence are:
1. Independence of provider
2. Effectiveness of client's internal controls
3. Auditor's direct knowledge
4. Qualifications of individuals providing the information
5. Degree of objectivity
6. Timeliness

b. and c.

SITUATION	TYPE OF EVIDENCE THAT IS MORE RELIABLE	FACTOR AFFECTING RELIABILITY
1	Confirmation with business organizations	Qualifications of provider
2	Physically examine three-inch steel plates	Qualifications of provider (in this case the auditor)
3	Examine documents when several competent people are checking each other's work	Effectiveness of internal controls
4	Examine inventory of parts for the number of units on hand	Degree of objectivity
5	Discuss potential lawsuits with CPA firm's legal counsel	Independence of provider
6	Confirm a bank balance	Degree of objectivity
7	Confirm a bank balance	Independence of provider
8	Physically count the client's inventory	Auditor's direct knowledge
9	Physically count the inventory	Independence of provider and auditor's direct knowledge

7-35

PROCEDURE	a. APPROPRIATE TERM	b. TYPE OF EVIDENCE
1	Recompute (e)	Recalculation
2	Observe (j)	Observation
3	Compute (d)	Analytical procedure
4	Foot (f), Trace (g)	Recalculation and reperformance
5	Scan (b)	Analytical procedure
6	Inquire (k)	Inquiry of client
7	Count (i)	Physical examination
8	Confirm (l)	Confirmation
9	Examine (a), Compare (h)	Documentation
10	Read (c)	Documentation

7-36 a. The purposes of analytical procedures are:

    1.   Understanding the client's business and industry.
    2.   Assessment of the entity's ability to continue as a going concern.
    3.   Indication of the presence of possible misstatements in the financial statements.
    4.   Reduction of detailed audit tests.

    b.   Analytical procedures are required in the planning and completion phases of the audit because of their importance in planning the audit, and as a final review for potential misstatements. Auditors use analytical procedures extensively because of their relatively low cost and effectiveness in identifying potential misstatements.

    c.   The extent to which the auditor will use the results of analytical procedures to reduce detailed tests depends on the effectiveness of the analytical procedure and whether it supports the correctness of the recorded account balance. The effectiveness of the analytical procedure is a function of the precision of the expectation developed by the auditor and whether it is based on objective data.

7-37 In general, the audit schedule is not set up in a logical manner to show what the auditor wants to accomplish. The primary objective of the audit schedule is to verify the ending balance in notes receivable and interest receivable. A secondary objective is to account for all interest income, cash received and cash disbursed for new notes, collateral as security, and other information about the notes for disclosure purposes.

    Specific deficiencies of the audit schedule presented in the question are included below.

    a. and b.

a. DEFICIENCY	b. IMPROVEMENT

1. Tick mark explanation "tested" does not indicate specifically what was done.	Should have separate tick marks meaning:
	    Agreed to confirmation
	    Footed
	    Traced to cash receipts journal
	    Recomputed, etc.

2. Explanation of some tick marks is not given.	Explain all tick marks on the same page of the audit schedule.
3. Classification of long-term portion indicates no verification.	Recompute portions of notes that are long-term.
4. Paid-to-date row is confusing.	Column should say "date paid to" and this should be confirmed.
5. Due dates are missing for J.J. Co., P. Smith, and Tent Co.	Include due dates on the audit schedule for these notes.

7-37 (continued)

c.   **Spreadsheet Solution**

The purpose of using an Excel spreadsheet in this problem is to give the student some experience in preparing a simple audit schedule using an Excel spreadsheet. It should be explained to students that this type of audit schedule may or may not be prepared in actual practice, and that often templates are used to prepare more time-consuming audit schedules. Also, whether or not tick marks are computerized is a matter to be decided. The advantage is that the completed audit work can then be stored and reviewed electronically. On the other hand, it may be more efficient to indicate audit work manually as it is performed, and a contrast in the color of the tick marks through use of a colored pencil may be desirable.

The following solution was prepared with Excel (Filename P737.xls). The formulas used are self-evident, so no listing is provided, although it is available on the Companion Website. Two items deserve comment:

1.   An advantage of using a spreadsheet program for these types of analyses is that footing and crossfooting are done automatically.

2.   When auditor tick marks are done by computer, a problem arises as to how to place them on the worksheet. One could use narrow columns inserted between the scheduled client data, or, as done here, the tick marks are placed in blank rows beneath the related data.

7-37 (continued)

VANDERVOORT COMPANY
A/C #110 - NOTES RECEIVABLE
12/31/11

Account #110 - Notes Receivable

Maker	Date Made/Due	Interest Rate/Date Paid to	Face Amount	Value of Security	Balance 12/31/10	Additions	Payments	Balance 12/31/11	Interest Receivable 12/31/10	Interest Earned	Interest Recd	Interest Receivable 12/31/11
Apex Co. c *	6/15/10 / 06/15/12	5% / None pd.	5000	None	4000 Tp	0	1000 r	3000	104 Tp	175 ˅	0	279
Ajax, Inc. c *	11/21/10 / Demand	5% / 12/31/11	3591	None	3591 Tp	0	3591 r	0	0 Tp	102 ˅	102 r	0
J.J. Co. c *	11/1/10 / 04/01/16 ($200/Mo.)	5% / 12/31/11	13180	24000	12780 Tp	0	2400 r	10380	24 Tp	577 ˅	601 r	0
P. Smith c *	7/26/11 / 08/01/13 ($1000/Mo.)	5% / 09/30/11	25000	50000	0	25000 r	5000 r	20000	0	468 ˅	200 r	268
Martin-Peterson c *	5/12/10 / Demand	5% / 12/31/11	2100	None	2100 Tp	0	2100 r	0	0 Tp	105 ˅	105 r	0
Tent Co. c *	9/3/11 / 02/01/14 ($400/Mo.)	6% / 11/30/11	12000	10000	0	12000 r	1600 r	10400	0	162 ˅	108 r	54
			22471 f Tp			37000 f	15691 f	43780 f,cf wtb	128 f Tp	1589 f op	1116 f	601 f,cf wtb

Legend of Auditor's Tick Marks

f Footed
cf Crossfooted
Tp Traced to prior year audit files
wtb Traced total to working trial balance
op Traced total to operations audit schedule - OP6
* Examined note for payee, made and due dates, interest rate, face amount, and value of security. No exceptions noted.
c Received confirmation, including date interest paid to, interest rate, interest paid during 2011, note balance, and security. No exceptions noted.
r Traced to cash receipts records
˅ Recomputed for the year

■ **Cases**

7-38 The following are deficiencies in the sufficiency and appropriateness of the evidence in the audit of accounts payable for Grande Stores:

McClure Advertising Credits – An insufficient number of confirmations (four) were sent. The use of alternative procedures is probably acceptable. However, one credit was confirmed by telephone, rather than by written confirmation. Although the differences found were immaterial, the auditors should have determined the reason for the differences, and any errors should have been projected to the population.

Twenty additional credits were selected for testing. Whether this is a sufficient number is a matter of judgment, and depends on several factors. With a fairly small sample, it is critical that the items selected for testing adequately represent the population. The testing relied on internal documentation, which is insufficient to support the credits. The placing of the ad is insufficient evidence without supporting evidence from the vendor supporting the reduction in accounts payable.

Springbrook Credits – These credits were confirmed by telephone, and were not supported by a written confirmation. The staff auditor was suspicious of the client's unwillingness to allow written confirmation of the amounts, as well as the client's changing explanation of the nature of the credits, but did not perform additional testing to resolve any doubts about the validity of the credits.

Ridolfi Credits – The auditor obtained an oral confirmation that these credits were not valid. The client indicated that the auditor's information was incorrect, but would not allow the auditor to obtain written confirmation for these credits. In addition, the credit memos had been altered, which should have further indicated to the auditor that the credits were not valid.

Accounts Payable Accrual – The auditors sent 50 accounts payable confirmations. Whether this is a sufficient number of confirmations is a matter of auditor judgment. However, the adequacy of the confirmations as evidence is significantly undermined by the knowledge that the client told suppliers how to respond. As a result, the auditor should have verified the confirmed balances using alternative procedures. There is no discussion of the performance of alternative procedures for nonresponses, or the resolution of the six responses that were not reconciled to Grande's records.

The auditors agreed to an adjustment of $260,000 when their cutoff tests indicated a potential liability of $500,000. It would be appropriate for the auditors to agree to a lower amount only if additional testing supported a lower accrued liability.

7-39 The audit schedule contains the following deficiencies:

1. There is no indication of follow-up on the identified error in the accrued interest payable computation.
2. There is no indication whether the confirmation exception was resolved.
3. The loan with an unwaived violation of a provision of the debt agreement is misclassified as long-term.
4. The liability activities of Lender's Capital Corp. and the audit schedule totals do not crossfoot.
5. There is no indication of cross-referencing of the stockholder loan to the related party transactions audit schedule.
6. There is no investigation of the payment on the stockholder loan that was reborrowed soon after year-end.
7. There is no consideration of the need to impute interest on the 0% stockholder loan.
8. There is no indication that the dates under "interest paid to" were audited.
9. There is no indication that the unusually high average interest rate ($281,333/$1,406,667 = 20%) was noted and investigated.
10. The audit schedule does not support the overall conclusions expressed.
11. The tick mark "R" is used but not explained in the tick mark legend.
12. There is no indication that the audit schedule was prepared by client personnel.

■ **7-40 – ACL Problem Solution**

a. There are 44 payroll transactions in the Payroll file. *(This is determined by reading the number at the bottom of the screen.)*
b. The largest and smallest gross pay amounts for September are $4,395.83 and $1,278.33, respectively. *(Use Quick Sort.)*
c. Total gross pay for September was $99,585.46. (*Use the Total command.*)
d. The report on the following page shows gross pay by department. (*Use the Summarize command on the Gross Pay column, save to a file, and print.*) Note that this screenshot was produced using the "Screen" option in the Output tab of the Summarize window. Students' hardcopy printouts will appear slightly different, but will contain the same departmental totals.

7-40 – ACL Problem (continued)

Report for requirement d:

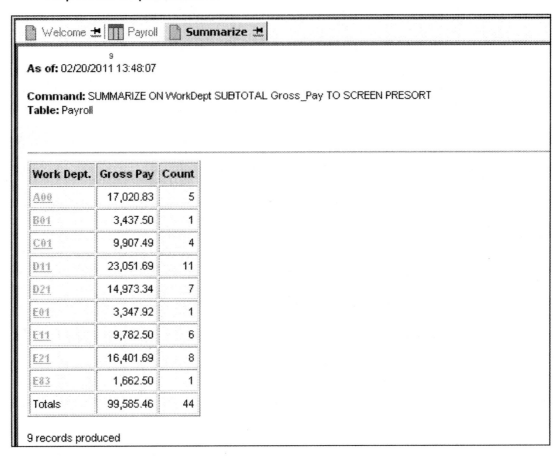

e. There are no exceptions in the calculation of net pay for September. (*Use the following Filter: Gross Pay – Taxes < > Net Pay.*)

f. There are no duplicate check numbers. (*Use the Duplicates command on the check [cheque] number column*). There are four missing checks (#12389 - #12392). The audit concern is that there may be unrecorded payroll transactions. (*Use the Gaps command on the check [cheque] number column.*)

■ **Internet Problem Solution: Use of Audit Software for Fraud Detection and Data Quality Assurance**

Internet Problem 7-1

a. ACL can be used to detect indicators of fraud for limitless volumes of transactions from many different types of data sources. Because companies generate very large amounts of data and use different information systems to generate that data, auditors must be able to overcome these potential constraints. ACL has the ability to handle huge volumes of data that are generated by various operating systems, database structures, and enterprise applications (e.g. ERP, CRM, SCM, and BI systems).

After data are captured, ACL can be used to independently test, reconcile, and validate transactional data. If performed manually, these types of procedures can take extraordinary amounts of time. ACL can identify trends, generate exception reports, and highlight potential areas of concern. Auditors can then use the information from the various analyses and conduct further audit procedures to determine whether a fraud has occurred.

b.   ACL's continuous monitoring software provides an independent mechanism to automatically monitor internal controls effectiveness within key business processes. Continuous monitoring allows companies to quickly identify issues and exceptions that might indicate control exposures. This will help companies identify risks and comply with testing requirements for management's report on the effectiveness of internal control.

(**Note**: Internet problems address current issues using Internet sources. Because Internet sites are subject to change, Internet problems and solutions may change. Current information on Internet problems is available at www.pearsonhighered.com/arens.)

Chapter 8

Audit Planning and Analytical Procedures

■ Review Questions

8-1 There are three primary benefits from planning audits: it helps the auditor obtain sufficient appropriate evidence for the circumstances, helps keep audit costs reasonable, and helps avoid misunderstandings with the client.

8-2 Eight major steps in planning audits are:

1. Accept client and perform initial planning
2. Understand the client's business and industry
3. Assess client business risk
4. Perform preliminary analytical procedures
5. Set materiality, and assess acceptable audit risk and inherent risk
6. Understand internal control and assess control risk
7. Gather information to assess fraud risks
8. Develop overall audit plan and audit program

8-3 The new auditor (successor) is required by auditing standards to communicate with the predecessor auditor. This enables the successor to obtain information about the client so that he or she may evaluate whether to accept the engagement. Permission must be obtained from the client before communication can be made because of the confidentiality requirement in the *Code of Professional Conduct*. The predecessor is required to respond to the successor's request for information; however, the response may be limited to stating that no information will be given. The successor auditor should be wary if the predecessor is reluctant to provide information about the client.

8-4 Prior to accepting a client, the auditor should investigate the client. The auditor should evaluate the client's standing in the business community, financial stability, and relations with its previous CPA firm. The primary purpose of new client investigation is to ascertain the integrity of the client and the possibility of fraud. The auditor should be especially concerned with the possibility of fraudulent financial reporting since it is difficult to uncover. The auditor does not want to needlessly expose himself or herself to the possibility of a lawsuit for failure to detect such fraud.

8-5 Auditing standards require auditors to document their understanding of the terms of the engagement with the client in an engagement letter. The engagement letter should include the engagement's objectives, the responsibilities of the auditor and management, and the engagement's limitations. An engagement letter is an agreement between the CPA firm and the client concerning the conduct of the audit and related services. It should state what services will be provided, whether any restrictions will be imposed on the auditor's work, deadlines for completing

8-5 (continued)

the audit, and assistance to be provided by client personnel. The engagement letter may also include the auditor's fees. In addition, the engagement letter informs the client that the auditor cannot guarantee that all acts of fraud will be discovered.

8-6 Because the Sarbanes-Oxley Act of 2002 explicitly shifts responsibility for hiring and firing of the auditor from management to the audit committee for public companies, the audit committee is viewed as "the client" in those engagements.

8-7 All audit and non-audit services must be preapproved in advance by the audit committee for public companies.

8-8 The second standard of fieldwork requires the auditor to obtain an understanding of the entity and its environment. Auditors need an understanding of the client's business and industry because the nature of the business and industry affect business risk and the risk of material misstatements in the financial statements. Auditors use the knowledge of these risks to assess the risk of material misstatement and to determine the appropriate extent of further audit procedures.

The five major aspects of understanding the client's business and industry, along with potential sources of information that auditors commonly use for each of the five areas are as follows:

1. *Industry and External Environment* – Read industry trade publications, AICPA Industry Audit Guides, and regulatory requirements.
2. *Business Operations and Processes* – Tour the plant and offices, identify related parties, and inquire of management.
3. *Management and Governance* – Read the corporate charter and bylaws, read minutes of board of directors and stockholders, and inquire of management.
4. *Client Objectives and Strategies* – Inquire of management regarding their objectives for the reliability of financial reporting, effectiveness and efficiency of operations, and compliance with laws and regulations; read contracts and other legal documents, such as those for notes and bonds payable, stock options, and pension plans.
5. *Measurement and Performance* – Read financial statements, perform ratio analysis, and inquire of management about key performance indicators that management uses to measure progress toward its objectives.

8-9 During the course of the plant tour the CPA will obtain a perspective of the client's business, which will contribute to the auditor's understanding of the entity and its environment. Remember that an important aspect of the audit will be an

8-9 (continued)

effective analysis of the inventory cost system. Therefore, the auditor will observe the nature of the company's products, the manufacturing facilities and processes, and the flow of materials so that the information obtained can later be related to the functions of the cost system.

The nature of the company's products and the manufacturing facilities and processes will reveal the features of the cost system that will require close audit attention. For example, the audit of a company engaged in the custom-manufacture of costly products such as yachts would require attention to the correct charging of material and labor to specific jobs, whereas the allocation of material and labor charges in the audit of a beverage-bottling plant would not be verified on the same basis. The CPA will note the stages at which finished products emerge and where additional materials must be added. He or she will also be alert for points at which scrap is generated or spoilage occurs. The auditor may find it advisable, after viewing the operations, to refer to auditing literature for problems encountered and solved by other CPAs in similar audits.

The auditor's observation of the manufacturing processes will reveal whether there is idle plant or machinery that may require disclosure in the financial statements. Should the machinery appear to be old or poorly maintained, the CPA might expect to find heavy expenditures in the accounts for repairs and maintenance. On the other hand, if the auditor determines that the company has recently installed new equipment or constructed a new building, he or she will expect to find these new assets on the books.

In studying the flow of materials, the auditor will be alert for possible problems that may arise in connection with the observation of the physical inventory, and he or she may make preliminary estimates of audit staff requirements. In this regard, the auditor will notice the various storage areas and how the materials are stored. The auditor may also keep in mind for further investigation any apparently obsolete inventory.

The auditor's study of the flow of materials will disclose the points at which various documents such as material requisitions arise. He or she will also meet some of the key manufacturing personnel who may give the auditor an insight into production problems and other matters such as excess or obsolete materials, and scrap and spoilage. The auditor will be alert for the attitude of the manufacturing personnel toward internal controls. The CPA may make some inquiries about the methods of production scheduling, timekeeping procedures and whether work standards are employed. As a result of these observations, the internal documents that relate to the flow of materials will be more meaningful as accounting evidence.

The CPA's tour of the plant will give him or her an understanding of the plant terminology that will enable the CPA to communicate fluently with the client's personnel. The measures taken by the client to safeguard assets, such as protection of inventory from fire or theft, will be an indication of the client's attention to internal control measures. The location of the receiving and shipping departments and the procedures in effect will bear upon the CPA's evaluation of internal control. The auditor's overall impression of the client's plant will suggest the accuracy and adequacy of the accounting records that will be audited.

8-10 One type of information the auditor obtains in gaining knowledge about the clients' industry is the nature of the client's products, including the likelihood of their technological obsolescence and future salability. This information is essential in helping the auditor evaluate whether the client's inventory may be obsolete or have a market value lower than cost.

8-11 A related party is defined by auditing standards as an affiliated company, principal owner of the client company, or any other party with which the client deals where one of the parties can influence the management or operating policies of the other.

Material related party transactions must be disclosed in the financial statements by management. Therefore, the auditor must identify related parties and make a reasonable effort to determine that all material related party transactions have been properly disclosed in the financial statements. Because instances of fraudulent financial reporting often involve transactions with related parties, auditors should be alert for the presence of fraud risk.

8-12 Because of the lack of independence between the parties involved, the Sarbanes-Oxley Act prohibits related party transactions that involve personal loans to executives. It is now unlawful for any public company to provide personal credit or loans to any director or executive officer of the company. Banks or other financial institutions are permitted to make normal loans to their directors and officers using market rates, such as residential mortgages.

8-13 The recent economic events have led to the collapse of several large financial services entities that has triggered a broader economic decline affecting all industries. The unstable economy has resulted in a significant slowdown in most businesses. These declines are likely to have a significant impact on financial reporting. First, severe market declines may impact the accounting for many types of investments and other assets that now may be impaired or may have experienced significant declines in their fair values. The determination of those accounts is largely dependent on numerous management judgments and estimates. Auditors should apply appropriate professional skepticism as they evaluate management's judgments and estimates. Second, the significant lack of sales and other revenues may be placing undue pressure on management to meet revenue targets, including the need for entity survival. Thus, there may be a greater presence of fraud risk due to these significant pressures. Third, auditors should closely evaluate the entity's ability to continue as a going concern. There may be several instances where the auditor's report should be modified to include an explanatory paragraph describing the auditor's substantial doubt about the entity's ability to continue as a going concern.

8-14 The information in a mortgage that is likely to be relevant to the auditor includes the following:

1. The parties to the agreement
2. The effective date of the agreement
3. The amounts included in the agreement
4. The repayment schedule required by the agreement
5. The definition and terms of default
6. Prepayment options and penalties specified in the agreement
7. Assets pledged or encumbered by the agreement
8. Liquidity restrictions imposed by the agreement
9. Purchase restrictions imposed by the agreement
10. Operating restrictions imposed by the agreement
11. Requirements for audit reports or other types of reports on compliance with the agreement
12. The interest rate specified in the agreement
13. Any other requirements, limitations, or agreements specified in the document

8-15 Information in the client's minutes that is likely to be relevant to the auditor includes the following:

1. Declaration of dividends
2. Authorized compensation of officers
3. Acceptance of contracts and agreements
4. Authorization for the acquisition of property
5. Approval of mergers
6. Authorization of long-term loans
7. Approval to pledge securities
8. Authorization of individuals to sign checks
9. Reports on the progress of operations
10. Discussion about outstanding litigation and other contingencies

It is important to read the minutes early in the engagement to identify items that need to be followed up on as a part of conducting the audit. For instance, if a long-term loan is authorized in the minutes, the auditor will want to make certain that the loan is recorded as part of long-term liabilities.

8-16 The three categories of client objectives are (1) reliability of financial reporting, (2) effectiveness and efficiency of operations, and (3) compliance with laws and regulations. Each of these objectives affects the auditor's assessment of inherent risk and evidence accumulation as follows:

1. *Reliability of financial reporting* – If management sees the reliability of financial reporting as an important objective, and if the auditor can determine that the financial reporting system is accurate and

8-16 (continued)

reliable, then the auditor can often reduce his or her assessment of inherent risk and planned evidence accumulation for material accounts. In contrast, if management has little regard for the reliability of management's financial reporting, the auditor must increase inherent risk assessments and gather more appropriate evidence during the audit.

2. *Effectiveness and efficiency of operations* – This area is of primary concern to most clients. Auditors need knowledge about the effectiveness and efficiency of a client's operations in order to assess client business risk and inherent risk in the financial statements. For example, if a client is experiencing inventory management problems, this would most likely increase the auditor's assessment of inherent risk for the planned evidence accumulation for inventory.

3. *Compliance with laws and regulations* – It is important for the auditor to understand the laws and regulations that affect an audit client, including significant contracts signed by the client. For example, the provisions in a pension plan document would significantly affect the auditor's assessment of inherent risk and evidence accumulation in the audit of unfunded liability for pensions. If the client were in violation of the provisions of the pension plan document, inherent risk and planned evidence for pension-related accounts would increase.

8-17 The purpose of a client's performance measurement system is to measure the client's progress toward specific objectives. Performance measurement includes ratio analysis and benchmarking against key competitors.

Performance measurements for a chain of retail clothing stores could include gross profit by product line, sales returns as a percentage of clothing sales, and inventory turnover by product line. An Internet portal's performance measurements might include number of Web site hits or search engine speed. A hotel chain's performance measures include vacancy percentages and supply cost per rented room.

8-18 *Client business risk* is the risk that the client will fail to achieve its objectives. Sources of client business risk include any of the factors affecting the client and its environment, including competitor performance, new technology, industry conditions, and the regulatory environment. The auditor's primary concern when evaluating client business risk is the risk of material misstatements in the financial statements due to client business risk. For example, if the client's industry is experiencing a significant and unexpected downturn, client business risk increases. This increase would most likely increase the risk of material misstatements in the financial statements. The auditor's assessment of the risk of material misstatements is then used to classify risks using the audit risk model to determine the appropriate extent of audit evidence.

8-19 Management establishes the strategies and business processes followed by a client's business. One top management control is management's philosophy and operating style, including management's attitude toward the importance of internal control. Other top management controls include a well-defined organizational structure, an effective board of directors, and an involved and effective audit committee. If the board of directors is effective, this increases management's ability to appropriately respond to risks. An effective audit committee can help management reduce the likelihood of overly aggressive accounting.

8-20 Analytical procedures are performed during the planning phase of an engagement to assist the auditor in determining the nature, extent, and timing of work to be performed. Preliminary analytical procedures also help the auditor identify accounts and classes of transactions where misstatements are likely. Comparisons that are useful when performing preliminary analytical procedures include:

- Compare client and industry data
- Compare client data with similar prior period data
- Compare client data with client-determined expected results
- Compare client data with auditor-determined expected results
- Compare client data with expected results, using nonfinancial data

8-21 Analytical procedures are required during two phases of the audit: (1) during the planning phase to assist the auditor in determining the nature, extent, and timing of work to be performed and (2) during the completion phase, as a final review for material misstatements or financial problems. Analytical procedures are also often done during the testing phase of the audit as part of the auditor's further audit procedures, but they are not required in this phase.

8-22 Gordon could improve the quality of his analytical tests by:

1. Making internal comparisons to ratios of previous years or to budget forecasts.
2. In cases where the client has more than one branch in different industries, computing the ratios for each branch and comparing these to the industry ratios.

8-23 Roger Morris performs ratio and trend analysis at the end of every audit. By that time, the audit procedures are completed. If the analysis was done at an interim date, the scope of the audit could be adjusted to compensate for the findings, especially when the results suggest a greater likelihood of material misstatements. Analytical procedures must be performed in the planning phase of the audit and near the completion of the audit.

The use of ratio and trend analysis appears to give Roger Morris an insight into his client's business and affords him an opportunity to provide excellent business advice to his client. It also helps provide a richer context for Roger to really understand his client's business, which should help Roger in assessing the risk of material misstatements.

8-24 The four categories of financial ratios and examples of ratios in each category are as follows:

1. *Short-term debt-paying ability* – Cash ratio, quick ratio, and current ratio.
2. *Liquidity activity* – Accounts receivable turnover, days to collect receivables, inventory turnover, and days to sell inventory.
3. *Ability to meet long-term debt obligations* – Debt to equity and times interest earned.
4. *Profitability* – Earnings per share, gross profit percent, profit margin, return on assets, and return on common equity

■ Multiple Choice Questions From CPA Examinations

8-25 a. (3)   b. (3)   c. (4)   d. (1)

8-26 a. (1)   b. (4)   c. (4)

8-27 a. (4)   b. (1)   c. (2)   d. (4)

■ Discussion Questions And Problems

8-28

Audit Activities	Related Planning Procedure
1. Send an engagement letter to the client.	(1) Accept client and perform initial audit planning
2. Tour the client's plant and offices.	(2) Understand the client's business and industry
3. Compare key ratios for the company to industry competitors.	(4) Perform preliminary analytical procedures
4. Review management's controls and procedures.	(3) Assess client's business risk
5. Review the accounting principles unique to the client's industry.	(2) Understand the client's business and industry.
6. Determine the likely users of the financial statements.	(1) Accept client and perform initial audit planning.
7. Identify potential related parties that may require disclosure.	(2) Understand the client's business and industry
8. Identify whether any specialists are required for the engagement.	(1) Accept client and perform initial audit planning

8-29 a.   A related party transaction occurs when one party to a transaction has the ability to impose contract terms that would not have occurred if the parties had been unrelated. Accounting standards conclude that related parties consist of all affiliates of an enterprise, including (1) its management and their immediate families, (2) its principal owners and their immediate families, (3) investments accounted for by the equity method, (4) beneficial employee trusts that are managed by the management of the enterprise, and (5) any party that may, or does, deal with the enterprise and has ownership, control, or significant influence over the management or operating policies of another party to the extent that an arm's-length transaction may not be achieved.

b.   (1)   Related party transaction. Canyon Outdoor has entered into an operating lease with a company owned by one of the directors on Canyon's board. Because the board has control and significant influence over management of Canyon, the lease transaction may not be at arm's length.

   (2)   Not a related party transaction. The fact that Canyon Outdoor has purchased inventory items for many years from Hessel Boating Company is a normal business transaction between two independent parties. Neither party has an ownership interest in the other party, and neither has an ability to exercise control or significance influence over the other.

   (3)   Related party transaction. The financing provided by Cameron Bank and Trust through the assistance of Suzanne may not be at arm's length given Suzanne's husband has control and significant influence over Canyon Outdoors and may have be able to influence the transaction through his wife's employment at the bank or through his influence over Canyon's management.

   (4)   Not a related party transaction. Just because the two owners are neighbors does not mean that either has significant influence or control over the other. Mere acquaintance does not suggest the transactions would not be at arm's length.

   (5)   Not a related party transaction. The declaration and approval of dividends payable to shareholders is a normal board function.

c.   When related party transactions or balances are material, the following disclosures are required:

   1.   The nature of the relationship or relationships.
   2.   A description of the transaction for the period reported on, including amounts if any, and such other information deemed necessary to obtain an understanding of the effect on the financial statements.

8-29 (continued)

3. The dollar volume of transactions and the effects of any change in the method of establishing terms from those used in the preceding period.
4. Amounts due from or to related parties, and if not otherwise apparent, the terms and manner of settlement.

d. Auditors can determine the existence of material transactions with related parties by performing the following procedures:

1. Obtain background information about the client in the manner discussed in this chapter to enhance understanding of the client's industry and business; i.e., examine corporate charter bylaws, minutes of board meetings, material contracts, etc.
2. Perform analytical procedures of the nature discussed in Chapters 7 and 8 to evaluate the possibility of business failure and assess areas where fraudulent financial reporting is likely.
3. Review and understand the client's legal obligations in the manner discussed in this chapter to become familiar with the legal environment in which the client operates.
4. Review the information available in the audit files, such as permanent files, audit programs, and the preceding year's audit documentation for the existence of material non-arm's-length transactions. Also discuss with tax and management personnel assigned to the client their knowledge of management involvement in material transactions.
5. Discuss the possibility of fraudulent financial reporting with company counsel after obtaining permission to do so from management.
6. When more than one CPA firm is involved in the audit, exchange information with them about the nature of material transactions and the possibility of fraudulent financial reporting.
7. Investigate whether material transactions occur close to year-end.
8. In all material transactions, evaluate whether the parties are economically independent and have negotiated the transaction on an arm's-length basis, and whether each transaction was transacted for a valid business purpose.
9. Whenever there are material non-arm's-length transactions, each one should be evaluated to determine its nature and the possibility of its being recorded at the improper amount. The evaluation should consider whether the transaction was transacted for a valid business purpose, was not unduly complex, and was presented in conformity with its substance.

8-29 (continued)

10. When management is indebted to the company in a material amount, evaluate whether management has the financial ability to settle the obligation. If collateral for the obligation exists, evaluate its acceptability and value.

11. Inspect entries in public records concerning the proper recording of real property transactions and personal property liens.

12. Make inquiries with related parties to determine the possibility of inconsistencies between the client's and related parties' understanding and recording of transactions that took place between them.

13. Inspect the records of the related party to a material transaction that is recorded by the client in a questionable manner.

14. When an independent party, such as an attorney or bank, is significantly involved in a material transaction, ascertain from them their understanding of the nature and purpose of the transaction.

8-30 a. First, the minutes of each meeting refer to the minutes of a previous meeting. The auditor should ensure that they have been provided access to all noted minutes, including the next year's minutes, probably for March 2012, to make sure the previous minutes referred to were those from October 21, 2011.

Additionally, the auditor will request the client to include a statement in the client representation letter stating that all minutes were provided to the auditor.

b.

INFORMATION RELEVANT TO 2011 AUDIT	AUDIT ACTION REQUIRED
March 5: 1. Increase in annual dividend payment.	Calculate the total dividends and determine that dividends paid to shareholders are properly reflected in the financial statements.
2. Approval of additional administration expenses to open offices in Portland.	During analytical procedures, an increase in administrative expenses should be included in the auditor's expectation of the expense balance. The auditor should be alert for other potential commitments that may have been made to open offices in the Northwest region.
3. Approval to engage in negotiations for a potential acquisition.	Determine the status of any potential acquisition or merger negotiations. Be alert for any commitments that may have been made as part of the negotiations process that may warrant financial statement disclosure.

8-30 (continued)

INFORMATION RELEVANT TO 2011 AUDIT	AUDIT ACTION REQUIRED
4. Potential negative findings from EPA investigation.	Evaluate the status of any resolution of negotiations with the EPA regarding findings in their report. Determine if any final determinations have been made about potential fines. Evaluate the need for recording any provisions for a loss contingency or disclosure of the status of the negotiations.
5. Officers' bonuses.	Determine whether bonuses were accrued at 12-31-10 and were paid in 2011. Consider the tax implications of unpaid bonuses to officers.
6. Discussion at the Audit Committee and Compensation Committee.	Determine what, if any, decisions made at either meeting have any impact on the audit of the financial statements.
October 21: 1. Reduction in sales and the related cutback in labor and shipping costs.	During analytical procedures, both the decrease in revenues and the decreases in labor and shipping costs should be included in the auditor's expectation of the related account balances. The auditor should be alert to the fact that the drop in operating performance might create undue incentives and pressures that could highlight the risk of fraud.
2. Approval of the acquisition and related financing.	Examine acquisition documentation and financing documentation to understand the impact to the financial statements for recording the acquisition and the debt transaction. Consider what commitments and contingencies exist and evaluate the appropriateness of the recording of the acquisition transaction and related disclosures.
3. Consideration of a new incentive stock option plan.	Determine if the new incentive stock option plan has been approved. If so, consider any accounting treatments required to reflect any commitments on the part of the company and evaluate the tax implication of the plan and need for related disclosure.
4. Identification of deficiencies in internal control.	Discuss with management the nature of the deficiencies in internal control and evaluate the impact of any remediation activities to address the deficiencies. Evaluate the impact of remediation on the auditor's tests of controls and need for substantive procedures.

8-30 (continued)

INFORMATION RELEVANT TO 2011 AUDIT	AUDIT ACTION REQUIRED
5. Resolution of the EPA report findings.	Examine the EPA resolution agreement and determine if the provision has been recorded for the expected costs to modify the air handling equipment . Consider the need for any additional disclosures of this resolution.
6. Discussion at the Audit Committee and Compensation Committee.	Determine what, if any, decisions made at either meeting have any impact on the audit of the financial statements.

    c.   The auditor should have obtained and read the March minutes, before completing the 12-31-10 audit. Two items were especially relevant and require follow-up for the 12-31-10 audit: the investigation by the EPA and approval for the 12-31-10 bonuses.

8-31

Statement	Related Stage of Audit
1. Not required during this stage.	2. Substantive testing
2. Should focus on enhancing the auditor's understanding of the client's business and the transactions and events that have occurred since the last audit date.	1. Planning the audit
3. Should focus on identifying areas that may represent specific risks relevant to the audit.	1. Planning the audit
4. Require documentation in the working papers of the auditor's expectation of the ratio or account balance.	2. Substantive testing
5. Do not result in detection of misstatements.	4. Statement is not correct concerning analytical procedures
6. Designed to obtain evidential matter about particular assertions related to account balances or classes of transactions.	2. Substantive testing

8-31 (continued)

Statement	Related Stage of Audit
7. Generally use data aggregated at a lower level than the other stages.	2. Substantive testing
8. Should include reading the financial statements and notes to consider the adequacy of evidence gathered.	3. Overall review
9. Involve reconciliation of confirmation replies with recorded book amounts.	4. Statement is not correct concerning analytical procedures
10. Use of preliminary or unadjusted working trial balance as a source of data.	1. Planning the audit
11. Expected to result in reduced level of detection risk.	2. Substantive testing

8-32 Here are expected values for each account except sales and the calculated difference between the expected value and actual recorded balance:

ACCOUNT	EXPECTED VALUE	DIFFERENCE IN EXPECTED AND RECORDED	REASONING TO SUPPORT EXPECTED VALUE
Executive salaries	**$563,348** ($546,940 x 103%)	-9.34% ($563,348 - $615,970) / $563,348	All executives received a 3 percent increase in salaries effective November 1, 2010. There were no additions to the number of executives in the current year.
Factory hourly payroll	**$11,167,246** Increase due to 3% payrate increase: ($10,038,877 x 3% =$301,166 increase due to payrate increase) 8% increase due to increased production ($10,038,877 + $301,166 = 10,340,043 x 108 % = $11,167,246)	-2.77% ($11,167,246-$11,476,319) / $11,167,246	The increase in factory hourly payroll is attributed to two primary factors. First, payroll expense would be expected to increase 3% over the prior year to account for the 3% wage increase for all employees (except executives). Second, payroll expense should increase 8% to account for the 8% increase in the number of units produced and sold.
Factory supervisors' salaries	**$809,400** ($785,825 x 103%)	-.15% ($809,400 - $810,588) / $809,400	All factory supervisors' salaries received a 3 percent increase effective November 1, 2010. There were no additions to the number of factory supervisors in the current year.
Office salaries	**$2,050,005** ($1,990,296 x 103%)	-.26% ($2,050,005 -$2,055,302) / $2,050,005	All office personnel received a 3 percent increase in salaries effective November 1, 2010. There were no additions to the number of office personnel in the current year.
Sales commissions	**$2,249,072** Increase in commissions due to increased sales: (5% x $4,618,461 = $230,923) $2,018,149 + $230,923 = 2,249,072	-5.3% $2,249,072 -$2,367,962) / $2,249,072	Sales increased by $6,157,948. Commissions are only earned on about 75% of the sales. Thus, only 75% of the increase ($4,618,461) would be considered in the calculation of commission expense. The fact that commissions are paid one month after they are earned does not affect commission expense for the year since management would have to accrue the expense for commissions earned but not paid as of October 31, 2011.

(Note: Sales have increased 12 percent over prior year. Four percent of that is due to an increase in the average selling price. The remaining 8 percent is attributed to an increase in the number of units sold.)

8-33 a. Gross margin percentage for drug and nondrug sales is as follows:

	DRUGS	NONDRUGS
2011	40.6%	32.0%
2010	42.2%	32.0%
2009	42.1%	31.9%
2008	42.3%	31.8%

The explanation given by Adams is correct in part, but appears to be overstated. The gross margin percentage for nondrugs is approximately consistent. For drugs, the percent dropped significantly in the current year, far more than industry declines. The percent had been extremely stable before 2011. In dollars, the difference is approximately $82,000 (42.2% - 40.6% x $5,126,000) which appears to be significant. Of course, the decline in Jones' prices may be greater than the industry due to exceptional competition.

b. As the auditor, you cannot accept Adams' explanation if $82,000 is material. The decline in gross margin could be due to an understatement of drug inventory, a theft of drug inventory, or understated sales. Further investigation is required to determine if the decline is due to competitive factors or to a misstatement of income.

8-34 a.
1. Commission expense could be overstated during the current year or could have been understated during each of the past several years. Or, sales may have been understated during the current year or could have been overstated in each of the past several years.
2. Obsolete or unsalable inventory may be present and may require markdown to the lower of cost or market.
3. Especially when combined with 2 above, there is a high likelihood that obsolete or unsalable inventory may be present. Inventory appears to be maintained at a higher level than is necessary for the company.
4. Collection of accounts receivable appears to be a problem. Additional provision for uncollectible accounts may be necessary.
5. Especially when combined with 4 above, the allowance for uncollectible accounts may be understated.
6. Depreciation expenses may be understated for the year.

8-34 (continued)

    b.   **ITEM 1** - Make an estimated calculation of total commission expense by multiplying the standard commission rate times commission sales for each of the last two years. Compare the resulting amount to the commission expense for that year. For whichever year appears to be out of line, select a sample of individual sales and recompute the commission, comparing it to the commission recorded.

        ITEMS 2 AND 3 - Select a sample of the larger inventory items (by dollar value) and have the client schedule subsequent transactions affecting these items. Note the ability of the company to sell the items and the selling prices obtained by the client. For any items that the client is selling below cost plus a reasonable markup to cover selling expenses, or for items that the client has been unable to sell, propose that the client mark down the inventory to market value.

        ITEMS 4 AND 5 - Select a sample of the larger and older accounts receivable and have the client schedule subsequent payments and credits for each of these accounts. For the larger accounts that show no substantial payments, examine credit reports and recent financial statements to determine the customers' ability to pay. Discuss each account for which substantial payment has not been received with the credit manager and determine the need for additional allowance for uncollectible accounts.

        ITEM 6 - Discuss the reason for the reduced depreciation expense with the client personnel responsible for the fixed assets accounts. If they indicate that the change resulted from a preponderance of fully depreciated assets, test the detail records to determine that the explanation is reasonable. If no satisfactory explanation is given, expand the tests of depreciation until satisfied that the provision is reasonable for the year.

8-35

RATIO NUMBER	NEED FOR INVESTIGATION	REASON FOR INVESTIGATION	NATURE OF INVESTIGATION
1.	Yes	Current ratio has decreased from previous year and is significantly lower than the industry averages. This could indicate a shortage of working capital required for competition in this industry.	Obtain explanation for the decrease in current ratio and investigate the effect on the company's ability to operate, obtain needed financing, and meet the requirements of its debt agreements.

8-35 (continued)

RATIO NUMBER	NEED FOR INVESTIGATION	REASON FOR INVESTIGATION	NATURE OF INVESTIGATION
2.	Yes	An 11-2/3% increase in the amount of time required to collect receivables provides less cash with which to pay bills. This change could represent a change in the collection policy, which could have a significant effect on the company in the future. It may also indicate that a larger allowance for uncollectible accounts may be needed if accounts receivable are less collectible than in 2010.	Determine the cause of the change in the time to collect and evaluate the long-term effect on the company's ability to collect receivables and pay its bills. The difference between the company's and the industry's days to collect could indicate a more strict credit policy for the company. The investigation of this possibility could indicate that the company is forfeiting a large number of sales and lead to a recommendation for a more lenient credit policy.
3.	Yes	The difference in the company's days to sell and the industry is significant. This could indicate that the company is operating with too low an inventory level causing stock-outs and customer dissatisfaction. In the long term, this could have a significant adverse effect on the company.	Investigate the reasons for the difference in the days to sell between the company and the industry. Determine the effect on the company in terms of customer dissatisfaction and lost customers due to stock-outs or long waits for delivery.
4.	No	N/A	N/A
5.	Yes	The industry average increased almost 10% indicating that the industry is building inventories either intentionally to fill an increased demand or unintentionally due to decreased demand and inability to dispose of inventory (as indicated further by significant decrease in the industry gross profit percent - see 8 below).	Investigate the market demand for the company's product to determine if a significant disposal problem may exist. There may be a net realizable value problem due to these conditions.

8-35 (continued)

RATIO NUMBER	NEED FOR INVESTIGATION	REASON FOR INVESTIGATION	NATURE OF INVESTIGATION
6.	No	N/A	N/A
7.	No	N/A	N/A
8.	Yes	The company appears to have raised prices during the past year to achieve the gross profit % of the industry. However, it appears that the industry's gross profit % has been reduced from either increased cost of goods which could not be passed on to customers in price increases or reduction in selling prices from competition, decreased demand for product, or overproduction. The result of these changes could be significant to the company's ability to produce a profit on its operations.	Determine the reason for the change in the industry's gross profit percent and the effect this might have on the company.
9.	No	N/A	N/A

b.   Mahogany Products operations differ significantly from the industry. Mahogany has operated in the past with higher turnover of inventory and receivables by selling at a lower gross margin and lower operating earnings. However, the company has changed significantly during the past year. The days to convert inventory to cash have increased 7% (11 days), while the current ratio has decreased by 15%. The company was able to increase its gross margin percent during the year when the industry was experiencing a significant decline in gross margin.

8-36 a.   The company's financial position is deteriorating significantly. The company's ability to pay its bills is marginal (quick ratio = 0.97) and its ability to generate cash is weak (days to convert inventory to cash = 266.7 in 2011 versus 173.8 in 2007). The earnings per share figure is misleading because it appears stable while the ratio of net income to common equity has been halved in two years. The accounts receivable may contain a significant amount of uncollectible

8-36 (continued)

accounts (accounts receivable turnover reduced 25% in four years), and the inventory may have a significant amount of unsalable goods included therein (inventory turnover reduced 40% in four years). The company's burden for increased inventory and accounts receivable levels has required additional borrowings. The company may experience problems in paying its operating liabilities and required debt repayments in the near future.

b.

ADDITIONAL INFORMATION	REASON FOR ADDITIONAL INFORMATION
1. Debt repayment requirements, lease payment requirements, and preferred dividend requirements	To project the cash requirements for the next several years in order to estimate the company's ability to meet its obligations.
2. Debt to equity ratio	To see the company's capital investment and ability of the company to exist on its present investment.
3. Industry average ratios	To compare the company's ratios to those of the average company in its industry to identify possible problem areas in the company.
4. Aging of accounts receivable, bad debt history, and analysis of allowance for uncollectible accounts	To see the collection potential and experience in accounts receivable. To compare the allowance for uncollectible accounts to the collection experience and determine the reasonableness of the allowance.
5. Aging of inventory and history of markdown taken	To compare the age of the inventory to the markdown experience since the turnover has decreased significantly. To evaluate the net realizable value of the inventory.
6. Short- and long-term liquidity trend ratios	To indicate whether the company may have liquidity problems within the next five years.

c. Based on the ratios shown, the following aspects of the company should receive special emphasis in the audit:

1. Ability of the company to continue to acquire inventory, replace obsolete or worn-out fixed assets, and meet its debt obligations based on its current cash position.

2. Reasonableness of the allowance for uncollectible accounts based on the reduction in accounts receivable turnover and increase in days to collect receivables.

8-36 (continued)

        3.   Reasonableness of the inventory valuation based on the decreased inventory turnover and increased days to sell inventory.

        4.   Computation of the earnings per share figure. It appears inconsistent that earnings per share could remain relatively stable when net earnings divided by common equity has decreased by 50%. This could be due to additional stock offerings during the period, or a stock split.

8-37 a.   eBay's decision to offer goods for sale at fixed prices in addition to goods offered through its Internet auctions may be related to any of these possible business strategies:

- *Match Competition.* Because other retailers offer products at fixed prices through the Internet, eBay's ability to offer products at fixed prices allows eBay to attract customers interested in purchasing goods offered by other retailers. Customers less interested in participating in online auctions may come to eBay to purchase items at fixed prices instead of visiting other retailer's Web sites. Thus, eBay may have decided that it needed to also offer products at fixed prices to match their competition and meet consumer expectations in the marketplace.

- *Target New Markets.* Many consumers may not be willing to participate in online auctions due to the inconvenience of refreshing their online bids during the auction period. By offering products at fixed prices to consumers through its Web site, eBay may be able to expand its market to consumers who do not choose to participate in the online auction.

       b.   Examples of business risks associated with the eBay's operations may include the following:

- *Insufficient Capacity to Handle Demand.* If demand for products through the eBay Web site exceeds expectations, internal systems may not be able to handle the volume of auctions and the processing of completed transactions in a timely fashion.

- *Customer Satisfaction with Product.* Because eBay products are offered by independent third parties, eBay faces risks related to product quality. If products acquired through eBay fail to meet consumer expectation for quality, customer use of eBay auctions may deteriorate over time.

■ *Consumer Privacy.* Given that online consumers will be providing confidential personal information, including credit card data, eBay's system must be designed to protect consumer privacy during transmission and processing of orders. Breaches in consumer privacy may affect future demand for online sales and may increase legal exposure to the company.

■ *Internet Availability.* eBay's business model is dependent solely on access to auctions through the Internet. During periods when the Internet is not available, eBay is unable to conduct business. If Internet outages are lengthy or frequent, consumers may be less interested in shopping on eBay.

c. The decision by eBay to acquire the online payment service, PayPal, streamlines the payment process between buyers and sellers on the eBay auctions. eBay's business risk may be affected if the payment process fails to work properly. PayPal enables customers, whether an individual or business, with an email address to securely, easily and quickly send and receive payments online. PayPal's service builds on the existing financial infrastructure of bank accounts and has tens of millions of registered accounts. Acquiring PayPal allows eBay to reduce business risk by ensuring they control this important aspect of the payment process in online commerce.

eBay's business model is totally dependent on buyer and seller easy access to the Internet. The decision to acquire the Internet communications company, Skype, may have been based on the view that the acquisition would strengthen eBay's access to the fastest growing Internet communications company. That helps ensure the company controls this important aspect of its business model.

d. The decision to sell most of its interest in Skype may been based on the company's desire to focus its strategy on facilitating online auctions. Skype's primary business model is to provide communications via the Internet. However, at this point in the online auction services market that type of communication is not critical to the service provided by eBay. Thus, the decision to streamline eBay's strategic focus may have actually reduced some aspects of business risk by allowing eBay management to be more focused on aspects related to online auctions rather than understanding the market for Internet based communications. However, eBay is assuming some business risk in the event Internet based communications in the future become critical to the online sales of products and services. Then, eBay's decision to exit the communications company may ultimately put them behind competitors who more successfully integrate online communications to the online sales and auction services.

8-37 (continued)

    e.   Each of the business risks identified in "b" may lead to an increased risk of material misstatements in the financial statements, if not effectively managed.

- *Insufficient Capacity to Handle Demand.* If demand for products through the eBay Web site exceeds the company's ability to process orders in a timely fashion, consumers may cancel earlier recorded orders or request returns when delivery occurs well beyond the expected delivery date. The accounting systems must be designed to accurately reflect cancellations and returns in a timely fashion consistent with GAAP. Additionally, if the processing of orders is significantly delayed, the accounting systems must be adequately designed to ensure sales are not recorded prematurely (e.g., not until delivery).

- *Customer Satisfaction with Product.* While the independent sellers who offer products on eBay auctions bear primary responsibility for product quality, some customers may seek financial reimbursement from eBay when products are not delivered or are in poor quality. Thus, eBay's financial statements may need to include reserves for product returns.

- *Consumer Privacy.* If consumer privacy is breached, existing sales may be cancelled or returns beyond the normal period may be requested. Such activity would need to be properly reflected in the financial statements. Additionally, legal exposures may increase, which may require additional financial statement disclosures.

- *Internet Availability.* The lack of Internet availability will may lead to penalties or fee payments to online sellers who use eBay to auction goods and to online advertising wanting to place advertisements on the eBay site. When the Internet is down, there may be fees owed to sellers and advertisers.

■ Cases

8-38 This case illustrates the common problem of an audit partner having to allocate his scarcest resource—his time. In this case, Winston Black neglects a new client for an existing one and causes himself several serious problems.

    a.   Auditing standards incorporate the AICPA's statement of quality control standards governing an audit practice. One of the quality control standards requires that firms maintain client acceptance procedures. Henson, Davis has such a policy; however, whatever enforcement mechanism for compliance with it must not be sufficient, as McMullan Resources was accepted without the procedures being completed. More to the point, auditing standards

8-38 (continued)

make the importance of adequate communication by a successor auditor with the predecessor auditor abundantly clear. In this case, Sarah Beale initiated a communication, but then left it incomplete when the predecessor auditor did not return her call. She rationalized this away by accepting representations from the new client. Of course, the predecessor auditor may be able to offer information that conflicts with the new client's best interest. It is not appropriate or in accordance with auditing standards to consider management's representations in lieu of a direct communication with the predecessor auditor. The client should not have been accepted until a sufficient communication occurred.

Can this be remedied? Yes and no. While AU auditing standards require communication with the predecessor auditor before accepting the engagement, a communication with the predecessor auditor should be conducted now, presumably by Black. However, if alarming information were obtained, Henson, Davis would find itself in the awkward position of having accepted a client it might not want. In that case, if it decides to withdraw from the engagement, it may be breaching a contractual obligation. If it continues, it may be taking an unwanted level of business and/or audit risk.

A related implication is the wisdom of Black's assumption about Beale's competence and how that affects her performance on the engagement. Black relied on Beale extensively, yet Beale's performance on the new client acceptance was deficient. Does this mean that Beale's performance in other areas was deficient as well? Certainly, Black can do a thorough review of Beale's work, but review may or may not reveal all engagement deficiencies.

Black's handling of this engagement also implies something about his attitude and objectivity. This was an initial engagement, yet he delegated almost all responsibility up to final review to Beale. He got credit for bringing in the new client, which directly benefited him in terms of his compensation. It would be against his best interest to not accept (withdraw from) this client. If he is unwilling to "do the right thing" here, how will he handle other difficult audit problems?

b.   In the audit of long-term contracts, it is essential to obtain assurance that the contract is enforceable so that income can be recognized on the percentage-of-completion basis. It is also important to consider other aspects of the contract that relate to various accounting aspects, such as price and other terms, cancellation privileges, penalties, and contingencies. In this case, Beale has concluded that the signed contract, written in French, is McMullan's "standard" contract, based on client representation. Of course, auditing standards require that management's representations, a weak form of evidence, be corroborated with other evidence where possible. Beale might argue that the confirmation obtained constitutes such evidence.

Beale's argument may seem logical with regard to enforcement, however, the confirmation form refers to existing disputes. It says nothing about contractual clauses that may foreshadow enforceability. For that reason the audit program requires the contract to be read. How would an auditor know whether the contract form was that of a standard contract without reading it? Furthermore, it may be unrealistic to assume there is such a thing as a "standard" contract in the first place. Long-term and short-term contracts are the result of negotiation and often contain special clauses and changed language.

In this case, not reading the contract was an insufficiency and the French-language copy should be translated by an independent translator and read by the auditors.

c. Compliance with GAAS is a matter that is always subject to professional judgment. One professional auditor may conclude he or she has complied with GAAS, and another would conclude that GAAS has been violated, so these matters are very seldom clear cut. However, in this case, it appears that Black and Beale may have violated GAAS in the following ways:

Standard of Field Work No. 1 - The auditor must adequately plan the work and must supervise any assistants. The requirements of predecessor and successor auditor communications discussed above relate to this standard. More generally, the audit partner should participate in planning, at least with a timely review. This would be more important than otherwise in the situation of a first-time engagement, as we have here. Similarly, some level of on-going partner supervision would seem prudent and logical. Black, apparently, did not really participate at all until final review.

Standard of Field Work No. 3 – The auditor must obtain sufficient appropriate audit evidence by performing audit procedures to afford a reasonable basis for an opinion regarding the financial statements under audit. As discussed above, the work on the Montreal contract was deficient and further evidence is required.

In addition, whenever the field work standards are violated there are implied violations of other standards. It might be argued that Beale was not proficient as an auditor because of her failures with the new client acceptance procedures and the Montreal contract. Similarly, it might be argued that due professional care was not taken both by Beale and by Black for delegating so much to Beale.

8-39 a. When the computer option is assigned, an Excel spreadsheet (Filename P839.xls) is used to compute a set of ratios as would be done manually (as shown below.) Five specific aspects of using the computer in doing this are discussed below. The first applies to both the manual and the computer approach.

    1.   Computation of ratios. The selection of ratios is arbitrary and should include a set that gives a good overview of all aspects of the company's financial statements that the user is interested in. And, in computing specific ratios, certain decisions must be made, such as whether to use net sales or gross sales. The formulas for the ratios selected for this solution are shown below. Note: where possible, the solution uses average balances (inventory and accounts receivable, for example) when required by the ratio formulas. Because 2007 balances are not available for computing 2008 average inventory and receivables, the solution does not calculate average inventory and calculate average inventory and accounts receivable turnover ratios for 2008.

Quick ratio = (cash + accounts receivable - allowance for doubtful accounts) / current liabilities

Gross margin/sales = gross margin / gross sales

Average inventory turnover = (cost of goods sold) / average inventory

Current ratio = Current assets / current liabilities

Average days to collect receivables = (average accounts receivable x 360) / (net sales)

Net income/total assets = (self-explanatory)

Net income/sales = net income / gross sales

Sales/equity = Gross sales / equity

Debt/equity = (total liabilities) / total equity

Net income/equity = (self-explanatory)

Allowance for doubtful accounts / accounts receivable = (self explanatory)

Bad debts/sales = bad debts / gross sales

Sales returns and allowances/sales = sales returns and allowances/gross sales

2. Set-up. Excel spreadsheets must be *planned* in advance. This can be referred to as "set-up." A useful technique is to use a block diagram to plan the set-up. This helps see the overall shape and content of the spreadsheet and is helpful for guiding its detailed preparation and how outputs will be controlled and formatted. A block diagram for this spreadsheet follows. It shows the spreadsheet divided into three sections: the heading, the input section, where data will be entered, and the results section where the ratios will be calculated. A vertical structure is used to facilitate printouts that will fit in an 8-1/2 x 14 inch format. The structure could just as easily be side-by-side.

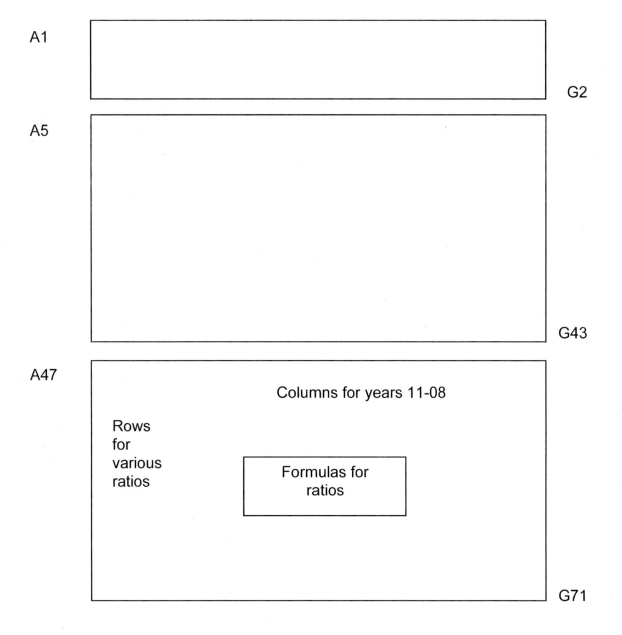

A1

G2

A5

G43

A47

Columns for years 11-08

Rows for various ratios

Formulas for ratios

G71

8-39 (continued)

3. Check on accuracy of inputs. A major concern is knowing that input data has been entered accurately. This can usually be achieved by two alternative procedures. The first is computing totals and comparing them to check figures. For example, the details of assets can be computed and added to 100. The second procedure is verification of details on a figure-by-figure basis back to the source.

4. Treatment of negative values. Negative values can be entered as negative inputs or positive inputs. It is important to respond properly to the treatment used when the values are included in computations.

5. Check on accuracy of formulas. One of the biggest problems with using spreadsheets is errors in the development of formulas. One use of each formula should be done manually to check its correctness and the formulas should receive a careful second party review. If this second step is impractical, a second party should at least review the results for reasonableness.

Templates for the computer solutions prepared using Excel are included on the Companion Website.

Solomon Bros. Manufacturing Co. Analytical Procedures				
	Calculated from adjusted year-end balances			
KEY RATIOS	**2011**	**2010**	**2009**	**2008**
Quick	.96	.83	.81	.74
Gross margin/sales	21.0%	22.1%	23.2%	25.0%
Average inventory turnover	1.79	1.82	1.93	NA
Current	2.19	1.96	1.91	1.75
Average days to collect receivables	131.10	123.94	116.06	NA
Net income/total assets	3.9%	3.9%	3.9%	4.3%
Net income/sales	5.0%	5.2%	5.3%	6.1%
Sales/equity	3.89:1	4.37:1	4.88:1	5.27:1
Debt/equity	4.02:1	4.82:1	5.64:1	6.42:1
Net income/equity	.19:1	.23:1	.26:1	.32:1
Allowance for doubtful accounts/ accounts receivable	10.6%	11.5%	12.5%	14.8%
Bad debts/sales	3.7%	4.0%	4.1%	4.6%
Sales returns and allowances/ gross sales	3.1%	3.0%	3.0%	2.9%

8-39 (continued)

        The Solomon brothers are considering going public to expand the business at a time that land and building costs in Boston are at extremely inflated values. Presently gross profit margins are 21% of sales and net income is 5% of sales. Both ratios decreased during the past year. To finance expansion, additional debt is out of the question because long-term debt is presently extremely high (debt to equity ratio is 4.02). Depreciation on new plant and equipment at the inflated prices will cause high depreciation charges, which may significantly reduce the profit margins.

b.   The account that is of the greatest concern is allowance for uncollectible accounts. The following are three key analytical procedures indicating a possible misstatement of allowance for uncollectible accounts:

1.	**Breakdown of the aging in percent**	**2011**	**2010**	**2009**	**2008**
	0 - 30 days	39.8%	42.1%	46.0%	49.9%
	31 - 60 days	33.5%	33.3%	32.0%	30.1%
	61 - 120 days	19.1%	17.6%	16.0%	15.0%
	over 120 days	7.6%	7.0%	6.0%	5.0%
		100.0%	100.0%	100.0%	100.0%
2.	Allowance/accounts receivable	10.6%	11.5%	12.5%	14.8%
3.	Bad debts/sales	3.7%	4.0%	4.1%	4.6%

It appears that the allowance is understated:

1.   If accounts were as collectible as before, allowance/accounts receivable should be about constant.
2.   If accounts become less collectible, allowance/accounts receivable should increase.
3.   Number 2 seems to be the case.

        The aging of accounts receivable shows a deterioration in the overall aging (0-30 decreased significantly in the past several years, while those in all other categories increased), while the allowance for uncollectible accounts as a percentage of accounts receivable has decreased from 14.8% to 10.6%. This indicates that the allowance for uncollectible accounts may be understated, especially considering the trend between 2008 and 2010.

Accounts Receivable.
The average days to collect receivables has increased steadily over the four-year period, which indicates that some accounts may not be collectible. This idea is supported by the deterioration in overall aging noted above.

8-39 (continued)

Sales.
Finally, gross margin as a percentage of sales has declined steadily over the four-year period from 25% to 21%. Net Income/Sales has also declined. The auditor should seek an explanation from the client for these trends.

■ **Integrated Case Application**

8-40

PINNACLE MANUFACTURING—PART I

a.

Account Balance	% Change 2010-2011	% Change 2009-2010
Net sales	1.45%	2.70%
Cost of goods sold	2.85%	4.18%
Operating expenses	-2.51%	2.40%
Income from operations	1.87%	-23.10%
Net receivables	51.30%	8.61%
Inventory	26.23%	1.05%
Accounts payable	37.09%	24.71%
Long-term debt	9.30%	- 0.17%

b.

Amounts (in thousands)

Ratios		2011	2010	2009
	Current assets	53,172	41,625	41,406
Current ratio:	Current liab.	30,413	21,527	18,942
		1.75	1.93	2.19
Debt to equity	Debt	54,833	43,868	41,322
	Equity	60,602	59,392	58,353
		90.5%	73.9%	70.8%
	Net income b/t	2,093	1,897	3,059
Net income bt/sales	Sales	150,738	148,586	144,686
		1.4%	1.3%	2.1%
Gross margin %	Gross profit	41,453	42,331	42,698
	Sales	150,738	148,586	144,686
		27.5%	28.5%	29.5%
Inventory turnover	COGS	109,285	106,255	101,988
	Ave. inventory	28,887	25,404	25,272
		3.8	4.2	4.0

c. While Pinnacle continues to experience some growth in net sales in 2011 over 2010, that growth is less than the growth in 2010 over 2009. Unfortunately, cost of goods sold continues to increase at higher rates than increases in sales resulting in lower gross margin percentages in

8-40 (continued)

2011, although the increase in cost of goods sold in 2011 over 2010 was not as significant as the increase in 2010 over 2009.

Apparently Pinnacle management made changes that have reduced overall operating expenses given the 2.51% decline in operating expenses in 2011 over 2010. Those changes resulted in an increase in income from operations in 2011 relative to the decrease experienced in 2010 and a slight increase in net income before taxes in 2011 over 2010.

While profitable, the review of changes in balance sheet accounts indicates that receivables are increasing at significant rates (51.30% in 2011) relative to increases in sales of only 1.45%. This buildup in receivables may lead to significant collection challenges in 2011 and beyond. Similarly, buildup of inventory may lead to excess amounts of inventory, especially if sales do not continue to increase beyond 2011. Concerns about inventory obsolescence are likely to be increasing given the slower inventory turnover in 2011.

The reduction in the current ratio suggests that liquidity is decreasing in 2011 relative to prior years. The increase in accounts payable to finance the inventory buildup in addition to increases in long-term debt suggests that management is increasing its borrowings to provide cash flow during a time where cash collections from receivables appear to be slowing as receivables continue to build. Increased borrowings (both short-term and long-term) will place greater needs on managing cash flow and liquidity in 2011 and beyond.

d. See page 8-33 for Pinnacle's common-size income statement. For the overall financial statements, the focus is on all accounts except direct expenses. For the direct expenses, it is better to use the disaggregated information. The suggested solution was prepared using Excel (Filename P840.xls).

Account Balance	Estimate of $ Amount of Potential Misstatement
Salaries & Wages	Salary and wages expenses are lower this year relative to prior years. Need to determine if salaried workers were laid off or terminated and extent that number of hourly workers or overtime was reduced in 2011.
Property taxes	Decrease of $155,000 when property increased
Bad debts	See requirement g for an analysis

8-40 (continued)

Depreciation expense	Increase of almost $700,000, perhaps partly due to new building and equipment purchases
Federal Income Taxes	FIT as a % of NIBT was 45% in 2010. 45% of 2011 NIBT is $941.9 million. Actual FIT for 2011 was $883.4 million. Difference of $585,000.
Interest expense	Short-term plus long-term interest bearing debt increased by 22%, from $32.6 million in 2010 to $39.8 million in 2011, but interest expense decreased. If interest rates have not changed, interest expense would be expected to increase by a similar amount to $2,804,800 ($2,299,000 x 1.22). Potential misstatement of $622,900 ($2,804,800 - $2,181,900).

e. See pages 8-34 to 8-36 for common-size income statement for each of Pinnacle's three divisions. The suggested solution was prepared using Excel (Filename P840.xls). For disaggregated information it is best to ignore the allocated expenses.

Account Balance	Estimate of $ Amount of Potential Misstatement
Welburn:	
Security	Decrease of $70,000 or 36% of sales relative to 43% in 2010 and 2009.
Solar Electro:	
Payroll benefits	Increased almost $50,000 while salaries and wages decreased. Potential misallocation between divisions.
Legal Service	Large increase may be indicative of other issues affecting disclosures and asset or liability valuation.
Miscellaneous	$200,000 increase needs investigation.

8-40 (continued)

(part of requirement d)

Pinnacle Manufacturing Company
Income Statement - All Divisions
For the Year Ended December 31

	2011 Dollar Value	2011 % of Sales	2010 Dollar Value	2010 % of Sales	2009 Dollar Value	2009 % of Sales
Sales	150,918,731	100.00%	148,764,555	100.00%	144,860,245	100.00%
Sales Returns and Allowances	181,103	0.12%	178,518	0.12%	173,832	0.12%
Cost of Sales*	109,284,780	72.41%	106,255,499	71.43%	101,988,165	70.40%
Gross Profit	41,452,848	27.47%	42,330,538	28.45%	42,698,248	29.48%
OPERATING EXPENSES-Allocated						
Salaries-Management	2,281,266	1.51%	2,387,993	1.61%	2,295,081	1.58%
Salaries-Office	315,169	0.21%	296,681	0.20%	306,856	0.21%
Licensing and certification fees	190,650	0.13%	172,883	0.12%	162,279	0.11%
Security	550,603	0.36%	637,580	0.43%	630,353	0.44%
Insurance	93,197	0.06%	103,842	0.07%	108,491	0.07%
Medical benefits	23,721	0.02%	29,453	0.02%	28,810	0.02%
Advertising	162,512	0.11%	178,009	0.12%	165,678	0.11%
Business publications	6,989	0.00%	5,555	0.00%	774	0.00%
Property taxes	22,585	0.01%	178,009	0.12%	175,692	0.12%
Bad debts	841,699	0.56%	1,034,060	0.70%	992,094	0.68%
Depreciation expense	5,336,783	3.54%	4,641,982	3.12%	4,367,565	3.02%
Accounting fees	273,956	0.18%	297,777	0.20%	299,789	0.21%
Total operating expenses-Allocated	10,099,130	6.69%	9,963,824	6.70%	9,533,462	6.58%
OPERATING EXPENSES-Direct						
Salaries-Sales	14,970,669	9.92%	15,327,777	10.30%	14,904,392	10.29%
Wages Rental	491,794	0.33%	595,389	0.40%	575,725	0.40%
Wages-Mechanics	1,113,539	0.74%	1,339,626	0.90%	1,333,411	0.92%
Wages-Warehouse	4,891,065	3.24%	5,340,271	3.59%	5,473,249	3.78%
Garbage collection	27,649	0.02%	29,771	0.02%	37,969	0.03%
Payroll benefits	2,657,889	1.76%	2,937,730	1.97%	2,894,300	2.00%
Rent- Warehouse	802,855	0.53%	764,346	0.51%	758,345	0.52%
Telephone	32,402	0.02%	45,173	0.03%	57,867	0.04%
Utilities	262,393	0.17%	267,005	0.18%	274,365	0.19%
Postage	89,763	0.06%	133,518	0.09%	151,278	0.10%
Linen service	17,282	0.01%	12,350	0.01%	16,083	0.01%
Repairs and maintenance	166,985	0.11%	168,405	0.11%	178,213	0.12%
Cleaning service	89,800	0.06%	81,589	0.05%	78,088	0.05%
Legal service	396,016	0.26%	190,540	0.13%	152,238	0.11%
Fuel	286,547	0.19%	341,192	0.23%	279,512	0.19%
Travel and entertainment	103,389	0.07%	103,842	0.07%	100,479	0.07%
Pension expense	228,555	0.15%	237,350	0.16%	127,011	0.09%
Office supplies	149,828	0.10%	148,340	0.10%	171,109	0.12%
Miscellaneous	300,188	0.20%	105,931	0.07%	144,012	0.10%
Total operating expenses-Direct	27,078,608	17.94%	28,170,145	18.94%	27,707,646	19.13%
Total Operating Expenses	37,177,738	24.63%	38,133,969	25.63%	37,241,108	25.71%
Operating Income	4,275,110	2.83%	4,196,569	2.82%	5,457,140	3.77%
Other Expense-Interest	2,181,948	1.45%	2,299,217	1.55%	2,397,953	1.66%
Income Before Taxes	2,093,162	1.39%	1,897,352	1.28%	3,059,187	2.11%
Federal Income Taxes	883,437	0.59%	858,941	0.58%	1,341,536	0.93%
Net Income	**1,209,725**	0.80%	**1,038,411**	0.70%	**1,717,651**	1.19%

* Details of manufacturing expenses are not
included in this schedule.

8-40 (continued)

(part of requirement e)

Pinncacle Manufacturing Company
Income Statement - Welburn Division
For the Year Ended December 31

	2011 $ Value	2011 % of Div. Sales	2010 $ Value	2010 % of Div. Sales	2009 $ Value	2009 % of Div. Sales
Sales	122,585,513	100.00%	120,830,903	100.00%	117,639,471	100.00%
Sales Returns and Allowances	127,673	0.10%	124,975	0.10%	121,694	0.10%
Cost of Sales*	90,373,709	73.72%	87,905,900	72.75%	84,375,503	71.72%
Gross Profit	32,084,131	26.17%	32,800,028	27.15%	33,142,274	28.17%
OPERATING EXPENSES-Allocated						
Salaries-Management	1,851,775	1.51%	1,934,168	1.60%	1,858,914	1.58%
Salaries-Office	255,833	0.21%	240,298	0.20%	248,539	0.21%
Licensing and certification fees	139,951	0.11%	127,659	0.11%	119,829	0.10%
Security	446,938	0.36%	516,406	0.43%	510,552	0.43%
Insurance	75,647	0.06%	84,103	0.07%	87,868	0.07%
Medical benefits	19,389	0.02%	24,032	0.02%	23,507	0.02%
Advertising	131,917	0.11%	144,181	0.12%	134,193	0.11%
Business publications	4,213	0.00%	2,981	0.00%	415	0.00%
Property taxes	17,873	0.01%	144,181	0.12%	142,304	0.12%
Bad debts	687,885	0.56%	831,572	0.69%	797,823	0.68%
Depreciation expense	4,206,533	3.43%	3,759,789	3.11%	3,537,525	3.01%
Accounting fees	223,534	0.18%	240,196	0.20%	241,817	0.21%
Total operating expenses-Allocated	8,061,488	6.58%	8,049,566	6.66%	7,703,286	6.55%
OPERATING EXPENSES-Direct						
Salaries-Sales	12,579,213	10.26%	12,694,443	10.51%	12,343,793	10.49%
Wages Rental	-		-		-	
Wages-Mechanics	-		-		-	
Wages-Warehouse	4,006,809	3.27%	4,325,377	3.58%	4,433,082	3.77%
Garbage collection	-		-		-	
Payroll benefits	2,039,389	1.66%	2,379,426	1.97%	2,344,248	1.99%
Rent- Warehouse	670,746	0.55%	623,389	0.52%	618,494	0.53%
Telephone	25,901	0.02%	36,045	0.03%	46,175	0.04%
Utilities	194,700	0.16%	216,266	0.18%	222,226	0.19%
Postage	77,924	0.06%	108,136	0.09%	122,519	0.10%
Linen service	14,126	0.01%	10,510	0.01%	13,685	0.01%
Repairs and maintenance	123,450	0.10%	117,538	0.10%	124,383	0.11%
Cleaning service	65,853	0.05%	66,085	0.05%	63,250	0.05%
Legal service	115,735	0.09%	131,334	0.11%	104,934	0.09%
Fuel	217,964	0.18%	276,343	0.23%	226,387	0.19%
Travel and entertainment	80,265	0.07%	84,103	0.07%	81,380	0.07%
Pension expense	187,891	0.15%	192,240	0.16%	102,872	0.09%
Office supplies	121,617	0.10%	120,149	0.10%	138,590	0.12%
Miscellaneous	57,147	0.05%	57,910	0.05%	78,729	0.07%
Total operating expenses-Direct	20,578,730	16.79%	21,439,294	17.74%	21,064,747	17.91%
Total operating expenses	28,640,218	23.36%	29,488,860	24.41%	28,768,033	24.45%
OPERATING INCOME	3,443,913	2.81%	3,311,168	2.74%	4,374,241	3.72%

* Details of manufacturing expenses are not included in this schedule.

8-40 (continued)

(part of requirement e)

Pinnacle Manufacturing Company
Income Statement - Solar-Electro Division
For the Year Ended December 31

	2011 $ Value	2011 % of Div. Sales	2010 $ Value	2010 % of Div. Sales	2009 $ Value	2009 % of Div. Sales
Sales	22,605,731	100.00%	21,680,289	100.00%	21,126,896	100.00%
Sales Returns and Allowances	43,825	0.19%	38,773	0.18%	37,756	0.18%
Cost of Sales*	17,008,377	75.24%	16,156,496	74.52%	15,507,635	73.40%
Gross Profit	5,553,529	24.57%	5,485,020	25.30%	5,581,505	26.42%
OPERATING EXPENSES-Allocated						
Salaries-Management	338,015	1.50%	352,230	1.62%	338,525	1.60%
Salaries-Office	46,697	0.21%	43,759	0.20%	45,259	0.21%
Licensing and certification fees	19,303	0.09%	15,287	0.07%	14,350	0.07%
Security	81,580	0.36%	94,046	0.43%	92,980	0.44%
Insurance	13,808	0.06%	15,319	0.07%	16,005	0.08%
Medical benefits	3,537	0.02%	4,376	0.02%	4,280	0.02%
Advertising	24,078	0.11%	26,255	0.12%	24,436	0.12%
Business publications	874	0.00%	542	0.00%	76	0.00%
Property taxes	3,264	0.01%	26,255	0.12%	25,913	0.12%
Bad debts	120,493	0.53%	157,730	0.73%	151,328	0.72%
Depreciation expense	889,483	3.93%	684,667	3.16%	644,192	3.05%
Accounting fees	39,666	0.18%	44,689	0.21%	44,992	0.21%
Total operating expenses-Allocated	1,580,798	6.99%	1,465,155	6.76%	1,402,336	6.64%
OPERATING EXPENSES-Direct						
Salaries-Sales	2,192,482	9.70%	2,402,414	11.08%	2,336,053	11.06%
Wages Rental	-		-		-	
Wages-Mechanics	-		-		-	
Wages-Warehouse	695,918	3.08%	787,698	3.63%	807,312	3.82%
Garbage collection	-		-		-	
Payroll benefits	478,669	2.12%	433,321	2.00%	426,916	2.02%
Rent- Warehouse	103,983	0.46%	109,403	0.50%	108,544	0.51%
Telephone	4,730	0.02%	6,567	0.03%	8,412	0.04%
Utilities	53,278	0.24%	39,383	0.18%	40,468	0.19%
Postage	7,131	0.03%	19,695	0.09%	22,315	0.11%
Linen service	2,578	0.01%	1,490	0.01%	1,941	0.01%
Repairs and maintenance	34,121	0.15%	39,383	0.18%	41,677	0.20%
Cleaning service	20,694	0.09%	12,033	0.06%	11,516	0.05%
Legal service	268,954	1.19%	45,950	0.21%	36,714	0.17%
Fuel	53,975	0.24%	50,326	0.23%	41,229	0.20%
Travel and entertainment	18,196	0.08%	15,319	0.07%	14,822	0.07%
Pension expense	34,297	0.15%	33,988	0.16%	18,187	0.09%
Office supplies	22,199	0.10%	21,880	0.10%	25,238	0.12%
Miscellaneous	234,892	1.04%	42,982	0.20%	58,433	0.28%
Total operating expenses-Direct	4,226,097	18.69%	4,061,832	18.74%	3,999,777	18.93%
Total operating expenses	5,806,895	25.69%	5,526,987	25.49%	5,402,113	25.57%
OPERATING INCOME	-253,366	-1.12%	-41,967	-0.19%	179,392	0.85%

* Details of manufacturing expenses are not
  included in this schedule.

8-40 (continued)

(part of requirement e)

Pinnacle Manufacturing Company
Income Statement - Machine-Tech Division
For the Year Ended December 31

	2011 $ Value	2011 % of Div. Sales	2010 $ Value	2010 % of Div. Sales	2009 $ Value	2009 % of Div. Sales
Sales	5,727,487	100.00%	6,253,363	100.00%	6,093,878	100.00
Sales Returns and Allowances	9,605	0.17%	14,770	0.24%	14,382	0.24
Cost of Sales*	1,902,694	33.22%	2,193,103	35.07%	2,105,027	34.54
Gross Profit	3,815,188	66.61%	4,045,490	64.69%	3,974,469	65.22
OPERATING EXPENSES-Allocated						
Salaries-Management	91,476	1.60%	101,595	1.62%	97,642	1.60
Salaries-Office	12,638	0.22%	12,624	0.20%	13,057	0.21
Licensing and certification fees	31,396	0.55%	29,937	0.48%	28,100	0.46
Security	22,086	0.39%	27,128	0.43%	26,820	0.44
Insurance	3,742	0.07%	4,420	0.07%	4,618	0.08
Medical benefits	795	0.01%	1044	0.02%	1022	0.02
Advertising	6,517	0.11%	7,573	0.12%	7,048	0.12
Business publications	1,902	0.03%	2,032	0.03%	283	0.00
Property taxes	1,448	0.03%	7,573	0.12%	7,475	0.12
Bad debts	33,321	0.58%	44,759	0.72%	42,942	0.70
Depreciation expense	240,767	4.20%	197,527	3.16%	185,850	3.05
Accounting fees	10,756	0.19%	12,891	0.21%	12,983	0.21
Total operating expenses-Allocated	456,844	7.98%	449,103	7.18%	427,840	7.02
OPERATING EXPENSES-Direct	198978					
Salaries-Sales	198,978	3.47%	230,922	3.69%	224,543	3.68
Wages Rental	491,794	8.59%	595,389	9.52%	575,724	9.45
Wages-Mechanics	1,113,539	19.44%	1,339,627	21.42%	1,333,411	21.88
Wages-Warehouse	188,339	3.29%	227,196	3.63%	232,853	3.82
Garbage collection	27,649	0.48%	29,771	0.48%	37,970	0.62
Payroll benefits	139,832	2.44%	124,984	2.00%	123,136	2.02
Rent- Warehouse	28,126	0.49%	31,554	0.50%	31,306	0.51
Telephone	1,771	0.03%	2,560	0.04%	3,280	0.05
Utilities	14,415	0.25%	11,357	0.18%	11,670	0.19
Postage	4,708	0.08%	5,688	0.09%	6,445	0.11
Linen service	579	0.01%	350	0.01%	457	0.01
Repairs and maintenance	9,414	0.16%	11,484	0.18%	12,153	0.20
Cleaning service	3,253	0.06%	3,472	0.06%	3,322	0.05
Legal service	11,327	0.20%	13,255	0.21%	10,590	0.17
Fuel	14,608	0.26%	14,522	0.23%	11,897	0.20
Travel and entertainment	4,928	0.09%	4,420	0.07%	4,277	0.07
Pension expense	6,368	0.11%	11,121	0.18%	5,951	0.10
Office supplies	6,012	0.10%	6,312	0.10%	7,281	0.12
Miscellaneous	8,141	0.14%	5,035	0.08%	6,856	0.11
Total operating expenses-Direct	2,273,781	39.70%	2,669,019	42.68%	2,643,122	43.37
Total operating expenses	2,730,625	47.68%	3,118,122	49.86%	3,070,962	50.39
OPERATING INCOME	1,084,563	18.94%	927,368	14.83%	903,507	14.83

* Details of manufacturing expenses are not
  included in this schedule.

8-40 (continued)

f. Both the companywide and the divisional income statements are useful, but for different purposes. The companywide information is useful for identifying material fluctuations in the financial statements. However, the disaggregated information is more helpful in identifying the source of the fluctuations.

g. **Estimate of Potential Understatement in Allowance**

	2011	2010	2009
A/R Turnover			
Sales	150,738	148,586	144,686
Average accounts receivable	10,831	8,278	7,936
Turnover	13.9	17.9	18.2
Days Sales Outstanding			
365	365	365	365
Turnover	13.9	17.9	18.2
Days	26.3	20.4	20.1

	2011	2010	2009
Bad Debt Expense as percentage of gross sales:	.56%	.70%	.68%

In the prior two years, bad debt expense as a percentage of gross sales has approximated .7%. In 2011, the days sales outstanding increased 28.92% from 20.4 days to 26.3 days. If you increase the .7% by 28.92%, bad debts as a percentage of sales would increase from .7% to .9%, which would suggest an estimated bad debt expense of $1,358,269.

The difference between recorded bad debt expense of $841,699 and the expected bad debt expense of $1,358,269 would require an increase of $516,570 to bad debt expense and the allowance for doubtful accounts.

Analysis of Inventory Balance

Account Balance	% Change 2010-2011	% Change 2009-2010
Net sales	1.45%	2.70%
Cost of goods sold	2.85%	4.18%
Inventory	26.23%	1.05%

8-40 (continued)

Ratios		2011	2010	2009
Gross margin %	Gross profit	41,453	42,331	42,698
	Sales	150,738	148,586	144,686
		27.5%	28.5%	29.5%
Inventory turnover	COGS	109,285	106,255	101,988
	Ave. inventory	28,887	25,404	25,272
		3.8	4.2	4.0
Days Inventory Outstanding				
		365	365	365
Inventory Turnover		3.8	4.2	4.0
		96.1	86.9	91.3

The significant buildup of inventories in 2011, despites slower growth in sales creates significant concerns about the potential for inventory obsolescence. Inventory is sitting in the warehouse longer in 2011 (by almost 10 days) relative to 2010. More extensive analysis regarding inventory obsolescence will be needed.

Analysis of Short-Term and Long-Term Debt

Account Balance	% Change 2010-2011	% Change 2009-2010
Accounts payable	37.09%	24.71%
Short-term/Current LTD	49.3%	6.47%
Long-term Debt	9.3%	-0.17%
Interest Expense	-5.1%	-4.1%

Accounts payable and short-term/current borrowings are up significantly. The increase of 37.09% in accounts payable is much greater than the increase in the ending inventory balance. And, short-term/Current LTD is up almost 50%, with long-term debt up about 9.3%. Despite increases in short-term and long-term debt, interest expense declined almost 5% in 2011. Additional work will be done to address the potential for material misstatements in these accounts.

h. There is a low risk that Pinnacle will fail financially in the next twelve months. The company has been profitable the past three years, is generating cash flows and most of the ratios indicate no severe financial difficulties. Several ratios, such as the current ratio and debt to equity have deteriorated somewhat, but not enough to cause significant concerns.

8-41 – ACL Problem Solution

a. The following is a printout of the Statistics command for Inventory Value at Cost:

```
Field       :   Value
                Number              Total       Average
Positive    :   145             694,361.94     4,788.70
Zeros       :    2
Negative    :    5              -13,882.00     2,776.40
Totals      :   152            680,479.94     4,476.84
Abs Value   :                  708,243.94
Range       :                  110,967.60
Highest     : 100,800.00 37,100.00 25,548.60 24,738.00
23,136.00
Lowest      : -10,167.60 -2,774.40 -595.20 -190.72 -154.08
```

There are 145 positive amounts, 2 zero amounts, and 5 negative amounts.

The following is a printout of the Statistics command for Market Value:

```
Field       :   MktVal
                Number              Total       Average
Positive    :   148           1,030,325.21     6,961.66
Zeros       :    2
Negative    :    2               -1,263.60      -631.80
Totals      :   152           1,029,061.61     6,770.14
Abs Value   :                 1,031,588.81
Range       :                   144,719.76
Highest     : 143,880.00 47,647.00 44,098.53 42,163.20
32,970.00
Lowest      : -839.76 -423.84 0.00 0.00 90.00
```

There are 148 positive amounts, 2 zero amounts, and 2 negative amounts.

b. There are several negative values in inventory, which is not possible. There is also one especially large item that should be verified.

c. There are alternative Expressions that can be used. One is Value/MktVal. Three items have market value less than cost. Several have a small difference between market value and cost that may night represent normal markups.

■ **Internet Problem Solution: Obtain Client Background Information**

Internet Problem 8-1

a. Students should have located the most recent Form 10-K filing for The Coca-Cola Company (search for "Coca Cola Co").

b.   *Item 1* of the Coca Cola Form 10-K provides an overview the company's business. In this section, management has included a general description of the Coca Cola Company, a list of its global operating units, descriptions of the products it manufactures and sales and its distribution processes, including seasonality issues and competition. Item 1 also includes discussion about raw materials, patents, copyrights, trade secrets, trademarks, government regulation, employee information, and information about its website and availability of SEC filings.

Item 1A includes management's disclosure of significant risk factors that may affect the Coca Cola Company. Management has identified over 30 categories of different risks and each is described in more depth. Some of the risks are likely to affect any large global company or other large beverage manufacturers, while others are more specific to the uniqueness of the Coca Cola Company.

Item 7 contains Management's Discussion and Analysis of the Financial Condition and Results of Operations. Management begins with an overview of its general business operations, followed by more in-depth discussions of its objectives, strategies, core capabilities, challenges and risks. This section also includes discussion about critical accounting policies and estimates, followed by more detailed analysis of changes in operations and financial position over the most recent year.

All this information would provide valuable insights to assist the auditor in obtaining a rich understanding of the entity and its environment for purposes of audit planning.

c.   The PepsiCo Form 10-K contains similar information about the overall business (Item 1), risk factors (Item 1A), and MDE&A (Item 7) for the PepsiCo Company. Auditors of Coca Cola would benefit from reading this information about PepsiCo in that it would inform them about the nature of the business for Coca Cola's chief competitor and it may raise awareness of other risks and current trends affecting the industry not disclosed in Coca Cola's Form 10-K. Understanding and awareness of the information provided by PepsiCo would assist the auditors of Coca Cola in their efforts to "obtain an understanding of the entity and its environment" as required by the second standard of fieldwork.

(**Note**: Internet problems address current issues using Internet sources. Because Internet sites are subject to change, Internet problems and solutions may change. Current information on Internet problems is available at www.pearsonhighered.com/arens).

Chapter 9

Materiality and Risk

■ Review Questions

9-1 The parts of planning are: accept client and perform initial planning, understand the client's business and industry, assess client business risk, perform preliminary analytical procedures, set materiality and assess acceptable audit risk and inherent risk, understand internal control and assess control risk, gather information to assess fraud risk, and develop overall audit plan and audit program. Evaluation of materiality is in the fifth part of planning. Risk assessment is in part three (client business risk), part five (acceptable audit risk and inherent risk), part six (control risk), and part seven (fraud risk).

9-2 Materiality is defined as: the magnitude of an omission or misstatement of accounting information that, in light of the surrounding circumstances, makes it probable that the judgment of a reasonable person relying on the information would have been changed or influenced by the omission or misstatement.

"Obtain reasonable assurance," as used in the audit report, means that the auditor does not *guarantee* or insure the fair presentation of the financial statements. There is some risk that the financial statements contain a material misstatement.

9-3 Materiality is important because if financial statements are materially misstated, users' decisions may be affected, and thereby cause financial loss to them. It is difficult to apply because there are often many different users of the financial statements. The auditor must therefore make an assessment of the likely users and the decisions they will make. Materiality is also difficult to apply because it is a relative concept. The professional auditing standards offer little specific guidance regarding the application of materiality. The auditor must, therefore, exercise considerable professional judgment in the application of materiality.

9-4 The preliminary judgment about materiality is the maximum amount by which the auditor believes the financial statements could be misstated and still not affect the decisions of reasonable users. Several factors affect the preliminary judgment about materiality and are as follows:

1. Materiality is a relative rather than an absolute concept.
2. Bases are needed for evaluating materiality.
3. Qualitative factors affect materiality decisions.

9-4 (continued)

4. Expected distribution of the financial statements will affect the preliminary judgment of materiality. If the financial statements are widely distributed to users, the preliminary judgment of materiality will probably be set lower than if the financial statements are not expected to be widely distributed.

5. The level of acceptable audit risk will also affect the preliminary judgment of materiality.

9-5 Because materiality is relative rather than absolute, it is necessary to have bases for establishing whether misstatements are material. For example, in the audit of a manufacturing company, the auditor might use as bases: net income before taxes, total assets, current assets, and working capital. For a governmental unit, such as a school district, there is no net income before taxes, and therefore that would not be an available base. Instead, the primary bases would likely be fund balances, total assets, and perhaps total revenue.

9-6 The following qualitative factors are likely to be considered in evaluating materiality:

a. Amounts involving fraud are usually considered more important than unintentional errors of equal dollar amounts.

b. Misstatements that are otherwise minor may be material if there are possible consequences arising from contractual obligations.

c. Misstatements that are otherwise immaterial may be material if they affect a trend in earnings.

9-7 A preliminary judgment about materiality is set for the financial statements as a whole. Tolerable misstatement is the maximum amount of misstatement that would be considered material for an individual account balance. The amount of tolerable misstatement for any given account is dependent upon the preliminary judgment about materiality. Ordinarily, tolerable misstatement for any given account would have to be lower than the preliminary judgment about materiality. In many cases, it will be considerably lower because of the possibility of misstatements in different accounts that, in total, cannot exceed the preliminary judgment about materiality.

9-8 There are several possible answers to the question. One example is:

Cash	$500	Overstatement
Fixed assets	$3,000	Overstatement
Long-term loans	$1,500	Understatement

Note: Cash and fixed assets are tested for overstatement and long-term loans for understatement because the auditor's objective in this case is to test for overstatements of owner's equity.

9-8 (continued)

The least amount of tolerable misstatement was allocated to cash and long-term loans because they are relatively easy to audit. The majority of the total allocation was to fixed assets because there is a greater likelihood of misstatement of fixed assets in a typical audit.

9-9   An estimate of the total misstatement in a segment is the estimate of the total misstatements based upon the sample results. If only a sample of the population is selected and audited, the auditor must project the total sample misstatements to the population to estimate the total misstatement. This is done for each audit area. The misstatements in each audit area must be totaled to make an estimate of the total misstatements in the overall financial statements. It is important to make these estimates so the auditor can evaluate whether the financial statements, taken as a whole, may be materially misstated.

The estimate for each segment is compared to tolerable misstatement for that segment and the estimate of the overall misstatement on the financial statements is compared to the preliminary judgment about materiality.

9-10   If an audit is being performed on a medium-sized company that is part of a conglomerate, the auditor must make a materiality judgment based upon the conglomerate. Materiality may be larger for a company that is part of a conglomerate because even though the financial statements of the medium-sized company may be misstated, the financial statements of the large conglomerate might still be fairly stated. If, however, the auditor is giving a separate opinion on the medium-sized company, the materiality would be lower than for the audit of a conglomerate.

9-11   The audit risk model is as follows:

$$PDR = \frac{AAR}{IR \times CR}$$

Where PDR = Planned detection risk
AAR = Acceptable audit risk
IR = Inherent risk
CR = Control risk

Planned detection risk A measure of the risk that audit evidence for a segment will fail to detect misstatements exceeding a tolerable amount, should such misstatements exist.

Acceptable audit risk A measure of how willing the auditor is to accept that the financial statements may be materially misstated after the audit is completed and an unqualified opinion has been issued.

9-11 (continued)

Inherent risk A measure of the auditor's assessment of the likelihood that there are material misstatements in a segment before considering the effectiveness of internal control.

Control risk A measure of the auditor's assessment of the likelihood that misstatements exceeding a tolerable amount in a segment will not be prevented or detected by the client's internal controls.

SAS 107 (AU 312) notes that the combination of inherent risk and control risk reflect the risk of material misstatement.

9-12 Planned detection risk is a measure of the risk that the audit evidence for a segment will fail to detect misstatements exceeding a tolerable amount, should such misstatements exist. When planned detection risk is increased from medium to high, the amount of evidence the auditor must accumulate is reduced.

9-13 An increase in planned detection risk may be caused by an increase in acceptable audit risk or a decrease in either control risk or inherent risk. A decrease in planned detection risk is caused by the opposite: a decrease in acceptable audit risk or an increase in control risk or inherent risk.

9-14 Inherent risk is a measure of the auditor's assessment of the likelihood that there are material misstatements in a segment before considering the effectiveness of internal control.
Factors affecting assessment of inherent risk include:

- Nature of the client's business
- Results of previous audits
- Initial vs. repeat engagement
- Related parties
- Nonroutine transactions
- Judgment required to correctly record transactions
- Makeup of the population
- Factors related to fraudulent financial reporting
- Factors related to misappropriation of assets

9-15 Inherent risk is set for segments rather than for the overall audit because misstatements occur in segments. By identifying expectations of misstatements in segments, the auditor is thereby able to modify audit evidence by searching for misstatements in those segments.
When inherent risk is increased from medium to high, the auditor should increase the audit evidence accumulated to determine whether the expected misstatement actually occurred. The effect on audit evidence is in the opposite direction compared to Review Question 9-12.

9-16 Extensive misstatements in the prior year's audit would cause inherent risk to be set at a high level (maybe even 100%). An increase in inherent risk would lead to a decrease in planned detection risk, which would require that the auditor increase the level of planned audit evidence.

9-17 Acceptable audit risk is a measure of how willing the auditor is to accept that the financial statements may be materially misstated after the audit is completed and an unqualified opinion has been issued.

Acceptable audit risk has an inverse relationship to evidence. If acceptable audit risk is reduced, planned evidence should increase.

9-18 When the auditor is in a situation where he or she believes that there is a high exposure to legal liability, the acceptable audit risk would be set lower than when there is little exposure to liability. Even when the auditor believes that there is little exposure to legal liability, there is still a minimum acceptable audit risk that should be met.

9-19 The first category of factors that determine acceptable audit risk is the degree to which users rely on the financial statements. The following factors are indicators of this:

- Client's size
- Distribution of ownership
- Nature and amount of liabilities

The second category of factors is the likelihood that a client will have financial difficulties after the audit report is issued. Factors affecting this are:

- Liquidity position
- Profits (losses) in previous years
- Method of financing growth
- Nature of the client's operations
- Competence of management

The third category of factors is the auditor's evaluation of management's integrity. Factors that may affect this are:

- Relationship with current or previous auditors
- Frequency of turnover of key financial or internal audit personnel
- Relationship with employees and labor unions

9-20 Exact quantification of all components of the audit risk model is not required to use the model in a meaningful way. An understanding of the relationships among model components and the effect that changes in the components have on the amount of evidence needed will allow practitioners to use the audit risk model in a meaningful way.

9-21 The auditor should revise the components of the audit risk model when the evidence accumulated during the audit indicates that the auditor's original assessments of inherent risk or control risk are too low or too high or the original assessment of acceptable audit risk is too low or too high.

The auditor should exercise care in determining the additional amount of evidence that will be required. This should be done without the use of the audit risk model. If the audit risk model is used to determine a revised planned detection risk, there is a danger of not increasing the evidence sufficiently.

■ **Multiple Choice Questions From CPA Examinations**

9-22 a. (4) b. (2) c (1)

9-23 a. (4) b. (3) c. (1)

9-24 a. (2) b. (1) c. (1)

■ **Discussion Questions And Problems**

9-25 a. The justification for a lower preliminary judgment about materiality for overstatements is directly related to legal liability and audit risk. Most auditors believe they have a greater legal and professional responsibility to discover overstatements of owners' equity than understatements because users are likely to be more critical of overstatements. That does not imply there is no responsibility for understatements.

b. There are two reasons for permitting the sum of tolerable misstatements to exceed overall materiality. First, it is unlikely that all accounts will be misstated by the full amount of tolerable misstatement. Second, some accounts are likely to be overstated while others are likely to be understated, resulting in net misstatement that is likely to be less than overall materiality.

c. This results because of the estimate of sampling error for each account. For example, the likely estimate of inventory is an overstatement of $4,500 + or - a sampling error of $9,500. You would be most concerned about overstatement for inventory because the estimated overstatement of $14,000 is close to tolerable misstatement and is the largest overstatement amount.

d. You would be most concerned about overstatement amounts since the total estimated overstatement amount ($26,000) exceeds the preliminary judgment about materiality for overstatements ($15,000). You would be most concerned about inventory since it has the largest overstatement amount.

9-25 (continued)

    e.   1.   This may occur because total tolerable misstatement was allowed to exceed the preliminary judgment (see Part b for explanation).

          2.   The auditor must determine whether the actual total overstatement amount actually exceeds the preliminary judgment by performing expanded audit tests or by requiring the client to make an adjustment for estimated misstatements.

9-26 a.   The direct projection of error = (misstatements/amount) sampled x population value.

        ($10,000/$1,000,000) x $2,500,000 = $25,000

    b.   No, the overall financial statements are not acceptable. Including the projected error for inventory, the total overstatement errors are $58,000 which exceeds materiality of $50,000.

    c.   The auditor should either propose an audit adjustment so that the unadjusted statement amount is less than materiality, and/or perform more testing to obtain a better estimate of the population misstatements. The additional testing will likely focus on receivables and inventory because they have the largest estimated misstatements.

9-27 a.   The profession has not established clear-cut guidelines as to the appropriate preliminary estimates of materiality. These are matters of the auditor's professional judgment.

        The illustrative materiality guidelines in Fig 9-2 (p. 253) are used in applying materiality for the problem. Other guidelines may be equally acceptable.

STATEMENT COMPONENT	PERCENT GUIDELINES	DOLLAR RANGE (IN MILLIONS)
Earnings from continuing operations before taxes	3 - 6%	$12.5 - $25.1
Current assets	3 - 6%	$67.6 - $135.2
Current liabilities	3 - 6%	$36.5 - $72.9
Total assets	1 - 3%	$38.6 - $115.8

    b.   The allocation to the individual accounts is not shown. The difficulty of the allocation is far more important than the actual allocation. There are several ways the allocation could be done. The most likely way would be to allocate only on the basis of the balance sheet rather than the income statement. Even then the allocation could vary significantly. One way would be to allocate the same

9-27 (continued)

amount to each of the balance sheet accounts on the consolidated statement of financial position. Using a materiality limit of $12,500,000 before taxes (because it is the most restrictive) and the same dollar allocation to each account excluding retained earnings, the allocation would be approximately $595,000,000 to each account. There are 21 account summaries included in the statement of financial position, which is divided into $12,500,000.

An alternative is to assume an equal percentage misstatement in each of the accounts. Doing it in that manner, total assets should be added to total liabilities and owners' equity, less retained earnings. The allocation would be then done on a percentage basis.

c. Auditors generally use *before* tax net earnings instead of *after* tax net earnings to develop a preliminary judgment about materiality given that transactions and accounts being audited within a segment are presented in the accounting records on a pretax basis. Auditors generally project total misstatements for a segment and accumulate all projected total misstatements across segments on a pretax basis and then compute the tax effect on an aggregate basis to determine the effects on after tax net earnings.

d. By allocating 75% of the preliminary estimate to accounts receivable, inventories, and accounts payable, there is far less materiality to be allocated to all other accounts. Given the total dollar value of those accounts, that may be a reasonable allocation. The effect of such an allocation would be that the auditor might be able to accumulate sufficient appropriate evidence with less total effort than would be necessary under part b. Under part b, it would likely be necessary to audit, on almost a 100% basis, accounts receivable, inventories, and accounts payable. On most audits it would be expensive to do that much testing in those three accounts.

It would likely be necessary to audit accounts such as cash and temporary investments on a 100% basis. That would not be costly on most audits because the effort to do so would be small compared to the cost of auditing receivables, inventories, and accounts payable.

e. It is necessary for you to be satisfied that the actual estimate of misstatements is less than the preliminary judgment about materiality for all of the bases. First you would reevaluate the preliminary judgment for earnings. Assuming no change is considered appropriate, you would likely require an adjusting entry or an expansion of certain audit tests.

9-28 a. The following terms are audit planning decisions requiring professional judgment:
- Preliminary judgment about materiality
- Control risk
- Risk of fraud
- Planned detection risk
- Acceptable audit risk
- Tolerable misstatement
- Inherent risk
- Risk of material misstatement

b. The following terms are audit conclusions resulting from application of audit procedures and requiring professional judgment:
- Estimated total misstatement in a segment
- Estimate of the combined misstatement
- Known misstatement

c. It is acceptable to change any of the factors affecting audit planning decisions at any time in the audit if indicated by changes in circumstances. The planning process begins before the audit starts and continues throughout the engagement.

9-29 Acceptable audit risk is a measure of how willing the auditor is to accept that the financial statements may be materially misstated after the audit is completed and an unqualified opinion has been issued.

a. True. A CPA firm should attempt to use reasonable uniformity from audit to audit when circumstances are similar. The only reasons for having a different audit risk in these circumstances are the lack of consistency within the firm, different audit risk preferences for different auditors, and difficulties of measuring audit risk.

b. True. Users who rely heavily upon the financial statements need more reliable information than those who do not place heavy reliance on the financial statements. To protect those users, the auditor needs to be reasonably assured that the financial statements are fairly stated. That is equivalent to stating that acceptable audit risk is lower. Consistent with that conclusion, the auditor is also likely to face greatest legal exposure in situations where external users rely heavily upon the statements. Therefore, the auditor should be more certain that the financial statements are correctly stated.

c. True. The reasoning for c is essentially the same as for b.

d. True. The audit opinion issued by different auditors conveys the same meaning regardless of who signs the report. Users cannot be expected to evaluate whether different auditors take different risk levels. Therefore, for a given set of circumstances, every CPA firm should attempt to obtain approximately the same audit risk.

1. Decrease — Healthier financial condition leads to a decrease in audit risk

2. Increase — Audit risk increases when management is dominated by a single person.

3. Increase — Audit risk increases when internal audit reports to top management rather than the audit committee.

4. Increase — Audit risk increases when there is turnover in key management positions.

5. Decrease — The monitoring by the bank loan officer decreases audit risk.

6. No effect — The timing of payments to employees has no effect on audit risk.

7. Decrease — Audit risk decreases due to the auditor's previous experience with the client.

8. Increase — A change in the method of accounting increases the risk of misstatements due to the new reporting method.

9. Increase — The unusual transaction increases audit risk.

10. Decrease — The resolution of the lawsuit decreases risk related to disclosure of the litigation.

11. Increase — Related party transactions increase audit risk.

12. No effect — The amount of insurance coverage has minimal effect on audit risk.

13. Increase — The potential for improper revenue recognition increases audit risk.

14. Increase — A planned stock offering increases incentives to misstate the financial statements and increases audit risk.

9-31 a. *Acceptable audit risk* A measure of how willing the auditor is to accept that the financial statements may be materially misstated after the audit is completed and an unqualified opinion has been issued. This is the risk that the auditor will give an incorrect audit opinion.

Inherent risk A measure of the auditor's assessment of the likelihood that there are material misstatements in a segment before considering the effectiveness of internal control. This risk relates to the auditor's expectation of misstatements in the financial statements, ignoring internal control.

Control risk A measure of the auditor's assessment of the likelihood that misstatements exceeding a tolerable amount in a segment will not be prevented or detected by the client's internal controls. This risk is related to the effectiveness of a client's internal controls.

Planned detection risk A measure of the risk that audit evidence for a segment will fail to detect misstatements exceeding a tolerable amount, should such misstatements exist. In audit planning, this risk is determined by using the other three factors in the risk model using the formula PDR = AAR / (IR x CR).

b.

	1	2	3	4	5	6
Acceptable Audit Risk	.05	.05	.05	.05	.01	.01
IR x CR	1.00	.24	.24	.06	1.00	.24
PDR = AAR / (IR x CR)	.05	.208	.208	.833	.01	.042
Planned Detection Risk in percent	5%	20.8%	20.8%	83.3%	1%	4.2%

c. Situation 5 will require the greatest amount of evidence because the planned detection risk is smallest. Situation 4 will require the least amount of evidence because the planned detection risk is highest. In comparing those two extremes, notice that acceptable audit risk is lower for situation 5, and both control and inherent risk are considerably higher.

d. 1. Increase; Compare the change from situation 5 to 1.
    2. Decrease; Compare the change from situation 2 to 1.
    3. Increase; Compare the change from situation 1 to 2.
    4. No effect; Compare the change from situation 2 to 3.

9-32 a. Low, medium, and high for the four risks and planned evidence have meaning only in comparison to each other. For example, an acceptable audit risk that is high means the auditor is willing to accept more risk than in a situation where there is medium risk without specifying the precise percentage of risk. The same is true for the other three risk factors and planned evidence.

b.

	1	2	3	4	5	6
Acceptable Audit Risk	H	H	L	L	H	M
IR x CR	L	M	H	M	M	M
PDR = AAR / (IR x CR)	H	M	L	L	M	M
Planned Evidence	L	M	H	H	M	M

L = low, M = medium, H = high

c.

	EFFECT ON PDR	EFFECT ON EVIDENCE
(1)	Decrease	Increase
(2)	Increase	Decrease
(3)	NA	Increase
(4)	Increase	Decrease
(5)	No effect	No effect

9-33

Risk Factor	Related Audit Risk Model Component
1.	Acceptable audit risk
2.	Control risk
3.	Acceptable audit risk
4.	Inherent risk
5.	Planned detection risk
6.	Acceptable audit risk
7.	Inherent risk
8.	Inherent risk
9.	Planned detection risk
10.	Control risk

9-34

	CONTROL RISK	INHERENT RISK	ACCEPTABLE AUDIT RISK	PLANNED EVIDENCE
a.	N	N	I	D
b.	N	N	D	I
c.	I	N	N	I
d.	N	I	N	I
e.	N	N	I	D
f.	D	D	N or I	D
g.	I	I	N	I
h.	I	N or I	D	I
i.	D	I	N	C
j.	I	I	D	I

- **Cases**

9-35

FACTOR	EFFECT ON THE RISK OF MATERIAL MISSTATEMENT	AUDIT RISK MODEL COMPONENT
1. Henderson is a new client.	Increases	Inherent risk
2. Henderson operates in a regulated industry, which increases regulatory oversight and need for compliance with regulations.	Increases	Acceptable audit risk
3. The company's stock is publicly traded.	Increases	Acceptable audit risk
4. The company is more profitable than competitors, but recent growth has strained operations.	Increases	Acceptable audit risk
5. The company has expanded its use of derivatives and hedging transactions.	Increases	Inherent risk
6. Henderson has added competent accounting staff and has an internal audit function with direct reporting to the audit committee.	Decreases	Control risk

9-35 (continued)

FACTOR	EFFECT ON THE RISK OF MATERIAL MISSTATEMENT	AUDIT RISK MODEL COMPONENT
7. The financial statements contain several accounting estimates that are based on management assumptions.	Increases	Inherent risk
8. The company has struggled in tracking property, plant & equipment.	Increases	Control risk
9. Henderson acquired a regional electric company.	Increases	Inherent risk
10. The audit engagement staff have experience in auditing energy and public companies.	Decreases	Planned detection risk
11. Partner review of key accounts will be extensive.	Decreases	Planned detection risk.

9-36 Computer prepared Excel worksheets (P936a.xls and P936b.xls) are contained on the Companion Website.

a. See Worksheet 9-36A on pages 9-18 and 9-19. It is important to recognize that there is no *one* solution to this requirement. The determination of materiality and allocation to the accounts is *always* arbitrary. In this illustration, the auditor makes estimated adjustments for problems noted by analytical procedures. This is an important step as the potential adjustments *reduce* income before taxes, and thus materiality. The illustrated solution recognizes that with downward adjustments, actual income may be much closer to the contractual amount required for an additional contribution to the employee's pension plan. This creates a sensitivity that will need to be watched carefully as the audit progresses. The allocation to the accounts is particularly arbitrary. It is noteworthy that the sum of allocated amounts equals 1.5 times materiality. It is assumed that this is consistent with the audit firm's internal policies.

b. The level of acceptable audit risk is based on an evaluation of three factors:

1. The degree to which external users rely on the statements.
2. The likelihood that the client will have financial difficulties after the audit report is issued.
3. The auditor's evaluation of management's integrity.

Stanton Enterprise is a public company and therefore has a high degree of reliance by external users on its financial statements. The Company's operating results and financial condition indicate that there is very little likelihood of financial difficulty in the immediate future. With regard to management's integrity, although there has been some concern with Leonard Stanton's past bankruptcy, the carefully monitored relationship has been good for the four years Stanton has been a client. On that basis, it appears management integrity is good.

Overall, then, an acceptable audit risk level of medium would seem appropriate.

c.   See Worksheet 9-36B on pages 9-20 and 9-21 that shows both horizontal and vertical analysis of the 2010 audited and the 2011 unaudited financial statements, as well as computation of applicable ratios. Following are the key observations to be made:

Overall Results Stanton Enterprises apparently had an extremely successful year in 2011. Sales increased by 36.4 percent, gross margin increased by 4 absolute percentage points, and income before taxes increased by 138.5 percent. Return on total assets and return on equity increased and are at admirable levels. These results allowed the Company to increase its dividends by 25 percent (recognizing that more shares were outstanding) and total stockholder's equity by 101.9 percent. Furthermore, the Company's current, quick, cash and times interest earned ratios are up, and its debt to equity ratio is down, indicating that the Company is extremely sound from a liquidity standpoint.

Trade Accounts Receivable In the face of such growth, trade accounts receivable increased by 59.3 percent, and at the same time, accounts receivable turnover slowed and days to collect increased somewhat. However, the allowance for uncollectible accounts was only .3 percent of gross receivables at the end of 2011, down from 1.0 percent at the end of 2010. This implies that the allowance may be significantly understated for 2011 and must be looked at very carefully during the current audit. This review would include considering whether a liberalization of credit policies was used to help increase sales.

Property, Plant and Equipment The Company made a significant additional investment in property, plant and equipment, increasing them by 30.5 percent. These new assets will need to be verified during the current audit. It is noteworthy that accumulated depreciation

9-36 (continued)

increased by only 16.1 percent. This could indicate that depreciation on the new assets was not recorded, but may not, depending on dates of acquisition and depreciation method used. Depreciation must be tested considering these facts as determined.

Goodwill Goodwill also increased significantly, by $855,000. This implies that the Company made an acquisition during the year. This could explain the increase in operating assets, and any such transaction must be examined in detail as part of the audit. Also, the goodwill from prior transactions must be considered during each audit and tested for possible impairment.

Accounts Payable Accounts payable went *down* from 2010 to 2011. This doesn't seem reasonable at all given an increase in business activity. It is very possible there are unrecorded liabilities at the end of 2011, and this must be an area of major emphasis during the audit.

Bank Loan Payable It seems somewhat strange for the Company to have an outstanding balance on its bank loan payable at the end of 2011 given its excellent operating results. This may be attributable to the growth in accounts receivable and inventory, or could be the result of an acquisition, or they simply haven't paid it off. In any case, verifying this balance is a relatively easy audit procedure.

Federal Income Taxes Payable and Income Tax Expense The Company's effective tax rate for 2010 was 34 percent. Income tax expense is only 22.5 percent of income before taxes for 2011. Federal income taxes payable on the balance sheet is significantly lower at 12-31-11 than would be expected based on 2010. These both indicate that the Company has not made its final tax accrual for 2011, and this area will require careful attention during the audit.

Common Stock Common stock increased by 25 percent. It is possible that this occurred in connection with an acquisition (see Goodwill), or in some other way. The issuance of new shares and surrounding circumstances will need to be understood and examined.

Sales Whenever there is a drastic increase in business activity, there is an increased risk of problems. It is possible that controls will lapse or not be carefully observed. It is possible that transactions will not be carefully accounted for. Therefore, in a situation such as Stanton's it is important to understand the nature of the changes that took place and to do a careful review of controls. It will be especially important to thoroughly test cutoffs if both sales and purchase transactions.

9-36 (continued)

Cost of Goods Sold and Gross Profit Consistent with the comments under sales, the auditors must determine why the gross profit percent has made such a significant improvement. Tests of costs and inventories will be more extensive than in more stable circumstances.

Pension Cost It appears that the Company exceeded the contractual amount for additional pension contribution. Yet, pension cost is a lesser percent of sales in 2011 than in 2010. This may indicate that an accrual for additional pension cost was not made. As pension cost is a complex and important area, it will be verified in detail during the audit.

d.

	ACCEPTABLE AUDIT RISK	INHERENT RISK	ANALYTICAL PROCEDURES
Detail tie-in	Medium	Medium	See Note 5
Existence	Medium	Medium	See Note 5
Completeness	Medium	Medium	See Note 5
Accuracy	Medium	Medium	See Note 5
Classification	Medium	Medium	See Note 5
Cutoff	Medium	High	High
Realizable value	Medium	High	High
Rights	Medium	Medium	See Note 5

Tolerable misstatement:	
Trade accounts receivable	$80,000
Allowance for uncollectible accounts	15,000
Total	$95,000

RATIONALE

1. Acceptable audit risk is medium for the engagement, therefore, it is medium for accounts receivable and all of its related objectives.
2. Inherent risk would be considered medium for most objectives given the significant changes in sales and accounts receivable.

9-36 (continued)

3.   Inherent risk for cutoff is considered high due to the Company's rapid growth in 2011 and the general frequency of cutoff errors.

4.   Inherent risk for realizable value is considered high because of the Company's rapid growth and the amount of judgment involved in establishing the allowance for uncollectible accounts.

5.   The analytical procedures performed are <u>preliminary</u> only, and don't provide substantive evidence. However, they can indicate areas where possible problems exist. In other words, they can't lower risk, but can increase it. In this case, they corroborate the high inherent risk level specified for cutoff and realizable value.

Stanton Enterprises
Worksheet 9-36A
Determination of Materiality and
Allocation to the Accounts
12/31/2011

DETERMINATION OF MATERIALITY:

Income before taxes	$8,004,277	
Possible adjustments - estimated. See Worksheet 9-36b:		
Increase allowance for uncollectible accounts	(220,000)	Increase to equal same % of trade accounts receivable as prior year.
Increase accounts payable	(1,070,000)	Reflect same increase as cost of goods sold.
Pension cost	NA	Can't estimate. May or may not be required.
Adjusted net income before taxes	$6,714,277	
5 percent	$ 335,714	
Round down to	$ 330,000	

  Note: A key consideration is whether the Company will be required to make its additional pension contribution. As more information is obtained, the amount considered material may be reduced to assure any possible misstatements in earnings are considered in light of that contractual obligation.

9-36 (continued)

Stanton Enterprises
Worksheet 9-36A, cont.
ALLOCATION TO THE ACCOUNTS:

	Prelim. 12/31/11	Tolerable Misstatement	
Cash	$243,689	5000	Easy to audit at low cost.
Trade accounts receivable	3,544,009	80000	Large tolerable misstatement (TM) because account is large and requires extensive sampling to audit.
Allowance for uncollectible accounts	(120,000)	15000	Fairly large TM because of inherent risk.
Inventories	4,520,902	100000	Large TM because account is large and requires extensive sampling to audit.
Prepaid expenses	29,500	5000	Easy to audit at low cost.
Total current assets	8,218,100		
Property, plant and equipment, at cost	12,945,255	100000	Small TM as a percent of account balance because most of balance is unchanged from prior year & audit of additions is relatively low cost.
Less: accumulated depreciation	(4,382,990)	40000	Fairly low TM due to possible risk of misstatement. See 9-36B.
	8,562,265		
Goodwill	1,200,000	20000	Fairly low TM due to possible risk of
Total assets	$17,980,365		misstatement. See 9-36B.
Accounts payable	$2,141,552	70000	Large TM because account is large and requires extensive sampling to audit.
Bank loan payable	150,000	0	Easy to audit at low cost.
Accrued liabilities	723,600	20000	Easy to audit at low cost.
Federal income taxes payable	1,200,000	40000	Fairly low TM due to possible risk of misstatement. See 9-35B.
Current portion of long-term	240,000	0	Easy to audit at low cost.
Total current liabilities	4,455,152		
Long-term debt	960,000	0	Easy to audit at low cost.
Stockholders' equity:			
Common stock	1,250,000	0	Easy to audit at low cost.
Additional paid-in capital	2,469,921	0	Easy to audit at low cost.
Retained earnings	8,845,292	NA	
Total stockholders' equity	12,565,213		
Total liabilities and stockholders' equity	$17,980,365	$495,000	(1.5 x $330,000)

9-36 (continued)

Stanton Enterprises
Worksheet 9-36B
Analysis of Financial Statements
and Audit Planning Worksheet
12/31/2011

BALANCE SHEET

	Preliminary 12/31/11	%	Audited 12/31/10	%	% Change
Cash	$243,689	1.4	$133,981	1.1	81.9
Trade accounts receivable	3,544,009	19.7	2,224,921	17.7	59.3
Allowance for uncollectible accounts	(120,000)	-0.7	(215,000)	-1.7	-44.2
Inventories	4,520,902	25.1	3,888,400	31.0	16.3
Prepaid expenses	29,500	0.2	24,700	0.2	19.4
Total current assets	8,218,100	45.7	6,057,002	48.3	35.7
Property, plant and equipment:					
At cost	12,945,255	72.0	9,922,534	79.1	30.5
Less, accumulated depreciation	(4,382,990)	-24.4	(3,775,911)	-30.1	16.1
	8,562,265	47.6	6,146,623	49.0	39.3
Goodwill	1,200,000	6.7	345,000	2.7	247.8
	$17,980,365	100.0	$12,548,625	100.0	43.3
Accounts payable	$2,141,552	11.9	$2,526,789	20.1	-15.2
Bank loan payable	150,000	0.8	0	0.0	--
Accrued liabilities	723,600	4.0	598,020	4.8	21.0
Federal income taxes payable	1,200,000	6.7	1,759,000	14.0	-31.8
Current portion of long-term debt	240,000	1.3	240,000	1.9	0.0
Total current liabilities	4,455,152	24.8	5,123,809	40.8	-13.0
Long-term debt	960,000	5.3	1,200,000	9.6	-20.0
Stockholder's equity:					
Common stock	1,250,000	7.0	1,000,000	8.0	25.0
Additional paid-in capital	2,469,921	13.7	1,333,801	10.6	85.2
Retained earnings	8,845,292	49.2	3,891,015	31.0	127.3
	12,565,213	69.9	6,224,816	49.6	101.9
	$17,980,365	100.0	$12,548,625	100.0	43.3

9-36 (continued)

Stanton Enterprises
Worksheet 9-36B, cont.
COMBINED STATEMENT OF INCOME
AND RETAINED EARNINGS

	Preliminary 12/31/11	%	Audited 12/31/10	%	% Change
Sales	$43,994,931	100.0	$32,258,015	100.0	36.4
Cost of goods sold	24,197,212	55.0	19,032,229	59.0	27.1
Gross profit	19,797,719	45.0	13,225,786	41.0	49.7
Selling, general and administrative expenses	10,592,221	24.1	8,900,432	27.6	19.0
Pension cost	1,117,845	2.5	865,030	2.7	29.2
Interest cost	83,376	0.2	104,220	0.3	-20.0
	11,793,442	26.8	9,869,682	30.6	19.5
Income before taxes	8,004,277	18.2	3,356,104	10.4	138.5
Income tax expense	1,800,000	4.1	1,141,000	3.5	57.8
Net income	6,204,277	14.1	2,215,104	6.9	180.1
Beginning retained earnings	3,891,015		2,675,911		
	10,095,292		4,891,015		
Dividends declared	(1,250,000)		(1,000,000)		
Ending retained earnings	$8,845,292		$3,891,015		

SIGNIFICANT RATIOS

Current ratio	1.84	1.18
Quick ratio	0.82	0.42
Cash ratio	0.05	0.03
Accounts receivable turnover	12.41	14.50
Days to collect	29.40	25.18
Inventory turnover	5.35	4.89
Days to sell	68.20	74.57
Days to convert to cash	97.60	99.75
Debt to equity ratio	0.43	1.02
Tangible net assets to equity	1.34	1.96
Times interest earned	97.00	33.20
Efficiency ratio	2.62	2.64
Profit margin ratio	0.18	0.11
Profitability ratio	0.48	0.28
Return on total assets	0.45	0.27
Return on equity	0.64	0.54

Note: Some ratios are based on
year-end balances, as 12-31-09
balances are not provided.

■ **Integrated Case Application**

9-37

PINNACLE MANUFACTURING—PART II

a.   Acceptable Audit Risk and Engagement Risk Issues:

External users' reliance on financial statements:

1.   The company is privately held, but there is a large amount of debt, therefore the financial statements will be used fairly extensively. Also, management is considering selling the Machine-Tech division, which has the potential to result in extensive use of the statements by the buyers.
2.   Item 6 in the planning phase indicates plans for additional debt financing.

Likelihood of financial difficulties:

1.   The solar power engine business revolves around constantly changing technology, thus making it inherently more risky than other businesses, with a better chance of subsequent bankruptcy. Item 1 in the planning issues raises a concern about the viability of the Solar-Electro division, but not necessarily the entire company.
2.   The conclusion in Part I of the case was that the likelihood of financial failure is low, even considering the issue with Solar-Electro.
3.   Item 9 in the planning phase indicates there is a debt covenant requiring a current ratio above 2.0 and a debt-to-equity ratio below 1.0. The current ratio has fallen below 2.0. This could result in the loan being called unless a waiver of the loan covenant is granted.

Management integrity:

No major issue exists that would cause the auditor to question management integrity, but the auditor should have done extensive client acceptance procedures before accepting the client. It is possible that Item 8 in the planning phase, turnover of internal audit personnel, could be intentional and increases the risk of fraudulent financial reporting.

b.   Acceptable audit risk is likely to be medium to low because of the factors listed previously, especially the planned increase in financing and the potential violation of the debt covenant agreement. Some might prefer an even lower acceptable risk because it is a first year audit.

9-37 (continued)

c. Inherent risks are addressed by examining each of the 11 items in the planning phase.

1. **Inherent Risk:** No effect on inherent risk

2. **Inherent Risk:** The primary concern is the possibility of obsolete inventory, which affects the valuation of inventory at the lower of cost or market.
   Accounts Affected: Inventory, cost of good sold

3. **Inherent Risk:** There is a potential related party transaction, which could affect the valuation of the transaction and may require disclosure as a related party transaction.
   Accounts Affected: Manufacturing equipment, footnote

4. **Inherent Risk:** This situation involves a nonroutine transaction where there is a risk that materials, labor and/or overhead are incorrectly applied to the property accounts.
   Accounts Affected: Property accounts, inventory and cost of sales.

5. **Inherent Risk:** A receivable outstanding for several months from a customer making up 15% of the company's outstanding accounts receivable balance may indicate a major collection problem, which could result in an understatement of the allowance for uncollectible accounts.
   Accounts Affected: Accounts receivable, bad debt expense, allowance for uncollectible accounts.

6. **Inherent risk:** No affect on inherent risk

7. **Inherent Risk:** There is a potential related party transaction, which could affect the valuation of the transaction and may require disclosure as a related party transaction.
   Accounts Affected: Repairs and maintenance expense and accounts payable

8. **Inherent Risk:** Although this does not directly affect inherent risk, it is possible that turnover of internal audit personnel could be intentional and increases the risk of fraudulent financial reporting. The turnover may also affect the auditor's assessment of control risk.
   Accounts Affected: All accounts

9. **Inherent Risk:** In addition to affecting acceptable audit risk, the auditor should be concerned about the risk of fraudulent financial reporting due to the incentive to make certain that all debt covenants have been met.
   Accounts Affected: All accounts

9-37 (continued)

10. **Inherent Risk:** An ongoing dispute with the Internal Revenue Service may require an adjustment to income tax liability or a disclosure in footnotes for a contingency, depending on the status of the dispute.
    Accounts Affected: Income tax expense and income taxes payable

11. **Inherent Risk:** This situation involves a related party transaction (Solar-Electro borrowed money from the Welburn division). Because this transaction was not conducted with an outside party, it is possible that the related receivable and payable might not have been properly eliminated on Pinnacle's consolidated financial statements.
    Accounts Affected: Notes payable, notes receivable, interest expense and interest income.

■ **Internet Problem Solution: Materiality and Tolerable Misstatement**

Internet Problem 9-1

a. Microsoft's income before taxes for 2009 was $19,821 million. Thus, engagement materiality could range from $594.6 million (3%) to $1.189 billion (6%). Although student responses will vary, a higher materiality seems appropriate given Microsoft's market position and overall financial condition.

b. The three largest asset line items are "Short-term investments" at $25.371 billion, "Goodwill" at $12.503 billion, and "Accounts Receivable" at $11.192 billion. These accounts would likely receive the largest allocation of tolerable misstatement. Of these three accounts, short-term investments would receive the smallest allocation because it is easy to audit at low cost. Accounts receivable is fairly costly to audit and would receive a larger allocation, as would goodwill due to the valuation issues.

(**Note**: Internet problems address current issues using Internet sources. Because Internet sites are subject to change, Internet problems and solutions may change. Current information on Internet problems is available at www.pearsonhighered.com/arens.)

Chapter 10

Section 404 Audits of Internal Control and Control Risk

■ **Review Questions**

10-1 Management typically has three broad objectives in designing effective internal controls.

1. **Reliability of Financial Reporting** Management is responsible for preparing financial statements for investors, creditors, and other users. Management has both a legal and professional responsibility to be sure that the information is fairly presented in accordance with reporting requirements such as GAAP or IFRS. The objective of effective internal control over financial reporting is to fulfill these financial reporting responsibilities.

2. **Efficiency and Effectiveness of Operations** Controls within an organization are meant to encourage efficient and effective use of its resources to optimize the company's goals. An important objective of these controls is accurate financial and non-financial information about the entity's operations for decision making.

3. **Compliance with Laws and Regulations** Section 404 of the Sarbanes-Oxley Act requires all public companies to issue a report about the operating effectiveness of internal control over financial reporting. In addition to the legal provisions of Section 404, public, nonpublic, and not-for-profit organizations are required to follow many laws and regulations. Some relate to accounting only indirectly, such as environmental protection and civil rights laws. Others are closely related to accounting, such as income tax regulations and fraud.

10-2 Management designs systems of internal control to accomplish three categories of objectives: financial reporting, operations, and compliance with laws and regulations. The auditor's focus in both the audit of financial statements and the audit of internal controls is on those controls related to the reliability of financial reporting plus those controls related to operations and to compliance with laws and regulations objectives that could materially affect financial reporting.

10-3 Section 404(a) requires management of all public companies to issue an internal control report that includes the following:

- A statement that management is responsible for establishing and maintaining an adequate internal control structure and procedures for financial reporting and
- An assessment of the effectiveness of the internal control structure and procedures for financial reporting as of the end of the company's fiscal year.

10-4 Management's assessment of internal control over financial reporting consists of two key characteristics. First, management must evaluate the *design* of internal control over financial reporting. Second, management must test the *operating effectiveness* of those controls. When evaluating the design of internal control over financial reporting, management evaluates whether the controls are designed to prevent or detect material misstatements in the financial statements. When testing the operating effectiveness of those controls, the objective is to determine whether the control is operating as designed and whether the person performing the control possesses the necessary authority and qualifications to perform the control effectively.

10-5 There are eight parts of the planning phase of audits: accept client and perform initial planning, understand the client's business and industry, assess client business risk, perform preliminary analytical procedures, set materiality and assess acceptable audit risk and inherent risk, understand internal control and assess control risk, gather information to assess fraud risks, and develop an overall audit plan and audit program. Understanding internal control and assessing control risk is therefore part six of planning. Only gathering information to assess fraud risk and developing an overall audit plan and audit program follow understanding internal control and assessing control risk.

10-6 The second GAAS field work standard states "The auditor must obtain a sufficient understanding of the entity and its environment, including its internal controls, to assess the risk of material misstatement of the financial statements whether due to error or fraud and to design the nature, timing, and extent of further audit procedures." The auditor obtains the understanding of internal control to assess control risk in every audit and that responsibility is the same for audits of both public and nonpublic companies. Auditors are primarily concerned about controls related to the reliability of financial reporting and controls over classes of transactions.

10-7 PCAOB Auditing Standard 5 requires that the auditor issue a report on the effectiveness of internal control over financial reporting. To express an opinion on internal controls, the auditor obtains an understanding of and performs tests of controls related to *all* significant account balances, classes of transactions, and disclosures and related assertions in the financial statements. PCAOB Auditing Standard 5 requires the auditor's independent assessment of the internal controls' design and operating effectiveness.

10-8   The six transaction-related audit objectives are:

1.   Recorded transactions exist (occurrence).
2.   Existing transactions are recorded (completeness).
3.   Recorded transactions are stated at the correct amounts (accuracy).
4.   Recorded transactions are properly included in the master files and correctly summarized (posting and summarization).
5.   Transactions are properly classified (classification).
6.   Transactions are recorded on the correct dates (timing).

10-9   COSO's *Internal Control–Integrated Framework* is the most widely accepted internal control framework in the U.S. The COSO framework describes internal control as consisting of five components that management designs and implements to provide reasonable assurance that its control objectives will be met. Each component contains many controls, but auditors concentrate on those designed to prevent or detect material misstatements in the financial statements.

10-10   The COSO *Internal Control – Integrated Framework* consists of the following five components:

1.   Control environment
2.   Risk assessment
3.   Control activities
4.   Information and communication
5.   Monitoring

10-11   The control environment consists of the actions, policies, and procedures that reflect the overall attitudes of top management, directors, and owners of an entity about internal control and its importance to the entity. The control environment serves as the umbrella for the other four components. Without an effective control environment, the other four are unlikely to result in effective internal control, regardless of their quality. The following are the most important subcomponents the control environment:

- Integrity and ethical values
- Commitment to competence
- Board of directors or audit committee participation
- Management's philosophy and operating style
- Organizational structure
- Assignment of authority and responsibility
- Human resource policies and practices

10-12 Internal control includes five categories of controls that management designs and implements to provide reasonable assurance that its control objectives will be met. These are called the components internal control, which consists of the following:

- The control environment
- Risk assessment
- Control activities
- Information and communication
- Monitoring

The control environment is the broadest of the five and deals primarily with the way management implements its attitude about internal controls. The other four components are closely related to the control environment. Risk assessment is management's identification and analysis of risks relevant to the preparation of financial statements in accordance with accounting standards. Management implements control activities and creates the accounting information and communication system in response to risks identified as part of its risk assessment in order to meet its objectives for financial reporting. Finally, management periodically assesses the quality of internal control performance to determine that controls are operating as intended and that they are modified as appropriate for changes in conditions (monitoring). All five components are necessary for effectively designed and implemented internal control.

10-13 The five categories of control activities are:

- Adequate separation of duties
  Example: The following two functions are performed by different people: processing customer orders and billing of customers.
- Proper authorization of transactions and activities
  Example: The granting of credit is authorized before shipment takes place.
- Adequate documents and records
  Example: Recording of sales is supported by authorized shipping documents and approved customer orders.
- Physical control over assets and records
  Example: A password is required before entry into the computerized accounts receivable master file can be made.
- Independent checks on performance
  Example: Accounts receivable master file contents are independently verified.

10-14 Separation of operational responsibility from record keeping is intended to reduce the likelihood of operational personnel biasing the results of their performance by incorrectly recording information.

10-14 (continued)

Separation of the custody of assets from accounting for these assets is intended to prevent misappropriation of assets. When one person performs both functions, the possibility of that person's disposal of the asset for personal gain and adjustment of the records to relieve himself or herself of responsibility for the asset without detection increases.

10-15 An example of a physical control the client can use to protect each of the following assets or records is:

1. Petty cash should be kept locked in a fireproof safe.
2. Cash received by retail clerks should be entered into a cash register to record all cash received.
3. Accounts receivable records should be stored in a locked, fireproof safe. Adequate backup copies of computerized records should be maintained and access to the master files should be restricted via passwords.
4. Raw material inventory should be retained in a locked storeroom with a reliable and competent employee controlling access.
5. Perishable tools should be stored in a locked storeroom under control of a reliable employee.
6. Manufacturing equipment should be kept in an area protected by security and fire alarms and kept locked when not in use.
7. Marketable securities should be stored in a safety deposit vault.

10-16 Independent checks on performance are internal control activities designed for the continuous internal verification of other controls. Examples of independent checks include:

- Preparation of the monthly bank reconciliation by an individual with no responsibility for recording transactions or handling cash.
- Recomputing inventory extensions for a listing of inventory by someone who did not originally do the extensions.
- The preparation of the sales journal by one person and the accounts receivable master file by a different person, and a reconciliation of the control account to the master file.
- The counting of inventory by two different count teams.
- The existence of an effective internal audit staff.

10-17 As illustrated by Figure 10-3, there are four phases in the process of understanding internal control and assessing control risk. In the first phase the auditor obtains an understanding of internal controls, which includes an understanding of their design and whether they have been implemented. Next the auditor must make a preliminary assessment of control risk (phase 2) and perform tests of controls (phase 3). The auditor uses the results of tests of controls to assess control risk and to ultimately decide planned detection risk and substantive tests for the audit of financial statements, which is phase 4.

10-18 When obtaining an understanding of internal control, the auditor must assess two aspects about those controls. First, the auditor must gather evidence about the *design* of internal controls. Second, the auditor must gather evidence about whether those controls have been *implemented*.

10-19 In a walkthrough of internal control, the auditor selects one or a few documents for the initiation of a transaction type and traces them through the entire accounting process. At each stage of processing, the auditor makes inquiries and observes current activities, in addition to examining completed documentation for the transaction or transactions selected. Thus, the auditor combines observation, documentation, and inquiry to conduct a walkthrough of internal control. PCAOB Auditing Standard 5 requires the auditor to perform at least one walkthrough for each major class of transactions.

10-20 Due to the nature of the subcomponents that constitute the control environment, such as integrity and ethical values and commitment to competence, the nature of evidence used to evaluate the control environment may differ somewhat from the nature of evidence used to evaluate control activities. While auditors examine similar types of evidence to assess both the control environment and control activities, they often perform more extensive inquires and observation to assess the design and implementation of control environment subcomponents, such as the entity's code of conduct and whistleblowing system, so they can evaluate whether employees understand those policies and procedures and to gain a sense as to the overall ethical tone and perception of management's integrity. Because of the more judgmental nature of many of the control environment subcomponents, auditors often make numerous inquiries and perform extensive observation of client personnel in the performance of policies and procedures to evaluate those subcomponents of the control environment. While inquiry and observation may also be performed to evaluate control activities, auditors frequently examine documentation that demonstrates a control activity was performed, such as examining signatures on documents or matching of documentation supporting a transaction, and they often reperform certain client performed procedures, such as the calculation of a transaction amount. For many control activities, documentation of their performance is more objectively evaluated in contrast to the evaluation of the control environment.

10-21 A significant deficiency exists if one or more control deficiencies exist that is less severe than a material weakness, but important enough to merit attention by those responsible for oversight of the company's financial reporting. A material weakness exists if a significant deficiency, by itself, or in combination with other significant deficiencies, results in a reasonable possibility that internal control will not prevent or detect material financial statement misstatements. The presence of one significant deficiency that is not deemed to be a material weakness may not affect the auditor's report. In that instance, the auditor's report on internal control over financial reporting would contain an unqualified opinion. However, if the deficiency is deemed to be a material weakness, the auditor must

10-21 (continued)

express an adverse opinion on the effectiveness of internal control over financial reporting.

10-22 The most important internal control deficiency which permitted the defalcation to occur was the failure to adequately segregate the accounting responsibility of recording billings in the sales journal from the custodial responsibility of receiving the cash. Regardless of how trustworthy James appeared, no employee should be given the combined duties of custody of assets and accounting for those assets.

10-23 Maier is correct in her belief that internal controls frequently do not function in the manner they are supposed to. However, regardless of this, her approach ignores the value of beginning the understanding of internal control by preparing or reviewing a rough flowchart. Obtaining an early understanding of the client's internal control will provide Maier with a basis for a decision about further audit procedures and sample sizes based on assessed control risk. By not obtaining an understanding of internal control until later in the engagement, Maier risks performing either too much or too little work, or emphasizing the wrong areas during her audit.

10-24 The extent of controls tested by auditors to express an opinion on internal controls for a public company is significantly greater than that tested solely to express an opinion on the financial statements. To express an opinion on internal controls for a public company, the auditor obtains an understanding of and performs tests of controls for *all* significant account balances, classes of transactions, and disclosures and related assertions in the financial statements. In contrast, the extent of controls tested by an auditor of a nonpublic company is dependent on the auditor's assessment of control risk. Whenever the auditor assesses control risk below maximum, the auditor must perform tests of controls to support that control risk assessment. The auditor *will not perform tests of controls* when the auditor assesses control risk at maximum. When control risk is assessed below the maximum, the auditor designs and performs a combination of tests of controls and substantive procedures. Thus, for a nonpublic company, the tests of controls vary based on the auditor's assessment of control risk.

10-25 Entity level controls, such as the effectiveness of the board of directors' and audit committee's oversight, can have a pervasive affect on many different transaction-level controls. If entity-level controls are deemed to be deficient, then there is greater likelihood that transaction-level controls may be ineffective in their design or operation. In contrast, if entity-level controls are deemed to be highly effective, the auditor may be able to place greater reliance on those controls, which may provide an opportunity to reduce testing of transaction-level controls thereby increasing the efficiency of the audit procedures.

10-26 Auditing standards indicate that reliance can be placed on controls that were tested in a prior year. Controls should be tested at least every three years, and whenever there is a significant change in the control. Continued reliance on the effectiveness of automated controls is appropriate if the auditor is satisfied that general controls over the computer applications are adequate to identify any changes to computerized processes. The ability to rely on prior year tests of automated controls is due to the systematic nature of IT-based procedures. That is, once an automated control is programmed to perform correctly, it should continue performing in that manner until the underlying software program is changed. In contrast, manual performed controls are generally tested each year because there is always a risk of human error occurring in the performance of a manual control.

10-27 When the auditor's risk assessment procedures identify significant risks, the auditor is required to test the operating effectiveness of controls that mitigate these risks in the current year audit, if the auditor plans to rely on those controls to support a control risk assessment below 100%. Thus, tests of controls are required in the current year audit for those controls the auditor plans to rely on to reduce control risk. The greater the risk, the more the audit evidence the auditor should obtain that controls are operating effectively.

10-28 The auditor may issue an unqualified opinion on internal control over financial reporting when two conditions are present:

- there are no identified material weaknesses; and
- there have been no restrictions on the scope of the auditor's work.

A scope limitation is the condition that would cause the auditor to express a *qualified opinion or a disclaimer of opinion* on internal control over financial reporting. This type of opinion is issued when the auditor is unable to determine if there are material weaknesses, due to a restriction on the scope of the audit of internal control over financial reporting or other circumstances where the auditor is unable to obtain sufficient appropriate evidence.

10-29 PCAOB Auditing Standard 5 requires that the audit of the financial statements and the audit of internal control over financial reporting be integrated. In an integrated audit, the auditor must consider the results of audit procedures performed to issue the audit report on the financial statements when issuing the audit report on internal control. For example, if the auditor identifies a material misstatement in the financial statements that was not initially identified by the company's internal controls, the auditor should consider this as at least a significant deficiency, if not a material weakness for purposes of reporting on internal control. In such circumstances, the auditor's report on the financial statements may be unqualified as long as management corrected the misstatement before issuing the financial statements. In contrast, however, the auditor's report on internal control must include an adverse opinion if the auditor concludes it is a material weakness.

■ Multiple Choice Questions From CPA Examinations

10-30   a. (3)   b. (1)   c. (4)   d. (4)

10-31   a. (3)   b. (2)   c. (4)   d. (2)

10-32   a. (2)   b. (4)   c. (4)   d. (2)

■ Discussion Questions and Problems

10-33
  1. Information and communication
  2. Control environment
  3. Risk assessment
  4. Monitoring
  5. Control activities
  6. Information and communication
  7. Control activities
  8. Control environment
  9. Risk assessment
 10. Control activities

10-34
  1. a. Adequate segregation of duties and proper authorization of transactions and activities.
      b. Recorded transactions exist.
      c. An unauthorized or invalid time card turned in by an existing employee. The time card may be for an employee who formerly worked for the company or one who is temporarily laid off.
      d. An employee could be claiming too many hours by having a friend punch him or her in early, or by making manual changes on time cards.
      e. Check to see that all employees that are punched in one day are physically present.

  2. a. Adequate documents and records.
      b. Existing transactions are recorded.
      c. A missing time card number never could be identified before preparation of payroll starts.
      d. An employee would not be paid for a time period. (The employee is almost certain to bring this to management's attention.) The primary benefit of the control would be to prevent misstatements for a short period of time and to prevent employee dissatisfaction from failure to pay them.
      e. Obtain a list of company employees and make sure that each one has received a paycheck for the time period in question.

3.   a.   Independent check on performance.
        b.   Recorded transactions are stated at the correct amounts.
        c.   Mechanical errors of adding up the number of hours, calculating the gross payroll incorrectly, or calculating withholding incorrectly.
        d.   Payroll checks incorrectly calculated could be paid to employees.
        e.   Recheck the amounts for gross payroll, withholding and net payroll.

4.   a.   Adequate documents and records.
        b.   Existing transactions are recorded.
        c.   Preparation of a check for an inappropriate person, the distribution of that check to that person, and the recording of that check in the cash disbursements journal as a voided check.
        d.   An employee who is supposed to void a check could record it as voided on the books and cash the check. At month-end the amount of the check could be covered by adjusting the bank reconciliation.
        e.   Test month-end bank reconciliations in detail to determine that the account reconciles properly, that all supporting documents are proper, looking especially for a check that cleared and was supposed to be voided, and that no alterations have been made to the bank statement.

5.   a.   Proper authorization of transactions and activities.
        b.   Recorded transactions exist and recorded transactions are stated at the correct amounts.
        c.   Both errors and fraud are likely to be prevented if competent trustworthy employees are hired. Hiring honest employees minimizes a likelihood of fraud. Hiring competent employees minimizes the likelihood of unintentional errors.
        d.   Several types of intentional misstatements could occur if a dishonest person is hired. Similarly, several types of unintentional errors could occur if an incompetent person is hired.
        e.   An examination of cancelled checks and supporting documents, including time cards and personnel records, is a test of the possibility of fraud. A test of the calculation of payroll is a test for an unintentional error caused by employees who are not competent.

10-34 (continued)

6. a. Proper authorization of transactions and activities.
    b. Recorded transactions exist.
    c. A paycheck cannot be processed for an invalid employee number.
    d. A fictitious payroll check could be processed for a fictitious employee if invalid employee numbers are included in the employee master file.
    e. Include test data transactions with invalid employee numbers in the data to be inputted into the payroll accounting system and determine that all invalid transactions are automatically rejected by the software application.

7. a. Adequate separation of duties.
    b. Recorded transactions exist.
    c. A fictitious payroll check that is originated by the person both preparing the payroll checks and distributing the payroll checks.
    d. If one person kept a record of time, prepared the payroll, and distributed the checks, that person could add a nonexistent employee to the payroll, process the information for the employee and deposit the paycheck in his or her own bank account without detection.
    e. Perform a surprise payoff in which the auditor accounts for all paychecks and distributes them to the employees, who must provide identification in order to receive their checks.

8. a. Proper authorization of transactions and activities, and adequate documents and records.
    b. Recorded transactions exist.
    c. The preparation of an inappropriate payroll check for a former employee is prevented.
    d. A terminated employee could be continued on the payroll with someone else obtaining the paycheck.
    e. Perform a surprise payoff in which the auditor accounts for all paychecks and distributes them to the employees, who must provide identification to receive their checks.

10-34 (continued)

9.   a.   Physical control over assets and records, and adequate segregation of duties.

     b.   Recorded transactions exist.

     c.   Checks prepared for nonexistent employees or employees on vacation, or absent for other reasons are controlled and safeguarded.

     d.   Checks could be lost which are intended for absent employees or a check could be taken by the person responsible for distributing the checks.

     e.   Examine cancelled checks to make certain that each check is properly endorsed, supported by a time card, and the person for whom the check is made out is still working for the company.

10.   a.   Proper authorization of transactions and activities and adequate separation of duties.

     b.   Recorded transactions exist and recorded transactions are stated at the correct amounts.

     c.   Preparation of a check for a fictitious employee or preparation of checks using an unapproved pay rate are prevented.

     d.   A fictitious payroll check could be processed for a fictitious employee if those with record keeping responsibilities are allowed to enter new employee numbers into the master file. Also, paychecks to valid employees could be overstated if unauthorized personnel have the ability to make changes to the pay rates in the master files.

     e.   Attempt to access the on-line payroll master file using a password that is not allowed access to that master file.

10-35 1.   a.   Adequate documents and records and independent checks on performance.

     b.   Transactions are stated at the correct amounts.

     c.   Changes to the computer master file of prices are reviewed when the master file is updated.

2.   a.   Proper authorization of transactions and adequate documents and records.

     b.   Recorded transactions exist.

     c.   Include a control in the accounts payable software that requires the input of a valid receiving report number before the software will process a payment on an accounts payable.

10-35 (continued)

3. a.   Adequate documents and records, physical control over assets and records, and independent checks on performance.

      b.   Recorded transactions exist.

      c.   1)   Fence in the physical facilities and prohibit employees from parking inside the fencing.

            2)   Require the accounting department to maintain perpetual inventory records and take physical counts of actual sides of beef periodically.

4. a.   Independent checks on performance.

      b.   Recorded transactions are stated at the correct amounts.

      c.   Counts by qualified personnel and independent checks on performance.

5. a.   Proper authorization of transactions and activities.

      b.   Transactions are stated at the correct amounts.

      c.   1)   Make sure that the salesman has a current price list.

            2)   Require independent approval of all transactions, including the price, before shipment is made.

6. a.   Adequate documents and records.

      b.   Recorded transactions exist.

      c.   (1)   Require that payments only be made on original invoices.

            2)   Require a receiving report be attached to the vendor's invoice before a payment is made.

7. a.   Adequate documents and records, and independent checks on performance.

      b.   Transactions are recorded on the correct dates.

      c.   Carefully coordinate the physical count of inventory on the last day of the year with the recording of sales to make certain counted inventory has not been billed and billed inventory has not been counted.

8. a.   Adequate separation of duties.

      b.   Recorded transactions exist.

      c.   Restrict the accounts payable clerk from being able to make changes to the approved vendor master file. Only allow purchasing personnel to input changes to that master file.

10-36   The criteria for dividing duties is to keep all asset custody duties with one person (Cooper). Document preparation and recording is done by the other person (Smith). Miller will perform independent verification. The two most important independent verification duties are the bank reconciliation and reconciling the accounts receivable master file with the control account, therefore they are assigned to Miller. The duties should be divided among the three as follows:

Robert Smith:	†2	4	†5	†7	†9	†11	14	16	17
James Cooper:	†1	†3	†6	†8	†10	†12	13		
Bill Miller:	15	18							

10-37   a.   The size of a company has a significant effect on the nature of the controls likely to exist. A small company has difficulty establishing adequate separation of duties and justifying an internal audit staff. However, a major type of control available in a small company is the knowledge and concern of the top operating person, who is frequently an owner-manager. His or her ability to understand and the entire operation of the company is potentially a significant compensating control. The owner-manager's interest in the organization and close relationship with the personnel enable him or her to evaluate the competence of the employees and the effectiveness of internal controls.

While some of the five control activities are unavailable in a small company, especially adequate segregation of duties, it is still possible for a small company to have proper authorization of transactions and activities, adequate documents and records, physical controls over assets and records, and, to a limited degree, independent checks on performance.

b.   Phersen and Collier take opposite and extreme views as to the credence to be given internal control in a small firm. Phersen seems to treat a small firm in the same manner as he would a large firm, which is inefficient. Because many types of controls are usually lacking in a small firm, especially one that is a nonpublic company, assessed control risk should be increased and more extensive substantive tests must be used. Because assessed control risk is higher, less emphasis is needed to identify the internal controls.

Collier is not meeting the standards of the profession in that she completely ignores the possibility of a severe deficiency in the system. She must obtain an understanding of internal control to determine whether it is possible to conduct an audit at all. Auditing standards require, at a minimum, an understanding of internal control.

10-37 (continued)

The auditor must understand the control environment and the flow of transactions. It is not necessary, however, for the auditor to prepare flowcharts or internal control questionnaires. The auditor of a nonpublic company is required to provide a written report about significant deficiencies or material weaknesses to those charged with governance, which may be common on many small audit clients.

c. Collier's approach is not acceptable when auditing either a public or non-public company. Collier must obtain an understanding of internal controls over financial reporting in all audits. When the auditor assesses control risk below the maximum, which is generally the case for public companies, the auditor must perform tests of controls to determine whether key controls over financial reporting are operating effectively. Those procedures must provide Collier a basis to express an opinion about internal controls over financial reporting for accelerated filer public companies.

d. While Pherson's approach includes procedures similar to those that would be performed to obtain an understanding of internal controls, if Pherson is auditing a public company, he may need to expand those procedures to ensure that enough information is obtained about the design and placed in operation status of internal controls over financial reporting. Furthermore, Pherson must perform tests of key controls over financial reporting to provide a basis for expressing an opinion on internal controls over financial reporting for accelerated filer public companies.

10-38 1. a. ■ Supplying the receiving department with the purchase order is regarded as a deficiency in that the department may be less careful in checking goods than they would be if they were working without a record of the quantities that should be received.

■ The failure to have the storekeeper receipt for the materials when they are sent to him or her from the receiving department or to tie in the items placed in storage with the acquisition constitutes a deficiency in control in that responsibility for shortages cannot be conclusively placed on either receiving or stores. The receiving department might, in collusion with a vendor, report receipts of materials that were never received. Also, either the receiving department or the stores department might fraudulently convert some of the materials and because of the lack of a record of responsibility, the company would be unable to determine which department was responsible.

10-38 (continued)

    b.   ■   This deficiency increases the likelihood of obsolete inventory and the possibility of theft of shipments larger than the amount ordered. It also increases the likelihood of inaccurate counts of inventory actually received and recorded.

          ■   The failure to isolate responsibility for shortages also increases the likelihood of obsolescence in that employees are likely to be less concerned when they are not held accountable. Because the company cannot isolate responsibility, it might also encourage receiving or stores to take goods.

    c.   Use a "blind" copy of the purchase order or a separate receiving report without a copy of the purchase order. Use perpetual inventory records to hold the storekeeper accountable. The storekeeper should also initial the receiving report or purchase order when he or she receives the goods.

2.   a.   ■   The payroll checks should not be returned to the computer department supervisor but should be distributed by persons independent of those having a part in generating the payroll data.

          ■   There is a lack of internal verification of the hours, rates, extensions or employees by above.

    b.   ■   Padding of payroll with fictitious names and extracting the checks made out to such names when they are returned after they have been signed.

          ■   There may be misstatements in hours, rates, extensions, and the existence of nonworking employees.

    c.   ■   Have the checks handed out by an independent person and not returned to Strode.

          ■   Internal verification of that information by Webber or someone else.

3.   a.   The bank statement and cancelled checks should not be reconciled by the manager, but should be sent by the bank directly to the home office, where the reconciliations should be made against the manager's report of cash disbursements.

    b.   The manager may draw checks to herself or others for personal purposes and omit them from her list of cash disbursements or inflate other reported disbursement amounts.

    c.   Have all bank statements sent directly to the home office and have Cooper report directly to the home office by use of a list of cash disbursements and all supporting documentation.

10-39 The following are deficiencies of internal control, by transaction-related audit objective.

Occurrence
- The receiving report is not sent to the stores department. A copy of the receiving report should be sent from the receiving room directly to the stores department with the materials received. The stores department, after verifying the accuracy of the receiving report, should indicate approval on that copy and send it to the accounts payable department. The copy sent to accounts payable will serve as proof that the materials ordered were received by the company and are in the user department.
- The controller should not be responsible for cash disbursements. The cash disbursement function should be the responsibility of the treasurer, not the controller, so as to provide proper segregation of duties between the custody of assets and the recording of transactions.
- The purchase requisition is not approved. The purchase requisition should be approved by a responsible person in the stores department. The approval should be indicated on the purchase requisition after the approver is satisfied that it was properly prepared based on a need to replace stores or the proper request from a user department.
- Preliminary review should be made before preparing purchase orders. Prior to preparation of the purchase order, the purchase office should review the company's need for the specific materials requisitioned and approve the request.

Completeness
- Purchase orders and purchase requisitions should not be combined and filed with the unmatched purchase requisitions, in the stores department. A separate file should be maintained for the combined and matched documents. The unmatched purchase requisitions file can serve as a control over merchandise requisitioned but not yet ordered.
- There is no indication of control over vouchers in the accounts payable department. A record of all vouchers submitted to the cashier should be maintained in the accounts payable department, and a copy of the vouchers should be filed in an alphabetical vendor reference file.
- There is no indication of any control over prenumbered documents. All prenumbered documents should be accounted for.

10-39 (continued)

Accuracy

■ Purchase requisitions and purchase orders are not compared in the stores department. Although purchase orders are attached to purchase requisitions in the stores department, there is no indication that any comparison is made of the two documents.

Prior to attaching the purchase order to the purchase requisition the requisitioner's functions should include a check that:

a. Prices are reasonable;
b. The quality of the materials ordered is acceptable;
c. Delivery dates are in accordance with company needs;
d. All pertinent data on the purchase order and purchase requisition (e.g., quantities, specifications, delivery dates, etc.) are in agreement.

Because the requisitioner will be charged for the materials ordered, the requisitioner is the logical person to perform these steps.

1. The purchase office does not review the invoice prior to processing approval. The purchase office should review the vendor's invoice for overall accuracy and completeness, verifying quantity, prices, specifications, terms, dates, etc., and if the invoice is in agreement with the purchase order, receiving report, and purchase requisition, the purchase office should clearly indicate on the invoice that it is approved for payment processing. The approved invoice should be sent to the accounts payable department.

2. The copy of the purchase order sent to the receiving room generally should not show quantities ordered, thus forcing the department to count goods received. In addition to counting the merchandise received from the vendor, the receiving department personnel should examine the condition and quality of the merchandise upon receipt.

3. There is no indication of control over dollar amounts on vouchers. Accounts payable personnel should prepare and maintain control sheets on the dollar amounts of vouchers. Such sheets should be sent to departments posting transactions to the general ledger and master files.

Note: Classification, timing, and posting and summarization are not applicable. Recording in journals is not included in the flowcharts.

10-40   1.   No testing is required in the December 31, 2011 audit because the auditor has determined that the automated control has not been changed since the prior year. The auditor obtains reasonable assurance that the automated control has not been changed due to the strong controls over IT security and software program changes. Thus, the auditor should consider the extent of testing of IT security and software changes that might be necessary in the current year audit due to the auditor's reliance on them to prevent changes to the underlying automated reconciliation control.

      2.   Testing is required in the December 31, 2011 audit because the underlying control is performed by a person and is not automated. Because the control is manually performed, there is a risk that the operation of the control may not be consistent with the design or the control may not have been performed. Thus, the auditor should test the control's operating effectiveness in the current year's audit.

      3.   Testing is required in the December 31, 2011 audit because the control is designed to mitigate a significant risk. Controls that mitigate significant risks must be tested each year.

      4.   Testing is required in the December 31, 2011 audit because the client made changes to the software system during the current year.

      5.   No testing is required in the December 31, 2011 audit because the auditor has determined that the automated control has not been changed since the prior year. The auditor obtains reasonable assurance that the automated control has not been changed due to the strong controls over IT security and software program changes. Thus, the auditor should consider the extent of testing of IT security and software changes that might be necessary in the current year audit due to the auditor's reliance on them to prevent changes to the underlying automated reconciliation control.

10-41 Following are the appropriate reporting formats for the five independent situations:

INDEPENDENT SITUATION	APPROPRIATE AUDIT REPORT	REASON FOR REPORT
1.	Adverse	The presence of a material misstatement not detected by the company's internal controls is considered at least a significant deficiency, if not a material weakness for purposes of reporting on internal controls.
2.	Qualified or disclaimer	The auditor's inability to obtain any evidence about the operating effectiveness of internal controls represents a scope limitation.
3.	Adverse	The detection of a deficiency that will not prevent or detect a material misstatement in the financial statements meets the definition of a material weakness, which requires an adverse opinion.
4.	Unqualified	The control deficiency was remediated and the auditor was able to obtain sufficient appropriate evidence that the new control operates effectively. Thus, an unqualified opinion on internal control is appropriate.
5.	Unqualified	Because the auditor does not believe the significant deficiency in internal control is a material weakness, the auditor's report would contain an unqualified opinion.

■ **Case**

10-42 a. **Sales**

TRANSACTION-RELATED AUDIT OBJECTIVE	CONTROL
Occurrence	■ Supervisor approves all invoices. ■ Accounts receivable clerk has no access to cash. ■ Monthly statements are sent to customers. ■ Supervisor approves all credit.
Completeness	■ Cash register is at the front of the store. ■ Sales clerks handle no cash. ■ Sales clerks summarize daily sales, which determine their commission. This summary is compared daily to total sales. ■ Sales transactions are used to update perpetuals and monthly physical inventory is taken.
Accuracy	■ Owner sets all prices. ■ Supervisor rechecks all calculations. ■ Accountant reconciles all computer totals to sales staff summary totals and supervisor's sales summary. ■ Monthly statements are sent to customers.
Posting and summarization	■ Computer is used to update records. ■ Monthly statements are sent. ■ The aged trial balance is compared to the general ledger.
Classification	None
Timing	■ Sales transactions are recorded daily.

10-42 (continued)

b. **Cash Receipts**

TRANSACTION-RELATED AUDIT OBJECTIVE	CONTROL
Occurrence	■ Monthly bank reconciliation is prepared. ■ Accounts receivable clerk compares duplicate deposit slip from bank to sales and cash receipts journal.
Completeness	■ Cash register is used for cash sales. ■ Cash collected on receivables is prelisted. ■ Supervisor deposits money in a locked box.
Accuracy	■ Supervisor recaps cash sales and compares totals to the cash receipts tapes. ■ Monthly bank reconciliation prepared. ■ Accounts receivable clerk compares duplicate deposit slip from bank to cash sales and cash receipts journal. ■ Monthly statements are sent to customers.
Posting and summarization	■ Computer is used to update records. ■ Monthly statements are sent. ■ The aged trial balance is compared to the general ledger.
Classification	None
Timing	■ Cash is deposited daily.

10-42 (continued)

    c. **Sales and Cash Receipts**

Deficiencies
- Supervisor enters all sales in the cash register, recaps sales and cash, and compares the totals to the tapes. She also receives all invoices from sales clerks. (This deficiency is offset by the daily summary form prepared by sales clerks and used to calculate sales clerks' commissions.)
- Lack of accounting for a numerical sequence of sales invoices. (Partially offset by control totals used by comparing sales clerks' and supervisor's control totals.)
- No internal verification of key entry for customer name, date, and sales classifications on either cash receipts or sales.
- There is no internal verification of general totals, posting to accounts receivable master file, or posting to the general ledger.
- There is a lack of internal verification of all of the accounting work done by the accounts receivable clerk.

- **Integrated Case Application**

10-43

PINNACLE MANUFACTURING—PART III

Following are control risk matrices and related notes that are used to direct a discussion of the requirements of the case. It should be understood that judgment is a critical element in this case, and accordingly, there often is no single right answer.

    Computer-prepared matrices using Excel (P1043.xls) are contained on the Companion Website and on the Instructor's Resource CD-ROM, which is available upon request. They are essentially the same as the matrices on the next two pages.

10-43 (continued)

PINNACLE MANUFACTURING - Part III
Control Risk Matrix – Acquisitions

Internal Controls	Recorded acquisitions are for goods and services received (occurrence).	Existing acquisition transactions are recorded (completeness).	Recorded acquisition transactions are stated at the correct amounts (accuracy).	Recorded acquisition transactions are properly included in the master files, and are properly summarized (posting and summarization).	Acquisition transactions are properly classified (classification).	Acquisition transactions are recorded on the correct dates (timing).
1. Required use of PO and receiving report with check of completeness	C					
2. Proper approval	C		C			
3. Segregation of functions	C					
4. Cancellation of documents	C					
5. Prenumbering of documents with accounting for sequence		C				
6. Internal verification of documents/records	C		C	C	C	C
7. Use of chart of accounts					C	
8. Procedures requiring prompt processing						C
9. Monthly reconciliation of A/P master file with general ledger				C		
Assessed control risk	Low	Low	Low	Low	Low	Low

PINNACLE MANUFACTURING - Part III
Control Matrix - Cash Disbursements

Internal Controls	Recorded cash disbursements are for goods and services actually received (occurrence).	Existing cash disbursement transactions are recorded (completeness).	Recorded cash disbursement transactions are stated at the correct amounts (accuracy).	Recorded cash disbursement transactions are properly included in the master file and are properly summarized (posting and summarization).	Cash disbursement transactions are properly classified (classification).	Cash disbursement transactions are recorded on the correct dates (timing).
1. Segregation of functions	C					
2. Review of support, signing of checks by authorized person	C					
3. Prenumbered checks; accounted for		C				
4. Use of chart of accounts					C	
5. Procedures for prompt recording						C
6. Monthly reconciliation of A/P master file with G/L				C		
Deficiencies						
1. Lack of an independent bank reconciliation (Done by Treasurer)		D	D			
2. Lack of internal verification of documentation package by cash disbursements clerk.			D		D	
3. Lack of internal verification of key entry into cash disbursements file.		D	D			
Assessed control risk	Medium	Medium	High	Low	Low	Low

10-43 (continued)

Notes to 10-43, Part III

1. The purpose of Part III is to:
   (a) have the students develop specific transaction-related audit objectives for a cycle,
   (b) obtain controls from a flowchart description,
   (c) relate controls to objectives,
   (d) evaluate a set of controls as a system.

2. Control is quite good for acquisitions. If misstatements in acquisitions occur, they will result from the incorrect application of controls, not their absence. This demonstrates the inherent deficiencies in any control system. It explains the reasons why some misstatements were found last year. However, they were not material. It also indicates the need for tests of controls and substantive tests of details of balances and/or transactions.

   Controls for cash disbursements are not nearly as good, given the three deficiencies. This provides an opportunity to discuss both fraud and errors. Given the deficiencies, there is potential for fraud in cash.

3. It is appropriate to use the matrices to consider whether all controls shown are important to both the client and to the auditor. Is it necessary to have all controls (e.g., prenumbering of requisitions)? Are the controls costly (e.g., internal verification of *all* acquisitions)? Should all controls be tested (e.g., cancellation of documents)?

■ **Internet Problem Solution: Disclosure of Material Weaknesses in Internal Control over Financial Reporting**

Internet Problem 10-1

   a. Students should have located the Form 10-K for Organic Alliance Inc. for the year ended 12-31-09. Instructors may want to encourage students to use the EDGAR Full-Text Search option to identify the company's filings more efficiently.

   b. Management's Annual Report on Internal Control Over Financial Reporting provides the following answers to the questions in a through f:
      1. Management is responsible for establishing and maintaining adequate internal control over financial reporting.
      2. Management's report is addressing internal control over financial reporting.

Internet Problem 10-1 (continued)

> 3. Management conducted its assessment of the effectiveness of internal control over financial reporting based on criteria established in COSO's Internal Control – Integrated Framework.
>
> 4. Management concluded that its internal control over financial reporting was not effective due to the existence of a material weakness as described in e. below.
>
> 5. Management arrived at its conclusion that internal control over financial reporting is not effective due to a material weakness that is the result of a lack of segregation of duties because of the limited number of Company personnel.
>
> 6. Management reports that it intends to hire a full time Chief Financial Officer to augment its internal control procedures and expand its accounting staff as the company grows and obtains a stronger cash position.

c. The report of the independent registered public accounting firm provides the following information about the auditor's evaluation of internal controls over financial reporting:

The company was not required to have, nor were the auditors engaged to perform, audits of its internal control over financial reporting, because Organic Alliance is not an accelerated filer public company. The auditor's report on the audit of the financial statements does note that while the consideration of internal control provides a basis for designing audit procedures, it does not provide evidence for the purpose of expressing an opinion on the effectiveness of the company's internal control over financial reporting.

(**Note**: Internet problems address current issues using Internet sources. Because Internet sites are subject to change, Internet problems and solutions may change. Current information on Internet problems is available at www.pearsonhighered.com/arens.)

Chapter 11

Fraud Auditing

■ **Review Questions**

11-1   Fraudulent financial reporting is an intentional misstatement or omission of amounts or disclosures with the intent to deceive users. Two examples of fraudulent financial reporting are accelerating the timing of recording sales revenue to increased reported sales and earnings, and recording expenses as fixed assets to increase earnings.

11-2   Misappropriation of assets is fraud that involves theft of an entity's assets. Two examples are an accounts payable clerk issuing payments to a fictitious company controlled by the clerk, and a sales clerk failing to record a sale and pocketing the cash receipts.

11-3   Fraudulent financial reporting is an intentional misstatement or omission of amounts or disclosures with the intent to deceive users, while misappropriation of assets is fraud that involves theft of an entity's assets. Frauds involving financial reporting are usually larger than frauds involving misappropriation of assets, usually involve top management, and do not directly involve theft of company assets.

11-4   The three conditions of fraud referred to as the "fraud triangle" are (1) Incentives/Pressures; (2) Opportunities; and (3) Attitudes/Rationalization. Incentives/Pressures are incentives of management or other employees to commit fraud. Opportunities are circumstances that allow management or employees to commit fraud. Attitudes/Rationalization are indications that an attitude, character, or set of ethical values exist that allow management or employees to commit a dishonest act or they are in an environment that imposes sufficient pressure that causes them to rationalize committing a dishonest act.

11-5   The following are example of risk factors for fraudulent financial reporting for each of the three fraud conditions:

- *Incentives/Pressures* - The company is under pressure to meet debt covenants or obtain additional financing.
- *Opportunities* – Ineffective oversight of financial reporting by the board of directors allows management to exercise discretion over reporting.
- *Attitudes/Rationalization* – Management is overly aggressive. For example, the company may issue aggressive earnings forecasts, or make extensive acquisitions using company stock.

11-6 The following are example of risk factors for misappropriation of assets for each of the three fraud conditions:

- *Incentives/Pressures* - The individual is unable to meet personal financial obligations.
- *Opportunities* – There is insufficient segregation of duties that allows the individual to handle cash receipts and related accounting records.
- *Attitudes/Rationalization* – Management has disregarded the inadequate separation of duties that allows the potential theft of cash receipts.

11-7 Auditors use several sources to gather information about fraud risks, including:

- Information obtained from communications among audit team members about their knowledge of the company and its industry, including how and where the company might be susceptible to material misstatements due to fraud.
- Responses to auditor inquiries of management about their views of the risks of fraud and about existing programs and controls to address specific identified fraud risks.
- Specific risk factors for fraudulent financial reporting and misappropriations of assets.
- Analytical procedures results obtained during planning that indicate possible implausible or unexpected analytical relationships.
- Knowledge obtained through other procedures such as client acceptance and retention decisions, interim review of financial statements, and consideration of inherent or control risks.

11-8 SAS 99 requires the audit team to conduct discussions to share insights from more experienced audit team members and to "brainstorm" ideas that address the following:

1. How and where they believe the entity's financial statements might be susceptible to material misstatement due to fraud. This should include consideration of known external and internal factors affecting the entity that might

    - create an incentive or pressure for management to commit fraud.
    - provide the opportunity for fraud to be perpetrated.
    - indicate a culture or environment that enables management to rationalize fraudulent acts.

11-8 (continued)

> 2. How management could perpetrate and conceal fraudulent financial reporting.
> 3. How assets of the entity could be misappropriated.
> 4. How the auditor might respond to the susceptibility of material misstatements due to fraud.

11-9   Auditors must inquire whether management has knowledge of any fraud or suspected fraud within the company. SAS 99 also requires auditors to inquire of the audit committee about its views of the risks of fraud and whether the audit committee has knowledge of any fraud or suspected fraud. If the entity has an internal audit function, the auditor should inquire about internal audit's views of fraud risks and whether they have performed any procedures to identify or detect fraud during the year. SAS 99 further requires the auditor to make inquiries of others within the entity whose duties lie outside the normal financial reporting lines of responsibility about the existence or suspicion of fraud.

11-10   The corporate code of conduct establishes the "tone at the top" of the importance of honesty and integrity and can also provide more specific guidance about permitted and prohibited behavior. Examples of items typically addressed in a code of conduct include expectations of general employee conduct, restrictions on conflicts of interest, and limitations on relationships with clients and suppliers.

11-11   Management and the board of directors are responsible for setting the "tone at the top" for ethical behavior in the company. It is important for management to behave with honesty and integrity because this reinforces the importance of these values to employees throughout the organization.

11-12   Management has primary responsibility to design and implement antifraud programs and controls to prevent, deter, and detect fraud. The audit committee has primary responsibility to oversee the organization's financial reporting and internal control processes and to provide oversight of management's fraud risk assessment process and antifraud programs and controls.

11-13   The three auditor responses to fraud are: (1) change the overall conduct of the audit to respond to identified fraud risks; (2) design and perform audit procedures to address identified risks; and (3) perform procedures to address the risk of management override of controls.

11-14   Auditors are required to take three actions to address potential management override of controls: (1) examine journal entries and other adjustments for evidence of possible misstatements due to fraud; (2) review accounting estimates for biases; and (3) evaluate the business rationale for significant unusual transactions.

11-15   Three main techniques use to manipulate revenue include: (1) recording of fictitious revenue; (2) premature revenue recognition including techniques such as bill-and-hold sales and channel stuffing; and (3) manipulation of adjustments to revenue such as sales returns and allowance and other contra accounts.

11-16   The handling of cash by individuals operating cash registers is particularly susceptible to theft. The notice "your meal is free if we fail to give you a receipt" is designed to ensure that every customer is given a receipt and all sales are entered into the register, establish accountability for the sale.

11-17   The three types of inquiry are informational, assessment, and interrogative. Auditors use informational inquiry to obtain information about facts and details that the auditor does not have. For example, if the auditor suspects financial statement fraud involving improper revenue recognition, the auditor may inquire of management as to revenue recognition policies. The auditor uses assessment inquiry to corroborate or contradict prior information. In the previous example, the auditor may attempt to corroborate the information obtained from management by making assessment inquiries of individuals in accounts receivable and shipping. Interrogative inquiry is used to determine if the interviewee is being deceptive or purposefully omitting disclosure of key knowledge of facts, events, or circumstances. For example, a senior member of the audit team might make interrogative inquiries of management or other personnel about key elements of the fraud where earlier responses were contradictory or evasive.

11-18   When making inquiries of a deceitful individual, three examples of verbal cues are frequent rephrasing of the question, filler terms such as "well" or "to tell the truth," and forgetfulness or acknowledgements of nervousness. Three examples of nonverbal cues by the individual are creating physical barriers by blocking their mouth, leaning away from the auditor, and signs of stress such as sweating or fidgeting.

11-19   When the auditor suspects that fraud may be present, SAS 99 requires the auditor to obtain additional evidence to determine whether material fraud has occurred. SAS 99 also requires the auditor to consider the implications for other aspects of the audit. When the auditor determines that fraud may be present, SAS 99 requires the auditor to discuss the matter and audit approach for further investigation with an appropriate level of management that is at least one level above those involved, and with senior management and the audit committee, even if the matter might be considered inconsequential. For public company auditors, the discovery of fraud of any magnitude by senior management is at least a significant deficiency and may be a material weakness in internal control over financial reporting. This includes fraud by senior management that results in even immaterial misstatements. If the public company auditor decides the fraud is a material weakness, the auditor's report on internal control over financial reporting will contain an adverse opinion.

Multiple Choice Questions From CPA Examinations

11-20   a. (3)   b. (4)   c. (1)   d. (2)

11-21   a. (1)   b. (2)   c. (4)

11-22   a. (1)   b. (1)   c. (1)

Discussion Questions and Problems

11-23

	INFORMATION	a. FRAUD RISK	b. FRAUD CONDITION
1.	Management has a strong interest in employing inappropriate means to minimize reported earnings for tax-motivated reasons.	Yes	Incentives/Pressures
2.	The company's board of directors includes a majority of directors who are independent of management.	No	N/A
3.	Assets and revenues are based on significant estimates that involve subjective judgments and uncertainties that are hard to corroborate.	Yes	Opportunities
4.	The company is marginally able to meet exchange listing and debt covenant requirements.	Yes	Incentives/Pressures
5.	New accounting pronouncements have resulted in explanatory paragraphs for consistency for the company and other firms in the industry.	No	N/A
6.	The company has experienced low turnover in management and its internal audit function.	No	N/A
7.	Significant operations are located and conducted across international borders in jurisdictions where differing business environments and cultures exist.	Yes	Opportunities
8.	There are recurring attempts by management to justify marginal or inappropriate accounting on the basis of materiality.	Yes	Attitudes/Rationalization
9.	The company's financial performance is threatened by a high degree of competition and market saturation.	Yes	Incentives/Pressures

11-24   a.   The purpose of the audit team's brainstorming session is for the audit team to exchange ideas about how and where they believe the entity's financial statements might be susceptible to material misstatement due to fraud, how management could perpetrate and conceal fraudulent financial reporting, and how assets of the entity could be misappropriated.

b.   The brainstorming meeting should ordinarily involve the key members of the audit team, ranging from audit staff members to partners on the engagement. This meeting would include audit team members located in other offices who work on the engagement as well as audit specialists, such as tax or IT specialists who work on the audit engagement. The meeting should be held during planning so that the audit plan can be adjusted to address the identified risks, and emphasize professional skepticism throughout the engagement.

c.   The two staff members on the engagement are just as responsible for engaging in the exchange of ideas as other members of the engagement team. While the two new staff accountants may not be familiar with engagement specifics, they do provide a fresh perspective of possible ways management might engage in fraud. More importantly, they will benefit from hearing the exchange of ideas from other members of the audit team. That should help heighten their professional skepticism as they perform the audit.

d.   The auditor has a responsibility to plan and perform the audit to obtain reasonable assurance about whether the financial statements are free of material misstatement, whether caused by error or fraud. Thus, the auditor's detection responsibility for fraud is no different from the auditor's detection responsibility for errors.

11-25   a.

	DEFICIENCY	RECOMMENDATION
1.	There is no basis for establishing the documentation of the number of paying patrons.	Prenumbered admission tickets should be issued upon payment of the admission fee.
2.	There is no segregation of duties between persons responsible for collecting admission fees and persons responsible for authorizing admission.	One clerk (hereafter referred to as the cash receipts clerk) should collect admission fees and issue prenumbered tickets. The other clerk (hereafter referred to as the admission clerk) should authorize admission upon receipt of the ticket or proof of membership.
3.	An independent count of paying patrons is not made.	The admission clerk should retain a portion of the prenumbered admission ticket (admission ticket stub).
4.	There is no proof of accuracy of amounts collected by the clerks.	Admission ticket stubs should be reconciled with cash collected by the treasurer each day.

11-25 (continued)

	DEFICIENCY	RECOMMENDATION
5.	Cash receipts records are not promptly prepared.	The cash receipts should be recorded by the cash receipts clerk daily on a permanent record that will serve as the first record of accountability.
6.	Cash receipts are not promptly deposited. Cash should not be left undeposited for a week.	Cash should be deposited at least once each day.
7.	There is no proof of the accuracy of amounts deposited.	Authenticated deposit slips should be compared with daily cash receipts records. Discrepancies should be promptly investigated and resolved. In addition, the treasurer should establish policy that includes a review of cash receipts.
8.	There is no record of the internal accountability for cash.	The treasurer should issue a signed receipt for all proceeds received from the cash receipts clerk. These receipts should be maintained and should be periodically checked against cash receipts and deposit records.

    b.   All of the deficiencies increase the likelihood of misappropriation of assets, by allowing individuals access to cash receipts or failing to maintain adequate records to establish accountability for cash receipts.

    c.   The deficiencies have less of an effect on the likelihood of fraudulent financial reporting than they do for misappropriation of assets. The first four deficiencies increase the likelihood of fraudulent financial reporting for reported revenues due to the lack of adequate records to establish the number of patrons.

11-26 1. a.   Error.

          b.   Use of prenumbered bills of lading that are periodically accounted for.

          c.   Trace a sequence of prenumbered bills of lading to recorded sales transactions. Confirm accounts receivable at year-end.

     2. a.   Error.

          b.   Internal verification of invoice preparation and posting by an independent person.

          c.   Test clerical accuracy of sales invoices.

3. a. Fraud.
    b. The prelisting of cash receipts should be compared to the postings in the accounts receivable master file and to the validated bank deposit slip.
    c. Trace cash received from prelisting to cash receipts journal. Confirm accounts receivable.

4. a. Fraud.
    b. Sales invoices are not recorded until receipt of shipping document indicating that the goods have been shipped.
    c. For sales before and after year end, examine shipping documents to verify the sale was recorded in the proper period. Confirm accounts receivable at year-end.

5. a. Error.
    b. No merchandise may leave the plant without the preparation of a prenumbered bill of lading.
    c. Trace credit entries in the perpetual inventory records to bills of lading and the sales journal. Confirm accounts receivable at year-end.

6. a. Error.
    b. Internal review and verification of account classification by an independent person.
    c. Test accuracy of invoice classification.

7. a. Fraud.
    b. Independent verification of packing slip.
    c. Reconcile inventory items on hand to perpetual inventory records and investigate any shortages.

8. a. Fraud.
    b. All payments from customers should be in the form of a check payable to the company. Monthly statements should be sent to all customers.
    c. Trace from recorded sales transactions to cash receipts for those sales; confirm accounts receivable balances at year-end.

11-27 a. The lack of separation of duties was the major deficiency that permitted the fraud for Appliance Repair and Service Company. Gyders has responsibility for opening mail, prelisting cash, updating accounts receivable, and authorizing sales allowances and write-offs for uncollectible accounts. It is easy for Gyders to take the cash before it is prelisted and to charge off an accounts receivable as a sales allowance or as a bad debt.

11-27 (continued)

    b.   The benefit of prelisting cash is to immediately document cash receipts at the time that they are received by the company. Assuming all cash is included on the prelisting, it is then easy for someone to trace from the prelisting to the cash receipts journal and deposits. Furthermore, if a dispute arises with a customer, it is easy to trace to the prelisting and determine when the cash was actually received. The prelisting should be prepared by a competent person who has no significant responsibilities for accounting functions. The person should not be in a position to withhold the recording of sales, adjust accounts receivable or sales for credits, or adjust accounts receivable for sales returns and allowances or bad debts.

    c.   Subsequent to the prelisting of cash, it is desirable for an independent person to trace from the prelisting to the bank statement to verify that all amounts were deposited. This can be done by anyone independent of whoever does the prelisting, or prepares or makes the deposit.

    d.   A general rule that should be followed for depositing cash is that it should be deposited as quickly as possible after it is received, and handled by as few people as possible. It is, ideally, the person receiving the cash that should prepare the prelisting and prepare the deposit immediately afterward. That person should then deposit the cash in the bank. Any unintentional errors in the preparation of the bank statement should be discovered by the bank. The authenticated duplicate deposit slip should be given to the accounting department who would subsequently compare the total to the prelisting. When an independent person prepares the bank reconciliation, there should also be a comparison of the prelisting to the totals deposited in the bank.

        Any money taken before the prelisting should be uncovered by the accounting department when they send out monthly statements to customers. Customers are likely to complain if they are billed for sales for which they have already paid. Thus, any pocketing of cash should be detected by customer complaints, as long as customer complaints are directed to someone other than individuals involved in prelisting cash.

11-28 a.

DEFICIENCIES	LIKELY MISSTATEMENTS
1. The foreman has the ability to hire employees and enter their names into the pay system with no other approval.	Nonexistent or incompetent employees may be hired at the foreman's option.
2. The foreman may make changes to salary rates without approval of company management.	Employees may be paid at rates that are higher than their skill warrants.
3. No investigation of new employees to determine background experience and dependability is performed.	Dishonest or unqualified employees may be hired.
4. No control exists over time cards and the completion thereof.	Employees may report and be paid for time that they did not work.
5. No review or internal verification of the amount on the payroll checks is performed.	Misstatements made by the payroll clerks in favor of employees would likely not be discovered.
6. Payroll checks are not prenumbered or controlled by the payroll clerks.	The chief accountant could prepare, sign, and cash an extra payroll check without detection.

  b. Deficiencies 1, 2, 4, 5, and 6 increase the likelihood of fraud involving misappropriation of assets. Fraud involving misappropriation of assets is relatively common for payroll, although the amounts are often not material. Fraudulent financial reporting involving payroll is less likely.

11-29 a. The auditor must conduct the audit to detect errors and fraud, including embezzlement, that are material to the financial statements. It is more difficult to discover embezzlements than most types of errors, but the auditor still has significant responsibility. In this situation, the deficiencies in internal control are such that it should alert the auditor to the potential for fraud. On the other hand, the fraud may be immaterial and therefore not be of major concern. The auditor of a public company must also consider the impact of noted deficiencies when issuing the auditor's report on internal control over financial reporting. When noted deficiencies are considered to be material weaknesses, whether individually or combined with other deficiencies, the auditor's report must be modified to reflect the presence of material weaknesses.

11-29 (continued)

    b.   The following deficiencies in internal control exist:

        1.   The person who reconciles the bank account does not compare payees on checks to the cash disbursements journal.

        2.   The president signs blank checks, thus providing no control over expenditures.

        3.   No one checks invoices to determine that they are cancelled when paid.

    c.   To uncover the fraud, the auditor could perform the following procedures:

        1.   Comparison of payee on checks to cash disbursements journal.

        2.   Follow up all outstanding checks that did not clear the bank during the engagement until they clear the bank. Compare payee to cash disbursements journal.

11-30   a.

	a. FRAUD?	b. TYPE OF FRAUD
1.	Yes	Fraudulent financial reporting
2.	Yes	Misappropriation of assets
3.	Yes	Fraudulent financial reporting
4.	Yes	Misappropriation of assets
5.	Yes	Fraudulent financial reporting
6.	Yes	Misappropriation of assets
7.	No *	N/A

*   Fraud involves intent. The circumstances suggest that there was no intent on the part of Franklin to be deceptive. If the purpose of omitting the footnote was to deceive the bank, then this case would represent fraudulent financial reporting.

11-31 1.   a.   Fraudulent financial reporting.
                b.   N/A
                c.   Confirm receivables, including the existence of any special terms with customers.

         2.   a.   Fraudulent financial reporting.
                b.   N/A
                c.   Test the accuracy of the aging by recalculating the number of days outstanding for a sample of accounts receivable.

         3.   a.   Misappropriation of assets.
                b.   Reconcile cash to amount recorded in the cash register.
                c.   N/A

         4.   a.   Fraudulent financial reporting.
                b.   N/A
                c.   Confirm accounts receivable at year end. Inquire about the existence of goods held for customers during inventory observation.

         5.   a.   Fraudulent financial reporting.
                b.   N/A
                c.   Confirm accounts receivable at year end. Obtain last receiving reports for returned goods from receiving department and trace to credit memos.

         6.   a.   Misappropriation of assets.
                b.   Credit memos are approved by an appropriate person independent of accounting for sales and cash receipts.
                c.   N/A

         7.   a.   Fraudulent financial reporting.
                b.   N/A
                c.   Confirm receivables, including the existence of any special terms with customers. Examine sales returns after year-end to see if they relate to sales recorded before year-end.

         8.   a.   Misappropriation of assets.
                b.   Require that all sales be supported by receipts recorded in the cash register.
                c.   N/A

11-32 1.   a.   There may be unrecorded cash disbursement transactions.

            b.   Because the transactions relate to cash disbursements, the cash account will be affected. The accounts payable account may be misstated if the disbursement is the payment on an account. If the disbursement is for the direct payment of an expense or is related to the purchase of assets, then expense or asset accounts will be affected. Payments on other liability accounts would impact those liability accounts.

            c.   Existing transactions are recorded (completeness).

      2.   a.   There may be fictitious accounts receivable accounts included in the master file.

            b.   Accounts receivable and sales are likely to be affected by fictitious receivables.

            c.   Amounts included exist (existence).

      3.   a.   Management may have manipulated key assumptions so that pension expense and pension liability amounts would be lower.

            b.   Pension expense and pension liability accounts are likely to be affected.

            c.   Amounts included are stated at the correct values (Accuracy).

      4.   a.   The client may have shipped and recorded large amounts of goods close to year end to third parties who may hold the goods on consignment or who have full rights of return. These shipments were made to record a fictitious sale and related receivable.

            b.   Accounts receivable and sales and the related costs of goods sold and ending inventory would be affected by this activity.

            c.   Recorded amounts existed (occurrence).

      5.   a.   Assets that were misappropriated may be concealed by recording purchase transactions using non-standard, fictitious vendor numbers.

            b.   Accounts payable would be overstated and the related asset account would be increased by the unauthorized transaction.

            c.   Recorded amounts existed (occurrence).

      6.   a.   Sales may be fictitiously recorded before any goods were shipped.

            b.   Sales and accounts receivable.

            c.   Recorded amounts existed (occurrence).

■   **Case**

11-33   a.   There are many fraud risk factors indicated in the dialogue. Among the fraud risk factors are the following:
- A significant portion of Mint's compensation is represented by bonuses and stock options. Although this arrangement has been approved by SCS's Board of Directors, this may be a motivation for Mint, the new CEO, to engage in fraudulent financial reporting.
- Mint's statement to the stock analysts that SCS's earnings would increase by 30% next year may be both an unduly aggressive and unrealistic forecast. That forecast may tempt Mint to intentionally misstate certain ending balances this year that would increase the profitability of the next year.
- SCS's audit committee may not be sufficiently objective because Green, the chair of the audit committee, hired Mint, the new CEO, and they have been best friends for years.
- One individual, Mint, appears to dominate management without any compensating controls. Mint seems to be making all the important decisions without any apparent input from other members of management or resistance from the Board of Directors.
- There were frequent disputes between Brown, the prior CEO, who like Mint apparently dominated management and the Board of Directors, and Jones, the predecessor auditor. This fact may indicate that an environment exists in which management will be reluctant to make any changes that Kent suggests.
- Management seems satisfied with an understaffed and ineffective internal audit department. This situation displays an inappropriate attitude regarding the internal control environment.
- Management has failed to properly monitor and correct a significant deficiency in its internal control—the lack of segregation of duties in cash disbursements. This disregard for the control environment is also a risk factor.
- Information about anticipated future layoffs has spread among the employees. This information may cause an increase in the risk of material misstatement arising from the misappropriation of assets by dissatisfied employees.

11-33 (continued)

b.   Kent has many misconceptions regarding the consideration of fraud in the audit of SCS's financial statements that are contained in the dialogue. Among Kent's misconceptions are the following:

- Kent states that the auditor does not have specific duties regarding fraud. In fact, an auditor has a responsibility to specifically assess the risk of material misstatement due to fraud and to consider that assessment in designing the audit procedures to be performed.

- Kent is not concerned about Mint's employment contract. Kent should be concerned about a CEO's contract that is based primarily on bonuses and stock options because such an arrangement may indicate a motivation for management to engage in fraudulent financial reporting.

- Kent does not think that Mint's forecast for 2012 has an effect on the financial statement audit for 2011. However, Kent should consider the possibility that Mint may intentionally misstate the 2011 ending balances to increase the reported profit in 2012.

- Kent believes the audit programs are fine as is. Actually, Kent should modify the audit programs because of the many risk factors that are present in the SCS audit.

- Kent is not concerned that the internal audit department is ineffective and understaffed. In fact, Kent should be concerned that SCS has permitted this situation to continue because it represents a risk factor for fraud.

- Kent states that an auditor provides no assurances about fraud because that is management's job. In fact, an auditor has a responsibility to plan and perform an audit to obtain reasonable assurance about whether the financial statements are free of material misstatement, whether caused by error or fraud.

- Kent is not concerned that the prior year's material weakness in internal control has not been corrected. However, Kent should be concerned that the lack of segregation of duties in the cash disbursements department represents a risk factor relating to misstatements arising from the misappropriation of assets. If the client was a publicly traded company, the presence of an uncorrected material weakness would significantly affect the auditor's report on internal control over financial reporting.

- Kent does not believe the rumors about big layoffs in the next month have an effect on audit planning. In planning the audit, Kent should consider this a risk factor because it may cause an increase in the risk of material misstatement arising from misappropriation of assets by dissatisfied employees.

11-33 (continued)

 c. SAS 99 requires that auditors document the following matters related to the auditor's consideration of material misstatements due to fraud:

- The discussion among engagement team personnel in planning the audit about the susceptibility of the entity's financial statements to material fraud.
- Procedures performed to obtain information necessary to identify and assess the risks of material fraud.
- Specific risks of material fraud that were identified, and a description of the auditor's response to those risks.
- Reasons supporting a conclusion that there is not a significant risk of material improper revenue recognition.
- Results of the procedures performed to address the risk of management override of controls.
- Other conditions and analytical relationships that indicated that additional auditing procedures or other responses were required, and the actions taken by the auditor.
- The nature of communications about fraud made to management, the audit committee, or others.

After fraud risks are identified and documented, the auditor should evaluate factors that reduce fraud risk. The auditor should then develop appropriate responses to the risk of fraud.

■ Integrated Case Application

11-34

PINNACLE MANUFACTURING—PART IV

 a. The following are some of the fraud risk triangle factors that students may identify from Parts I through III:

Incentives/Pressures
1. Pinnacle's board is considering selling the Machine-Tech division, and the president of the division is committed to making it profitable (Part I).
2. Pinnacle is in danger of violating its debt covenants (Part II).

Opportunities
1. Pinnacle engages in a number of related party transactions (Part I)
2. Realizable value issues exist with inventory and receivables (Part I and II).
3. There has been turnover in internal audit personnel (Part II).

11-34 (continued)

Attitudes/Rationalizations
1. Pinnacle has had disputes with the IRS (Part II).

b. The company is in the engine manufacturing business, and has recently expanded into solar engines. The engine manufacturing business is competitive and increasingly outsourced. The solar business depends on developing technology. These characteristics are most likely to affect inventory, and to a lesser extent accounts receivable and fixed assets.

c. Pinnacle could overstate revenues in several ways. The auditor would especially focus on the Machine-Tech division because of the incentives identified in part a.

Technique to overstate revenue	Audit technique to determine if fraud is occurring
Record sales in subsequent period as current sales.	Examine shipping documents for sales recorded before year end.
Ship goods to customers that were not ordered.	1. Examine customer orders for goods shipped before year-end 2. Confirm accounts receivable.

d. Several changes in account balances suggest the potential for fraud:
1. Revenues increased by 8%. If this increase was not expected, it could suggest revenue recognition fraud.
2. The decline in depreciation and bad debt expense, which are management estimates, could suggest the use of estimates to overstate income.

e. Potential fraud risks from Part II

	Fraud risk	Fraud Triangle Element (if yes)
1.	Yes	Motivation (justify commitment to solar)
2.	Yes	Opportunity
3.	Yes	Opportunity (related party transaction)
4.	Yes	Opportunity
5.	Yes	Opportunity
6.	No	
7.	Yes	Opportunity (related party transaction)
8.	Yes	Opportunity
9.	Yes	Incentives
10.	Yes	Attitude/rationalization
11.	Yes	Opportunity (related party transaction)

11-35 – ACL Problem Solution

  a. The invoice amount column totals $278,641.33.
  b. There are no exceptions in the calculation of unit cost x quantity. (Create a filter with the expression Unit_Cost * Quantity <> Invoice_Amount.)
  c. There are three items where the unit cost exceeds $100 (product # 090584072, 090585322, and 090081001). See the following printout. (Filter used Unit Cost >100.)

```
Page             1                      02/10/2011      14:10:33
Produced with ACL by: ACL Educational Edition - Not For Commercial Use
INV.DATE    INVNO   PRODNO    QUANTITY   VENDOR_NO   INVOICE_AMT   UNIT_COST
10/21/2002   87   090584072     41        11475        7125.80      173.80
10/21/2002   22   090585322     29        11837        3996.20      137.80
04/09/2002        090081001      3        10134         467.40      155.80
                                73                     11589.40      467.40
```

  d. The three vendors with the largest total dollars for 2002 were: vendor #s 10025, 11475, and 12130. (Summarize by vendor number, then Quick Sort to find the largest three.)
  e. The following amounts are over $15,000: vendor #10025 for $56,767.20, vendor #11475 for $20,386.19, and vendor #12130 for $15,444.80. [Filter used is (VENDOR_NO = "10025" OR VENDOR_NO = "11475" OR VENDOR_NO = "12130") AND INVOICE_AMOUNT > 15000.]
  f. See the following printout. (Filter, then print report). Total transactions for vendor #10134 = $22.618.62. (Edit filter to include only vendor #10134 and use Total command)

```
Page       1                        02/10/2011      15:45:19
Produced with ACL by: ACL Educational Edition - Not For Commercial Use
INV._DATE    INV._NO PRODNO    QTY   VENDOR_NO   INVOICE_AMOUNT   UNITCOST

09/29/2002   030303343    100   10134        883.00         8.83
11/12/2002   0302303      458   10134      18883.34        41.23
04/09/2002   090081001      3   10134        467.40       155.80
09/30/2002   010551340    278   10134       1823.68         6.56
02/14/2002   052484405    115   10134        561.20         4.88
10/15/200255 060102096    286   13440      11068.20        38.70

                        1240               33686.82       256.00
```

■ **Internet Problem Solution: Brainstorming About Fraud Risks**

Internet Problem 11-1

    a.   Common pitfalls of brainstorming include group domination, social loafing, groupthink and groupshift. Each of these problems can generally be avoided through adequate planning and session facilitation.

    b.   The following techniques can improve the effectiveness of a brainstorming session: assign homework to participants, establish ground rules for everyone to follow, set the proper tone so that everyone is comfortable, allow no criticism of ideas during the idea generation phase, encourage participants to generate as many ideas as possible, give credit to the group for the work, and manage the group size and composition to maximize the session's effectiveness.

(**Note**: Internet problems address current issues using Internet sources. Because Internet sites are subject to change, Internet problems and solutions may change. Current information on Internet problems is available at www.pearsonhighered.com/arens.)

Chapter 12

The Impact of Information Technology
on the Audit Process

■ **Review Questions**

12-1   The proper installation of IT can lead to internal control enhancements by replacing manually-performed controls with computer-performed controls. IT-based accounting systems have the ability to handle tremendous volumes of complex business transactions cost effectively. Computer-performed controls can reduce the potential for human error by replacing manual controls with programmed controls that apply checks and balances to each transaction processed. The systematic nature of IT offers greater potential to reduce the risk of material misstatements resulting from random, human errors in processing.

   The use of IT based accounting systems also offers the potential for improved management decisions by providing more and higher quality information on a more timely basis than traditional manual systems. IT-based systems are usually administered effectively because the complexity requires effective organization, procedures, and documentation. That in turn enhances internal control.

12-2   When entities rely heavily on IT systems to process financial information, there are new risks specific to IT environments that must be considered. Key risks include the following:

   ■   *Reliance on the functioning capabilities of hardware and software.* The risk of system crashes due to hardware or software failures must be evaluated when entities rely heavily on IT to produce financial statement information.
   ■   *Systematic versus random errors.* Due to the uniformity of processing performed by IT based systems, errors in computer software can result in incorrect processing for all transactions processed. This increases the risk of many significant misstatements.
   ■   *Unauthorized access.* The centralized storage of key records and files in electronic form increases the potential for unauthorized on-line access from remote locations.
   ■   *Loss of data.* The centralized storage of data in electronic form increases the risk of data loss in the event the data file is altered or destroyed.
   ■   *Visibility of audit trail.* The use of IT often converts the traditional paper trail to an electronic audit trail, eliminating source documents and paper-based journals and records.

12-2 (continued)

- *Reduced human involvement.* The replacement of traditional manual processes with computer-performed processes reduces opportunities for employees to recognize misstatements resulting from transactions that might have appeared unusual to experienced employees.
- *Lack of traditional authorization.* IT-based systems can be programmed to initiate certain types of transactions automatically without obtaining traditional manual approvals.
- *Reduced segregation of duties.* The installation of IT-based accounting systems centralizes many of the traditionally segregated manual tasks under the authority of the IT function now that those functions are mainly performed by the computer.
- *Need for IT experience.* As companies rely to a greater extent on IT-based systems, the need for personnel trained in IT systems increases in order to install, maintain, and use systems.

12-3 The audit trail represents the accumulation of source documents and records maintained by the client to serve as support for the transactions occurring during the accounting period. The integration of IT can change the audit trail by converting many of the traditionally paper-based source documents and records into electronic files that cannot be visually observed. Because many of the transactions are entered directly into the computer as they occur, some of the documents and records are even eliminated.

12-4 Random error represents errors that occur in an inconsistent pattern. Manual accounting systems are especially prone to random errors that result from honest mistakes that occur as employees perform day-to-day tasks. When those mistakes do not consistently occur while performing a particular task, errors are distributed randomly into the accounting records. An example of a random error is when an employee accidentally pulls the wrong unit price off the approved price list when preparing a sales invoice for a particular customer.

Systematic error represents errors that occur consistently across all similar transactions. Because IT-based systems perform tasks uniformly for all transactions submitted, any mistake in software programming results in the occurrence of the same error for every transaction processed by the system. An example of a systematic error occurs when a program that is supposed to post sales amounts to the accounts receivable subsidiary records actually posts the sales amount twice to customers' accounts.

12-5 In most traditional accounting systems, the duties related to authorization of transactions, recordkeeping of transactions, and custody of assets are segregated across three or more individuals. As accounting systems make greater use of IT, many of the traditional manually performed tasks are now performed by the computer. As a result, some of the traditionally segregated duties, particularly authorization and recordkeeping, fall under the responsibility of IT personnel who

12-5 (continued)

oversee IT operations. To compensate for the collapsing of duties under the IT function, key IT tasks related to programming, operation of hardware and software, and data control are segregated. Separation of those IT functions restricts an IT employee's ability to inappropriately access software and data files in order to misappropriate assets.

12-6 *General controls* relate to all aspects of the IT function. They have a global impact on all software applications. Examples of general controls include controls related to the administration of the IT function; software acquisition and maintenance; physical and on-line security over access to hardware, software, and related backup; back-up planning in the event of unexpected emergencies; and hardware controls. *Application controls* apply to the processing of individual transactions. An example of an application control is a programmed control that verifies that all time cards submitted are for valid employee id numbers included in the electronically accessible employee master file.

12-7 The typical duties often segregated within an IT function include systems development, computer operations, and data control. Systems development involves the acquisition or programming of application software. Systems development personnel work with test copies of programs and data files to develop new or improved application software programs. Computer operations personnel are responsible for executing live production jobs in accordance with a job schedule and for monitoring consoles for messages about computer efficiency and malfunctions. Data control personnel are responsible for data input and output control. They often independently verify the quality of input and the reasonableness of output. By separating these functions, no one IT employee can make changes to application software or underlying master files and then operate computer equipment to use those changed programs or data files to process transactions.

12-8 If general controls are ineffective, there is a potential for material misstatement in each computer-based accounting application, regardless of the quality of automated application controls. If, for example, the systems development process is not properly controlled, there is a greater risk that unauthorized and untested modifications to accounting applications software have occurred that may have affected the automated control. If general controls are strong, there is a greater likelihood of placing greater reliance on automated application controls. Stronger general controls should lead to greater likelihood that underlying automated application controls operate effectively and data files contain accurate, authorized, and complete information. When general controls are effective, the auditor may not have to test the automated application control in the current year, as long as the automated control has not changed since it was last tested by the auditor and that test was performed within the last three years.

12-9 Application controls apply to the processing of specific individual transactions within a transaction cycle, such as a computer performed credit approval process for sales on account. Due to the nature of these types of controls, application controls generally link directly to one or more specific transaction objectives. For example, the credit approval application control directly links to the occurrence objective for sales. Auditors typically identify both manual and computer-performed application controls for each transaction-related objective using a control risk matrix similar to the one discussed in Chapter 10.

12-10 "Auditing around the computer" represents an audit approach whereby the auditor does not use computer controls to reduce control risk. Instead, the auditor uses non-IT controls to support a reduced control risk assessment. In these situations, the use of IT does not significantly impact the audit trail. Typically, the auditor obtains an understanding of internal control and performs tests of controls, substantive tests of transactions, and account balance verification procedures in the same manner as if the accounting system was entirely manual. The auditor is still responsible for gaining an understanding of general and application computer controls because such knowledge is useful in identifying risks that may affect the financial statements.

12-11 The test data approach involves processing the auditor's test data using the client's computer system and the client's application software program to determine whether the computer-performed controls correctly process the test data. Because the auditor designs the test data, the auditor is able to identify which test items should be accepted or rejected by the computer. When using this approach the auditor should assess the following:

■ How effectively does the test data represent all relevant conditions that the auditor wants to test?
■ How certain is the auditor that the application programs being tested by the auditor's test data are the same programs as those used by the client throughout the year to process actual transactions?
■ How certain is the auditor that test data is effectively eliminated from the client's records once testing is completed?

Parallel simulation with audit software involves the auditor's use of an auditor-controlled software program to perform parallel operations to the client's software by using the same data files. Because the auditor's software is designed to parallel an operation performed by the client's software, this strategy is referred to as parallel simulation testing. Parallel simulation could be used in the audit of payroll by writing a program that calculates the accrued vacation pay liability for each employee using information contained in the employee master file. The total liability calculated by the auditor's software program would then be compared to the client's calculation to determine if the liability for accrued vacation pay is fairly stated at year-end.

12-12 Often companies that purchase and install vendor developed software applications on computer hard drives rely on IT consultants to assist in the installation and maintenance of that software because those companies do not have dedicated IT personnel. Also, assignment of responsibility may reside with user departments. Companies can reduce these risks related to not having IT personnel by performing sufficient reference and background checks about software vendor and IT consultant reputations. In addition, companies can load software programs onto hard drives in a format that does not permit changes by client personnel, particularly non-IT user department personnel who may have primary responsibility for the system. Companies should also consider segregating key duties related to access to master files and responsibilities for processing transactions.

12-13 Because many companies that operate in a network environment decentralize their network servers across the organization, there is an increased risk for a lack of security and lack of overall management of the network operations. The decentralization may lead to a lack of standardized equipment and procedures. In many instances responsibility for purchasing equipment and software, maintenance, administration, and physical security, often resides with key user groups rather than with a centralized IT function. Also, network-related software often lacks the security features, including segregation of duties, typically available in traditionally centralized environments because of the ready access to software and data by multiple users.

12-14 In database management systems, many applications share the same data files. This increases risks in some cases given that multiple users, including individuals outside accounting, access and update data files. Without proper database administration and access controls, risks of unauthorized, inaccurate, and incomplete data files increase. The centralization of data also increases the need to properly back-up data information on a regular basis.

12-15 An online sales ordering system poses many potential risks for an audit client. Risks that may exist include:

1. Customer data is susceptible to interception by unauthorized third parties.
2. The client company's data, programs, and hardware are susceptible to potential interception or sabotage by external parties.
3. An unauthorized third party may attempt to transact business with the client company.

These risks can be addressed by the use of firewalls, encryption techniques, and digital signatures. A *firewall* is a system of hardware and software that monitors and controls the flow of e-commerce communications by channeling all network connections through a control gateway. A firewall protects data, programs, and other IT resources from external users accessing the

12-15 (continued)

system through networks, such as the Internet. *Encryption techniques* are based on computer programs that transform a standard message into a coded (encrypted) form. One key (the public key) is used for encoding the message and the other key (the private key) is used to decode the message. Encryption techniques protect the security of electronic communication during the transmission process. Finally, the use of *digital signatures* can enhance internal controls over the online sales order system by authenticating the validity of customers and other trading partners who conduct business with the client company.

12-16 The fact that your client has outsourced the majority of its accounting information system to a third-party data center does not change your professional responsibilities. The second standard of fieldwork requires the auditor to obtain an understanding of internal controls in all audits. Thus, the auditor would need to perform procedures to obtain information to provide an understanding of internal controls that may reside at the data center. The auditor would benefit greatly from a service auditor's report, if one is available. Because the client has outsourced a majority of the accounting information system, the auditor is likely to identify controls that may support lower assessments of control risk that must be tested. Either the auditors may decide to conduct their own testing of those controls or they may be able to obtain a Report on Controls that Have Been Implemented and Tested for Operating Effectiveness.

■ Multiple Choice Questions From CPA Examinations

12-17 a. (2)   b. (1)   c. (3)   d. (3)

12-18 a. (1)   b. (3)   c. (3)   d. (3)

■ **Discussion Questions and Problems**

12-19 A schedule showing the pertinent transaction-related audit objectives and application controls for each type of misstatement is below and on the following two pages.

MISSTATEMENT	TRANSACTION-RELATED AUDIT OBJECTIVE	COMPUTER-BASED CONTROLS
1. A customer number on a sales invoice was transposed and, as a result, charged to the wrong customer. By the time the error was found, the original customer was no longer in business.	■ Recorded transactions exist ■ Transactions are properly posted and summarized	■ Key verification ■ Check digit ■ Reconciliation to customer number on purchase order and bill of lading
2. A former computer operator, who is now a programmer, entered information for a fictitious sales return and ran it through the computer system at night. When the money came in, he took it and deposited it in his own account.	■ Recorded transactions exist	■ Input security controls over cash receipts records ■ Scheduling of computer processing ■ Controls over access to equipment ■ Controls over access to live application programs
3. A nonexistent part number was included in the description of goods on a shipping document. Therefore, no charge was made for those goods.	■ Existing transactions are recorded	■ Preprocessing review ■ Programmed controls (e.g., compare part no. to parts list master file)

12-19 (continued)

MISSTATEMENT	TRANSACTION-RELATED AUDIT OBJECTIVE	COMPUTER-BASED CONTROLS
4. A customer order was filled and shipped to a former customer that had already filed bankruptcy.	■ Recorded transactions exist	■ Preprocessing authorization ■ Preprocessing review ■ Programmed controls (e.g., comparison to customer file)
5. The sales manager approved the price of goods ordered by a customer, but he wrote down the wrong price.	■ Transactions are stated at the correct amounts	■ Preprocessing review ■ Programmed controls (e.g., comparison to the on-line authorized price list)
6. A computer operator picked up a computer-based data file for sales of the wrong week and processed them through the system a second time.	■ Recorded transactions exist ■ Transactions are recorded on the correct dates	■ Correct file controls ■ Cutoff procedures ■ Programmed controls (e.g., check for sequence of dates)
7. For a sale, a data entry operator erroneously failed to enter the information for the salesman's department. As a result, the salesman received no commission for that sale.	■ Existing transactions are recorded	■ Conversion verification (e.g., key verification) ■ Programmed controls (e.g., check field for completeness)
8. Several remittance advices were batched together for inputting. The cash receipts clerk stopped for coffee, set them on a box, and failed to deliver them to the data input personnel.	■ Existing transactions are recorded ■ Transactions are recorded on the correct dates	■ Control totals reconciled to manual totals of all batches ■ Computer accounts for numerical sequence of batches submitted

	PERSON 1	PERSON 2	PERSON 3	PERSON 4
a.	■ Systems analyst ■ Programmer	■ Computer operator	■ Librarian	■ Data control
b.	■ Systems analyst ■ Programmer	■ Computer operator	■ Librarian ■ Data control	N/A
c.	■ Systems analyst ■ Programmer ■ Data control*	■ Computer operator ■ Librarian*	N/A	N/A

* This solution assumes the data control procedures will serve as a check on the computer operator and will allocate work across both persons.

      d.   If all five functions were performed by one person, internal control would certainly be weakened. However, the company need not be unauditable, for two reasons: First, there may be controls outside the IT function which constitute effective control. For example, users may reconcile all input and output data on a regular basis. Second, the auditor of a non-public entity is not required to rely on internal control. He or she may take a substantive approach to the audit assuming adequate evidence is available in support of transactions and balances.

12-21   a.   The important controls and related sales transaction-related audit objectives are:

CONTROL	SALES TRANSACTION-RELATED AUDIT OBJECTIVE
1. Use of prenumbered sales orders	■ Existing sales transactions are recorded
2. Segregated approval of sales by credit department; customer purchase orders are attached to sales orders; approval is noted on form	■ Recorded sales are for shipments made to existing customers

12-21 (continued)

3.	Segregated entry of approved sales orders	■ Recorded sales are for shipments made to existing customers ■ Recorded sales are posted to correct customer account
	Prices are entered using an approved price list	■ Recorded sales are at the correct price
	Sales invoices are prepared from the data file created from sales order entry; hash totals are generated and used; sales invoices are prenumbered; control totals are reconciled by an independent person	■ Recorded sales are for shipments made to existing customers ■ Existing sales transactions are recorded ■ Recorded sales are at the correct amount ■ Sales transactions are properly included in the master files
4. & 5.	Bills of lading are produced with sales invoices and eventually filed with the sales invoice in numerical order; differences in quantities are corrected and transaction amounts are adjusted	■ Existing sales transactions are recorded ■ Recorded sales are for the correct quantity of goods shipped
6.	Hash totals of daily processing matched to hash and control totals generated by independent person	■ Existing sales transactions are recorded. ■ Recorded transactions are for shipments made to existing customers

b. Among the audit procedures to be applied to a sample of the invoices and source documents are the following:

1. Account for the sequence of prenumbered sales order forms.
2. Review the sales order forms for agreement with purchase orders from customers.
3. Determine that evidence of approval by the credit department appears on all sales order forms.
4. Account for the sequence of prenumbered sales invoices.
5. Ascertain that bills of lading have been prepared for all invoices and are in agreement therewith.
6. Determine that the price list used by the billing clerk has been properly authorized. Trace prices on the list to invoices, and test the extensions and additions on the invoices.
7. Ascertain that the sales invoices are in agreement with the data on the sales order forms.

Among the audit procedures to be applied to the data file are the following:

1. Verify the company's predetermined "hash" totals and control amounts by computing similar totals on selected batches of invoices and items from the data file.
2. Compare totals and see that they reconcile.
3. Arrange for a tabulating run to be made of selected test transactions. Compare the items in this printout with the totals previously compiled from the test transactions.

12-22

1. Wilcoxon Sports should strengthen several of its IT general controls. The fact that the programmer was able to access the current live version of the sales application program suggests that there are breakdowns in appropriate segregation of duties among IT personnel. Programmers should be restricted from access to actual software used in production. The librarian function should protect access to live versions of the programs and only provide access to operators that allows them to use actual live versions of software to process transactions.

   Wilcoxon should consider strengthening its processes for authorizing and approving software changes. More extensive procedures should be implemented regarding requests and approvals for software changes. Only upon the presentation of adequate documentation and approvals should the librarian provide access of a test copy of the software programs to the programmers. Without adequate documentation and approvals, the programmers should not be granted access to software. Furthermore, the librarian should never accept revised programs back from the programmers when there is no supporting documentation that a change was authorized. Approvals for software changes should include user department approvals, such as those responsible for the sales function.

   For larger IT functions, programmers are split into subgroups with some programmers only authorized to address programming issues for application software (e.g., the sales application) while other programmers are only authorized to address programming issues for systems software, such as operating software.

2. Strengthening IT general controls over program changes, restricting access to live software versions, and enhancing segregation of duties will significantly reduce the programmer's ability to make unauthorized changes to software as was done at Wilcoxon Sports. If all program changes must be accompanied by extensive documentation and approvals for those changes, it will be more difficult for programmers to make an

12-22 (continued)

unauthorized change. Furthermore restricting programmer access to only test copies of software that have been approved for modification makes it much more difficult for programmers to implement a change in software without someone's knowledge. If the librarian only accepts revised programs for properly authorized changes, then the programmer will be prevented from sneaking a changed program back into live production.

If programmer functions are separated among programmers such that only a subset is authorized to modify application programs and not system software, then it will require collusion among programmers to implement a change in application software that also requires modification to system software. That segregation would prevent situations like the one at Wilcoxon whereby the programmer was able to make unauthorized changes to both the sales application and the operating system software.

12-23   a.   The major problems the auditor faces in verifying sales and accounts receivable include:

1.   Determining that both cash and credit sales are valid, and that all were recorded in the proper amount.
2.   Determining that accounts receivable balances are proper and that transactions were recorded in the proper amount and to the proper customer.
3.   Determining whether the internal controls are adequate, so that he or she may rely on the system to provide correct information.

In this case, meeting some of these objectives is complicated by the fact that much of the pertinent information is in machine-readable form only.

b.   The concept of test data can be employed by having the auditor make test purchases in different departments of the store and observing whether the sales are recorded properly in the appropriate records. The auditor may also wish to enter invalid data to see that programmed controls reject the transactions. Difficulties the auditor would have to overcome in using test data are:

1.   The test data must comprise all relevant conditions that the auditor desires to test so as to test every conceivable deficiency possible in the system.
2.   The program tested by the auditor's test data must be the same program that is used throughout the year by the client to ensure the validity of results.
3.   The test data will probably have to be eliminated from most of the client's records since the auditor's purchases would not be part of the company's regular business.

12-23 (continued)

  c. Generalized audit software can be employed in this audit by following these steps:

    1. Decide the objectives of the test—e.g., to select and analyze a random sample of sales invoices or to compare the totals of master files to the entries into the general ledger.
    2. Begin to design the application by identifying and selecting pertinent data from the client's files.
    3. Design the most useful format and contents of the auditor's generalized audit software reports.
    4. Complete the application design by developing the logical and programmed approach to extract and manipulate the data to produce reports.
    5. Process the program and information to produce the reports.

  Several tests that can be conducted using a generalized audit program are:

    1. Select accounts according to certain selection criteria for accounts receivable confirmation and print the confirmations.
    2. Prepare an analysis of sales and cost of sales.
    3. Test the year-end cutoff of sales.
    4. Review all intercompany sales transactions.
    5. Foot the various files and select unusual or large transactions according to certain criteria.
    6. Age accounts receivable.
    7. Test the recording of sales transactions by parallel simulation.

  d. Several ways to reduce the information entered into the cash register are:

    1. By setting the date in the register for the day, there will be no need to enter the date.
    2. Same as 1 for store code number and sales clerk number.
    3. There is no need to enter cash sale or credit sale since entering the customer account number implies a credit sale.
    4. Install optical scanning point of sale equipment.
    5. Have the computer pull unit prices based on product number from price list master file.

12-24 a. The nature of generalized audit software is to provide computer programs that can process a variety of file media and record formats to perform a number of functions using computer technology.

    There are several types of generalized audit software packages. Usually, generalized audit software is a purchased audit software program that is Windows-based and easily operated on

12-24 (continued)

the auditor's desktop or laptop computer. Other generalized audit software exists that contain programs that create or generate other programs, programs that modify themselves to perform requested functions, or skeletal frameworks of programs that must be completed by the user.

A package can be used to perform or verify mathematical calculations; to include, exclude, or summarize items having specified characteristics; to provide subtotals and final totals; to compute, select, and evaluate statistical samples for audit tests; to print results or sequence that will facilitate an audit step; to compare, merge, or match the contents of two or more files, and to produce machine-readable files in a format specified by the auditor.

b. Ways in which a generalized audit software package can be used to assist in the audit of inventory of Boos & Baumkirchner, Inc., include the following:

1. Compare data on the CPA's set of preprinted inventory count cards to data on the disk inventory master file and list all differences. This will assure that the set of count cards furnished to the CPA is complete.
2. Determine which items and parts are to be test-counted by making a random selection of a sample from the audit deck of count cards or the disk inventory master file. Exclude from the population items with a high unit cost or total value that have already been selected for test counting.
3. Read the client's disk inventory master file and list all items or parts for which the date of last sale or usage indicates a lack of recent transactions. This list provides data for determining possible obsolescence.
4. Read the client's disk inventory master file and list all items or parts of which the quantity on hand seems excessive in relation to quantity used or sold during the year. This list provides data for determining overstocked or slow-moving items or parts.
5. Read the client's disk inventory master file and list all items or parts of which the quantity on hand seems excessive in relation to economic order quantity. This list should be reviewed for possible slow-moving or obsolete items.
6. Enter the audit test-count quantities onto the cards. Match these cards against the client's adjusted disk inventory master file, comparing the quantities on the cards to the quantities on the disk file and list any differences. This will indicate whether the client's year-end inventory counts and the master file are substantially in agreement.

7. Use the adjusted disk inventory master file and independently extend and total the year-end inventory and print the grand total on an output report. When compared to the balance determined by the client, this will verify the calculations performed by the client.

8. Use the client's disk inventory master file and list all items with a significant cost per unit. The list should show cost per unit and both major and secondary vendor codes. This list can be used to verify the cost per unit.

9. Use the costs per unit on the client's disk inventory master file, and extend and total the dollar value of the counts on the audit test count cards. When compared to the total dollar value of the inventory, this will permit evaluation of audit coverage.

12-25 a. Strengths of current systems development and program change processes at Granger Container:

- Eric Winecoff's extensive knowledge of the software being used helps lead to effective program changes and new application software developments.

- The small size of the IT staff and its team oriented approach allows the IT team to respond quickly to meet Granger's needs for system change.

- The IT programming staff tests applications using test copies of data files before implementation of the new system.

- Original data files are locked in the file storage room, which can only be accessed by Eric.

- Some documentation is maintained for each program change.

b. Deficiencies in current systems development and program change processes:

- Most program change requests are generated by IT personnel, with few program change requests generated by user department personnel who rely on the system to perform day-to-day tasks.

- No user personnel are involved in the program design and testing processes. Users have less ability to make suggestions of useful programmed controls to be performed automatically by the computer.

- Over reliance on Eric and the software package purchased from Eric's former employer may not always lead to the most effective and efficient system.

- No written requests for program changes are maintained. Thus, there is no audit trail of program changes that occur over time.

- No documented approval of program changes is maintained. Eric merely extends verbal approval. Again, the lack of documented approval increases the difficulty in determining that only authorized program changes occur.
- Periodic progress reports and approvals are not documented. This lack of documentation increases the potential for mismanaged program development. The lack of documentation makes future changes of those programs more difficult and time-consuming.
- The current review process is dependent on a programmer's willingness to bring issues to Eric's attention. Eric only becomes involved if a programmer approaches him for input. Too much reliance and trust is placed on programmers.
- There is no standardized format for designing programs. Rather, each programmer is able to employ his or her own programming style. Thus, it is more difficult to review current programs under development to determine that only authorized changes are being made. And, future changes involving those programs will be more difficult than if a standardized programming format was employed.
- Programmers have access to the computer room to load programs for testing. That access may allow a programmer to load a live copy of a program for processing. That could lead to inappropriate processing and manipulation of data, which in turn may lead to misstatements in the financial statements due to unauthorized or inaccurate processing.
- Programmers make changes directly into the live copies of actual programs that are currently in use. That could result in inaccurate processing of transactions when operators use that program to process actual data before all program changes have been thoroughly tested and debugged.
- Only Eric reviews test results. Users, internal auditors, and quality assurance personnel should also participate in designing test data and reviewing test results. Users are particularly most knowledgeable of the types of transaction data that the system should be capable of handling.
- Only Eric generates a limited amount of program change documentation. User and operation manuals and systems flowcharts and narratives are not updated for the change.
- There is no formal conversion plan developed that includes pilot testing and parallel testing before and during conversion.
- No user or operator training occurs.

    c.   Recommendations to improve processes:

- Encourage user personnel to submit written requests for change on a pre-printed program change request form. Change requests should contain the written approval of user department supervisors before submission to IT.
- Log all program change request forms by assigning a numerical sequence to all program change forms. Maintain a log of all approved and denied program change requests to generate an audit trail of the program change process.
- Develop a team approach to systems development and program changes. Require teams of programmers, user department personnel, internal audit, and a systems analyst to work on the program change from start to finish.
- Institute an IT Steering Committee that approves all significant program change requests. Eric should be required to formally report to this committee on a regular basis. For all other program changes, documented approvals should be obtained from Eric and the user department supervisory personnel for the department affected by the application program subject to change.
- Develop a formal Systems Development Methodology (SDM) that is to be used for all program development projects. When designing the SDM, build in required checkpoints for review and approval for each stage of development.
- Develop standardized programming formats and style to ensure consistent and accurate programming across programmers.
- Only provide test copies of application programs and data files for use by programmers. Never give the programming staff the actual application program currently in use.
- Prohibit programming staff from entering the computer operating room or secondary storage. Require programmers to submit test copies of programs and master files to the operations staff for testing.
- Only accept newly developed software into live production if accompanied by all required authorizations and documentation.
- Develop extensive documentation of the entire development process.
- Ensure that all user and operations manuals, systems flowcharts and narratives are updated.
- Develop a formal conversion plan that outlines the planned approach to implementing the new program. The plan should include extensive pilot and parallel testing, if possible.
- Train operators and users on the new system features before relying on the new system to process transactions.

INTERNAL CONTROL	a. TYPE OF CONTROL	b. TRANSACTION-RELATED AUDIT OBJECTIVE	c. OPPORTUNITY TO RELY ON PRIOR YEAR TESTING
1	AC	Recorded payroll transactions exist for valid employees	Yes
2	AC	Recorded payroll transactions exist (i.e. are for currently employed personnel)	Yes
3	AC	Recorded payroll transactions are classified into the correct accounts	Yes
4	AC	Recorded payroll transactions are at the correct amounts	Yes
5	AC	Recorded payroll transactions are summarized and posted to the correct general ledger account at the correct amounts	Yes
6	MC	Recorded payroll transactions exist; existing payroll transactions are recorded	No, since manual control
7	AC	Recorded payroll transactions exist (i.e., are for time actually worked)	Yes
8	MC	Recorded payroll transactions exist (i.e., are for time actually worked)	No, since manual control
9	MC	Recorded payroll transactions are at the correct amounts	No, since manual control
10	AC	Recorded payroll transactions exist (i.e., for valid work performed); recorded payroll transactions are at the correct amounts	Yes

12-27 Recommendations to improve Hardwood Lumber Company's Information Systems function:

- The Vice President of Information Systems (VP of IS) should report on a day-to-day basis to senior management (i.e. the president) and should not be under the authority of user personnel. This ensures that the IS function is not subordinate to a user function, which might inappropriately allocate IS resources to that user function's projects.

- The VP of IS should have access to the board of directors and should be responsible for periodically updating the board on significant IS projects. Perhaps, the board should create an IS Steering Committee to oversee IS activities (like the Audit Committee oversees the financial reporting process).

- Operations staff should not have responsibility for maintaining the operating software security features. This responsibility should be assigned to a more senior, trusted IS individual, such as the VP of IS.

- Video monitors should be examined continually. The actual monitors could be viewed on an ongoing basis by building security guards. Hardwood should consider taping what the cameras are viewing for subsequent retrieval in the event of a security breach.

- Consider requiring the use of card-keys and passwords to grant entrance to the computer room to enhance security surrounding unauthorized access to the computer room.

- Hardwood may consider purchasing a vendor developed access security software package to strengthen on-line security beyond the features currently provided by the operation software's security features.

- Restrict programmer access to test copies of software programs for only those programs that have been authorized for program change. Access to copies of other programs may not be necessary when those programs have not been authorized for change.

- Grant systems programmers access only to approved test copies of systems software, and grant application programmers access only to approved copies of application software.

- Consider hiring a systems analyst to coordinate all program development projects. Systems analysts can strengthen communications between user and programming personnel, and they can increase the likelihood that a strong systems development process is followed.

- Develop a weekly Job Schedule that outlines the order in which operators should process jobs. The VP of IS should review computer output to determine that it reconciles to the approved Job Schedule. This will increase the likelihood that only approved jobs are processed and that they are processed in the correct sequence.

- Relocate the secondary storage to a physically secure room separate from the computer room. Only grant the librarian access to this room. This will prevent the unauthorized removal of program and data files.

12-27 (continued)

- Remove the librarian's CHANGE rights to program and data files. The librarian should not be able to make changes to those files. The librarian should only be able to copy the contents of those files.
- Develop regular procedures for preparing backup copies of programs and data files and ensure those copies are sent to off-site storage.
- Use internal header and trailer labels on program tapes to ensure that the proper tapes are mounted for processing.
- Consider purchasing a vendor-developed librarian software package to assist the librarian in maintaining complete and accurate records of secondary storage programs and data files.
- Make sure only user department personnel have the ability to authorization additions or changes to data files.

12-28 a. The following deficiencies in the Parts for Wheels, Inc. online sales system may lead to material misstatements in the financial statements:

1. *Lack of Sales System Interface.* The lack of automatic interface between the online sales ordering system and the sales accounting system may increase the risk of material misstatements for sales. Sales orders printed from the online system may be lost and not recorded, or they may be recorded more than once if not properly controlled. Additionally, because each sale must be manually entered, there is increased risk that sales may be processed or recorded inaccurately.

2. *Lack of Inventory System Interface.* The lack of automatic interface between the online sales ordering system and the inventory management system may increase the risk that processed sales may not be properly reflected in the inventory accounting records. Given manual processing, there may be some risk that shipments occurred without completion of a proper bill of lading, which is required to adjust inventory records. As a result, shipments will not be accurately deducted from inventory records. Also, if bills of lading are not properly numbered and accounted for, there is a possibility that completed bills of lading are not entered or are entered more than once. Furthermore, the manual process of recording inventory transactions increases the risk of inaccurate posting of bills of lading into the inventory records.

3. *Manual Credit Approval.* The process of verifying credit authorization with the credit card agency is dependent on human processing. The lack of automatic electronic credit authorization may increase the risk of sales to unauthorized customers. This may lead to an increase risk of collection problems from credit card receivables.

12-28 (continued)

    4.   *Premature Recording.* Currently, sales are entered into the sales journal on the date credit is authorized, which is often the date the order is placed. This may result in premature recording of sales, given that sales are recorded before shipment has occurred. As a result, sales may be recorded in accounting periods different from when inventory records are updated for the shipment. Cutoff problems may occur.

    5.   *Inadequate Tracking of Returns.* If systems for tracking and estimating online sales returns are inadequate, Parts for Wheels, Inc. may understate estimates of customer returns, including estimated costs for refunding shipping costs. This could result in overstated net sales and understated shipping costs.

b.   Below are suggested changes that could be made to the existing manual system to enhance internal control, without re-designing the online system:

    1.   When the accounting department prints submitted orders from the online system, each order should be numbered sequentially with the range of used numbers logged daily. When the sales orders are recorded, the order number should be recorded.

    2.   Pre-numbered bills of lading should be used. All bills of lading should be accompanied by the sales order used by warehouse personnel to process shipment. All bills of lading should be forwarded to accounting on the date of shipment.

    3.   Accounting should match the bills of lading with the accounting department's copy of the sales orders before any entries are recorded in the sales journal and inventory system. Entries to the sales journal and inventory records should be made on the same day to ensure consistent cutoff of the recording of transactions.

c.   Customers may have these concerns about ordering parts through the Parts for Wheels Web site:

    1.   *Consumer Privacy.* Customers may be concerned about providing credit card information over the Parts for Wheels Web site. The company may consider disclosing information about company policies and procedures designed to reduce risks of breaches of consumer privacy. The company may implement encryption technologies to increase security of the information during transmission. The company may also consider obtaining a *WebTrust* seal of assurance for its online sales system.

12-28 (continued)

    2.   *Lack of Transaction Confirmation.* Given that sales orders are not processed until printed by the accounting department, customers do not receive an electronic confirmation that the sales order has been approved for processing. So, as consumers exit the Web site, they do not have complete confidence that their order will be processed. To address this concern, Parts for Wheels could notify customers via email when the credit authorization occurs. That would indicate the sale is approved for processing.

    3.   *Inaccurate Inventory Listing Information.* Consumers may be concerned that the online information about product descriptions and prices is inaccurate. For example, inventory descriptions may be outdated or insufficient and prices may be incorrect. Furthermore, on-hand quantities may be misstated, resulting in unexpected back-orders of *products. Parts for Wheels could disclose* information about how often the inventory database information is updated and posted. In addition, they could consider more frequent updates than weekly.

    4.   *Lack of Contact Information.* Online consumers may want information about how company officials can be reached in the event there are questions and disputes surrounding orders. Parts for Wheels could disclose appropriate contact information, in addition to enabling complaints to be registered online through its Web site.

12-29 a. Anytime an organization outsources its information technology functions to a third party, there are several inherent risks that arise. For First Community Bank, management is totally reliant on Technology Solutions' internal controls designed to protect IT hardware, operations, software, and data maintained at the data center. In essence, the design and operation of most of the IT general controls necessary to reduce IT related risks to acceptable levels are under direct control of Technology Solutions. Thus, the bank's management is reliant on Technology Solutions' implementation of effective IT related general controls.

    Because First Community must transmit transaction related data between the bank and the Technology Solutions data center, there is a risk that data may be lost, corrupted, or stolen during the communication transfer process.

    Also, like First Community, other organizations that use Technology Solutions to manage IT have access to servers located at Technology Solutions. There is some risk that other customers of Technology Solution might negatively affect IT operations of First Community.

12-29 (continued)

b. As noted in the answer to part a., the outsourcing of the IT function to Technology Solutions means that most of the IT general controls are now under the direct supervision of management at Technology Solutions. While management at First Community continues to be responsible for the design and operation of internal controls, including those related to IT, they are now dependent on Technology Solutions' design and operation of effective IT controls, especially those related to IT general controls.

c. The use of Technology Solutions is likely to have a significant effect on the audit of the financial statements of First Community Bank. Because the bank has outsourced all of the bank's financial reporting applications to Technology Solutions, most of the IT related controls and underlying applications and data files now reside at Technology Solutions. The auditors for First Community will need to understand all IT related operations, including those at Technology Solutions, so that they can understand internal control, assess the risks of material misstatements, and perform appropriate tests of controls and substantive tests. Most likely the auditors of First Community will seek a SAS 70 report on controls that have been implemented and tested for operating effectiveness.

■ **Case**

12-30 1. Strengths in lines of reporting from IS to senior management at Jacobsons:

■ Melinda Cullen (IS Manager) and the chief operating officer (COO) work closely on identifying hardware and software needs.
■ Melinda's boss, the COO, has access to the board of directors and provides periodic updates about IS issues, if needed.

Deficiencies in lines of reporting from IS to senior management:

■ The chief IS person (Melinda) is relegated to a manager level and is not considered a part of the senior executive team. This signals a potential lack of adequate support extended by top management to the IS function.
■ The IS Manager reports to a key user, the COO. The COO may place undue pressure on IS to work on IS related projects that affect the COO's areas of responsibility. Thus, other areas, such as those under the chief financial officer's control (i.e., the accounting system), may not receive adequate IS resources.

- Melinda and the COO make all major hardware and software decisions without input from other user personnel and the board of directors.
- There does not appear to be a written IS strategic plan that sets direction for the IS function.

Recommendations related to the lines of reporting from IS to senior management:

- The IS Manager should report directly to the president and be considered a part of senior management (i.e. on equal footing relative to the COO, CFO, etc.).
- The board of directors should receive regular input from the IS Manager about the status of IS projects.
- A written strategic plan should be developed and reviewed annually by the board.
- Significant hardware and software changes should be approved by the board or its IS Steering Committee. Other changes to application software should also be approved by affected user departments.

2. Assessment of Melinda's fulfillment of IS Manager responsibilities, including her strengths:

- Melinda is actively involved in the IS function and closely monitors day-to-day IS activities.
- Melinda is experienced in Jacobson's IS function, having been employed by the company for 12 years. She has served in several IS roles at Jacobsons. Thus, she offers stability for the IS function.
- Melinda performs extensive background checks before offering candidates employment in IS functions.
- Melinda has successfully maintained a fairly stable IS staff.
- Melinda conducts weekly IS departmental meetings to discuss issues affecting the performance of the department.
- Apparently the IS department is functioning well, given that few IS-related problems must be reported by the COO to the board.

Concerns about current management of the IS function:

- Melinda may be over delegating tasks to IS personnel without maintaining close accountability for employee actions. For example, programmers are given extensive leeway in programming changes to software and operators check each other's work to ensure that Melinda's job schedule was properly followed.

■ Melinda spends too much of her time in the systems analyst role, which leaves little time for her to adequately monitor all IS tasks.

Recommendations for change related to the management of the IS department:

■ Consider assigning systems analyst responsibilities to a senior programmer.

■ Establish standardized programming procedures and have Melinda review changed programs for compliance with those procedures.

■ Melinda should reconcile the Job Processed Log to the job schedule developed by her.

■ Melinda should assign or at least approve the assignment of programmer staff responsibilities.

3. Assessment of the strengths of the programming function at Jacobsons:

■ The programming staff is experienced with both systems software and Jacobsons' application software.

■ The assignment of projects based on time availability of programmers ensures that each programmer stays familiar with all types of software in use at Jacobsons.

■ Programmers regular attend continued professional education courses.

■ Extensive logs of tape use and of changes made to programs are maintained.

Concerns about the programming function:

■ Programmers work with both systems and application software program changes. Thus, a programmer is more likely to be able to implement an unauthorized change to an application program that also requires an unauthorized change to systems software.

■ Programmers are responsible for maintaining secondary storage of live programs and data files. Thus, programmers are able to make unauthorized changes to live production copies of programs and data files.

12-30 (continued)

Recommendations for change related to the programming function at Jacobsons:

- Divide programmers into systems programmers and application programmers. Only assign system software changes to systems programmers and application software changes to application programmers.
- Reassign responsibility for maintaining secondary storage to either the computer operators or to data control personnel.

4. Assessment of the strengths of the IS operations function at Jacobsons:

- Melinda prepares a job schedule which operators follow to process transactions. Day-shift operators reconcile Job Processed Logs generated during the night shift to the job schedule, and night shift operators do the same type of reconciliation for jobs processed during the day.
- Operators perform routine monthly backup procedures.
- Input batch controls are generated to verify the accuracy and completeness of processing.

Concerns about the IS operations function:

- Backup procedures only occur monthly, which increases the risk of data loss.
- No one, other than operators, verifies that only jobs included on the job schedule are processed. Melinda depends totally on the completeness of the operators' identification of exceptions noted by operators.
- Jobs Processed Logs are generally discarded, unless the output does not reconcile to the job schedule.
- Operators have the authority to make small changes to application programs.
- Comparison of batch input control totals to computer processing is not performed by someone independent of the operator responsible for the processing.

Recommendations for change related to the management of the IS operations function:

- Update key data files and program tapes on a more periodic basis (perhaps daily). Store backup copies offsite.
- Prohibit operators from performing any programming tasks. Restrict access to program files to a READ/USE only capability.

12-30 (continued)

> 5. Assessment of the strengths of the IS data control function at Jacobsons:
>
> - Data control personnel review exception listings and submit requests for correction on a timely basis.
> - Data control clerks monitor the distribution of output.
>
> Concerns about the IS data control function:
>
> - Data control personnel have the authority to approve changes to master files. Thus, they could add a fictitious employee to the employee master file to generate a payroll check for a non-existent employee.
>
> Recommendations for change related to the management of the IS data control function:
>
> - Restrict data control personnel from being able to authorize changes to master files. Only allow the respective user department to authorize changes to master files. Data control clerks should be held accountable for only inputting user department authorized changes to master files.
>
> 6. Users should be responsible for approving changes to master files. They should actively compare authorized input to output to ensure the accuracy, completeness, and authorization of output. Users should also be an active participant in the program systems development process. They should participate in program development design, testing, and implementation. In addition, users should have a voice in establishing the job schedule, given that users understand their processing needs best.

12-31 – ACL Problem Solution

> a. There are three transactions with missing dates. There are several negative balance transactions with no indication that they are purchase returns.
>
> b. Total purchases are $300,682.04 (use the Total command on the Amount column).

12-31 – ACL Problem (continued)

c. There are twelve gaps and many duplicates (Gaps and Duplicates commands). For gaps, the auditor is concerned that there may be unrecorded purchases. For duplicates, the auditor is concerned that purchases may be recorded more than once. In this case, no duplicate has the same amount as the transaction with the same document number.

d. Using the Summarize command to summarize total purchases by product, the total is the same as in requirement b: $300,682.04. See printout below and on the pages that follow.

Printout for requirement d:

Page 1   04/05/2011   17:35:00
Produced with ACL by: ACL Educational Edition
- Not For Commercial Use

PRODNO	AMOUNT	COUNT
010102710	65.89	2
010102840	11859.40	3
010134420	7107.44	11
010155150	3183.60	2
010155170	5858.55	2
010207220	3223.22	2
010226620	5594.40	2
010310890	735.28	2
010311990	2157.52	1
010551340	974.96	1
010631190	1483.70	5
010803760	-2481.33	6
023946372	270.06	2
023973042	5323.64	6
024104312	435.60	2
024121332	39.20	1
024128712	3609.69	26
024128812	1271.00	2
024128932	177.99	2
024130572	31.80	1
024133112	18497.00	9
024139372	148.50	1
030030323	1210.00	3
030303343	35.32	1
030305603	310.69	3
030321663	291.27	4
030321683	946.68	3
030324883	874.20	1
030364163	644.80	1
030412553	1625.73	6
030412903	12.40	2
030934423	4407.30	2
034255003	6627.20	8
040224984	44.00	2

12-31 – ACL Problem (continued)

PRODNO	AMOUNT	COUNT
040225014	208.80	2
040226054	43.50	1
040240284	10293.40	4
040240664	3552.00	1
040240884	3967.50	1
040241754	6029.24	4
040247034	7650.80	3
040270354	1242.56	5
040276054	4124.50	2
052204515	1997.94	1
052208805	10618.25	3
052210545	0.00	1
052484425	726.24	1
052484435	864.00	5
052504005	200.94	3
052530155	122.88	32
052720305	164.00	1
052720615	15826.00	2
052770015	90.52	2
060100306	190.40	2
060100356	318.00	2
060102066	39.80	1
060102106	5014.80	2
060112296	10964.80	2
060217066	2359.80	3
070104177	-6155.52	4
070104347	144.27	1
070104397	4046.43	1
070104657	185.49	2
080101018	8.14	1
080102618	3595.20	4
080102628	413.00	2
080123438	700.29	1
080123938	2798.64	1
080126008	7919.26	31
080126308	381.12	10
080935428	20438.93	5
080938748	5.98	1
090010011	330.67	2
090069591	3647.52	4
090081001	6282.00	2
090501051	1688.80	3
090501551	2774.28	11
090504761	376.37	4
090506331	-27.20	1
090507811	7425.52	7
090508191	101.06	2
090509561	664.02	4
090585322	58702.80	3
090599912	2803.40	7
090669611	7317.00	4
093788411	907.20	8
	300682.04	339

12-31 – ACL Problem (continued)

e. Product #024133112 represents 6.15% of total purchases. See report below and at the top of page 12-31. See highlighted amount for product #024133112.

Printout for requirement e:

PRODNO	COUNT	Percent of Count	Percent of Field	AMOUNT
010102710	2	0.59	0.02	65.89
010102840	3	0.88	3.94	11859.40
010134420	11	3.24	2.36	7107.44
010155150	2	0.59	1.06	3183.60
010155170	2	0.59	1.95	5858.55
010207220	2	0.59	1.07	3223.22
010226620	2	0.59	1.86	5594.40
010310890	2	0.59	0.24	735.28
010311990	1	0.29	0.72	2157.52
010551340	1	0.29	0.32	974.96
010631190	5	1.47	0.49	1483.70
010803760	6	1.77	-0.83	-2481.33
023946372	2	0.59	0.09	270.06
023973042	6	1.77	1.77	5323.64
024104312	2	0.59	0.14	435.60
024121332	1	0.29	0.01	39.20
024128712	26	7.67	1.20	3609.69
024128812	2	0.59	0.42	1271.00
024128932	2	0.59	0.06	177.99
024130572	1	0.29	0.01	31.80
024133112	9	2.65	6.15	18497.00
024139372	1	0.29	0.05	148.50
030030323	3	0.88	0.40	1210.00
030303343	1	0.29	0.01	35.32
030305603	3	0.88	0.10	310.69
030321663	4	1.18	0.10	291.27
030321683	3	0.88	0.31	946.68
030324883	1	0.29	0.29	874.20
030364163	1	0.29	0.21	644.80
030412553	6	1.77	0.54	1625.73
030412903	2	0.59	0.00	12.40
030934423	2	0.59	1.47	4407.30
034255003	8	2.36	2.20	6627.20
040224984	2	0.59	0.01	44.00
040225014	2	0.59	0.07	208.80
040226054	1	0.29	0.01	43.50
040240284	4	1.18	3.42	10293.40
040240664	1	0.29	1.18	3552.00
040240884	1	0.29	1.32	3967.50
040241754	4	1.18	2.01	6029.24
040247034	3	0.88	2.54	7650.80
040270354	5	1.47	0.41	1242.56
040276054	2	0.59	1.37	4124.50
052204515	1	0.29	0.66	1997.94
052208805	3	0.88	3.53	10618.25
052210545	1	0.29	0.00	0.00
052484425	1	0.29	0.24	726.24
052484435	5	1.47	0.29	864.00
052504005	3	0.88	0.07	200.94
052530155	32	9.44	0.04	122.88
052720305	1	0.29	0.05	164.00
052720615	2	0.59	5.26	15826.00
052770015	2	0.59	0.03	90.52
060100306	2	0.59	0.06	190.40

12-31 – ACL Problem (continued)

PRODNO	COUNT	Percent of Count	Percent of Field	AMOUNT
060100356	2	0.59	0.11	318.00
060102066	1	0.29	0.01	39.80
060102106	2	0.59	1.67	5014.80
060112296	2	0.59	3.65	10964.80
060217066	3	0.88	0.78	2359.80
070104177	4	1.18	-2.05	-6155.52
070104347	1	0.29	0.05	144.27
070104397	1	0.29	1.35	4046.43
070104657	2	0.59	0.06	185.49
080101018	1	0.29	0.00	8.14
080102618	4	1.18	1.20	3595.20
080102628	2	0.59	0.14	413.00
080123438	1	0.29	0.23	700.29
080123938	1	0.29	0.93	2798.64
080126008	31	9.14	2.63	7919.26
080126308	10	2.95	0.13	381.12
080935428	5	1.47	6.80	20438.93
080938748	1	0.29	0.00	5.98
090010011	2	0.59	0.11	330.67
090069591	4	1.18	1.21	3647.52
090081001	2	0.59	2.09	6282.00
090501051	3	0.88	0.56	1688.80
090501551	11	3.24	0.92	2774.28
090504761	4	1.18	0.13	376.37
090506331	1	0.29	-0.01	-27.20
090507811	7	2.06	2.47	7425.52
090508191	2	0.59	0.03	101.06
090509561	4	1.18	0.22	664.02
090585322	3	0.88	19.52	58702.80
090599912	7	2.06	0.93	2803.40
090669611	4	1.18	2.43	7317.00
093788411	8	2.36	0.30	907.20
	339	99.79	99.90	300682.04

f.   Starting with the classified table from requirement e, students should filter out items less than $1000. Next, run the Stratify command using a minimum value of $1210 (smallest amount in table) and a maximum value of $20,439 (second largest amount in table). See report below.

Printout for requirement f:

```
Page  1                                    04/05/2011        18:26:44
Produced with ACL by: ACL Educational Edition - Not For Commercial Use
  <<< STRATIFY over 1,210.00-> 20,439.00 >>>
  >>> Minimum encountered was 1,210.00
  >>> Maximum encountered was 58,702.80
```

AMOUNT			COUNT	<-- %	% -->	AMOUNT
1,210.00	->	3,132.89	12	28.57%	7.91%	23413.37
3,132.90	->	5,055.79	11	26.19%	14.31%	42371.76
5,055.80	->	6,978.69	6	14.29%	12.06%	35715.03
6,978.70	->	8,901.59	5	11.90%	12.64%	37420.02
8,901.60	->	10,824.49	2	4.76%	7.06%	20911.65
10,824.50	->	12,747.39	2	4.76%	7.71%	22824.20
12,747.40	->	14,670.29	0	0.00%	0.00%	0.00
14,670.30	->	16,593.19	1	2.38%	5.34%	15826.00
16,593.20	->	18,516.09	1	2.38%	6.25%	18497.00
18,516.10	->	20,439.00	1	2.38%	6.90%	20438.93
> 20,439.00			1	2.38%	19.82%	58702.80
			42	100.00%	100.00%	296120.76

■ Internet Problem Solution: Assessing IT Governance

Internet Problem 12-1

    a.   Successful organizations understand that the use of technologies leads to different risks that need to be managed to ensure that IT supports the implementation of the organization's strategy and goals. Those organizations realize the importance of maintaining proper governance and oversight over IT functions.

    b.   IT governance is an integral part of the enterprise governance. Boards and senior executives need to extend governance already exercised by the organization to include IT. Consistent with overall organizational governance, IT governance is the responsibility of the board and senior management.

    d.   If an organization's board and senior management were actively overseeing IT governance, an auditor would likely have greater confidence in the company's commitment to governance generally and the oversight and management of IT in particular. This information would likely be used in the auditor's evaluation of the company's control environment and the general controls over IT.

(**Note**: Internet problems address current issues using Internet sources. Because Internet sites are subject to change, Internet problems and solutions may change. Current information on Internet problems is available at www.pearsonhighered.com/arens.)

Chapter 13

Overall Audit Plan and Audit Program

■ **Review Questions**

13-1 The five types of tests auditors use to determine whether financial statements are fairly stated include the following:

- ■ Risk assessment procedures
- ■ Tests of controls
- ■ Substantive tests of transactions
- ■ Analytical procedures
- ■ Tests of details of balances

While risk assessment procedures (procedures to gain an understanding of the entity and its environment, including internal control) help the financial statement auditor obtain information to make an initial assessment of control risk, tests of controls must be performed to support an assessment of control risk that is below maximum. The purpose of tests of controls is to obtain evidence regarding the effectiveness of controls in support of an assessment of control risk below maximum. If controls are found to be effective and functioning, the substantive evidence may be reduced. Substantive evidence is obtained to reduce detection risk. Substantive evidence includes evidence from substantive tests of transactions, analytical procedures, and tests of details of balances.

For audits of internal control over financial reporting, the auditor only performs the first two types of audit tests: procedures to obtain an understanding of internal control and tests of controls. Because a public company auditor must issue a report on internal control over financial reporting, the extent of the auditor's tests of controls must be sufficient to issue an opinion about the operating effectiveness of those controls. That generally requires a significant amount of testing of controls over financial reporting.

13-2 Risk assessment procedures are performed to assess the risk of material misstatement in the financial statements. Risk assessment procedures include procedures performed to obtain an understanding of the entity and its environment, including internal controls. Auditors use the results of the risk assessment procedures to design and perform further audit procedures. Further audit procedures (not risk assessment procedures) provide the auditor sufficient appropriate evidence.

13-3 Tests of controls are audit procedures to test the operating effectiveness of control policies and procedures in support of a reduced assessed control risk, and provide the primary basis for the auditor's report on internal controls over financial reporting. Specific accounts affected by performing tests of controls

13-3 (continued)

for the acquisition and payment cycle include the following: cash, accounts payable, purchases, purchase returns and allowances, purchase discounts, manufacturing expenses, selling expenses, prepaid insurance, leasehold improvements, and various administrative expenses.

13-4 Tests of controls are audit procedures to test the operating effectiveness of control policies and procedures in support of a reduced assessed control risk. Examples include:

1. The examination of vendor invoices for indication that they have been clerically tested, compared to a receiving report and purchase order, and approved for payment.
2. Examination of employee time cards for approval of overtime hours worked.
3. Examination of journal entries for proper approval.
4. Examination of approvals for the write-off of bad debts.

Substantive tests of transactions are audit procedures testing for monetary misstatements to determine whether the six transaction-related audit objectives have been satisfied for each class of transactions. Examples are:

1. Recalculation of amounts (quantity times unit selling price) on selected sales invoices and tracing of amounts to the sales journal.
2. Examination of vendor invoices in support of amounts recorded in the acquisitions journal for purchases of inventories.
3. Recalculation of gross pay for selected entries in the payroll journal.
4. Tracing of selected customer cash receipts to the accounts receivable master file, agreeing customer names and amounts.

13-5 A test of control audit procedure to test that approved wage rates are used to calculate employees' earnings would be to examine rate authorization forms to determine the existence of authorized signatures.

A substantive test of transactions audit procedure would be to compare a sample of rates actually paid, as indicated in the earnings record, to authorized pay rates on rate authorization forms.

13-6 The auditor resolves the problem by making assumptions about the results of the tests of controls and performing both the tests of controls and substantive tests of transactions on the basis of these assumptions. Ordinarily the auditor assumes an effective system of internal control with few or no exceptions planned. If the results of the tests of controls are as good as or better than the assumptions that were originally made, the auditor can be satisfied with the substantive tests of transactions, unless the substantive tests of transactions themselves indicate the existence of misstatements. If the tests of controls results were not as good as the auditor assumed in designing the original tests, expanded substantive tests must be performed.

13-7   The primary purpose of testing sales and cash receipts transactions is to evaluate the internal controls so that the scope of the substantive tests of the account balances may be set. If the auditor performs the tests of details of balances prior to testing internal controls, no benefit will be derived from the tests of controls. The auditor should attempt to understand the entity and its environment, including internal controls, as early as practical through the analysis of the accounting system, tests of controls, and substantive tests of transactions.

13-8   When the results of analytical procedures are different from the auditor's expectations and thereby indicate that there may be a misstatement in the balance in accounts receivable or sales, the auditor should extend the tests to determine why the ratios are different from expectations. Confirmation of accounts receivable and cutoff tests for sales are two procedures that can be used to do this. On the other hand, if the ratios are approximately what the auditor expects, the other tests can be reduced. This means that the auditor can satisfy the evidence requirements in different ways and that analytical procedures and confirmation are complementary when the results of the tests are both good.

13-9   Substantive tests of transactions are performed to verify the accuracy of a client's accounting system. This is accomplished by determining whether individual transactions are correctly recorded and summarized in the journals, master files, and general ledger. Substantive tests of transactions are also concerned with *classes* of transactions, such as payroll, acquisitions, or cash receipts. Tracing amounts from a file of vouchers to the acquisitions journal is an example of a substantive test of transactions for the acquisition and payment cycle. Tests of details of balances verify the ending balance in an *individual* account (such as inventory, accounts receivable, or depreciation expense) on the financial statements. An example of a test of details of balances for the acquisition and payment cycle is to physically examine a sample of the client's fixed assets.

13-10   1.   *Control #1 -- Computer verification of the customer's credit limit.* The presence of effective general controls over software programs and master file changes can significantly reduce the auditor's testing of automated controls such as control #1. Once it is determined that control #1 is functioning properly, the auditor can focus subsequent tests on assessing whether any changes have occurred that would limit the effectiveness of the control. Such tests might include determining whether any changes have occurred to the program and whether these changes were properly authorized and tested prior to implementation. These are all tests of general controls over software programs and master file changes.

2.   *Control #2 – The accounts receivable clerk matches bills of lading, sales invoices, and customer orders before recording in the sales journal.* This control is not an automated control, but is rather a manual control performed by an employee. General controls over

13-10 (continued)

software programs and master file changes would have little effect on the auditor's testing of control #2. If the auditor identifies control #2 as a key control in the sales and collection cycle, he or she would most likely examine a sample of the underlying documents for the accounts receivable clerk's initials and reperform the comparisons.

13-11 The audit of fixed asset additions normally involves the examination of invoices in support of the additions and possibly the physical examination of the additions. These procedures are normally performed on a test basis with a concentration on the more significant additions. If the individual responsible for recording new acquisitions is known to have inadequate training and limited experience in accounting, the sample size for the audit procedures should be expanded to include a larger sample of the additions for the year. In addition, inquiry as to what additions were made during the year may be made by the auditor of plant managers, the controller, or other operating personnel. The auditor should then search the financial records to determine that these additions were recorded as fixed assets.

Care should also be taken when the repairs and maintenance expense account is analyzed since lack of training may cause some depreciable assets to be expensed at the time of acquisition.

13-12 The following shows which types of evidence are applicable for the five types of tests (see Table 13-2 on. p. 408).

TYPE OF EVIDENCE	TYPES OF TESTS
Physical examination	Tests of details of balances
Confirmation	Tests of details of balances
Documentation	All except analytical procedures
Observation	Risk assessment procedures and tests of controls
Inquiries of the client	All five types
Reperformance	Tests of controls, substantive tests of transactions, and tests of details of balances
Analytical procedures	Analytical procedures
Recalculation	Substantive tests of transactions and tests of details of balances

13-13 Going from most to least costly, the types of tests are:

- Tests of details of balances
- Substantive tests of transactions
- Tests of controls
- Risk assessment procedures
- Analytical procedures

13-14 C represents the auditor's assessment of the effectiveness of internal control. C_3 represents the idea that it is not cost-effective to test internal controls and all assurance must come from substantive testing.

Tests of controls at the C_1 level would provide minimum control risk. This would require more testing of the controls than would be required at either C_2 or C_3. Testing controls at the C_1 level allows the auditor to obtain assurance from the controls, thereby allowing for a reduction in the amount of substantive testing which must be performed to meet the level of acceptable audit assurance. C_1 reflects the level of testing of controls necessary for the audit of internal controls over financial reporting required by PCAOB Standard 5.

It would be a good decision to obtain assurance from tests of controls at point C_1 especially if the cost of substantive testing is considerably greater than tests of controls.

At point C_2, the auditor performs some tests of controls and is able to reduce control risk below maximum. Point C_2 would be appropriate if it is cost beneficial for the auditor to obtain assurance at a level between the two extremes mentioned above (C_1 and C_3).

13-15 By identifying the best mix of tests the auditor can accumulate sufficient appropriate evidence at minimum cost. The auditor can thereby meet the standards of the profession and still be cost effective and competitive.

13-16 The four-step approach to designing tests of controls and substantive tests of transactions is as follows:

1. Apply the transaction-related audit objectives to the class of transactions being tested.
2. Identify specific control policies and procedures that should reduce control risk for each transaction-related audit objective.
3. Develop appropriate tests of controls for each key control.
4. Design appropriate substantive tests of transactions considering deficiencies in internal control and expected results from 3 above.

13-17 The approach to designing tests of controls and substantive tests of transactions (Figure 13-4) emphasizes satisfying the transaction-related audit objectives developed in Chapters 6 and 10. Recall that these objectives focus on the proper functioning of the accounting system.

13-17 (continued)

The methodology of designing tests of details of balances (Figure 13-6) emphasizes satisfying the balance-related audit objectives developed in Chapter 6. The primary focus of these objectives is on the fair presentation of account balances in the financial statements. The extent of testing depends, in part, on the results of the tests of controls and substantive tests of transactions.

13-18 It is desirable to design tests of details of balances before performing tests of controls and substantive tests of transactions to enable the auditor to determine if the overall planned evidence is the most efficient and effective in the circumstances. In order to do this, the auditor must make assumptions about the results of the tests of controls and substantive tests of transactions. Ordinarily the auditor will assume no significant misstatements or control problems in tests of controls and substantive tests of transactions unless there is reason to believe otherwise. If the auditor determines that the tests of controls and substantive tests of transactions results are different from those expected, the amount of testing of details of balances must be altered.

13-19 If tolerable misstatement is low, and inherent risk and control risk are high, planned tests of details of balances which the auditor must perform will be high. An increase in tolerable misstatement or a reduction of either inherent risk or control risk will lead to a reduction in the planned tests of details of balances.

13-20 The eight balance-related audit objectives and related procedures are as follows:

GENERAL BALANCE-RELATED AUDIT OBJECTIVE	SPECIFIC OBJECTIVE	AUDIT PROCEDURE
Detail tie-in	Inventory on the inventory summary agrees with the physical count, the extensions are correct, and the total is correctly added and agrees with the general ledger.	Check extensions of price times quantity on a sample basis, foot the detailed inventory summary, and trace the balance to the general ledger and financial statements.
Existence	Inventory as stated in financial statements actually exists.	Trace inventory from final inventory summary to actual inventory and physically count selected items.
Completeness	Existing inventory items have been counted and included in the financial statements.	Select items from the physical inventory and trace to the client's final summary to make sure that all items are included.

13-20 (continued)

GENERAL BALANCE-RELATED AUDIT OBJECTIVE	SPECIFIC OBJECTIVE	AUDIT PROCEDURE
Accuracy	Inventory items included in the financial statements are stated at the correct amounts.	Perform price tests of inventory by examining supporting vendors' invoices for selected inventory items and reverify price times quantity.
Classification	Inventory as included in the financial statements is properly classified.	Compare the classification of inventory into raw materials, work in process, and finished goods by comparing the description on physical inventory count tags with the client's final inventory listing.
Cutoff	Inventory cutoff is properly recorded at the balance sheet date.	Trace selected receiving reports several days before and after the balance sheet date to determine whether inventory purchases are recorded in the proper period and related physical inventory counts are included or excluded from inventory.
Realizable value	Inventory on the financial statements excludes unusable items.	Inquire of factory employees and management regarding obsolescence of inventory, and examine storeroom for evidence of damaged or obsolete inventory.
Rights and obligations	Inventory items in the financial statements are owned by the client.	Review contracts with suppliers and customers for the possibility of the inclusion of consigned or other non-owned inventory.

13-21 Auditors frequently consider it desirable to perform audit tests throughout the year rather than waiting until year-end because of the CPA firm's difficulty of scheduling personnel and the client's need for timely financial statements. Due to the uneven distribution of the year-end dates of their clients, there is a shortage of personnel during certain periods of the year and excess available time at other periods. The procedures that are performed at a date prior to year-end are often dependent upon adequate internal controls and when the client will have the information available. Additionally, public company auditors must begin their testing of controls earlier in the year to ensure they are able to test a sufficient sample of controls for operating effectiveness. Some controls may only be performed monthly

13-21 (continued)

or quarterly. Thus, the public company auditor must begin testing early in the year so that there is a sufficient number of months or quarters to test.

Procedures that may be performed prior to the end of the year are:

1. Update fixed asset schedules.
2. Examine new loan agreements and other legal records.
3. Vouch certain transactions.
4. Analyze changes in the client's accounting systems.
5. Review minutes of board of directors' meetings.
6. If the client has effective internal control, the following procedures may be performed with minor review and updating at year-end:
    (a) Observation of physical inventories;
    (b) Confirmation of accounts receivable balances;
    (c) Confirmation and reconciliation of accounts payable balances.

■ Multiple Choice Questions From CPA Examinations

13-22   a. (2)   b. (2)   c. (1)   d. (4)

13-23   a. (2)   b. (3)   c. (1)   d. (3)

■ Discussion Questions and Problems

13-24

a.	b.	a.	b.
1. TD of B	Recalculation	7. ST of T	Documentation
2. TD of B	Confirmation	8. AP	Analytical procedures
3. T of C	Documentation	9. TD of B	Documentation
4. TD of B	Documentation	10. T of C	Inquiry and observation
5. AP	Analytical procedures	11. T of C	Inquiry
6. T of C	Documentation		

13-25

a.		b.
1.	T of C	Accuracy
2	ST of T	Accuracy
3.	ST of T	Posting and summarization
4.	T of C	Classification
5.	ST of T	Completeness
6.	T of C	Occurrence
7.	ST of T	Posting and summarization
8.	ST of T	Accuracy

13-26

a.	b.	c.	d.	e.	f.
1. Acquisition and Payment	Recalculation	Substantive	S T of T	Posting and summarization	N/A
2. Acquisition and Payment	Documentation	Test of control or Substantive	S T of T	Occurrence	N/A
3. Acquisition and Payment	Documentation	Substantive	T D of B	N/A	Cutoff
4. Sales and Collection	Inquiry	Substantive	T D of B	N/A	Realizable value
5. Inventory and Warehousing	Analytical procedure	Substantive	A P	N/A	Realizable value
6. Capital Acquisition and Repayment	Confirmation	Substantive	T D of B	N/A	Existence Accuracy
7. Sales and Collection	Recalculation	Substantive	T D of B	N/A	Detail tie-in

13-27

a. TRANSACTION-RELATED AUDIT OBJECTIVE	b. TEST OF CONTROL PROCEDURE	c. SUBSTANTIVE TEST
1. Existing acquisition transactions are recorded. (Completeness)	Account for numerical sequence of receiving reports and trace to acquisitions journal entry.	Reconcile vendor statements to accounts payable listing.
2. Existing cash disbursement transactions are recorded, recorded transactions exist, and recorded transactions are stated at the correct amounts. (Completeness, Occurrence, and Accuracy).	Observe cash handling procedures and examine bank reconciliation to determine if was prepared by an independent person.	Perform tests of bank reconciliation as of the balance sheet date.
3. Recorded transactions exist, recorded transactions are stated at the correct amounts, and transactions are properly classified. (Occurrence, Accuracy, and Classification)	Examine invoice packages for initials indicating that review has been performed.	Examine supporting invoices and recheck items checked by the clerk.
4. Recorded transactions exist. (Occurrence)*	Examine invoices for the controller's initials.	Examine supporting invoices for same information examined by the controller.
5. Recorded transactions exist. (Occurrence)	Examine invoices for indication of check number and date.	Examine supporting invoices, purchase orders, and receiving reports containing the proper check number and date for each cash disbursement.

* The objectives satisfied depend upon what she examines. She might, for example, examine supporting documents for accuracy and even for account classification. In that event, those two objectives would be added.

(a) CONTROL ACTIVITY	(b) TRANSACTION-RELATED AUDIT OBJECTIVE(S)	(c) TEST OF CONTROL	(d) POSSIBLE MISSTATEMENT	(e) SUBSTANTIVE AUDIT PROCEDURE
1. Separation of duties	Occurrence	Observe check mailing procedures and inquire about normal procedures	Bookkeeper takes signed check and changes payee name	Compare payee name on cancelled check to supporting documents
2. Adequate documents or records	Occurrence	Examine supporting documents for indication of cancellation	Duplicate payment for an acquisition	Examine supporting documents for every payment to selected vendors
3. Independent checks on performance	Occurrence Accuracy	Examine vendors' invoices for indication of comparison	Invalid or unauthorized payment	Examine supporting documents for appropriateness of expenditures
4. Independent checks on performance	Accuracy	Examine vendors' invoices for indication of recalculation	A misstatement in calculation of a vendor's invoice	Recalculation of vendors' invoices
5. Proper authorization	Occurrence	Examine approved purchase orders for a sample of acquisitions	Unauthorized acquisitions of goods	Examine supporting documents for appropriateness of expenditures
6. Adequate documents or records	Occurrence Completeness	Account for a numerical sequence of receiving reports	Unrecorded acquisitions exist	Confirm accounts payable, especially vendors with small or zero balances
7. Independent checks on performance	Timing	Examine vendors' invoices for indication of comparison	Cutoff misstatements	Perform search for unrecorded liabilities
8. Independent checks on performance	Posting and summarization	Examine indication of reconciliation of the master file and control account	Misstatements in master file or control account	Foot subsidiary records and compare to control account
9. Independent checks on performance	Classification	Examine vendors' invoices for indication of internal verification	Account classification misstatements	Compare vendors' invoices to acquisitions journal for reasonableness of account classification
10. Proper authorization	Occurrence	Examine cancelled checks for signature	Invalid or unauthorized payment	Examine supporting documents for appropriateness of expenditures

13-29 a. 1. Automated control embedded in computer software
2. Manual control whose effectiveness is based significantly on IT-generated information
3. Automated control embedded in computer software
4. Manual control whose effectiveness is based significantly on IT-generated information
5. Manual control whose effectiveness is not significantly reliant on IT-generated information

b. 1. The extent of testing of this control could be significantly reduced in subsequent years if effective controls over program and master file changes are in place. Such controls would increase the likelihood that the inventory software program that contains the automated control and the related inventory master file are not subject to an unauthorized change. If the auditor determines that no changes have been made to the automated control, the auditor can rely on prior year audit tests of the controls as long as the control is tested at least once every third year audit. If the control mitigates a significant risk, the control must be tested in the current year's audit.
2. The extent of testing of this control could be moderately reduced in subsequent years if effective controls over program and master file changes are in place. Such controls would increase the likelihood that the printout of prices accurately reflects actual prices used by the system to record inventory transactions. Adequate controls over the master file decrease the likelihood that prices approved by the sales and purchasing department managers have been changed without authorization. However, because this control is also dependent on manager review of computer generated output, some testing may be required each year, although the amount of testing may be reduced by effective general controls.
3. The extent of testing of this control could be significantly reduced in subsequent years if effective controls over program and master file changes are in place. Such controls would increase the likelihood that the inventory software program that processes the automatic purchase order and the related inventory master file of product numbers are not subject to an unauthorized change.
4. The extent of testing of this control could be moderately reduced in subsequent years if effective controls over program changes are in place. Such controls would increase the likelihood that the purchasing system software program that identifies purchases exceeding $10,000 per vendor functions

13-29 (continued)

> accurately. However, because this control is also dependent on manager review of the computer generated exception listing, some testing may be required each year.
>
> 5. Because this control is not dependent on technology processes, the strength of general controls over program and master file changes is likely to not have an impact on the extent of testing of this review by the sales department manager.

13-30 a. Although a client may have very effective internal controls, the auditor cannot place complete reliance on them in evaluating whether the financial statements are fairly stated. This reflects the inherent limitations of internal control, and the need under auditing standards to perform certain tests of balances such as confirmation of receivables and observation of inventory.

b. The auditor may decide not to place the maximum reliance on internal control if it is not cost-beneficial. The auditor may decide that it is more cost-effective to reduce reliance on controls and perform more substantive tests.

c.
1. A
2. B
3. B, C
4. A, B, C
5. B (assuming similar other client characteristics)
6. B, C (depending on auditor's judgment)
7. C
8. B, C

13-31 a. The sequence the auditor should follow is:

3. Assess control risk.
1. Determine whether it is cost effective to perform tests of controls.
4. Perform tests of controls.
2. Perform substantive tests of details of balances.

The only logical sequences for parts b through e are shown as follows:

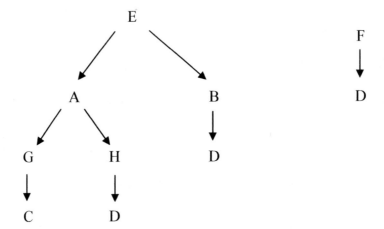

Any other sequence is not cost effective or incorrect. For example: E, A, G, C would be the sequence when there is planned reduced assessed control risk and effective results of tests of controls.

b.   The sequence is E, A, H, D. The logic was reasonable. The auditor believed the internal controls would be effective and it would be cost effective to perform tests of controls. In performing the tests of controls the auditor concluded the controls were not effective. Therefore, expanded substantive tests of details of balances were needed.

c.   The sequence is E, B, G, C. The auditor concluded the internal controls may be effective, but it was not cost effective to reduce assessed control risk. The auditor should not have performed tests of controls. It would have been more cost effective to skip performing tests and instead follow the sequence E, B, D.

d.   The sequence is F, A, G, C. The logic is not reasonable. When the auditor concluded the controls were not effective he or she should have gone immediately to D and performed expanded substantive tests of details of balances.

e.   The sequence is F, D. The logic was reasonable. The auditor concluded that internal controls were not effective, therefore the auditor went directly to substantive tests of details of balances and performed expanded tests.

AUDIT	PROCEDURES TO OBTAIN AN UNDERSTANDING OF INTERNAL CONTROL	TESTS OF CONTROLS	SUBSTANTIVE TESTS OF TRANSACTIONS	ANALYTICAL PROCEDURES	TESTS OF DETAILS OF BALANCES
1	E	E	S	E	S
2	M	N	S	M	E
3	E	E	M	E	S, E*

E   =   Extensive amount of testing.
M   =   Medium amount of testing.
S   =   Small amount of testing.
N   =   No testing.
S,E* =   Small amount of testing for the gross balance in accounts receivable; extensive testing done for the collectibility of the accounts.

a.   For audit 1 the recommended strategy is to maximize the testing of internal controls and minimize the testing of the details of all ending balances in inventory. The most important objective would be to minimize the number of locations that need to be visited. The justification for doing this is the quality of the internal controls and the results of prior years' audits. Assuming that some of the locations have a larger portion of the ending inventory balance than other locations, the auditor can likely completely eliminate tests of physical counts of some locations and emphasize the locations with larger dollar balances. The entire strategy is oriented to minimizing the need to visit locations.

b.   Audit risk for this audit should be low because of the plans to sell the business, severe under-financing and a first year audit. The lack of controls over accounts payable and the large number of adjusting entries in accounts payable indicate the auditor cannot consider the internal controls effective. Therefore the plan should be to do extensive tests of details of balances, probably through accounts payable confirmation and other end of year procedures. No tests of controls are recommended because of the impracticality of reduced assessed control risk. Some substantive tests of transactions and analytical procedures are recommended to verify the correctness of acquisitions and to obtain information about the reasonableness of the balances.

13-32 (continued)

    c.   The most serious concern in this audit is the evaluation of the allowance for uncollectible accounts. Given the adverse economic conditions and significant increase of loans receivable, the auditor must be greatly concerned about the adequacy of the allowance for uncollectible accounts and the possibility of uncollectible accounts being included in loans receivable. Given the internal controls, the auditor is not likely to be greatly concerned about the gross accounts receivable balance, except for accounts that need to be written off. Therefore, for the audit of gross accounts receivable there will be a greatly reduced assessed control risk and relatively minor confirmation of accounts receivable. In evaluating the allowance for uncollectible accounts, the auditor should test the controls over granting loans and following up on collections. However, given the changes in the economy, it will be necessary to do significant additional testing of the allowance for uncollectible accounts. Therefore an "S" is included for tests of details of balances for gross accounts receivable and an "E" for the tests of net realizable value.

13-33 a.   Factors which could explain the difference in the amount of evidence accumulated in different parts as well as the total time spent on the engagement are:

        1.   Internal control
        2.   Materiality of the account balance
        3.   Size of the populations
        4.   Makeup of populations
        5.   Initial vs. repeat engagement
        6.   Results of the current and previous audits
        7.   Existence of unusual transactions
        8.   Motivation of the client to misstate the financial statements
        9.   Degree of client integrity
     10.   Reliance by third parties on the audited financial statements

        For an example, in the first audit, the partner has apparently made the decision to emphasize tests of controls and substantive tests of transactions and minimize tests of details of balances. That implies effective internal controls and a low expectation of misstatement (low inherent and control risk.) In the third audit, the partner apparently has a high expectation of misstatements, and therefore believes it is necessary to do extensive tests of controls and substantive tests of transactions, as well as extensive tests of details of balances. Audit two is somewhere between audit one and three.

    b.   The audit partners could have spent time discussing the audit approach and scope with Bryan prior to the beginning of the field work.

13-33 (continued)

c.   The nature of these three engagements and the different circumstances appear to be excellent examples of the tailoring of audit procedures to appropriate levels considering the circumstances. Bryan's judgment could have been improved on each engagement if the audit partner discussed the audit approach with her during the engagement.

d.   The first audit is most likely the integrated audit of a public company because of the emphasis on tests of controls. The third audit also involves extensive tests of transactions, but the size of the company and extensive tests of balances suggest it is not a integrated audit.

13-34 a.   Phase I – Procedures 5, 9, 7
Phase II – Procedure 2
Phase III – Procedures 8, 1, 3
Phase IV – Procedures 4, 6

b.   The following is a time line for the audit procedures, showing the sequence of the parts of a typical audit.

	July 31				Audit Report Date	
5, 9, 7, 2		8	1	3	4	6

Parts 5, 9, and 7 are all a part of planning and are therefore done early. These are in the sequence shown in Chapter 8. As part of planning the audit, the auditor obtains an understanding of internal control and initially assesses control risk. The auditor then performs tests of controls and substantive tests of transactions and reassesses control risk.

Ideally, most analytical procedures are performed after the client has prepared financial statements, but before tests of details of balances are performed. Therefore, they should be done before confirmation of accounts payable to provide information about the expectation of misstatement.

Confirmation of accounts payable should be done as early as possible after the balance sheet date to facilitate getting responses back, performing alternative procedures for nonresponses, and reconciling differences before the audit is completed.

Tests for review of subsequent events are normally the last procedures done on the engagement before the audit report date. The audit report is issued after the audit report date.

c.   The time line shows that 5, 9, 7 and 2 are frequently done before the balance sheet date.

■ **Cases**

13-35 a.   The major deficiencies in the audit and the reasons for their occurrence are:

    1.   The change in the accounting system to computerize the inventory, a change in accounting personnel, and the existence of a few more errors in the tests of controls should have alerted the auditors to expand the scope of the work. It was questionable to conclude that the internal controls were effective.

    2.   Reduction in the scope of the inventory work based on the lack of errors last year was improper since new internal controls were in use with new personnel this year and the inventory balance was higher.

    3.   The new division should have been audited more thoroughly. It came to Merkle through merger and was likely to have different operating characteristics and internal controls.

    4.   The determination that the errors in the sample were immaterial was improper. The errors should have been projected from the sample to the population, and the projected error should have been compared to tolerable misstatement, after considering risk. The obsolescence problem uncovered in the audit should have been evaluated carefully to consider the implications on potential obsolescence of inventory.

    5.   Given the new personnel on the engagement, Brewer apparently failed to adequately supervise and review the work of assistants.

    6.   There was an apparent lack of the use of analytical procedures. A decline in sales should have warned the auditor to a potential decline in profits and obsolete inventory.

    b.   Brewer should have been aware that the inventory internal controls and the personnel in that department were new, that the interim tests revealed more errors than normal, and that the inventory tests revealed more errors than normal despite the reduction in scope. In this situation, the scope of the inventory work should have been increased to reveal the magnitude of the problems encountered. In addition, because of the staff turnover on this engagement, Brewer should have devoted more of his time to supervising the work of the staff on this engagement.

    c.   The likelihood of Brewer losing the suit is high. The auditors appear not to have followed general standards 1 and 3 and standards of field work 1, 2, and 3 in the performance of the engagement. Although the misstatements result from fraud, the auditors may be held responsible because apparently the audit was not conducted in accordance with auditing standards.

a. (1) *Assess inherent risk.* This would be done under both approaches.

   (2) *Obtain an understanding of internal control.* This would be done under both approaches, however, it may be more extensive where control risk is reduced below the maximum due to the knowledge gained through testing.

   (3) *Perform tests of controls.* This would be done only under the "reducing control risk" approach, given that the client is a non-public entity.

   (4) *Perform analytical procedures.* This would be done under both approaches, although such procedures may be more extensive where control risk is reduced below the maximum.

   (5) *Assess planned detection risk.* This would be done under both approaches.

b. The "reducing control risk" approach has several advantages:

   1. It should result in lower overall audit cost. This will occur where the client's business activity is complex and its volume of transactions is large. In this type of situation, internal controls can provide a great deal of assurance that many of the financial statement assertions are correct, and the audit effort to test those controls can be significantly less than full-scale substantive tests of balances would require.

   2. For very large audits, it would be impossible to complete the audit on time and at an acceptable cost without relying on controls. Large clients are usually publicly held and must file their Form 10-K with the SEC within 60 days of their fiscal year end. These large companies generally have many locations, including worldwide operations. Controls must be relied upon to do these audits.

   3. The more detailed investigation of controls that is required to reduce control risk, including testing, provides a better understanding of the system. This not only may provide a more concrete basis for conducting substantive tests, it creates more opportunities to make useful recommendations to the client.

   4. Performance of detailed tests of transactions creates the opportunity to reveal employee defalcations that would otherwise not be discovered. In addition, employee knowledge that transactions will be examined serves as a deterrent to defalcation in the first place.

13-36 – Part I (continued)

    c.   The primary advantage of the "substantive" approach is one of efficiency. Where clients are smaller, there is less opportunity to adequately segregate core duties, which makes it more difficult to rely on controls. Thus, the auditor focuses the audit work on the balance sheet as of the end of the client's fiscal year. Furthermore, by going into the client's office at one point in time and doing the entire audit, auditor scheduling problems are reduced and there is less disruption to the client.

13-36 – Part II

    a.   For this audit, .17 is the level of detection risk for tests of the inventory balance that will provide an overall audit risk of .05 assuming tests of controls and analytical procedures are conducted as planned and achieve the expected results (i.e., don't indicate any misstatements exceeding a tolerable amount). Thus, as individual tests of details of inventory are planned, their design would be based on that level of risk of failing to reveal a greater-than-tolerable misstatement.

    b.

$$TDR = \frac{.05}{1.0 \times 1.0 \times .6}$$

$$TDR = .08$$

    c.   The reduction of risk for detailed tests of the inventory balance means that more reliance must be placed on those detailed tests. In this case, the degree of allowable risk is cut in half. In terms of sample size, this will result in a significant increase (the exact impact will depend on the sampling method used). It is also possible the auditor may feel less comfortable relying on analytical procedures to the extent otherwise planned, and may believe some other detailed tests are appropriate.

13-36 Part III

It is not appropriate to "rework" the Audit Risk Model as proposed by the staff person. The Audit Risk Model is a planning model that is based on testing the hypothesis that the financial statements do not contain a material misstatement. If an indication of a possible misstatement is revealed by applying the model at *any stage*, the hypothesis must be rejected and the audit plan revised to assume there is a material misstatement that must be subjected to measurement. The staff person should independently evaluate whether the increase in control risk requires an increase in substantive tests.

- **Internet Problem Solution: Assessing Effects of Evidence Mix**

Internet Problem 13-1

a. Cisco's fiscal 2009 year-end was July 31, 2010. The company appears to have a 52-53 week year ending on the last Saturday in July. McDonald's Corporation and Google Inc. have December 31st year-ends. The year-end should not impact the audit procedures performed, but it may impact the timing. Since the majority of public companies have December 31st year-ends, more procedures may need to be performed before year end to deliver the audit report on a timely basis.

b. Google Inc.   43 days
    Cisco Systems, Inc.   51 days
    McDonald's Corporation   57 days

    The company's year-end, as well as the need to perform extensive procedures such as confirmation of receivables and inventory testing likely affect the number of days to issue the report.

c. Although the report for Cisco Systems Inc. report was issued in 52 days compared to 57 days for the audit report for McDonald's Corporation, Cisco is larger and has more inventory and accounts receivable. Auditor's likely placed greater emphasis on tests of details of balances for this audit. However, the size of the three companies and the number of days to the issuance of the audit report suggests extensive reliance on controls and testing before year-end for all three companies.

(**Note**: Internet problems address current issues using Internet sources. Because Internet sites are subject to change, Internet problems and solutions may change. Current information on Internet problems is available at www.pearsonhighered.com/arens.)

Chapter 14

Audit of the Sales and Collection Cycle:
Tests of Controls and Substantive
Tests of Transactions

■ **Review Questions**

14-1 a. The *bill of lading* is a document prepared at the time of shipment of goods to a customer indicating the description of the merchandise, the quantity shipped, and other data. Formally, it is a written contract of the shipment and receipt of goods between the seller and carrier. It is also used as a signal to bill the client. The original is sent to the customer and one or more copies are retained.

      b. A *sales invoice* is a document indicating the description and quantity of goods sold, the price including freight, insurance, terms, and other relevant data. It is the method of indicating to the customer the amount owed for the sale and the due date of the payments. The original is sent to the customer and one or more copies are retained. The sales invoice is the document for recording sales in the accounting records.

      c. The *credit memo* is a document indicating a reduction in the amount due from a customer because of returned goods or an allowance granted. It often takes the same general form as a sales invoice, but it reduces the customer's accounts receivable balance rather than increasing it.

      d. The remittance advice is a document that accompanies the sales invoice mailed to the customer and can be returned to the seller with the payment. It is used to indicate the customer name, sales invoice number, and the amount of the invoice when the payment is received. A remittance advice is used to permit the immediate deposit of cash receipts as a means of improving control over the custody of assets.

      e. The *monthly statement to customers* is the document prepared monthly and sent to each customer indicating the beginning balance of that customer's accounts receivable, the amount and date of each sale, cash payments received, credit memos issued, and the ending balance due. It is, in essence, a copy of the customer's portion of the accounts receivable master file.

14-2 Proper credit approval for sales helps minimize the amount of bad debts and the collection effort for accounts receivable by requiring that each sale be evaluated for collection potential.

      Adequate controls in the credit function enable the auditor to place more reliance on the client's estimate of uncollectible accounts. Without these controls, the auditor would have to make his or her own credit checks on the customers in order to be convinced that the allowance for uncollectible accounts is reasonable.

14-3   The sales journal contains the record of each sales transaction that includes the customer name, date, amount, and the account classification for each transaction. The sales journal generally represents the record of each individual transaction. Typically, the sales journal accumulates transactions for a period of time, which is often monthly. Transactions recorded in the sales journal are then posted to the general ledger, and if the transaction is for sales on account the accounts receivable master file is updated for each transaction.

The accounts receivable master file is used to record individual sales, cash receipts, and sales returns and allowances for each customer and to maintain customer account balances. The master file is updated using data from the sales journal, sales return journal, cash receipts journal. The total in the accounts receivable master file equals the total in the accounts receivable general ledger account.

14-4   BestSellers.com could integrate its online ordering system with its inventory system so that a book shipment is made only after the customer's credit card company approves the customer's purchase. Because credit card issuers often transfer funds electronically almost immediately after a sale, BestSellers.com could also set up their system to ship books only after payment has been received by the credit card issuer. Finally, BestSellers.com could arrange with an online credit service bureau to run credit checks on customers purchasing over a preset minimum amount. Although BestSellers.com sells its goods through the Internet, the company should still record sales revenue when the books are shipped to customers.

14-5

TRANSACTION-RELATED AUDIT OBJECTIVE	KEY INTERNAL CONTROLS
1. Recorded sales are for shipments actually made to existing customers (occurrence).	■ Recording of sales is supported by authorized shipping documents and approved customer orders. ■ Credit is authorized before shipment takes place. ■ Sales invoices are prenumbered and properly accounted for. ■ Only customer numbers existing in the computer data files are accepted when they are entered. ■ Monthly statements are sent to customers; complaints receive independent follow-up.
2. Existing sales transactions are recorded (completeness).	■ Shipping documents are prenumbered and accounted for. ■ Sales invoices are prenumbered and accounted for.

14-5 (continued)

TRANSACTION-RELATED AUDIT OBJECTIVE	KEY INTERNAL CONTROLS
3. Recorded sales are for the amount of goods shipped and are correctly billed and recorded (accuracy).	■ Determination of prices, terms, freight, and discounts is properly authorized. ■ Internal verification of invoice preparation. ■ Approved unit selling prices are entered into the computer and used for sales. ■ Batch totals are compared with computer summary reports.
4. Sales transactions are properly included in the accounts receivable master file and are correctly summarized (posting and summarization).	■ Regular monthly statements sent to customers. ■ Internal verification of accounts receivable master file contents. ■ Comparison of accounts receivable master file or trial balance with general ledger balance.
5. Sales transactions are properly classified (classification).	■ Use of adequate chart of accounts. ■ Internal review and verification of the account classifications.
6. Sales are recorded on the correct dates (timing).	■ Procedures requiring billing and recording of sales on a daily basis as close to the time of occurrence as possible. ■ Internal verification of timely recording of transactions.

14-6

Tests of controls:

1. On a sample of sales invoices, examine proper authorization and indication of internal verification of sales amounts.
2. Examine approved computer printout of unit selling prices.
3. Examine file of batch totals for initials of data control clerk; compare totals to summary reports.

Substantive tests of transactions:

1. Recompute information on sales invoices.
2. Trace entries in sales journal to related sales invoices.
3. Trace detail on sales invoices to shipping documents, approved price lists, and customers' orders.

14-7 The most important duties that should be segregated in the sales and collection cycle are:

1. Receiving orders for sales
2. Shipping goods
3. Billing customers and recording sales
4. Maintaining inventory records
5. Maintaining general accounting records
6. Maintaining detailed accounts receivable records
7. Processing cash receipts
8. Granting credit and pursuing unpaid accounts

Segregation of duties should be used extensively in the sales and collection cycle for two reasons. First, cash receipts are subject to easy manipulation. Second, the large number and nature of transactions within the cycle make the procedure of cross-checking, where one employee's duties automatically serve to verify the accuracy of another's, highly desirable.

If the asset-handling activities (shipping goods and processing cash receipts) are combined with their respective accountability activities (maintaining inventory, accounts receivable, and general accounting records), a serious deficiency with respect to safeguarding those assets exists. It would be easy for an employee, by either omitting or adding an entry, to use the company's assets for his or her own purpose. If the credit granting function is combined with the sales function, there may be a tendency of sales staff to optimize volume even at the expense of high bad debt write-offs.

14-8 The use of prenumbered documents is meant to prevent the failure to bill or record sales as well as to prevent duplicate billings and recordings. An example of a useful control to provide reasonable assurance that all shipments are billed is for the billing clerk to file a copy of all shipping documents in sequential order after a shipment has been billed. Periodically, someone can account for all numbers in the sequence and investigate the reason for missing documents. Computer programs can be used to identify gaps and duplicates in the sequence. The same type of a useful test in this area is to account for the sequence of duplicate sales invoices in the sales journal, watching for omitted numbers, duplicate numbers, or invoices outside the normal sequence. This test simultaneously provides evidence of both the occurrence and completeness objectives.

14-9   1.   Credit is authorized before a sale takes place.

  Test: Analyze the allowance for uncollectible accounts and write-offs of accounts receivable during the period to determine the effectiveness of the credit approval system.

2.   Goods are shipped only after proper authorization.

  Test: Review physical inventory shortages to determine the effectiveness of inventory control.

3.   Prices, including payment terms, freight, and discounts, are properly authorized.

  Test: Compare actual price charged for different products, including freight and terms, to the price list authorized by management.

14-10   The purpose of footing and crossfooting the sales journal and tracing the totals to the general ledger is to determine that sales transactions are properly included in the accounts receivable master file and are correctly summarized. The auditor will make a sample selection from the sales journal to perform tests of controls and substantive tests of transactions, so he or she must determine that the general ledger agrees with the sales journal.

14-11   The verification of sales returns and allowances is quite different from the verification of sales for three primary reasons:

1.   Sales returns and allowances are normally an insignificant portion of operations and therefore receive little attention from the auditor.
2.   The primary emphasis the auditor places on sales returns and allowances is to determine that returns and allowances are properly authorized and that sales are not overstated at year-end and subsequently reversed by the issuance of returns.
3.   The completeness objective cannot be ignored because unrecorded sales returns and allowances can materially overstate net income.

14-12   Cash is the most liquid asset that a company owns and thus it is the most likely target of misappropriation. The emphasis the auditor places on the possibility of misappropriation of cash is not inconsistent with his or her responsibility, which is to determine the fairness of the presentation of the financial statements. If material fraud has occurred, and it is not fully disclosed in the financial statements, those statements are not fairly presented.

TRANSACTION-RELATED AUDIT OBJECTIVE	KEY INTERNAL CONTROLS
1. Recorded cash receipts are for funds actually received by the company (occurrence).	■ Separation of duties between handling cash and record keeping. ■ Independent reconciliation of bank accounts.
2. Cash received is recorded in the cash receipts journal (completeness).	■ Separation of duties between handling cash and record keeping. ■ Use of remittance advices or a prelisting of cash. ■ Immediate endorsement of incoming checks. ■ Internal verification of the recording of cash receipts. ■ Regular monthly statements to customers.
3. Cash receipts are deposited and recorded at the amounts received (accuracy).	■ Same as 2 above. ■ Approval of cash discounts. ■ Regular reconciliation of bank accounts. ■ Batch totals are compared with computer summary reports.
4. Cash receipts are properly included in the accounts receivable master file and are correctly summarized (posting and summarization).	■ Regular monthly statements to customers. ■ Internal verification of accounts receivable master file contents. ■ Comparison of accounts receivable master file or trial balance totals with general ledger balance.
5. Cash receipts transactions are properly classified (classification).	■ Use of adequate chart of accounts. ■ Internal review and verification.
6. Cash receipts are recorded on the correct dates (timing).	■ Procedure requiring recording of cash receipts on a daily basis. ■ Internal verification.

14-14 Audit procedures that the auditor can use to determine whether all cash receipts were recorded are:

- Discussion with personnel and observation of the separation of duties between handling cash and record keeping.
- Account for numerical sequence of remittance advices or examine prelisting of cash receipts.
- Observe immediate endorsement of incoming checks.
- Examine indication of internal verification of the recording of cash receipts.
- Observe whether monthly statements are sent to customers.
- Trace from remittance advices or prelisting to cash receipts journal.

14-15 Proof of cash receipts is a procedure to test whether all recorded cash receipts have been deposited in the bank account. In this test, the total cash receipts recorded in the cash receipts journal for a period of time, such as a month, are reconciled to the actual deposits made to the bank during the same time period. The procedure is not useful to discover cash receipts that have not been recorded in the journals or time lags in making deposits, but it is useful to discover recorded cash receipts that have not been deposited, unrecorded deposits, unrecorded loans, bank loans deposited directly into the bank account, and similar misstatements.

14-16 Lapping is the postponement of entries for the collection of receivables to conceal an existing cash shortage. The fraud is perpetrated by someone who records cash in the cash receipts journal and then enters them into the computer system. The person defers recording the cash receipts from one customer and covers the shortage with receipts from another customer. These in turn are covered by the receipts from a third customer a few days later. The employee must either continue to cover the shortage through lapping, replace the stolen money, or find another way to conceal the shortage.

This fraud can be detected by comparing the name, amount and dates shown on remittance advices to cash receipts journal entries and related duplicate deposit slips. Since the procedure is relatively time-consuming, auditors ordinarily perform the procedure only where there is a specific concern with fraud because of internal control deficiencies discovered.

14-17 The audit procedures most likely to be used to verify accounts receivable charged off as uncollectible and the purpose of each procedure are as follows:

- Examine approvals by the appropriate persons of individual accounts charged off. The purpose is to determine that charge-offs are approved.
- Examine correspondence in client's files that indicates the uncollectibility of the accounts for a selected number of write-offs. The purpose is to determine that the account appears to be uncollectible.

14-17 (continued)

- Examine Dun and Bradstreet credit records as an indication of the uncollectibility of an account. The purpose is the same as the previous procedure.
- Consider the reason for the charge-off compared to the company policy for writing off uncollectible accounts. The purpose is to determine whether or not company policy is being followed.

14-18   The primary objective of the tests of controls and substantive tests of transactions for sales and cash receipts is to determine whether or not the auditor may rely on internal controls to produce accurate information. If it is determined through tests of controls and substantive tests of transactions that the system provides reliable information as to accounts receivable balances, the auditor may reduce the sample size for the confirmation of accounts receivable and adjust the type of confirmation and timing of the tests. If the system is not considered effective because of deficiencies in internal control, the sample size must be increased, positive confirmations will probably be necessary, and the confirmations will most likely be as of the balance sheet date.

14-19   It is often acceptable to perform tests of controls and substantive tests of transactions at an interim date. The auditor may decide it is necessary to test the untested period at year-end. It is acceptable to perform tests of controls and substantive tests of transactions for sales and cash receipts at an interim date and not perform additional tests of the system at year-end under the following circumstances:

- The auditor believes that internal controls are effective.
- The auditor does not anticipate significant changes in the internal controls during the remaining period.
- The transactions normally occurring between the completion of the tests of controls and substantive tests of transactions and the end of the year are similar to the transactions prior to the test date.
- The remaining period is not too long.

14-20   Generally, successful tests of controls and substantive tests of transactions allow for a reduction of tests of details of balance at year-end. However, Diane Smith chose the month of March, which only represents one-twelfth of the year, as her test period. With such a short test period, Diane cannot conclude that she has selected a representative sample from the total population; therefore, without testing additional months (consensus of several CPA firms requires at least nine months coverage), Diane should not change the scope of her tests of details of balances at year-end.

14-21 a. (2)   b. (1)   c. (3)   d. (4)

14-22 a. (4)   b. (3)   c. (1)   d. (2)

14-23 a. (4)   b. (4)   c. (2)

■ **Discussion Questions and Problems**

14-24 1. a. Recorded sales are to valid customers who are able to pay (Occurrence).
          b. Select a sample of sales recorded in the sales journal and determine if the appropriate individuals approved the corresponding customer order.
          c. Sales may be overstated if customer is unable to pay for the goods.
          d. Examine sales returns and write-offs of accounts during the year to determine if returns and write-offs are the result of customers unable to pay. Review aging of accounts receivable to determine if accounts in older aging categories include sales transactions that are unlikely to be collected.

          2. a. Online sales are recorded in the sales system (Completeness).
          b. Review online sales system documentation and make inquiries of client personnel to determine that the automatic interface is a part of the system design. Enter a sample of test transactions of online sales to determine if test data included in the sales journals. Reverse all test data items.
          c. Online sales may not be recorded in the sales account, which would understates sales.
          d. Trace a sample of online sales transactions to the sales journal.

          3. a. Recorded sales are billed using approved prices (Accuracy).
          b. Obtain a list of pre-approved unit prices in the master file. Enter product numbers into the sales system to determine if the unit price presented is correct. Inquire about access privileges to the master file. Attempt to login to access the master file.
          c. Sales transactions could be recorded using incorrect amounts.
          d. Compare a sample of prices on a sample of sales invoices to the approved prices lists at the time the sale occurred.

4. a. Existing sales transactions are recorded (Completeness) and sales are recorded on the correct dates (Timing).

    b. Inquire of shipping personnel about the process they use to forward shipping documents to accounting and observe the timeliness of when that occurs.

    c. Goods shipped may not be recorded in the sales journal at all or in the wrong time period.

    d. Compare date per shipping order to date of posting in sales journal for a sample of shipments.

5. a. Recorded sales are for shipments actually made (Occurrence) and all shipments are recorded as sales (Completeness).

    b. Review the client's documentation for the sequence of bills of lading.

    c. Shipments could be recorded twice (due to duplicate bills of lading) which would overstate sales or shipments may not be recorded (due to missing bills of lading) which would understate sales.

    d. Review the list of bills of lading to determine if there are duplicates or missing documents.

6. a. Recorded sales are for shipments actually made (Occurrence).

    b. Review systems documentation and make inquiries of personnel to determine if the sales application is programmed to only allow recording of sales with a valid bill of lading number. Attempt to enter a sales transaction into the sales journal without a bill of lading number to determine if the transaction is rejected.

    c. Sales could be recorded even though goods have not been shipped to customers.

    d. Review the sales journal to determine if there is a corresponding bill of lading for a sample of sales journal entries.

7. a. Recorded sales are for the correct amounts (Accuracy).

    b. Review a sample of sales transactions to determine if there is documentation of the independent verification.

    c. Sales could be misstated because they are recorded at inaccurate amounts.

    d. For a sample of sales transactions, verify the accuracy of the sales amount.

8. a. All cash sales are recorded (Completeness).
    b. Inquire about duties for individuals responsible for cash collections and observe whether they have access to accounting or shipping functions.
    c. The person handling cash collections may misappropriate cash and not record the cash sale in accounting records.
    d. Trace a sample of shipments to determine if they have been recorded as sales in the accounting records.

9. a. Sales transactions are correctly included in the accounts receivable master file and are correctly summarized (Posting and Summarization).
    b. Examine evidence that the accounts receivable master file to the general ledger for accounts receivable.
    c. The accounts receivable master file does not reflect transactions that are included in the ending accounts receivable general ledger balance.
    d. Compare the dates of entry in the sales journal for a sample of sales transactions to the date the transactions are posted in the accounts receivable master file.

14-25

1. a. Test of control
    b. Existing sales transactions are recorded. (Completeness)
    c. Documentation

2. a. Test of control
    b. Recorded sales are for shipments actually made to existing customers. (Occurrence)
    c. Documentation

3. a. Substantive test of transactions
    b. Recorded sales are for the amount of goods shipped. (Accuracy)
    c. Documentation

4. a. Substantive test of transactions
    b. Sales transactions are properly included in the accounts receivable master file and are correctly summarized. (Posting and summarization)
    c. Reperformance

5. a. Test of control
    b. Recorded sales returns are for returns from existing customers. (Occurrence)
    c. Documentation

      6.   a.   Test of control

           b.   (1)   Cash received is recorded in the cash receipts journal. (Completeness)

                    (2)   Cash receipts are recorded on the correct dates. (Timing)

           c.   Observation or documentation

      7.   a.   Substantive test of transactions

           b.   (1)   Recorded receipts are for funds actually received by the company. (Occurrence)

                    (2)   Cash received is recorded in the cash receipts journal. (Completeness)

                    (3)   Cash receipts are deposited at the amount received. (Accuracy)

                    (4)   Cash receipts are recorded on the correct dates. (Timing)

           c.   Documentation

14-26 a.   *Objective 1*   A given sale is recorded more than once, or a sale is recorded for which a shipment was not made.

               Objective 2   A shipment took place for which no sale was recorded.

               Objective 3   A sales journal was incorrectly footed, or a sales transaction was posted to the incorrect customer account.

        b.   The first objective deals with overstatement of sales resulting from recording sales for which no shipment had occurred. The second objective concerns understatement of sales. It results from a shipment that has not been recorded.

        c.   Procedures 2, 3, and 4 are tests of controls. Procedures 1, 5, and 6 are substantive tests of transactions.

        d.

	(1) OCCURRENCE	(2) COMPLETENESS	(3) POSTING AND SUMMARIZATION
SUBSTANTIVE TEST OF TRANSACTIONS	Procedure 6	Procedure 1	Procedure 5
TEST OF CONTROL	Procedure 2	Procedure 4	Procedure 3

14-26 (continued)

e.

PROCEDURE	CONTROL BEING TESTED	NATURE OF MISSTATEMENT TRYING TO PREVENT
2	A shipping document is attached to each duplicate sales invoice.	To prevent billing to a customer or recording a sale for which no shipment has been made.
3	An independent person traces from the sales journal to the accounts receivable master file. A tick mark is shown in the margin of the sales journal after a transaction is traced.	Preventing misstatements in failure to post to the accounts receivable master file, posting to the wrong customer, at the wrong amount, or at the wrong date.
4	At the time of billing, the duplicate sales invoice number is written on the bottom left-hand corner of each shipping document. Periodically, the entire sequence of shipping documents is accounted for and each is examined to make certain there is an invoice number, which indicates that a given shipment has been billed.	The failure to bill customers for shipments actually made.

14-27   a.   (4)   b.   (2)   c.   (3)

TEST OF CONTROL OR SUBSTANTIVE TEST OF TRANSACTIONS	TRANSACTION-RELATED AUDIT OBJECTIVE(S)	SUBSTANTIVE TEST
1. S T of T	Accuracy	Not applicable
2. S T of T	Posting and summarization	Not applicable
3. T of C	Accuracy	Compare unit selling prices on duplicate sales invoices to the approved price list.
4. T of C	Classification	Examine a sample of sales transactions to determine if each one is correctly classified in the sales journal.
5. S T of T	Classification	Not applicable
6. S T of T	Completeness Accuracy Timing Posting and summarization	Not applicable
7. S T of T	Occurrence Completeness Accuracy Timing	Not applicable
8. T of C	Accuracy	Recalculate the cash discounts for a sample of remittances and determine whether each one was consistent with company policy.
9. T of C	Completeness	Trace from a sample of remittance advices to the cash receipts journal to determine if the related cash is recorded.

14-29

POSSIBLE ERROR OR FRAUD	CONTROL
1. Customer checks are properly credited to customer accounts and are properly deposited, but errors are made in recording receipts in the cash receipts journal.	c. Remittance advices are separated from the checks in the mailroom and forwarded to the accounting department.
2. Customer checks are misappropriated before being forwarded to the cashier for deposit.	f. Monthly statements are mailed to customers with outstanding balances.
3. Customer checks are received for less than the customers' full account balances, but the customers' full account balances are credited.	e. Total amounts posted to the accounts receivable subsidiary records from remittance advices are compared to the validated deposit slip.
4. Customer checks are credited to incorrect customer accounts.	f. Monthly statements are mailed to customers with outstanding balances.
5. Different customer accounts are each credited for the same cash receipt.	g. An employee, other than the bookkeeper, periodically prepares a bank reconciliation.

14-30 a.

DEFICIENCY	RECOMMENDED IMPROVEMENT
1. Financial secretary exercises too much control over collections.	To extent possible, financial secretary's responsibilities should be confined to record keeping.
2. Finance committee is not exercising its assigned responsibility for collection.	Finance committee should assume a more active supervisory role.
3. The finance committee is responsible for the auditing function and administration of the cash function. Moreover, the finance committee has not performed the auditing functions.	An audit committee should be appointed to perform periodic auditing procedures or engage outside auditors.
4. The head usher has sole access to cash during the period of the count. One person should not be left alone with the cash until the amount has been recorded or control established in some other way.	The number of counters should be increased to at least two, and cash should remain under joint surveillance until counted and recorded so that any discrepancies will be brought to attention.
5. The collection is vulnerable to robbery while it is being counted and from the church safe prior to its deposit in the bank.	The collection should be deposited in the bank's night depository immediately after the count. Physical safeguards, such as locking and bolting the door during the period of the count, should be instituted. Vulnerability to robbery will also be reduced by increasing the number of counters.
6. The head usher's count lacks usefulness from a control standpoint because he surrenders custody of both the cash and the record of the count.	The financial secretary should receive a copy of the collection report for posting to the financial records. The head usher should maintain a copy of the report for use by the audit committee.

DEFICIENCY	RECOMMENDED IMPROVEMENT
7. Contributions are not deposited intact. There is no assurance that amounts withheld by the financial secretary for expenditures will be properly accounted for.	Contributions should be deposited intact. If it is considered necessary for the financial secretary to make cash expenditures, he should be provided with a petty cash fund. The fund should be replenished by a check based upon a properly approved reimbursement request and satisfactory support.
8. Members are asked to enter "cash" on the payee line, thus making the checks completely negotiable and vulnerable to misappropriation.	Members should be asked to make checks payable to the church. At the time of the count, ushers should stamp the church's restrictive endorsement (For Deposit Only) on the back of the check.
9. No mention is made of bonding.	Key employees and members involved in receiving and disbursing cash should be bonded.
10. Written instructions for handling cash collections apparently have not been prepared.	Especially because much of the work involved in cash collections is performed by unpaid, untrained church members, often on a short-term basis, detailed written instructions should be prepared.
11. The envelope system has not been encouraged. Control features that it could provide have been ignored.	The envelope system should be encouraged. Ushers should indicate on the outside of each envelope the amount contributed. Envelope contributions should be reported separately and supported by the empty collection envelopes. Prenumbered envelopes will permit ready identification of the donor by authorized persons without general loss of confidentiality.

INTERNAL CONTROL	a. STRENGTH OR DEFICIENCY	b. TRANSACTION RELATED AUDIT OBJECTIVE	c. NATURE OF DEFICIENCY
1. Credit is granted by a credit department.	Strength	Occurrence of sales.	
2. Once shipment occurs and is recorded in the sales journal, all shipping documents are marked "recorded" by the accounting staff.	Strength	Completeness of sales.	
3. Sales returns are presented to a sales department clerk who prepares a written, prenumbered receiving report.	Deficiency		Prenumbered receiving reports should be prepared by receiving department clerks immediately upon receipt of returned goods. A duplicate copy of the receiving report should be sent to the credit department for approval and preparation of a credit memorandum that is then forwarded to accounting to record the sales return.
4. Cash receipts received in the mail are received by a secretary with no record-keeping responsibility.	Strength	Completeness of cash receipts.	
5. Cash receipts received in the mail are forwarded unopened with remittance advices to accounting.	Deficiency		This represents inadequate segregation of duties because it gives custody of the cash to those in accounting who are responsible for recordkeeping activities. Personnel in accounting could misappropriate cash receipts and alter accounting records to hide the fraud.

INTERNAL CONTROL	a. STRENGTH OR DEFICIENCY	b. TRANSACTION RELATED AUDIT OBJECTIVE	c. NATURE OF DEFICIENCY
6. The cash receipts journal is prepared by the treasurer's department	Deficiency		The cash receipts journal represents the primary accounting record for all cash received. It should be prepared by personnel within the accounting function, not the treasury function. The treasury function has primarily responsibilities surrounding the custody of cash. Thus, they should not have any recordkeeping responsibilities.
7. Cash is deposited weekly.	Deficiency		Cash should be deposited at least daily to prevent loss or theft of cash.
8. Statements are sent monthly to customers.	Strength	• Occurrence of sales • Accuracy of sales • Posting and summarization of sales • Completeness of cash receipts • Accuracy of cash receipts Posting and summarization of cash receipts	
9. Write-offs of accounts receivable are approved by the controller.	Deficiency		This is an inappropriate segregation of duties. The controller has recordkeeping responsibilities. The write-off of accounts involves authorization responsibilities. The write-offs should be approved by the credit department, not the controller.
10. The bank reconciliation is prepared by individuals independent of cash receipts recordkeeping.	Strength	• Occurrence of cash receipts • Completeness of cash receipts Accuracy of cash receipts	

CONTROL	TRANSACTION-RELATED AUDIT OBJECTIVE	POTENTIAL FINANCIAL STATEMENT MISSTATEMENT IF CONTROL IS ABSENT
1.	Occurrence	Sales may be recorded for invalid or non-existent products.
	Accuracy	Sales may be processed based on inaccurate price information.
2.	Occurrence	Sales may be recorded for non-existent products.
	Accuracy	Sales may be processed for existing products using quantities ordered, even when ordered quantities are not on hand.
3.	Occurrence	Sales may be processed for customers who are unable to pay.
4.	Occurrence	Shipments may be made to persons making an unauthorized credit card purchase (e.g., with a stolen credit card).
5.	Accuracy	Sales may be processed inaccurately (e.g., wrong product, wrong price, wrong quantity).
6.	Occurrence	Sales may be recorded even though shipment has not occurred.
	Timing	Sales may be recorded in the wrong time period.

■ **Case**

14-33 a.

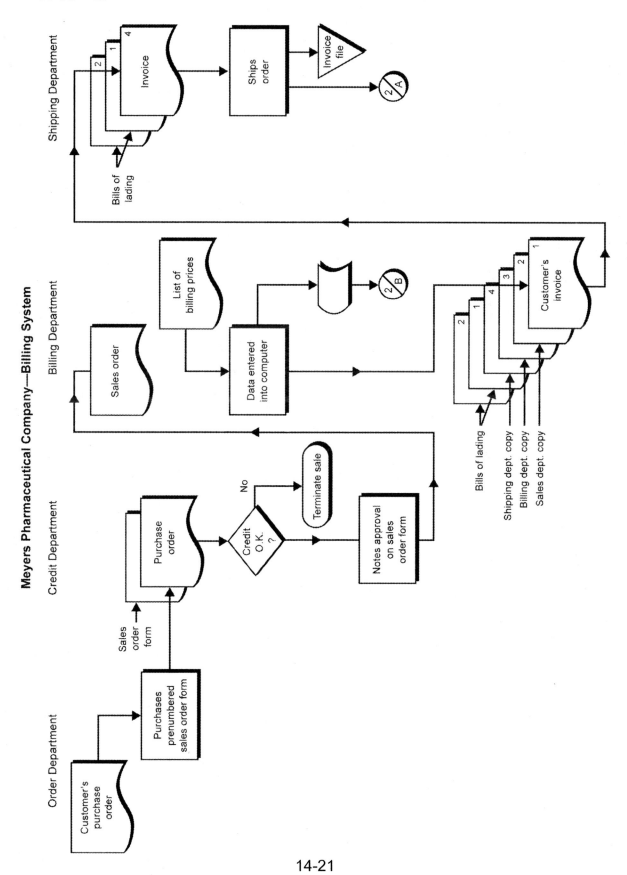

Meyers Pharmaceutical Company—Billing System

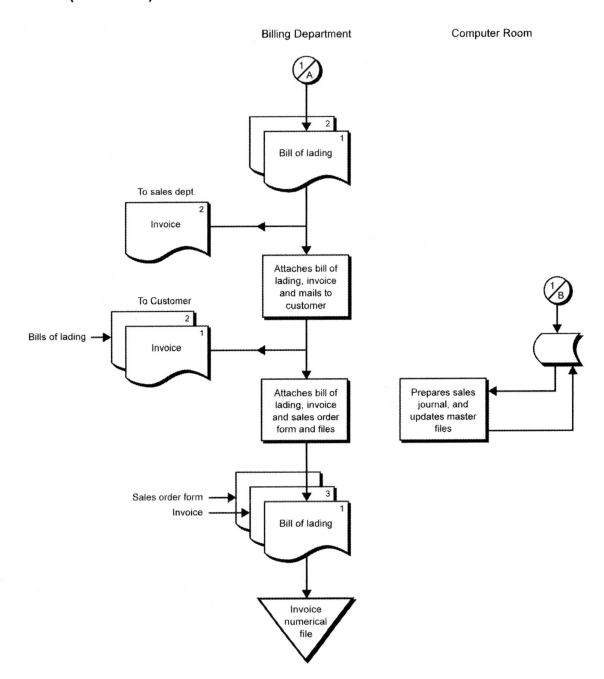

14-33 (continued)

b. and c.

TRANSACTION-RELATED AUDIT OBJECTIVE	INTERNAL CONTROLS	TEST OF CONTROL
1. Recorded sales occurred.	Bill of lading and sales order form are attached to invoice. Sales are initiated by sales order form from customer. Credit department investigates customer credit and approves sales before shipment of merchandise is authorized.	Examine invoice package for presence of bill of lading and sales order form. Examine sales order form for indication of credit approval. Review client's credit approval system for effectiveness.
2. Existing sales transactions are recorded.	Bill of lading and invoices are prenumbered (numerical sequence is not accounted for) and must be prepared before merchandise is shipped.	Account for numerical sequences of bills of lading and sales invoices and determine that all have been recorded.
3. Recorded sales are at the correct amounts.	Control totals are prepared and checked by computer. (No verification of the sales price is performed.)	Examine computer edit reports for indication of errors and disposition thereof.
4. Sales transactions are properly included in the accounts receivable master file and are correctly summarized.	Sales transactions are simultaneously recorded in sales, accounts receivable, cost of sales, and relieved from the perpetual inventory.	Trace sales transactions to sales journal.
5. Recorded sales are properly classified.	None.	Not applicable.
6. Sales are recorded on the correct dates.	None.	Not applicable.

14-33 (continued)

     d.

TRANSACTION-RELATED AUDIT OBJECTIVE	SUBSTANTIVE TEST OF TRANSACTIONS AUDIT PROCEDURES
1. Recorded sales occurred.	Select a sample of sales from sales journal and examine customer's purchase order, sales order form, and bill of lading to determine that the goods were ordered and shipped.
2. Existing sales transactions are recorded.	Perform analytical tests, including comparisons of operating statistics to prior years and month to month at year-end.
3. Recorded sales transactions are stated at the correct amounts.	Compare sales prices to price lists. Examine customer correspondence indicating pricing disputes. Test clerical accuracy of a sample of sales invoices.
4. Sales transactions are properly included in the accounts receivable master file and are correctly summarized.	Foot the sales journal and trace the balance to the general ledger.
5. Recorded sales are properly classified.	Examine sales documents to determine that sales transactions are properly classified.
6. Sales are recorded on the correct dates.	Compare dates on bills of lading to the sales journal to determine that sales are recorded on a timely basis. Compare sales month to month and investigate any significant fluctuations, especially near year-end.

     e.   An audit program for conducting the audit of sales is as follows:

          1.   Obtain the sales journal for the year and perform the following procedures:
              (a)   Foot the journal for one month and reconcile to the general ledger balance.
              (b)   From the journal, select a sample of invoices and perform the following:

         (1)   See that the customer's purchase order, sales order form, and bill of lading are available. Compare quantity, sales price, customer name, and date of shipment to sales journal. Obtain explanation of any differences.

         (2)   Examine sales order form for indication of credit approved.

         (3)   Compare sales price to price list.

         (4)   Test clerical accuracy of sales invoices.

         (5)   Determine propriety of classification of sales transactions.

2.   Select a sample of bill of lading numbers. Locate the corresponding bills of lading and trace them to the sales journal to determine that the shipments were recorded. Compare the date per the bill of lading to the date per the sales journal to determine the promptness of recording.

3.   Examine customer correspondence during the year for disputes on pricing of invoices.

4.   Prepare a schedule of sales, cost of sales, and gross margin percentage, showing comparison between recent years and month to month. Obtain explanation of any significant fluctuations.

■ **Integrated Case Application**

14-34   a., b., c., and d.

PINNACLE MANUFACTURING—Part V

#	a. Key Internal Control	b. Transaction Related Audit Objectives	c. Test of Control	d. Substantive Test of Transaction
1.	Segregation of the purchasing, receiving, and cash disbursements functions.	Recorded acquisitions are for goods and services actually received (occurrence). Recorded cash disbursements are for goods and services actually received (occurrence).	Discuss segregation of duties with personnel and observe activities.	Trace entries in the acquisitions journal to related vendors' invoices, receiving reports, and purchase orders.
2.	Use of prenumbered voucher packages, properly accounted for.	Existing acquisition transactions are recorded (completeness).	Account for a sequence of voucher packages.	Trace from a file of vendors' invoices to the acquisitions journal.
3.	Use of prenumbered checks, properly accounted for.	Existing cash disbursement transactions are recorded (completeness).	Account for a sequence of checks.	Reconcile recorded cash disbursements with the cash disbursements on the bank statement (proof of cash disbursements).
4.	Use of prenumbered receiving reports, properly accounted for.	Existing acquisition transactions are recorded (completeness).	Account for a sequence of receiving reports.	Trace from a file of receiving reports to the acquisitions journal.
5.	Internal verification of document package before check preparation.	• Recorded acquisitions are for goods and services actually received (occurrence). • Recorded acquisitions are stated at the correct amounts (accuracy). • Acquisition transactions are properly included in the master files, and are properly summarized (posting and summarization). • Acquisitions are properly classified (classification). Acquisitions are recorded on the correct dates (timing).	Examine document package for indication of internal verification.	Examine supporting documents for propriety and recompute information on the supporting documents.

14-26

a., b., c., and d.

#	a. Key Internal Control	b. Transaction Related Audit Objectives	c. Test of Control	d. Substantive Test of Transaction
5.	Internal verification of document package before check preparation.	• Recorded acquisitions are for goods and services actually received (occurrence). • Recorded acquisitions are stated at the correct amounts (accuracy). • Acquisition transactions are properly included in the master files, and are properly summarized (posting and summarization). • Acquisitions are properly classified (classification). • Acquisitions are recorded on the correct dates (timing).	Examine document package for indication of internal verification.	Examine supporting documents for propriety and recompute information on the supporting documents.
6.	Review of supporting documents and signing of checks by an independent, authorized person.	Recorded cash disbursements are for goods and services actually received (occurrence).	Examine checks for signature.	Trace the cancelled check to the related acquisitions journal entry and examine for payee name and amount.
7.	Cancellation of documents prior to signing of the check.	Recorded acquisitions are for goods and services actually received (occurrence).	Examine indication of cancellation.	Examine the acquisitions journal for duplicate entries to a vendor.
8.	Monthly reconciliation of the accounts payable master file with the general ledger.	• Acquisition transactions are properly included in the master files, and are properly summarized (posting and summarization). • Cash disbursement transactions are properly included in the master file, and are properly summarized (posting and summarization).	Inquire of client about monthly reconciliation procedures.	Foot acquisitions and cash disbursements journals and trace postings to the general ledger and accounts payable and inventory master files.
9.	Independent reconciliation of the monthly bank statements.	Existing cash disbursement transactions are recorded (completeness). • Recorded cash disbursement transactions are stated at the correct amounts (accuracy).	Examine file of completed bank reconciliations.	Reconcile recorded cash disbursements with the cash disbursements on the bank statement (proof of cash disbursements).

14-34 (continued)

e.

Acquisitions Substantive Tests of Transactions

Note: More than one audit procedure is listed for certain objectives even though the requirement is for only one procedure.

TRANSACTION-RELATED AUDIT OBJECTIVES	SUBSTANTIVE AUDIT PROCEDURES
Occurrence	• Compare prices on vendor invoices with approved price limits established by management. • Review the acquisitions journal, general ledger, and accounts payable master file for large or unusual amounts.
Completeness	• Trace a sample of receiving reports to the acquisitions journal. • Trace from a file of vendors' invoices to the acquisitions journal. • Trace from additions in perpetual inventory records to recorded acquisitions.
Accuracy	• Compare amounts for entries in acquisitions journal to related vendors' invoices, purchase orders and receiving reports. • Recompute information on vendor invoices. • Compare prices on vendor invoices with approved price limits established by management.
Posting and Summarization	• Trace individual entries in accounts payable master file to acquisitions journal.
Classification	• Examine vendors' invoices for proper classification. • Compare classification with chart of accounts by reference to vendors' invoices.
Timing	• Compare dates of receiving reports and vendors' invoices with dates in the acquisitions journal.

14-28

14-34 (continued)

f.

Cash Disbursements Substantive Tests of Transactions

Note: More than one audit procedure is listed for certain objectives even though the requirement is for only one procedure.

TRANSACTION-RELATED AUDIT OBJECTIVES	SUBSTANTIVE AUDIT PROCEDURES
Occurrence	• Trace cancelled check numbers in the cash disbursements journal to related cancelled checks and examine for payee, name, and amount. • Examine cancelled check for authorized signature, proper endorsement, and cancellation by the bank. • Review the cash disbursements journal, general ledger, and accounts payable master file for large or unusual amounts. • Trace cancelled check to the related acquisitions journal entry and examine for payee name and amount.
Completeness	• Trace entries in acquisitions journal to subsequent payment in cash disbursements journal.
Accuracy	• Compare cancelled checks with the related acquisitions journal and cash disbursements journal entries. • Recompute cash discounts.
Posting and Summarization	• Trace individual entries in accounts payable master file to cash disbursements journal.
Classification	• Compare classification with chart of accounts by reference to vendors' invoices and acquisitions journal.
Timing	• Compare dates on cancelled checks with cash disbursements journal. • Compare dates on cancelled checks with the bank cancellation date.

14-34 (continued)

g. *Note: Student answers will depend on answers in requirements b through f.*

General

1. Discuss the following items with client personnel and observe activities:
   a. Segregation of duties
   b. Monthly reconciliation of accounts payable master file with the general ledger.
2. Test journal summarization and posting for a test month:
   a. Foot acquisition journal and trace postings to the general ledger and accounts payable and inventory master files.
   b. Foot cash disbursements journal and trace postings to general ledger and accounts payable master file.
3. Examine file of completed bank reconciliations.
4. Account for a sequence of cancelled checks.
5. Reconcile recorded cash disbursements with cash disbursements on the bank statement.
6. Review the acquisitions journal, cash disbursements journal, general ledger, and accounts payable master file for large or unusual amounts.
7. Examine underlying documents (vendors' invoices, receiving reports, purchase orders, and purchase requisitions) for indication of cancellation and reasonableness.

Acquisitions

8. Trace entries in the acquisitions journal to related vendors' invoices, receiving reports, and purchase orders.
   a. Examine indication of internal verification of dates, unit costs, prices, extensions and footings, account classification, recording in the journal, and posting and summarization.
   b. Examine supporting documents for propriety.
   c. Compare prices on vendors' invoices with approved price limits established by management.
   d. Recompute information on vendors' invoices.
   e. Examine vendors' invoices for proper classification.
   f. Compare dates on recorded acquisitions with dates on receiving reports and vendors' invoices.
   g. Examine document package for indication of internal verification.

14-34 (continued)

9.   Account for a sequence of receiving reports and voucher packages.

10.   Trace a sample of receiving reports and vendors' invoices to the acquisitions journal.

Cash Disbursements

11.   Select a sample of cancelled checks and:
   a.   Trace cancelled check to the related cash disbursements journal entry and acquisitions journal entry and examine for payee, name, amount, and date.
   b.   Examine check for signature, proper endorsement, and cancellation by the bank.
   c.   Compare date on cancelled check with bank cancellation date.
   d.   Recompute cash discounts.

14-35 – ACL Problem Solution

a.   There are 112 transactions in the month of September, 2002. The total amount of these transactions is $127,941.13 (Filter expression is DATE1 >= '20020901' AND DATE1 <= '20020930'; Count command; then Total command).

b.   Type "IN" has the highest count. See the following report created using the Summarize command:

```
Page    1                         04/10/2011  12:09:18
Produced with ACL by: ACL Educational Edition -
Not For Commercial Use

TYPE            AMOUNT      COUNT
 AA             -533.59         1
 CN            -9025.02       108
 IN           525259.16       588
 PM           -45281.38        71
 TR            -1538.48         4

              468880.69       772
```

c.   There are 588 sales invoices (IN), totaling $525,259.16. The largest single invoice amount is $5,549.19 and the average invoice amount is $893.30. (Filter by invoice type = IN; then use Statistics command on the Amount column.)

d. Leaving the filter from part c intact, create a computed field with the following expression: DUE – DATE1 and then add this column to the table view. Several of the invoices have negative results, which means that possibly the wrong year was used for the due date. Also, some are 90 days old, which indicates potential collection problems.

e. See the following printout:, which is the result of using the Stratify command after a filter is applied to isolate "IN" transactions greater than or equal to $300.

As of: 04/10/2011 12:31:28

Command: STRATIFY ON AMOUNT SUBTOTAL AMOUNT INTERVALS 10 TO SCREEN
Table: Metaphor_AR_2002

Filter: TYPE = "IN" AND AMOUNT >= 300 (509 records matched)

Minimum encountered was 303.99
Maximum encountered was 5,549.19

AMOUNT	Count	Percent of Count	Percent of Field	AMOUNT
303.99 - 828.50	262	51.47%	28.24%	145,800.02
828.51 - 1,353.02	146	28.68%	30.41%	157,026.25
1,353.03 - 1,877.54	53	10.41%	16.23%	83,783.99
1,877.55 - 2,402.06	23	4.52%	9.24%	47,727.14
2,402.07 - 2,926.58	9	1.77%	4.59%	23,696.18
2,926.59 - 3,451.10	9	1.77%	5.56%	28,689.86
3,451.11 - 3,975.62	4	0.79%	2.84%	14,640.60
3,975.63 - 4,500.14	1	0.2%	0.86%	4,426.14
4,500.15 - 5,024.66	1	0.2%	0.96%	4,954.64
5,024.67 - 5,549.19	1	0.2%	1.07%	5,549.19
Totals	509	100%	100%	516,294.01

■ **Internet Problem Solution: Point of Sales Systems Controls**

Internet Problem 14-1

The following answers are based on the SEC's Litigation Release No. 20470 and related press releases associated with the fraud at Bally Total Fitness Holding Corporation:

a. According to the SEC press releases and Litigation Release No. 20470, Bally fraudulently accounted for three types of revenue it received from members: initiation fees, prepaid dues, and reactivation fees.

Internet Problem 14-1 (continued)

Initiation fees: Bally fraudulently and prematurely recognized revenue from initiation fees. Part of the price of a Bally health club membership was a one-time initiation fee that was either paid in full when the member joined or was financed over a period of time, typically 36 months. Regardless of how the initiation fee was paid, accounting standards prohibit Bally from recognizing all the revenues from initiation fees immediately. Instead, accounting standards require that Bally recognize initiation fee revenue over the entire membership life. This means that for members who maintained their memberships beyond the financing period, or initial period of membership, Bally was required to defer initiation fee revenue and recognize it over the estimated membership life, not over the term of the initial period of membership. However, Bally prematurely recognized its members' initiation fee revenue over a period that was not only shorter than the estimated membership life, but in most instances even shorter than the initial period of membership.

Personal Training Services: In addition to selling health club memberships, Bally also sold personal training services (i.e., exercise sessions with personal trainers). Some customers prepaid for sessions with personal trainers. Accounting standards require that revenue from prepaid personal training services be recognized only when earned, which is when the personal training services were actually provided. Bally, however, recognized revenue related to personal training services before those services were actually provided.

Reactivation Fees: Bally also fraudulently recognized revenue from unpaid dues on inactive memberships. Not all Bally members who completed their initial membership contract term renewed their membership. Instead, they ceased paying dues. Those members who had paid all amounts due under the initial membership contract, but who had then stopped paying monthly dues for six months or longer, were solicited by Bally for "reactivation." Under that offer, lapsed members could rejoin by paying a "reactivation fee," which was lower than an "initiation fee."

Accounting standards prohibit Bally from recognizing any revenue from "reactivation fees" until after the reactivating members had entered into binding contracts. Rather than comply with accounting standards, Bally simply projected the number of reactivating members that it anticipated rejoining up to three years into the future, and then recognized those anticipated but hypothetical reactivation fees as revenue. The company recognized that hypothetical revenue over a period composed of (a) the average delinquent period (that is, the period between when members stopped paying their monthly dues and when they reactivated) plus (b) the average reactivation period. In later years, they abandoned this methodology and adopted a modified cash basis of accounting for reactivation fees.

b.   Students should have located the December 17, 2009 press release.

c.   The press release notes that the SEC's order against the audit firm (Ernst & Young) finds that the firm identified Bally as a risky audit because its managers were former E&Y audit partners who had "historically been aggressive in selecting accounting principles and determining estimates," and whose compensation plans placed "undue emphasis on reported earnings." Out of more than 10,000 audit clients in North America, E&Y identified Bally as one of E&Y's riskiest 18 accounts and as the riskiest account in the Lake Michigan area.

d.   Students should have located the complaint against John M. Kiss who served as the engagement partner for the 2001 and 2002 audits.

According to the complaint, E&Y recognized Bally as a risky audit and designated Bally as a "close monitoring account" from at least 1996 through 2003. A "close monitoring account" represented one that presented a risk that created a "significant chance the firm [E&Y] will suffer damage to its reputation, monetarily, or both." Bally was designated as a close monitoring account for several reasons, including, among other things, that Bally's manager's were former E&Y audit partners who were "difficult" and had "historically been aggressive in selecting accounting principles and determining estimates." The complaint notes that the managers had placed undue emphasis on maintaining stock prices and that management used "(un)reliable ... estimation process[es] or questionable judgments." Bally's compensation plans placed undue emphasis on reported earnings. E&Y's internal guidance notes that a "history of 'aggressive' applications of accounting policies could indicate a predisposition to misstate the financial statements."

(**Note**: Internet problems address current issues using Internet sources. Because Internet sites are subject to change, Internet problems and solutions may change. Current information on Internet problems is available at www.pearsonhighered.com/arens.)

Chapter 15

Audit Sampling for Tests of Controls and Substantive Tests of Transactions

■ **Review Questions**

15-1   A representative sample is one in which the characteristics of interest for the sample are approximately the same as for the population (that is, the sample accurately represents the total population). If the population contains significant misstatements, but the sample is practically free of misstatements, the sample is nonrepresentative, which is likely to result in an improper audit decision. The auditor can never know for sure whether he or she has a representative sample because the entire population is ordinarily not tested, but certain things, such as the use of random selection, can increase the likelihood of a representative sample.

15-2   Statistical sampling is the use of mathematical measurement techniques to calculate formal statistical results. The auditor therefore quantifies sampling risk when statistical sampling is used. In nonstatistical sampling, the auditor does not quantify sampling risk. Instead, conclusions are reached about populations on a more judgmental basis.

For both statistical and nonstatistical methods, the three main parts are:

1.   Plan the sample
2.   Select the sample and perform the tests
3.   Evaluate the results

15-3   In replacement sampling, an element in the population can be included in the sample more than once if the random number corresponding to that element is selected more than once. In nonreplacement sampling, an element can be included only once. If the random number corresponding to an element is selected more than once, it is simply treated as a discard the second time. Although both selection approaches are consistent with sound statistical theory, auditors rarely use replacement sampling; it seems more intuitively satisfying to auditors to include an item only once.

15-4   A simple random sample is one in which every possible combination of elements in the population has an equal chance of selection. Two methods of simple random selection are use of a random number table, and use of the computer to generate random numbers. Auditors most often use the computer to generate random numbers because it saves time, reduces the likelihood of error, and provides automatic documentation of the sample selected.

15-5 In systematic sampling, the auditor calculates an interval and then methodically selects the items for the sample based on the size of the interval. The interval is set by dividing the population size by the number of sample items desired.

To select 40 numbers from a population of 2,800, the auditor divides 40 into 2,800 and gets an interval of 70. He or she then selects a random number between 0 and 69. Assume the auditor chooses 17. The first item is the number 17. The next is 87, then 157, 227, and so on.

The advantage of systematic sampling is its ease of use. In most populations a systematic sample can be drawn quickly, the approach automatically puts the numbers in sequential order and documentation is easy.

A major problem with the use of systematic sampling is the possibility of bias. Because of the way systematic samples are selected, once the first item in the sample is selected, other items are chosen automatically. This causes no problems if the characteristics of interest, such as control deviations, are distributed randomly throughout the population; however, in many cases they are not. If all items of a certain type are processed at certain times of the month or with the use of certain document numbers, a systematically drawn sample has a higher likelihood of failing to obtain a representative sample. This shortcoming is sufficiently serious that some CPA firms prohibit the use of systematic sampling.

15-6 The purpose of using nonstatistical sampling for tests of controls and substantive tests of transactions is to estimate the proportion of items in a population containing a characteristic or attribute of interest. The auditor is ordinarily interested in determining internal control deviations or monetary misstatements for tests of controls and substantive tests of transactions.

15-7 A block sample is the selection of several items in sequence. Once the first item in the block is selected, the remainder of the block is chosen automatically. Thus, to select 5 blocks of 20 sales invoices, one would select one invoice and the block would be that invoice plus the next 19 entries. This procedure would be repeated 4 other times.

15-8   The terms below are defined as follows:

TERM	DEFINITION
a. Acceptable risk of assessing control risk too low (ARACR)	The risk the auditor is willing to take of accepting a control as effective or a rate of monetary misstatements as tolerable, when the true population exception rate is greater than the tolerable exception rate.
b. Computed upper exception rate (CUER)	The highest estimated exception rate in the population at a given ARACR.
c. Estimated population exception rate (EPER)	The exception rate the auditor expects to find in the population before testing begins. It is necessary to plan the appropriate sample size.
d. Sample exception rate (SER)	The actual rate of exception discovered in the sample. It is calculated by dividing the actual number of exceptions in the sample by the sample size.
e. Tolerable exception rate (TER)	The exception rate the auditor will permit in the population and still be willing to use the assessed control risk and/or the amount of monetary misstatements in the transactions established during planning.

15-9   The sampling unit is the population item from which the auditor selects sample items. The major consideration in defining the sampling unit is making it consistent with the objectives of the audit tests. Thus, the definition of the population and the planned audit procedures usually dictate the appropriate sampling unit.

The sampling unit for verifying the occurrence of recorded sales would be the entries in the sales journal since this is the document the auditor wishes to validate. The sampling unit for testing the possibility of omitted sales is the shipping document from which sales are recorded because the failure to bill a shipment is the exception condition of interest to the auditor.

15-10   The tolerable exception rate (TER) represents the exception rate that the auditor will permit in the population and still be willing to use the assessed control risk and/or the amount of monetary misstatements in the transactions established during planning. TER is determined by choice of the auditor on the basis of his or her professional judgment.

The computed upper exception rate (CUER) is the highest estimated exception rate in the population, at a given ARACR. For nonstatistical sampling, CUER is determined by adding an estimate of sampling error to the SER (sample exception rate). For statistical sampling, CUER is determined by using a statistical sampling table after the auditor has completed the audit testing and therefore knows the number of exceptions in the sample.

15-11 Sampling error is an inherent part of sampling that results from testing less than the entire population. Sampling error simply means that the sample is not perfectly representative of the entire population.

Nonsampling error occurs when audit tests do not uncover errors that exist in the sample. Nonsampling error can result from:

1. The auditor's failure to recognize exceptions, or
2. Inappropriate or ineffective audit procedures.

There are two ways to reduce sampling risk:

1. Increase sample size.
2. Use an appropriate method of selecting sample items from the population.

Careful design of audit procedures and proper supervision and review are ways to reduce nonsampling risk.

15-12 An attribute is the definition of the characteristic being tested and the exception conditions whenever audit sampling is used. The attributes of interest are determined directly from the audit program. In a test of control, that attribute is evidence of the operation of the control consistent with the design. In a substantive test, the attribute is the absence of monetary misstatement.

15-13 An attribute is the characteristic being tested for in a population. An exception occurs when the attribute being tested for is absent. The exception for the audit procedure, the duplicate sales invoice has been initialed indicating the performance of internal verification, is the lack of initials on duplicate sales invoices.

15-14 Tolerable exception rate (TER) is the result of an auditor's judgment. The suitable TER is a question of materiality and is therefore affected by both the definition and the importance of the attribute in the audit plan. It represents the exception rate that the auditor will permit in the population and still be willing to conclude that the control is operating effectively and/or the amount of monetary misstatements in the transactions established during planning is acceptable.

The sample size for a TER of 7% would be smaller than that for a TER of 4%, all other factors being equal.

15-15 The appropriate ARACR is a decision the auditor must make using professional judgment. The degree to which the auditor wishes to reduce assessed control risk below the maximum is the major factor determining the auditor's ARACR.

The auditor will choose a smaller sample size for an ARACR of 10% than would be used if the risk were 5%, all other factors being equal.

15-16 The relationship between sample size and the four factors determining sample size are as follows:

    a.   As the ARACR increases, the required sample size decreases.

    b.   As the population size increases, the required sample size is normally unchanged, or may increase slightly.

    c.   As the TER increases, the sample size decreases.

    d.   As the EPER increases, the required sample size increases.

15-17 In this situation, the sample exception rate (SER) is 4%, the sample size is 100 and the ARACR is 10%. From the 10% ARACR table (Table 15-9) then, the CUER is 7.9%. This means that the auditor can state with a 10% risk of being wrong that the true population exception rate does not exceed 7.9%.

15-18 Analysis of exceptions is the investigation of individual exceptions to determine the cause of the breakdown in internal control. Such analysis is important because by discovering the nature and causes of individual exceptions, the auditor can more effectively evaluate the effectiveness of internal control. The analysis attempts to tell the "why" and "how" of the exceptions after the auditor already knows how many and what types of exceptions have occurred.

15-19 When the CUER exceeds the TER, the auditor may do one or more of the following:

1.   Revise the TER or the ARACR. This alternative should be followed only when the auditor has concluded that the original specifications were too conservative, and when he or she is willing to accept the risk associated with the higher specifications.

2.   Expand the sample size. This alternative should be followed when the auditor expects the additional benefits to exceed the additional costs. That is, the auditor believes that the sample tested was not representative of the population and that exceptions are not expected in the expanded sample.

3.   Revise assessed control risk upward. This is likely to increase substantive procedures. Revising assessed control risk may be done if 1 or 2 is not practical and additional substantive procedures are possible.

4.   Write a letter to management. This action should be done in conjunction with each of the three alternatives above. Management should always be informed when its internal controls are not operating effectively. If a deficiency in internal control is considered to be a significant deficiency in the design or operation of internal control, professional standards require the auditor to communicate the significant deficiency to the audit committee or its equivalent in writing. If the client is a publicly traded company, the auditor must evaluate the deficiency to determine the impact on the auditor's

15-19 (continued)

report on internal control over financial reporting. If the deficiency is deemed to be a material weakness, the auditor's report on internal control would contain an adverse opinion.

15-20 Random (probabilistic) selection is a part of statistical sampling, but it is not, by itself, statistical measurement. To have statistical measurement, it is necessary to mathematically generalize from the sample to the population.

Probabilistic selection must be used if the sample is to be evaluated statistically, although it is also acceptable to use probabilistic selection with a nonstatistical evaluation. If nonprobabilistic selection is used, nonstatistical evaluation must be used.

15-21 The decisions the auditor must make in using attributes sampling are:
- What are the objectives of the audit test?
- Does audit sampling apply?
- What attributes are to be tested and what exception conditions are identified?
- What is the population?
- What is the sampling unit?
- What should the TER be?
- What should the ARACR be?
- What is the EPER?
- What generalizations can be made from the sample to the population?
- What are the causes of the individual exceptions?
- Is the population acceptable?

In making the above decisions, the following should be considered:

- The individual situation.
- Time and budget constraints.
- The availability of additional substantive procedures.
- The professional judgment of the auditor.

■ **Multiple Choice Questions From CPA Examinations**

15-22 a. (3) b. (1) c. (1) d. (1)

15-23 a. (1) b. (3) c. (4) d. (4)

15-24 a. (4) b. (3) c. (2)

■ Discussion Questions and Problems

15-25   a.

SAMPLING UNIT	NUMBERING SYSTEM FOR THE POPULATION	EXCEL SELECTION FORMULA
1. Sales invoice	All invoices numbered 0001 to 8274	=RANDBETWEEN(1,8274)
2. Bill of lading	All bills of lading numbered 18221 through 29427 (if a random number table is used, the left-most digit "2" can be dropped)	=RANDBETWEEN(18221, 29427)
3. Customer	A pair of random numbers, where the first random number is the page number (1-20), and the second random number is the line number on the page (1-50)	=RANDBETWEEN(1,20) and =RANDBETWEEN(1,50)
4. Line numbers on the sales journal that have a sales invoice recorded on them	A pair of random numbers, where the first random number is the page number (1-215), and the second random number is the invoice as counted down from the top of the page (1-100)	=RANDBETWEEN(1,215) and =RANDBETWEEN(1,100)

15-25 (continued)

An example random sampling plan prepared in Excel (P1525.xls) is available on the Companion Website. The command for selecting the random number can be entered directly onto the spreadsheet, or can be selected from the function menu (math & trig) functions. It may be necessary to add the analysis tool pack to access the RANDBETWEEN function. Once the formula is entered, it can be copied down to select additional random numbers. When a pair of random numbers is required, the formula for the first random number can be entered in the first column, and the formula for the second random number can be entered in the second column.

    b.   First five numbers using systematic selection:

SAMPLING UNIT	INTERVAL	RANDOM STARTING POINT	FIRST 5 SAMPLE ITEMS
1. Sales invoice	110 (8274/75)	39	39 149 259 369 479
2. Bill of lading	149 [(29427-18221) = 11206/75]	18259	18259 18408 18557 18706 18855
3. Customer	13 (979 lines/75)	Page 1, line #11	**Page** **Line** 1 11 1 24 1 37 1 50 2 13

Using systematic selection, the definition of the sampling unit for determining the selection interval for population 3 is the total number of lines in the population. The length of the interval is rounded down to ensure that all line numbers selected are within the defined population.

15-26   a.   To test whether shipments have been billed, a sample of warehouse removal slips should be selected and examined to see if they have the proper sales invoice attached. The sampling unit will therefore be the warehouse removal slip.

15-26 (continued)

b.   *Attributes sampling method*: Assuming the auditor is willing to accept a TER of 4% at a 5% ARACR, expecting no exceptions in the sample, the appropriate sample size would be 74, determined from Table 15-8.

   Nonstatistical sampling method: There is no one right answer to this question because the sample size is determined using professional judgment. Due to the relatively small TER (4%), the sample size should not be small. It will most likely be similar in size to the sample chosen by the statistical method.

c.   Systematic sample selection:

   ■   22946   =   Population size of warehouse removal slips (34687-11741).
   ■   74   =   Sample size using statistical sampling (students' answers will vary if nonstatistical sampling was used in part b.
   ■   310   =   Interval (22946/74) if statistical sampling is used (students' answers will vary if nonstatistical sampling was used in part b).
   ■   11878   =   Random starting point.

   Select warehouse removal slip 11878 and every 310th warehouse removal slip after (12188, 12498, etc.)

   Computer generation of random numbers using Excel (P1526.xls):

   =RANDBETWEEN(11741,34687)

   The command for selecting the random number can be entered directly onto the spreadsheet, or can be selected from the function menu (math & trig) functions. It may be necessary to add the analysis tool pack to access the RANDBETWEEN function. Once the formula is entered, it can be copied down to select additional random numbers.

d.   Other audit procedures that could be performed are:
   1.   Test extensions on attached sales invoices for clerical accuracy. (Accuracy)
   2.   Test time delay between warehouse removal slip date and billing date for timeliness of billing. (Timing)
   3.   Trace entries into perpetual inventory records to determine that inventory is properly relieved for shipments. (Posting and summarization)

15-26 (continued)

  e. The test performed in part c cannot be used to test for occurrence of sales because the auditor already knows that inventory was shipped for these sales. To test for occurrence of sales, the sales invoice entry in the sales journal is the sampling unit. Since the sales invoice numbers are not identical to the warehouse removal slips it would be improper to use the same sample.

15-27 a. It would be appropriate to use attributes sampling for all audit procedures except audit procedures 1 and 3. Procedure 1 involves recalculation of just one month's sales journal's mathematical accuracy. The auditor would judgmentally select the month to test. Procedure 3 involves the performance of an analytical procedure for which the auditor is doing a 100% review of the entire sales journal.

  b. The appropriate sampling unit for audit procedures 2, and 4-6 is a sales invoice number, date, or line item in the sales journal. The primary emphasis in the test is the occurrence and accuracy objectives.

  c. The attributes for testing are as follows:

AUDIT PROCEDURE	ATTRIBUTE
2	Entries in the sales journal have been shipped as evidence by the existence of a related shipping document.
4	Prices used to calculate the sales amount on the invoice match those on the approved price list.
5	The date that credit approval is documented on the sales order precedes the date on the shipping document.
6	The calculation of the sales amount on the sales invoice is mathematically accurate.

  d. The sample sizes for each attribute are as follows:

AUDIT PROCEDURE	TEST OF CONTROL OR SUBSTANTIVE TEST OF TRANSACTIONS	SAMPLE SIZE			SAMPLE SIZE
		ARACR	TER	EPER	
2	S T of T	5%	5%	0.5%	93
4	T of C	5%	7%	1.5%	66
5	T of C	5%	7%	1.5%	66
6	ST of T	5%	5%	0.5%	93

15-28 a. Because the sample sizes under nonstatistical sampling are determined using auditor judgment, students' answers to this question will vary. They will most likely be similar to the sample sizes chosen using attributes sampling in part b. The important point to remember is that the sample sizes chosen should reflect the changes in the four factors (ARACR, TER, EPER, and population size). The sample sizes should have fairly predictable relationships, given the changes in the four factors. The following reflects some of the relationships that should exist in student's sample size decisions:

	SAMPLE SIZE	EXPLANATION
1.	90	Given
2.	> Column 1	Decrease in ARACR
3.	> Column 2	Decrease in TER
4.	> Column 1	Decrease in ARACR (column 4 is the same as column 2, with a smaller population size)
5.	< Column 1	Increase in TER-EPER
6.	< Column 5	Decrease in EPER
7.	> Columns 3 & 4	Decrease in TER-EPER

b. Using the attributes sampling table in **Table 15-8**, the sample sizes for columns 1-7 are:
   1. 88
   2. 127
   3. 181
   4. 127
   5. 25
   6. 18
   7. 149

c.

CHANGE IN FACTORS	EFFECT ON SAMPLE SIZE	ILLUSTRATION IN PART a or b
1. Increase in ARACR.	Decrease	Compare columns 4 and 1
2. Increase in TER.	Decrease	Compare columns 3 and 2 (population sizes are not consistent, but this has little effect on sample size)
3. Increase in EPER.	Increase	Compare columns 6 and 5
4. Increase in population size.	No effect or slight increase	Compare columns 4 and 2

15-28 (continued)

d. The difference in the sample size for columns 3 and 6 result from the larger ARACR and larger TER in column 6. The extremely large TER is the major factor causing the difference.

e. *The greatest effect on the sample size is the difference between TER and EPER.* For columns 3 and 7, the differences between the TER and EPER were 3% and 2% respectively. Those two also had the highest sample size. Where the difference between TER and EPER was great, such as columns 5 and 6, the required sample size was extremely small.

    Population size had a relatively small effect on sample size. The difference in population size in columns 2 and 4 was 99,000 items, but the increase in sample size for the larger population was marginal (actually the sample sizes were the same using the attributes sampling table).

f. The sample size is referred to as the initial sample size because it is based on an estimate of the SER. The actual sample must be evaluated before it is possible to know whether the sample is sufficiently large to achieve the objectives of the test.

15-29 a.

	SER	TER-SER	ALLOWANCE FOR SAMPLING ERROR SUFFICIENT?
1.	2%	3%	Probably*
2.	2%	3%	No (due to smaller sample size)*
3.	2%	3%	Yes
4.	2%	3%	Probably*
5.	2%	3%	No (due to small sampling size)
6.	10%	NA	No (SER exceeds TER)
7.	0%	5%	Yes
8.	0%	5%	No due to small sample size

* Students' answers as to whether the allowance for sampling error risk is sufficient will vary, depending on their judgment. However, they should recognize the effect that lower sample sizes have on the allowance for sampling risk in situations 1, 5 and 8.

15-29 (continued)

b. Using the attributes sampling table in Table 15-9, the CUERs for columns 1-8 are:

1. 4.6%
2. 6.2%
3. 4.0%
4. 4.6%
5. 9.2%
6. 16.4%
7. 3.0%
8. 11.3%

c.

	CHANGE IN FACTORS	EFFECT ON CUER	ILLUSTRATIONS IN PART a or b
1	Decrease in ARACR	Increase	Compare columns 3 and 4
2	Decrease in population size	No effect or minor decrease	Compare columns 1 and 4
3	Decrease in sample size	Increase	Compare columns 4 and 5 (both sample exception rates are 2%)
4	Decrease in the number of exceptions in the sample	Decrease	Compare columns 6 and 7

d. The factor that appears to have the greatest effect is the number of exceptions found in the sample compared to sample size. For example, in columns 2 and 6, the increase from 2% to 10% SER dramatically increased the CUER. Population size appears to have the least effect. For example, in columns 1 and 4, the CUER was the same using the attributes sampling table even though the population in column 1 was 10 times larger.

e. The CUER represents the results of the actual sample whereas the TER represents what the auditor will allow. They must be compared to determine whether or not the population is acceptable.

15-30 a. and b. The sample sizes and CUERs are shown in the following table:

	ACTUAL SAMPLE SIZE	INITIAL SAMPLE SIZE FROM TABLE 15-8	SER	CUER FROM TABLE 15-9	TER
1	100	127	2.0%	6.2%	6.0%
2	100	93	4.0	9.0	5.0
3	20	18	5.0	18.1	20.0
4	100	99	0.0	3.0	3.0
5	60	65	1.7	6.4	8.0
6	60	60	13.3	>20.0	15.0

a. The auditor selected a sample size smaller than that determined from the tables in populations 1 and 5. The effect of selecting a smaller sample size than the initial sample size required from the table is the increased likelihood of having the CUER exceed the TER. If a larger sample size is selected, the result may be a sample size larger than needed to satisfy TER. That results in excess audit cost. Ultimately, however, the comparison of CUER to TER determines whether the sample size was too large or too small.

b. The SER and CUER are shown in columns 4 and 5 in the preceding table.

c. The population results are unacceptable for populations 1, 2, and 6. In each of those cases, the CUER exceeds TER.

   The auditor's options are to change TER or ARACR, increase the sample size, or perform other substantive tests to determine whether there are actually material misstatements in the population. An increase in sample size may be worthwhile in population 1 because the CUER exceeds TER by only a small amount. Increasing sample size would not likely result in improved results for either population 2 or 6 because the CUER exceeds TER by a large amount.

d. Analysis of exceptions is necessary even when the population is acceptable because the auditor wants to determine the nature and cause of all exceptions. If, for example, the auditor determines that a misstatement was intentional, additional action would be required even if the CUER were less than TER.

15-30 (continued)

e.

TERM	NATURE OF TERM
1. Estimated population exception rate	Nonstatistical estimate made by auditor.
2. Tolerable exception rate	Audit decision.
3. Acceptable risk of assessing control risk too low	Audit decision.
4. Actual sample size	Audit decision (determined by other audit decisions).
5. Actual number of exceptions in the sample	Sample result.
6. Sample exception rate	Sample result.
7. Computed upper exception rate	Statistical conclusion about the population.

15-31 a. The actual allowance for sampling risk is shown in the following table:

	SER	CUER	ACTUAL ALLOWANCE FOR SAMPLING RISK (CUER-SER)
1	4.0%	10.3%	6.3%
2	4.0	7.9	4.9
3	4.0	12.1	8.1
4	3.0	7.6	4.6

   b. The CUER is higher for attribute 1 than attribute 2 because the sample size is smaller for attribute 1, resulting in a larger allowance for sampling risk.

   c. The CUER is higher for attribute 3 than attribute 1 because the auditor selected a lower ARACR. This resulted in a larger allowance for sampling risk to achieve the lower ARACR.

   d. If the auditor increases the sample size for attribute 4 by 50 items and finds no additional exceptions, the CUER is 5.1% (sample size of 150 and three exceptions). If the auditor finds one exception in the additional items, the CUER is 6.0% (sample size of 150, four

15-31 (continued)

exceptions). With a TER of 6%, the sample results will be acceptable if one or no exceptions are found in the additional 50 items. This would require a lower SER in the additional sample than the SER in the original sample of 3.0 percent. Whether a lower rate of exception is likely in the additional sample depends on the rate of exception the auditor expected in designing the sample, and whether the auditor believe the original sample to be representative.

15-32 a. The following shows which are exceptions and why:

INVOICE NUMBER	EXCEPTION?	TYPE OF EXCEPTION
5028	No	Error was detected and corrected by client.
6791	No	Sales invoice was voided.
6810	Yes	Proof of shipment not presented.
7364	No	Credit collection problem; should be noted for review of allowance for doubtful accounts.
7625	Yes	Duplicate sales invoice not properly filed.
8431	Yes	Invoices not recorded by proper date; represents potential cutoff problem.
8528	Yes	Customer orders not included in invoice package to verify compliance with the order.
8566	Yes	Error in pricing. No internal verification.
8780	Yes	Duplicate sales invoice not properly filed.
9169	Yes	Credit not authorized.
9974	Yes	Internal verification of price extensions and postings of sales invoices was not included.

b. It is inappropriate to set a single acceptable tolerable exception rate and estimated population exception rate for the combined exceptions because each attribute has a different significance to the auditor and should be considered separately in analyzing the results of the test.

c. The CUER assuming a 5% ARACR for each attribute and a sample size of 150 is as follows:

INVOICE NUMBER	DESCRIPTION OF ATTRIBUTE	NUMBER OF EXCEPTIONS	SER
6810	Shipping document not located	1	.67%
7625 8780 8528	Duplicate sales invoice/customer order not located	3	2.00%
8431	Invoice date improper	1	.67%
8566	Price extensions postings incorrect	1	.67%
8566 9974	Price extensions and postings not internally verified	2	1.33%
9169	Credit not authorized	1	.67%

d.

INVOICE NUMBER	TER-SER	SAMPLING ERROR SUFFICIENT?
6810	5.33%	Yes
7625 8780 8528	4.0%	Probably*
8431	5.33%	Yes
8566	5.33%	Yes
8566 9974	4.67%	Probably*
9169	5.33%	Yes

* Students' answers will most likely vary for this attribute.

15-32 (continued)

e. For each exception, the auditor should check with the controller to determine an explanation for the cause. In addition, the appropriate analysis for each type of exception is as follows:

INVOICE NUMBER	EXCEPTION ANALYSIS
6810	Confirm the account balances to the customers; examine the reduction in the perpetual inventory records.
7625	Trace the amount to the sales journal and accounts receivable master file; examine the shipping document and recompute the sale amount.
8431	Determine who recorded the invoice and check several others prepared by him or her to determine if the problem consistently occurs.
8528	Examine the accounts receivable master file for subsequent cash receipt; examine sales invoices for other invoices to the same customer to determine if customer orders were attached.
8566	Check the price on other invoices to the same customer. Check the price on other invoices that have the same product.
8780	See 7625
9169	Check credit history of customer and evaluate collectibility of the customer's account.
9974	Recheck actual price, extensions and postings; determine who the clerk was and check several other invoices for proper indication of performance.

15-33 a.

Attribute	Missing element
1	CUER is 9.2%
2	Initial sample size is 77
3	Tolerable exception rate is 7%
4	The actual number of exceptions in the sample was 1
5	ARACR is 5%
6	Sample size is 70

b. The sample results are unacceptable for Attributes 1 and 6 because CUER exceeds TER for those attributes.

15-33 (continued)

  c. The sample size for attribute 1 is smaller than the sample size for attribute 3 because the estimated population exception rate is 0% for attribute 1 but 1% for attribute 3. Because there is no expectation of errors in the population, the sample size is smaller for attribute 1.

  d. The CUER is smaller for attribute 2 relative to attribute 5 for two primary reasons. First, ARACR is higher in attribute 2 relative to attribute 5, which means the auditor has a greater willingness to accept the risk that the assessment of control risk is too low for attribute 2. Second, the difference between TER and EPER is slightly higher for attribute 2 relative to attribute 5.

■ **Case**

15-34 a. Audit sampling could be conveniently used for procedures 3 and 4 since each is to be performed on a sample of the population.

  b. The most appropriate sampling unit for conducting *most* of the audit sampling tests is the shipping document because most of the tests are related to procedure 4. Following the instructions of the audit program, however, the auditor would use sales journal entries as the sampling unit for step 3 and shipping document *numbers* for step 4. Using shipping document numbers, rather than the documents themselves, allows the auditor to test the numerical control over shipping documents, as well as to test for unrecorded sales. The selection of numbers will lead to a sample of actual shipping documents upon which tests will be performed.

  c. *Note: The sampling data sheet that follows assumes an attributes sampling approach.* The only difference between the sampling data sheet for attributes sampling and for nonstatistical sampling is the actual determination of sample size. For nonstatistical sampling, students' answers will vary, but will most likely be comparable to the sample sizes determined under attributes sampling.

15-34 (continued)

DESCRIPTION OF ATTRIBUTES	EPER	TER	ARACR	INITIAL SAMPLE SIZE*
A duplicate sales invoice exists for the shipping document selected.	1.0	5.0	10	77
Shipping document agrees with related duplicate sales invoice.	0.0	4.0	10	57
The duplicate sales invoice has attached a copy of the shipping document, shipping order, and customer order.	1.0	5.0	10	77
The shipping order has proper credit approval.	1.0	5.0	10	77
The duplicate sales invoice has internal verification of computations.	1.0	5.0	10	77
The duplicate sales invoice has the same price and quantity as approved price list and shipping document.	0.0	4.0	10	57
Customer name, amount and date agrees between duplicate sales invoice and sales journal and subsidiary ledger.	0.0	4.0	10	57

*   assumes the shipping document is the sampling unit.

■ **Integrated Case Application**

15-35   a. and d.

PINNACLE MANUFACTURING—PART VI

Client: Pinnacle Manufacturing

Audit Area: Tests of Controls and Substantive Test of Transactions—Acquisitions.

Define the Objective(s): Examine vendors' invoices, receiving reports, purchase orders, and other related documents to determine whether the system has functioned as intended and as described in the audit program.

Define the population precisely (including stratification, if any): Vouchers from 1/1/2011 to 10/31/2011. First voucher number – 6734. Last voucher number – 33722.

15-35 (continued)

Define the sampling unit, organization of population items, and random selection procedures: Voucher number, recorded sequentially in the acquisitions journal; random number function in electronic spreadsheet.

Description of Attributes	Planned Audit				Actual Results			
	EPER	TER	ARACR	Initial Sample Size	Sample Size	Number of Exceptions	SER	Calculated Sampling Error (TER-SER)
1. Evidence of internal verification of voucher package including propriety of purchase, dates, unit costs, prices, extensions, footings, account classification, recording in journal, and posting and summarization. (6a, b)	0	6%	10%	30	30	2	6.7%	-.7% (note SER exceeds TER)
2. Prices on vendors' invoices conform to approved price limits established by management. (6c)	0	5%	10%	40	40	0	0	5%
3. Price times quantity and other calculations on the vendor's invoice are correct. (6d)	1%	5%	10%	50	50	0	0	5%
4. Evidence of proper account classification on vendors' invoices. (6e)	2%	5%	10%	70	70	0	0	5%
5. Dates on entries in purchases journal agree with dates on receiving reports. (6f)	1%	5%	10%	50	50	2	4%	1%
6. Evidence of internal verification of each purchase voucher. (6g)	0	6%	10%	30	30	0	0%	6%

Results: Based on the results of the tests, all controls appear effective except for evidence of internal verification. Since there were also two errors on timing and an error in comparing the vendor's invoice amount to the acquisitions journal that is not included as an attribute, a larger than normal sample in year-end testing of accounts payable is appropriate.

Notes:
1. The planned audit variables are judgmental. The results of the prior year from part III were used to decide EPER. Initial sample size and CUER are judgments.
2. There was an error discovered where there was no attribute. This happens in practice too. The auditor should not ignore the exception even though it is an unplanned discovery.

b.

Client: Pinnacle Manufacturing

Audit Area: Tests of Controls and Substantive Test of Transactions—Cash Disbursements

Define the Objective(s): Examine cancelled checks and other related documents to determine whether the system has functioned as intended and as described in the audit program.

15-35 (continued)

Define the population precisely (including stratification, if any): Cancelled checks from 1/1/2011 to 10/31/2011. First check number – 12376. Last check number – 37318.

Define the sampling unit, organization of population items, and random selection procedures: Check number, recorded sequentially in the cash disbursements journal; random number function in electronic spreadsheet.

	Planned Audit				Actual Results			
Description of Attributes	**EPER**	**TER**	**ARACR**	**Initial Sample Size**	**Sample Size**	**Number of Exceptions**	**SER**	**Calculated Sampling Error (TER-SER)**
1. Payee, name, amount, and date on cancelled check agrees with related purchases journal and cash disbursements entry. (9a)	0	5%	10%	40				
2. Evidence of signature, proper endorsement and cancellation of each check. (9b)	0	5%	10%	40				
3. Date on cancelled check agrees with bank cancellation date. (9c)	2	5%	10%	70				
4. Cash discounts are correct. (9d)	0	5%	10%	40				

    c.   Population = voucher numbers 6734 to 33722

Sample size = 50

Random Selection:

If random selection is performed using Excel, the command to select numbers randomly from the population is:

=RANDBETWEEN(6734, 33722)

The command for selecting the random number can be entered directly onto the spreadsheet, or can be selected from the function menu (math & trig) functions under the "insert" menu. It may be necessary to add the analysis tool pack to access the RANDBETWEEN function. Once the formula is entered, it can be copied down to select additional random numbers. The random numbers will vary for each student, so they are not listed in this solution.

■ Internet Problem Solution: Applying Statistical Sampling

Internet Problem 15-1

   a.   The primary difference between nonstatistical and statistical sampling is that statistical sampling allows the auditor to quantitatively measure sampling risk using the laws of probability. In non-statistical sampling, the auditor is only able to qualitatively assess sampling risk using auditor judgment.

   b.   Auditors frequently justify the use of nonstatistical sampling by noting the additional costs associated with the use of statistical sampling. They argue that statistical sampling is more costly due to the cost of training auditors on the use of statistical sampling, costs of selecting the sample using random selection, and the cost of sampling evaluation that requires the quantification of sampling risks using formulas based on probability theory. The article highlights, however, that the ready availability of computers and off-the-shelf software with statistical sampling applications built in have virtually mitigated most of these concerns.

   c.   The primary advantage of statistical sampling is the ability to quantitatively measure sampling risk within a specific confidence interval. The ability to quantitatively measure sampling risk distinguishes statistical sampling from nonstatistical sampling, where the auditor is left to judgment as to the extent of sampling risk present.

   d.   In probability sampling, every item in the population under audit has a known chance of selection. The decision as to which items in the population to select is left to the laws of chance, not to auditor judgment.

   e.   The upper confidence limit is the projected misstatement plus the allowance for sampling risk. The auditor uses the upper confidence limit to evaluate whether the sample result is acceptable or not. If the upper confidence limit exceeds the maximum tolerable misstatement amount, the auditor decides that the misstatement in the population may exceed the tolerable amount. If the upper confidence limit is less than the maximum tolerable misstatement, the auditor decides that the potential misstatement in the population is acceptable (tolerable).

(**Note**: Internet problems address current issues using Internet sources. Because Internet sites are subject to change, Internet problems and solutions may change. Current information on Internet problems is available at www.pearsonhighered.com/arens.)

Chapter 16

Completing the Tests in the
Sales and Collection Cycle:
Accounts Receivable

■ Review Questions

16-1   Tests of details of balances are designed to determine the reasonableness of the balances in sales, accounts receivable, and other account balances that are affected by the sales and collection cycle. Such tests include confirmation of accounts receivable, and examining documents supporting the balance in these accounts.

Tests of controls and substantive tests of transactions for the sales and collection cycle are intended to determine the effectiveness of internal controls and to test the substance of the transactions that are produced by this cycle. Such tests consist of activities such as examining sales invoices in support of entries in the sales journal, reconciling cash receipts, or reviewing the approval of credit.

The results of the tests of controls and substantive tests of transactions affect the procedures, sample size, timing and items selected for the tests of details of balances (i.e., effective internal controls will result in reduced testing when compared to the tests of details required in the case of inadequate internal controls).

16-2   The negative form requests the recipient to respond only if he or she disagrees with the information stated on the request. Negative confirmation requests may be used to reduce audit risk to an acceptable level when:

1. The auditor has assessed the risk of material misstatement as low and has obtained sufficient appropriate evidence regarding the design and operating effectiveness of controls relevant to the assertion being tested by the confirmation procedure.
2. The population of items subject to negative confirmation procedures is made up of a large number of small, homogenous, account balances, transactions, or other items.
3. The auditor expects a low exception rate.
4. The auditor reasonably believes that recipients of negative confirmation requests will give the requests adequate consideration.

For example, in the examination of demand deposit accounts in a financial institution, it may be appropriate for an auditor to include negative confirmation requests with the customers' regular statements when the combined assessed level of inherent and control risk is low and the auditor has no reason to believe that the recipients will not consider the requests.

16-2 (continued)

The preceding requirement that negative confirmations are considered appropriate where the internal controls of the sales and collection cycle are effective is violated by Cynthia Roberts' approach. Not only is her approach questionable from the standpoint that nonresponses have not necessarily proved the existence of the receivable, but her confirmation at an interim date requires her to assume an assessed control risk less than maximum, but she has not tested the related internal controls to justify this assumption.

16-3 The following are analytical procedures for the sales and collection cycle, and potential misstatements uncovered by each test. Each ratio should be compared to previous years.

ANALYTICAL PROCEDURE	POTENTIAL MISSTATEMENT
1. Gross margin by product line	Sales cutoff errors or other misstatements involving sales; purchase cutoff errors or other misstatements involving inventory or purchases.
2. Sales returns and allowances as a percentage of gross sales by product line or segment	All returns were not recorded, or shipments to customers were not in accordance with specifications and were returned (this could result in significant operating problems).
3. Trade discounts taken as a percentage of net sales	Discounts that were taken by customers and allowed by the company were not recorded.
4. Bad debts as a percentage of gross sales	Misstatement in determining the allowance for uncollectible accounts.
5. Days sales in receivables outstanding	A problem with collections, an understatement of bad debts and allowance for uncollectible accounts.
6. Aging categories as a percentage of accounts receivables	Collection problems and understatement of allowance for uncollectible accounts.
7. Allowance for uncollectible accounts as a percentage of accounts receivable	Misstatement in determining the allowance for uncollectible accounts.
8. Comparison of the balances in individual customers' accounts over a stated amount with their balances in the previous year	A problem with collections and therefore a misstatement of the allowance for uncollectible accounts, or cutoff errors or other misstatements in customer accounts.

16-4   The following are balance-related audit objectives and related audit procedures for the audit of accounts receivable.

BALANCE-RELATED AUDIT OBJECTIVE	AUDIT PROCEDURE
Accounts receivable in the aged trial balance agree with related master file amounts; the total is correctly added and agrees with the general ledger (detail tie-in).	■ Trace twenty accounts from the trial balance to the related accounts in the master file. ■ Foot two pages of the trial balance, total all pages, and trace totals to the general ledger.
The accounts receivable in the aged trial balance exist (existence).	Confirm accounts receivable using positive confirmations. Confirm all amounts over $15,000 and a nonstatistical sample of the remainder.
Existing accounts receivable are included in the aged trial balance (completeness).	Trace ten accounts from the accounts receivable master file to the aged trial balance.
Accounts receivable in the trial balance are accurately recorded (accuracy).	Confirm accounts receivable using positive confirmations. Confirm all amounts over $15,000 and a nonstatistical sample of the remainder.
Accounts receivable in the aged trial balance are properly classified (classification).	Review the receivables listed on the aged trial balance for notes and related party receivables.
Transactions in the sales and collection cycle are recorded in the proper period (cutoff).	Select the last 10 sales transactions from the current year's sales journal and the first 10 from the subsequent year's and trace each one to the related shipping documents, checking for the date of actual shipment and the correct recording.
Accounts receivable in the trial balance are owned (rights).	Review the minutes of the board of directors for any indication of pledged or factored accounts receivable.
Accounts receivable in the trial balance are stated at realizable value (realizable value).	Discuss with the credit manager the likelihood of collecting older accounts. Examine subsequent cash receipts and the credit file on older accounts to evaluate whether receivables are collectible.

16-5   The most important objectives satisfied by confirmations are existence, rights, and accuracy. In extreme cases, confirmations are also useful tests for cutoff. Sometimes confirmations may also help the auditor satisfy the completeness objective.

16-6   A necessary audit procedure is to test the information on the client's trial balance for detail tie-in. The footing in the total column and the columns depicting the aging must be checked and the total on the trial balance reconciled to the general ledger to determine that all accounts are included in the listing.

The master file records are the tie-in between tests of controls, substantive tests of transactions, and tests of details of balances. The aged trial balance is the listing of the master file. Since the auditor uses the aged trial balance in tests of details, he or she must be sure that information is the same as that tested in tests of controls and substantive tests of transactions. In addition to tests of computerized controls over the master file and aged trial balance, the auditor usually traces a sample of individual balances to the master file to determine that the trial balance has been properly summarized from the master file. In most cases, it will not be necessary to trace each amount to the master file unless a significant number of misstatements is noted and it is determined that reliance cannot be place upon the trial balance with less than 100% testing.

16-7   The purpose of the accuracy tests of gross accounts receivable is to determine the correctness of the total amounts receivable from customers. These tests normally consist of confirmation of accounts receivable or examination of shipping documents in support of the shipment of goods to customers.

The purpose of the test of the realizable value of receivables is to estimate the amount of the accounts receivable balance that will not be collected. To estimate this amount, the auditor normally reviews the aging of the accounts receivable, analyzes subsequent cash payments by customers, discusses the collectibility of individual accounts with client personnel, and examines correspondence and financial statements of significant customers.

16-8   In most audits it is more important to carefully test the cutoff for sales than for cash receipts because sales cutoff misstatements are more likely to affect net earnings than are cash receipt cutoff misstatements. Cash receipt cutoff misstatements generally lead to a misclassification of accounts receivable and cash and, therefore, do not affect income.

To perform a cutoff test for sales, the auditor should obtain the number of the last shipping document issued before year-end and examine shipping documents representing shipments before and after year-end and the related sales invoices to determine that the shipments were recorded as sales in the appropriate period.

The propriety of the cash receipts cutoff is determined through tests of the year-end bank reconciliation. Deposits in transit at year-end should be traced to the subsequent bank statement. Any delays in crediting deposits by the bank should be investigated to determine whether the cash receipts books were held open.

16-9   The value of accounts receivable confirmation as evidence can be visualized more clearly by relating it to tests of controls and substantive tests of transactions. If the beginning balance in accounts receivable can be assumed to be correct and careful tests of the controls have been performed, the auditor should be in an excellent position to evaluate the fairness of the ending balance in accounts receivable.

16-9 (continued)

Confirmations are typically more effective than tests of controls and substantive tests of transactions for discovering certain types of misstatements. These include invalid accounts, disputed amounts, and uncollectible accounts resulting from the inability to locate the customer. Although confirmations cannot guarantee the discovery of any of these types of misstatements, they are more reliable than tests of controls and substantive tests of transactions, because tests of controls and substantive tests of transactions rely upon internally created documents, whereas confirmations are obtained from independent sources.

There are two instances in which confirmations are less likely to uncover omitted transactions and amounts than tests of controls and substantive tests of transactions. First, in order to send a confirmation, it is necessary to have a list of accounts receivable from which to select. Naturally, an omitted account will not be included in the population from which the auditor is selecting the sample. Second, if an account with an omitted transaction is confirmed, customers are less likely to respond to the confirmation, or, alternatively, will state that it is correct. Tracing shipping documents or sales orders to the related duplicate sales invoice and the accounts receivable master file is an effective method of discovering omitted transactions.

Clerical errors in billing customers and recording the amounts in the accounts can be effectively discovered by confirmation, tests of controls, or substantive tests of transactions. Confirmations are typically more effective in uncovering overstatement of accounts receivable than understatements, whereas tests of controls and substantive tests of transactions are effective for discovering both types. The important concept in this discussion is the existence of both a complementary and a substitute relationship between tests of controls and substantive tests of transactions, and confirmations. They are complementary in that both types of evidence, when combined, provide a higher level of overall assurance of the fair presentation of sales, sales returns and allowances, and accounts receivable than can result from either type considered separately. The strengths of tests of controls and substantive tests of transactions combined with the strengths of confirmation result in a highly useful combination. The two types of evidence are substitutes in the sense that the auditor can obtain a given level of assurance by decreasing the tests of controls and substantive tests of transactions if there is an offsetting increase in the confirmation of accounts receivable. The extent to which the auditor should rely upon the tests of controls and substantive tests of transactions is dependent upon his or her evaluation of the effectiveness of internal controls. If the auditor has carefully evaluated internal control, tested internal controls for effectiveness, and concluded that the internal controls are likely to provide correct results, it is appropriate to reduce the confirmation of accounts receivable. On the other hand, it would be inappropriate to bypass confirmation altogether.

In the situation being addressed in this problem, the auditor will want to put more emphasis on tests of controls and substantive tests of transactions than confirmations because of the nature of the customers and the effectiveness of internal control. Nevertheless, both types of tests should be used.

16-10 There are two common types of confirmations used for confirming accounts receivable: "positive" confirmations and "negative" confirmations. A positive confirmation is a letter, addressed to the debtor, requesting that the recipient indicate directly on the letter whether the stated account balance is correct or incorrect and, if incorrect, by what amount. A negative confirmation is also a letter, addressed to the debtor, but it requests a response only if the recipient disagrees with the amount of the stated account balance. A positive confirmation is more reliable evidence because the auditor can perform follow-up procedures if a response is not received from the debtor. With a negative confirmation, failure to reply must be regarded as a correct response, even though the debtor may have ignored the confirmation request.

Offsetting the reliability disadvantage, negative confirmations are less expensive to send than positive confirmations, and thus more of them can be distributed for the same total cost. The determination of which type of confirmation to be sent is an auditor's decision, and it should be based on the facts in the audit. Auditing standards indicate that it is acceptable to use negative confirmations only when all of the following circumstances are present:

1. The auditor has assessed the risk of material misstatement as low and has obtained sufficient appropriate evidence regarding the design and operating effectiveness of controls relevant to the assertion being tested by the confirmation procedure.
2. The population of items subject to negative confirmation procedures is made up of a large number of small, homogenous, account balances, transactions, or other items.
3. The auditor expects a low exception rate.
4. The auditor reasonably believes that recipients of negative confirmation requests will give the requests adequate consideration.

Typically, when negative confirmations are used, the auditor is using a reduced control risk assessment in the audit of accounts receivable. It is also common to use negative confirmations for audits of hospitals, retail stores, and other industries where the receivables are due from the general public. In these cases, far more assurance is obtained from tests of controls and substantive tests of transactions than from confirmations.

It is also common to use a combination of negative and positive confirmations by sending the positives to accounts with large balances and negatives to those with small balances. This allows the auditor to focus the confirmation testing on large account balances, while still testing a representative sample from the rest of the population at minimal cost.

16-11 It is acceptable to confirm accounts receivable prior to the balance sheet date if the internal controls are adequate and can provide reasonable assurance that sales, cash receipts, and other credits are properly recorded between the date of the confirmation and the end of the accounting period.

16-11 (continued)

Other factors the auditor is likely to consider in making the decision are the materiality of accounts receivable and the auditor's exposure to lawsuits because of the possibility of client bankruptcy and similar risks. If the decision is made to confirm accounts receivable prior to year-end, it is necessary to test the transactions occurring between the confirmation date and the balance sheet date by examining internal documents and performing analytical procedures at year-end.

16-12 The most important factors affecting the sample size in confirmations of accounts receivable are:

- Tolerable misstatement
- Inherent risk (relative size of total accounts receivable, number of accounts, prior year results, and expected misstatements)
- Control risk
- Achieved detection risk from other substantive tests (extent and results of substantive tests of transactions, analytical procedures, and other tests of details)
- Type of confirmation (negatives normally require a larger sample size)

16-13 Auditing standards indicate an oral response, including a response received over the telephone, is not considered a confirmation, but constitutes other evidence in support of a receivable balance. Email responses are considered to be valid confirmation responses if the auditor can be confident in the identity of the confirmation respondent. Auditors can verify mailing addresses to phone directories, or to information in the client's accounts receivable master file if the client has adequate controls over the master file. Email responses can be verified by third party intermediaries, or by verifying the domain of the email address.

16-14 In most confirmations of accounts receivable, some type of stratification is desirable. A typical approach to stratification is to consider both the size of the outstanding balance and the length of time an account has been outstanding as a basis for selecting the balances for confirmation, since these are the accounts that are more likely to include a significant misstatement. It is also important to sample some items from every material stratum of the population. Using this approach, the auditor will pay careful attention to the accounts in which misstatements are most likely to occur and will follow the guidelines set forth in Chapter 15 regarding the need to obtain a representative sample of the population.

16-15 Alternative procedures are procedures performed on a positive confirmation not returned by the debtor using documentation evidence to determine whether the recorded receivable exists and is collectible. It is common to send second requests for confirmations and sometimes even third requests.

16-15 (continued)

Even with these efforts, some customers do not return the confirmations, so it is necessary to follow up with alternative procedures. The objective of the alternative procedures is to determine, by a means other than confirmation, whether the unconfirmed account existed and was properly stated at the confirmation date. For any confirmation not returned, the following documentation can be examined to verify the existence and accuracy of amounts making up the ending balance in accounts receivable:

1. *Subsequent cash receipts* Evidence of the receipt of cash subsequent to the confirmation date includes examining remittance advice, entries in the cash receipts records, or perhaps even subsequent credits in the accounts receivable master file. The examination of evidence of subsequent cash receipts is usually the most useful alternative procedure because it is reasonable to assume that a customer would not make a payment unless it was a valid receivable. On the other hand, the fact of payment does not establish whether there was an obligation on the date of the confirmation. In addition, care should be used to match each unpaid sales transaction with evidence of its payment as a test for disputes or disagreements over individual outstanding invoices.

2. *Duplicate sales invoices* These are useful to verify the actual issuance of a sales invoice and the actual date of the billing

3. *Shipping documents* These are important to establish whether the shipment was actually made and as a test of cutoff.

4. *Correspondence with the client* Usually it is unnecessary to review correspondence as a part of alternative procedures, but it can be used to disclose disputed and questionable receivables not uncovered by other means.

The extent and nature of the alternative procedures depends primarily upon the materiality of the unconfirmed accounts, the nature and extent of the misstatements discovered in the confirmed responses, the subsequent cash receipts of the unconfirmed accounts, and the auditor's evaluation of the effectiveness of internal controls. It is normally desirable to account for all unconfirmed balances with alternative procedures, even if the amounts are small, as a means of properly generalizing from the sample to the population.

16-16 Confirmation of accounts receivable is normally performed on only a sample of the total population. The purpose of the confirmation is to obtain outside verification of the balance of the account and to obtain an indication of the rate of occurrence of misstatements in the accounts. Most misstatements indicated by differences on the confirmation replies will not be material; however, differences must be analyzed individually and in total to determine their effect on the total accounts receivable balance. Though the individual differences may not be material, they may indicate a material problem when extended to the entire population, and with regard to the internal controls over the accounts receivable.

16-17   Three differences that may be observed in the confirmation of accounts receivable that do not constitute misstatements, and an audit procedure that would verify each difference are as follows:

1.   Payment has been made by the customer, but not received by the client at the confirmation date. The subsequent payment should be examined as to the date deposited.
2.   Merchandise shipped by the client has not been received by the customer at the confirmation date. The shipping documents should be examined to verify that the goods were shipped prior to confirmation date.
3.   Merchandise has been returned, but has not been received by the client at the confirmation date. Receiving documents and the credit memo should be examined.

16-18   With regard to the sales and collection cycle, the auditor uses flowcharts, assessing control risk for the accounting cycle, tests of controls, and tests of details of balances in the determination of the likelihood of a material misstatement in the accounts affected by the sales and collection cycle. The flowcharts provide a means for the auditor to document and analyze the accounting systems as represented by the client. The auditor would then make an initial assessment of control risk based on the controls which are present in the accounting cycle as documented in the flowcharts, and would plan the tests of controls based upon the selection of the significant controls. The auditor would then perform the tests of the significant controls to determine the effectiveness of the controls and to plan the substantive tests that are necessary based upon the revised assessment of control risk for this accounting cycle. Finally, after considering the results of tests of controls and substantive tests of transactions, the auditor would perform tests of details of balances to determine whether material misstatements exist in the account balances.

16-19   Accounting standards require that sales returns and allowances be matched with the related sales if the amounts are material. However, most companies record sales returns and allowances in the period in which they occur, under the assumption of approximately equal, offsetting amounts at the beginning and end of each accounting period. This approach is acceptable, if the amounts are not significant.

■ **Multiple Choice Questions From CPA Examinations**

16-20   a.   (4)   b.   (4)   c.   (2)

16-21   a.   (4)   b.   (2)   c.   (2)

16-22   a.   (3)   b.   (1)   c.   (3)

▪ Discussion Questions and Problems

16-23
1. Detail tie-in
2. Detail tie-in
3.   a.   Existence
     b.   Accuracy
     c.   Realizable value (if cash receipts relate to older accounts)
4.   a.   Existence
     b.   Accuracy
5.   a.   Existence
     b.   Accuracy
     c.   Realizable value (if cash receipts relate to older accounts)
6. Cutoff
7. Rights
8. Classification

16-24

a. BALANCE-RELATED AUDIT OBJECTIVE	b. PREVENTIVE INTERNAL CONTROL	c. TESTS OF DETAILS OF BALANCES AUDIT PROCEDURES
1. Accounts receivable in the aged trial balance agree with related master file amounts, and the total is correctly added and agrees with the general ledger (detail tie-in).	The client should foot the trial balance and reconcile the total to the balance in the general ledger.	The auditor should foot the trial balance of accounts receivable and reconcile it to the balance per the general ledger.
2. Existing accounts receivable are included in the aged trial balance (com-pleteness).	The accounts receivable master file should be reconciled to the control account periodically by an independent person.	Foot the aged trial balance and compare the total to the general ledger. Trace a sample of accounts from the master file to the aged trial balance to determine if all are included.

16-24 (continued)

a. BALANCE-RELATED AUDIT OBJECTIVE	b. PREVENTIVE INTERNAL CONTROL	c. TESTS OF DETAILS OF BALANCES AUDIT PROCEDURES
3. Accounts receivable exist (existence).	The accounts receivable master file should be reconciled to the control account periodically by an independent person.	Foot the aged trial balance and compare the total to the general ledger. Trace from the aged trial balance to the master file, looking for duplicates.
4. Transactions are recorded in the proper period (cutoff).	The client should establish cutoff procedures so that only shipments made before year-end are recorded as current period sales.	Examine shipping documents for sales recorded immediately before and after year-end to test whether sales are recorded in the proper period.
5. Accounts receivable are stated at realizable value (realizable value)	The client should perform an analysis of the collectibility of accounts receivable at the end of the year and should communicate with its customers to determine the likelihood of the collectibility of individual accounts.	The auditor should keep informed of current economic conditions and consider their effect on collectibility of accounts receivable for the client. The auditor may compare cash receipts after year-end to the cash receipts of the similar period of the previous year and consider any changes as to their effect on the collectibility of the accounts receivable.
6. Accounts receivable are stated at the correct amounts (accuracy).	The client should record claims for defective merchandise as soon as possible after the claim is received to keep accounts receivable balances as accurate as possible.	The auditor should note any replies to the confirmation of accounts receivable which indicate disputes between a customer and client. The auditor should review the client's correspondence files from customers.

a. BALANCE-RELATED AUDIT OBJECTIVE	b. PREVENTIVE INTERNAL CONTROL	c. TESTS OF DETAILS OF BALANCES AUDIT PROCEDURES
7. The company has rights to accounts receivable (rights and obligations) (also presentation and disclosure).	The controller should maintain a schedule containing all required disclosure information, including pledging or other restrictions on accounts receivable.	The auditor's standard bank confirmation should contain an inquiry as to assets pledged for loans from that institution. When loan confirmations are sent by the auditor, they should contain an inquiry as to any assets pledged for the indebtedness.
8. Transactions are recorded in the proper period (cutoff).	The client should follow a policy of holding open the books to record any returns in the subsequent period which apply to goods shipped and sales recorded in the current period.	The auditor should review returns recorded in the subsequent period to determine if they apply to goods shipped and sales recorded prior to year-end. The auditor should perform an analytical test to determine whether or not returns in the first month of the next year are similar in magnitude to those experienced in the same period of previous years.
9. Accounts receivable are properly classified (classification).	The client should maintain separate accounts for the recording of receivables due from affiliated companies.	The auditor should review the trial balance of accounts receivable to determine whether or not accounts from affiliated companies are included in the customer accounts. The auditor should be aware of affiliated companies and the transactions between them and the client, and should inquire and follow up to determine that accounts receivable from affiliates are not included in the accounts receivable from customers.

16-25

a. TYPE OF EVIDENCE	b. TYPE OF TEST	c. and d. OBJECTIVE(S)
1. Reperformance	(4) Test of details of balances	Detail tie-in
2. Documentation	(1) Test of control	Completeness
3. Documentation	(1) Test of control	Occurrence
4. Documentation	(4) Test of details of balances	Cutoff
5. Inquiry	(4) Test of details of balances	Cutoff
6. Observation	(1) Test of control	Posting and summarization
7. Documentation	(2) Substantive test of transactions	Timing
8. Analytical procedure	(3) Analytical procedure	N/A

16-26

PROCEDURE	a. TYPE OF TEST	b. BALANCE-RELATED AUDIT OBJECTIVE
1	Test of details	Existence and accuracy
2	Test of details	Cutoff
3	S T of T	Cutoff
4	Test of details	Accuracy and existence (may also include realizable value if cash receipts examined are for older accounts)
5	S T of T	Classification
6	S T of T	Rights
7	Test of details	Completeness
8	Test of control	Existence
9	Test of control	Accuracy
10	S T of T	Completeness
11	Test of details	Detail tie-in
12	S T of T	Detail tie-in
13	Test of details	Classification

16-27 a. A shipment should be recorded as a sale on the date of shipment or the passing of title, whichever occurs first. Ordinarily, a shipment is considered a sale when it is shipped, picked up, or delivered by a common carrier.

b. The sales invoice number can be ignored, except to determine the shipping document number.

INVOICE NO.	SHIPPING DOCUMENT NO.	MISSTATEMENT IN SALES CUTOFF	OVERSTATEMENT OR UNDERSTATEMENT OF AUG. 31 SALES
August sales			
5431	2164	none	
5434	2169	4,214.30	overstatement
5432	2165	none	
5433	2168	1,620.22	overstatement
5435	2166	none	
		5,834.52	
September sales			
5437	2163	2,541.31	understatement
5436	2167	106.39	understatement
5438	2170	none	
5440	2171	none	
5439	2172	none	
		2,647.70	
Net overstatement		3,186.82	
Adjusting entry			
Sales		3,186.82	
Accounts receivable			3,186.82

c. After making the type of cutoff adjustments shown in part b, current year sales would be overstated by:

Amount of sale

2168	2,541.31
2169	106.39
2170	852.06
2171	1,250.50
2172	646.58
	5,396.84

The best way to discover the misstatement is to be on hand on the balance sheet date and record in the audit working papers the last shipping document issued in the current period. Later, the auditors can examine shipping documents before and after the balance sheet date to determine if they were correctly dated.

An alternative, if there are perpetual records, is to follow up differences between physical inventory counts and perpetual record balances to determine if the cause was end of the period cutoff misstatements. Assume, for example, that there were 626 units of part X263 on hand August 31, but the perpetual records showed a total of 526, and a shipment of 100 units included on the perpetual August 31. This is a likely indication of a September shipment that had been dated August 31.

d. The following procedures are usually desirable to test for sales cutoff.

1. Be present during the physical count on the last day of the accounting period to determine the shipping document number for the last shipment made in the current year. Record that number in the working papers.

2. During year-end field work, select a sample of shipping documents preceding and succeeding those selected in procedure 1. Shipping documents with the same or with a smaller number than the one determined in procedure 1 should be included in current sales. Those with document numbers larger than that number should have been excluded from current sales.

3. During year-end field work, select a sample of sales from the sales journal recorded in the last few days of the current period, and a sample of those recorded for the first few days in the subsequent period. Trace sales recorded in the current period to related shipping documents to make sure that each one has a number equal to or smaller than the one in procedure 1. Similarly, trace sales recorded in the subsequent period to make sure each sale has a related shipping document number greater than the one in procedure 1.

16-27 (continued)

e. The following are effective controls and related tests of controls to help prevent cutoff misstatements.

	CONTROL	TEST OF CONTROL
(1)	Policy requiring the use of prenumbered shipping documents.	Examine several documents for prenumbering.
(2)	Policy requiring the issuance of shipping documents sequentially.	Observe issuance of documents, examine document numbers and inquiry.
(3)	Policy requiring recording sales invoices in the same sequence as shipping documents are issued.	Observe recording of documents, examine document numbers and inquiry.
(4)	Policy requiring dating of shipping documents, immediate recording of sales, and dating sales on the same date as the shipment.	Observe dating of shipping documents and sales invoices, and timing of recording.
(5)	Use of perpetual inventory records and reconciliation of differences between physical and perpetual records.	Examine worksheets reconciling physical counts and perpetual records.

16-28 a. The two types of confirmations used for confirming accounts receivable are "positive" and "negative" confirmations. A positive confirmation is a letter, addressed to the debtor, requesting that the recipient indicate directly on the letter whether the stated account balance is correct or incorrect and, if incorrect, by what amount. A negative confirmation requests a response from the debtor only when the debtor disagrees with the stated amount.

When deciding which type of confirmation to use, the auditor should consider the assessed control risk in the sales and collection cycle, the make-up of the population, cost/benefit relationship, and any information about the existence of the accounts. Positive confirmations are more reliable but more expensive than negative confirmations. Positive confirmations should be used when the population is comprised of a small number of large accounts, and when there are suspected conditions of dispute or inaccuracy. When negative confirmations are used, the auditor has normally assessed control risk below maximum and tested the internal controls for effectiveness. Negative confirmations are often used when accounts receivable are comprised of a large number of small accounts receivable from the general public.

16-28 (continued)

b.   When evaluating the collectibility of accounts receivable, the auditor may review the aging of accounts receivable, analyze subsequent cash receipts from customers, discuss the collectibility of individual accounts with client personnel, and examine correspondence and financial statements of significant customers. Changes in the aging of receivables should be analyzed in view of any changes in the client's credit policy and in the current economic conditions.

c.   When customers fail to respond to positive confirmation requests, the CPA may not assume with confidence that these customers checked the request, found no disagreement, and therefore did not reply. Some busy customers will not take the time to check confirmation requests and will not respond, hence obvious exceptions may exist without being reported to the CPA. In the case of fraud or embezzlement, the perpetrators could perhaps prevent exceptions from being reported and prevent letters addressed to nonexistent customers from being returned from the post office as undeliverable. Confirmations returned as undeliverable by the post office will require appropriate action to obtain better addresses.

Follow-up is necessary when customers do not reply because the CPA has selected the positive confirmation route for certain receivables, and the most logical step to follow first is to mail second requests.

d.   When no response is received to the second request for positive confirmation, the auditor should use alternative procedures. These normally include examination of the customer's remittance advice and related cash receipt. This is often a simple and effective check where cash receipts were received subsequent to the balance sheet date. Correspondence in the client's files will also sometimes offer satisfactory evidence. The auditor should also examine shipping documents, sales invoices, contracts, or other documents to substantiate that the charges were proper.

In unusual cases, the CPA should mail a third request and possibly make telephone calls in an effort to get a reply directly from the customer. The CPA may find it necessary, where significant amounts are involved and circumstances are not clear, to investigate the existence and/or financial status of a customer.

16-29   a.   Tests of controls and substantive tests of transactions related to the allowance for doubtful accounts include the following:

1.   Test of controls for customer authorization and credit approval.
2.   Substantive tests of transactions for posting and summarization and aging of accounts receivable.
3.   Substantive tests of transactions for bad debt charge-offs.
4.   Tests of controls over follow-up on past due accounts.

   b.   An analysis of the allowance for doubtful accounts as a percentage of accounts receivable and the percentage of receivables in each aging category follows.

	12/31/2011	12/31/2010
Allowance as a % of accounts receivable	6.25%	7.27%
Charge-offs as a % of sales	0.94%	0.99%
Percentage of receivables in each aging category		
0-30 days	62.28%	67.42%
30-60 days	17.65%	15.62%
60-90 days	11.93%	10.28%
Over 90 days	8.14%	6.68%
Total	100.00%	100.00%

Despite the increased in the allowance account from $75,000 in 2010 to $90,000 in 2011, the analysis suggests the account is understated. Whether the allowance is misstated by more than $15,000 is a matter of judgment. Although the allowance increased from $75,000 to $90,000 it decreased as a percentage of accounts receivable from 7.27% in 2010 to 6.25% in 2011. An increase in the allowance of almost $15,000 would be necessary maintain the allowance at the same percentage of accounts receivable as the prior year.

In addition, current accounts receivable decreased from 67.42% to 62.28% of accounts receivable. The amount of past due receivables increased from $335,892 to $543,346. The allowance is 16.56% of past due receivables for 2011 and 22.33% for 2010. To maintain the allowance as the same percentage of past due receivables would require an increase in the allowance of more than $30,000.

16-30 a. Yes, it is acceptable for the controller to review the list of accounts the auditor intends to confirm. The confirmations will be sent to the company's customers, and the auditor must be sensitive to the client's concern with the treatment of their customers. At the same time, if the client refuses permission to confirm receivables, the auditor must consider the effect on the audit opinion. If the restriction is material, a qualified or disclaimer of opinion may be needed.

b. The auditor should be willing to perform special procedures that the client requests if the client is in agreement that these procedures may not necessarily be considered within the scope of the auditor's engagement. In the case of the 20 additional confirmations which the controller requested that the auditor send, the auditor should be willing to send the confirmations; however, these confirmations should not be considered in the evaluation of the results of the accounts receivable confirmations sent by the auditor.

c. If the auditor complies with the controller's request to eliminate six of the accounts from the confirmation tests, the auditor must perform alternative procedures on the six accounts. These procedures would normally be more extensive than the alternative procedures performed for nonresponses. The auditor should evaluate whether not confirming the receivables is significant to the scope of the audit. If the auditor believes that the impact of not confirming these accounts is material, he or she must qualify the scope and opinion paragraphs of the auditor's report to indicate the restriction of scope imposed by the client. If the auditor believes that the impact of omitting the six accounts from testing is highly material, a disclaimer of opinion is appropriate.

16-31 a. Confirmation responses that represent timing differences are due to such items as payments and shipments in transit. Responses that represent likely timing differences are:

#2 – represents a likely payment in transit
#5 – represents a likely shipment in transit

Item #3 refers to a payment after-year end. This is not a timing difference, but an apparent misunderstanding by the customer as to the required response.

#4 could represent a payment in transit, and #10 could represent a credit in transit. However, this is unlikely given the date of the transactions.

16-31 (continued)

b.   It is difficult to determine whether a confirmation difference is a misstatement without further investigation.

#6 appears to represent a misstatement as the client does not appear to have properly accounted for the advance payment.

For response #8, the customer is contesting the charge. The auditor will need to investigate whether the customer's balance is likely to be adjusted.

#9 indicates that goods were shipped on consignment, and appears to represent a misstatement.

c.   For all of the exceptions, the auditor is concerned about four principal things:

(1)   Whether there is a client error. Many times the confirmation response differences are due to timing differences for deposits in the mail and inventory in transit to the customer. Sometimes customers misunderstand the confirmation or the information requested. The auditor must distinguish between those and client errors.

(2)   The amount of the client error if any.

(3)   The cause of the exception. It could be intentional, a misunderstanding of the proper way to record a transaction, or a breakdown of internal control.

(4)   Potential misstatements in the sample not tested. The auditor must estimate the misstatement in the untested population, based on the results of the tests of the sample.

Suggested steps to clear each of the comments satisfactorily are:

1.   (a)   Examine supporting documents, including the sales invoices and applicable sales and shipping orders, for propriety and accuracy of the sales.

(b)   Review the cash receipts books for the period after December 31, 2010, and note any cash receipts from the PDQ Company. The degree of internal control over cash receipts should be an important consideration in determining the reliance that can be placed on the cash receipts entries. In addition, because there is no assurance that cash receipts after December 31 represent the payment of invoices supporting the December 31 trial balance, consideration should be given to requesting a confirmation from the PDQ Company of the invoices paid by their checks.

2. This is an apparent timing difference. The auditor should examine the date of receipt of payment on the client's book to see if the time was in fact a payment in transit at December 31.

3. This is a confirmation of the balance with an additional comment about a subsequent payment. Since the customer has given us the data, it is preferable to check to see that the information agrees with the company's records.

4. (a) The cause should be investigated thoroughly. If the cash receipt was posted to the wrong account, it may indicate merely a clerical error. On the other hand, posting to the wrong account may indicate lapping.

    (b) Such a comment may also indicate a delay in posting and depositing of receipts. If this is the case, the company should be informed immediately so that it can take corrective steps.

5. This appears to represent a shipment in transit. The auditor should evaluate the shipping document and evaluate whether in the circumstances it is reasonable that the customer received the goods on January 5th.

6. (a) Determine if such advance payment has been received and that it has been properly recorded. A review should be made of other advance payments to ascertain that charges against such advances have been properly handled.

    (b) If the advance payment was to cover these invoices, the auditor should propose a reclassification of the $1,350, debiting the advance payment account and crediting accounts receivable–trade.

7. (a) The auditor should be alert to the possibility of a fictitious sale or receivable. The auditor should verify the address of the company to determine if the confirmation was sent to the correct address. It is possible the company has moved, or is no longer in business. If the address used was incorrect, a revised confirmation should be sent.

    (b) Examine the shipping order for indications that the goods were shipped and, if available, carrier's invoice and/or bill of lading for receipt of the goods.

8. This should be discussed with the appropriate officials and correspondence with the customer should be reviewed to allow determination whether an adjustment should be made in the amount receivable or if an allowance for uncollectible accounts should be set up.

9. As title on any goods shipped on consignment does not pass until those goods are sold, the sales entry should be reversed, the inventory reduction reversed, and cost of sales credited if it is actually a consignment sale. Other so-called sales should be reviewed and

16-31 (continued)

company officials queried to determine if other sales actually represent consignment shipments; if so, a similar adjustment should be made for all consignment shipments.

10. This may indicate a misposting of the credit or a delay in posting the credit. Comments under 4 above would also apply to credits.

16-32

CHANGE IN CIRCUMSTANCE	LIKELY TEST OF DETAILS OF BALANCES RESPONSE
1. Analytical procedures indicated a significant slowing in accounts receivable turnover.	d. Expand the review of cash receipts after year-end to evaluate the collectibility of accounts receivable.
2. The client entered into sales contracts with new customers that differ from the client's standard sales contracts.	b. Send positive confirmations that include requests for information on side agreements and special terms.
3. The client had a significant increase in sales near year-end.	e. Increase the sample size for sales cutoff testing for sales recorded before year-end.
4. Accounts receivable confirmations were ineffective due to a very low response rate in the prior year audit.	i. Perform alternative procedures to test the existence and accuracy of accounts receivable instead of sending positive confirmations.
5. The client began experiencing an increase in returns due to product changes that resulted in increased defects.	a. Expand testing of sales returns after year-end and compare the level of returns with the prior year.
6. You found several pricing errors in your substantive tests of transactions for sales.	g. Increase the sample size for positive confirmations of accounts receivable.
7. In performing substantive test of transactions for cash receipts, you found that receipts were promptly recorded in customer accounts, but there were delays in depositing the receipts at the bank.	h. While at the client's premises at year-end, obtain information on the last few cash receipt at year-end for cash receipts cutoff testing.
8. The client entered into a new loan agreement with the bank. Accounts receivable are pledged as collateral for the loan.	f. Send a confirmation to the bank confirming amounts pledged as collateral under loan agreements.
9. The client did not reconcile the accounts receivable subledger with the accounts receivable balance in the general ledger on a regular basis.	c. Increase the number of accounts traced from the accounts receivable trial balance to the accounts receivable subledger.

16-33 a.   If called upon to evaluate the adequacy of the sample size, the type of confirmation used, and the percentage of accounts confirmed, the following additional information would be required:

- The number of accounts that had positive balances at 12/31/11
- The materiality of total accounts receivable
- The distribution and size of the accounts receivable
- The assessment of control risk based on the understanding obtained of internal control and tests of controls
- The results of the confirmation tests in previous years
- The risk of exposure to bankruptcy and similar risks (audit risk)
- Expected misstatements

b.   If the amounts are material, it is necessary to perform follow-up procedures for positive confirmations not returned by the debtor. It is common to send second requests for confirmations and sometimes even third requests. Even with these efforts, some customers do not return the confirmation, so it is necessary to follow up on all nonresponses with a method referred to as "alternative procedures."

c.   The alternative procedures used for verifying the two nonresponses do not appear to be adequate. In scheduling the subsequent cash receipts, for confirmation request no. 9, the auditor should have indicated which invoices the payments applied to and whether or not the invoices were included in the balance at 12/31/11. In addition, the auditor should have examined copies of checks or remittance advices if they were available or traced the amounts to the bank deposit slip and into the bank statement. The cash receipts listed for confirmation request no. 9 total in excess of the balance due at 12/31/11; the auditor should have indicated what portion of this balance applies to the balance at 12/31/11.

The alternative procedures for confirmation request no. 26 show a small payment for which no indication of the invoice to which it applies is given. The auditor examined a duplicate sales invoice, which may or may not support the balance at 12/31/11. The auditor must determine which sales invoices are represented by the $2,500 balance at 12/31/11 and then examine a shipping document to support the shipment of goods to the customer. The even amount of the balance and periodic payments also raise a question about the possibility of a note outstanding rather than an account receivable.

■ **Case**

16-34 a. There are four major factors affecting acceptable audit risk for the audit of Smalltown Regional Hospital.

   1. There are several large loans to two local banks, both which have said they are reluctant to extend more credit.
   2. A modern hospital is being built in a nearby city, which affects the competitive environment, and therefore the likelihood of financial failure.
   3. The hospital has been incurring significant deficits in the past.
   4. County taxes may not be able to make up the deficits, as they have in the past.

   Considering the combined effect of these factors, the auditor should set a low acceptable audit risk.

   b. The following are major inherent risks:

   1. In the audit of accounts receivable and property, plant and equipment, the amounts are highly material.
   2. Misstatements are common in billings, cash receipts, accounts receivable balances, and bad debts.
   3. Due to the high unemployment rate, there is a significant risk of increased bad debts.

   c. The major difficulty the auditor faces is the ineffective controls over sales and the unreliability of confirmations because of the nature of the customers. The auditor should therefore plan to emphasize substantive tests of transactions for sales and alternative procedures, especially subsequent cash receipts. The controls over cash receipts are such that it is practical to reduce assessed control risk after a proper understanding is obtained of internal control and tests of controls are performed. A likely approach is the following:

   1. Test internal controls over cash receipts using tests of controls to make sure that the controls are effective to prevent fraud.
   2. Do substantive tests of transactions for revenues, with emphasis on tests for unrecorded revenues, billing misstatements, and recording misstatements. The sample for sales should be traced to subsequent cash receipts to test whether each receipt has been correctly recorded. One important test is to select a sample of patient charts and trace transactions through to the revenue journal. The patient chart is a reliable indicator of services provided to patients.

16-34 (continued)

    3.   The accounts receivable aged trial balance should be tested for detail tie-in. Minimal confirmations should be sent, with emphasis on large or unusual balances. The emphasis should be on subsequent cash receipts.

    4.   A careful evaluation of all older, outstanding accounts is essential due to the likelihood of bad debts. The high unemployment rate in the community increases the likelihood of a material misstatement of the allowance for uncollectible accounts.

    d.   The following emphasis is appropriate for each type of test:

TYPE OF TEST	EMPHASIS	REASON
1. Test of controls	None, except control of cash receipts.	Controls are deficient in all areas except cash receipts.
2. Substantive test of transactions	Extensive	Tests of details of balances evidence (confirmation) is not reliable, therefore substantive tests of transactions are the most important evidence. Substantive tests of transactions are even more important because of potential for misstatement for the completeness objective. Tests of details of balances are unlikely to uncover any existing misstatements for this objective.
3. Analytical procedure	Extensive	An indication of misstatements may result from these tests.
4. Tests of details of balances	Reasonably extensive, except confirmations which should be minimal.	Confirmations are not emphasized because of the lack of reliability in the situation. Tests of details of balances are used most extensively for bad debts and the allowance for uncollectible accounts.

■ **Integrated Case Application**

16-35

PINNACLE MANUFACTURING - PART VII

a. Relationships, ratios, and trends:

   1. Comparison of current listing of accounts payable with that of the previous audit date, noting significant changes in amounts and makeup, e.g., changes in major suppliers.

   2. Ratios:
      ■ Accounts payable / purchases
      ■ Gross profit ratio
      ■ Overhead / materials cost
      ■ Material / total product cost: total dollar basis and unit cost basis
      ■ Overhead / direct labor
      ■ Units purchased / units sold
      ■ Specific expense items / sales

   3. Trends:
      ■ Purchases by month
      ■ Gross profit by month
      ■ Other recurring expenses by month

b. 1. Re-add or use the computer to total the accounts payable list and trace the total to the general ledger.

Ending balance tests

   2. Select a sample of 51 vendors and request that they send a copy of their year-end statement directly to you. Examine the vendors' statements and reconcile these to the accounts payable list. (Note: student sample sizes will vary.)

   3. Trace from the accounts payable list to vendors' invoices and statements for any non-responses.

Cutoff tests

   4. Obtain number of last receiving report issued as part of physical observation of inventory.

   5. Examine subsequent cash disbursements greater than $50,000 and examine related documentation to determine if such disbursements were properly recorded as liabilities as of the balance sheet date. (Note: student sample sizes or selection criteria will vary.)

6.   Trace a sample of receiving reports issued just before and after year-end to the appropriate journal and vendor invoice.

7.   Examine vendor invoices for merchandise received shortly after year-end to determine whether they were on an FOB origin basis.

Disclosure and classification tests

8.   Review the list and master file for related parties, notes or other interest-bearing liabilities, long-term payables, and debit balances.

9.   Review financial statements to make sure that material related parties, long-term, and interest-bearing liabilities are segregated.

c.   Audit procedures would be conducted more extensively and sample sizes would increase in a situation where assessed control risk and inherent risk were high and analytical procedures indicated a high potential for misstatements. It is likely that there would be confirmation of accounts payable whereas in part b that may not have been necessary. There would also be more extensive out-of-period liability tests.

d, e, and f: *See pages 16-28 and 16-29.*

g.   Students' conclusion about whether accounts payable is materially misstated will depend on their estimate of the allowance for sampling risk in part e. The projected error in accounts payable affecting the income statement is an overstatement of $124,915 compared to tolerable misstatement of $250,000. The total projected error in accounts payable is an understatement of $171,607. Students should also recognize that some of the errors in accounts payable do not affect net income, and tolerable misstatement for the balance sheet and accounts payable is likely to be larger than tolerable misstatement for accounts payable as it relates to the income statement.

The presence of potentially material misstatements in accounts payable suggests that control risk may need to be increased for one or more objectives and substantive tests of balances increased. Most of the errors in year-end accounts payable relate to cutoff. In this case, the auditor may decide that year-end cutoff tests should be expanded.

16-35 (continued)

Requirements d, e, and f

Vendor Key Accounts (>$250,000)

Vendor Key Accounts (>$250,000)	Balance Per Books	Amount Confirmed by Vendor	Difference: Books Over (Under) Amount Confirmed	Timing Difference: No Misstatement	Misstatement in Accounts Payable o/s (u/s)	Misstatement in Related Accounts		Brief Explanation
						Other Balance Sheet Misstatement o/s (u/s)	Income Stmt misstatement o/s (u/s)	
FiberChem	793,050	825,550	(32,500)		(32,500)	(32,500)		FOB Origin (Inventory and A/P)
Total	793,050	825,550	(32,500)	--	(32,500)	(32,500)	--	

Accounts in Stratum $50,001 - $250,000

	Balance Per Books	Amount Confirmed by Vendor	Difference: Books Over (Under) Amount Confirmed	Timing Difference: No Misstatement	Misstatement in Accounts Payable o/s (u/s)	Other Balance Sheet Misstatement o/s (u/s)	Income Stmt misstatement o/s (u/s)	Brief Explanation
Mobil	93,210	131,022	(37,812)	(37,812)				Timing difference – shipment in transit
Norris	88,315	205,611	(117,296)		(117,296)		117,296	Unrecorded A/P (Purchases and A/P)
Remington	123,411	123,411	--		53,529		(53,529)	Pinnacle recorded FOB shipment before received (Purchases and A/P)
Advent	51,750	59,250	(7,500)		(7,500)	(7,500)		B/S fixed asset error
Total	356,686	431,137	(162,608)	(37,812)	(71,267)	(7,500)	63,767	

Accts in Stratum less than or equal to $50000

	Balance Per Books	Amount Confirmed by Vendor	Difference: Books Over (Under) Amount Confirmed	Timing Difference: No Misstatement	Misstatement in Accounts Payable o/s (u/s)	Other Balance Sheet Misstatement o/s (u/s)	Income Stmt misstatement o/s (u/s)	Brief Explanation
Fuller	32,470	39,570	(7,100)	(7,100)				Timing difference – payment in transit
Total	32,470	39,570	(7,100)	(7,100)	--	--	--	

16-28

16-35 (continued)

Estimate of m/s in the income statement

Misstatements in sample-Stratum $50,000-$250,000		63,767
Dollars sampled-Stratum $50,001-$250,000		2,660,879
Dollars in Pop-Stratum $50,001-$250,000		5,212,467
Income statement m/s - Point estimate		124,915	(63,767/2,660,879*5,212,467)
Estimate of sampling error		100,000	Highly judgmental
Total Estimate		**224,915**

Estimate of m/s in accounts payable

Misstatements in key items		**(32,500)**

Misstatements in stratum $50,001-$250,000:

Misstatements in sample	(71,267)	
Dollars sampled	2,660,879	
Dollars in Pop-Stratum $50,001-$250,000	5,212,467	
Point estimate		**(139,607)**	(-71,267/2,660,879*5,212,467)
Accounts payable m/s-Point estimate		**(171,607)**
Estimate of sampling error		**(150,000)**	Highly judgmental
Total Estimate		**(321,607)**

16-36 – ACL Problem Solution

a. There are 201 invoices in the file, totaling $286,315.79. (Read count at bottom of table; use Total command on NEWBAL column.)

b. 78 records contain finance charges, totaling $3,872.20 of finance charges. (Filter expression is FINCHG > .0, then run Count and Total commands.)

c. Customer #812465 has the largest balance outstanding: $47,598.10. (Remove filter from part b, summarize by customer number and print to an ACL table.) See the following report:

```
Page    1                       04/11/2011  09:30:51
Produced with ACL by: ACL Educational Edition -
Not For Commercial Use
```

CUSTNO	NEWBAL	COUNT
	0.00	1
051593	34931.05	29
202028	44678.85	18
250402	33716.00	14
284354	21767.54	15
359310	421.15	7
444413	27277.99	13
503458	22558.65	23
778088	14271.03	21
812465	47598.10	27
878035	4111.82	2
925007	18286.53	15
962353	16697.08	16
	286315.79	201

d. The largest amount is $47,598.10 and the smallest non-zero amount is $421.15. (Use Quick Sort on the ACL table created in step c.)

e. See the following printout of the aging of customer #812465. (Return to the original table, create a filter expression of CUSTNO = "812465", then run the Age command.)

```
Page    1                       02/11/2011    09:38:49
Produced with ACL by: ACL Educational Edition -
Not For Commercial Use
  <<< AGE over 0-> 10,000 >>>
  >>> Minimum encountered was 10
  >>> Maximum encountered was 34
```

STMTDT		COUNT	<-- %	% -->	NEWBAL
0 ->	29	18	66.67%	84.36%	40154.38
30 ->	59	9	33.33%	15.64%	7443.72
60 ->	89	0	0.00%	0.00%	0.00
90 ->	119	0	0.00%	0.00%	0.00
120 ->	10,000	0	0.00%	0.00%	0.00
		27	100.00%	100.00%	47598.10

16-36 – ACL Problem (continued)

f.   See the following printout. There are 10 customers with balances over $5000. (Go back to the summarized table from part c, create a filter expression to exclude balances > $5,000). Then stratify these balanced into two intervals. (Do Quick Sort to find minimum and maximum amounts, then run Stratify command using two intervals and the minimum and maximum amounts from the Quick Sort results.)

```
Page    1                        02/11/2011    10:05:13
Produced with ACL by: ACL Educational Edition -
Not For Commercial Use
  <<< STRATIFY over 14,271.03-> 47,598.10 >>>
  >>> Minimum encountered was 14,271.03
  >>> Maximum encountered was 47,598.10

NEWBAL                   COUNT  <-- %    % -->   NEWBAL
14,271.03 -> 30,934.56     6    60.00%   42.89%  120858.82
30,934.57 -> 47,598.10     4    40.00%   57.11%  160924.00
                          10   100.00%  100.00%  281782.82
```

■ **Internet Problem Solution: Revenue Recognition**

Internet Problem 16-1

a.   The SEC states that "revenue generally is realized or realizable and earned when all of the following criteria are met:

- Persuasive evidence of an arrangement exists,
- Delivery has occurred or services have been rendered,
- The seller's price to the buyer is fixed or determinable, and
- Collectibility is reasonably assured.

b.   The SEC states that the following are important criteria:

- The risks of ownership must have passed to the buyer;
- The customer must have made a fixed commitment to purchase the goods, preferably in written documentation;
- The buyer, not the seller, must request that the transaction be on a bill and hold basis. The buyer must have a substantial business purpose for ordering the goods on a bill and hold basis;
- There must be a fixed schedule for delivery of the goods. The date for delivery must be reasonable and must be consistent with the buyer's business purpose (e.g., storage periods are customary in the industry);

Internet Problem 16-1 (continued)

- The seller must not have retained any specific performance obligations such that the earning process is not complete;
- The ordered goods must have been segregated from the seller's inventory and not be subject to being used to fill other orders; and
- The equipment [product] must be complete and ready for shipment.

(**Note**: Internet problems address current issues using Internet sources. Because Internet sites are subject to change, Internet problems and solutions may change. Current information on Internet problems is available at www.pearsonhighered.com/arens.)

Chapter 17

Audit Sampling for
Tests of Details of Balances

■ **Review Questions**

17-1   The most important difference between (a) tests of controls and substantive tests of transactions and (b) tests of details of balances is in what the auditor wants to measure. In tests of controls and substantive tests of transactions, the primary concern is testing the effectiveness of internal controls and the rate of monetary misstatements. When an auditor performs tests of controls and substantive tests of transactions, the purpose is to determine if the exception rate in the population is sufficiently low to justify reducing assessed control risk to reduce substantive tests. When statistical sampling is used for tests of controls and substantive tests of transactions, attributes sampling is ideal because it measures the frequency of occurrence (exception rate). In tests of details of balances, the concern is determining whether the monetary amount of an account balance is materially misstated. Attributes sampling, therefore, is seldom useful for tests of details of balances.

17-2   Stratified sampling is a method of sampling in which all the elements in the total population are divided into two or more subpopulations. Each subpopulation is then independently sampled, tested and the results projected to the population. After the results of the individual parts have been computed, they are combined into one overall population measurement. Stratified sampling is important in auditing in situations where the misstatements are likely to be either large or small.

In order for an auditor to obtain a stratified sample of 30 items from each of three strata in the confirmation of accounts receivable, he or she must first divide the population into three mutually exclusive strata. A random sample of 30 items is then selected independently for each stratum.

17-3   The point estimate is an estimate of the total amount of misstatement in the population as projected from the known misstatements found in the sample. The projection is based on either the average misstatement in the sample times the population size, or the net percent of misstatement in the sample times the population book value.

The true value of misstatements in the population is the net sum of all misstatements in the population and can only be determined by a 100% audit.

17-4   The statement illustrates how the misuse of statistical estimation can impair the use of an otherwise valuable audit tool. The auditor's mistake is that he or she treats the point estimate as if it is the true population value, instead of but one possible value in a statistical distribution. Rather than judge whether the point

17-4 (continued)

estimate is material, the auditor should construct a statistical confidence interval around the point estimate, and consider whether the interval indicates a material misstatement. Among other factors, the interval will reflect appropriate levels of risk and sample size.

17-5   Monetary unit sampling is a method whereby the population is defined as the individual dollars (or other currency) making up the account balance. A random sample is drawn of these individual monetary units and the physical audit units containing them are identified and audited. The results of auditing the physical audit units are applied, pro rata, to the random monetary units, and a statistical conclusion about all population monetary units is derived.

Monetary unit sampling is the most commonly used method of statistical sampling for tests of details of balances. This is because it uses the simplicity of attributes sampling yet still provides a statistical result expressed in dollars. It does this by using attribute tables to estimate the total proportion of population dollars misstated, based on the number of sample dollars misstated, and then modifies this amount by the amounts of misstatements found. This latter aspect gives monetary unit sampling its "variables" dimension, although normal distribution theory is not used; rather an arbitrary rule of thumb is applied to make the adjustment.

17-6   Sampling risk is the risk that the characteristics in the sample are not representative of those in the population. The two types of sampling risk faced by the auditor testing an account balance are:

   a.   The risk of incorrect acceptance (ARIA)—this is the risk that the sample supports the conclusion that the recorded account balance is not materially misstated when it is materially misstated.
   b.   The risk of incorrect rejection (ARIR)—this is the risk that the sample supports the conclusion that the recorded account balance is materially misstated when it is not materially misstated.

Sampling risk occurs whenever a sample is taken from a population and therefore applies to all sampling methods. While ARIA applies to all sampling methods, ARIR is only used in variables sampling and difference estimation.

17-7   The steps in nonstatistical sampling for tests of details of balances and for tests of controls are almost identical, as illustrated in the text. The major differences are that sampling for tests of controls deals with exceptions and sampling for tests of details of balances concerns dollar amounts. This results in differences in the application of the two methods, but not the steps.

17-8   The two methods of selecting a monetary unit sample are random sampling and systematic sampling. Under random sampling, in this situation, 57 random numbers would be obtained (the sample size in 17-14) between 1 and 12,625,000. These would be sorted into ascending sequence. The physical audit units in the inventory listing containing the random monetary units would then be identified by cumulating amounts with an adding machine or spreadsheet if the data is in machine-readable form. As the cumulative total exceeds a successive random number, the item causing this event is identified as containing the random dollar unit.

When systematic sampling is used, the population total amount is divided by the sample size to obtain the sampling interval. A random number is chosen between 1 and the amount of the sampling interval to determine the starting point. The dollars to be selected are the starting point and then the starting point plus the interval amount applied successively to the population total. The items on the inventory listing containing the dollar units are identified using the cumulative method described previously.

In applying the cumulative method under both random sampling and systematic sampling, the page totals can be used in lieu of adding the detailed items if the page totals are considered to be reliable.

17-9   A unique aspect of monetary unit sampling is the use of the preliminary judgment about materiality, as discussed in Chapter 9, to directly determine the tolerable misstatement amount for the audit of each account. Most sampling techniques require the auditor to determine tolerable misstatement for each account by allocating the preliminary judgment about materiality. This is not required when monetary unit sampling is used. The preliminary judgment about materiality is used.

17-10   Acceptable risk of incorrect acceptance (ARIA) is the risk the auditor is willing to take of accepting a balance as correct when the true misstatement in the balance is greater than tolerable misstatement. ARIA is the equivalent term to acceptable risk of assessing control risk too low for audit sampling for tests of controls and substantive tests of transactions.

The primary factor affecting the auditor's decision about ARIA is control risk in the audit risk model, which is the extent to which the auditor relies on internal controls. When internal controls are effective, control risk can be reduced, which permits the auditor to increase ARIA, which in turn reduces the required sample size. Besides control risk, ARIA is also affected directly by acceptable audit risk and inversely by inherent risk and other substantive tests already performed on the account balance, assuming effective results. For example, if acceptable audit risk is reduced, ARIA must also be reduced. If analytical procedures were performed and there is no indication of problem areas, there is a lower likelihood of misstatements in the account being tested, and ARIA can be increased.

17-11 The statement reflects a misunderstanding of the statistical inference process. The process is based on the long-run probability that the process will produce correct results in a predictable proportion of the times it is applied. Thus, a random sampling process that produces a 90% confidence interval will produce intervals that do, in fact, contain the true population value 90% of the time. However, the confidence limits of each interval will not all be the same.

17-12 ARIA for tests of details of balances is the equivalent of ARACR for tests of controls and substantive tests of transactions. If internal controls are considered to be effective, control risk can be reduced. A lower control risk requires a lower ARACR, which requires a larger sample size for testing. If controls are determined to be effective after testing, control risk can remain low, which permits the auditor to increase ARIA. An increased ARIA allows the auditor to reduce sample sizes for tests of details of balances.

17-13 In using the binomial distribution, monetary unit sampling estimates the proportion of all population dollars misstated *by some amount*. For the sample items actually misstated, the amounts of those misstatements are used. However, many items in the population have a statistical probability of being misstated by some other amount. An assumption must be made as to what this amount is in order to compute the monetary unit sampling results. This is called the "percent of misstatement assumption."

Since the purpose of monetary unit sampling is to estimate the most the misstatements in the population are likely to be, there is an inherent need for conservatism in the MUS process. Since account balance details if they are overstated, are unlikely to be overstated by more than their recorded value, a 100% assumption is a conservative choice. On this basis it is easier to justify the 100% misstatement assumption than a less conservative amount, and thus it is commonly used.

17-14 The preliminary sample size is calculated as follows:

Tolerable misstatement	500,000
÷ Average misstatement percent assumption	÷ 1.00
	500,000
÷ Recorded population value	12,625,000
= Tolerable exception rate	4%

Using the table for a 10% ARACR with an expected population exception rate of zero and a tolerable exception rate of 4%, the preliminary sample size is 57.

17-15 Misstatement bounds using the attributes tables

MISSTATE-MENT	RECORDED VALUE	AUDITED VALUE	MISSTATE-MENT	MISSTATE-MENT/ RECORDED AMOUNT
1	897.16	609.16	288.00	.321
2	47.02	0	47.02	1.000
3	1,621.68	1,522.68	99.00	.061

Using the attributes sampling table for a sample size of 100, and an ARIA of 10%, the CUER is:

NO. OF MISSTATEMENTS	CUER	INCREASE IN BOUND RESULTING FROM AN ADDITIONAL MISSTATEMENT
0	.023	
1	.039	.016
2	.053	.014
3	.066	.013

In order to calculate the upper and lower misstatement bounds, it will be assumed that for a zero misstatement rate the percent of misstatement is 100%.

The upper misstatement bound:

NO. OF MISSTATE-MENTS	RECORDED VALUE	x	CUER PORTION	x	UNIT MISSTATE-MENT	=	MIS-STATE-MENT BOUND PORTION
0	12,625,000		.023		1.000		290,375
1	12,625,000		.016		1.000		202,000
2	12,625,000		.014		.321		56,737
3	12,625,000		.013		.061		10,012
					Upper Misstatement Bound		559,124

17-15 (continued)

The lower misstatement bound:

Before adjustment:

NO. OF MISSTATE-MENTS	RECORDED VALUE	x	CUER PORTION	x	UNIT MISSTATE-MENT	=	MIS-STATE-MENT BOUND PORTION
0	12,625,000		.023		1.000		<u>290,375</u>

Adjustment:

Point estimate for overstatements = sum of misstatement percents x recorded value / sample size

= (.321 + 1.000 + .061) x (12,625,000 / 100)

= 1.382 x 126,250

= 174,478

Adjusted lower misstatement bound = initial bound - point estimate for overstatements

= 290,375 - 174,478

= <u>115,897</u>

Based on this calculation method, the population is not acceptable as stated since the upper misstatement bound exceeds the $500,000 materiality limit.

17-16 The difficulty in determining sample size lies in estimating the number and amount of misstatements that may be found in the sample. The upper bound of a monetary unit sample is sensitive to these factors. Thus, sample size varies a great deal with differing assumptions about them.

Generally, the auditor will determine sample size by making reasonable but conservative assumptions about the sample exception rate and average misstatement amount. In the absence of information about misstatement amount, which is most difficult to anticipate, a 100% assumption is often used.

17-17 The decision rule for difference estimation is:

If the two-sided confidence interval for the misstatements is completely within plus or minus tolerable misstatements, accept the hypothesis that the book value is not misstated by a material amount. Otherwise, accept the hypothesis that the book value is misstated by a material amount. For example, assume the LCL is -10,000, the UCL is 40,000 and tolerable misstatement is $45,000. The following illustrates the decision rule:

```
     - TM                                          + TM
   - 45,000 _____ 0 _____ + 45,000

              - 10,000 _____ + 40,000
                LCL                        UCL
```

The auditor can conclude that the population is not materially misstated since both LCL and UCL are within the tolerable misstatement limits.

17-18 When a population is not considered acceptable, there are several possible courses of action:

1. Perform expanded audit tests in specific areas. If an analysis of the misstatements indicates that most of the misstatements are of a specific type, it may be desirable to restrict the additional audit effort to the problem area.

2. Increase the sample size. When the auditor increases the sample size, sampling error is reduced if the rate of misstatements in the expanded sample, their dollar amount, and their direction are similar to those in the original sample. Increasing the sample size, therefore, may satisfy the auditor's tolerable misstatement requirements.

    Increasing the sample size enough to satisfy the auditor's tolerable misstatement standards is often costly, especially when the difference between tolerable misstatement and projected misstatement is small.

3. Adjust the account balance. When the auditor concludes that an account balance is materially misstated, the client may be willing to adjust the book value.

4. Request the client to correct the population. In some cases the client's records are so inadequate that a correction of the entire population is required before the audit can be completed.

5. Refuse to give an unqualified opinion. If the auditor believes the recorded amount in accounts receivable or any other account is not fairly stated, it is necessary to follow at least one of the above alternatives or to qualify the audit opinion in an appropriate manner.

17-19   The population standard deviation is a measure of the difference between the individual values and the mean of the population. It is calculated for all variables sampling methods but not for monetary unit sampling. For the auditor, it is usually estimated before determining the required sample size, based on the previous year's results or on a preliminary sample.

The population standard deviation is needed to calculate the sample size necessary for an acceptable precision interval when variable sampling methods are used. After the sample is selected and audited, the population standard deviation is estimated from the standard deviation calculated from the values in the sample.

The required sample size is directly proportional to the square of the population standard deviation.

17-20   This practice is improper for a number of reasons:

1.   No determination was made as to whether a random sample of 100 inventory items would be sufficient to generate an acceptable precision interval for a given confidence level. In fact, a confidence limit was not even calculated.
2.   The combined net amount of the sample misstatement may be immaterial because large overstatement amounts may be offsetting large understatement amounts resulting in a relatively small combined net amount.
3.   Although no misstatement by itself may be material, other material misstatements might not have exhibited themselves if too small of a sample was taken.
4.   Regardless of the size of individual or net amounts of misstatements in a sample, the effect on the overall population cannot be determined unless the results are evaluated using a statistically valid method.

17-21   Difference estimation is a method for estimating the total misstatement in a population by multiplying the average misstatement (the audited value minus the recorded value) in a random sample by the number of items in the entire population.

Ratio estimation is quite similar to difference estimation. However, instead of basing the estimate of total misstatement on the difference between audited and recorded values, it uses the ratio of misstatement amounts to recorded amounts. This ratio for the sample is multiplied times the total population recorded amount to estimate total misstatement. Mean-per-unit estimation is a method of estimating the total audited value of the population by multiplying the arithmetic average, or mean, audited value of the sample times the number of items in the population.

Stratified mean-per-unit estimation is similar to mean-per-unit estimation except that the population is divided into groups of homogeneous items, called strata, for purposes of sample design. A separate random sample is selected from each stratum and the estimate of the total population audited amount is computed by determining an estimate for each stratum and adding the results.

17-21 (continued)

The following are examples where each method could be used:

a. Difference estimation can be used in computing the balance in accounts receivable by using the misstatements discovered during the confirmation process, where a significant number of misstatements are found.

b. Ratio estimation can be used to determine the amount of the LIFO reserve where internal inventory records are maintained on a FIFO basis but reporting is on LIFO.

c. Mean-per-unit estimation can be used to determine total inventory value where the periodic inventory method is employed.

d. Stratified mean-per-unit estimation can be used to determine total inventory value where there are several locations and each is sampled separately.

Monetary unit sampling would generally be preferable to any of these where few or no misstatements are expected. Difference and ratio estimation are not reliable where the exception rate is low, and mean-per-unit is generally not as efficient. However, in item "c" above, mean-per-unit must be used because there is only one value per sample item.

17-22 Tolerable misstatement (Chapter 9) represents the portion of overall materiality allocated to each individual account. It is the amount of misstatement the auditor believes can be present in an account and the account balance still be acceptable for audit purposes.

Since hypothesis testing requires a decision rule based on materiality, that amount should be tolerable misstatement for an individual account balance. If test results provide a confidence limit greater than tolerable misstatement, the auditor would conclude the account is misstated. This would result in one or more of several actions:

1. Perform expanded audit tests in specific areas.
2. Increase the sample size.
3. Adjust the account balance.
4. Request the client to correct the population.
5. Refuse to give an unqualified opinion.

In addition, it may be possible to adjust tolerable misstatement (upward) and remake the decision. The basis for this would be a reconsideration of the original judgment concerning determining overall materiality and allocation to the accounts. For example, audit work completed on another account may indicate that a much lower tolerable misstatement exists for that account then originally planned. This would allow a reallocation providing a larger tolerable misstatement to the subject account.

17-23 Difference estimation can be very effective and very efficient where (1) an audited value and a book value is available for each population item, (2) a relatively high frequency of misstatements is expected, and (3) a result in the form of a confidence interval is desired. In those circumstances, difference estimation far outperforms both MUS and mean-per-unit estimation. It may or may not outperform ratio estimation, depending on the relationship of misstatement amounts to recorded amounts. If focus on large dollar value items is required, difference estimation can be used with stratification.

17-24 Examples of audit conclusions resulting from the use of attributes, monetary unit, and variables sampling are as follows:

> Use of attributes sampling in a test of sales transactions for internal verification:
>
>> We have examined a random sample of 100 sales invoices for indication of internal verification; two exceptions were noted. Based on our sample, we conclude, with a 5% risk, that the proportion of sales invoices to which internal verification has not been applied does not exceed 6.2%.
>
> Use of monetary unit sampling in a test of sales transactions for existence:
>
>> We have examined a random sample of 100 dollar units of sales transactions for existence. All were supported by properly prepared sales orders and shipping documents. Based on our sample, we conclude, with a 20% risk, that invalid sales do not exceed $40,000.
>
> Use of variables sampling in confirmation of accounts receivable (in the form of an interval estimate and a hypothesis test):
>
>> We have confirmed a random sample of 100 accounts receivable. We obtained replies or examined satisfactory other evidence for all sample items. A listing of exceptions is attached. Based on our sample, we estimate, with 10% risk, that the true population misstatement is between $20,000 understatement and $40,000 overstatement. Since tolerable misstatement for accounts receivable is judged to be $50,000, we conclude, with a risk of 5%, that accounts receivable are not materially misstated.

■ Multiple Choice Questions from CPA Examinations

17-25	a. (4)	b. (2)	c. (3)
17-26	a. (3)	b. (1)	c. (4)
17-27	a. (4)	b. (3)	c. (4)

■ Discussion Questions and Problems

17-28 a. 92 (Book value/tolerable misstatement) x assurance factor =
(6,900,000/150,000) x 2

b. If poor results were obtained for tests of controls and substantive tests of transactions for sales, sales returns and allowances, and cash receipts, the required sample size for tests of details of balances would need to be increased. Using the formula in the problem, the auditor would increase sample size by increasing the assurance factor. This has the same effect has specifying a lower acceptable risk of incorrect acceptance (ARIA).

c. A systematic sample can be selected based on the number of accounts, or the dollar value of the population. To select a systematic sample based on the number of accounts, the total number of accounts in the population is divided by the required sample size to determine the interval. A random number is then selected between one and the interval as the starting point. Because each account has an equal likelihood of selection, this method is appropriate if all the accounts are similar in size, or if the population is stratified into two or more samples.

To select a systematic sample based on the dollar value of the population, the population value is divided by the required sample size to obtain the appropriate interval. A random number is then selected between one and the interval as the starting point. The interval is added to the starting point to determine the dollar units selected. Accounts are selected for testing where the cumulative total of accounts receivable includes the random number. This method of selection is similar to monetary unit selection, and accounts greater than the amount of the interval are automatically selected using this method.

d. The direct projection of error for the sample can be computed as follows:

(Errors in sample/sample book value) x population book value = (1,500/230,000) x 6,900,000 = $45,000 overstatement

The projected error of $45,000 is well below tolerable misstatement of $150,000 and provides an allowance for sampling risk of $105,000. Accordingly, the population is deemed to be fairly stated.

17-29   a.   The following summarizes the confirmation responses:

	Recorded Value	Confirmation Response	Misstatement	
Acct. 147	$ 24,692	$ 23,597	$ 1,095	Pricing error
Acct. 228	183,219	157,216	26,003	Cutoff error
Acct. 278	7,546	5,546	0	Timing difference
Acct. 497	15,319	0	15,319	Cutoff error
Acct. 564	8,397	7,858	539	Error in quantity shipped
Acct. 653	32,687	19,328	13,359	Cutoff error
Acct. 839	5,286	0	0	Timing difference
Total misstatement			$56,315	

b.   Estimate of total misstatement

	Sample Value	Sample Misstatements	Book Value	Projected Misstatement
Stratum 1	$1,287,643	$26,003	$1,287,643	$ 26,003
Stratum 2	1,349,678	29,773	4,348,268	95,920
Stratum 3	94,637	539	947,682	5,397
Totals	$2,731,958	$56,315	$6,583,593	$127,320

c.   The population is not acceptable since the projected misstatement of $127,320 exceeds tolerable misstatement of $100,000. The auditor is likely to propose an adjustment and/or increase testing. In this situation, many of the errors involved cutoff, so the auditor could expand testing in this area and propose an adjustment for the errors found. Because the cutoff errors were isolated and testing expanded in this area, the cutoff errors would not be included in the projection of error for each stratum.

17-30   a.   If random selection is performed using Excel (P1730.xls), the command to select numbers randomly from the population is:

=RANDBETWEEN(1,207295)

The 10 random numbers selected using this approach will vary for each student.

The command for selecting the random numbers can be entered directly onto the spreadsheet, or can be selected from the function menu (math & trig) functions. It may be necessary to add the analysis tool pack to access the RANDBETWEEN function. Once the formula is entered, it can be copied down to select additional random numbers.

NOTE: Random dollar items are matched with population item numbers where the cumulative book value of the population includes the random dollar selected.

17-30 (continued)

b.

$$\text{Interval} = \frac{\text{Population total}}{\text{Number of items selected}}$$

$$= \frac{207,295}{10}$$

$$= \underline{20,729} \text{ Interval}$$

Using 1857 as a starting point, we have:

	SYSTEMATIC DOLLAR	POPULATION ITEM NO.
1	1,857	2
2	22,586	6
3	43,315	8
4	64,044	8
5	84,773	15
6	105,502	20
7	126,231	26
8	146,960	30
9	167,689	30
10	188,418	35

NOTE: Systematic dollar items are related to population item numbers in the same manner as for part a above.

c. All items larger than the interval will be automatically included. If the interval is 20,729 item 30 will be included at least once, and item 8 at least twice.

   The same is not necessarily true for random number selection, but the probability is high. Note that for item 8, there is a probability of approximately 22% (44,110/207,295) of its being included in a given sample draw. It was included twice in a sample of 10.

d. There is no significant difference in ease of selection between computer generation of random numbers and systematic selection. Some auditors prefer the use of random numbers because they believe this helps ensure an unbiased sample.

e. Monetary unit sampling would be used because (1) it is efficient and (2) it focuses on large dollar items.

17-31 a. The differences that were uncovered include only five misstatements rather than seven. Items 2 and 7 are not misstatements, but only timing differences. Therefore, only the five misstatements are summarized in order to compute the upper and lower misstatement bounds. These misstatements are summarized below.

ITEM	RECORDED VALUE	AUDITED VALUE	MISSTATE-MENT	MISSTATE-MENT/ RECORDED VALUE
1	$2,728.00	$2,498.00	$ 230.00	.084
3	3,890.00	1,190.00	2,700.00	.694
4	791.00	815.00	(24.00)	(.030)
5	548.00	1,037.00	(489.00)	(.892)
6	3,115.00	3,190.00	(75.00)	(.024)

Upper misstatement bound before adjustment:

NO. OF MISSTATE-MENTS	RECORDED VALUE	x	CUER PORTION	x	MISSTATE-MENT % ASSUMPTION	=	MIS-STATE-MENT BOUND
0	$1,975,000		.023		1.000		$45,425
1	1,975,000		.016		.694		21,930
2	1,975,000		.014		.084		2,323
			.053				$69,678

Lower misstatement bound before adjustment:

NO. OF MISSTATE-MENTS	RECORDED VALUE	x	CUER PORTION	x	MISSTATE-MENT % ASSUMPTION	=	MIS-STATE-MENT BOUND
0	$1,975,000		.023		1.000		$45,425
1	1,975,000		.016		.892		28,187
2	1,975,000		.014		.030		830
3	1,975,000		.013		.024		616
			.066				$75,058

17-31 (continued)

> **Adjustment of upper misstatement bound:**
>
> > Point estimate for understatement amounts = sum of misstatement percents x recorded value / sample size
> >
> > > = (.892 + .030 + .024) x (1,975,000 / 100)
> > >
> > > = .946 x 19,750
> > >
> > > = 18,684
> >
> > Adjusted bound = initial bound - point estimate for understatement amounts
> >
> > > = 69,678 - 18,684
> > >
> > > = <u>50,994</u>
>
> **Adjustment of lower misstatement bound:**
>
> > Point estimate for overstatement amounts = sum of misstatement percents x recorded value/sample size
> >
> > > = (.694 + .084) x (1,975,000 / 100)
> > >
> > > = .778 x 19,750
> > >
> > > = 15,366
> >
> > Adjusted bound = initial bound - point estimate for overstatements
> >
> > > = 75,058 - 15,366
> > >
> > > = <u>59,692</u>

b. The population is not acceptable as stated because both the lower misstatement bound and upper misstatement bound exceed materiality. In this situation, the auditor has the following options:

1. Segregate a specific type of misstatement and test it separately (for the entire population). The sample would then not include the specified type of misstatement since it is being tested separately.
2. Increase the sample size.

17-31 (continued)

3. Adjust the account balance (i.e., propose an adjustment).
4. Request the client to review and correct the population.
5. Consider qualifying the opinion is the client refuses to correct the problem.
6. Consider the criteria used in the test, possibly in connection with additional audit work in areas outside of accounts receivable.

Of these options, segregating a specific type of misstatement may prove to be the most beneficial. In this problem, items 3 and 5 are cutoff misstatements. Segregating these items, testing cutoff more extensively, and eliminating them from the sample would result in the following bounds:

Upper misstatement bound:

NO. OF MISSTATE-MENTS	RECORDED VALUE	x	CUER PORTION	x	MISSTATE-MENT % ASSUMPTION	=	MIS-STATE-MENT BOUND
0	$1,975,000		.023		1.000		$45,425
1	1,975,000		.016		.084		2,654
			.039				$48,079
Less adjustment [(.030 + .024) (19,750)]							(1,067)
							$47,012

Lower misstatement bound:

NO. OF MISSTATE-MENTS	RECORDED VALUE	x	CUER PORTION	x	MISSTATE-MENT % ASSUMPTION	=	MIS-STATE-MENT BOUND
0	$1,975,000		.023		1.000		$45,425
1	1,975,000		.016		.030		948
2	1,975,000		.014		.024		664
			.053				$47,037
Less adjustment [(.084) (19,750)]							(1,659)
							$45,378

17-31 (continued)

It can be seen that both misstatement bounds are now within materiality after cutoff misstatements were segregated. These misstatements were significant in two ways. Their existence increased the overall estimated population exception rate, and their magnitude contributed to the amount of estimated misstatements in the portion of the population represented by the misstatements in the sample.

17-32 a. The audit approach of testing all three account balances is acceptable. This approach is also desirable when the following conditions are present:

1. The auditor can obtain valid, reliable information to perform the required tests in all of the areas.
2. The internal controls for each of the three areas are comparable.
3. Misstatements are expected to occur evenly over the entire population. For instance, the auditor does not expect a large number of misstatements in accounts receivable and few, if any, in inventory.

b. The required sample size for all three accounts is:

$$\frac{\text{Tolerable misstatement}}{\text{Recorded population value}} \quad \frac{100{,}000}{10{,}000{,}000} = .01$$

From the attributes table sample size n cannot be determined, but using interpolation it is approximately $114 + (114 - 76) = 152$. (This is not an appropriate method to determine sample size in practice.)

c. The required sample sizes if each account is tested separately are:

ACCOUNT	FACTOR		APPROX. SAMPLE SIZE
Accounts receivable	$n = \dfrac{100{,}000}{3{,}600{,}000}$	$= .03$	76
Inventory	$n = \dfrac{100{,}000}{4{,}800{,}000}$	$= .02$	114
Marketable securities	$n = \dfrac{100{,}000}{1{,}600{,}000}$	$= .06$	38

The important point is that sample size under b is much smaller than for the sum of the individual samples in c.

17-32 (continued)

d. The population would be arranged so that all accounts receivable would be first, followed by inventory and marketable securities. The items would be identified by the cumulative totals. In the example, the number 4,627,871 would relate to an inventory item since it is between the cumulative totals of $3,600,000 and $8,400,000. Accordingly, for this number the inventory audit procedures would be performed.

e. The misstatement data are as follows:

RECORDED AMOUNT	AUDITED AMOUNT	DIFFERENCE	MISSTATEMENT/ RECORDED AMOUNT
$987.12	$887.12	$100.00	10.1%

Assuming a 100% average misstatement in the population when there are no misstatements found and an ARIA of 10%, the misstatement bounds are:

Upper misstatement bound:

$$\$10,000,000 \times .012 \times 1.0 = \$120,000$$

$$\$10,000,000 \times .008 \times .101 = \underline{\quad 8,080}$$
$$\underline{\$128,080}$$

Lower misstatement bound:

Before adjustment:

$$\$10,000,000 \times .012 \times 1.0 = \$120,000$$

Adjustment:

$$.101 \times \frac{\$10,000,000}{200} = \underline{(5,050)}$$
$$\underline{\$114,950}$$

Based on the sample results and the stated combined acceptable misstatement of $100,000, the population (i.e., accounts receivable, inventory, and marketable securities *combined*) should not be accepted as stated without further testing.

17-33   1. (a)   2. (c)   3. (a)   4. (d)   5. (d)

17-34

Computer Solution. This is an excellent problem to use a spreadsheet to solve, as it requires a great deal of computational work. A solution prepared using Excel is included on the Companion Website (Filename P1734.xls). Important points to stress are:

1. The spreadsheet program is set up in two sections: one for data entry and one for computations.
2. Cells are set up for variables by name, and the values for the variables are then entered in those cells (e.g., sample size =_____). _____ Computations are then done by reference to the cells rather than by entering values in the formulas. This allows the worksheet to be used as a general program for similar problems.
3. Although the program assures computational accuracy, the formulas *must be correct*. They should always be reviewed and double checked, and test data should be processed to assure accuracy.

     a.   Calculating the point estimate:

$$\hat{E} = N \bullet \Sigma \frac{e_j}{n}$$

$$\hat{E} = 1840 \bullet \frac{173.69}{80}$$

$$\hat{E} = 3994.87$$

Before computing the computed precision interval, we must compute the standard deviation:

	e_j	$(e_j)^2$
$SD = \sqrt{\dfrac{\Sigma\,(e_j)^2 - n(\bar{e})^2}{n-1}}$	$(72.00)	5,184.00
	65.70	4,316.49
	41.10	1,689.21
	36.10	1,303.31
$=\sqrt{\dfrac{16,521.79 - 80\left(\dfrac{173.69}{80}\right)^2}{80-1}}$	51.80	2,683.24
	(.12)	.01
	30.00	900.00
	21.11	445.63
$= 14.30$	$173.69	16,521.79

17-34 (continued)

Computed precision interval:

$$CPI = NZ_A \bullet \frac{SD}{\sqrt{n}} \bullet \sqrt{\frac{N-n}{N}}$$

$$CPI = 1{,}840 \bullet 1.64 \bullet \frac{14.30}{\sqrt{80}} \bullet \sqrt{\frac{1{,}840 - 80}{1{,}840}}$$

$$CPI = \$4{,}718.46$$

The confidence interval is expressed as $3{,}994.87 \pm 4{,}718.46$.

To compute the confidence limits,

UCL $= \hat{E} + CPI = 3{,}994.87 + 4{,}718.46 = 8{,}713.33$

LCL $= \hat{E} - CPI = 3{,}994.87 - 4{,}718.46 = -723.59$

b. The auditor should not accept the book value of the population since the maximum misstatement in the population that she was willing to accept, $6,000, at a risk level of 5%, is less than the possible amount of true misstatement indicated by the UCL of $8,713.33.

c. The options available to the auditor at this point are:

1. Perform expanded audit tests in specific areas.
2. Increase the sample size.
3. Adjust the account balance.
4. Request the client to correct the population.
5. Refuse to give an unqualified opinion.

17-35 a. It would be desirable to use unstratified difference estimation when the auditor believes that there is not a small number of misstatements in the population that are in total material, and the population has a large number of small misstatements that in total could be material.
Unstratified difference estimation would not be appropriate when either of the above characteristics is not present. For example, if the auditor believes that certain large accounts payable may contain large misstatements that are material, they should be tested separately.
A significant consideration in this situation is whether the auditor can identify the entire population. This consideration applies whether using stratified or unstratified difference estimation. The auditor in this instance is identifying the population based upon an accounts payable list. If this list includes only those accounts with

17-35 (continued)

an outstanding balance, the sample is ignoring those accounts that have a recorded balance of zero.

Thus, many accounts could be understated but not considered in the sample or the statistical inferences drawn from the sample.

b. Ignoring the ARIR, the required sample size may be computed as follows:

$$n = \left[\frac{SD^* \bullet Z_A \bullet N}{TM - E^*} \right]^2$$

where

$$TM - E^* \quad = \quad 45,000 - 20,000 = \$25,000$$

$$n = \left[\frac{280 \bullet 1.28 \bullet 610}{25,000} \right]^2 = 76$$

c. In order to determine whether the population is fairly stated, the computed precision interval must be calculated.

$$CPI = N \bullet Z_A \bullet \frac{SD}{\sqrt{n}} \bullet \sqrt{\frac{N-n}{N}}$$

$$CPI = 610 \bullet 1.28 \bullet \frac{267}{\sqrt{76}} \bullet \sqrt{\frac{610-76}{610}} = 22,374.33$$

CI   = $\hat{E} \pm CPI$

CI   = $21,000 \pm 22,374$

UCL =   43,374

LCL =   -1,374

Since both UCL and LCL are less than tolerable misstatement, the auditor can conclude that the population is fairly stated.

The primary reasons the population is acceptable is that (1) the actual point estimate is reasonably close to the expected misstatement, and (2) the actual sample standard deviation is less than the estimated standard deviation.

17-35 (continued)

    d.   Considering the ARIR, the sample size may be computed from the following formula:

$$n = \left[\frac{SD^{*}(Z_A + Z_R)N}{TM - E^{*}} \right]^2$$

$$n = \left[\frac{280\,(1.28 + 1.28)\,610}{45{,}000 - 20{,}000} \right]^2 = 306$$

    e.   The sample size increases significantly with the inclusion of the ARIR because by including it the auditor is establishing the risk he or she will take of rejecting an acceptable population, as well as considering the risk of accepting an unacceptable population. It takes more effort (sample items) to control two risks, rather than just one. The effect can be seen from reviewing the formula for calculating the sample size.

■   **Cases**

17-36 a.   *Determination of ARIA* - Note that there are many ways to estimate ARIA. One method is as follows:

        ARIA =   AAR / (IR x CR x APR)
                =   .05 / (.8 x .5 x 1.0)
                =   .05 / .4
                =   .13 rounded to .10 (to be conservative)

Tolerable misstatement as a percent:

        TER =   TM / Population
               =   800,000 / 12,000,000
               =   .067 rounded to .06 (to be conservative)

Sample size determined using Table 15-8 (assumes an expected misstatement of zero and a misstatement percent of 100%):

        n   =   38

17-36 (continued)

b.   *Determination of ARIA* - Note that there are many ways to estimate ARIA. One method is as follows:

$$
\begin{aligned}
ARIA &= AAR / (IR \times CR \times APR) \\
&= .05 / [1.0 \times .8 \times (1 - .6)] \\
&= .05 / .32 \\
&= .16 \text{ rounded to } .15
\end{aligned}
$$

Tolerable misstatement as a percent:

$$
\begin{aligned}
TER &= TM / Population \\
&= 800,000 / 23,000,000 \\
&= .035 \text{ rounded to } .03 \text{ (to be conservative)}
\end{aligned}
$$

There is no table available for an ARIA of 15%. Inherent risk and control risk for inventory are greater than for accounts receivable. However, due to the inclusion of a component for analytical procedures risk, ARIA for inventory is not significantly greater than ARIA for accounts receivable. Because the book value of the population for inventory is much larger, the tolerable misstatement as a percent is much lower for inventory. As a result, the sample size for inventory should be larger than the sample size for accounts receivable in requirement a.

c.   The same ARIA must be used for the entire combined test. It would be most prudent to use the lower of the ARIAs calculated for the separate tests, (i.e. 10% from the examples shown in requirements a and b).

Tolerable misstatement as a percent:

$$
\begin{aligned}
TER &= TM / Population \\
&= 800,000 / (12,000.000 + 23,000,000) \\
&= 800,000 / 35,000,000 \\
&= .023 \text{ (rounded to } .02)
\end{aligned}
$$

Sample size computed using Table 15-8 (allows for a .005 exception rate—an average of the expected misstatements for accounts receivable and inventory—and assumes misstatement percent of 100%):

$$
n = 194
$$

17-36 (continued)

    d.   The generation of random numbers using Excel (P1736.xls) to obtain the sample of 38 accounts receivable for confirmation would be obtained as follows:

Population book value = $12,000,000

Command to obtain each random number:

=RANDBETWEEN(1,12000000)

Once the formula is entered, it can be copied down to select additional random numbers. To obtain a sorted list, the list of random numbers should be copied to a separate column, and pasted as a value (use the "Paste Special" command and select "value"). Then use the "Data Sort" command to obtain a sorted list.

The command for selecting the random numbers can be entered directly onto the spreadsheet, or can be selected from the function menu (math & trig) functions. It may be necessary to add the analysis tool pack to access the RANDBETWEEN function.

An example prepared using Excel is included on the Companion Website (filename P1736.xls).

17-37   a.   This nonstatistical (i.e., nonprobabilistic or judgmental) sample is a stratified sample. All 23 items over $10,000 were examined 100%. The remaining 7,297 items were tested with a sample of 77 items. Although this was not a probabilistic sample, auditing standards require that in the auditor's judgment, it is a representative one. Accordingly, the results must be projected to the population and a judgment made about sampling risk, although sampling risk and precision cannot be measured.

Projection of the total population misstatement would be as follows:

Items over $10,000:

Projected Misstatement = Audited value - Recorded value
                             = 432,000 - 465,000
                             = (33,000) overstatement

Items under $10,000 - average misstatement amount method:

Projected Misstatement = Average sample misstatement
                              x population size
                             = [(4,350) / 77] x (7,320 - 23)
                             = (56.49) x 7297
                             = (412,207) overstatement

17-37 (continued)

Items under $10,000 - proportional amount method:

Projected Misstatement = Sample misstatement ratio x population book value
= [(4,350) / 81,500] x (2,760,000 - 465,000)
= (.053) x 2,295,000
= (121,635) overstatement

Where sample misstatements are:

ITEM	AUDITED VALUE	RECORDED VALUE	MISSTATEMENT
12	4,820	5,120	(300)
19	385	485	(100)
33	250	1,250	(1,000)
35	3,875	3,975	(100)
51	1,825	1,850	(25)
59	3,780	4,200	(420)
74	0	2,405	(2,405)
Totals	14,935	19,285	(4,350)

Note that the sample misstatements are divided by the sample book value of $81,500 to calculate the sample misstatement ratio. The projected misstatement is significantly lower using the proportional amount method because the average account size in the sample is large than the average account size in the population.

Total misstatement is either:

(33,000) + (412,207) = (445,207) overstatement
or
(33,000) + (121,635) = (154,635) overstatement

In either case, the following can be said: There are a significant number of misstated items in the sample, and the amount is quite large. Since the sample is representative, it is clear that there is a material misstatement of the population. The amount of misstatement is not easily estimable from the sample. It could be significantly higher or lower than either point estimate. At this point, the best course of action would be to ask the client to make a study of their records for all population items to identify more accurately the misstatements that exist and correct them.

17-37 (continued)

b. If this were a PPS sample, the sampled portion would be evaluated as follows:

Misstatement taintings:

ITEM	AUDITED VALUE	RECORDED VALUE	MIS-STATEMENT	PERCENT
12	4,820	5,120	(300)	(.059)
19	385	485	(100)	(.206)
33	250	1,250	(1,000)	(.800)
35	3,875	3,975	(100)	(.025)
51	1,825	1,850	(25)	(.014)
59	3,780	4,200	(420)	(.100)
74	0	2,405	(2,405)	(1.000)

Calculation of overstatement bound:

OVER-STATE-MENT	UPL	RECORDED VALUE	UNIT MISSTATE-MENT ASSUMPTION	MIS-STATE-MENT BOUND PORTION
0 [1]	.040	2,295,000	1.0	91,800
1	.022	2,295,000	1.0	50,490
2	.020	2,295,000	.800	36,720
3	.019	2,295,000	.206	8,983
4	.017	2,295,000	.100	3,902
5	.018	2,295,000	.059	2,437
6	.016	2,295,000	.025	918
7	.017	2,295,000	.014	546

[1] From Table 15-9 using an ARIA of 5 percent and a sample size of 75.

Overstatement bound from sample	195,796
Misstatement of 100% items	33,000
Total overstatement bound	228,796

17-37 (continued)

An adjusted understatement bound is calculated as follows:

Initial understatement bound = .040 x 2,295,000
= 91,800

Point estimate for overstatements = sum of unit misstatement assumptions / sample size x recorded population amount

= 2.204 / 77 x 2,295,000
= 65,691

Adjusted understatement bound = initial bound - point estimate for overstatements

= 91,800 - 65,691
= 26,109

As would be expected, this is very small. Since all misstatements were overstatements, one wouldn't expect a net understatement to occur.

The results of a PPS sample indicate that the accounts receivable balance is overstated by as much as $228,796. This is about 8 percent of the recorded book amount. It is significantly greater than tolerable misstatement, indicating that the population is unacceptable and must be subject to more scrutiny either by the client and/or the auditor.

c. A template for the PPS portion of the problem is prepared using Excel on the Companion Website (Filename P1737.xls). This template is a complete worksheet for MUS, including appropriate tables for various exception rates and risk levels. You will note that the results are very similar to those computed manually, the differences being due to rounding.

17-38 – ACL Problem Solution

a. The sampling interval is $15,606.03. The sample size will be 43 based on the population size ($680,479.94) divided by the sampling interval.
b. The revised sampling interval is $20,691.03 and the revised sample size will be 32.

17-38 – ACL Problem (continued)

    c.   The first four columns of the sample items are as follows:

	PRODNO	PRODCLS	LOCATION	PRODDESC
1	070104347	07	06	LATEX SEMI-GLOSS ORANGE
2	070104177	07	06	LATEX SEMI-GLOSS LILAC
3	070104657	07	06	LATEX SEMI-GLOSS PINK
4	070104327	07	06	LATEX SEMI-GLOSS YELLOW
5	070104377	07	06	LATEX SEMI-GLOSS GREEN
6	030414283	03	03	METRIC SOCKET SET 11 PC
7	030321663	03	03	SCREW DRIVER 1/8 X 4 SL
8	030030323	03	03	LONG NOSE PLIERS 7"
9	030303343	03	03	STRAIGHT CLAW HAMMER
10	030309373	03	03	HEAVY DUTY BRACE
11	030302303	03	03	MITRE BOX 21"
12	090506331	09	04	5 PIECE GARDEN TOOL SET
13	090508191	09	04	PISTOL GRIP NOZZLE
14	090509931	09	04	OSCILLATING SPRINKLER
15	090584072	09	04	22" SELF-PROPELLED MOW
16	090585322	09	04	18" REEL MOWER
17	010803760	01	01	7 PC KITCHEN TOOL SET
18	010102840	01	01	PRESSURE COOKER 8QT
19	052720305	05	05	1X8 SHIPLAP PER MFBM
20	052484425	05	05	PLYWOOD 4X8X 3/4 GIS
21	052504005	05	05	5/16 SHEATHING
22	080102618	08	02	1/2" SOFT TUBING 30'COIL
23	080102628	08	02	R161D TUBING 1/2" -12'
24	080126008	08	02	1/2" CPVC PLASTIC PIPE
25	080123968	08	02	REDVGING TY 3"X3"X1"
26	080512778	08	02	COMPACT DOUBLE BOWEL SNK
27	024144812	02	02	TRUNK SKI CARRIER
28	060102096	06	02	SEVILLE ENTRANCE SET BR
29	060112296	06	02	LION DOOR KNOCKER BR
30	060221506	06	02	BLACK ENAMEL GRILL
31	060217066	06	02	ALUMINUM DOOR
32	040225014	04	03	6 PC WOODBORIN SET
33	040232194	04	03	12 SP AUTO SCROLLER SAW
34	040240664	04	03	SHAPENER FOR 1/4" BITS
35	040247034	04	03	SET OF 6 ROTARY CUTTERS
36	040277154	04	03	ADJUSTABLE DADO

    d.   Thirty-size items were selected for testing. This is less than the sample size in part a since larger items will be represented in the item more than once.

    e.   Product #080102618 with a value at cost of $100,800.00 is the largest item in the sample. Ten items have a value larger than the sampling interval in the sample and in the population.

■ Internet Problem Solution: Monetary Unit Sampling Considerations

Internet Problem 17-1

   a.   The three steps in applying MUS are:
   1.   Determining the proper sample size;
   2.   Selecting the sample and performing the audit procedures; and
   3.   Evaluating the results and arriving at a conclusion about the recorded population value.

   b.   According to the paper's authors "Because MUS is based on attribute sampling, the sample size may be determined by the same basic procedures as for a statistical sample size for tests of controls."

   c.   The authors state that two factors must be considered when evaluating results. These factors are: the **type** of exception meaning whether it is an understatement or an overstatement and the **extent** of the exception must be measured and considered in estimating the misstatement.

(**Note**: Internet problems address current issues using Internet sources. Because Internet sites are subject to change, Internet problems and solutions may change. Current information on Internet problems is available at www.pearsonhighered.com/arens.)

Chapter 18

Audit of the Acquisition and Payment Cycle: Tests of Controls, Substantive Tests of Transactions, and Accounts Payable

■ **Review Questions**

18-1   a.   Asset accounts:

- Office supplies
- Delivery equipment
- Machinery and equipment
- Land
- Cash in bank
- Prepaid expenses

   b.   Liability accounts:

- Accounts payable
- Accrued property taxes
- Accrued insurance
- Other accrued liabilities

   c.   Expense accounts:

- Purchases, purchase returns & allowances, purchases discounts (COGS accounts)
- Rent expense
- Legal expense
- Fines and penalties
- Advertising expense
- Repairs and maintenance
- Depreciation expense
- Utilities expense
- Property tax expense
- Administrative expenses
- Income tax expense

TRANSACTION-RELATED AUDIT OBJECTIVE	POSSIBLE INTERNAL CONTROLS	COMMON TESTS OF CONTROLS
1. Recorded cash disbursements are for goods and services actually received (occurrence).	■ There is adequate segregation of duties between accounts payable and custody of signed checks. ■ Supporting documentation is examined before signing of checks by an authorized person. ■ Approval of payment on supporting documents at the time checks are signed.	■ Discuss with personnel and observe activities. ■ Discuss with personnel and observe activities. ■ Examine indication of approval.
2. Existing cash disbursement transactions are recorded (completeness).	■ Checks are prenumbered and accounted for. ■ The bank reconciliation is prepared monthly by an employee independent of recording cash disbursements or custody of assets.	■ Account for a sequence of checks. ■ Examine bank reconciliations and observe their preparation.
3. Recorded cash disbursement transactions are accurate (accuracy).	■ Calculations and amounts are internally verified. ■ The bank reconciliation is prepared monthly by an independent person.	■ Examine indication of internal verification. ■ Examine bank reconciliations and observe their preparation.
4. Cash disbursement transactions are properly included in the accounts payable master file and are properly summarized (posting and summarization).	■ Accounts payable master file contents are internally verified. ■ Accounts payable master file or trial balance totals are compared with general ledger balances.	■ Examine indication of internal verification. ■ Examine initials on general ledger accounts indicating comparison.
5. Cash disbursement transactions are properly classified (classification).	■ An adequate chart of accounts is used. ■ Account classifications are internally verified.	■ Examine procedures manual and chart of accounts. ■ Examine indication of internal verification.
6. Cash disbursement transactions are recorded on the correct dates (timing).	■ Procedures require recording of transactions as soon as possible after the check has been signed. ■ Dates are internally verified.	■ Examine procedures manual and observe whether unrecorded checks exist. ■ Examine indication of internal verification.

TRANSACTION-RELATED AUDIT OBJECTIVE	POSSIBLE INTERNAL CONTROLS	COMMON TESTS OF CONTROLS
1. Recorded acquisitions are for goods and services received, consistent with the best interests of the client (occurrence).	■ Purchase requisition, purchase order, receiving report, and vendor's invoice are attached to the voucher. ■ Acquisitions are approved at the proper level. ■ Computer accepts entry of purchases only from authorized vendors in the vendor master file. ■ Documents are cancelled to prevent their reuse. ■ Vendors' invoices, receiving reports, purchase orders, and purchase requisitions are internally verified.	■ Examine documents in voucher package for existence. ■ Examine indication of approval. ■ Attempt to input transactions with valid and invalid vendors. ■ Examine indication of cancellation. ■ Examine indication of internal verification.
2. Existing acquisition transactions are recorded (completeness).	■ Purchase orders are prenumbered and accounted for. ■ Receiving reports are prenumbered and accounted for. ■ Vouchers are prenumbered and accounted for.	■ Account for a sequence of purchase orders. ■ Account for a sequence of receiving reports. ■ Account for a sequence of vouchers.
3. Recorded acquisition transactions are accurate (accuracy).	■ Calculations and amounts are internally verified. ■ Batch totals are compared with computer summary reports. ■ Acquisitions are approved for prices and discounts	■ Examine indication of internal verification. ■ Examine file of batch totals for initials of data control clerk; compare totals to summary reports. ■ Examine indication of approval.
4. Acquisition transactions are properly included in the accounts payable and inventory master files, and are properly summarized (posting and summarization).	■ Accounts payable master file contents are internally verified. ■ Accounts payable master file or trial balance totals are compared with general ledger balances.	■ Examine indication of internal verification. ■ Examine initials on general ledger accounts indicating comparison.

18-3 (continued)

TRANSACTION-RELATED AUDIT OBJECTIVE	POSSIBLE INTERNAL CONTROLS	COMMON TESTS OF CONTROLS
5. Acquisition transactions are properly classified (classification).	■ Adequate chart of accounts is used. ■ Account classifications are internally verified.	■ Examine procedures manual and chart of accounts. ■ Examine indication of internal verification.
6. Acquisition transactions are recorded on the correct dates (timing).	■ Procedures require recording transactions as soon as possible after the goods and services have been received. ■ Dates are internally verified.	■ Examine procedures manual and observe whether unrecorded vendors' invoices exist. ■ Examine indication of internal verification.

18-4   Auditing standards require that the tests of controls and substantive tests of transactions cover the entire accounting period in order to determine that the system was operating in a consistent manner throughout the period. In selecting the number of items for testing, the auditor must determine the sample size, statistically or nonstatistically, such that it is likely to be representative of the actual conditions of the population of all transactions.

In testing items that are periodic procedures rather than individual transactions (such as monthly bank reconciliations), the auditor must determine the appropriate timing to determine that those procedures are operating properly.

18-5   The importance of cash discounts to the client is that the client can produce a substantial savings if it makes use of the cash discounts available. The auditor should examine vouchers and invoices to determine whether discounts are being taken in accordance with the terms available.

18-6   The difference in the purpose of the steps is that Procedure 1 ascertains whether all existing acquisitions are recorded properly (completeness and accuracy), whereas Procedure 2 is designed to determine whether recorded acquisitions are proper (occurrence and accuracy). Although the two procedures test opposite objectives (completeness and occurrence), they are similar in that each is designed to determine that the vendor's name, type of material and quantity purchased, and total amount of the acquisition agree with the receiving report, vendor's invoice, and acquisitions journal entries.

18-7   It is difficult to control blank or voided checks (as well as checks issued before they are mailed) without having a printed prenumbered system of blank checks. Without prenumbering, unauthorized and unrecorded checks may be more easily issued without detection until after they have cleared the bank. The auditor can compensate for poor control over checks by reconciling recorded cash disbursements with cash disbursements on the bank statement for a test period.

18-8 A voucher is a document used by an organization to establish a formal means of recording and controlling acquisitions. A voucher register is a journal for recording the vouchers for the acquisition of goods and services. The use of a voucher system improves control over the recording of purchases by facilitating the recording in numerical order at the earliest possible date, the point at which the invoice is received.

18-9 The point at which goods and services are received is ordinarily when title to the goods and services passes and a liability that should be included in the financial statements is established.

18-10 The acquisition and payment cycle is related to the inventory accounts in that normally all purchases of raw materials in the case of a manufacturing operation or merchandise in the case of a distribution company are recorded through this cycle. If the tests of internal controls of the acquisition and payment cycle indicate that proper controls exist to ensure that the proper cost is used in valuing the inventory and that new purchases of inventory are recorded at the proper time, in the proper amount, and in the proper account, tests concerned with the accuracy and cutoff of the inventory accounts may be reduced from that level required if the controls were not adequate.

18-11 The acquisition and payment cycle includes the recording of liabilities that are set up in the accounts payable account. If the auditor finds that the internal controls in the acquisition and payment cycle are sufficient to ensure that accounts payable are recorded in the proper amount and at the proper time, reconciling the vendors' statements and testing the cutoff as year-end procedures of the accounts payable balance may be greatly reduced.

18-12 The procedure will most likely uncover the misstatement in item b. The search for unrecorded invoices is designed to detect an understatement of accounts payable.

18-13 Unless evidence is discovered which indicates that a different approach should be followed, auditors traditionally follow a conservative approach in selecting vendors for accounts payable confirmations and customers for accounts receivable confirmations. The auditor assumes that the client is more likely to understate accounts payable, and therefore concentrates on the vendors with whom the client deals actively, especially if that vendor's balance appears to be lower than normal on the client's accounts payable listing at the confirmation date. In verifying accounts receivable, the auditor assumes that the client is more likely to overstate account balances; and for that reason concentrates more on the larger dollar balances and is not as concerned with "zero balances."

18-14 A vendor's invoice is sent with or at the same time as the order and states the amount of goods shipped, the price, and other details. This is the vendor's bill for the goods shipped. A vendor's statement contains the individual open items and the ending balance due in the account. A vendor's statement is not as

18-14 (continued)

meaningful as an invoice to verify individual transactions because a statement includes only the total amount of the transactions and not the details making up the shipment, such as unit price and freight. The vendor's statement can be used to verify the correct balance in accounts payable for an individual vendor. The statement contains the ending balance and the individual transactions required to reconcile the accounts payable listings and determine the propriety of the balances shown for individual vendors.

18-15 There are several reasons why it is not as common to confirm accounts payable at an interim date as it is for accounts receivable:

- Less reliance is placed on accounts payable systems than accounts receivable systems for most audits. For accounts payable, it is common to rely heavily on the search for unrecorded accounts payable to test the balance. When control risk is assessed at the maximum, it is inappropriate to confirm at an interim date.
- In auditing accounts payable, it is common for the auditor to confirm only those accounts for which vendors' statements are not available (received by the client) at year-end. Hence, the auditor will not know which accounts will be confirmed until the end of the year.
- Accounts payable confirmation is usually a less important and less time consuming task than confirmation of receivables; therefore, it is less important to confirm the accounts payable early for purposes of reducing year-end audit time.

18-16 It is important that the cutoff of accounts payable be coordinated with that of the physical inventory to determine that they are established at the same point in time. If these cutoffs are not consistent, goods may be counted in the physical inventory for which no liability in accounts payable has been recorded, or vice versa. Such a situation would result in an understatement of accounts payable and cost of goods sold or an overstatement of these two accounts, respectively. During the physical inventory, the auditor should gather cutoff information (such as the last several receiving reports and shipping documents) to assist in the determination that an accurate cutoff was established.

18-17 F.O.B. destination means that the title to the goods passes when they are received by the purchaser. F.O.B. origin signifies that the title passes to the buyer when the goods are shipped by the seller.

The auditor should be aware that the client might receive inventory subsequent to year-end that legally was the property of the client at year-end. When receiving reports near year-end are being examined and tested in connection with inventory cutoff tests, the auditor should search for goods that were shipped prior to year-end F.O.B. origin and received after the closing date. Examination of bills of lading will substantiate the date of shipment.

■ Multiple Choice Questions From CPA Examinations

18-18 a. (2)   b. (2)   c. (2)   d. (4)

18-19 a. (3)   b. (3)   c. (3)

18-20 a. (4)   b. (1)

■ Discussion Questions and Problems

18-21

QUESTION	a. TRANSACTION-RELATED AUDIT OBJECTIVE(S)	b. TEST OF CONTROL	c. POTENTIAL MIS-STATEMENT(S)	d. SUBSTANTIVE PROCEDURE
1	Recorded acquisitions and payments are for goods and services received, consistent with the best interests of the client (occurrence).	Observe and inquire about personnel performing purchasing, shipping, payables and disbursing functions.	Goods received and not recorded or recorded and not received. Disbursements made for goods not received.	Vendor statement reconciliation. Review of physical inventory shortages.
2	Acquisitions are recorded on the correct dates (timing). Existing acquisitions are recorded (completeness).	Observe and inquire about the procedure performed by mail clerk. Compare date mail is received to date accounting received invoices.	Late recording or non-recording of liabilities to suppliers.	Vendor statement reconciliation. Search for unrecorded liabilities.
3	Existing acquisitions are recorded (completeness).	Account for numerical sequence of receiving reports and determine that all were recorded.	Receiving reports are misplaced and acquisitions not recorded.	Vendor statement reconciliation.
4	Acquisitions are recorded at the proper amounts (accuracy).	Examine cancelled invoices for indication of checking for clerical accuracy.	Acquisitions from vendors are recorded at improper amounts.	Test extensions, footings, discounts, and freight terms on vendors' invoices.

18-21 (continued)

QUESTION	a. TRANSACTION-RELATED AUDIT OBJECTIVE(S)	b. TEST OF CONTROL	c. POTENTIAL MIS-STATEMENT(S)	d. SUBSTANTIVE PROCEDURE
5	Acquisition transactions are properly classified (classification).	Examine indication of approval.	Acquisitions are recorded in the wrong account.	Examine supporting invoice for reasonableness of accounting distribution.
6	Payments are recorded on the correct dates (timing). Existing payments are recorded (completeness).	Observe whether the system automatically posts checks when they are prepared.	Checks are disbursed and not recorded.	Examine checks clearing the bank prior to year-end to determine that they were recorded in the cash disburse-ments journal prior to year-end.
7	Acquisitions are for goods and services received, consistent with the best interests of the client (occurrence).	Examine invoices for which checks have been disbursed to determine that they have been cancelled.	Invoices are recorded and paid more than once.	Examine vendor statements, noting any unrecorded payments appearing on the statement.
8	Recorded cash disbursements are for goods and services actually received (occurrence).	Observe and inquire about the handling of checks from the time they are mailed to suppliers.	Checks are disbursed and no merchandise is received. Checks are received by other than the supplier for whom they are intended.	Trace checks to supporting invoice and determine reasonableness of expenditure. Reconcile vendors' statements.

QUESTION	a. TYPE OF TEST	b. PURPOSE OF PROCEDURE
1	Both (test of authorization is a test of control)	■ To determine that the amount recorded in the acquisitions journal is correct (accuracy). ■ To determine that recorded purchases are for goods and services actually received (occurrence).
2	Both (accounting for sequence is a test of control)	■ To determine that all receiving reports were eventually entered into the system as liabilities (completeness). ■ To determine that acquisitions were recorded at the proper amounts, considering the goods received (accuracy).
3	Substantive test of transactions	■ To determine that the amount recorded is accurate, that the classification is proper, and that the acquisition is for goods and services received, consistent with the best interests of the company (accuracy, classification and occurrence).
4	Test of control	■ To determine that the vendors' invoices are approved for payment, and that receiving reports and purchase orders are all attached (occurrence).
5	Substantive test of transactions	■ To determine that postings to the cash disbursements journal are properly summarized and posted to the general ledger and are posted to the accounts payable master file (posting and summarization).
6	Test of control	■ To determine that all check numbers are included to the cash disbursements journal, no check number is included more than once and voided checks are accounted for (completeness and occurrence).
7	Substantive test of transactions	■ To determine that the proper amount of cash disbursements are recorded during the test month. Checks are not recorded more than once and checks are not omitted (accuracy, occurrence and completeness).
8	Substantive test of transactions	■ To determine that checks are recorded on the correct dates (timing).

18-23   a.   Here are advantages for purchasing raw material jewelry items online through supplier Web sites:

- *Increased Product Selection.* Donnen Design purchasing personnel may be able to locate new products only offered through the Internet that they may not be able to obtain through normal purchasing channels.
- *Faster Delivery of Purchases.* Because Donnen Design purchasing agents may be able to purchase raw material jewelry items with company credit cards, shipment of the products to Donnen warehouses can occur at the point of sale. Thus, raw materials may be received by Donnen more quickly.
- *More Product Information.* Most jewelry suppliers post pictures of the products for sale on the Internet. Thus, Donnen purchasing personnel may have greater opportunities to pre-screen items before purchase than they do through traditional ordering sources.

b.   Here are potential risks associated with online purchases of raw material jewelry items:

- *Unauthorized Purchases Using Donnen Credit Cards.* Given that all online sales must be made using a company credit card, purchasing agents may have an opportunity to make unauthorized purchases that are charged to Donnen credit cards but shipped to purchasing agent addresses.
- *Privacy Protection for Donnen Credit Cards.* Because the reputation of the online vendors is unknown, there is some risk that Donnen credit card information will not be adequately protected by vendors from unauthorized use.
- *Inconsistent Product Quality.* Because Donnen purchasing agents will be buying products from a wide variety of new vendors, they have less information about product quality across vendors. As a result, the quality of the products purchased may vary extensively.
- *Reliability of Supplier.* Because Donnen purchasing agents will be buying products from a wide variety of new vendors, the reliability of those suppliers may vary extensively. There is no certainty that orders placed with each vendor will be processed completely and accurately.

c.   The primary advantage of allowing Donnen Design purchasing agents to acquire products using company credit cards is that the products will be shipped and delivered on a more timely basis than if they pay by company check.

18-23 (continued)

d. The primary advantages of restricting purchases to only those that can be paid by company check are that it (1) decreases the risk that Donnen personnel use company credit cards to make unauthorized purchases and (2) decreases the risk that online vendors fail to adequately protect Donnen credit card information.

e. Suggested internal controls:

(1) To prevent purchasing agents from making unauthorized purchases of non-jewelry items using Donnen credit cards, the company could:

- Request through the credit card agency that only selected types of products are authorized for purchase (for example, the credit card would not be allowed for any services, such as travel, food, hotel, etc).
- Send all credit card billing statements directly to accounting for reconciliation to receiving reports of inventory products.
- Separate credit cards may be issued to purchasing personnel with pre-specified spending limits.

(2) To prevent purchasing agents from ordering jewelry items for shipment to an agent's home address, the company could:

- Send all credit card billing statements directly to accounting for reconciliation to receiving reports.
- Only allow purchases from selected online vendors whose policies indicate that products may only be shipped to the credit card billing address (which would be a Donnen Design address).

(3) To prevent a buildup of unused credits with online vendors for returned goods, the company could:

- Only allow purchases from selected online vendors whose policies indicate that products may be returned for credit to the credit card account.
- Pre-screen product quality from all vendors before authorizing the use of that vendor for online purchasing.
- Establish purchasing limits for each online vendor so that the amount of purchases at a single vendor are not excessive.

MISSTATE-MENT	a. TRANSACTION-RELATED AUDIT OBJECTIVE NOT MET	b. PREVENTIVE CONTROL	c. SUBSTANTIVE PROCEDURE
1	Recorded cash disbursements are for goods and services actually received (occurrence).	Once checks are signed by the treasurer, they are returned to someone independent of purchasing and accounts payable for mailing. All supporting documents are cancelled to prevent reuse.	Review physical inventory shortages for unusual or inconsistent occurrences. Compare payee on the check to the company name on the vendor's invoice.
2	Recorded cash disbursement transactions are correctly stated (accuracy).	Checks are prepared using a computer process, which assures simultaneous preparation of check and journal. Reconcile bank account on a timely basis at the end of each month.	Compare check amounts to entries in the cash disbursements journal. Test bank reconciliation.
3	Cash disbursement transactions are recorded on the correct dates (timing).	Transactions are recorded automatically using a computer process with the same information as the check preparation.	Trace last checks written to cash disbursements journal. Examine date checks cancelled at bank to determine if checks were held by the client.
4	Recorded acquisitions are for goods and services received, consistent with the best interests of the client (occurrence).	Require that an authorized purchase order and/or approval of each invoice by the ordering department head be required before payments are made for goods received.	Examine underlying documents for reasonableness and authenticity.

MISSTATE-MENT	a. TRANSACTION-RELATED AUDIT OBJECTIVE NOT MET	b. PREVENTIVE CONTROL	c. SUBSTANTIVE PROCEDURE
5	Acquisition transactions are properly classified (classification).	Account distributions are reviewed by a responsible individual prior to entry into the system.	Examination of supporting invoices for entries into the repairs and maintenance account to verify the proper account distribution.
6	Acquisition transactions are recorded on the correct dates (timing).	Receiving reports to be delivered to accounting at the end of the day on which the raw materials are received. Accounting department accounts for numerical sequence of receiving reports after obtaining the last number used from receiving personnel.	At the date on which the cutoff test is to be performed, the auditor obtains the number of the last receiving report(s) that should have been recorded and accounts for the numerical sequence of all previous receiving report(s) that should have been recorded.

18-25 a. The type of audit evidence used for each procedure is as follows:

AUDIT PROCEDURE	TYPE OF AUDIT EVIDENCE
1	Reperformance
2	Internal documentation
3	External documentation (exchange rate); reperformance
4	Inquiries of client
5	External documentation
6	Confirmation
7	Internal and external documentation
8	Analytical procedure

18-25 (continued)

b.

AUDIT PROCEDURE	BALANCE-RELATED AUDIT OBJECTIVE						
	Detail tie-in	Existence	Completeness	Accuracy	Classification	Cutoff	Obligations
1	X						
2					X		
3				X			
4					X		
5		X	X	X		X	
6		X	X	X		X	
7			X			X	
8		X	X			X	

Note: Rights and Realizable value are not applicable to accounts payable.

c. Auditing standards require that all audit objectives be met by gathering sufficient appropriate evidence. Auditor judgment is required to determine the appropriate evidence to satisfy each objective. For example, where an objective is contributed to by an audit procedure that uses less reliable evidence, the audit objective will not be completely met. In such a case, additional evidence will be gathered using other audit procedures.

In this case, the evidence used in procedure 4 is from inquiries of the client, which is generally a weak form of evidence. Thus, the classification objective could require more reliable evidence from other audit procedures to be fully met.

Procedure 2 uses internal documentation as its primary evidence. The reliability of this procedure would depend on the effectiveness of the client's internal controls in producing the internal documents.

EXCEPTION	a. TYPE OF EXCEPTION	b. TRANSACTION-RELATED AUDIT OBJECTIVE NOT MET	c. AUDIT IMPORTANCE	d. FOLLOW-UP	e. EFFECT ON AUDIT	f. PREVENTIVE CONTROLS
1	Monetary misstatement	Acquisition transactions are properly classified (classification).	Indicates that no one is effectively reviewing the accounting distribution. Auditor must consider the effect of the exceptions on determining the amount of reliance that he or she may place on the system.	Determine the significance of the misclassifications and plan any required additional steps that are deemed appropriate.	If considered significant, the exceptions could prevent reliance on the system of internal controls and require the auditor to perform additional tests of the classification of items within the financial statements.	Have someone review the account distribution of invoices that enter the system.
2	Control deviation	Recorded acquisitions and related cash disbursements are for goods and services received, consistent with the best interests of the client (occurrence).	Indicates that the controller is not following the procedure of initialing invoices. This may indicate that he or she is not effectively reviewing invoices and other supporting documents prior to payment.	Determine whether or not the controller is effectively reviewing invoices and other supporting documents.	If determination is made that controller does not review supporting documents, the audit tests should be increased to determine the significance of the deficiency.	A competent independent person should review supporting documents for approval of controller and test items to determine effectiveness of controller's review.

EXCEPTION	a.\n\nTYPE OF EXCEPTION	b.\n\nTRANSACTION-RELATED AUDIT OBJECTIVE NOT MET	c.\n\nAUDIT IMPORTANCE	d.\n\nFOLLOW-UP	e.\n\nEFFECT ON AUDIT	f.\n\nPREVENTIVE CONTROLS
3	Monetary misstatement	Acquisition transactions are recorded on the correct dates (timing).	At the date of the physical inventory, this situation will be critical in that any items counted in physical inventory and not recorded in the acquisitions journal will cause an understated cost of sales and accounts payable.	Determine whether or not this situation persists throughout the year and whether it is rectified at physical inventory date and year-end.	Require expansion of purchase cutoff work at physical inventory date and year-end.	Require that copies of all receiving reports be routed directly to accounting and that accounting account for numerical sequence of receiving reports on a regular basis.
4	Monetary misstatement	Recorded cash disbursements are for goods and services actually received (occurrence).	It could be a fraudulent payment or it could result in an overstatement of perpetual inventory records. If the payment is fraudulent, there are serious audit ramifications. If it is unintentional, the situation is wasteful of company assets and must be brought to the client's attention.	First determine whether it is fraudulent. If not, investigate the frequency of occurrence of duplicate payments to determine their significance.	The duplicate payments result in recording of nonexistent inventory. If the company performs an interim physical inventory, the auditor could experience a problem relying on the system of internal control between the physical inventory date and year-end.	Invoices must be matched with an original receiving report and purchase order prior to approval for payment. All duplicate invoices are marked "duplicate" upon receipt.

18-26 (continued)

EXCEPTION	a. TYPE OF EXCEPTION	b. TRANSACTION- RELATED AUDIT OBJECTIVE NOT MET	c. AUDIT IMPORTANCE	d. FOLLOW-UP	e. EFFECT ON AUDIT	f. PREVENTIVE CONTROLS
5	Monetary misstatement	Recorded cash disbursement transactions are correctly stated (accuracy).	Results in $100 liability, which may or may not be recorded on the books.	Investigate the exception rate to determine the possible effect of unrecorded liabilities on the financial statements.	Probably none, since occurrence rate is low. If amount is significant, then expansion of reconciliation of vendor statements may be appropriate.	An independent person should compare checks to invoice amount prior to signing checks.
6	Control deviation	Existing cash disbursement transactions are recorded (completeness).	The check may not actually have been voided. It could represent the disbursement of cash if a check was prepared.	Determine company policy for voided checks and evaluate the potential for unrecorded checks.	Auditor should examine the bank cutoff statement for the possibility that the voided check and other checks may have been issued and cashed but not recorded.	Require that all voided checks be properly voided and saved.

18-26 (continued)

EXCEPTION	a. TYPE OF EXCEPTION	b. TRANSACTION- RELATED AUDIT OBJECTIVE NOT MET	c. AUDIT IMPORTANCE	d. FOLLOW-UP	e. EFFECT ON AUDIT	f. PREVENTIVE CONTROLS
7	Control deviation and Monetary misstatement	Recorded acquisitions are for goods and services received, consistent with the best interests of the client (occurrence). Recorded acquisition transactions are correctly stated (accuracy).	Absence of receiving reports prevents the auditor from determining whether or not the goods were received and processed on a timely basis. The extension error indicates that the clerical accuracy of invoice tests are ineffective.	Obtain bill of lading copy from vendor to determine whether or not the merchandise was received. Determine if the absence of receiver indicates that they are not compared to the invoice. Determine the exception rate by expanding the tests if the misstatement noted is considered significant.	If either of the problems is considered significant to the auditor, he or she should expand the scope of his or her tests of controls or substantive tests of transactions to determine the effect on the financial statements.	Require that copies of receiving reports must be present before invoices are approved for payment. Have an independent person test extensions to determine that the clerical tests are effective.

NOTE: For all monetary misstatements that are potential frauds, the auditor should evaluate whether a fraud occurred. Even one fraud is sufficient for the auditor to consider the potential impact on the audit, primarily because materiality is normally smaller for fraud than for errors.

a. Vouchers 2528 and 2531 were incorrectly included in the June 2011 acquisitions journal. The associated goods were received after June 30, 2011.

As for July 2011, voucher numbers 2527 and 2530 were incorrectly included because the goods were actually received before the end of June 2011.

Let's assume the corrections were made in two journal entries as follows:

Accounts payable	$11,687.99	
Inventory		$11,687.99
Inventory	$ 6,935.73	
Accounts payable		$ 6,935.73

b. Improper dating of dating of receiving reports 7280 through 7282 would result in the improper recording of vouchers 2528, 2529, and 2531 in the June 2011 acquisitions journal. That would result in the overstatement of inventory and accounts payable as of June 30, 2011 by $16,576.32. The auditor might catch this by comparing receiving reports recorded just before year end to vendor invoices or vendor statements to determine if the items reflected as being received by the client just prior to year end are included in the vendor invoice or vendor statement as a balance owed as of June 30.

c. To verify the appropriateness of the cutoff of inventory acquisitions and the related accounts payable balance at year end, the auditor examines receipts of goods before and after the balance sheet date to ensure those items received before year end are included in the acquisitions journal (and thus the accounts payable balance) in the last month of the fiscal year. The auditor also determines that receipts of goods after year end are not reflected in the acquisitions journal (and thus the accounts payable balance) as of year end.

d. Possible internal controls that would prevent the errors noted at The Broughton Cap Company include the following:

- Require that receiving reports be completed in sequential order as goods are received.
- Require receiving reports to be to accounts payable daily for immediate voucher preparation.
- Accounts payable clerks account for the numerical sequence of receiving reports and prepare voucher packages in numerical sequence starting based on the order of receiving reports received.

18-27 (continued)

- An independent person matches the purchase order, receiving report, and voucher package and verifies accuracy and correctness of dates of receipts relative to dates of recording of voucher in the acquisitions journal.
- Vendor statements are reconciled on a monthly basis with the accounts payable master file.

18-28 a. The fact that the client made a journal entry to record vendors' invoices which were received late should simplify the CPA's test for unrecorded liabilities and reduce the possibility of a need for a further adjustment, but the CPA's test is nevertheless required. Clients normally are expected to make necessary adjustments to their books so that the CPA may audit financial statements that the client believes are complete and correct. If the client has not recorded late invoices, the CPA is compelled in his or her testing to substantiate what will ultimately be recorded as an adjusting entry. In this audit, the CPA should test entries in the 2012 voucher register to ascertain that all items that were applicable to 2011 have been included in the journal entry recorded by the client.

b. No. Response to inquiry alone generally does not constitute sufficient appropriate evidence. The CPA should obtain a letter in which responsible executives of the client's organization represent that to the best of their knowledge all liabilities have been recognized. However, this is done as a normal audit procedure to remind the client of his or her responsibilities and the statements that have been made. It does not relieve the CPA of the responsibility for making his or her own tests.

c. Whenever a CPA is justified in relying on work done by an internal auditor he or she can reduce (but not eliminate) his or her own audit work. In this case, the CPA should have determined early in his or her audit that Ozine's internal auditor is qualified by being both technically competent and reasonably independent. Once satisfied as to these points, the CPA should discuss the nature and scope of the internal audit program with the internal auditor and review his or her internal audit schedules in order that the CPA may properly coordinate his or her own program with that of the internal auditor. If the Ozine internal auditor is qualified and has made tests for unrecorded liabilities, the CPA may limit his or her work to a less extensive test in this audit area if the results of the internal auditor's tests were satisfactory.

18-28 (continued)

    d.   Work done by an auditor for a federal agency will normally have no effect on the scope of the CPA's audit, since the concern of government auditors is usually limited to matters which are unrelated to the financial statements. Nevertheless, the CPA should discuss the government auditor's work program with him or her, as there are isolated situations where specific procedures followed to a satisfactory conclusion by a government auditor will furnish the CPA with added assurance and therefore permit him or her to reduce certain work in an area. However, government auditors are usually interested primarily in substantiating as valid and allowable those costs which a company has allocated against specific government contracts or sales to the government, and consequently there is little likelihood that the auditor for a federal agency at Ozine would check for unrecorded liabilities.

        (Another reason for discussing the federal auditor's results with him or her is that his or her findings may affect the financial statements in other ways.)

    e.   In addition to the 2012 acquisitions journal, the CPA should consider the following sources for possible unrecorded liabilities:

        1.   If a separate cash disbursements journal exists, examine underlying documentation for disbursements recorded during the first part of 2012. Determine if any of the disbursements relate to acquisitions that should have been recorded in 2011.

        2.   Vendors' invoices that have not been entered in the acquisitions journal.

        3.   Status of tax returns for prior years still open.

        4.   Discussions with employees.

        5.   Representations from management.

        6.   Comparison of account balances with preceding year.

        7.   Examination of individual accounts during the audit.

        8.   Existing contracts and agreements.

        9.   Minutes.

      10.   Attorneys' bills and letters of representation.

      11.   Status of renegotiable business.

      12.   Correspondence with principal suppliers.

      13.   Audit testing of cutoff date for reciprocal accounts, e.g., inventory and fixed assets.

a. **Bergeron Internal Controls**	b. **Transaction Related Audit Objective(s)**	c. **Test of Controls**
1. Prenumbered purchase orders are used and accounted for.	Occurrence, Completeness	Review Bergeron's accounting for the sequence of purchase orders to determine if all are properly accounted for.
2. All purchase orders must be approved by the vice president of finance.	Occurrence	Examine a sample of purchase orders and verify that all are properly approved by the vice president of finance.
3. Prenumbered receiving reports are prepared upon receipt of goods.	Completeness	Review Bergeron's accounting for the sequence of receiving reports to determine if all are properly accounted for.
4. Goods are stored in a warehouse that is under the control of the shipping manager.	Completeness	Observe whether access to the inventory in the warehouse is properly restricted. Inquire as to how the shipping manager restricts access to inventory.
5. Perpetual inventory records are updated upon receipt of goods as evidenced by the receiving report.	Completeness, Accuracy, Timing	Examine a sample of receiving reports and verify that the perpetual inventory records were updated on a timely basis.

18-29 (continued)

a. Bergeron Internal Controls	b. Transaction Related Audit Objective(s)	c. Test of Controls
6. Chief accountant matches vendor invoices to purchase order and receiving reports (If related to goods purchased), checking for accuracy and appropriateness. Chief accountant documents review by initialing documents.	Occurrence, Completeness, Accuracy	Examine a sample of matched documents and verify that all are properly initialed by the chief accountant and that amounts are accurate and appropriate.
7. Access to accounting records is restricted by password to the chief accountant.	Occurrence	Attempt to access the accounting records with an invalid password.
8. Accounting records are updated timely based on matching of documentation.	Timing	Examine a sample of matched documents and verify that entries were made in the accounting records in the correct time period.
9. President reviews all documentation before approving cash disbursements and controls signed checks until mailing.	Occurrence	Examine a sample of cash disbursement transactions and verify that all are properly approved by the president.
10. Controller performs a monthly bank reconciliation.	Occurrence, Completeness, Accuracy, Timing	Examine a sample of monthly bank reconciliations to verify they were performed and properly completed.

a. Bergeron Internal Controls	b. Transaction Related Audit Objective(s)	c. Test of Controls
11. Controller reconciles on a monthly basis the accounts payable listing to the accounts payable general ledger account. Controller initials reconciliation upon completion.	Posting and summarization	Examine a sample of monthly reconciliations to determine they are initialed and prepared properly.
12. Independent inventory counts are obtained quarterly and reconciled to the perpetual inventory records.	Occurrence, Completeness, Accuracy	Observe client inventory count teams during one of the quarterly inventory counts to determine whether they are following the client's inventory counting procedures.

18-30 a.   It is an appropriate procedure to have the client perform the reconciliations of vendors' statements as long as the auditor maintains control over the statements which have been received directly from the vendor and the auditor performs adequate tests to determine that the reconciling items shown on the reconciliations are proper.

b.   On Statement 1, the auditor must determine that the payment was recorded on the company's books prior to June 30. The auditor may also want to examine the cutoff bank statement to determine if the check to this vendor cleared the bank within a reasonable amount of time.

On Statement 2, the auditor must determine that the payment was recorded on the company's records prior to June 30 and investigate the reason that the vendor had not received the payment at the time his or her statement was prepared. The auditor must determine whether or not the goods represented on the invoices that Milner had not received were in the company's inventory at June 30. This may be accomplished by requesting that the vendor send proof of shipment for the goods invoiced.

For Statement 3, the auditor should request that the vendor provide additional details of the account balance. Otherwise, the auditor will not be able to use the vendor's statement and will have to include the $5,735.69 as a potential misstatement.

18-30 (continued)

For Statement 4, the auditor must determine whether or not the item for which the credit memo was issued by the vendor on July 15 was appropriately recorded on the company's records at June 30, including consideration of inventory.

The Statement 5 reconciliation is incorrect. The payment by Milner on July 3 should not have been deducted from the accounts payable balance per the master file. The auditor should investigate the unlocated difference, since it could be comprised of two much larger offsetting amounts that the auditor may wish to test.

c. The auditor must consider whether the coverage achieved by the 18 confirmations that were received directly from the vendors is sufficient outside verification of the accounts payable balance at June 30. If the auditor is satisfied with this coverage, he or she may wish to support the four nonresponses by examining vendor invoices in support of the amount recorded in the master file. If the client has received vendor statements from any of these four suppliers, the auditor may wish to reconcile these statements.

18-31 a. It is essential to coordinate the cutoff tests with the physical observation of inventory. If the cutoff is inconsistent with the physical inventory there can be significant misstatements in the income statement and the balance sheet. For example, assume an inventory acquisition for $40,000 is received late in the afternoon of December 31, after the physical inventory is completed. If the acquisition is included in accounts payable and purchases but excluded from inventory, the result is an understatement of net earnings of $40,000. On the other hand, if the acquisition is excluded from both inventory and accounts payable, there is a misstatement in the balance sheet, but the income statement is correct.

b.

RECEIVING REPORT NO.	DESCRIPTION OF MISSTATEMENT(S)	ADJUSTING ENTRY			
		DEBIT		CREDIT	
		ACCOUNT	AMOUNT	ACCOUNT	AMOUNT
2631	None				
2632	Received prior to year-end and not recorded	Inventory	6,320.54	Accounts payable	6,320.54

18-31 (continued)

| RECEIVING REPORT NO. | DESCRIPTION OF MISSTATEMENT(S) | ADJUSTING ENTRY | | | |
| | | DEBIT | | CREDIT | |
		ACCOUNT	AMOUNT	ACCOUNT	AMOUNT
2633	Included in accounts payable and not inventory	Inventory	3,761.22	Purchases	3,761.22
2634	Received prior to year-end and not recorded	Inventory	7,832.18	Accounts payable	7,832.18
2635	Included in accounts payable and not inventory	Inventory	6,847.77	Purchases	6,847.77
2636	None				
2637	Title passed prior to year-end and not recorded	Inventory	5,878.36	Accounts payable	5,878.36
2638	None				

    c.   Typically, misstatements that have an effect on earnings are most important because of the importance of earnings to users of financial statements. Receiving report numbers 2633 and 2635 affect earnings. In addition, these misstatements are more important because they represent the recording of part of the entry. If they are not adjusted, the inventory balance the following year will be understated by $10,608.99 (3,761.22 + 6,847.77). For the other three items (receiving report numbers 2632, 2634 and 2637), the misstatement is less important because they would be recorded the following year and the account balances would then be proper.

■ **Case – Ward Publishing Company**

18-32

Part I

Computer Solution. Computer prepared data sheets using Excel are contained on the Companion Web site (Filename P1832.xls).

    Application of audit sampling is not appropriate for Procedures 1-8 due to the nature of the procedures. In this case, audit sampling is also not appropriate for

18-32 - Part I (continued)

Procedure 10 because the sampling unit is a line item in the cash disbursements journal. The sampling data sheet that follows represents an attributes sampling approach. The only differences between this approach and a nonstatistical sampling approach are the estimate of ARACR and the determination of sample sizes. See the footnotes to the sampling data sheet for further explanations. A sampling data sheet using attributes sampling follows:

	DESCRIPTION OF ATTRIBUTE	PLANNED AUDIT			
		EPER	TER	ARACR*	INITIAL SAMPLE SIZE**
9.a.	Entry in CD journal agrees with details on cancelled check.	0%	6%	10%	38
9.b.(1)	All supporting documents attached to vendor's invoice.	1%	5%	10%	77
9.b.(2)	Documents agree with disbursements.	0%	6%	10%	38
9.b.(3)	Entry in CD journal agrees with details on vendor's invoice.	0%	6%	10%	38
9.b.(4)	Discount was taken as appropriate.	0%	6%	10%	38
9.b.(5)	Vendor's invoice initialed.	1%	5%	10%	77
9.b.(6)	Account coding reasonable.	0%	6%	10%	38
9.b.(7)	Purchases approved by Ward.	1%	5%	10%	77
9.b.(8)	P.O. or P.R. properly approved.	1%	5%	10%	77
9.b.(9)	Prices, footings and extensions are correct.	0%	6%	10%	38
9.b.(10)	Details on supporting documents agree.	0%	6%	10%	38
9.b.(11)	Documents properly completed and cancelled upon payment.	1%	5%	10%	77

*   For a nonstatistical sampling data sheet, ARACR columns should indicate "medium" for all attributes.

**   For a nonstatistical sampling data sheet, students' determination of sample size will vary. While no one answer is correct, the sample size chosen for each attribute should reflect the EPER, TER and ARACR for that attribute.

18-32 (continued)

Part II

a. *Attributes sampling approach*: The results portion of the sampling data sheet are as follows:

ATTRIBUTE NO.		SAMPLE SIZE	EXCEPTIONS	EXCEPTION RATE	CUER
9.a.		50	0	0	4.6%
9.b.	(1)	50	1*	2%	7.6%
	(2)	50	0	0	4.6%
	(3)	50	0	0	4.6%
	(4)	50	0	0	4.6%
	(5)	50	6*	12%	over 17.8%
	(6)	50	3**	6%	12.9%
	(7)	50	0	0	4.6%
	(8)	50	0	0	4.6%
	(9)	50	0	0	4.6%
	(10)	50	0	0	4.6%
	(11)	50	0	0	4.6%
* Control deviations					
** Monetary misstatements					

Nonstatistical approach: Because CUER under nonstatistical sampling is estimated using auditor judgment, students' answers to this question will vary. They will most likely be similar to the CUERs calculated using attributes sampling.

Because the SER is zero for attributes 9.a., 9.b.(2)-(4), and 9.b.(7)-(11), it is unlikely that students will estimate CUER greater than the TER of 5% (tests of controls) or 6% (substantive tests of transactions). For attribute 9.b.(5) students should conclude that the results are not acceptable because the SER of 12% clearly exceeds the TER of 5%. For attribute 9.b.(6), even though the SER equals the TER of 6%, the results are not acceptable because sampling error must be considered in determining CUER. For attribute 9.b.(1), students' estimates of CUER will be more variable since the SER is only 2%. Some students will find the results acceptable, and some will not, depending on their estimates of sampling error.

b. Exception 1 is not an exception, and has no effect on tests of details of accounts payable.

Exception 2 is a control deviation. Even though it is not a monetary misstatement, controls require the presence of all supporting documents before a purchase and the related disbursement are processed. If an invalid purchase is recorded, the liability and the related debited account may be overstated. If an invalid disbursement is recorded, accounts payable may be inappropriately reduced.

18-32 - Part II (continued)

Thus, misstatements in the occurrence of those transactions could actually result in both overstatements and understatements of accounts payable. Tests for occurrence include tracing items on the accounts payable listing to supporting documents and confirmation of accounts payable and reconciliation to vendor's statements.

Exception 3 is a control deviation where one-half of those items also contain monetary misstatements. Misclassification is a serious misstatement. However, it relates to the debit entry, not the credit to accounts payable. Tests supporting charges to assets and expense accounts will need to be increased, but tests of accounts payable will probably not be affected.

c. On the following page is an audit program for accounts payable. The balance-related audit objectives tested by each procedure are indicated. Because the appropriate audit risk for accounts payable is high and inherent risk is low, and because analytical review procedures were excellent, detailed tests should be held to a minimum. The exception to this is for procedure 3; this has not been reduced because of the exception in procedure 9.b.(1).

	BALANCE-RELATED AUDIT OBJECTIVES						
	Detail tie-in	Existence	Completeness	Accuracy	Classification	Cutoff	Obligations
1. Obtain list of accounts payable. Foot the list and agree to general ledger.	X						
2. Trace all items on the list over $10,000 to vendor's invoice and supporting documents.		X		X			
3. Obtain vendor's statements for 20 vendors with greatest volume of purchases, plus 10 others, by confirmation. Reconcile statements to accounts payable list.		X	X	X		X	
4. Examine all subsequent period disbursements and payments in process of amounts over $5,000 to determine if they were recorded in the proper period.			X			X	
5. Review the list of accounts payable for proper classification of accounts due to related parties, debit balances, or items with unusual terms.					X		

Note: Rights and Realizable value are not applicable to accounts payable. No audit work was considered necessary for obligations.

■ **Internet Problem Solution: Identifying Accounts Payable Fraud**

Internet Problem 18-1

a. Most often the cause of a duplicate payment is due to error versus fraud. While many of the accounting software packages have controls to identify duplicate payments, slight differences in duplicate invoices can prevent the software controls from detecting a duplicate payment. For example, duplicate invoices from the same vendor with slightly different invoice numbers of #3454 and #3454-A may not be recognized by the software controls. The most common cause of duplicate invoice numbers is having duplicate vendor numbers for the same vendor. Because duplicate invoices from the same vendor are applied to different vendor accounts, the duplicates aren't easily detected because it appears that the two invoices are from different vendors.

b. Dupe searches look for duplicate elements within two or more invoices. If several elements match, then there may be a greater likelihood that duplicate invoices might be present. Another technique is the use of "fuzzy-matching," which is similar to dupe searches except that the comparison is focused on "similarities" in elements rather than exact matches.

c. Benford's Law can be used to predict the frequency of certain numbers in a pattern of digits. For example, Benford's law predicts that, out of a group of numbers, the first digit will be a "1" about 30% of the time, whereas it will be an "8" about 5.1% of the time. So, if an individual who records fictitious accounts payable transactions includes an excessive amount of fictitious transactions beginning with the number "1" in the first digits column, the use of Benford's Law may detect that activity when it reveals unexpected pattern of transactions beginning with the number "1".

d. A common fraud technique is to process transactions at amounts that are just below limits that require management approval. For example, spending limits may require higher level management approval for transactions greater than or equal to $5,000. So, an individual may record a fictitious transaction that has an amount of $4,950.

   To detect that kind of fraudulent activity, transactions that are just below the approval limits could be flagged for review. For example, all transactions that are 5% or less than the approval limit could be flagged for review. In our example, all transactions between $4,750 and $5,000 would be reviewed. Thus, the $4,950 transaction would be selected for review.

Internet Problem 18-1 (continued)

    e.   One control to detect payments made falsely to employees due to the inclusion of employees in the vendor master file is to perform a cross-check of the vendor and employee master files. By merging the vendor and employee master files, an organization can match certain variables (or do a fuzzy match) in the files such as:

- Address
- Tax ID numbers
- Phone numbers
- Bank routing numbers

Matches of these variables between the two files should be investigated to determine if employees are falsely included in the vendor master file.

(**Note**: Internet problems address current issues using Internet sources. Because Internet sites are subject to change, Internet problems and solutions may change. Current information on Internet problems is available at www.pearsonhighered.com/arens.)

Chapter 19

Completing the Tests in the
Acquisition and Payment Cycle:
Verification of Selected Accounts

■ **Review Questions**

19-1   Because the source of the debits in the asset account is the acquisitions journal (or similar record), the current period acquisitions of property, plant and equipment have already been partially verified as part of the acquisition and payment cycle. In that testing, the occurrence, completeness, accuracy, cutoff, and classification of acquisitions of property, plant, and equipment would have been examined. The disposal of assets, depreciation and accumulated depreciation are not tested as a part of the acquisition and payment cycle.

19-2   The reason for the emphasis on current period acquisitions in auditing property, plant, and equipment is that there is an expectation that permanent assets will be kept and maintained on the records for several years. The assets carried over from the preceding years can be assumed to have been verified in the prior years' audits.

      If tests of controls and substantive tests of transactions do not show that all disposals have been recorded, additional testing of the prior balance could be required. A first year audit also necessitates tests of the beginning balance.

19-3   Many clients may accidentally or intentionally record purchases of assets in the repair and maintenance account. The misstatement is caused by a lack of understanding of accounting standards and some clients' desire to avoid income taxes. Repair and maintenance accounts are verified primarily to uncover unrecorded property purchases. In other cases, however, management has fraudulently capitalized repair and maintenance expenses to boost profitability and assets.

      The auditor typically vouches the larger amounts debited to those expense accounts at the same time that property accounts are being audited.

19-4   The audit procedures that may be applied to determine that all property, plant and equipment retirements have been recorded are as follows:

    1.   Review whether newly acquired assets replace existing assets and inquire as to whether the old asset has been removed from the books.
    2.   Analyze gains on the disposal of assets and miscellaneous income for receipts from the disposal of assets. Compare these to property, plant and equipment accounts to see whether the asset has been removed from the books.

19-4 (continued)

3. Review planned modification and changes in product lines, taxes, or insurance coverage for indications of deletions of equipment.
4. Make inquiries of management and production personnel about the disposal of assets.

19-5 The two considerations to be kept in mind in auditing depreciation expense are:

1. Whether the client is following a consistent depreciation policy from period to period.
2. The accuracy of the client's calculations.

An overall reasonableness test can be made by calculating the depreciation rate for the year times the undepreciated fixed assets. In addition, it is desirable to check the accuracy of the depreciation calculation. The extent of the accuracy tests will vary depending on the engagement circumstances.

19-6 Since the source of the debits to prepaid insurance is the acquisitions journal or similar record (assuming all insurance premiums are charged to prepaid insurance rather than insurance expense), the current period premiums have already been partially verified as a part of the acquisition and payment cycle. The allocation of the premium between prepaid insurance is not tested as a part of the acquisition and payment cycle.

19-7 The audit of prepaid insurance should ordinarily take a relatively small amount of audit time because:

1. The balance in prepaid insurance is normally immaterial;
2. There are ordinarily few transactions during the year and most transactions are immaterial;
3. The transactions are ordinarily not complex.

19-8 The evaluation of the adequacy of insurance is a test of reasonable protection against the loss of existing assets. The verification of prepaid insurance is performed to determine whether:

1. The balances represent proper charges against future operations.
2. The additions represent charges to these accounts and are reflected at actual cost.
3. Amortization or write-off is reasonable under the circumstances.

The evaluation of adequacy of insurance coverage is more important because of the potential loss due to under-insurance. Verification of prepaid insurance usually involves an immaterial amount and is not emphasized in most audits.

19-9 The audit of prepaid expenses differs from the audit of other asset accounts, such as accounts receivable or property, plant, and equipment, because prepaid expenses are often immaterial. Analytical procedures are often sufficient for auditing prepaid expenses, while tests of details of balances are usually required for other accounts such as accounts receivable and property, plant, and equipment.

19-10 Debits to accrued rent arise from the cash disbursements journal, which is verified as a part of tests of controls and substantive tests of transactions for cash disbursements. The credits typically arise from the general journal and may not have been verified as a part of these tests. Furthermore, tests of controls and substantive tests of transactions do not include verification of the inclusion of accruals on all existing property and verification of the consistent treatment of the accruals from year to year.

19-11 Property tax accruals take little audit time for most audits, and since there are relatively few transactions to test and they are typically material in amount, it is common to verify the accounts 100 percent. On the other hand, accounts payable takes quite a bit of audit time and since there are usually a large number of transactions to test and they are typically varied in amount, it is common to verify the account on a test basis.

19-12 The following documents will be used to verify accrued property taxes and related expense accounts:

1. Deeds to properties
2. Property tax returns
3. Cancelled checks
4. Invoices from the taxing authority

19-13 Three expense accounts that are tested as part of the acquisition and payment cycle or the payroll and personnel cycle are:

1. Property tax expense
2. Payroll expense
3. Rent expense

Three expense accounts that are not directly verified as part of either of these cycles are:

1. Depreciation expense
2. Amortization of patents
3. Year-end bonuses to officers

19-14 The analysis of expense accounts is a procedure by which selected expense accounts are verified by examining underlying supporting vendors' invoices or other documentation to determine if the transactions making up the total are correctly stated. The emphasis in most expense account analysis is on the occurrence of recorded amounts, accuracy, and classification.

Potentially the same objectives are accomplished in tests of controls and substantive tests of transactions as for expense account analysis. The major differences are that tests of controls and substantive tests of transactions are selected from all of the acquisitions and cash disbursements journals for the entire period whereas transactions examined for expense analysis are limited to the account being analyzed. Nevertheless, the procedures are closely related, and if the tests of controls and substantive tests of transactions procedures results are satisfactory, reduced expense account analysis is implied.

19-15 The approach for verifying depreciation expense should emphasize the consistency of the method of depreciation used and the related computations, since these aspects of depreciation expense are the main determinants of the account balance. The use of analytical procedures and reperformance tests is important for depreciation expense.

In verifying repair expense, the emphasis should be on vouching transactions that may be capital items; therefore, examining supporting documentation for transactions from months with unusually large totals or transactions that are themselves large or unusual is the normal audit approach followed.

The approach is different because in repairs and maintenance the primary objective is to locate improperly classified fixed assets, whereas in depreciation the emphasis is on consistency from period to period and accurate depreciation calculations.

19-16 The factors that should affect the auditor's decision whether or not to analyze an account balance are:

1. The analytical procedures indicate there is a high likelihood of misstatement in an account.
2. The tests of controls and substantive tests of transactions indicate there is a high likelihood of misstatement in an account.
3. The account is likely to contain misstatements because it is difficult for the client to properly classify or value the transactions.
4. The auditor knows that the account is frequently subject to abuse or misstatement.
5. The analysis of the account might disclose a contingency.
6. Tax returns and the SEC require the disclosure of certain information, which the account is likely to provide.

Four expense accounts that are commonly analyzed in audit engagements are:

1. Legal expense
2. Travel and entertainment expense
3. Tax expense
4. Repair and maintenance expense

■ Multiple Choice Questions From CPA Examinations

19-17 a. (1)   b. (1)   c. (3)

19-18 a. (3)   b. (4)   c. (2)

19-19 a. (1)   b. (4)   c. (3)

19-20 a. (4)   b. (4)   c. (4)

■ Discussion Questions and Problems

19-21

ITEM NO.	INTERNAL CONTROL	SUBSTANTIVE AUDIT PROCEDURE
1	Use of government study depreciation tables.	Compare to government study depreciation table.
2	Establish a policy for deciding which items require capitalization and establish an internal verification procedure.	Test all expense charges to these accounts that exceed a certain amount.
3	Require internal verification in the recording of property acquisitions.	Compare supporting documentation on property acquisitions to the recorded value.
4	Require the deposit of all cash directly into the bank account.	(1) Confirm loans with the bank and perform other tests for unrecorded loans. (2) Examine plant asset additions and agree to recorded amounts and dete
5	Have office manager periodically report to the accounting department whether or not there have been abandonments or replacements.	Trace from equipment recorded on the accounting records to the equipment.
6	Internally verify charges for depreciation expenses.	Compare depreciation expense for administration and manufacturing to previous years.
7	Assign tools to individual foreman and periodically count the tools.	Check the client's physical count of the tools.

19-22

a. PURPOSE	b. TEST OF CONTROL TO TEST FOR EXISTENCE OF CONTROL	c. SUBSTANTIVE PROCEDURE TO TEST FOR MISSTATEMENTS
1. To assure that recording asset misstatements are minimized. (Existence, completeness)	Verify that master file exists and is used.	Physically examine fixed assets and trace to master file.
2. To minimize accounting classification misstatements. (Classification)	Verify that written policies exist.	Examine supporting documentation for transactions to determine if policies are followed for account classification.
3. To minimize depreciation calculation and recording misstatements. (Accuracy)	Examine records for indication of periodic verification of master file.	Test calculations and postings of depreciation charges.
4. To minimize improper purchases. (Existence)	Examine a sample of purchase invoices of fixed assets in excess of $20,000 for Board of Directors' approval.	Examine a sample of purchase invoices of fixed assets for propriety and reasonableness.
5. To provide a record of fixed assets and protect against their loss. (Completeness and existence)	Examine the company's physical count of equipment that compares tags on the equipment to records of tags.	Trace a sample of recorded equipment to the related equipment to make sure it exists.

19-23

ITEM NO.	a. TYPE OF EVIDENCE USED	b. TYPE OF PROCEDURE	c. & d. OBJECTIVE(S)
1	Analytical procedure	Analytical procedure	Not applicable
2	Confirmation	Test of details of balances	Existence Completeness Accuracy Cutoff
3	Internal documentation	Test of control	Completeness
4	Physical examination	Test of details of balances	Existence Accuracy
5	Recalculation	Substantive test of transactions	Posting and summarization
6	Analytical procedure	Analytical procedure	Not applicable
7	Inquiry of client	Test of details of balances	Completeness Accuracy
8	External documentation (cancelled checks)	Substantive test of transactions	Completeness Timing Accuracy
9	External documentation	Substantive test of transactions	Occurrence Accuracy Timing Classification
10	External documentation	Test of details of balances	Completeness Cutoff Accuracy
11	Recalculation	Test of details of balances	Accuracy
12	Observation	Test of control	Occurrence

19-24 a. The amounts listed in the beginning balance column would be verified by examining the ending audited balances in the prior year audit files. Each ending balance for land, building-office, production equipment, office equipment, and IT hardware would be verified in addition to the mathematical accuracy of the beginning balance column.

b. To obtain evidence about the items in the additions column, the auditor would obtain detailed information of what individual additions comprise the additions amount for each account category and then examine supporting documentation, such as invoices, purchase contracts, and receiving reports, for some or all of the individual items that make up the additions amount on the schedule. For large purchases, the auditor may want to examine approvals noted in board of director minutes or on purchase orders. The auditor should be alert for whether an addition to these accounts is associated with the disposal of an existing asset that should be considered as part of the steps in c. below.

c. To obtain evidence about the items in the disposal column, the auditor would obtain detailed information of what individual disposals comprise the disposal amounts for each category and then examine supporting documentation, such as shipping documents and cash receipts for disposal transactions. The auditor should determine if any disposals noted as part of the procedures performed in step b are included as disposals in this schedule.

d. The auditor would verify the mathematical accuracy of the summation of the beginning balances plus additions less disposals crossfoots to the ending balance for each property item listed on the schedule. The auditor would also recalculate the summation of the amounts listed in the ending balance column to the total shown on the schedule. Each ending balance would be tied to the general ledger balances and the total would be traced to the line item in the balance sheet.

e. The following accounts may be affected by additions and disposals of property, plant, and equipment:

   (1) Additions of buildings and equipment may impact short-term and long-term debt on the balance sheet. Many large purchases of buildings and equipment must be financed with the issuance of debt or creation of long-term capital leases that must be reflected as liabilities on the balance sheet. That would then impact interest expense and depreciation expense accounts.

19-24 (continued)

> (2) Disposals of equipment are likely to impact the cash accounts for cash received from the sale of disposed items, accumulated depreciation accounts for equipment, and other income and expenses due to any gain or loss on the sale.

19-25

PURPOSE	EVALUATION OF ADEQUACY
1. To assure that the clients' detailed schedule equals the total in the general ledger. (Detail tie-in)	This procedure is necessary as a starting point to perform detailed tests.
2. To assure that taxes on property included on the schedule of accrued taxes are not over- or underpaid. (Accuracy)	This procedure is adequate for its purpose.
3. To assure that the accrued/prepaid account is correctly stated. (Accuracy)	This procedure is adequate for its purpose.

Overall, the program fails to emphasize the possibility of omitted property from the list. The key to an adequate audit of accrued property taxes is making sure all owned property and only owned property is included and on the list.

19-26

LIABILITY THAT COULD BE UNCOVERED	AUDIT PROCEDURE TO UNCOVER LIABILITY
a. Contingent liability related to a Lawsuit	Review minutes of the Board of Directors' meetings.
b. Building used as collateral for a loan or a mortgage tied to the building's purchase	Examine documents of ownership to determine if the loan is collateralized and send confirmations to major banks.
c. Unrecorded lease	Examine lease agreements.
d. Note payable	Examine underlying records for loans related to the interest expense and send confirmations to major banks.
e. Loan by borrowing against an insurance policy	Obtain a confirmation from the life insurance company.
f. Note payable	Obtain confirmation from bank for loans.
g. Income taxes payable for nondeductible expenses	Examine a sample of travel and expense reports to make sure they comply with IRS requirements.

19-27 The banker has failed to recognize that the audit tests discussed relate as much to the income statement as to the balance sheet. For example, obtaining an understanding of internal control and the tests of controls and substantive tests of transactions are heavily income statement oriented, analytical procedures are more closely related to the income statement than to the balance sheet, and even tests of details of the balance sheet help to uncover misstatements in the income statement. The typical audit recognizes the interrelationship between the income statement and the balance sheet and uses this interrelationship to help design more effective tests to uncover misstatements in both statements. The auditor is and should be greatly concerned about the fair presentation of the income statement.

■ **Case – Ward Publishing Company**

19-28 a. The tests of acquisition and cash disbursement transactions have two purposes: to determine whether related internal accounting controls are functioning (tests of controls), and to determine whether the transactions actually contain any monetary misstatements (substantive). The results of the tests apply to the population of all acquisitions and cash disbursements, including plant and equipment and lease acquisitions and cash disbursements, even though the specific sample tested does not include any such transaction. Thus, if the results of the tests are favorable, it is concluded that there is a lower expectation of misstatements in plant and equipment and lease transactions, and vice-versa.

   b. A summary of the results from tests of controls and substantive tests of transactions for acquisitions and cash disbursements from Case 18-32 is: all transaction-related audit objectives are being met at a satisfactory level except:

   1. All supporting documents are not always attached to the vendor's invoice. *Note: Students using a* **nonstatistical** *approach to Case 18-32 may not conclude that the results for this attribute [9.b.(1)] are unacceptable, depending on their estimate of CUER. However, most students will likely conclude that the results are unacceptable.*
   2. All vendors' invoices are not initialed for internal verification. Half of those not initialed had account classification errors.

   The impact of these results and the results from items 1 through 7 affect the balance-related audit objectives for plant and equipment in the following way:

19-28 (continued)

BALANCE-RELATED AUDIT OBJECTIVE	RESULTS OF TESTS OF CONTROLS AND SUBSTANTIVE TESTS OF TRANSACTIONS	RESULTS FROM CONCLUSIONS 1-7
Detail tie-in	Misstatements unlikely	—
Existence	Misstatements moderately likely	—
Completeness	Misstatements unlikely	Conclusion 1 supports
Accuracy	Misstatements moderately likely	Conclusion 4 indicates a need for additional evidence
Classification	Misstatements highly likely	Conclusion 6 indicates a need for additional evidence
Cutoff	Misstatements unlikely	—
Realizable value	No significant evidence provided	Conclusion 3 indicates a need for additional evidence
Rights and obligations	Misstatements unlikely	—

Conclusions 3, 5, and 7 indicate a need for more extensive auditing for existence, completeness, accuracy, and classification. All large items should be verified and samples should be larger than normal. All other tests can be performed at minimum levels.

c. The results of tests of controls and substantive tests of transactions are directly related to the tests of many expense accounts, primarily through tests for account classification, but also through tests of accuracy and existence. For example, if the auditor concludes that the internal controls are effective for recording acquisition transactions, the likelihood of misstatements for accounts such as supplies, purchases, and repairs and maintenance is greatly reduced. The auditor must keep in mind, however, that certain expense accounts are not usually verified as a part of tests of controls and substantive tests of transactions. An example is depreciation expense. Similarly, certain accounts may have a higher inherent risk such as legal expense and therefore require additional testing even if tests of controls and substantive tests of transactions results are satisfactory. Also, analytical procedures and tests of details of balances for balance sheet accounts results affect the extent of auditing needed for expense accounts.

19-28 (continued)

    d.   The results of tests of controls and substantive tests of transactions indicate the potential for significant classification misstatements. (See the results for Audit Procedure 9b(5) for classification in Part 2 of Case 18-32.) This potential for misclassification misstatement combined with the analytical procedures results in Conclusion 6 indicate a need for more extensive account analysis for repairs and maintenance, small tools expense, and the three other accounts where there are significant changes from prior years. No other conclusions should cause the auditor significant concern in the audit of expense accounts.

19-29   a.   Items 1 through 6 would have been found in the following way:

    1.   The company's policies for depreciating equipment are available from several sources:

        a)   The prior year's audit schedules and permanent file.

        b)   Footnote disclosure in the annual report and SEC Form 10-K.

        c)   Company procedures manuals.

        d)   Detailed fixed asset records.

    2.   The ten-year lease contract would be found when supporting data for current year's equipment additions were examined. Also, it may be found by a review of company lease files, contract files, or minutes of meetings of the board of directors. The calculations would likely be shown on a supporting schedule and can be traced to the general journal.

    3.   The building wing addition would be apparent by the addition to buildings during the year. The use of the low construction bid amount would be found when support for the addition was examined. When it was determined that this inappropriate method was followed, the actual costs could be determined by reference to construction work orders and supporting data. The wing could also be examined.

    4.   The paving and fencing could be discovered when support was examined for the addition to land.

    5.   The details of the retirement transactions could be determined by examining the sales agreement, cash receipts documentation, and related detailed fixed asset record. This examination would be instigated by the recording of the retirement in the machinery account or the review of cash receipts records.

19-29 (continued)

6. The auditor would become apprised of a new plant in several ways:

   a) Volume would increase.
   b) Account details such as cash, inventory, prepaid expenses, and payroll would be attributed to the new location.
   c) The transaction may be indicated in documents such as the minutes of the board, press releases, and reports to stockholders.
   d) Property tax and insurance bills examined show the new plant.

   One or more of these occurrences should lead the auditor to investigate the reasons and circumstances involved. Documents from the city and appraisals could be examined to determine the details involved.

b. The appropriate adjusting journal entries are as follows:

1. No entry necessary.

2. This is an operating lease and should not have been capitalized.

Prepaid rent	$ 50,000	
Lease liability	354,000	
Allowance for depreciation-machinery and equipment	20,200	
Machinery and equipment		$404,000
Depreciation expense		20,200

   To correct initial recording of lease:

Equipment rent expense	$37,500	
Prepaid rent		$37,500

   To record nine months rent:

   9/12 x $50,000 = $37,500

3. The wing should have been recorded at its cost to the company.

(Accounts originally credited)	$15,000	
Buildings		$15,000

19-29 (continued)

To correct initial recording of new wing:

Depreciation expense	$3,167	
Allowance for depreciation—		
Buildings		$3,167

To correct depreciation for excess cost.

Depreciation on beginning balance
1,200,000/25 = 48,000

Depreciation recorded on addition
51,500 - 48,000 = 3,500

Correct depreciation for addition:

Remaining useful life of addition is 12 years
(600,000/1,200,000 x 25 = 12-1/2 years;
12-1/2 - ½ = 12 years)

Depreciation = $160,000/12 x ½ = $6,667
Correction = $6,667 - $3,500 = $3,167

4.   The paving and fencing are land improvements and should be depreciated over their useful lives.

Land improvements (may be	$50,000	
combined with buildings		
with buildings account—		
buildings and improvements)		
Land		$50,000

To correct initial recording of paving and fencing:

Depreciation expense	$2,500	
Allowance for depreciation—		
Land Improvements		$2,500

To record first year's depreciation on paving and fencing:

$50,000/10 x ½ = $2,500

19-29 (continued)

5. The cost and allowance for depreciation should have been removed from the accounts and a gain or loss on sale recorded.

Cost of asset	$480,000

Allowance for depreciation:
To 12/31/10 –
480,000/10 x 3-1/2 168,000
For 2011 –
480,000/10 x ½ 24,000
192,000

Net book value	288,000
Cash proceeds	260,000
Loss on sale	$28,000

The correcting entry is:

Allowance for depreciation—		
Machinery and Equipment	$203,000	
Loss on sale of assets	28,000	
Machinery and Equipment		$220,000
Depreciation expense		11,000

6. Donated property should be capitalized at its fair market value.

Land	$100,000	
Buildings	400,000	
Contributed capital-Donated Property		$500,000

To record land and building for new plant donated by Crux City:

Depreciation expense	$8,000	
Allowance for depreciation—Buildings		$8,000

To record depreciation on new plant:

$400,000/25 x ½ = $8,000

19-30 a.

To: In-Charge Auditor

From: Audit Manager

Subject: Concerns about the schedule prepared by the client and the staff assistant in the audit of Vernal Manufacturing Company

The analytical procedures schedule for the audit of Vernal Manufacturing Company is completely inadequate and needs to be redone. There are several deficiencies:

1.   The headings, references, and indexing on the audit schedule are incomplete. It appears that the schedule was prepared by the client, but it is not possible to determine from the schedule.

2.   A classified income statement would provide more useful information than the single-step statement provided.

3.   The schedule should include the additional columns showing the percent of net sales for 12-31-10 and 12-31-11. This information would permit us to more effectively evaluate the relative change in each account.

4.   There is no indication that the general ledger totals were compared to general ledger balances or that calculations were tested.

5.   There is no identification of accounts that we are concerned may be materially misstated. For example, the $1,381 change in insurance expense appears immaterial but the 427% change in other expense may be significant.

6.   There is no indication of specific accounts that require additional investigation and the nature of such investigation.

7.   There is no indication that the client's explanations have been evaluated and supported by evidence. Management inquiry is a weak form of evidence and unsatisfactory by itself.

19-30 (continued)

b. For every explanation provided by the client, an alternative possibility is a misstatement in the financial statements. The auditor must be satisfied that significant differences are not material misstatements. The following are a few examples:

ACCOUNT	POSSIBLE MISSTATEMENT
Sales	Cutoff error for sales
Sales returns and allowances	Returns due to technological deficiencies in products that may indicate obsolete inventory
Miscellaneous income	Including proceeds of the sale of equipment as income rather than decreasing the equipment account
Cost of goods sold	Small increase in cost of goods sold compared to net sales may indicate an overstatement of ending inventory or understatement of any of the accounts making up cost of goods sold

c. To perform a meaningful determination of the most important variances, an alternative design of the audit schedule follows. It is much easier to determine relevant variances with an adequate analytical procedures schedule.

19-30 (continued)

	PER G/L 12-31-10	PERCENT 12-31-10	PER G/L 12-31-11	PERCENT 12-31-11	CHANGE Amount	Percent
Sales	$8,467,312	100.8%	$9,845,231	102.5%	$1,377,919	16.3%
Sales returns and allowances	(64,895)	(0.8%)	(243,561)	(2.5%)	(178,666)	275.3%
Net Sales	8,402,417	100.0%	9,601,670	100.0%	1,199,253	14.3%
Cost of goods sold:						
Beginning inventory	1,487,666	17.7%	1,389,034	14.5%	(98,632)	(6.6%)
Purchases	2,564,451	30.5%	3,430,865	35.7%	866,414	33.8%
Freight-in	45,332	0.5%	65,782	0.7%	20,450	45.1%
Purchase returns	(76,310)	(0.9%)	(57,643)	(0.6%)	18,667	(24.5%)
Factory wages	986,755	11.7%	1,145,467	11.9%	158,712	16.1%
Factory benefits	197,652	2.4%	201,343	2.1%	3,691	1.9%
Factory overhead	478,659	5.7%	490,765	5.1%	12,106	2.5%
Factory depreciation	344,112	4.1%	314,553	3.3%	(29,559)	(8.6%)
Ending inventory	(1,389,034)	(16.5%)	(2,156,003)	(22.5%)	(766,969)	55.2%
Total	4,639,283	55.2%	4,824,163	50.2%	184,880	4.0%
Gross margin	3,763,134	44.8%	4,777,507	49.8%	1,014,373	27.0%
Selling, general and administrative:						
Executive salaries	167,459	2.0%	174,562	1.8%	7,103	4.2%
Executive benefits	32,321	0.4%	34,488	0.4%	2,167	6.7%
Office salaries	95,675	1.1%	98,540	1.0%	2,865	3.0%
Office benefits	19,888	0.2%	21,778	0.2%	1,890	9.5%
Travel and entertainment	56,845	0.7%	75,583	0.8%	18,738	33.0%
Advertising	130,878	1.6%	156,680	1.6%	25,802	19.7%
Other sales expense	34,880	0.4%	42,334	0.4%	7,454	21.4%
Stationery and supplies	38,221	0.5%	21,554	0.2%	(16,667)	(43.6%)
Postage	14,657	0.2%	18,756	0.2%	4,099	28.0%
Telephone	36,551	0.4%	67,822	0.7%	31,271	85.6%
Dues and memberships	3,644	0.0%	4,522	0.0%	878	24.1%
Rent	15,607	0.2%	15,607	0.2%	0	0.0%
Legal fees	14,154	0.2%	35,460	0.4%	21,306	150.5%
Accounting fees	16,700	0.2%	18,650	0.2%	1,950	11.7%
Depreciation, SG&A	73,450	0.9%	69,500	0.7%	(3,950)	(5.4%)
Bad debt expense	166,454	2.0%	143,871	1.5%	(22,583)	(13.6%)
Insurance	44,321	0.5%	45,702	0.5%	1,381	3.1%
	961,705	11.4%	1,045,409	10.9%	83,704	8.7%
Total operating income	2,801,429	33.3%	3,732,098	38.9%	930,669	33.2%
Other expenses:						
Interest expense	120,432	1.4%	137,922	1.4%	17,490	14.5%
Other	5,455	0.1%	28,762	0.3%	23,307	427.3%
Total	125,887	1.5%	166,684	1.7%	40,797	32.4%
Other income:						
Gain on sale of assets	43,222	0.5%	(143,200)	(1.5%)	(186,422)	(431.3%)
Interest income	243	0.0%	223	0.0%	(20)	(8.2%)
Miscellaneous income	6,365	0.1%	25,478	0.3%	19,113	300.3%
Total	49,830	0.6%	(117,499)	(1.2%)	(167,329)	(335.8%)
Income before taxes	2,725,372	32.4%	3,447,915	35.9%	722,543	26.5%
Income taxes	926,626	11.0%	1,020,600	10.6%	93,974	10.1%
Net income	$1,798,746	21.4%	$2,427,315	25.3%	$ 628,569	34.9%

19-30 (continued)

The following are variances of special significance to the audit that have been determined from the revised analytical procedures worksheet. Before doing additional work, there should be further discussion with knowledgeable management about the variances identified. After investigating management's explanations, the following additional audit procedures may be appropriate:

ACCOUNT	POTENTIAL ADDITIONAL AUDIT PROCEDURES
1. Sales	Perform extensive cutoff tests and other tests for possible overstatements.
2. Sales returns and allowances	Examine supporting documents for the largest sales returns and allowances and consider the effect on inventory valuation.
3. Cost of goods sold. Cost of goods sold increased only $185,000, but sales increased 1.2 million.	Do careful tests of physical counts, costing, cutoff, inventory, and tests for obsolescence.
4. Travel and entertainment	Examine supporting documentation for large travel and entertainment expenses.
5. Telephone	Compare telephone expense by month to determine the possibility of a misclassification.
6. Legal expense	Analyze legal expense to determine the possibility of lawsuits or other legal actions that might affect the financial statements.
7. Depreciation expense	Compare depreciation by month to determine the possibility of the failure to record one month's depreciation.
8. Bad debt expense	Performed detailed analytical procedures and other tests of accounts receivable to evaluate the adequacy of the allowance for uncollectible accounts.
9. Other expense	Analyze other expense to determine the nature of other expense and the possibility of misclassification or incorrect accounting.
10. Gain on the sale of assets	Analyze the account to determine the nature of the transactions and any misclassification or incorrect accounting.

■ Internet Problem Solution: Centerpulse Ltd. Fraud

Internet Problem 19-1

a. According to the SEC's complaint, the members allegedly involved in the fraud include Urs Kamber, chief financial officer, Stephan Husi, controller, and Richard Jon May, group vice president of finance, tax counsel, and treasurer.

b. The primary incentives for engaging in the fraud were to present a more favorable financial position to ensure its banks would extend a $635 million credit facility needed to cover the costs associated with the settlement of outstanding litigation linked to several product recalls. Management wanted to ensure that its actual results closely matched budgets and forecasts they had previously provided the bank as part of its credit facility negotiations.

c. Management delayed recording $25 million of expenses associated with attorneys' fees arising from the recall litigation settlement.

d. According to the SEC complaint, management failed to write-off an impaired asset linked to its "Global Supply Chain" software system. The asset reflected costs incurred on the development of this project. When the company's European Orthopedics Division, abandoned this project the underlying software had no value and thus should have been written off.

e. According to the Complaint, when Centerpulse filed its 2002 financial statements with the SEC, the impact of all their fraudulent actions resulted in their reporting 2002 pre-tax income of $244 million instead of $217.6 million, an overstatement of approximately 11 percent..

(**Note**: Internet problems address current issues using Internet sources. Because Internet sites are subject to change, Internet problems and solutions may change. Current information on Internet problems is available at www.pearsonhighered.com/arens.)

Chapter 20

Audit of the Payroll and Personnel Cycle

■ **Review Questions**

20-1   General ledger accounts that are likely to be affected by the payroll and personnel cycle in most audits include the following:

Cash	Direct labor
Inventory	Salary expense
Construction in progress	Commission expense
Wages payable	Payroll tax expense
Payroll taxes withheld	
Accrued payroll taxes	

20-2   In companies where payroll is a significant portion of inventory, as in manufacturing and construction companies, the improper account classification of payroll can significantly affect asset valuation for accounts such as work in process, finished goods, and construction in process. For example, if the salaries of administrative personnel are incorrectly charged to indirect manufacturing overhead, the overhead charged to inventory on the balance sheet can be overstated. Similarly, if the indirect labor cost of individual employees is charged to specific jobs or processes, the valuation of inventory is affected if labor is improperly classified. When some jobs are billed on a cost plus basis, revenue and the valuation of inventory are both affected by improperly classifying labor to jobs.

20-3   Five tests of controls that can be performed for the payroll and personnel cycle are:

1.   *Examine time card for indication of approval to ensure that payroll payments are properly authorized.* The purpose of this test is to determine that recorded payroll payments are for work actually performed by existing employees (occurrence).
2.   *Account for a sequence of payroll checks to ensure existing payroll payments are recorded.* The purpose of this test is to determine that existing payroll transactions are recorded (completeness).
3.   *Examine time cards to ensure that recorded payroll payments are for work actually performed by existing employees.* The purpose of this test is the same as in item 1 above.
4.   *Compare postings to the chart of accounts to ensure that payroll transactions are properly classified.* (Classification)
5.   *Observe when recording takes place to ensure that payroll transactions are recorded on a timely basis.* (Timing)

20-4   The percentage of total audit time in the cycle devoted to performing tests of controls and substantive tests of transactions is usually far greater in the payroll and personnel cycle than for the sales and collection cycle because year-end balances in payroll-related accounts are often immaterial. Also, there is relatively little independent third party evidence, such as confirmations, to verify the related payroll accounts. In contrast, the accounts related to the sales and collection cycle can usually be verified for the most part by confirmations from customers. In addition, in the sales and collection cycle, verification of the realizability of receivables and sales cutoff tests are important and time- consuming tasks.

20-5   The auditor should be concerned with whether the human resources department is following the proper hiring and termination procedures. An obvious reason for this would be to ensure that there are adequate safeguards against hiring and retaining incompetent and untrustworthy people. The ramifications of hiring such people can range from simple inefficiency and waste to outright fraud or theft. More importantly, though, it is necessary for the auditor to assure himself or herself that the client is hiring and terminating according to operations standards and procedures. It is necessary to see if the internal controls are working as planned before they can be effectively evaluated. To say that the auditor doesn't care who is hired and who is fired is to suggest that he or she doesn't care if the internal controls work according to any standards. Failure to follow proper termination procedures could lead to fraudulent payments for work not performed.

20-6   To trace a random sample of prenumbered time cards to the related payroll payments in the payroll register and compare the hours worked to the hours paid is to test if payroll payments have been recorded (completeness) and if those employees who worked are being paid for their time actually worked. Employees are likely to inform management if they are not paid, or underpaid. To trace a random sample of payroll payments from the payroll register and compare the hours worked to the hours paid is to test if the recorded payroll payments are for work actually performed by existing employees (occurrence). This test, in effect, attempts to discover nonexistent employees or duplicate payments, if there are any. For this reason, the second procedure is typically more important to the audit of payroll.

20-7   In auditing payroll withholding and payroll tax expense, the emphasis should normally be on evaluating the adequacy of the payroll tax return preparation procedures rather than the payroll tax liability, because a major reason for misstatements in the liability account is incorrect preparation of the returns in the past. If the preparation procedures are inadequate, and the amounts do not appear reasonable, then the auditor should expand his or her work and recompute the withholding and expense amounts to determine that the proper amount has been accrued. In addition, the auditor should consider the amount of penalties which may be assessed for inadequate withholdings and include these amounts in the accrual if they are significant.

20-8 Several analytical procedures for the payroll and personnel cycle and misstatements that might be indicated by significant fluctuations are as follows:

ANALYTICAL PROCEDURE	MISSTATEMENT TYPES
1. Comparison of payroll expense accounts to amounts in prior years.	Cutoff misstatements or improper amounts recorded in a period.
2. Direct labor divided by sales compared to industry standards in prior years.	Cutoff misstatements or amounts charged to improper payroll accounts.
3. Commission expense divided by sales compared to industry standards, prior years, or sales agreements.	Failure to record commission on sales, or recording the improper commission amount.
4. Payroll tax expense divided by salaries and wages compared to prior year balances adjusted for changes in the tax rate and not including officers' salaries.	Failure to record payroll taxes or recording of the improper amount.
5. Comparison of accrued payroll and payroll tax accounts to prior years.	Failure to record payroll accruals or recording improper amounts at the end of a period.
6. The percentage of labor included in work in process and finished goods inventories compared to prior years.	Use of improper labor standards, or classification misstatements.
7. Analysis of direct labor variances.	Use of improper labor standards, or classification misstatements.

20-9 An auditor should perform audit tests primarily designed to uncover fraud in the payroll and personnel cycle when he or she has determined that internal controls are deficient (or the opportunity exists for management to override the internal controls) or when there are other reasons to suspect fraud. Audit procedures that are primarily for the detection of fraud in the payroll and personnel cycle include:

1. Examine cancelled payroll checks for employee name, authorized signature, and proper endorsement (especially for second endorsements) to discover checks going to nonexistent employees. The endorsement should be compared to signatures on W-4 forms.
2. Trace selected transactions recorded in the payroll journal or listing to the human resources department files to determine whether the employees were actually employed during the period.
3. Select several terminated employees from payroll records to determine whether each former employee received his or her termination pay in accordance with company policy and to determine that the employee's pay was discontinued on the date of termination.

20-9 (continued)

4. Examine the subsequent payroll periods of terminated employees to ascertain that the employees are no longer being paid.
5. Request a surprise payroll payoff to observe if any unclaimed checks result, which will necessitate extensive investigation.

20-10 The *Payroll Master File* is maintained for each employee indicating the gross pay for each payment period, deductions from the gross pay, the net pay, the check number, and the date. The purpose of this record is to provide detailed information for federal and state income tax purposes, and to serve as the final record of what each employee was actually paid.

The *W-2 Form* is issued to each employee at the end of each calendar year and indicates his or her gross pay, income taxes withheld, and FICA withheld for the year. In serving as a summary of the employee's earnings record, the W-2 form conveniently provides information necessary for the employee to fill out his or her income tax returns.

A *Payroll Tax Return* is the form required by and submitted to the local, state and federal governments for the payment of withheld taxes and the employer's portion of FICA taxes and state and federal unemployment compensation taxes.

20-11 Where the primary objective is to detect fraud, the auditor will examine the following supporting documents and records:

1. Cancelled payroll checks for employee name, authorized signature and proper endorsement, watching specifically for unusual or recurring second endorsements.
2. Payroll journal or listing, tracing transactions to the personnel files to determine whether the employees were actually employed during the payroll period.
3. Payroll journal or listing and individual payroll records, selecting terminated employees to determine whether each terminated employee received his or her termination pay in accordance with company policy and whether each employee was paid in the subsequent payroll period.
4. Payroll checks, observing each employee as he or she picks up and signs for his or her check.
5. Time cards, testing them for reasonableness or observing whether they are being punched by the proper employees.

20-12 Types of authorizations in the payroll and personnel cycle are:

1. Deduction authorization, without which the wrong amount (or no deduction) may be deducted from the employee's paycheck.
2. Rate authorizations, without which the employee may be getting paid at the wrong rate.
3. Time card authorization, without which the employee may be getting paid for the wrong quantity of hours worked.

20-12 (continued)

4. Payroll check authorization, without which unauthorized funds may be paid out.
5. Commission rate authorization, without which the salespeople might be improperly compensated for their sales efforts.
6. Authorization to hire a new employee, without which nonexistent or unqualified personnel may be added to the payroll.

20-13   It is common to verify total officers' compensation even when the tests of controls and substantive tests of transactions results in payroll are excellent because the salaries and bonuses of officers must be included in filings with the SEC and IRS (e.g., the Form 10-K Report, proxy, and the federal income tax return) and because management may be in a position to pay themselves more than the authorized amount, since the controls over the officers' payroll are typically weaker and therefore easier to override than those of the normal payroll.

The usual audit procedure used to verify the officers' compensation is to obtain the authorized salary of each officer from the minutes of the board of directors and compare it to the related earnings record.

20-14   An imprest payroll account is a separate payroll bank account in which a constant balance, either zero or small, is maintained. When a payroll is paid, the exact amount of the net payroll is transferred by check or electronic funds transfer from the general account to the imprest account. The purpose and advantage of an imprest payroll account is that it limits the company's exposure to payroll fraud by limiting the amount that may be misappropriated.

20-15   Several audit procedures the auditor can use to determine whether recorded payroll transactions are recorded at the proper amounts are:

1. Recompute hours worked from time cards.
2. Compare pay rates with union contract, approval by the board of directors, or other source.
3. Recompute gross pay.
4. Check withholdings by reference to tax tables and authorization forms in personnel files.
5. Recompute net pay.
6. Compare cancelled check with payroll journal or listing for amount.

20-16   Attributes sampling can be used in the payroll and personnel cycle in performing tests of controls and substantive tests of transactions with the following objectives:

1. Time card hours agree with payroll computations.
2. Overtime hours are approved.
3. Foreman approves all time cards.
4. Hourly rates agree with personnel files and union contracts.

20-16 (continued)

5. Gross pay calculation is verified.
6. Exemptions taken agree with W-4.
7. Income tax, other deductions, and net pay calculations are verified.
8. Authorizations are available for voluntary withholdings and miscellaneous deductions.
9. Paycheck endorsement is same as signature on W-4 form.

The frequency of control deviations or monetary errors must be estimated prior to performing the tests. This estimate together with the acceptable risk of assessing control risk too low (ARACR) and the tolerable exception rate will enable the auditor to determine the sample size required. Once the tests are performed on the sample, evaluation of the results will indicate whether the exception rate is lower than, equal to, or higher than that anticipated. The auditor must then use this judgment to decide the appropriate action to take.

■ **Multiple Choice Questions From CPA Examinations**

20-17 a. (2)   b. (3)   c. (3)

20-18 a. (4)   b. (4)   c. (4)

■ **Discussion Questions and Problems**

20-19

TRANSACTION-RELATED AUDIT OBJECTIVE	TEST OF CONTROL	POTENTIAL MISSTATEMENT	SUBSTANTIVE AUDIT PROCEDURE
1. Recorded payroll transactions are stated at the proper pay rates (accuracy).	Examine authorizations in personnel files.	Employees are paid the wrong rate.	Compare rates in payroll journal or listing to rates in personnel files.
2. Hours worked are correctly recorded (accuracy).	Examine time cards and observe preparation.	Incorrect recording of time.	Randomly sample workers and trace to time cards for hours worked.

TRANSACTION-RELATED AUDIT OBJECTIVE	TEST OF CONTROL	POTENTIAL MISSTATEMENT	SUBSTANTIVE AUDIT PROCEDURE
3. Recorded payroll payments are for work actually performed by existing employees (occurrence).	Examine time cards for approval.	Incorrect times are used in computing employees' pay.	Analyze payroll records of a sample of employees for reasonableness.
4. Recorded payroll transactions are for proper rate and amount (accuracy).	Examine payroll journal or listing for indication of internal verification.	Employees' pay is miscalculated.	Recompute employees' pay, compare pay rates to personnel files, and hours worked to time cards.
5. Time records are properly classified by job (classification).	Examine system of identifying jobs by number.	Direct labor is charged to wrong jobs.	Trace entries from job summaries to time cards, job cards, etc.
6. Recorded payroll checks are for work performed by existing employees (occurrence).	Observe and discuss payroll system with employees.	Payroll payments are made to nonexistent employees.	Trace payroll payments to employees, to determine if employee exists.
7. Payments are made to actual employees (occurrence).	Observe payments and discuss with employees.	Payments are made to wrong employees.	Examine cancelled checks for endorsements, and compare to personnel file.
8. Recorded payroll transactions exist (occurrence).	Examine personnel files for termination notices.	Employees are improperly terminated and payment continues.	Compare termination dates from personnel files to date of last paycheck.

20-20

TYPE OF TEST	TRANSACTION-RELATED AUDIT OBJECTIVE(S)
1. Substantive test of transactions	To determine if monthly payroll costs have been correctly allocated (accuracy).
2. Test of control	To determine if recorded payroll transactions are for work actually performed by existing employees (occurrence).
3. Substantive test of transactions	To determine if employees are paid for the hours they have worked (accuracy).
4. Substantive test of transactions	To determine if the appropriate person is paid and amount and time are correct (accuracy and timing).
5. Substantive test of transactions	To determine if the correct job is charged for labor and if the amount is recorded correctly for each job (classification and accuracy).
6. Test of control	To determine if all payroll checks are recorded (completeness).
7. Substantive test of transactions	To determine whether terminated employees were subsequently paid for work not performed (occurrence). To determine whether an obligation may exist for unpaid severance pay (completeness).

20-21

RECOMMENDED CONTROL	SUBSTANTIVE AUDIT PROCEDURE
1. Approval of time cards by foreman and observation of use of time clock by the foreman.	Observe employees punching in—only one card per employee—to see whether any employee punches two cards (normally not an effective or practical audit procedure).
2. Paychecks distributed by someone other than the foreman.	Perform payroll payoff, requiring identification from all employees prior to payment.
3. Pay employees only for time charged to jobs. Reconcile payroll expense to amounts charged to jobs.	Compare total hours worked from payroll journal or listing to total hours worked as recorded on job cost tickets.
4. Internal verification of classification.	Trace labor distribution to supporting job input forms.
5. Payroll checks not returned to payroll clerk after signing.	Perform payoff as described in 2 above.
6. Internal verification of calculations and amounts.	Recompute federal withholding taxes and trace to employee earnings record.
7. Payroll checks are prenumbered and accounted for. Use an imprest bank account where the amount to be deposited is taken from the payroll journal or listing.	Reconcile the disbursements in the payroll journal or listing to the disbursements on the payroll bank statement.

	TYPE OF TEST	TRANSACTION-RELATED AUDIT OBJECTIVE(S)	BALANCE-RELATED AUDIT OBJECTIVE(S)
1.	(3) Analytical procedure	N/A	N/A
2.	(1) Test of control; (2) STOT	Occurrence and accuracy	N/A
3.	(4) TDB	N/A	Completeness
4.	(1) Test of control	Accuracy	N/A
5.	(4) TDB	N/A	Detail tie-in
6.	(1) Test of control	Completeness	N/A
7.	(2) STOT	Posting and summarization	N/A
8.	(3) Analytical procedure	N/A	N/A
9.	(2) STOT	Occurrence, timing and accuracy	N/A
10.	(3) Analytical procedure	N/A	N/A
11.	(1) Test of control	Accuracy	N/A
12.	(4) TDB	N/A	Completeness, accuracy, and cutoff

20-23   A flowchart of steps for each type of test is given below (requirements a, b, and c):

TESTS OF CONTROLS OR SUBSTANTIVE TESTS OF TRANSACTIONS	TESTS OF DETAILS OF BALANCES
6	2
5	9
3	7
8	4
	1

20-24 a. Brendin's approach to determining why this year's payroll tax expense was so high suffers from two serious deficiencies: First, it lacks relevance, and second, it is too narrowly focused. The approach lacks relevance in that he is testing payroll *withholding* which is not the same as payroll tax expense. Some payroll taxes are related to withholding such as FICA, but income tax withheld does not give rise to an expense, and certain payroll taxes, such as unemployment compensation, are not withheld. The approach is too narrowly focused in that the analytical test results could have resulted from a misstatement of the payroll itself; Brendin does not appear to be considering this possibility.

b. A more suitable approach for determining whether payroll tax was properly stated in the current year would be to evaluate the reasonableness of the total payroll, reconcile the payroll to amounts shown on payroll tax reports, and check computations as shown on those reports for reasonableness.

20-25

	a. INTERNAL CONTROL DEFICIENCY	b. TYPE OF MISSTATEMENT
1.	The foreman should not hire employees.	The foreman may hire unqualified employees, friends or possibly a fictitious person to be paid through the payroll system.
2.	The foremen should not recommend wages for employees.	The foreman may provide inappropriate pay rates or pay rates that are split between an employee and the foreman.
3.	Time cards should not be left in a box that employees have access to.	Employees, including the foreman, can take extra time cards and clock in for other employees or fictitious employees.
4.	The foreman collects and approves the time cards as well as the duties described in 1-3. (Note: It is appropriate for the foreman to approve times cards if he has none of the other duties described in 1-3.)	The foreman can include fictitious time cards for check preparation.
5.	There is no internal verification of the payroll clerk's input of names or hours into the payroll system.	The payroll clerk can make mistakes entering the hours or names.

20-25 (continued)

	a. INTERNAL CONTROL DEFICIENCY	b. TYPE OF MISSTATEMENT
6.	The controller compares two output records and fails to compare the output to any input records.	The controller will not find any existing mistakes made by the payroll clerk.
7.	The foreman receives the payroll checks for distribution.	The foreman can keep checks for which he has submitted time cards for nonexistent employees.
8.	The foreman mails checks to absent employees.	Nonexistent or former employees who had someone else prepare their time cards will receive a check in the mail.
9.	The controller hires and approves wages for salaried employees and signs their checks.	The controller can submit information for a nonexistent employee, open a checking account in the person's name and receive the direct deposit. She can also submit the improper salary rate to the payroll clerk and split the payment with the employee.
10.	The controller has sole access to pay rates.	The controller can include any pay rates she desires, for herself or others, including fictitious employees and friends who will split the amounts with her.
11.	The payroll clerk can add names to the payroll records.	The payroll clerk can add fictitious names for either salaried or hourly employees. She can set up a checking account in the same manner discussed in 9.
12.	An accounting clerk does the bank reconciliation each month.	The person is unlikely to be qualified to do quality bank reconciliation and will thereby be unlikely to find the frauds included previously.

20-26

	a. TRANSACTION-RELATED AUDIT OBJECTIVE NOT MET	b. CONTROL EFFECTIVE IN PREVENTING OR DETECTING MISAPPROPRIATION
1.	Occurrence (fictitious employee)	Only the human resource function which is separate from the payroll function can add employees to payroll.
2.	Accuracy (fictitious hours)	All payroll hours or payroll overtime hours must be approved by the employee's supervisor.
3.	Accuracy (fictitious hours)	Approval of time records by supervisor. Require employees to sign in using personal identification.
4.	Occurrence (failure to remove a terminated employee)	Require notification of human resources on termination of employees. Surprise payroll payoff.
5.	Accuracy (unauthorized pay rates)	Only the human resource function which is separate from the payroll function can change employee pay rates.

c.   The surprise payroll payoff is effective in detecting fictitious employees that have been placed on the payroll, or terminated employees that were not properly removed from the payroll (occurrence). If payroll is directly deposited, a surprise payoff can still be performed by requiring employees to sign for payroll stubs or other acknowledgement of payment.

20-27

DEPARTMENT	EXTENT OF INCREASE OR DECREASE IN PAYROLL EXPENSE	EXPLANATION FOR EXPECTED CHANGE IN DEPARTMENT'S PAYROLL EXPENSE
Warehouse and Shipping Department	Extensive Increase	Each online sale must be individually processed for shipment to single, stand-alone customers. The time and effort to process, package, and ship goods to each online customer will significantly increase the warehouse and shipping department payroll expense.

20-27 (continued)

DEPARTMENT	EXTENT OF INCREASE OR DECREASE IN PAYROLL EXPENSE	EXPLANATION FOR EXPECTED CHANGE IN DEPARTMENT'S PAYROLL EXPENSE
IT Department	Little Change	Because the company outsourced the creation and support of the online sales system, payroll expense would likely increase minimally (e.g., some increase would occur despite the outsourcing). However, consulting expense would be expected to increase extensively.
Accounts Receivable Department	Little to Moderate Increase	Because online sales are applied to customer credit cards, most of the collection of the receivables would be handled by the credit card agencies, not by Archer Uniform's accounts receivable department. Some increase in payroll expense may occur, if there are disputes between Archer Uniforms and the credit card agencies over the amounts processed throughout the month. Additional time may be required to reconcile the processing of cash payments by the credit card agencies and the recording of sales in Archer Uniform's financial statements.
Accounts Payable Department	Moderate Increase	Assuming total sales significantly increase due to the new online offering, the volume of inventory purchases will increase. This increase in inventory purchasing will result in an increase in vendor payments to be processed. Thus, payroll expense for the accounts payable department may increase moderately. Some efficiencies may be obtained by processing larger bulk orders in a single vendor payment. However, new products may be offered and additional vendors may be used, which in turn will increase the volume of processing required in accounts payable.
Receiving Department	Extensive Increase	Assuming total sales significantly increase due to the new online offering, the volume of inventory purchases to be received and processed into the inventory warehouse will correspondingly increase.
Executive Management	Little Change	Most of the work associated with the new online sales offerings will be the responsibility of other employees.

20-27 (continued)

DEPARTMENT	EXTENT OF INCREASE OR DECREASE IN PAYROLL EXPENSE	EXPLANATION FOR EXPECTED CHANGE IN DEPARTMENT'S PAYROLL EXPENSE
Marketing	Moderate Increase	The extent of increase in payroll expense for this department will be dependent on the amount of advertising that Archer Uniforms creates to promote its new Web site. Assuming some advertising is created, there would be a moderate increase in marketing payroll expense. Other advertising expenses may increase for ads generated through external ad agencies and through Web site ad contracts.

20-28 a. An audit program to verify sales commission expense is as follows:

   1. Select a sample of office copies of sales invoices.
      a. Check commissions rate to commissions rate file.
      b. Check computation of sales commissions.
      c. Examine invoices for internal verification by accounts receivable clerk.
      d. Trace sales commission amounts to sales commission ledger.
   2. Foot the sales commission ledger for one or more months, and trace the total to the general ledger.
   3. Compare totals for periods in the sales commission ledger to period balances of sales commission expense.

   b. An audit program to verify accrued sales commissions is:

   1. Compare the accrual with that of the previous year. Investigate any significant change.
   2. Compare the amount of commissions paid to the salesmen on the fifteenth of the month following year-end to the total accrued commissions at year-end. Obtain a reconciliation and explanation for any reconciling items.
   3. Send confirmations to salesmen for the larger amounts of accrued commissions and a sample of the smaller amounts.

20-29   a.   Conventional forms and documents in a payroll system include the following:

- ■ Personnel records
- ■ Deduction authorization forms
- ■ Rate authorization forms
- ■ Time cards and job time tickets
- ■ Payroll checks
- ■ Payroll journal or listing and labor distribution
- ■ Earnings record
- ■ W-2 form
- ■ Payroll tax returns

In using the computer service center, it appears that there is no loss in documentation in substance; however, the *earnings record* is not printed out each pay period, thus, the current version is usually in *machine readable form*. (This assumes that authorization forms exist although they are not discussed in the case.) The fact that the earnings record is in magnetic form is not a problem, as long as the service bureau has adequate backup and recovery controls.

The above analysis reflects the fact that Leggert's internal controls in the payroll area are generally good. There is good segregation of duties between the President and Clark, assuming both are trustworthy, honest people. Procedures, forms, records, and reports are comprehensive and well-designed.

The only potential deficiency in internal control is that errors in details could be made by the service bureau and not necessarily be caught. It is difficult to imagine that these would be material.

20-29 (continued)

b.

PAYROLL TRANSACTION-RELATED AUDIT OBJECTIVE	PROCEDURES	TYPE OF PROCEDURE
1. Recorded payroll payments are for work performed by existing employees (occurrence).	a. Observe existence of personnel files in President's care.	Test of control
	b. Observe use of time clock and control of time cards by clerk.	Test of control
	c. Examine time cards for President's approval.	Test of control
	d. Observe distribution of payroll checks by President.	Test of control
	e. Examine cancelled checks for proper endorsement.	Substantive test of transactions
	f. Compare cancelled checks with personnel records.	Substantive test of transactions
	g. Examine cancelled check for President's signature.	Test of control
2. Existing payroll transactions are recorded (completeness).	a. Account for the numerical sequence of payroll checks.	Test of control and substantive test of transactions
	b. Observe preparation of payroll bank reconciliation by President.	Test of control
3. Recorded payroll transactions are for the amount of time actually worked and at the proper pay rate; withholdings are properly calculated (accuracy).	a. Observe use of time clock and control of time cards by Clark.	Test of control
	b. Observe Clark rechecking hours.	Test of control
	c. Recompute gross pay, deductions and net pay.	Substantive test of transactions
	d. Trace rates and authorizations to personnel file.	Substantive test of transactions
	e. Examine payroll journal or listing for approval by Clark.	Test of control
	f. Compare rates in payroll journal or listing with personnel files to determine that rate actually paid is authorized.	Substantive test of transactions

20-29 (continued)

PAYROLL TRANSACTION-RELATED AUDIT OBJECTIVE	PROCEDURES	TYPE OF PROCEDURE
4. Payroll transactions are properly classified (classification).	a. Review chart of accounts.	Test of control
	b. Examine payroll journal or listing for approval by Clark.	Test of control
	c. Compare classification with chart of accounts or procedures manual.	Substantive test of transactions
5. Payroll transactions are recorded on the correct dates (timing).	a. Observe collection and processing of time cards by Clark.	Test of control
	b. Examine payroll journal or listing for approval by Clark.	Test of control
	c. Observe posting of ledger by Clark.	Test of control
	d. Observe preparation of payroll bank reconciliation by President.	Test of control
	e. Compare date of check recorded in payroll journal with date on cancelled checks and time cards.	Substantive test of transactions
6. Payroll transactions are properly included in the employee earnings record; they are properly summarized.	a. Observe re-adding of payroll journal or listing and posting by Clark.	Test of control
	b. Examine payroll journal or listing for approval by Clark.	Test of control
	c. Observe posting of ledger by Clark.	Test of control
	d. Trace postings from payroll journal to general ledger.	Substantive test of transactions

    c.   Procedures in performance format:

        1.   Make observations of the following activities by Mary Clark:
            a)   Control, collection and processing of time cards.
            b)   Rechecking of hours on time cards.
            c)   Processing and approval of payroll journal or listing.
            d)   Posting of general ledger.

20-29 (continued)

2. Make observations of the following activities by the President:
    a) Maintenance of personnel files.
    b) Distribution of paychecks.
    c) Processing and approval of payroll journal or listing.
    d) Posting of general ledger.

3. Make observations of the following general matters and activities:
    a) Use of time clock by employees.
    b) Existence and use of adequate chart of accounts.

4. Select a sample of payroll check numbers and:
    a) Account for existence and recording of paychecks.
    b) Examine paychecks for President's signature.
    c) Examine checks for proper endorsement.
    d) Compare cancelled checks with personnel records.
    e) Compare date on check with date recorded in payroll journal or listing and on the time card.

5. Select a sample of payroll entries from the payroll journal or listing and perform the following steps:
    a) Obtain time cards, examine for President's approval, and trace hours to payroll journal or listing.
    b) Examine personnel files and authorization for rates and deductions.
    c) Recompute gross pay, deductions, and net pay.
    d) Compare account classification with chart of accounts or procedures manual.

6. Select a sample of payroll journals and perform the following steps:
    a) Examine payroll journal for approval by Clark.
    b) Trace postings to general ledger.

d. A sampling data sheet follows. Note that this sampling data sheet was prepared using attributes sampling. The only difference between this approach and a nonstatistical approach is the determination of sample size. Under nonstatistical sampling, students' sample sizes will vary.

20-29 (continued)

DESCRIPTION OF ATTRIBUTES	PLANNED AUDIT			INITIAL SAMPLE SIZE***
	EPER*	TER**	ARACR**	
1. Payroll check number accounted for	0%	5%	5%	59
2. Payroll check signed by President	0%	4%	5%	74
3. Time card approved by President	1%	6%	5%	78
4. Time card hours agree with payroll journal or listing	1%	6%	5%	78
5. Personnel file is complete	0%	6%	5%	49
6. Pay rate and deductions supported by authorization	1%	4%	5%	156
7. Gross pay, deductions, and net pay correctly computed	0%	5%	5%	59

*	These amounts are arbitrary to complete data sheet. Information to determine actual appropriate amounts is not given in problem.
**	These amounts are judgments and are not the only acceptable amounts.
***	Determined from attributes sampling tables.

■ **Internet Problem Solution: Risks of Outsourcing the Payroll Function**

Internet Problem 20-1

     a.   The employer, not the third party, is ultimately responsible for the deposit and payment of federal tax liabilities. Even thought the third party is making the deposits, the employer is the responsible party. If the third party fails to make the federal tax payments, the IRS may assess penalties and interest on the employer's account.

     b.   If there are any issues with an account, the IRS will send correspondence to the employer at the address of record. The IRS strongly recommends that the employer not change their address of record to that of the payroll service provider. That way, the employer can stay informed of matters involving their business.

     c.   The investigation report noted the following: Richley, the owner of Payroll Data Services Inc. (PDS), "pleaded guilty on April 11, 2008 to three counts of mail fraud, four counts of tax evasion, and one count of money laundering. Richley admitted that between January 2000 and April 2003, he received approximately $4.3 million of employment taxes from at least 36 PDS clients by falsely representing that he would pay the funds to the IRS on the companies' behalf. Rather than remitting the employment taxes to the IRS, Richley used the money for other purposes, including buying multiple luxury vehicles, spending $360,000 in hotels and casinos in Las Vegas, and buying a residence in Lawrenceburg, Indiana. Richley also filed false employment tax returns on behalf of his clients, and false personal income tax returns, in an effort to conceal his embezzlement scheme."

d. In addition to the case involving Payroll Data Services Inc. noted in c above (in the 2009 report), one case in fiscal 2009 and one case in fiscal 2010 involved a payroll service or other benefits provider:

■ **Ex-Benefits Firm CFO Sentenced for Tax Fraud**

On September 9, 2009, in Raleigh, N.C., James McLamb was sentenced to 30 months in prison and ordered to pay nearly $8 million in restitution for tax fraud. McLamb, CFO for the Castleton Group, administered payroll and benefits for about 100 small and mid-size companies in North Carolina's Triangle area. According to court documents, McLamb collected federal withholding taxes from employees of the Castleton's clients and then provided the IRS with phony information so Castleton could keep the money. North Carolina's Department of Insurance determined the company never paid at least $8 million in payroll taxes from client companies to the IRS. Castleton shut down suddenly in December 2007 amid state and federal investigations into its finances. The closure left about 3,500 area employees, whose health benefits Castleton handled, without insurance coverage and left the companies that contracted with Castleton liable for the unpaid taxes.

■ **Owner of Defunct Payroll Services Company Sentenced for Embezzlement of $2.65 Million in FICA Taxes**

March 12, 2010, in Trenton, N.J., Joshua Schechter, owner of a defunct payroll services company in San Antonio, Texas, was sentenced to 30 months in prison for embezzling $2.65 million in FICA taxes that client companies owed to the Internal Revenue Service (IRS). Schechter pleaded guilty in October 2008, to a two-count Information charging him with filing false tax returns. Robert Stockton, Schechter's business partner, was previously sentenced to 18 months in prison for his role. At his plea hearing, Stockton stated that in 1985 he

Internet Problem 20-1 (continued)

established a business called The Business Office to provide payroll services to client businesses. In August 2003, Stockton reached an agreement to sell his business to Online Business Services (OBS) based in San Antonio, Texas. OBS was owned and operated by Joshua Schechter and was also in the payroll services business. According to court document, from 2003 through 2005, the two firms contracted with business clients to provide payrolls services. Schechter, along with Stockton and others, intentionally filed and cause to be filed numerous false IRS Form 941s which indicated that the victim clients were responsible for paying only a fraction of the tax actually due. Both defendants admitted that they did not forward to the IRS the actual amount of payroll tax for each victim and instead kept the money in OBS accounts to be used for illegal purposes.

(**Note**: Internet problems address current issues using Internet sources. Because Internet sites are subject to change, Internet problems and solutions may change. Current information on Internet problems is available at www.pearsonhighered.com/arens.)

Chapter 21

Audit of the Inventory and Warehousing Cycle

■ **Review Questions**

21-1 Inventory is often the most difficult and time consuming part of many audit engagements because:

    1.   Inventory is generally a major item on the balance sheet and often the largest item making up the accounts included in working capital.

    2.   The need for organizations to have the inventory in diverse locations makes the physical control and counting of the inventory difficult.

    3.   Inventory takes many different forms that are difficult for the auditor to fully understand.

    4.   The consistent application of different valuation methods can be fairly complicated.

    5.   The valuation of inventory is difficult due to such factors as the large number of different items involved, the need to allocate the manufacturing costs to inventory, and obsolescence.

21-2 The acquisition and payment cycle includes the system for purchasing all goods and services, including raw materials and purchased parts for producing finished goods. Purchase requisitions are used to notify the purchasing department to place orders for inventory items. When inventory reaches a predetermined level or automatic reorder point, requisitions may be initiated by stockroom personnel or by computer. In other systems, orders may be placed for the materials required to produce a customer order, or orders may be initiated upon periodic evaluation of the situation in light of the prior experience of inventory activity. After receiving the materials ordered, as part of the acquisition and payment cycle, the materials are inspected with a copy of the receiving document used to book perpetual inventory. In a standard cost inventory system, the acquisition and payment cycle computes any inventory purchase variances, which then enter the inventory system.

    The following audit procedures in the acquisition and payment cycle illustrate the relationship between that cycle and the inventory and warehousing cycle.

    1.   Compare the inventory cost entered into the inventory system to the supporting invoice to determine that it was properly recorded and the purchase variance (standard cost system), if any, was properly reflected.

    2.   Test the purchase cutoff at the physical inventory date and year-end to determine whether or not the physical inventory and year-end inventory cutoffs are proper from a purchase standpoint.

21-3 Cost accounting records are those which are concerned with the processing and storage of raw materials, work in process, and finished goods, insofar as these activities constitute internal transfers within the inventory and warehousing cycle. These records include computerized files, ledgers, worksheets and reports which accumulate material, labor, and overhead costs by job or process as the costs are incurred.

Cost accounting records are important in conducting an audit because they indicate the relative profitability of the various products for management planning and control, and determine the valuation of inventories for financial statement purposes.

21-4 The most important tests of the perpetual records the auditor must make before assessed control risk can be reduced, which may permit a reduction in other audit tests are:

1. Tests of the purchases of raw materials and pricing thereof.
2. Tests of the cost accounting documents and records by verifying the reduction of the raw material inventory for use in production and the increase in the quantity of finished goods inventory when goods have been manufactured.
3. Tests of the reduction in the finished goods inventory through the sale of goods to customers.

Assuming the perpetuals are determined to be effective, physical inventory tests may be reduced, as well as tests of inventory cutoff. In addition, an effective perpetual inventory will allow the company to test the physical inventory prior to the balance sheet date.

21-5 The continuation of shipping operations during the physical inventory will require the auditor to perform additional procedures to insure that a proper cutoff is achieved. The auditor must conclude that merchandise shipped is either included in the physical count or recorded as a sale, but not both.

Since no second count is taken, the auditor must increase the number of test counts to determine that the counts recorded are accurate.

21-6 The auditor must not give the controller a copy of his or her test counts. The auditor's test counts are the only means of controlling the original counts recorded by the company. If the controller knows which items were test counted, he or she will be able to adjust other uncounted items without detection by the auditor.

21-7 The most important audit procedures to test for the ownership of inventory during the observation of the physical counts and as a part of subsequent valuation tests are:

1. Discuss with the client.
2. Obtain an understanding of the client's operations.
3. Be alert for inventory set aside or specially marked.

21-7 (continued)

   4. Review contracts with suppliers and customers to test for the possibility of consigned inventory or inventory owned by others that is in the client's shop for repair or some other purpose.
   5. Examine vendor invoices indicating that merchandise on hand was sold to the company.
   6. Test recorded sales just before and just after the physical inventory to determine that the items were or were not on hand at the physical inventory date and that a proper cutoff was achieved.

21-8   Auditing procedures to determine whether slow-moving or obsolete items have been included in inventory are:

   1. Obtain a sufficient understanding of the client's business to aid in recognizing inventory that is no longer useful in the client's business.
   2. Review the perpetual records for slow-moving items.
   3. Discuss the quality of the inventory with management.
   4. Ask questions of production personnel during physical inventory observation about the extent of the use or nonuse of inventory items.
   5. Make observations during the physical inventory for rust, damaged inventory, inventory in unusual locations, and unusual amounts of dust on the inventory.
   6. Be aware of inventory that is tagged obsolete, spoiled, or damaged, or is set aside because it is obsolete or damaged.
   7. Examine obsolescence reports, scrap sales, and other records in subsequent periods that may indicate the existence of inventory that should have been excluded from the physical inventory or included at a reduced cost.
   8. Calculate inventory ratios, by type of inventory if possible, and compare them to previous years or industry standards.

21-9   The auditor could have uncovered the misstatement if there were adequate controls over the use of inventory tags. More specifically, the auditor should have assured himself or herself that the client had accounted for all used and unused tag numbers by examining all tags, if necessary. In addition, the auditor should have selected certain tags (especially larger items) and had the client show him or her where the goods were stored. The tag numbers used and unused should have been recorded in the auditor's working papers for subsequent follow-up. As part of substantive procedures, the auditor could have performed analytical tests on the inventory and cost of sales. A comparison of ratios such as gross margin percentage and inventory turnover could have indicated that a problem was present.

21-10 A proper cutoff of purchases and sales is heavily dependent on the physical inventory observation because a proper cutoff of sales requires that finished goods inventory included in the physical count be excluded from sales and all inventory received be included in purchases.

To make sure the cutoff for sales is accurate, the following information should be obtained during the taking of the physical inventory:

1. The last shipping document number should be recorded in the working papers for subsequent follow-up to sales records.
2. A review should be made of shipping to test for the possibility of shipments set aside for shipping and not counted or other potential cutoff problems.
3. When prenumbered shipping documents are not used, a careful review of the client's method of getting a proper sales cutoff is the first step in testing the cutoff.
4. A list of the most recent shipments should be included in the working papers for subsequent follow-up to sales records.

For the purchase cutoff, the following information should be noted:

1. The last receiving report number should be noted in the working papers for subsequent follow-up to purchase records.
2. A review should be made of the receiving department to make sure all inventory has been properly included in the physical inventory.

21-11 Compilation tests are the tests of the summarization of physical counts, the extension of price times quantity, footing the inventory summary, and tracing the totals to the general ledger.

Several examples of audit procedures to verify compilation are:

1. Trace the tag numbers used to the final inventory summary to make sure they were properly included and the numbers not used to the final inventory summary to make sure no tag numbers have been added.
2. Trace the test counts recorded in the working papers to the final inventory summary to make sure they are correctly included.
3. Trace inventory items on the final inventory list to the tags as a test of the existence of recorded inventory.
4. Test the extensions and footings of the physical inventory summary.

21-12

	ANALYTICAL PROCEDURE	TYPE OF POTENTIAL MISSTATEMENT
1.	Compare gross margin percentage with previous years.	Overstatement or understatement of inventory amounts (prices and/or quantities).
2.	Compare inventory turnover with previous years.	Obsolete inventory.
3.	Compare unit costs with previous years.	Overstatement or understatement of unit costs.
4.	Compare extended inventory value with previous years.	Errors in compilation, unit costs, or extensions.
5.	Compare current year manufacturing costs with previous years.	Misstatement of unit costs of inventory, especially direct labor and manufacturing overhead.

21-13

DATE	PURCHASE QUANTITY	PRICE	TO BE INCLUDED IN 12-31-09 INVENTORY	EXTENSION
11-26-11	2,400	$2.07	700 @ $2.07	$1,449.00
12-06-11	1,900	$2.28	1,900 @ $2.28	4,332.00
				$5,781.00

Assuming FIFO inventory valuation, the 12-31-11 inventory should be valued at $5,781, and is thus currently overstated by $121.

If the 1-26-12 purchase was for 2,300 binders at $2.12 each, the 12-31-11 inventory should be valued at $5,477.00 (1,900 @ $2.12 + 700 @ $2.07) and is thus currently overstated by $425. The reason is the lower of cost or market rule, with the $2.12 being the replacement cost.

21-14 The direct labor hours for an individual inventory item would be verified by examining engineering specifications or similar information to determine whether the number of hours to complete a unit of finished goods was correctly computed. Ordinarily it is difficult to test the number of hours to an independent source.

The manufacturing overhead rate is calculated by dividing the total annual number of labor hours into total manufacturing overhead. These two totals are verified as a part of the payroll and personnel and acquisition and payment cycles.

Once these two numbers are verified (overhead rate per direct labor hour and the number of direct labor hours per unit of each type of inventory), it is not difficult to verify the overhead cost in inventory.

21-15 With a job cost system, labor charged to a specific job is accumulated on a job cost sheet. The direct labor dollars included on the job cost sheet can be traced to the employee "job time sheet" to make sure the hours are correctly included on the job cost sheet. The labor rate can be verified by comparing it to the amount on the employee's earnings record.

21-16 Assuming the auditor properly documents receiving report numbers as a part of the physical inventory observation procedures, the auditor should verify the proper cutoff of purchases as a part of subsequent tests by examining each invoice to see if a receiving report is attached. If the receiving report is dated on or before the inventory date and the last recorded number, the received inventory must have been included in the physical inventory; therefore the invoice should be included in accounts payable. Those invoices that are received after the balance sheet date but shipped F.O.B. shipping point on or before the close of the year would indicate merchandise in transit.

■ Multiple Choice Questions From CPA Examinations

21-17 a. (3) b. (2) c. (1)

21-18 a. (1) b. (2) c. (2)

21-19 a. (4) b. (3) c. (2)

■ Discussion Questions and Problems

21-20

PURPOSE OF INTERNAL CONTROL	TEST OF CONTROL	POTENTIAL FINANCIAL MISSTATEMENT	SUBSTANTIVE AUDIT PROCEDURE
1. For a proper valuation of inventory. (Accuracy)	Examine receiving and requisition documents, trace to perpetual records.	Misstatement of inventory.	Compare physical count to perpetual inventory record.
2. To make sure physical inventory counts are accurate. (Accuracy, existence and completeness)	Observe counting personnel and discuss with client.	Misstatement of inventory.	Compare physical count to perpetual inventory record.
3. To make sure inventory compilation is accurate. (Accuracy)	Observe who compiles the inventory and discuss with client.	Misstatement of inventory.	Reperform clerical tests of inventory compilation.

21-20 (continued)

PURPOSE OF INTERNAL CONTROL	TEST OF CONTROL	POTENTIAL FINANCIAL MISSTATEMENT	SUBSTANTIVE AUDIT PROCEDURE
4. To ensure inventory is recorded when received, payments made are for goods received, and quantities and descriptions are accurate. (Completeness, existence and accuracy)	Account for a numerical sequence of receiving reports and observe matching invoices received from vendors.	Understatement of inventory or payment for goods not received.	Trace quantity and description on vendor's invoice to receiving report.
5. To minimize theft or unrecorded shipments of inventory. (Existence)	Discuss with client and observe whether personnel prepare shipping documents.	Overstatement of inventory.	Compare physical count to perpetual records.
6. To ensure inventory shipments are recorded as sales. (Completeness)	Account for a numerical sequence of shipping orders.	Understatement of sales.	Trace quantity and description on bills of lading to recorded sales.
7. To assure reasonable costs are used for inventory and cost of goods sold. (Accuracy)	Review procedures for determining standard costs.	Misstatement of inventory.	Trace costs from supporting documents to development of standards.
8. To make sure obsolete goods are classified as such. (Accuracy)	Read policy and discuss procedures with client.	Misstatement of inventory.	Analytical procedures for inventory.

a. TRANSACTION-RELATED AUDIT OBJECTIVE	b. RELATED RISK	c. TEST OF CONTROL
1. Recorded transactions represent valid, approved purchases (Occurrence).	If purchasing agents can make purchases from any vendor, there is a risk that purchasing agents may make unauthorized purchases of items not approved (for personal use).	Enter non-valid vendor numbers into the purchasing system to see if the related transaction is rejected.
2. Recorded inventory may not be recorded at appropriate amounts, due to obsolescence (Accuracy).	Without information about the amount of time inventory is in the warehouse, management is less likely to identify slow moving items that should be recorded at the lower of cost or market.	Select a sample of inventory items from the perpetual inventory system and recalculate the number of days each item has been present in the warehouse.
3. Actual shipments of inventory are recorded in the perpetual inventory records (Completeness).	Shipments of inventory may occur but not be recorded.	Select a sample of items in the warehouse and physically move them to the shipping areas to see if the microchip correctly removes those items from the perpetual inventory records.
4. Inventory recorded in the perpetual records physically exists (Occurrence).	Non-inventory warehouse individuals may remove inventory without authorization.	Observe client personnel in the inventory warehouse and determine if each person is authorized to be in the warehouse.
5. Inventory transactions are properly classified (Classification).	Equipment or supplies may be inaccurately classified as inventory if they are not physically separated from the inventory.	Observe whether equipment or supplies are stored in the same physical space as inventory.

21-21 (continued)

a. TRANSACTION- RELATED AUDIT OBJECTIVE	b. RELATED RISK	c. TEST OF CONTROL
6. Recorded inventory items are physically present (Occurrence) and recorded at correct amounts (Accuracy).	If periodic reconciliations of inventory records to physical counts are not performed, there is a risk that items may be removed from the warehouse without knowledge, which would result in overstated inventory amounts.	Inspect the client's test samples for accuracy and reasonableness. Inquire about the nature of discrepancies identified.
7. Actual inventory on hand may not be recorded in the perpetual inventory listing (Completeness).	There is a risk that inventory on hand is not included in the inventory records.	Inspect the client's test samples for accuracy and reasonableness. Inquire about the nature of discrepancies identified.
8. The perpetual inventory records are accurately summarized and posted to the general ledger accounts (Posting and Summarization)	There could be errors in the mathematical formulas of the inventory records.	Recalculate the inventory amounts and determine that the totals agree to the general ledger balances.
9. Recording inventory transactions represent actual receipts of inventory items (Occurrence).	Inventory could be added to the inventory account balance before actual goods are received.	Enter an addition to the perpetual inventory system without a valid receiving report number to determine if the system rejects the transaction.
10. Recording of inventory in the client's records is valid (Occurrence)	Inventory held on consignment may be recorded as the client's inventory.	Observe whether inventory held on consignment is stored in the same physical space as inventory.

21-22   a.   It is important to review the cost accounting records and test their accuracy for the following reasons:

1. The cost accounting records determine unit costs that are applied to derive inventory values. Since inventory is usually material, unit costs must be verified.

2. In many companies, there are many types of inventory items with complex cost structures. The potential for misstatement is great in determining costs. The auditor would need to go to an extreme effort to verify such costs without being able to rely on the cost accounting records which provides the costs, (i.e., it is far more efficient to test the cost accounting records than the costs themselves).

3. The cost accounting records also deal with transferring inventories through the production cycle and then from finished goods for sales. These transfers must be handled accurately for inventory to be properly stated.

b.   1.   Examine engineering specifications for expected (standard) labor hours. Examine time records for hours worked on part during measured period. Divide by units produced to test reasonableness of standard.

2. Review specifications for types of labor required to produce parts, or observe production. Review union contracts or earnings records to develop reasonable rate for this labor mix.

3. Identify appropriate overhead accounts, paying careful attention to consistent application. Determine amounts for these accounts for a measured period. Determine direct labor hours from payroll records from the same period. Compute the overhead rate per direct labor hour.

4. Review engineering specifications. Review material usage variance.

5. Trace to vendor's invoices. Review material price variance.

6. Sum individual components.

AUDIT PROCEDURE	TYPE OF TEST	PURPOSE
1	Test of Control	To make sure that proper controls exist and are being followed in the taking of the physical inventory. (Existence, completeness, accuracy and classification)
2	Substantive Test	To ensure that all inventory represented by an inventory tag actually exists. (Existence)
3	Substantive Test	To test the accuracy of the client's perpetual inventory records. (Existence, completeness, and accuracy)
4	Substantive Test	To test client's final inventory compilation. (Existence, completeness, accuracy and classification)
5	Substantive Test	To test that the final inventory was valued at its proper cost. (Accuracy)
6	Test of Control	To ensure that no raw material was issued without proper approval. (Existence)
7	Test of Control or Substantive Test	To ensure that additions recorded on the finished goods perpetual records were recorded on the books as completed production. (Accuracy and classification)

MISSTATEMENT	a. CONTROL THAT SHOULD HAVE PREVENTED THE MISSTATEMENT FROM OCCURRING	b. SUBSTANTIVE AUDIT PROCEDURE THAT COULD BE USED TO UNCOVER THE MISSTATEMENT
1	Internal verification by another person.	Examine vendors' invoices in support of prices used.
2	Keep a record of the last shipping report number shipped before the inventory count.	Examine bills of lading for first shipments recorded after the physical inventory to determine that they were shipped after year-end.
3	Perform independent second counts on all merchandise. All persons responsible for inventory tags and compilation of physical inventory should be independent of custody of perpetual inventory records.	Record test counts and trace to compiled inventory.
4	Use of prenumbered tags and accounting for numerical sequence.	Account for all prenumbered tags during the physical examination and during compilation tests.
5	Internal verification of perpetual inventory prices.	Compare vendor invoice prices to perpetual inventory prices.
6	Segregation of obsolete inventory.	Perform net realizable value and lower of cost or market tests of inventory, including tests of the perpetual inventory.
7	Periodic review of reasonableness of manufacturing overhead rate.	Test reasonableness of manufacturing overhead rate.

	Internal Controls	Tests of Controls
1.	Inventory purchases are used to update the perpetual Atlanta inventory records.	Trace inventory quantities for a sample of purchase transactions to the perpetual inventory records as a part of tests of controls and substantive tests of acquisition transactions.
2.	Transfers of inventory are used to update the Atlanta and local distribution center perpetual inventory records.	Trace inventory quantities for a sample of shipments from Atlanta to local distribution centers to the perpetual inventory records.
3.	Inventory sales are used to update the local distribution center perpetual inventory records.	Trace inventory quantities for a sample of sales transactions to the perpetual inventory records as a part of tests of controls and substantive tests of sales transactions.
4.	Local distribution centers access to perpetual records is restricted to processing sales transactions.	Test the effectiveness of the perpetual records access restrictions using the CPA firm's computer audit specialists.
5.	Quarterly physical inventory is taken for comparison to and adjustment of perpetual records.	Examine local distribution center physical inventory count records and adjustments to the perpetual records.
6.	Internal auditors test the perpetual records continuously.	Examine internal auditor audit programs and working papers for their tests of the perpetual records and the findings.
7.	Internal auditors sample inventory counts and test inventory adjustments.	Examine internal auditor audit programs and working papers for their tests of the physical observation of inventory and the findings.

b.   There are four ways to reduce physical observation of inventory. Auditors will use their judgment to decide which combination of these to use.

1.   Reduce the number of local warehouses to observe inventory counting and do test counts of inventory.
2.   Reduce the number of auditors who observe the inventory counting at each location.
3.   Reduce the sample sizes for test counts inventory.
4.   Perform the physical observation of inventory at an interim date.

21-26 a.

Inventory Description	Units on Hand	Dollars	Number of Units Requiring Floor Space	Per Unit Required Sq. Footage	Total Square Footage Required to Store Inventory (Units x Sq ft)
AC Unit – Model 635	1240	$806,000	413.333333[a]	16	6613.33333
AC Unit – Model 770	1733	$1,940,960	577.666667[a]	16	9242.66667
Furnace – Model 223	1992	$2,589,600	996[b]	16	15936
Furnace – Model 225	2008	$2,761,000	1004[b]	16	16064
Air Handling Ducts	11883	$1,485,400	2970.75[c]	25	74,268.75
		$9,582,960			122,124.75

[a] 2 pallets of AC units sit on top of 1 pallet that rests on the floor (1240/3 = 413.33; 1733/3 = 577.66667.

[b] 1 furnace can sit on top of the unit that rests on the floor (1992/2 = 996; 2008/2 = 1004)

[c] 3 boxes can be stored on top of the box that rests on the floor (11883/4 = 2971)

.

b. .The above analytical procedure suggests that inventory may be significantly overstated. The amount of square footage that would be needed (122,124.75 square feet) to store the stated amount of inventory is 22.1% greater than the amount of square footage (100,000 square feet) available in the warehouse facility. The auditor would need to design further substantive tests to examine the existence of inventory at year end.

21-27 a. The auditor in this situation should observe the recording of the shipments on the day of occurrence and record these details in the working papers so a determination can be made as to whether the shipments affected the physical inventory count.

b. 1. There is no clear-cut answer to sample size for inventory counts. The answer to the question depends on additional factors, such as the randomness of your test counts and whether the values of the merchandise are relatively stratified. It also depends on inherent risk for inventory physical counts and the materiality of inventory compared to total assets.

2. Request a recount by the client or greatly expand your tests to determine whether a material misstatement exists.

21-27 (continued)

    c.   The auditor should determine how this inventory is valued and after discussion with the client it may be well to classify it as obsolete. In all cases, the auditor must specifically identify the merchandise in the working papers for subsequent evaluation. The auditor should also be aware that this could be an indication of widespread obsolescence problems in other parts of the inventory.

    d.   One of the important tasks the auditor undertakes during the observation is to determine that inventory tags are physically controlled. This assures that the inventory is not understated because tags are lost, or overstated because falsified tags are added. In this situation, the auditor should recover the discarded tags and request that the practice be stopped, and that control of tags be established under the auditor's direct observation.

21-28   The following procedures should be established to insure that the inventory count includes all items that should be included and that nothing is counted twice:

    1.   All materials should be cleared from the receiving area and stored in the appropriate space before the count.

    2.   Incoming shipments of unassembled parts and supplies should be held in the receiving area until the end of the day and then inventoried.

    3.   If possible, the day's shipments of finished appliances should be taken to the shipping area before the count. (Unshipped items remaining in the shipping area should be inventoried at the end of the day.)

    4.   Great care must be exercised over goods removed from the warehouse itself. These may be unassembled parts and supplies requisitioned on an emergency basis or unscheduled shipments of finished appliances. Alternative methods for recording these removals are:

        a)   Keep a list of all items removed and indicate on the list whether the item had been counted.

        b)   Record the removal on the inventory tag if the item has been inventoried.

        c)   Indicate on the material requisition or the shipping order that the item had been inventoried. For any of these alternatives, a warehouse employee or the perpetual inventory clerk must adjust the recorded counts.

    5.   The finished appliances remaining in the warehouse should be inventoried at the end of the day.

21-28 (continued)

> 6. The warehouse should be instructed to date all documents as of the day the materials are received, issued, or shipped.

> 7. The inventory clerk should post the May 31 production and shipment of finished goods to the inventory record based upon the dates shown on the plant production report and the shipping report. This will provide a proper cutoff because provisions have been made to adjust all counts for goods manufactured and shipped on May 31.

> 8. The listing of inventory differences should be reviewed by the controller and warehouse supervisor prior to booking the adjustment. Abnormal differences should be investigated, and recounts (with appropriate reconciliation) should be made where appropriate.

21-29

Computer Solution. Computer solutions in Excel are contained on the companion Website (Filename is P2129.xls).

> a.

	2011	2010	2009	2008
Gross margin %	26.3%	22.6%	22.4%	22.4%
Inventory turnover	6.6	7.6	7.6	7.9

> b. Logical causes of the changes in the gross margin as a percent of sales include:

>> 1. Selling prices were raised without a corresponding increase in cost of sales.
>> 2. The method of accounting for inventory was changed, causing a higher ending inventory (more expenses absorbed into inventory) and lower cost of sales.
>> 3. Inventory cutoff was improper, causing sales to be recorded without the corresponding entry to cost of sales.
>> 4. The product mix of the company changed. More high markup items were sold than in previous years.
>> 5. An improper journal entry was recorded which adjusted the gross margin upward.

21-29 (continued)

Logical causes of the changes in the inventory turnover include:

1. The increased selling prices, which caused the gross margin percent to increase, reduced demand for the product, and decreased the inventory turnover.
2. The company is building its inventory supply in anticipation of increased sales in the future.
3. The company's inventory contains obsolete or unsalable merchandise, which is affecting the turnover rate.

c. 26.3% - 22.6% = 3.7% increase in gross margin %

   3.7% x sales of $92.8 million =
   $3,433,600 potential misstatement

   $68.4 million (2009 COGS) / 7.6 inventory turnover =
   $9.0 million

   $11.6 million - 9.0 million =
   $2,600,000 potential misstatement

   Both calculations indicate a potential misstatement exceeding $2,000,000.

d. The auditor should discuss the two changes with the client and obtain a reasonable explanation for them. He or she should then perform appropriate procedures to verify the validity of the explanation. Ultimately, the auditor must be confident the change does not result from a misstatement in the financial statements.

21-30 a.

1. Exclude
2. Exclude
3. Include
4. Include
5. Exclude

b. 1. This merchandise would be excluded because title does not pass to buyer on an F.O.B. destination shipment until delivery to the buyer. Since it was not received until January 2012, there is no basis for including it in inventory.
2. Goods held "on consignment" do not belong to the consignee, and should not be included in inventory.
3. Normally title to a stock item does not pass to the customer until shipment, even though it has been set aside. Therefore it should be included in inventory.

21-30 (continued)

4.   Title to goods shipped F.O.B. shipping point normally passes to the buyer on delivery to the transportation agency, and in this instance the goods belong to your client at December 31, 2011. There is an error in recording the acquisition.

5.   Since this machine is fabricated to the customer's order, title to customer made-merchandise passes to the buyer as materials and labor are appropriated to the job. When the job is completed and ready for shipment as in this case, it may be considered as a completed sale.

21-31 a. 1.   Extension errors are as follows:

DESCRIPTION	EXTENSION AS RECORDED	ACTUAL EXTENSION	OVER (UNDER) STATEMENT
Wood	$ 11.04	$ 110.40	$=(99.36)
Metal cutting tool	1,740.00	1,470.00	270.00
Cutting fluid	240.00	1,040.00	(800.00)
Sandpaper	579.00	5.70	573.30
			$ (56.06)

2.   The differences in the previous year's and this year's cost indicate a problem. The auditor should attempt to obtain support for the current year's cost if the effect of the differences noted seems significant (considering that the test only covered 20% of the dollar items). A review for reasonableness indicates the following:

a)   Precision cutting torches are expensive. Maybe $800 each is a reasonable price. Examine a vendor's invoice or a price list.

b)   Aluminum scrap values may fluctuate significantly. The two prices may be reasonable. Look at sales invoices for the two years.

c)   Lubricating oil cost appears unreasonable for this year and for the previous year. The auditor should examine invoices for both years. If the previous year's costs were incorrect, determination of the effect of the misstatements on the prior year's and this year's financial statements must be completed to determine the need for disclosure of the misstatements.

21-31 (continued)

3. Investigate the reasons for the omission of these tags from final inventory compilation. If it is determined that the omission of two tags is significant based on the number of tags used and tested, the auditor should account for all tags to determine the total extent of omissions.

4. Page total footing errors are as follows:

PAGE NO.	CLIENT TOTAL	CORRECT TOTAL	OVER- (UNDER-) STATEMENT
14	$2,375.36	$2,375.30	$ 0.06
82	6,721.18	6,421.18	300.00
			$300.06

b. First, the auditor should keep in mind that only 20% of the inventory was tested. If sampling were random, a direct extrapolation would magnify projected misstatements by five. In addition, the auditor must consider sampling error.

The net effect of the misstatements for which we were able to compute the actual misstatement was an overstatement of inventory by $244.00 a small amount (see items 1 and 4). However, the exceptions resulted from various causes including incorrect decimal placement, mathematical errors, and unit of measure errors. The auditor should determine that the net effect of the misstatements is not significant; in addition, to insure against other individual misstatements that might be significant, the auditor should review the extensions and other computations for reasonableness and obvious misstatements.

For the items for which the amount of the misstatement could not be determined, the auditor should follow up as described in 2 and 3 above. From the results of the follow-up, the effect of the misstatements noted should be assessed and determination made as to the need for expansion of scope for the tests considered.

c. Prior to compiling the inventory next year, Martin Manufacturing should implement the following internal controls:

1. Review formulas in schedule for inventory compilation. Accuracy of spreadsheet should be independently reviewed.
2. Someone familiar with the inventory should review the compilation schedules for reasonableness of quantities, prices, and extensions.
3. All inventory tags should be accounted for prior to posting to the compilation schedules and a control total compared to the total on the compilation sheets after the compilation is complete.

21-32 a. Necessary adjustments to client's physical inventory:

Material in Car #AR38162 — received in warehouse on January 2, 2012	$ 8,120
Materials stranded en route (Sales price $19,270 / 125%)	15,416
Total	23,536
Less unsalable inventory	1,250*
Total adjustment	$22,286

> * If freight charges have been included in the client's inventory, the amount would be $1,600 and the amount of the total adjustment would be $21,936. Journal entry 6 probably would have a credit to purchases of $1,600 in this case.

b. Auditor's worksheet adjusting entries:

1.

Purchases	$ 2,183	
Accounts Payable		$ 2,183

To record goods in warehouse but not invoiced–received on RR 1060.

2. No entry required. Title to goods had passed.

3.

Accounts receivable	12,700	
Sales		12,700

To record goods as sold which were loaded on December 31 and not inventories-SI 968.

4.

Sales	19,270	
Accounts receivable		19,270

To reverse out of sales material included in both sales (SI 966) and in physical inventory (after adjustment).

5. No adjustment required.

6.

Claims receivable	1,600	
Purchases		1,250
Freight In		350

To record claim against carrier for merchandise damaged in transit.

7. Inventory   22,286
        Cost of goods sold   22,286

    To adjust accounts for changes
    in physical inventory quantities.

8. Sales   15,773
        Accounts receivable   15,773

    To reverse out of sales invoices
    #969, 970, 97l. The sales book
    was held open too long. This
    merchandise was in warehouse
    at time of physical count and so
    included therein.

■ Case

21-33

Computer Solution. Computer solutions in Excel are contained on the Companion Website (Filename P2133.XLS).

A. A price of $8 is proper for pricing L37 spars at 12-31-11 since the next shipment of spars was not received until 1-06-12. However, the next invoice shows a lower cost, which indicates a decline in the value of this product. If the net realizable value (selling price less cost to sell) is less than the $8 per meter cost, the spars should be revalued to net realizable value at 12-31-11.

B. The total is 10,000/12 feet times $1.20 per foot = $1,000. In addition, the freight of $200 should have been as follows:

$$\frac{\$200}{(12{,}800 \text{ inches} / 12 \text{ inches per foot})} = \$0.1875 \text{ per ft.}$$

Total inventory cost should be ($1.20 + 0.1875 per foot) times 833 feet (10,000/12) = $1,155.79 or an overstatement of inventory by $10,844.21.

C. FIFO value would be:

Voucher 12-61   1,000 yards at $10.00 per yard = $10,000
Voucher 11-81   500 yards at $ 9.50 per yard =   4,750
        Inventory is overstated by $250 $14,750

Voucher number 12-81 is not used because the receiving date is after year-end.

21-33 (continued)

    D.   FIFO value would be:

Voucher 12-61	800 feet at $8.00 per foot	=	$6,400
Voucher 11-81	200 feet at $8.20 per foot	=	1,640
			$8,040

        Inventory is understated by $40. However, if the reduction in cost on voucher #12-61 indicates that the net realizable value of the struts is below the cost on voucher #11-81, then the net realizable value of the struts should be used as the cost.

    E.   Pricing is correct if the item is for inventory. It is possible that this item should be capitalized.

    F.   Proper FIFO cost is 40 pair x 2 = 80 springs x $69.00 each = $5,520. Inventory is understated by $5,244.

    G.   Pricing is correct. However, the fasteners were purchased in 2004 five years ago, and only eleven or 14% have been used. Consideration should be given as to whether net realizable value is less than cost.

21-33 (continued)

SEA GULL AIRFRAMES, INC.
SUMMARY OF INVENTORY MISSTATEMENTS

Item No. and Description	Quantity			Price			Recorded Amount	Correct Amount	Amount of Misstatement
	Per Inventory	Correct	Difference	Per Inventory	Correct	Difference			
A. L37 Spars	3,000	3,000	0	8.00	8.00	0.00	24,000.00	24,000.00	0.00
B. B68 Metal Formers	10,000	833	9,167	1.20	1.3875	– 0.1875	12,000.00	1,155.79	– 10,844.21
C. R01 Metal Ribs	1,500	1,500	0	10.00	10/9.50	.50	15,000.00	14,750.00	– 250.00
D. St26 Struts	1,000	1,000	0	8.00	8/8.20	– .20	8,000.00	8,040.00	40.00
E. Industrial hand drills	45	45	0	20.00	20.00	0.00	900.00	900.00	0.00
F. L803 Steel Leaf Springs	40	80	– 40	69.00	69.00	0.00	276.00	5,520.00	5,244.00
G. V16 Fasteners	5.50	5.50	0	10.00	10.00	0.00	55.00	55.00	0.00
Total misstatement									– 5,810.21
Items over $5,000									– 11,054.21
Items under $5,000									5,244.00
									– 5,810.21

CONCLUSION: (see next page for calculations)

There is a material potential misstatement due to the number and size of misstatements found relative to the sample chosen. In order to determine a more accurate estimate of the actual misstatement, additional tests are necessary.

REMARKS
A. NRV [assumed] exceeds cost.
B. Quantity based on inches, not feet; freight not included.
C. 500 yards overpriced.
D. 200 feet underpriced. NRV [assumed] O.K.
E. [Assumed] not capitalizable.
F. Includes extension error in inventory.
G. Consider separately for obsolescence.

21-33 (continued)

PROJECTED MISSTATEMENTS

Dollars tested

Sample items	Over 5,000	Under $5,000
No exceptions	360,000	2,600
A	24,000	
B	12,000	
C	15,000	
D	8,000	
E		900
F		276
G		55
Dollars tested	419,000	3,831

PROJECTED MISSTATEMENT IGNORING SAMPLING ERROR*

More than $5,000 $\dfrac{4,150,000}{419,000}$ X −11,054.21 = − $109,486

Less than $5,000 $\dfrac{4,125,000}{3,831}$ X 5,244 = $5,646,436

*   Used ratio estimation for projected misstatement. Difference estimation
    results are equally unacceptable.

■ **Internet Problem Solution: Using Inventory Count Specialists**

Internet Problem 21-1

a.   RGIS has assisted Hines Horticulture in the physical inventory counts
     of Hines' products held on consignment at Home Depot stores. Hines
     maintains ownership of the inventory until it is scanned and sold at a
     Home Depot store. RGIS helps Hines maintain its perpetual inventory
     records by providing coverage on a wide geographic basis.

b.   The business arrangement between Hines and Home Depot involves
     Hines' products being on consignment at numerous Home Depot
     stores. Because Hines maintains ownership, it must maintain accurate
     counts of inventory located at numerous Home Depot stores that
     span a wide geographic area. Hines doesn't have the workforce
     needed to verify accurate counts of items on consignment at Home
     Depot. RGIS, as an outsourced inventory count specialist, is able to
     assist Hines in the inventory count procedures.

Internet Problem 21-1 (continued)

c. The auditor has a responsibility to obtain sufficient appropriate evidence about inventory related assertions. That responsibility would not differ for inventory counted by count specialists or client personnel. The auditor would need to obtain evidence about inventory balances counted by RGIS and Hines employees.

d. The fact that some of Hines' inventory is counted by RGIS, a reputable inventory count specialists company, may be viewed by the auditor as an effective internal control to support a lower control risk assessment than when the inventory is counted by Hines personnel. The auditor may also be able to send requests to RGIS to confirm directly to the auditor inventory counts at a sample of Home Depot stores.

e. **Advantages**: Experienced inventory specialists; No or very limited management time required to train employees on inventory procedures; Ability to continue business while the counting proceeds; Company employees are free to continue with their daily tasks, etc.

Disadvantages: Company may lose control over the counting process; Management may experience a disconnect from the inventory counting process which might lead to a loss of information; Inventory specialists may not be familiar with inventory if the company is in a unique industry; etc.

(**Note**: Internet problems address current issues using Internet sources. Because Internet sites are subject to change, Internet problems and solutions may change. Current information on Internet problems is available at www.pearsonhighered.com/arens.)

Chapter 22

Audit of the Capital Acquisition and Repayment Cycle

- **Review Questions**

22-1   Four examples of interest bearing liability accounts commonly found on balance sheets are:

1.   Notes payable
2.   Contracts payable
3.   Mortgages payable
4.   Bonds payable

These liabilities have the following characteristics in common:

1.   Relatively few transactions affect the account balance, but each transaction is often highly material in amount.
2.   The exclusion of a single transaction could be material in itself.
3.   There is a legal relationship between the client entity and the holder of the stock, bond, or similar ownership document.
4.   There is a direct relationship between interest and dividend accounts and debt and equity.

These liabilities differ in what they represent and the nature of their respective liabilities.

22-2   The characteristics of the liability accounts in the capital acquisition and repayment cycle that result in a different auditing approach than the approach followed in the audit of accounts payable are:

1.   Relatively few transactions affect the account balance, but each transaction is often highly material in amount.
2.   The exclusion of a single transaction could be material in itself.
3.   There is a legal relationship between the client entity and the holder of the stock, bond, or similar ownership document.
4.   There is a direct relationship between interest and dividend accounts and debt and equity.

22-3   It is common to audit the balance in notes payable in conjunction with the audit of interest expense and interest payable because it minimizes the verification time and reduces the likelihood of overlooking misstatements in the balance. Once the auditor is satisfied with the balance in notes payable and the related interest rates and due dates for each note, it is easy to test the accuracy of accrued interest. If the interest expense for the year is also tested at the same time, the likelihood of omitting a note from notes payable for which interest has been paid is minimized. When there are a large number of notes or a large number of transactions during the year, it is usually too time consuming to completely tie out interest expense as a part of the audit of the notes payable and related accrued interest. Normally, however, there are only a few notes and few transactions during the year.

22-4   The most important controls the auditor should be concerned about in the audit of notes payable are:

1.   The proper authorization for the issuance of new notes (or renewals) to insure that the company is not being committed to debt arrangements that are not authorized.
2.   Controls over the repayment of principal and interest to insure that the proper amounts are paid.
3.   Proper records and procedures to insure that all amounts in all transactions are properly recorded.
4.   Periodic independent verification to insure that all the controls over notes payable are working.

22-5   The most important analytical procedures used to verify notes payable is a test of interest expense. By the use of this test, auditors can uncover misstatements in interest calculations or possible unrecorded notes payable.

22-6   It is more important to search for unrecorded notes payable than unrecorded notes receivable because the omission of an asset is less likely to occur than the omission of a debt. Several audit procedures the auditor can use to uncover unrecorded notes payable are:

1.   Examine the notes paid after year-end to determine whether they were liabilities at the balance sheet date.
2.   Obtain a standard bank confirmation that includes specific reference to the existence of notes payable from all banks with which the client does business.
3.   Review the bank reconciliation for new notes credited directly to the bank account by the bank.
4.   Obtain confirmation from creditors who have held notes from the client in the past and are not currently included in the notes payable schedule.

> 5. Analyze interest expense to uncover a payment to a creditor who is not included on the notes payable schedule.
> 6. Review the minutes of the board of directors for authorized but unrecorded notes.

22-7 The primary purpose of analyzing interest expense is to uncover a payment to a creditor who is not included on the notes payable schedule. The primary considerations the auditor should keep in mind when doing the analysis are:

> 1. Is the payee for the interest payment listed in the cash disbursements journal also included in the notes payable list?
> 2. Has a confirmation for notes payable been received from the payee?

22-8 The tests of controls and substantive tests of transactions for liability accounts in the capital acquisition and repayment cycle consists of tests of the control and substantive tests over the payment of principal and interest and the issuance of new notes or other liabilities, whereas the tests of details of balances concern the balance of the liabilities, interest payable, and interest expense. A unique aspect of the capital acquisition and repayment cycle is that auditors normally verify the transactions and balances in the account at the same time, as described in the solution to Review Question 22-3.

22-9 Four types of restrictions long-term creditors often put on companies in granting them a loan are:

> 1. Financial ratio restrictions
> 2. Payment of dividends restrictions
> 3. Operations restrictions
> 4. Issue of additional debt restrictions

The auditor can find out about these restrictions by examining the loan agreement and related correspondence associated with the loan, and by confirmation. The auditor must perform calculations and observe activities to determine whether the client has observed the restrictions.

22-10 The primary objectives in the audit of owners' equity accounts are to determine whether:

> 1. The internal controls over capital stock and related dividends are adequate.

2. Owners' equity transactions are recorded properly, as defined by the following six transaction-related audit objectives:

    ■ Occurrence
    ■ Completeness
    ■ Accuracy
    ■ Posting and summarization
    ■ Classification
    ■ Timing

3. Owners' equity balances in the financial statements satisfy the following balance-related audit objectives:

    ■ Detail tie-in
    ■ Existence
    ■ Completeness
    ■ Accuracy
    ■ Classification
    ■ Cutoff

4. Owners' equity balances are properly presented and disclosed to satisfy the following presentation and disclosure-related audit objectives:

    ■ Occurrence and Rights and Obligations
    ■ Completeness
    ■ Accuracy and Valuation
    ■ Classification and Understandability

22-11 Although the corporate charter and bylaws are legal documents, their legal nature is not being judged by the auditor. They are being used only to reference transactions being tested by the auditor and provide insight into some of the key control features of the company. The auditor should consult an attorney if the information the auditor needs from the documents is not clear or if a legal interpretation is needed.

22-12 The major internal controls over owners' equity are:

1. Proper authorization of transactions
2. Proper record keeping
3. Adequate segregation of duties between maintaining owners' equity records and handling cash and stock certificates
4. The use of an independent registrar and stock transfer agent

22-13   The audit of owners' equity for a closely held corporation differs from that for a publicly held corporation in that the amount of time spent in verifying owners' equity in a closely held corporation is usually minimal because of the relatively few transactions for capital stock accounts that occur during the year. For publicly held corporations, the audit of owners' equity is more complex due to the existence of a larger number of shareholders and frequent changes in the individuals holding stock.

The audits are not significantly different in regard to whether the transactions in the equity accounts are properly authorized and recorded and whether the amounts in the accounts are properly classified, described, and stated in accordance with generally accepted accounting principles.

22-14   The duties of a stock registrar are to make sure that stock is issued by a corporation in accordance with the capital authorization of the board of directors, to sign all newly issued stock certificates, and to make sure old certificates are received and cancelled before a replacement certificate is issued when there is a change in the ownership of the stock.

The duties of a transfer agent are to maintain the stockholder records, and in some cases, disburse cash dividends to shareholders.

The use of the services of a stock registrar improves the effectiveness of the client's internal controls by preventing the improper issuance of stock certificates. Along similar lines, the use of the services of an independent transfer agent improves the control over the stock records by putting them in the hands of an independent organization.

22-15   The number of shares outstanding, the correct valuation of capital stock transactions, and par value can all be confirmed with a transfer agent. The balance can then be easily recalculated from this information.

22-16   Because it is important to verify that properly authorized dividends have been paid to owners of stock as of the dividend record date, a comparison of a random sample of cancelled dividend checks to a dividend list prepared by management would be inadequate. Such an audit step is useless unless the dividend list has first been verified to include all stockholders of record at the dividend record date. A better test is to determine the total number of shares outstanding at the dividend date from the stock registrar and recompute the total dividends that should have been paid for comparison with the total amount actually paid. A random sample of cancelled checks should then be compared to the independent registrar's records to verify that the payments were actually made to valid shareholders.

22-17   If a transfer agent disburses dividends for a client, the total dividends declared can be verified by tracing the amount to a cash disbursement entry to the agent and also confirming the amount. There should ordinarily be no need to test individual dividend disbursement transactions if a stock transfer agent is used.

22-18 The major emphasis in auditing the retained earnings account should be on the recorded changes that have taken place during the year, such as net earnings for the year, dividends declared, prior period adjustments, extraordinary items charged or credited directly to retained earnings, or setting up or elimination of appropriations. Except for dividends declared, the other items should be verified during other parts of the engagement. This is especially true of the net earnings for the year. Therefore, the audit of retained earnings primarily consists of an analysis of the changes in retained earnings and the verification of the authorization and accuracy of the underlying transactions.

22-19 For auditing owners' equity and calculating earnings per share, it is crucial to verify that the number of shares used in each is accurate. Earnings are verified as an integral part of the entire audit and should require no additional verification as a part of owners' equity. The auditor should consider relevant accounting standards to verify that the earnings per share figure and the disclosures of descriptions of the various classes of stock noted in the corporate charter and minutes of the board of directors conform to those standards.

■ Multiple Choice Questions From CPA Examinations

22-20 a. (2)   b. (2)   c. (1)   d. (3)

22-21 a. (4)   b. (3)   c. (1)   d. (1)

■ Discussion Questions and Problems

22-22

a. PURPOSE OF CONTROL	b. POTENTIAL FINANCIAL STATEMENT MISSTATEMENT	c. AUDIT PROCEDURE TO DETERMINE EXISTENCE OF MATERIAL MISSTATEMENT
1. To insure that all note liabilities are actual liabilities of the company.	Loss of assets through payment of excess interest rates or the diversion of cash to unauthorized persons.	Examine note request forms for proper authorization and discuss terms of note with appropriate management personnel.
2. To insure that note transactions are recorded in full and in detail.	Improper disclosure or misstatements in notes payable through duplication.	Reconcile detailed contents of master file or other records to control account.

22-22 (continued)

a. PURPOSE OF CONTROL	b. POTENTIAL FINANCIAL STATEMENT MISSTATEMENT	c. AUDIT PROCEDURE TO DETERMINE EXISTENCE OF MATERIAL MISSTATEMENT
3. To insure that all note-related transactions agree with account balances.	Misstatement of notes payable.	Reconcile master file with outstanding notes payable.
4. To prevent misuse of notes and funds earmarked for notes.	Misstatement of liabilities and cash.	Perform all substantive procedures on extended basis. Trace from paid notes file to cash receipts to determine that the appropriate amount of cash was received when the note was issued.
5. To insure that notes are not paid more than once.	Loss of cash.	Examine outstanding notes and paid notes for similarities and the potential for reusing the notes.
6. To insure that only the proper interest amount is paid and recorded.	Misstatement of interest expense and related accrual.	Recompute interest on a test basis.

22-23 a.

AUDIT PROCEDURE	PURPOSE
1	To determine if the account balances are reasonable as related to each other and to examine for unreasonable changes in the account balances.
2	To obtain independent confirmation of bond indebtedness and collateral.
3	To determine the nature of restrictions on client as a means of verifying whether the restrictions have been met and to insure they are adequately disclosed.
4	To insure that the bonds are not subject to unnecessary early retirement by bondholders and that proper disclosures are made.
5	To determine if the calculations are correct and accounts are accurate.

22-23 (continued)

b. The auditor should be alert for the following provisions in the bond indenture agreement:

1. Restrictions on payment of dividends
2. Convertibility provisions
3. Provisions for repayment
4. Restrictions on additional borrowing
5. Required maintenance of specified financial ratios

c. The auditor can determine whether the above provisions have been met by the following procedures:

1. Audit of payments of dividends
2. Determine if the appropriate stock authorizations are adequate
3. Determine if sinking fund is adequate
4. Search for other liabilities
5. Calculate ratios and compare to agreement

d. The auditor should verify the unamortized bond discount or premium on a bond that was in force at the beginning of the year by recalculation. This is done by dividing the premium or discount by the number of total months the bonds will be outstanding and multiplying by the number of months remaining. For bonds issued in the current year, the bond premium or discount must first be verified. The monthly premium or discount is then calculated and multiplied by the number of months still outstanding.

e. The following information should be requested from the bondholder in the confirmation of bonds payable:

1. Amount of bond
2. Maturity date
3. Interest rate
4. Payment dates
5. Payment amounts
6. Assets pledged as security
7. Restrictions on client activities

22-24 a. The amounts listed in the beginning balance column would be verified by examining the ending audited balances in the prior year audit files. The ending balance for each type of long-term debt would be verified in addition to the mathematical accuracy of the beginning balance column.

b. To obtain evidence about the items in the additions column, the auditor would obtain detailed information of what individual additions comprise the additions amount for each account category and then examine supporting documentation, such as the long-term debt contracts and bond or debenture agreements, and the auditor would examine evidence of proper approval, such as minutes documenting board of director approval. The auditor would also verify whether cash was received and deposited in company cash accounts if the debt was tied to cash financing. For some types of long-term debt, such as a mortgage, the company would not receive cash given that the debt is linked to the purchase of an asset. Thus, the auditor would verify that the acquired property is included as an addition in the audit schedule reflecting property, plant and equipment or other asset account.

c. To obtain evidence about the items in the payments column, the auditor would review the related debt contract to determine if the amounts paid are reasonable. The auditor would also verify that the payment amounts agree with cash disbursement records and associated bank statements. The auditor may consider confirming the payment information with the bond trustee.

d. The auditor would verify the mathematical accuracy of the summation of the beginning balances plus additions less payments to ensure it crossfoots to the ending balance for each long-term debt category listed on the schedule. The auditor would also recalculate the summation of the amounts listed in the ending balance column to the total shown on the schedule. Each ending balance would be tied to the general ledger balances and the total would be traced to the line item in the balance sheet.

e. The auditor would verify interest rates and due dates by examining the long-term debt contracts, such as the bond or debenture agreement.

22-24 (continued)

    f,   The auditor could use the information in the schedule to develop a substantive analytical procedure related to interest expense. The auditor could calculate an average long-term debt balance for each type of debt listed on the schedule that would be multiplied by that debt's interest rate to develop an expectation of interest expense for each debt category. The auditor would then compare the summation of those expectations for all debt types to the recorded interest expense in the general ledger.

    To audit interest payable, the auditor would verify, by review of the debt agreements, the interest payment due dates and interest rates to determine the appropriate period of time for which interest expense requires accrual. For example, the debt agreement for the convertible debentures may indicate that interest is due quarterly on the first day of April, July, October, and January. Thus, the auditor would expect that that one quarter's interest expense ($131,250) requires accrual as of December 31, 2011 ($10,000,000 times 5.25% divided by 4 = $131,250). That expectation would be compared to the amount recorded in the general ledger as accrued interest for that debt type. The auditor would also need to determine that prior interest payments have been made and recorded, thus not requiring any additional accrual at December 31.

22-25 a. The emphasis in the verification of notes payable in this situation should be in determining whether all existing notes are included in the client's records. The four audit procedures listed do not satisfy this emphasis.

    b.

AUDIT PROCEDURE	PURPOSE
1	To determine if the notes payable list reconciles to the general ledger.
2	To determine if the notes payable on the list are correctly recorded and disclosed.
3	To verify that all recorded notes payable are properly recorded and disclosed.
4	To insure that interest expense is properly recorded on the books.

c.   Procedure 2 is not necessary in light of procedure 3. They both perform the same function and the confirmation is from an independent source. The sample sizes for the procedures are probably appropriate, considering the deficiencies in record keeping procedures.

d.   In addition to the procedures mentioned, the following ones are essential because there must be a search for unrecorded notes:

1.   Analyze interest expense and send a confirmation for notes payable to all payees not receiving a confirmation for notes.
2.   Confirm the balance in notes payable to payees included in last year's notes payable list but not confirmed in the current year.
3.   Examine notes paid after year-end to determine whether they were liabilities at the balance sheet date.
4.   Obtain a standard bank confirmation that includes a specific reference to notes payable from all banks with which the client does business.
5.   Review the minutes of the board of directors.

22-26   In each case, any actual failure to comply would have to be reported in a footnote to the statements in view of the possible serious consequences of advancing the maturity date of the loan. The individual audit steps that should be taken are as follows:

a.   Calculate the working capital ratio at the beginning of and through the previous fiscal year. If it is under 2 to 1, determine compensation of officers for compliance with the limitation.

b.   Examine the client's copies of insurance policies or certificates of insurance for compliance with the covenant, preparing a schedule of book value, appraised or estimated value, and coverage for the report. Confirm policies held with trustee.

c.   Examine vouchers supporting tax payments on all property covered by the indenture. By reference to the local tax laws and the vouchers, determine that all taxes have been paid before the penalty-free period expired. If the vouchers in any case are inadequate, confirm with the trustee who holds the tax receipts.

d.   Vouch the payments to the sinking fund. Confirm bond purchases and sinking fund balance with trustee. Observe evidence of destruction of bonds for bonds cancelled. Report the fund as an asset, preferably giving the composition as to cash and bonds held alive, if any.

22-27 a. It is desirable to prepare an audit schedule for the permanent file for the mortgage so that the appropriate information concerning the mortgage will be conveniently available for future years' audits. This information should include all the provisions of the mortgage as well as the purchase price, date of purchase, and a list of items pledged as collateral. It may also contain an amortization schedule of principal and interest (especially if the auditor has access to a computer program for preparation of such a schedule).

b. The audit of mortgage payable, interest expense, and interest payable should all be done together since these accounts are related and the results of testing each account have a bearing on the other accounts. The likelihood of misstatement in the client's records is determined faster and more effectively by doing them together.

c. The audit procedures that should ordinarily be performed to verify the issue of the mortgage, the balance in the mortgage and interest payable, and the balance in the interest expense accounts are:

1. Determine if the mortgage was properly authorized.
2. Obtain the mortgage agreement and schedule the pertinent provisions in the permanent file, including the face amount, payments, interest rate, restrictions, and collateral.
3. Confirm the mortgage amount, terms, and collateral with the lending institution.
4. Recompute interest payable at the balance sheet date and reconcile interest expense to the decrease in principal and the payments made.
5. Test interest expense for reasonableness.

d. Accounting standards require disclosures related to long-term debt. The terms of the debt agreement are to be disclosed, including interest rates, maturity dates, five-year payment information, assets pledged as collateral, among other items. Significant restrictions on the activities of the company, such as maintaining cash or other compensating balances or restricting the amount of dividends that can be paid, should be disclosed. Thus, auditors obtain copies of long-term debt agreements to determine that the client's disclosures are complete and accurate.

a. PURPOSE OF CONTROL	b. POTENTIAL FINANCIAL STATEMENT MISSTATEMENT	c. AUDIT PROCEDURES TO DETERMINE EXISTENCE OF MATERIAL MISSTATEMENT
1. To insure that records are properly maintained.	Misstatement of owners' equity and the disbursement of dividends and capital to the wrong people.	Determine if company uses services of an independent registrar, or transfer agent. Confirm details of equity accounts with them.
2. To insure that records are properly maintained.	Misstatement of owners' equity and earnings per share.	Account for all unissued certificates and account for all cancelled certificates and their mutilation.
3. To insure that the general ledger reflects the balance of supporting records.	Misstatement of owners' equity and earnings per share.	Trace postings from master file and stock certificates into general ledger. Reconcile master file to general ledger.
4. To insure that the dividends declared are paid to the proper individuals.	Misstatement of dividends declared on balance sheet or payment to the wrong people, which could result in a liability.	Obtain confirmation of paid dividends from independent transfer agent.
5. To insure that stock is issued and retired only at the discretion of the board.	Illegal payments of cash and issue of shares.	Examine cancelled shares and newly issued ones to make sure they are included in the board of directors minutes.
6. To insure that all shares issued or retired are properly authorized.	Misstatement of dividends declared on balance sheet or payment to the wrong people, which could result in a liability.	Verify authenticity of all changes in owners' equity account.

a. **PURPOSE OF AUDIT PROCEDURES**	b. **MISSTATEMENTS THAT MAY BE UNCOVERED**
1. To determine what type of stock may be issued, under what circumstances, and its description.	Unauthorized outstanding stock or improper description of stock.
2. To determine the propriety of changes in the accounts and to verify their accuracy.	The issuance or retirement of stock without proper authorization, improper valuation, or incorrect dividend calculations.
3. To determine if there were any shares issued or retired during year, or if any certificates are missing.	Unrecorded or unauthorized transactions, or transactions not handled in a legal manner.
4. To determine if all retired stock has been cancelled.	Same as 3.
5. To determine if any stock issues, retirements, or dividends were authorized.	Unauthorized or omitted equity transactions.
6. To verify that earnings per share has been correctly computed.	Incorrect earnings per share computation.
7. To determine that dividends are legal and disclosure in the financial statements is proper.	Illegal payments of dividends and improper disclosure of the information in the financial statements.

22-30 The proposal for the limitation of procedure is not justified by the stated facts. Although the transfer agent and the registrar know the number of shares issued, they do not necessarily know the number of shares outstanding. Furthermore, the audit of capital stock includes more than determining the number of shares outstanding. For example, the auditor must determine what authorizations exist for the issuance of shares, what assets were received in payment of shares, how the transactions were recorded, and what subscription contracts have been entered into. Confirmation from the registrar could not help in determining these things.

In addition to confirmation from the registrar, the audit of capital stock might include the following procedures, the purposes of which are briefly indicated:

1. Examine the corporation charter—to determine the number of shares authorized and the special provisions for each class of stock if more than one class is authorized.
2. Examine minutes of stockholders' and directors' meetings—to determine authorization for appointments of the registrar and the transfer agent; to determine authorization for the issuance or reacquisition of shares.

22-30 (continued)

3. Examine provisions regarding capital stock in the corporation law of the state of incorporation—to determine any special provisions, such as those for the issuance of no par stock.

4. Analyze the capital stock accounts to obtain an orderly picture of stock transactions for use as a guide to other auditing procedures and as a permanent record.

5. Trace the consideration received for capital stock into the records—to determine what consideration has been received and how it has been recorded.

6. Examine and schedule treasury stock and review entries for treasury stock—to determine the existence of treasury stock as authorized and to determine that a proper record has been made.

7. Review registrar's invoices and cash disbursements—to determine that original issue taxes have been paid.

8. Compare dividends with stock outstanding at dividend dates—to determine that dividends have been properly paid and also to substantiate the stock outstanding.

9. Review subscription and option contracts, etc.—to determine the facts in regard to subscriptions and options and to determine that these facts have been properly recorded and that they are adequately disclosed.

22-31 a. The audit program for the audit of Pate Corporation's capital stock account would include the following procedures:

1. Examine the articles of incorporation, the bylaws, and the minutes of the board of directors from the inception of the corporation to determine the provisions or decisions regarding the capital stock, such as classes of stock, par value or stated value, authorized number of shares, authorization for the sale of new issues or additional sales of unissued stock, declarations of stock splits and dividends in the form of cash or stock, and granting of stock options or stock rights. Determine that the accounting records are in accordance with these provisions or decisions and that appropriate disclosure is made by footnote if necessary. Extract pertinent data for the auditor's permanent file.

2. Examine the stock certificate stub book and determine whether the total of the open stubs agrees with the Capital Stock account in the general ledger. Examine cancelled stock certificates, which are generally attached to the corresponding stub.

   Information on the stubs regarding the number of shares, date, etc. for both outstanding and cancelled stock certificates should be compared with the Capital Stock account. All certificate numbers should be accounted for and, if the CPA deems it necessary, confirmation of the number of certificates printed should be obtained from the printer. A test check should be made to determine that the proper amounts of original issue and capital stock transfer taxes have been affixed to the stubs and the cancelled certificates. The stockholders shown in the stock certificate stub book should be compared with the stockholders' master file if one is maintained.

3.   Analyze the Capital Stock account from the corporation's inception and verify all entries. Trace all transactions involving the transfer of cash either to the cash receipts or the cash disbursements records. If property other than cash was received in exchange for capital stock, trace the recording of the property to the proper asset account and consider the reasonableness of the valuation placed on the property. Transactions showing the sale of stock at a discount or premium should be traced to the Capital Contributed in Excess of Par Value account. If capital stock has been sold at a discount, consideration should be given to the possible violation of state laws and the client's attention should be directed to the matter. Should the analysis of the Capital Stock account disclose that the corporation has engaged in treasury stock transactions, determine that the increase or decrease in net assets resulting from these transactions has not been placed in the Retained Earnings account.

The audit procedures to be applied to the audit of the Capital Contributed in Excess of Par Value account are usually applied at the same time that the Capital Stock account is being audited because the two accounts are interrelated. The accounts should be analyzed and the entries verified when the related entries in the Capital Stock account are verified. If an entry is not related to Capital Stock account entries, as in the case of a write-off of a deficit as the result of a quasi reorganization, authorization for the entry and the supporting material should be examined.

4.   The following audit procedures would be applied to the Retained Earnings account:

i.   Analyze the account from its inception. Consider the validity of the amounts representing income or loss that were closed from the Profit and Loss account. Amounts representing appraisal increments or writing up of assets should be considered for reasonableness, and the increase should be reported separately from retained earnings in the stockholders' equity section of the balance sheet.

      ii.   Any extraordinary gains or losses carried directly to the Retained Earnings account should be investigated and their treatment reviewed in relation to accounting standards.

      iii.   Entries recording the appropriation of retained earnings or the return of such appropriations should be reviewed for reasonableness, and authorization for the entries should be traced to the proper authority. Similarly, actions of the board of directors that affected retained earnings should be traced to the account analysis.

      iv.   Conditions such as loan covenants or contingent liabilities that were uncovered during the audit that might require or make desirable the placing of restrictions on retained earnings should be reviewed for proper disclosure in the financial statements.

      v.   Entries recording cash or stock dividends should be traced to the minutes of the board of directors for authorization and traced to the Cash account or the Capital Stock account. A separate computation should be made by the CPA of the total amount of dividends paid based upon his or her schedules of outstanding stock as an overall test of the existence of the distributions. If stock dividends have been distributed, the amount removed from retained earnings should be reviewed for compliance with accounting standards.

b.   In conducting his or her audit, the CPA verifies retained earnings as he or she does other items on the balance sheet for several reasons. A principal reason is that the verification is an assurance or double check that no important item was overlooked in the audit of the accounts that were the contra or balancing part of the entry recorded in retained earnings. An example of an important item that may be overlooked would be a balance sheet account that was closed during the year under audit and the account removed from the general ledger current file. Another reason is that, though the entry in the contra account may have been examined, the auditor may have overlooked that the balancing part of the entry was to retained earnings, a treatment that may have been contrary to accounting standards; his or her audit of retained earnings would bring this noncompliance to his or her attention.

    Still another reason for verifying the retained earnings account is to determine whether any portion of the balance in the account may be subject to restriction by state law or other authority. Since the account is the basis for the payment of dividends, it is important to determine that the balance is composed of income realized from transactions free from any restrictions.

22-32 a.

ACCOUNT	EXPECTED CHANGE IN BALANCE 2009 TO 2010	EXPLANATION FOR EXPECTED CHANGE IN BALANCE
Cash	Increase	While much of the proceeds were used to reduce debt and purchase hardware and software, unused proceeds were deposited in company bank accounts.
Accounts Receivable	Little Change	The process of becoming publicly held would likely have minimal impact on accounts receivable, unless the volume of business on the E-Antiques Web site significantly grows as a result of going public.
Property, Plant, and Equipment	Increase	Because stock proceeds were used to purchase hardware and software, the balance in property, plant, and equipment would be expected to increase.
Accounts Payable	Increase	Assuming the purchase of hardware and software is made on account, the balance in accounts payable would be expected to increase.
Long-Term Debt	Decrease	Because stock proceeds were used to payoff loans, the balance in long-term debt would be expected to decrease.
Common Stock	Increase	Despite using stock proceeds to acquire original shares from company founders, the issuance of stock through the process of going public would result in a significant increase in the common stock account.
Additional Paid in Capital	Increase	Despite using stock proceeds to acquire original shares from company founders, the issuance of stock through the process of going public would result in a significant increase in the additional paid in capital account, assuming the stock was issued at a price above par value.
Retained Earnings	No Change	The transactions associated with going public would not affect the retained earnings account.
Treasury Stock	Increase	The acquisition of the original shares from the company founders would be treated as a purchase of treasury stock, thereby increasing the account balance.
Dividends	No Change	The transactions associated with going public would not directly affect the dividends account. If the company pays dividends, the account would increase because of the increase in the number of shares outstanding.
Revenues	Little Change	The process of becoming publicly held would likely have minimal impact on revenues for the current year, unless the volume of business on the E-Antiques Web site significantly grows as a result.

22-32 (continued)

    b.   While the decline in stock market price to $19 share is not favorable news for E-Antiques, that decline would have no impact on the common stock, additional paid-in capital, or retained earnings accounts since the company did not engage in any stock related transactions during 2011. Rather, the decline in market value impacts E-Antiques investors.

    c.   The decline in stock price would likely increase the auditor's assessment of business risk and audit risk. The decline is likely to place significant pressure on management to generate favorable financial results in order to boost stock prices to earlier highs. That pressure may create a strong enough incentive for management to engage in activities that may lead to an increased likelihood of material misstatements in the financial statements due to fraud.

■ **Internet Problem Solution: Overview of the NYSE**

Internet Problem 22-1

    a.   The NYSE Group operates the New York Stock Exchange (NYSE) and the NYSE Arca. The NYSE is the world's largest and most liquid cah equities exchange. It provides a reliable, orderly, liquid and efficient marketplace where investors buy and sell listed company's common stock and other securities. NYSE Arca operates the first open, all-electronic stock exchange in the United States and has a leading position in trading exchange-traded funds and exchange-listed securities. NYSE Arca is also an exchange for trading equity options.

    b.   To be able to trade securities on the Trading Floor, an Exchange-issued trading license is required. Only qualified and approved NYSE broker-dealer entities may acquire and hold trading licenses.

    c.   The Exchange has the capacity to trade up to 10 billion shares per day. The record for shares traded in one day was 3.1 billion on June 24, 2005.

    d.   At the NYSE, 100% of orders are electronically delivered directly to trading posts, booths, or handheld computers on the Trading Floor. More than 95% of orders to buy or sell reach the specialist's workstation directly at the trading post through the Exchange's SuperDOT electronic order-routing system.

    e.   The U.S. Securities and Exchange Commission (SEC) oversees the NYSE and it member organizations.

Internet Problem 22-1 (continued)

    f.   The three widely cited stock indexes include the Dow Jones Industrial Average (DJIA), the NYSE Composite Index, and Standard & Poor's 500 (S&P 500). The DJIA is an index of 30 "blue chip" U.S. stocks used to measure the performance of the U.S. financial markets. It is the oldest stock price measure in continuous use and has become the most widely recognized market indicator in the world. The NYSE Composite Index closely reflects the broader market, as it represents 77% of the total market capitalization of all publicly traded companies in the United States. It encompasses 61% of the total market capitalization of all publicly traded companies around the world. The S&P 500 is an index of 500 stocks that represents the price trend movements of the major common stock of U.S. public companies.

    g.   According to the NYSE Guide, there are five basic categories of stock:

        1.   Income stocks pay unusually large dividends that can be used as a means of generating income without selling stock, but the price of the stock does not rise very quickly.

        2.   Blue-chip stocks are issued by very solid and reliable companies with long histories of consistent growth and stability. Blue-chip stocks usually pay small but regular dividends and maintain a fairly steady price throughout ups and downs.

        3.   Growth stocks are issued by young, entrepreneurial companies that are experiencing a faster growth rate than their general industries. These stocks normally pay little or no dividend because the company needs all of its earnings to finance expansion.

        4.   Cyclical stocks are issued by companies that are affected by general economic trends. The prices of these stocks tend to go down during recessionary periods and increase during economic booms.

        5.   Defensive stocks are the opposite of cyclical stocks. They tend to be issued by companies producing staples such as food, beverages, drugs, and insurance. They tend to maintain their value during recessionary periods.

(**Note**: Internet problems address current issues using Internet sources. Because Internet sites are subject to change, Internet problems and solutions may change. Current information on Internet problems is available at www.pearsonhighered.com/arens.)

Chapter 23

Audit of Cash Balances

■ **Review Questions**

23-1   The appropriate tests for the ending balance in the cash accounts depend heavily on the initial assessment of control risk, tests of controls, and substantive tests of transactions for cash receipts. The company's controls over cash receipts assist the auditor in determining that cash received is promptly deposited, that receipts recorded are proper, that customer accounts are promptly updated, and that the cash cutoff at year-end is proper. If the results of the evaluation of internal control, the tests of controls, and the substantive tests of transactions are adequate, it is appropriate to reduce the tests of details of balances for cash, especially for the detailed tests of bank reconciliations. On the other hand, if the tests indicate that the client's controls are deficient, extensive year-end testing may be necessary.

23-2   The appropriate tests for the ending balance in the cash accounts depend heavily on the initial assessment of control risk, tests of controls, and substantive tests of transactions for cash disbursements. The company's controls over cash disbursements assist the auditor in determining that cash disbursed is for approved company purposes, that cash disbursements are promptly recorded in the proper amount, and that cash cutoff at year-end is proper. If the results of the evaluation of internal control, the tests of controls, and the substantive tests of transactions are adequate, it is appropriate to reduce the tests of details of balances for cash, especially for the detailed tests of bank reconciliations. On the other hand, if the tests indicate that the client's controls are inadequate, extensive year-end testing may be necessary.

An example in which the conclusions reached about the controls in cash disbursements would affect the tests of cash balances would be:

> If controls over the issuance of blank checks, the review of payees, amounts, and supporting documentation, the signing of checks, and the reconciliation of bank statements and vendors' statements are adequate, the auditor's review of outstanding checks on the year-end bank reconciliation may be greatly reduced. The year-end outstanding checks can be verified by testing a sample of checks returned with the cutoff bank statement rather than tracing all paid outstanding checks and the final monthly checks in the cash disbursements journal to the last month's cleared checks and the bank reconciliation.

23-3   The monthly reconciliation of bank accounts by an independent person is an important internal control over cash balances because it provides an opportunity for an internal verification of the cash receipts and cash disbursements transactions, investigation of reconciling items on the bank reconciliation, and the verification of the ending cash balance. Anyone responsible for the following duties would not be considered independent for the purposes of preparing monthly bank reconciliations:

- Issuance of checks
- Receipt and deposit of cash
- Other handling of cash
- Record keeping

23-4   The controller's approach is to reconcile until the balance agrees. The shortcoming of this approach is that it does not include a review of the items that flow through the account and it opens the door for the processing of improper items. Such items as checks payable to improper parties, reissuance of outstanding checks to improper parties, and kiting of funds would not be discovered with the controller's approach. The controller's procedures should include the following:

a.   Examination of all checks clearing with the statement (including those on the previous month's outstanding check list) and comparison of payee and amount to the cash disbursements journal.

b.   Test of cash receipts to determine that they are deposited within a reasonable amount of time.

c.   Follow-up on old outstanding checks so that they can be recognized as income after it is determined that they will not be cashed, and no liability exists.

23-5   Bank confirmations differ from positive confirmations of accounts receivable in that bank confirmations request several specific items of information, namely:

1.   The balances in all bank accounts.
2.   Restrictions on withdrawals.
3.   The interest rate on interest-bearing accounts.
4.   Information on liabilities to the bank for notes, mortgages, or other debt.

Positive confirmations of accounts receivable request the customer to confirm an account balance stated on the confirmation form or designate a different amount with an explanation. The auditor anticipates few exceptions to accounts receivable confirmations, whereas with bank confirmations he expects differences between the balance per bank and balance per the books that the client must reconcile. Bank confirmations should be requested for all bank accounts, but positive confirmations of accounts receivable are normally requested only for a sample of accounts. If bank confirmations are not returned, they must be pursued until the auditor is satisfied as to what the requested information is. If positive confirmations of accounts receivable are not returned, second and maybe third requests may be made, but thereafter, follow-ups are not likely to be pursued. Alternative procedures, such as examination of subsequent payments or other support of customers' accounts may then be used.

23-5 (continued)

The reason why more importance is placed on bank confirmations than accounts receivable confirmations is that cash, being the most liquid of assets, must be more closely controlled than accounts receivable. In addition, other information— such as liabilities to the bank must be known for purposes of the financial statements. Finally, there are usually only a few bank accounts and most bank accounts have a large volume of transactions during the year.

23-6   This is a good auditing procedure that attempts to discover if any accounts that should have been closed are still being used, such as by a company employee to deposit customer remittances. The procedure may also discover unrecorded and contingent liabilities.

23-7   A cutoff bank statement is a partial period bank statement with the related cancelled checks, duplicate deposit slips, and other documents included in bank statements, which is mailed by the bank directly to the auditor. The purpose of the cutoff bank statement is to verify the reconciling items on the client's year-end reconciliation with evidence that is inaccessible to the client.

23-8   Auditors are usually less concerned about the client's cash receipts cutoff than the cutoff for sales, because the cutoff of cash receipts affects only cash and accounts receivable and not the income statement, whereas a misstatement in the cutoff of sales affects accounts receivable and the income statement.

For the purpose of detecting a cash receipt cutoff misstatement, there are two useful audit procedures. The first is to trace the deposits in transit to the cutoff bank statement to determine the date they were deposited in the bank account. Because the recorded cash will have to be included as deposits in transit on the bank reconciliation, the auditor can test for the number of days it took for the in-transit items to be deposited. If there is more than a two or three day delay between the balance sheet date and the subsequent deposit of all deposits in transit, there is an indication of a cutoff misstatement. The second audit procedure requires being on the premises at the balance sheet date and counting all cash and checks on hand and recording the amount in the audit files. When the bank reconciliation is tested, the auditor can then check whether the deposits in transit equal the amount recorded.

23-9   An imprest bank account for a branch operation is one in which a fixed balance is maintained. After authorized branch personnel use the funds for proper disbursements, they make an accounting to the home office. After the expenditures have been approved by the home office, a reimbursement is made to the branch account from the home office's general account for the total of the cash disbursements. The purpose of using this type of account is to provide controls over cash receipts and cash disbursements by preventing the branch operators from disbursing their cash receipts directly, and by providing review and approval of cash disbursements before more cash is made available.

23-10 The purpose of the four-column proof of cash is to verify:

- Whether all recorded cash receipts were deposited.
- Whether all deposits in the bank were recorded in the accounting records.
- Whether all recorded cash disbursements were paid by the bank.
- Whether all amounts that were paid by the bank were recorded as cash disbursements in the accounting records.

Two types of misstatements that the four-column proof of cash is meant to uncover are:

- Cash received that was not recorded in the cash receipts journal
- Checks that cleared the bank but have not been recorded in the cash disbursements journal

23-11 Whenever a cutoff bank statement is not received directly from the bank, the auditor may verify the bank statement for the month subsequent to year-end. The audit procedures used for the verification are as follows:

1. Foot all of the cancelled checks, debit memos, deposits, and credit memos.
2. Check to see that the bank statement balances when the totals in 1 are used.
3. Review the items included in 1 to make sure they were cancelled by the bank in the proper period and do not include any erasures or alterations.

The purpose of this verification is to test whether the client's employees have omitted, added, or altered any of the documents accompanying the statement.

23-12 Lapping is a defalcation in which a cash shortage is concealed by delaying the crediting of cash receipts to the proper accounts receivable. The first step in the fraud is to withhold cash remitted by a customer from a bank deposit. A few days later, because the customer must receive credit for the remittance, the first customer's account is credited with an amount from a remittance made by a second customer. The process requires the continuous shifting of shortages from account to account and the crediting of subsequent receipts to the wrong accounts receivable.

Kiting is a procedure used to conceal cash shortages from employers and auditors, to conceal bank overdrafts from the bank or banks affected, or to pad a cash position. All kiting procedures are designed to take advantage of the "float" period during which a check is in transit between banks.

A shortage in the cash in bank account may be concealed by depositing in the bank a transfer check drawn on another bank. The transfer check, not recorded as a deposit or a cash disbursement, brings the bank account into agreement with

23-12 (continued)

the books of account. The check is recorded a few days later and the shortage "reappears" unless the process is repeated. A similar effect may be obtained by depositing unrecorded fictitious N.S.F. checks.

If a depositor desires to write a check for which he does not have funds on deposit, he can deposit a transfer check large enough to cover the payment, even though the transfer check itself creates an overdraft. The transfer process may be repeated indefinitely or may be terminated by a deposit of sufficient funds to cover the overdraft. Because the purpose of this procedure is to conceal an overdraft from the bank, the transfer check may or may not be recorded on the books on the date that it was drawn.

Kiting to pad a cash position typically occurs at the end of a fiscal period; a check transferring funds from one bank to another is deposited and recorded on the date drawn but is not recorded as a cash disbursement until the following period. In this case, the credit on the books would probably be made to a revenue account and the subsequent debit to an expense account.

The following audit procedures would be used to uncover lapping:

- Confirm accounts receivable and give close attention to exceptions made by customers about payment dates. The confirmation procedure is better applied as a surprise at an interim date so that if a person is engaged in lapping, he or she will not have been able to bring the "lapped" accounts up to date. If the confirmations are always prepared at year-end, the audit step may be anticipated by the person doing the lapping and the shortage given a different form such as kiting of checks.
- Make a surprise count of the cash and customers checks on hand. The deposit of these funds should be made under the auditor's control, and the details of the deposit should later be compared with the cash receipts book and the accounts receivable records.
- Compare the details of remittance lists (if prepared), stamped duplicate deposit slips, and entries in the cash receipts book. Because deposit slips are easily altered, some auditors prepare duplicate deposit slips for deposits made a few days before and after the audit date and have these slips authenticated by the bank. These authenticated duplicate deposit slips are compared to remittance lists and to entries in the cash book.
- Compare the check vouchers received with the customers' checks with stamped duplicate deposit slips, the entries in the cash book, and postings to the accounts receivable records. If the client stamps the voucher with the date it was received, the auditor should make careful comparisons of the stamped dates to the dates recorded in the cash receipts journal.

23-12 (continued)

Kiting might be uncovered by the following audit procedures:

- As a surprise count of cash and customers' checks on hand is made as a test for lapping, determine that checks representing transfers of funds are properly recorded on the books.
- Prepare a schedule of the interbank transfers made for a few days before and after the audit date. The schedule should show, for each check, the date that the cash disbursement was recorded on the books, and the dates of withdrawal and deposit shown on the bank statements.
- Obtain cutoff bank statements directly from the bank covering the seven to ten day period after the balance sheet date. Examine the checks returned with the cutoff statements and pay attention to dates of the transactions stamped by the banks on the backs of the checks. These stamped dates should not be earlier than the dates of the checks or the dates of cash disbursements recorded on the books. Protested (N.S.F.) checks should be investigated to determine they are not fictitious checks deposited temporarily to cover a shortage.

23-13   Assuming a client with excellent internal controls uses an imprest payroll bank account, the verification of the payroll bank reconciliation ordinarily takes less time than the tests of the general bank account even though the number of payroll disbursements exceeds those for the general account because an imprest payroll account has no activity other than payroll disbursements and deposits made to reestablish the standard minimum account balance. Furthermore, most employees cash their checks quickly, so there usually are few outstanding checks, especially older ones, and no other reconciling items. On the other hand, the general bank account will include all regular activity plus bank charges, notes, other liabilities, etc., which must be reconciled and verified.

23-14   The verification of petty cash reimbursements consists of footing the petty cash vouchers supporting the amounts of the reimbursements, accounting for a sequence of petty cash vouchers, examining the petty cash vouchers for authorization and cancellation, and examining the supporting documentation attached to the vouchers for reasonableness. The balance in the fund is verified by a count of the petty cash. Testing of petty cash transactions is more important than the ending balance in the account, because even if the amount of the petty cash fund is small, there is potential for a large number of improper transactions if the fund is frequently reimbursed.

23-15 There is a greater emphasis on the detection of fraud in tests of details of cash balances than for other balance sheet accounts because the amount of cash flowing into and out of the cash account is frequently larger than for any other account in the financial statements. Furthermore, the susceptibility of cash to misappropriation is greater than other types of assets because most other assets must be converted to cash to make them usable.

This emphasis affects the auditor's evidence accumulation in auditing year-end cash as in these examples:

- Verifying whether cash transactions are properly recorded
- Testing of bank reconciliations
- Obtaining bank confirmations

23-16 The misstatements that are of the greatest concern to auditors in bank reconciliations are intentional ones to cover up a cash shortage, usually resulting from a defalcation. A fraudulent deposit in transit or an omitted outstanding check will both cover up a cash shortage. Omitted deposits in transit or inclusion of a nonexistent outstanding check are likely misstatements only when the bank balance, after reconciling items are accounted for, is greater than the book balance, a highly unlikely occurrence.

23-17 This questions deals with a situation where a company's bank received an electronic deposit of cash from credit card agencies making payments on behalf of customers purchasing products from the company's online Web site. The company does not have the electronic deposit recorded in the general ledger. The company's bank reconciliation should include an adjustment for this transaction, which would increase the book balance of cash and decrease accounts receivable from credit card agencies.

- **Multiple Choice Questions From CPA Examinations**

23-18 a. (3) b. (2) c. (1)

23-19 a. (4) b. (2) c. (4)

23-20

MOTIVATION	INTERNAL CONTROL	AUDIT PROCEDURE
1. To cover a shortage.	Internal verification of bank reconciliation.	Foot outstanding check list.
2. To cover a cash shortage or to improve the current ratio.	Independent bank reconciliation.	Obtain bank confirmation.
3. To cover a shortage.	Internal verification of bank reconciliation, including accounting for all checks recorded in the cash disbursements journal as cleared or still outstanding.	Trace all checks dated on or before June 30 that cleared with the cutoff bank statement to the June 30 outstanding check list.
4. Same as 3.	Same as 3.	Verify the bank reconciliation by tracing checks dated on or before June 30 in the cash disbursements journal to checks clearing with the June 30 bank statement. Any checks not clearing should be included on the June 30 outstanding check list.
5. Hold open books to improve cash position.	Independent bank reconciliation.	Trace deposits in transit to cutoff bank statements to determine deposit date.
6. Kiting-covering a defalcation or padding a cash position.	Independent bank reconciliation.	Trace all interbank transfers to accounting records.
7. Original check was unauthorized and illegal. Outstanding check made the bank reconcile.	Independent bank reconciliation that includes accounting for all cash disbursement transactions.	Verify the bank reconciliation, including cash disbursements for all material uncleared outstanding checks.

23-21 The objectives of each of the audit procedures are:

1. To ascertain all cash balances and liabilities to banks that might exist. The verification includes amounts and descriptions.
2. To assure that the client is using the correct balance from the bank in preparing its reconciliation.
3. To determine which checks on the outstanding check list have since cleared and to uncover checks that should have been included on the outstanding check list, but were not. These could represent a cover-up of a cash shortage.
4. To create a list of outstanding checks for follow-up to determine why they have not cleared and to investigate the possibility of a misstatement of cash and accounts payable.
5. To assure that all loans, terms, and arrangements with the bank were properly authorized by the board of directors and are disclosed in the financial statements.
6. To reconcile the recording of cash receipts and cash disbursements between the bank and the client's books and to prepare a bank reconciliation at the same time. This may disclose existence, completeness, accuracy, cutoff, or posting and summarization misstatements.
7. To determine if there is a cutoff misstatement in cash disbursements.
8. To make sure the cash receipts were recorded by the bank shortly after the beginning of the new year *and* recorded in the current year's cash receipts journal. A misstatement in either of these could indicate the cover-up of a cash shortage or a cash receipts cutoff misstatement.

23-22 a. Bank reconciliation:

Balance per bank		$ 1,522
Add:		
Deposits in transit		2,000
Check erroneously charged to Pittsburgh Supply		646
Less: outstanding checks		(2,218)
Adjusted bank balance		$ 1,950
Balance per books before adjustments	$10,103	
Adjustments to books:		
July bank service charge	(107)	
Note payment (6,000 principal, 400 interest)	(6,400)	
NSF check	(516)	
Unrecorded check	(1,130)	
Balance per books after adjustments	$ 1,950	

23-22 (continued)

(1)	6/30 DIT		600
	July deposits per books		26,874
	July deposits per bank		(25,474)
	7/31 DIT		$ 2,000
(2)	6/30 O/S checks		$ 2,578
	July checks per books		23,171
	July checks clear		(25,307)
	Erroneous check charged		646
	Unrecorded check		$ 1130
	7/31 O/S checks		$ 2,218

b.   Adjusting entry:

Miscellaneous expense	$ 107	
Interest expense	400	
Note payable	6,000	
Allowance for doubtful accounts	516	
Purchases	1,130*	
Cash in bank		$ 8,153

To record adjustments arising from
7/31/11 bank reconciliation.

*   Will require reversal on August 1 because of recording in
cash disbursements journal.

23-23   a.   In verifying the interbank transfers, the following audit procedures should
be performed:

1.   List interbank transfers made a few days before and after the
balance sheet date (already done).
2.   Trace these interbank transfers to the appropriate accounting
records, bank reconciliations, and bank records to verify proper
recording.

b.   **For December 2011**

Cash in bank	$16,000	
Branch bank clearing account		$16,000
Cash in bank	21,000	
Branch bank clearing account		21,000
Cash in bank	22,000	
Branch bank clearing account		22,000

Only the first entry is essential because the same entry is also
being made on the branch bank for the other two entries.

23-23 (continued)

For January 2012

Eliminate corresponding entries already made for the above.

c. **For December 2011**

Home office clearing account	$28,000	
Cash in bank		$28,000
Home office clearing account	21,000	
Cash in bank		21,000
Home office clearing account	22,000	
Cash in bank		22,000

For January 2012

Eliminate corresponding entries already made for the above.

d. and e.

HOME OFFICE RECORDS		BRANCH ACCOUNT RECORDS
17,000	No DIT*	No OC**
28,000	No DIT	No OC
16,000	No DIT	No OC
10,000	No DIT	OC
21,000	No DIT	No OC
22,000	No DIT	OC
39,000	No DIT	No OC

*   DIT = Deposit in transit
** OC = Outstanding check

	POSSIBLE MISSTATEMENTS DUE TO ERRORS OR FRAUD		AUDIT PROCEDURE TO PROVIDE EVIDENCE
1.	The auditor suspects that a lapping scheme exists because an accounting department employee who has access to cash receipts also maintains the accounts receivable ledger and refuses to take any vacation or sick days.	b.	Compare the details of the cash receipts journal entries with the details of the corresponding daily deposit slips.
2.	The auditor suspects that the entity is inappropriately increasing the cash reported on its balance sheet by drawing a check on one account and not recording it as an outstanding check on that account and simultaneously recording it as a deposit in a second account.	h.	Prepare a bank transfer schedule.
3.	The entity's cash receipts of the first few days of the subsequent year were properly deposited in its general operating account after the year-end. However, the auditor suspects that the entity recorded the cash receipts in its books during the last week of the year under audit.	b.	Compare the details of the cash receipts journal entries with the details of the corresponding daily deposit slips.
4.	The auditor noticed a significant increase in the number of times that petty cash was reimbursed during the year and suspects that the custodian is stealing from the petty cash fund.	f.	Examine invoices, receipts, and other documentation supporting reimbursement of petty cash.
5.	The auditor suspects that a kiting scheme exists because an accounting department employee who can issue and record checks seems to be leading an unusually luxurious lifestyle.	e.	Obtain the cutoff bank statement and compare the cleared checks to the year-end reconciliation.
6.	During tests of the reconciliation of the payroll bank account, the auditor notices that a check to an employee is significantly larger than other payroll checks.	d.	Agree gross amount on payroll checks to approved hours and pay rates.
7.	The auditor suspects that the controller wrote several checks and recorded the cash disbursements just before year-end but did not mail the checks until after the first week of the subsequent year.	e.	Obtain the cutoff bank statement and compare the cleared checks to the year-end reconciliation.

23-25 a.

CORRECTED RECONCILIATION
December 31, 2011

Balance per bank 12-31-11		$26,978.41
Add:		
Deposits in transit		3,715.27
Less: Outstanding checks*		(3,121.83)
Balance per bank - adjusted		$27,571.85
Balance per books - before adjustments		$27,253.85
Add: proceeds of note collected by bank		1,200.00
Less:		
Dishonored check	$450,00	
Unrecorded bank service charge	35,00	
Error in recording check	397.00	(882.00)
Balance per books - adjusted		$27,571.85

*List of checks totals $3,121.83 not $3,295.15.

b.

Cash	$1,200.00	
Notes receivable		$1,200.00
To record collection of a note left for collection.		
Accounts receivable	450.00	
Cash		450.00
To charge dishonored check to accounts receivable.		
Miscellaneous expense	35.00	
Cash		35.00
To charge December bank service charge to expense.		
Accounts payable	397.00	
Cash		397.00
To charge to accounts payable (or to receivables) the actual amount of a check drawn which was recorded for a lower amount.		

23-26   a.

	Cash 9/30/11	Receipts	Disburse-ments	Cash 10/31/11
Balance per bank	$6,915	$28,792	$27,431	$8,276
Deposits in transit				
9/30/11	5,621	(5,621)		
10/31/11		996		996
Outstanding checks				
9/30/11	(1,811)		(1,811)	
10/31/11			2,615	(2,615)
Bank error — check charged				
to wrong account			(1,144)	1,144
NSF checks		(600)	(1,335)	735
Balance per bank — adjusted	$10,725	$23,567	$25,756	$8,536
Balance per books — unadjusted	$10,725	$20,271	$25,160	$5,836
Adjustments to be made				
Interest charged			596	(596)
Note proceed		3,296		3,296
Balance per books — adjusted	$10,725	$23,567	$25,756	$8,536

b.   Adjusting journal entries:

Dr. Cash in bank	$ 3,296	
Cr. Notes receivable		$2,900
Cr. Interest income		396
Dr. Interest expense	596	
Cr. Cash in Bank		596

To record adjustments resulting
from Oct. 31, 2009 reconciliation
of bank account.

■ **Internet Problem Solution: Check Clearing for the 21st Century Act**

Internet Problem 23-1

a.   A substitute check is a special paper copy of the front and back of an
original check, and is specially formatted so it can be processed as if it
were an original check. The front of a substitute check should state:
"This is a legal copy of your check. You can use it the same way you
would use the original check."

b.   Because of Check 21 and other check-system improvements, checks
may be processed faster. The majority of consumers do not receive
their canceled checks with their account statements, but instead may
receive "pictures" (known as digital images), a list of paid checks, or a
combination of these items. Check 21 will have little or no effect on
these practices.

Internet Problem 23-1 (continued)

Individuals who do receive canceled checks back in their account statements, may notice some changes under Check 21. For example, the bank may send a combination of original checks and substitute checks. A canceled substitute check can be used as proof of payment just like a canceled original check.

The account agreement with the bank governs whether the customer receives canceled checks with their account statements. If they currently receive canceled checks back with their statements, they will continue to receive the checks unless the bank notifies the customer it is changing the account agreement.

c.   No. In general, the law does not require the bank to return original checks. Many banks destroy original paper checks. Other banks may store original checks for some period of time and then destroy them. Check 21 ensures that customers have the same legal protections when they receive a substitute check from the bank as when they receive an original check.

(**Note**: Internet problems address current issues using Internet sources. Because Internet sites are subject to change, Internet problems and solutions may change. Current information on Internet problems is available at www.pearsonhighered.com/arens.)

Chapter 24

Completing the Audit

■ **Review Questions**

24-1   There are four presentation and disclosure-related audit objectives:

PRESENTATION AND DISCLOSURE-RELATED AUDIT OBJECTIVES	DESCRIPTION
Occurrence and rights and obligations	Account-related information as described in the footnotes exists and represents the rights and obligations of the company.
Completeness	All required disclosures are included in the financial statement footnotes.
Accuracy and valuation	Footnote disclosures are accurate and valued correctly.
Classification and understandability	Account balances are appropriately classified and related financial statement disclosures are understandable.

24-2   A financial statement disclosure checklist is an audit tool that summarizes all disclosure requirements contained in accounting standards. Auditors use the disclosure checklist to determine that all required disclosures are completely presented and disclosed in the financial statements and accompanying footnotes. This helps the auditor obtain sufficient appropriate evidence about the completeness objective for the presentation and disclosure-related audit objective.

24-3   A contingent liability is a potential future obligation to an outside party for an unknown amount resulting from activities that have already taken place. Some examples would be:

- ■   Pending litigation
- ■   Income tax disputes
- ■   Product warranties
- ■   Notes receivable discounted
- ■   Guarantees of obligations of others
- ■   Unused balances of outstanding letters of credit

24-3 (continued)

An actual liability is a real future obligation to an outside party for a known amount from activities that have already taken place. Some examples would be:

- Notes payable
- Accounts payable
- Accrued interest payable
- Income taxes payable
- Payroll withholding liabilities
- Accrued salaries and wages

24-4 If you are concerned about the possibility of contingent liabilities for income tax disputes, there are various procedures you could use for an intensive investigation in that area. One approach would be an analysis of income tax expense. Unusual or nonrecurring amounts should be investigated to determine if they represent situations of potential tax liability. Another helpful procedure for uncovering potential tax liabilities is to review the general correspondence file for communication with attorneys or IRS agents. This might give an indication that the potential for a liability exists even though no actual litigation has begun. Finally, an examination of internal revenue agent reports from prior years may provide the most obvious indication of disputed tax matters.

24-5 The auditor would be interested in a client's future commitments to purchase raw materials at a fixed price so that this information could be disclosed in the financial statements. The commitment may be of interest to an investor as it is compared to the future price movements of the material. A future commitment to purchase raw materials at a fixed price may result in the client paying more or less than the market price at a future time.

24-6 The analysis of legal expense is an essential part of every audit engagement because it may give an indication of contingent liabilities which may become actual liabilities in the future and require disclosure in the current financial statements. Since any single contingency could be material, it is important to verify all legal transactions, even if the amounts are small. After the analysis of legal expense is completed, the attorneys to whom payment was made should be considered for letters of confirmation for contingencies (attorney letters).

24-7 Pyson should determine the materiality of the lawsuits by requesting from Merrill's attorneys an assessment of the legal situations and the probable liabilities involved. In addition, Pyson may have his own attorney assess the situations. Proper disclosure in the financial statements will depend on the attorneys' evaluations of the probable liabilities involved. If the evaluations indicate highly probable, material amounts, disclosure will be necessary in the form of a footnote, assuming the amount of the probable material loss cannot be reasonably estimated. If the client refuses to make adequate disclosure of the contingencies, a qualified or adverse opinion may be necessary.

24-8   An asserted claim is an existing legal action that has been taken against the client, whereas an unasserted claim represents a *potential* legal action. The client's attorney may not reveal an unasserted claim for fear that the disclosure of this information may precipitate a lawsuit that would be damaging to the client, and that would otherwise not be filed.

24-9   If an attorney refuses to provide the auditor with information about material existing lawsuits or likely material unasserted claims, the audit opinion would have to be modified to reflect the lack of available evidence. This is required by auditing standards, and has the effect of requiring management to give its attorneys permission to provide contingent liability information to auditors and to encourage attorneys to cooperate with auditors in obtaining information about contingencies.

24-10   The first type of subsequent event is one that has a direct effect on the financial statements and requires adjustment. Examples of this type of subsequent event are as follows:

- Declaration of bankruptcy by a customer with an outstanding accounts receivable balance due to the deteriorating financial condition
- Settlement of a litigation for an amount different from the amount recorded on the books
- Disposal of equipment not being used in operations at a price below the current book value
- Sale of investments at a price below recorded cost
- Sale of raw material as scrap in the period subsequent to the balance sheet date

The second type of subsequent event is one that has no direct effect on the financial statements but for which disclosure is advisable. Examples include the following:

- Decline in the market value of securities held for temporary investment or resale
- Issuance of bonds or equity securities
- Decline in the market value of inventory as a consequence of government action barring further sale of a product
- Uninsured loss of inventories as a result of fire

24-11   Malano's approach does not take into consideration the need to obtain letters from attorneys as near the end of field work as possible. If the letters are received near the balance sheet date, the period from the balance sheet to the end of the auditor's field work will not be included in the attorneys' letters. His procedure would not obtain the most current information regarding contingent liabilities, and would not provide adequate information for disclosure of pertinent subsequent events.

24-12   The major considerations the auditor should take into account in determining how extensive the subsequent events review should be are:

- The company's financial strength and stability of earnings
- The effectiveness of the company's internal controls
- The number and significance of the adjustments made by the auditor
- The length of time between the balance sheet date and the completion of the audit
- Changes in key personnel

Auditors of public companies should be aware that PCAOB Standard 5 requires them to also inquire about changes in internal control over financial reporting occurring subsequent to the end of the fiscal period that might significantly affect internal control over financial reporting.

24-13   Audit procedures normally performed as a part of the review for subsequent events are:

- Cutoff and valuation tests of various balances and related transactions; e.g., sales cutoff tests
- Inquire of management
- Correspond with attorneys
- Review internal statements prepared subsequent to the balance sheet date
- Review records prepared subsequent to the balance sheet date
- Examine minutes of meetings of board of directors and stockholders subsequent to the balance sheet date
- Obtain a letter of representation

24-14   Subsequent events occurring between the balance sheet date and the date of the auditor's report are those transactions and events which might affect the financial statements being audited (either adjustment, disclosure, or both). Examples of these types of events would be:

- Declaration of bankruptcy by a customer with an outstanding accounts receivable balance due because of a deteriorating financial condition
- Settlement of a litigation for an amount different from the amount recorded on the books
- Disposal of equipment not being used in operations at a price below the current book value
- Sale of investments at a price below recorded cost
- Sale of raw material as scrap in the period subsequent to the balance sheet date
- Decline in the market value of securities held for temporary investment or resale

24-14 (continued)

- Issuance of bonds or equity securities
- Decline in the market value of inventory as a consequence of government action barring further sale of a product
- Uninsured loss of inventories as a result of fire

If these events and transactions have a material effect on the financial statements, they may require adjustment of the current period financial statements or disclosure. Auditors of larger public companies should also be alert for subsequent changes in internal control over financial reporting.

The subsequent discovery of facts existing at the date of the auditor's report occurs when the auditor becomes aware that some information included in the financial statements was materially misleading after the audited financial statements have been issued. Some examples of such facts would be:

- Subsequent discovery of the inclusion of fraudulent sales
- Subsequent discovery of the failure to write-off obsolete inventory
- Omission of an essential footnote

In such cases when the auditor discovers the statements to be misleading, he or she should request the client to issue a revised set of financial statements as soon as possible containing a new audit report and an explanation of the reasons for the revisions to the financial statements.

24-15 The weakness in Lawson's approach is the danger of discovering an inadequacy in one audit area which could affect other areas of the audit. For example, if misstatements were discovered as part of the tests of controls for sales, the initial plans for the tests of details of balances for accounts receivable may have been insufficient and should have been revised. Similarly, the audit of fixed assets is related to the contracts and notes payable whenever fixed assets are used as collateral.

Another difficulty with Lawson's approach is that there is no combining of the misstatements in different audit areas to determine if the combined misstatements are material. If the combined misstatements are considered material, it may be necessary to expand the testing in certain areas or require adjusting entries to some balances.

24-16 The accumulation of audit evidence is crucial to the auditor in determining whether the financial statements are stated in accordance with relevant accounting standards, applied on a basis consistent with the preceding year. The evaluation of the adequacy of the disclosures in financial statements is made to determine that the account balances on the trial balance are properly aggregated and disclosed on the financial statements.

24-16 (continued)

Examples where adequate disclosure could depend heavily upon the accumulation of evidence are:

- The disclosure of declines in inventory values below cost
- The segregation of current from noncurrent receivables
- The segregation of trade accounts receivable from amounts due from affiliates
- The disclosure of contingent liabilities that the auditor has not been informed of by the client

Examples where audit evidence does not normally significantly affect the adequacy of the disclosure are:

- Deciding whether a disposal of equipment should be recorded as an extraordinary item
- The disclosure of an acquisition made subsequent to year end
- The disclosure of contingencies that the auditor was informed of by the client

24-17 A letter of representation is a written communication from the client to the auditor which formalizes statements that the client has made about matters pertinent to the audit. Auditing standards suggest four categories of items that should be included in the letter. Below are those four items with examples in each category follow (refer students to auditing standardsfor a comprehensive list):

1. *Financial statements*
    - Management's acknowledgment of its responsibility for the fair presentation in the financial statements of financial position, results of operations, and cash flows in conformity with generally accepted accounting principles
    - Management's belief that the financial statements are fairly presented in conformity with generally accepted accounting principles

2. *Completeness of information*
    - Availability of all financial records and related data
    - Completeness and availability of all minutes or meetings of stockholders, directors, and committees of directors
    - Absence of unrecorded transactions

24-17 (continued)

    3.   *Recognition, measurement, and disclosure*
- Management's belief that the effects of any uncorrected financial statement misstatements are immaterial to the financial statements
- Information concerning fraud involving (1) management, (2) employees who have significant roles in internal control, or (3) others where the fraud could have a material effect on the financial statements
- Information concerning related party transactions and amounts receivable from or payable to related parties
- Unasserted claims or assessments that the entity's lawyer has advised are probable of assertion and must be disclosed in accordance with accounting standards
- Satisfactory title to assets, liens or encumbrances on assets, and assets pledged as collateral
- Compliance with aspects of contractual agreements that may affect the financial statements

    4.   *Subsequent events*
- Bankruptcy of a major customer with an outstanding account receivable at the balance sheet date
- A merger or acquisition after the balance sheet date

For audits of public companies, PCAOB Standard 5 requires the auditor to obtain specific representations from management about internal control over financial reporting. Some of those representations are noted below:

    5.   *Internal controls*
- Management's acknowledgement of its responsibility for establishing and maintaining effective internal controls over financial reporting.
- Management's conclusion about the effectiveness of internal control over financial reporting as of the end of the fiscal period.
- Disclosure to the auditor of all deficiencies in the design or operation of internal control over financial reporting identified as part of management's assessment, including separate disclosure of significant deficiencies and material weaknesses.
- Management's knowledge of any material fraud or other fraud involving senior management or other employees who have a significant role in the company's internal control over financial reporting.

Auditors of accelerated filer public companies may obtain a combined representation letter for both the audit of the financial statements and the audit of internal control over financial reporting.

24-17 (continued)

A management letter is a letter directed to the client to inform management of certain recommendations about the business which the CPA believes would be beneficial to the client.

Items that might be included in a management letter are:

- Recommendation to switch inventory valuation methods
- Recommendation to install a formal security system
- Recommendation to prepare more timely bank reconciliations
- Recommendation to segregate duties
- Recommendation to have certain types of transactions authorized by specific individuals

24-18 Information accompanying basic financial statements is any and all information prepared for management or outside users included with the basic financial statements. Examples include detailed comparative statements supporting control totals in the basic statements, supplementary information required by the SEC, statistical data such as ratios and trends, and specific comments on the changes that have taken place in the financial statements.

The auditor can provide one of two levels of assurance for information accompanying basic financial statements. The auditor may issue a positive opinion indicating a high level of assurance, or a disclaimer indicating no assurance.

24-19 Auditing standards require the auditor to read information in annual reports containing audited financial statements for consistency with the financial statements and the auditor's report. Types of information the auditor examines include statements about financial condition in the president's letter and displays and summaries of statistical financial information.

24-20 A regular audit documentation review is the one that is done by someone who is knowledgeable about the client and the unique circumstances in the audit.

The purposes of this review are to:

- Evaluate the performance of inexperienced personnel
- To make sure that the audit meets the CPA firm's standard of performance
- To counteract the bias that frequently enters into the auditor's judgment.

Examples of important potential findings in a regular audit documentation review are:

- Incorrect computations
- Inadequate scope
- Lack of proper documentation for audit decisions

24-20 (continued)

An independent review is one done by a completely independent person who has no experience on the engagement. The purpose is to have a competent professional from within the firm who has not been biased by the ongoing relationship between the regular auditors and the client perform an independent review. Examples of important potential findings in an independent review are:

■ A number of small adjustments waived that should have been accumulated into an adjusting journal entry due to materiality
■ Too narrow and too biased of a scope in an audit area
■ Inadequate disclosure of contingencies

24-21 In addition to the required communications to those charged with governance required by auditing standards, the Sarbanes-Oxley Act expands these communications requirements by also requiring public company auditors to timely report the following items to the audit committee:

■ All critical accounting policies and practices to be used.
■ All alternative treatments of financial information within generally accepted accounting principles that have been discussed with management, ramifications of the use of such alternative disclosures and treatments, and the treatment preferred by the auditor.
■ Other material written communications between the auditor and management, such as any management letter or schedule of unadjusted differences.

As the audit of the public company is completed, the auditor should determine that the audit committee is informed about the initial selection of and changes in significant accounting policies or their application during the current audit period. When changes have occurred, the auditor should inform the committee of the reasons for the change. The auditor should also communicate information about methods used to account for significant unusual transactions and the effect of significant accounting policies in controversial or emerging areas.

■ **Multiple Choice Questions From CPA Examination**

24-22   a.   (2)   b.   (2)   c.   (1)

24-23   a.   (4)   b.   (2)   c.   (3)   d.   (4)

24-24   a.   (3)   b.   (4)   c.   (2)

24-25   a.   (3)   b.   (3)   c.   (2)

■ Discussion Questions And Problems

24-26 a. A contingent liability is a potential future obligation to an outside party for an unknown amount arising from activities that have already taken place. A commitment is an agreement to commit the entity to a set of fixed conditions in the future, regardless of what happens to profits or the economy as a whole.

Knowledge of both contingencies and commitments is extremely important to users of financial statements because they represent the encumbrance of potentially material amounts of resources during future periods, and thus affect the future cash flows available to creditors and investors. Because of this, accounting standards require that material contingencies and commitments be disclosed. The auditor has an obligation to discover the existence of such items to determine that they are properly disclosed in order to have complied with auditing standards.

b. Johnson's tests of controls and substantive tests of transactions related to payments of notes payable and related interest expense would provide her information about scheduled debt payments and related interest rate terms, which are required footnote disclosure related items. Similarly, substantive tests of transactions would reveal additions and retirements of notes payable, which both affect notes payable disclosures. Tests of details of balances, such as notes payable confirmations, would provide sufficient appropriate evidence about the existence of ending balances and related notes payable terms, such as interest rates and required collateral.

c. Three useful audit procedures for uncovering contingencies that Johnson would likely perform in the normal conduct of the audit, even if she had no responsibility for uncovering contingencies, are:

  ■ Review internal revenue agent reports of income tax settlements
  ■ Review minutes of meetings of board of directors and stockholders
  ■ Confirm used and unused balances of lines of credit

d. Three other procedures Johnson is likely to perform specifically for the purpose of identifying undisclosed contingencies are:

  ■ Make inquiries of management
  ■ Analyze legal expenses for indication of contingent liabilities
  ■ Request letters from attorneys regarding the existence and status of litigation and other potential contingent liabilities

24-27 a. A contingent liability is a potential future obligation to an outside party for an unknown amount resulting from activities that have already taken place. The most important characteristic of a contingent liability is the uncertainty of the amount; if the amount were known it would be included in the financial statements as an actual liability rather than as a contingency.

b. Audit procedures to learn about these items would be as follows:

The following procedures apply to all three items:

- Discuss the existence and nature of possible contingent liabilities with management and obtain appropriate written representations.
- Review the minutes of directors' and stockholders' meetings for indication of lawsuits or other contingencies.
- Analyze legal expense for the period under audit and review invoices and statements of legal counsel for indications of contingent liabilities.
- Obtain letters from all major attorneys performing legal services for the client as to the status of pending litigation or other contingent liabilities.

The following are additional procedures for individual items:

Lawsuit Judgment — no additional procedures; see above list of procedures applicable to all three items.

Stock dividend
- Confirm details of stock transactions with registrar and transfer agent.
- Review records for unusual journal entries subsequent to year-end.

Guarantee of interest payments
- Discuss, specifically, any related party transactions with management and include information in letter of representation.
- Review financial statements of affiliate, and where related party transactions are apparent, make direct inquiries of affiliate management, and perhaps even examine records of affiliate if necessary.

c. Nature of adjusting entries or disclosure, if any, would be as follows:

1. The lawsuit should be described in a footnote to the balance sheet. In view of the court decision, retained earnings may be restricted for $4,000,000, the amount of the first court decision. Also, in view of the court decision any reasonable estimate of the amount the company expects to pay as a result of the suit might be used in lieu of the $4,000,000. A current liability will be set up as soon as a final decision is rendered or if an agreement as to damages is reached. If liability is admitted to by Marco, and only the amount is in dispute, a liability can be set up for the amount admitted to by the company with a corresponding charge to expense or shown as an extraordinary item if the amount is material.

2. The declaration of such a dividend does not create a liability that affects the aggregate net worth in any way. The distribution of the dividend will cause a reduction in retained earnings and an increase in capital stock. No entry is necessary, but an indication of the action taken, and that such a transfer will subsequently be made, should be shown as a footnote or as a memorandum to Retained Earnings and Common Stock in the balance sheet.

3. If payment by Newart is uncertain, the $137,500 interest liability for the period June 2 through December 1, 2011, could be reflected in the Marco Corporation's accounting records by the following entry:

Interest Payments for Newart Company $137,500
    Accrued Interest Payable — Newart Bonds $137,500

The debit entry should be included as other assets. Collection is uncertain and the Marco Corporation may not have a right against the Newart Company until all interest payments have been met and the bonds retired. If this treatment is followed, the balance sheet should be footnoted to the effect that the Marco Corporation is contingently liable for future interest payments on Newart Company bonds in the amount of $2,200,000.

If the interest has been paid by the time the audit is completed, or if for other reasons it seems certain that the payment will be made by Newart on January 15, no entry should be made by Marco. In this circumstance a footnote disclosing the contingent liability of $2,337,500 and the facts as to the $137,500 should be included with the statements.

24-28 a. In this situation, Little need only send requests for letters to those attorneys who are involved with legal matters directly affecting the financial statements. The letters should be sent reasonably near to the completion of the field work, but the follow-up on nonresponses and unsatisfactory responses should not be deferred until the last day of field work. She should have examined the letters when they were returned and performed follow-up work at that time. Furthermore, the third letter should have addressed the lawsuit if the client informed the auditor of its existence.

b. The auditor would be required to follow up on the first attorney's letter by sending a second request or calling the attorney to solicit a response. The second letter would not require any additional follow-up due to the nature of the work performed by this attorney. Regarding the third attorney's letter, it is necessary to have a conference with the attorney, client, and auditor to determine the nature and significance of the lawsuit.

It would be a serious violation of due care to ignore the information in the third attorney's letter. In rare circumstances, a disclaimer of opinion is necessary if the information cannot be obtained.

24-29 1. A retroactive pay increase could be uncovered by reading the minutes of the board of directors' or stockholders' meetings, examining contracts, holding discussions with management, reading the local newspaper, and analyzing internal financial statements prepared subsequent to the balance sheet date.

Granting of a retroactive pay increase is likely to create a liability at the balance sheet date for the earned but unpaid wages in the year under audit. A liability clearly exists if a union contract was under negotiation at the balance sheet date but not settled until later. If the retroactive pay increase was unexpected at the balance sheet date, the expense could be related to the date of the settlement, but even then, most auditors would require that retroactive wages be accrued at the balance sheet date. The liability and related expense that should be accrued at the balance sheet date is the amount of unpaid wages existing at the balance sheet date assuming the pay increase is accrued. No mention in the audit report is necessary.

2. The declaration of a stock dividend subsequent to the balance sheet date could be uncovered by reading the minutes of the board of directors or stockholders subsequent to the balance sheet date, by confirmation with the independent stock registrar, or through discussion with management.

24-29 (continued)

The stock dividend should be disclosed in a footnote, including the date of declaration, the percent of the stock dividend, and the effect on issued shares, capital stock, paid-in capital and retained earnings. No audit report modification is necessary.

3. The sale of a major fixed asset at a substantial profit could be uncovered by reviewing minutes of the board of directors, reviewing correspondence files, reviewing cash receipts records of the subsequent period, or through discussions with management. The sale should be disclosed in a footnote, and the explanation should include the amount of the gain and the effect, if any, on future operations of the company. No audit report modification is necessary.

4. An additional tax assessment could be uncovered by examining subsequent cash disbursements, review of the minutes of the board of directors or stockholders, examining internal revenue agent reports for all expenses not cleared by the Internal Revenue Service, requesting letters from attorneys near the end of the field work, and through discussions with management.

The tax assessment should be accrued as a tax expense and a liability for the year under audit and clearly disclosed if the amount is material. If the tax assessment is accrued and adequately disclosed, no audit report modification is necessary.

5. The antitrust suit may have been uncovered through inquiries of the client, the client representation letter, or letters from client's legal counsel. The antitrust suit should be disclosed in a footnote.

24-30

a. 3 — Amount should have been determined to be uncollectible before end of field work, but it was discovered after the issuance of the statements. The financial statements should have been known to be misstated on 8-19-11.

b. 4 — The amount appeared collectable at the end of the field work.

c. 1 — The uncollectible amount was determined before end of field work.

d. 2 — The cause of the bankruptcy took place after the balance sheet date, therefore the balance sheet was fairly stated at 6-30-11. Most auditors would probably require that the account be written off as uncollectible at 6-30-11, but they are not required to do so. Footnote disclosure is necessary because the subsequent event is material.

e. 2 — The sale took place after the balance sheet date but, since the loss was material and will affect future profits, footnote disclosure is necessary.

24-30 (continued)

    f.   1 — The settlement should be reflected in the 6-30-11 financial statement as an adjustment of current period income and not a prior period adjustment.

    g.   4 — The financial statements were believed to be fairly stated on 6-30-11 and 8-19-11.

    h.   2 — The cause of the lawsuit occurred before the balance sheet date and the lawsuit should be included in the 6-30-11 footnotes. Note: If the loss is both probable and can be reasonably estimated, then answer 1 is correct - adjust the 6-30-11 financial statements for the amount of the expected loss.

    i.   2 — The lawsuit originated in the current year, but the amount of the loss is unknown.

24-31   a.   It is desirable to have a letter of representation in spite of the accumulated audit evidence to impress upon management its responsibility for the representations in the financial statements and to formally document the responses from the client to auditor inquiries about various aspects of the audit.

    b.   The letter of representation is not very useful as audit evidence since it is a written statement from a nonindependent source. In effect, the client being audited makes certain representations related to the audit of itself.

    c.   Several categories of information commonly included in a letter of representation with examples in each category follow (See auditing standards for a complete list):

        1.   *Financial statements*
- Management's acknowledgment of its responsibility for the fair presentation in the financial statements of financial position, results of operations, and cash flows in conformity with accounting standards
- Management's belief that the financial statements are fairly presented in conformity with accounting standards

        2.   *Completeness of information*
- Availability of all financial records and related data
- Completeness and availability of all minutes or meetings of stockholders, directors, and committees of directors
- Absence of unrecorded transactions

24-31 (continued)

      3.   *Recognition, measurement, and disclosure*
- Management's belief that the effects of any uncorrected financial statement misstatements are immaterial to the financial statements
- Information concerning fraud involving (1) management, (2) employees who have significant roles in internal control, or (3) others where the fraud could have a material effect on the financial statements
- Information concerning related party transactions and amounts receivable from or payable to related parties
- Unasserted claims or assessments that the entity's lawyer has advised are probable of assertion and must be disclosed in accordance with accounting standards
- Satisfactory title to assets, liens or encumbrances on assets, and assets pledged as collateral
- Compliance with aspects of contractual agreements that may affect the financial statements

      4.   *Subsequent events*
- Bankruptcy of a major customer with an outstanding account receivable at the balance sheet date
- A merger or acquisition after the balance sheet date

For audits of public companies, PCAOB Standard 5 requires the auditor to obtain specific representations from management about internal control over financial reporting. Some of those representations are noted below:

      5.   *Internal controls*
- Management's acknowledgement of its responsibility for establishing and maintaining effective internal controls over financial reporting.
- Management's conclusion about the effectiveness of internal control over financial reporting as of the end of the fiscal period.
- Disclosure to the auditor of all deficiencies in the design or operation of internal control over financial reporting identified as part of management's assessment, including separate disclosure of significant deficiencies and material weaknesses.
- Management's knowledge of any material fraud or other fraud involving senior management or other employees who have a significant role in the company's internal control over financial reporting.

Auditors of larger public companies may obtain a combined representation letter for both the audit of the financial statements and the audit of internal control.

24-32 a. A typical additional information report includes the financial statements associated with a short-form report plus additional information likely to be useful to management and other statement users. The statements included with short form audit reports are defined by the profession, but the additional information included in additional information reports varies considerably.

b. The purpose of additional information reports is to provide management and other users information that is useful for their decision making that has not been included in the basic financial statements.

c. It would be appropriate to include all of the items as additional information except the following:

    2. The adequacy of insurance coverage. The auditor is not an insurance professional, and any comments about the insurance coverage should be factual. For example, it would be appropriate to state that the insurance coverage is less than the recorded book value.

    3. Adequacy of the allowance for uncollectible accounts. Comments that an account balance is correctly stated are inappropriate. The auditor has already issued an auditor's opinion on the statements as a whole. If an opinion on a specific account balance is desired, it should be done in accordance with a special report.

    5. Material weaknesses in internal control. These should be identified and communicated to management as a part of the auditor's internal control deficiencies letter to those charged with governance (e.g., the audit committee).

d. The following could also be included as additional information:

- Detailed breakdown of sales and expenses by month
- Detailed financial statements making up cost of goods sold, selling and administrative expenses
- A detailed breakdown of inventory

e. The following would be added to the standard audit report:

Our audit was made for the purpose of forming an opinion on the basic financial statements taken as a whole. The accompanying information on pages x through y is presented for purposes of additional analysis and is not a required part of the basic financial statements. Such information has not been subjected to the auditing procedures applied in the audit of the basic financial statements, and, accordingly, we express no opinion on it.

a.

		Possible Misstatement – Overstatement (Understatement)				
Item	Total Amount	Current Assets	Noncurrent Assets	Current Liabilities	Noncurrent Liabilities	Income Before Tax
1	$125,000			($125,000)		$125,000
2	85,000	(85,000)	60,000			(25,000)
3	44,000	(44,000)				(44,000)
4	52,000		52,000			52,000
5	43,000					0
6	Not known		0		0	
		(129,000)	112,000	(125,000)	0	108,000

b. The net effect of the adjustments to the balance sheet and income statement are material to the financial statements. Pretax income would be overstated by $108,000, which is in excess of the income statement materiality, as a result of these items if they are not properly reflected in the accounting records. Likewise, current assets are misstated by more than materiality. Even though the net effect of adjustments to current assets and noncurrent assets is less than materiality for total assets, the fact that a major financial statement line item, such as current assets, is misstated by more than materiality, the adjustments would need to be made to fairly state the financial statements. Note, the problem fails to provide information about the dollar amounts involved in Item 6. Most likely the nature of that item consists of a large dollar amount, which would need to be reflected in the financial statements given the impact it would have on noncurrent assets and noncurrent liabilities.

24-34 a. Schwartz's legal and professional responsibility in the issuance of management letters is only to make sound recommendations based on his professional interpretation of the audit evidence accumulated and to not omit information of serious systems deficiencies. He must follow due care in management letters and management services in the same manner as is required for audits.

b. Major considerations that will determine whether Schwartz is liable in this situation are whether the client installed the system according to Schwartz's instructions or whether they deviated from his instructions and whether they could have foreseen the possibility of the erased master file based on their understanding of the system. Another major consideration is the degree to which Schwartz followed due care considering the needs of the client and the competence of existing employees of Cline Wholesale Co.

■ Case

24-35   a.   See the "Summary of Possible Adjustments" on page 24-21 that follows.

         b.   Aviary's management may refuse to make some or all of the proposed adjustments because all of the adjustments except (4) reduce net income. Management will most likely be reluctant to make any adjustments that will make the company look less profitable. Aviary's management may also refuse to make some or all of the proposed entries because they do not want to admit that their records contain misstatements.

         c.   As indicated on the "Summary of Possible Adjustments" on page 24-21, you should attempt to have Aviary's management record all of the potential adjustments found. However, at a minimum, entries (5) and (6) should be recorded. One positive way for you to convince Aviary's management to make these entries would be to stress that (1) considerable judgment is required to determine the allowances for inventory obsolescence and doubtful accounts and (2) it is not uncommon for auditors to assist clients in adjusting these accounts. This may help minimize management's reluctance to admit making a mistake.

              You should also stress that it would be wise to adjust the allowance accounts in a year with substantial net income. The allowance accounts will most likely increase in future years, especially if entries (5) and (6) are not made in the current year. Since management cannot be sure that the company will generate substantial net income in future years, it would be best to adjust the allowance accounts in the current year and avoid a substantial reduction to net income in a future year that is not as profitable as the current year.

         d.   Your responsibility related to unadjusted misstatements that management has determined are immaterial individually and in the aggregate is to determine *for yourself* whether the combined effect of these unadjusted misstatements are material for the audit. The combined effect of the unadjusted misstatements must be compared to overall materiality. Assuming that the remaining unadjusted misstatements are well below your materiality threshold, you do not need to qualify your audit opinion. You should consider having the client include a summary of this audit schedule in the management representation letter, along with management's representation that the uncorrected misstatements are immaterial.

24-35 (continued)

e. Auditors of larger public companies must evaluate the noted adjustments to determine their impact on the auditor's report on internal control over financial reporting. As discussed in Chapter 10, the audit of the financial statements and the audit of internal control over financial reporting for a large public company are to be integrated. Public company auditors must consider the results of audit procedures performed to issue the audit report on the financial statements when issuing the audit report on internal control. For example, if the possible adjustments identified by Aviary Industries' auditor are deemed to be material misstatements that were not initially identified by the company's internal controls, the auditor should consider this as at least a significant deficiency, if not a material weakness for purposes of reporting on internal control. In this case, the auditor's report on Aviary's financial statements would be unqualified as long as management corrected the misstatement before issuing the financial statements. However, the auditor's report on internal control over financial reporting would include an adverse opinion if the auditor concludes that it is a material weakness.

a.

Client Name Aviary Industries

SUMMARY OF POSSIBLE ADJUSTMENTS
Year-ended December 31, 2011

Description	A/C Dr. A/C Cr.	Total Amount	Possible Adjustments - Dr (CR)						
			Current Assets	Non-Current Assets	Current Liabilities	Non-Current Liabilities	Beginning Equity	Income	Expenses
(1) Unrecorded credit memos*	Sales R&A A/R	26,451	(26,451)					26,451	
(2) Unrecorded inventory purchases	Purchases A/P	25,673			(25,673)				25,673
(3) Sales recorded in wrong period	Sales A/R	41,814	(41,814)					41,814	
(4) Held checks	Cash A/P	43,671	43,671		(43,671)				
(5) Obsolete inventory**	Loss A/C Inventory Allow. A/C	15,000	(15,000)						15,000
(6) AFDA understated**	Bad debt exp. AFDA	35,000	(35,000)						35,000
Totals			(74,594)		(69,344)			68,265	75,673

Conclusions:
The net effect of the above items is as follows:

Working capital $143,938 decrease
Total assets: $ 74,594 decrease
Net income: $143,938 decrease

Opinion as to need for AJE: Preliminary materiality was $100,000. However, revised materiality based on 5% of actual income before taxes = $1,508,929 x 5% = $75,446.45. Rounded = $75,000. The combined effect of the above proposed entries on net income exceeds revised materiality. Propose that all entries be recorded. However, at a minimum, entries (5) and (6) should be recorded in order to decrease the effect of the above entries to a level below revised materiality of $75,00000. Entry (1) or (2) may also have to be recorded in order to have some cushion between the net income misstatement and revised materiality after recording entries (5) and (6).

* Entry assumes that items were returned prior to 12-31-11 and counted in inventory at year-end (no COGS/inventory misstatement).

** Because entry deals with an accounting estimate, the lower end of the range would be sufficient.

■ Internet Problem Solution: Audit Committee Responsibilities

Internet Problem 24-1

a. According to the company's website: "The Audit Committee of the Board of Directors assists the Board of Directors in fulfilling its responsibility for oversight of the quality and integrity of the accounting, auditing, and reporting practices of the Company, and such other duties as directed by the Board. The Committee's purpose is to oversee the accounting and financial reporting processes of the Company, the audits of the Company's financial statements, the qualifications of the public accounting firm engaged as the Company's independent auditor to prepare or issue an audit report on the financial statements of the Company and internal control over financial reporting, and the performance of the Company's internal audit function and independent auditor. The Committee reviews and assesses the qualitative aspects of financial reporting to shareholders, the Company's processes to manage business and financial risk, and compliance with significant applicable legal, ethical, and regulatory requirements. The Committee is directly responsible for the appointment (subject to shareholder ratification), compensation, retention, and oversight of the independent auditor."

b. The Audit Committee oversees the audits of the Company's financial statements and the qualifications of the public accounting firm engaged as the Company's independent auditor. The independent auditor reports directly to the Committee, which has responsibility for hiring and terminating the auditor, and for approving the audit fee paid to the auditor.

c. The committee meets at least eight times a year with additional meetings occurring as necessary.

d. According to the Responsibilities Calendar, the Committee prepares the agenda for Committee meetings in consultation between the Committee chair, Finance management, senior internal audit employee designated by the Committee, and the independent auditor. The Committee also reviews the following with Finance management and the auditor:

   ■ Matters related to the effectiveness of its internal controls and the independent auditor's attestation, including any noted "material weaknesses" or "significant deficiency" in the design or operation of internal control over financial reporting.

- Matters related to the audit, including significant changes to the audit plan or serious difficulties or disputes with management encountered by the auditor, and any steps taken to resolve the issue.
- Critical accounting policies (at least annually)
- Review of the earnings release prior to issuance
- Review of the Company's quarterly financial statements and analyses prepared by management
- Alternative treatments of financial information within GAAP related to material items that have been discussed with management.
- Review of periodic reports of the Company, including MD&A disclosures.
- Any significant findings and recommendations of the independent auditor and internal audit together with management's responses.

e. The Committee will periodically meet in executive session without Company management present. When in executive session, the meeting may only include Committee members or it may also include Committee members and external advisors, such as the independent auditor. The purpose of meeting in executive session is to give Committee members and external advisors an opportunity to share information or concerns without management being present. This provides an opportunity for open and frank communications about matters that may be of concern to the Committee, such as any suspicions of senior management engagement in fraudulent or otherwise unethical activities.

(**Note**: Internet problems address current issues using Internet sources. Because Internet sites are subject to change, Internet problems and solutions may change. Current information on Internet problems is available at www.pearsonhighered.com/arens.)

Chapter 25

Other Assurance Services and Nonassurance Services

■ **Review Questions**

25-1 Levels of assurance represent the degree of certainty the practitioner has attained, and wishes to convey, that the conclusions stated in his or her report are correct.

Audits of historical financial statements prepared in accordance with accounting standards are one type of examination. They are governed by auditing standards. An audit results in a conclusion that is in a positive form. In this type of report, the practitioner makes a direct statement as to whether the presentation of the assertions, taken as a whole, conforms to the applicable criteria. The level of assurance is high.

In a review, the practitioner provides a conclusion in the form of a negative assurance. In this form, the practitioner's report states whether any information came to the practitioner's attention to indicate that the assertions are not presented in all material respects in conformity with the applicable criteria. The level of assurance is limited.

A compilation is defined in SSARS as presenting, in the form of financial statements, information that is the representation of management *without undertaking to express any assurance* on the statements.

25-2 A negative assurance states, along with factual statements, that nothing came to the accountant's attention that would lead the accountant to believe that the financial statements were not prepared in accordance with accounting standards. The reason for including such a statement in a review report is to provide financial statement users with some level of assurance that the financial statements are fairly stated. The level of assurance is less than that for an audit of historical financial statements, but more than the zero-level assurance for a compilation.

25-3 Compilation is defined in SSARS No. 1 as presenting in the form of financial statements information that is the representation of management, without undertaking to express any assurance on the statements. Review is defined by SSARS No. 1 as performing inquiry and analytical procedures that provide the accountant with a reasonable basis for expressing limited assurance that there are no material modifications that should be made to the statements in order for them to be in conformity with accounting standards.

There is no level of assurance provided by a compilation. Reviews provide limited assurance, but considerably less than a typical audit.

25-4 One of three forms of compilation can be provided to clients:

- *Compilation With Full Disclosure* Compilation of this type requires disclosures in accordance with accounting standards, the same as for audited statements.
- *Compilation That Omits Substantially All Disclosures* This type of compilation is acceptable if *the report indicates the lack of disclosures* and the absence of disclosures is not, to the CPA's knowledge, undertaken with the intent to mislead users.
- *Compilation Without Independence* A CPA firm can issue a compilation report even if it is not independent with respect to the client, as defined by the *Code of Professional Conduct*. However, the CPA firm must state its lack of independence in the report.

25-5 The following five things are required by SSARS No. 1 for compilation. The preparer of the statements must:

- Know something about the accounting principles and practices of the client's industry.
- Know the client, the nature of its business transactions, accounting records and employees, and the basis, form, and content of the financial statements.
- Make inquiries to determine if the client's information is satisfactory.
- Read the compiled financial statements and be alert for any obvious omissions or errors in arithmetic and generally accepted accounting principles.
- Disclose in the report any omissions or departures from accounting standards of which the accountant is aware. This requirement does not apply to a compilation that omits substantially all disclosures.

25-6 For a compilation, the accountant does not have to make inquiries or perform other procedures to verify information supplied by the entity beyond those identified in the answer to Review Question 25-5. But if the accountant becomes aware that the statements are not fairly presented, he or she should obtain additional information. If the client refuses to provide the information, the accountant should withdraw from the compilation engagement.

25-7 The following types of procedures are emphasized for review services:

■ Obtain knowledge of the accounting principles and practices of the client's industry. The level of knowledge for reviews should be somewhat higher than that for compilation.

■ Obtain knowledge of the client. The information should be about the nature of the client's business transactions, its accounting records and employees, and the basis, form, and content of the financial statements. The level of knowledge should be higher than that for compilation.

■ Make inquiries of management. The objective of these inquiries is to determine whether the financial statements are fairly presented, assuming that management does not intend to deceive the accountant. Inquiry is the most important of the review procedures. The following are illustrative inquiries:

• Inquire as to the company's procedures for recording, classifying, and summarizing transactions, and disclosing information in the statements.

• Inquire into actions taken at meetings of stockholders and board of directors.

• Inquire of persons having responsibility for financial and accounting matters whether the financial statements have been prepared in conformity with accounting standards.

■ Perform analytical procedures. The analytical procedures are meant to identify relationships and individual items that appear to be unusual. The appropriate analytical procedures are no different from the ones already studied in Chapters 7 and 8 and in those chapters dealing with tests of details of balances.

25-8 For review services, if a client fails to follow applicable accounting standards, a modification of the report is needed. The accountant is not required to determine the *effect of a departure* if management has not done so, but that fact must also be disclosed in the report. For example, the use of replacement cost rather than FIFO for inventory valuation would have to be disclosed, but the effect of the departure on net earnings does not require disclosure.

25-9 Compilations and reviews under SSARS No. 1 can only be issued for nonpublic companies for which an audit has not been performed. They may be for monthly, quarterly, or annual statements.

Reviews are issued on quarterly information of publicly held companies as a part of the client's reporting requirements to the SEC and are subject to PCAOB standards. Although there are some minor differences in the wording on a review report for a nonpublic company and a public company review report, they are substantively the same.

25-10   The review procedures are essentially the same for public company and SSARS 1 reviews. Some additional procedures are required for public company reviews that are beyond the scope of SSARS 1 as follows:

- The level of knowledge the accountant has about the client's internal control is likely to be higher for public company reviews. Because an annual audit is done for public companies that have an interim review, the accountant must also obtain sufficient information about the client's internal control for both annual and interim financial information.
- The auditor's knowledge of the results of the audit procedures performed during the annual audit will affect the scope of the procedures performed during the review of interim financial information.
- The accountant will also have a good idea whether the quarterly statements were accurate after the annual audit is complete. This information will be useful in determining the review procedures in subsequent years.
- Under SSARS, the auditor makes inquiries about actions of directors and stockholder meetings; for public companies the auditor reads the minutes of those meetings.
- For public companies, the accountant must also obtain evidence that the interim financial information agrees or reconciles with the accounting records.

25-11   Attestation standards provide a general framework for and set reasonable boundaries around the attestation function. They provide guidance to AICPA standard-setting bodies for establishing detailed standards and interpretations of standards for specific types of services. They also provide practitioners useful guidance in performing new and evolving attestation services where no specific guidance exists.

The attestation standards, therefore, provide a conceptual framework for various types of services. Auditing standards do the same thing for the conduct of the ordinary audit of financial statements prepared in accordance with accounting standards.

25-12   In a *WebTrust* assurance services engagement, a client engages a CPA to provide reasonable assurance that a company's Web site complies with one or more of the following *five Trust Services* principles:

1.   *Security* – Security practices ensuring that the system is protected against authorized access (both physical and logical).
2.   *Availability* – Availability practices, ensuring that the system is available for operation and use as committed or agreed.
3.   *Processing Integrity* – Processing integrity, ensuring that system processing is complete, accurate, timely, and authorized.

25-12 (continued)

> 4. *Online Privacy* – Online privacy practices, ensuring that personal information obtained as a result of e-commerce is collected, used, disclosed, and retained as committed or agreed.
>
> 5. *Confidentiality* – Confidentiality practices, ensuring that information designated as confidential is protected as committed or agreed.

A licensed CPA can issue a *WebTrust* opinion on an individual principle or on combinations of principles.

25-13 The purpose of a *SysTrust* engagement is for the licensed accountant to evaluate a company's information technology system using *Trust Services* principles and criteria and to determine whether controls over the system exist. The accountant then performs tests to determine whether those controls were operating effectively during a specified period. See the solution to Review Question 25-12 for the five *Trust Services* principles.

25-14 One option would be for you to visit the service organization to obtain evidence about the design and operating effectiveness of internal controls at the service organization. However, a more efficient option may be for the service organization to engage its auditor to provide a Type 1 report that provides an opinion about the fairness of the description of the service organization's system and opinion about the suitability of the design of the controls in that system. Or, the service organization may engage its auditor to provide a Type 2 report that provides the opinions contained in a Type 1 report, plus an opinion on the operating effectiveness of controls at the service organization.

25-15 A *prospective financial statement* is a predicted or expected financial statement in some future period or at some future date. There are two general types of prospective financial statements: forecasts and projections. A *forecast* is a prospective financial statement that presents an entity's expected financial position, results of operations, and cash flows for future periods, to the best of the responsible party's knowledge and belief. A *projection* is a prospective financial statement that presents an entity's financial position, results of operations, and cash flows, to the best of the responsible party's knowledge and belief, given one or more hypothetical assumptions.

An examination of prospective financial statements involves:

- Evaluating the preparation of the prospective financial statements.
- Evaluating the support underlying assumptions.
- Evaluating the presentation of the prospective financial statements for conformity with AICPA presentation guidelines.
- Issuing an examination report.

25-16 The reporting requirements for statements prepared on a basis other than GAAP include the following paragraphs: introductory, scope, middle, opinion, and restriction of distribution paragraph. The introductory, scope, and opinion paragraphs are essentially the same as for statements prepared in conformity with GAAP. The middle paragraph states the basis of presentation and refers to a note to the financial statements that describes the basis of accounting followed. The restriction of distribution (final) paragraph is used when the financial statements are prepared in conformity with requirements of a governmental regulatory agency. Distribution of the report is then restricted to those within the entity and for filing with the regulatory agency.

25-17 It would be appropriate for Germany to provide a report to Northern State Bank on all of the conditions except the competency of management. Reports on the working capital ratio, dividends paid on preferred stock, and aging of accounts receivable are factual matters within a normal auditor's competence. Reporting on the competence of management is highly subjective and should not ordinarily be in a debt compliance letter.

■ Multiple Choice Questions From CPA Examinations

25-18 a. (4) b. (2) c. (2)

25-19 a. (3) b. (1) c. (2)

25-20 a. (1) b. (2) c. (1)

■ Discussion Questions and Problems

25-21 The accountant is responsible for the care in the preparation of compiled financial statements. The accountant must perform all five steps identified in the answer in Review Question 25-5 with due care. The report must also be properly prepared and reflect the findings of the accountant.

Users other than management are not prohibited from using compiled financial statements. They can expect the accountant to meet the standards set by the profession.

The courts have not established the responsibilities of accountants for compilations. Presumably, the responsibilities should be far less than for audits and somewhat less than for reviews. Responsibilities exist, but the level has yet to be finalized.

25-22 a. The primary procedures performed in a review engagement consist of performing analytical procedures and inquiries of management. But, in addition to those procedures, the accountant should also perform the following:

- Obtain knowledge of the accounting principles and practices of the client's industry.
- Obtain knowledge of the client's business
- Obtain a letter of representation
- Perform additional procedures if the accountant becomes concerned that information is incorrect, incomplete or otherwise unsatisfactory.
- Issue the review report.

b. 1. Inquire about the nature of repairs made to determine if any represent expenses that should be capitalized. Ask about whether any of the related property, plant, and equipment should be adjusted to reflect permanent impairment and inquire if any equipment that is currently included in the financial statements has been disposed of during the year.

2. Inquire about whether management has documentation in the contract of the real estate taxes not being the responsibility of the client until next year and ask to review that contract. Perhaps examine any public records of tax obligations for the county or municipality to determine the status of outstanding taxes due.

3. Ask management to provide invoices from most recent purchases of pipes for construction and estimate the inventory values based on the most recent prices to determine the impact of changes in market conditions on the ending inventory balance.

4. Calculate days sales in inventory and compare trends to prior years to determine whether collections are slowing. Analyze aging categories of accounts receivable relative to prior years to evaluate whether receivables are older.

5. Make inquiries of the client's legal counsel to obtain their views of the likely outcome of the lawsuit.

PROCEDURE	a. REQUIRED ON A COMPILATION ENGAGEMENT	b. REQUIRED ON A REVIEW ENGAGEMENT
1.	X	X
2.	X	X
3.	X	X
4.		X
5.	X	X
6.		
7.		
8.		X
9.	X	X
10.		X

X = Required procedure

25-24   a.   In addition to the inquiries listed, the accountant must understand the client's business to facilitate evaluating whether the statements are reasonable. Analytical procedures must also be performed. It may also be appropriate to inquire about such things as the possibility of unbilled sales, authorization procedures for sales, whether the accounts receivable control account has been reconciled with the master file records, and the possible inclusion of consignment shipments as sales.

   b.   In reviews, no procedures such as tests of controls, substantive tests of transactions, cutoff tests, or confirmation requests are done. The only things that are done are inquiries and analytical tests. An examination of the procedures for sales and receivables discussed in Chapters 14 and 16 shows that there is considerable difference between an audit and those review procedures listed in this problem.

   c.   Inquiries would ordinarily be made of the chief financial officer in a small or large business. Ordinarily the chief financial officer in a small business is the owner, but it may also be a controller or vice-president.

25-24 (continued)

    d.   Additional procedures should be performed when the accountant believes, based on the information obtained through inquiry and analytical procedures, that the financial statements may be materially misstated. Examples where this could be the case are:

- A material increase in the gross margin percent
- A material decrease in allowance for uncollectible accounts divided by accounts receivable
- A statement by a bookkeeper that leads the accountant to believe the client's personnel do not fully understand correct sales cutoff procedures

    e.   The achieved level of assurance for audits is ordinarily much higher than for reviews. The differences in the procedures identified in this problem and those studied in Chapters 14 and 16 are significant and result in large differences in the achieved levels of assurance.

25-25   a.   It is *not* appropriate to do a SSARS review service for a publicly held company. SSARS engagements are restricted to nonpublic companies. Annual statements of public companies must either be audited or unaudited in accordance with PCAOB auditing standards and requirements of the Securities and Exchange Commission. This provides a clearer definition in the level of assurance for the financial statements of public companies. However, a review-type service can be provided for interim financial statements of public companies.

    b.   There are some deficiencies in the approach taken:

- Because Tidwell is a high risk client, indicating a high likelihood of misstatement, and because the required review procedures include inquiries and analytical procedure, the review should, at least in part, be performed by the more experienced member of the engagement team, and not be so completely delegated.
- Because there are some differences between an SSARS 1 review and a public company review, use of the firm's standard procedures for SSARS reviews without modification is inappropriate. Additional procedures to be performed include (at a minimum):
  - Relating inquiries to findings in the recent audit
  - Reading minutes

25-25 (continued)

   c.   The following problems exist with regard to the report:

- Pages should be marked "unaudited" not "reviewed."
- The report should be addressed to the client, not the Securities and Exchange Commission.
- The wording of the report should be changed from the SSARS review to the required wording for public companies, including reference to PCAOB standards.

25-26

   a.   A client may request a *SysTrust* engagement for a system that is in the pre-implementation phase. In this engagement, the CPA would report on the suitability of the design of the controls and the report would be as of a point in time rather than for a period of time.

   b.   The CPA cannot perform *WebTrust* assurance services without being licensed by the AICPA to provide such services. CPAs seeking to provide *WebTrust* services must attend training, apply for the *WebTrust* license, and satisfy other quality control requirements.

   c.   The CPA can perform the requested *SysTrust* assurance service on compliance with the Availability principle. CPAs can provide assurance about an entity's compliance with a single *Trust Services* principle or a combination of two or more principles.

   d.   The *WebTrust* seal cannot remain on the company's Web site through May 31, 2012 without the CPA updating his or her work to support the seal. The *WebTrust* service requires the CPA to update his or her testing once every twelve months to ensure the entity continues to comply with *Trust Services* principles and criteria.

25-27   a.   It would be acceptable to undertake the engagement only if all of the following conditions exist:

- The accountant has sufficient competence to properly complete an examination of the forecasted financial statements.
- The client is willing to take responsibility for preparation (with the accountant's assistance) of the forecast in accordance with guidelines, established by the AICPA in *Statements on Standards for Accountant's Services on Prospective Financial Statements*.
- The accountant believes a reasonably accurate forecast is practicable in the circumstances.
- The client understands and agrees to the examination procedures and reporting requirements the accountant must comply with.

25-27 (continued)

    b.   If Monson believes the accountant can issue an opinion about the achievability of the forecast, but later finds that such an opinion cannot be given, Monson is likely to be unhappy. The result would be a loss of fee, loss of a client for other services, and perhaps even a lawsuit. Similarly, Monson must understand his responsibilities concerning the forecast of the assumptions and other aspects of the report, again to avoid a misunderstanding later.

    c.   The primary information the CPA firm will need to help in completing the forecast are the following:

- Audited financial statements for the past several years. (Easily available because Monson is an audit client.)
- Information about the economic conditions of the industry. The CPA firm will likely need knowledge beyond that required for performing the audits.
- Information about the offer he has made for the new business and the offer he has received for the existing assets. Because the financial statements will be a forecast, and not a projection, it is necessary to determine that there is a reasonable likelihood of the transaction being completed and the forecasted result, assuming both transactions are finalized.

    d.   The report will be a report on a forecast and will include the following components:

- An identification of the prospective financial statements presented.
- A statement that the examination of the prospective financial statements was made in accordance with AICPA standards and a brief description of the nature of such examination.
- The accountant's opinion that the prospective financial statements are presented in conformity with AICPA presentation guidelines and that the underlying assumptions provide a reasonable basis for the forecast.
- A caveat that the prospective results may not be achieved.
- A statement that the accountant assumes no responsibility to update the report for events and circumstances occurring after the date of the report.

25-28   a.   The purpose of a debt compliance letter is to provide the lender with an independent opinion of the existence or nonexistence of some condition. The lender usually will request a CPA to determine whether certain loan covenants are being adhered to by the debtor.

25-28 (continued)

    b.   An audit of the company is necessary before a debt compliance letter is issued because a compliance letter would be difficult to prepare without an audit. This stems from the fact that the CPA is usually concerned with financial balances and ratios of the company when preparing a debt compliance letter. An audit is virtually required in order to verify these amounts.

    c.   A CPA firm could issue a debt compliance letter on the amount of the current ratio and the owner's equity. The firm may report on these two aspects because it is qualified to evaluate such matters. However, the other three requests require legal expertise and subjective judgment that a CPA firm does not claim to possess. Therefore, the CPA should restrict the debt compliance letter to the two quantitative requests.

25-29 a.   *We have audited, in accordance with generally accepted auditing standards, the balance sheet of Pollution Control Devices, Inc. as of _____ and the related statements of income, retained earnings, and cash flows for the year then ended, and have issued our report thereon dated _____.*

        In connection with our audit, nothing came to our attention that caused us to believe that the Company failed to comply with any of the provisions of the indenture dated _____ with (lender) insofar as they relate to accounting matters. However, our audit was not directed primarily toward obtaining knowledge of such noncompliance.

        This report is intended solely for the information of the boards of directors and management of Pollution Control Devices, Inc. and (lender) and should not be used for any other purpose.

    b.   The supplemental report would have to state that the company was not in compliance with the provisions of the indenture because net earnings did not exceed dividends by at least $1,000,000.

    c.   The supplemental report would be the same as discussed in b. Assuming that a default in the provisions of the indenture results in the loan becoming due immediately, the auditor's report would have to include either an adverse or qualified opinion depending upon the materiality of the misstatement. Because the mortgage is for $4 million, which is material to the client, violation of the indenture and potential default cannot be dismissed as being immaterial.

    d.   Contingencies due to a lawsuit may affect the liabilities of the client that will affect the indenture provisions. The auditor will be unable to express an opinion in the debt compliance letter because of this uncertainty. This should be disclosed in the supplemental report.

25-30 a. Jones will probably have to conduct additional audit tests in order to report on these items individually. It will be necessary for Jones to accumulate additional evidence because the materiality of the individual items is much lower than for the overall financial statements. The additional evidence will enable the auditor to obtain a higher level of assurance regarding the items than is attained without expanding the audit procedures. The individual items have a lower level of materiality because their magnitude is less than the overall financial statements. Therefore, an amount that is not considered material to the financial statements as a whole may be material when applied to the three accounts being considered.

b. The following additional tests are likely to be needed before the special report can be issued:

Sales
■ Cutoff tests of sales may be expanded
■ Depending upon the previous results, tests of controls and substantive tests of transactions for sales may be increased

Net fixed assets
■ Examine physical existence of a sample of fixed assets
■ Determine if fixed assets are still on the books but not being used
■ Recalculate depreciation
■ Increase vouching of additions in the current year

Inventory
■ Increase the price test coverage of inventory value

It should be noted that the extent of these tests depends on the results attained in these areas in the audit, the amount of evidence gathered in the audit, and the client's internal controls. The audit procedures above are vague because of this and are intended to be illustrative of the type of procedures that should be considered. After-the-fact auditing has limitations in that some information cannot feasibly be recreated. For instance, the auditor cannot extend test counts of inventory in order to verify the quantity of inventory. In these cases the auditor must attempt to satisfy the objective by alternative methods.

c. *We have audited the schedules of sales, net fixed assets, and inventory valued at FIFO (as defined in the lease agreement dated _____ between (lessor) and Sarack Lumber Supply Co.) of Sarack Lumber Supply Co. for the year-ended _____. These schedules are the responsibility of Sarack Lumber Supply Co's. management. Our responsibility is to express an opinion on the schedules based on our audit.*

25-30 (continued)

We conducted our audit in accordance with auditing standards generally accepted in the United States. Those standards require that we plan and perform the audit to obtain reasonable assurance about whether the schedules of sales, net fixed assets, and inventory valued at FIFO are free of material misstatement. An audit includes examining, on a test basis, evidence supporting the amounts and disclosures in the schedules. An audit also includes assessing the accounting principles used and significant estimates made by management, as well as evaluating the overall schedule presentation. We believe that our audit provides a reasonable basis for our opinion.

In our opinion, the schedules of sales, net fixed assets, and inventory valued at FIFO present fairly, in all material respects, the sales, net fixed assets, and inventory valued at FIFO of Sarack Lumber Supply Co. for the year-ended _____, on the basis specified in the lease agreement referred to above.

This report is intended solely for the information and use of the boards of directors and management of Sarack Lumber Supply Co. and (lessor) and should not be used for any other purpose.

■ **Internet Problem Solution: Accounting and Review Services Committee**

Internet Problem 25-1

a. ARSC consists of 7 members, all of whom are AICPA members. ARSC members are appointed to achieve appropriate representation among small and medium firms actively involved in the provision of compilation and review services. The Director of AICPA Audit and Attest Standards nominates the ARSC Chair and in consultation with the ARSC Chair, nominates members of the ARSC. The AICPA Board of Directors approves nominations of the ARSC Chair and members.

b. ARSC executes an established due process to develop standards that includes deliberations in meetings open to the public, public exposure of proposed SSARS, and a formal vote.

c. Circumstances surrounding the need for a new standard.

Internet Problem 25-1 (continued)

    d.   Issuance of an exposure draft of a proposed SSARS or a final SSARS requires written affirmative approval of two-thirds of all ARSC members.

    e.   Yes, all meetings of ARSC are open to the public except for sessions dealing with administrative or confidential matters.

(**Note**: Internet problems address current issues using Internet sources. Because Internet sites are subject to change, Internet problems and solutions may change. Current information on Internet problems is available at www.pearsonhighered.com/arens.)

Chapter 26

Internal and Governmental Financial Auditing and Operational Auditing

■ Review Questions

26-1 Internal auditors who perform financial auditing are responsible for evaluating whether their company's internal controls are designed and operating effectively and whether the financial statements are fairly presented. This responsibility is essentially the same as the responsibility of external auditors who perform financial audits. The two types of auditors are also similar in that they both must be competent and must remain objective in performing their work and reporting their results. Despite these similarities, the role of the internal auditor in financial auditing differs from that of an external auditor in the following ways:

- Because internal auditors spend all of their time with one company, their knowledge about the company's operations and internal controls is much greater than the external auditor's knowledge.
- Guidelines for performing internal audits are not as well defined as the guidelines for external auditors.
- Internal auditors are responsible to the management of the companies that they work for, while external auditors are responsible to financial statement users.
- Because internal auditors are responsible to management, their decisions about materiality and risks may differ from the decisions of external auditors.

26-2 The two categories of standards in the IIA International Standards for the Professional Practice of Auditing are (1) Attribute Standards and (2) Performance Standards.

The *Attribute Standards* are:

- Purpose, authority, and responsibility
- Independence and objectivity
- Proficiency and due professional care
- Quality assurance and improvement program

The *Performance Standards* are:

- Managing the internal audit activity
- Nature of work
- Engagement planning
- Performing the engagement
- Communicating results
- Monitoring progress
- Management's acceptance of risks

26-3   External auditors are considered more independent than internal auditors for the audit of historical financial statements because their audit report is intended for the use of external users. From an internal user's perspective, internal auditors are employees of the company being audited.

Internal auditors can achieve independence by reporting to the board of directors or president. The responsibilities of internal auditors affect their independence. The internal auditor should not be responsible for performing operating functions in a company or for correcting deficiencies when ineffective or inefficient operations are found.

26-4   Governmental financial audits are similar to audits of commercial companies in that both types of audits require the auditor to be independent, to accumulate and evaluate evidence, and to apply generally accepted auditing standards (GAAS). The two types of audits are different because governmental financial audits also require the auditor to apply generally accepted governmental auditing standards (GAGAS), which are broader than GAAS and include testing for compliance with laws and regulations. Governmental financial auditing can be done either by auditors employed by federal and state governments (governmental auditors) or by CPA firms.

26-5   The Single Audit Act was created in 1984 to eliminate redundancy in the audits of governmental agencies. The Single Audit Act provides for a single coordinated audit to satisfy the audit requirements of all federal funding agencies. The Single Audit Act was originally only applicable to audits of state and local governments, but the requirements of the Act were extended in 1990 to higher-education institutions and other not-for-profit organizations through the issuance of OMB Circular A-133.

26-6   The auditing standards of the Yellow Book are consistent with the ten generally accepted auditing standards of the AICPA.

Some important additions and modifications are as follows:

- *Materiality and significance.* The Yellow Book recognizes that acceptable audit risk and tolerable misstatement may be lower in governmental audits than in audits of commercial enterprises.
- *Quality control.* Organizations that audit government entities must have an appropriate system of internal quality control and must participate in an external quality control review program.
- *Compliance auditing.* The Yellow Book requires that the audit be designed to provide reasonable assurance of detecting material misstatements resulting from noncompliance with provisions of contracts or grant agreements that have a material and direct effect on the financial statements.
- *Reporting.* The audit report must state that the audit was made in accordance with generally accepted government auditing standards. In addition, the report on financial statements must describe the scope of the auditors' testing of compliance with laws and regulations and internal controls and present the results of those tests, or refer to a separate report containing that information.

26-6 (continued)

■ *Audit files.* The Yellow Book indicates that audit files should contain sufficient information to enable an experienced reviewer with no previous connection to the audit to ascertain from the audit files evidence that supports the auditors' significant conclusions and judgments.

26-7 The primary specific objectives that must be incorporated into the design of audit tests under the Single Audit Act are as follows:

■ Amounts reported as expenditures were for allowable services.
■ Records indicate that those who received services or benefits were eligible to receive them.
■ Matching requirements, levels of effort, and earmarking limitations were met.
■ Federal financial reports and claims for advances and reimbursements contain information that is supported by the records from which financial statements were prepared.
■ Amounts claimed or used for matching were determined in accordance with relevant OMB circulars.

26-8 The revised OMB Circular A-133 greatly simplified reporting under the Single Audit Act. The following reports are required:

1. An opinion on whether the financial statements are in accordance with GAAP.
2. An opinion as to whether the schedule of federal awards is presented fairly in all material respects in relation to the financial statements as a whole.
3. A report on internal control related to the financial statements and major programs.
4. A report on compliance with laws, regulations and the provisions of contracts or grant agreements, noncompliance with which could have a material effect on the financial statements. This report can be combined with the report on internal control.
5. A schedule of findings and questioned costs.

26-9 An operational audit is the review of any part of an organization's operating procedures and methods for the purpose of evaluating efficiency and effectiveness.

26-10 The three major differences between financial and operational auditing are:

- *Purpose of the audit.* Financial auditing emphasizes whether historical information was correctly recorded. Operational auditing emphasizes effectiveness and efficiency. The financial audit is oriented to the past, whereas an operational audit concerns operating performance for the future.
- *Distribution of the reports.* For financial auditing, the report is typically distributed to many users of financial statements, such as stockholders and bankers. Operational audit reports are intended primarily for management.
- *Inclusion of nonfinancial areas.* Operational audits cover any aspect of efficiency and effectiveness in an organization and can therefore involve a wide variety of activities. Financial audits are limited to matters that directly affect the fairness of financial statement presentations.

26-11 Effectiveness refers to the accomplishment of objectives, whereas efficiency refers to the resources used to achieve those objectives. An example of an operational audit for effectiveness would be to assess whether a governmental agency has met its assigned objective of achieving elevator safety in a city. An example of efficiency is when two different production processes manufacture a product of identical quality, the process with the least cost is considered to be most efficient.

26-12 The following are the distinctions between the three kinds of operational audits and an example of each for a not-for-profit hospital:

TYPES OF OPERATIONAL AUDIT	EXAMPLE FOR A HOSPITAL
Functional Functions are a means of categorizing the activities of a business, such as the billing function or production function. A functional operational audit deals with any of these functions.	Review of the payroll department to determine if the operations are effectively and efficiently performed.
Organizational An operational audit of an organization deals with an entire organizational unit, such as a department, branch, or subsidiary.	Review of the entire hospital for inefficiencies found in any department in the hospital.
Special assignment Special operational auditing assignments arise at the request of management for anything of concern to management.	Review of the IT system for failure to bill insurance companies for reimbursable charges.

26-13 Internal auditors are in a unique position to perform operational audits. They spend all of their time working for the company they are auditing. They therefore develop considerable knowledge about the company and its business, which is essential to effective operational auditing.

26-14 Different federal and state government auditors perform operational auditing, often as a part of doing financial audits. The most widely recognized government auditors group is the United States Government Accountability Office (GAO). In addition, each state has an Auditor General's office that has similar responsibilities to the GAO. There are also auditors for most state treasury departments and various other state government auditors.

There are no significant differences between internal and governmental auditors' roles and opportunities for operational auditing. Internal auditors ordinarily do operational audits of for-profit organizations, whereas governmental auditors perform the same role for governmental units.

26-15 It is common, as a part of doing an audit of historical financial statements, for CPA firms to also identify operational problems and make recommendations that may benefit the audit client. The recommendations can be made orally, but they are typically made by use of a *management letter*.

It is also common for the client to engage a CPA firm to do operational auditing of one or more specific parts of its business. Usually, such an engagement would occur only if the company does not have an internal audit staff or if the internal audit staff lacks expertise in a certain area. In most cases, specialized management services staff of the CPA firm, rather than the auditing staff, performs these services. For example, a private company may ask the CPA firm to evaluate the efficiency and effectiveness of its computer systems. Auditors of public companies have to be especially cautious due to the prohibition of many non-audit services for public company audit clients.

26-16 Criteria for evaluating efficiency and effectiveness in operational auditing means deciding the specific objectives that should have been achieved in the operation being audited. Usually, it is insufficient to state that the criteria are efficient and effective operations. More specific criteria are usually described. The following are five possible specific criteria for evaluating effectiveness of an IT system for payroll:

- Was payroll completed and computer generated payroll checks prepared at least twelve hours before the payroll distribution deadline in each of the past 26 weeks?
- Were there two or less complaints by employees each week in the past 26 weeks concerning incorrect paychecks that are attributable to the IT system?
- Is there a weekly review of the completed payroll by a person who is qualified to evaluate whether the payroll is reasonable?
- Is the weekly error listing reviewed by the payroll system's analyst to evaluate whether the payroll system should be changed?
- Does the IT payroll system for each branch office include the specific application controls for payroll that are recommended by the home office?

26-17 The three phases of operational auditing are planning, evidence accumulation and evaluation, and reporting and follow-up. These phases have equivalents in historical financial statement audits, but each phase is, of course, somewhat different, given the focus on the audit of operations rather than the audit of historical financial statements.

26-18 Planning in an operational audit is similar to the audit of historical financial statements. Like audits of financial statements, the operational auditor must determine the scope of the engagement and communicate that to the organizational unit. It is also necessary to properly staff the engagement, obtain background information about the organizational unit, evaluate internal controls, and decide the appropriate evidence to accumulate.

The major difference between planning an operational audit and a financial audit is the extreme diversity in operational audits. Because of the diversity, it is often difficult to decide on specific objectives of an operational audit. Another difference is that staffing is often more complicated in an operational audit than in a financial audit. This is because the areas covered by operational audits are diverse and often require special technical skills.

26-19 Two major differences in operational and financial auditing affect operational auditing reports. First, in operational audits, the report is usually sent only to management, with a copy to the unit being audited. The lack of third party users reduces the need for standardized wording in operational auditing reports. Second, the diversity of operational audits requires a tailoring of each report to address the scope of the audit, findings, and recommendations.

■ **Multiple Choice Questions from CPA Examinations**

26-20   a.   (3)   b.   (4)   c.   (2)

26-21   a.   (2)   b.   (1)   c.   (3)

26-22   a.   (4)   b.   (1)   c.   (4)

26-23   a.   (2)   b.   (1)   c.   (3)

■ **Cases**

26-24   a.   Objectivity means that the internal auditor must have, and maintain, an unbiased and independent viewpoint in the performance of audit tests, evaluation of the results, and issuance of the audit findings. Objectivity would not exist if the internal auditor were to audit his/her own work. Objectivity implies no subordination of judgment to another and a lack of influence by others over the internal auditor.

26-24 (continued)

b. 1. Objectivity is not impaired. Development of written policies and procedures to guide Lajod's staff is a responsibility of the internal audit staff. The internal auditors are responsible for the independent evaluation and verification of proper internal controls.

2. Objectivity is impaired. The preparation of bank reconciliations is an internal check over cash. In order to maintain objectivity, the auditor should not perform assignments that are included as part of the independent evaluation and verification of proper internal controls. Separation of duties should be maintained.

3. Objectivity is not impaired in the review of the budget for reasonableness if the internal auditor has no responsibility for establishing or implementing the budget. Objectivity is also not impaired if the internal auditor merely reviews budget variances and explanations for those variances. Objectivity would be impaired, however, if the internal auditor makes managerial decisions concerning performance in the review of variances.

4. Objectivity is impaired in that the internal auditor will be called upon to evaluate the design and implementation of the system in which the auditor played a significant role. Testing of the internal controls would not impair objectivity because this activity is necessary for determining the adequacy of accounting and administrative controls.

5. Objectivity is impaired. The internal auditors should not be involved in the record keeping process.

c. 1. Yes, the reporting relationship results in an objectivity problem. The controller is responsible for the accounting system and related transactions.

   The internal audit staff is responsible for independent and objective review of the accounting system and related transactions. Independence and objectivity may not exist because the internal audit staff is responsible for reviewing the work of the corporate controller, the person to whom it reports.

2. No, the responses for requirement b would not be affected by the internal audit staff reporting to an audit committee rather than the controller. In order to maintain objectivity, the internal audit staff should refrain from performing non-audit functions such as management decision-making, design and installation of systems, record keeping, etc. Ideally, the internal audit staff should perform only audit functions to avoid being called upon to evaluate its own performance. This is true without regard to organizational reporting relationships.

26-25 a. Additional steps that ordinarily should be taken by Weston Corporation's internal auditors as a consequence of finding excessive turnover in a department of White Division are categorized and explained below.

Field Work The department turnover rate should be compared with rates in other departments of White Division, other divisions of Weston Corporation, and industry rates if available. The present department turnover rate should be compared with previous rates in the department.

The nature of skills needed in the department should be reviewed and compared to job descriptions, if job descriptions exist. The hiring procedures employed by the human resource department should be reviewed as well as Lado's wages and benefits to determine if they are competitive.

The labor efficiency variance should be examined in an attempt to determine the portion attributable to inadequate training. Multiple standards or a new standard may be appropriate. Present and former departmental workers should also be interviewed in an attempt to get additional points of view on the problems of the department.

Recommendations The information gathered during the performance of field work would form the basis for any recommendations. Audit findings would be included in the audit report and unfavorable findings would lead, in most cases, to recommendations. Recommendations likely to result from the audit findings might include the preparation/revision of job descriptions and the establishment of formal training programs.

Operating Management Review The internal auditors should adopt a participatory or problem-solving approach in reviewing audit findings and making recommendations to the department being reviewed. The report should be discussed with the departmental supervisor before the report is finalized. The comments and suggestions of the supervisor should be considered and, if appropriate, included in the report.

26-25 (continued)

b.   The participation of the internal audit department in the computer feasibility study, including advising and concurring with the system selected, creates an objectivity problem. The internal audit department could not accept an audit assignment involving the problems of the existing computer system without placing themselves in a position of conflict of interest.

   To eliminate the existing objectivity problem, outside consultants should be used to study the problems with the computer system. To reduce future objectivity problems, the internal audit department should not perform functions that may place it in a position of auditing its own work. Auditors should not assume a decision making role as this will negate their future independence from those decisions.

c.   1.   The location of Weston Corporation's internal audit department is inappropriate. Independence is the key to the work of the internal auditor and is achieved through organizational status and objectivity. A Director of Internal Auditing should report to a high level management executive in order to promote independence, ensure adequate audit coverage, and to assure the proper consideration of audit reports.

   Having the Director of Internal Audits directly report to the Corporate Controller is inappropriate. A major portion of the internal auditor's responsibility involves the review of the accounting function. Thus, the Director may be far less than objective in evaluating the work of a superior.

   2.   Reports of Weston's Internal Audit Department should be distributed to all those having a direct interest in the audit, including:

   ■   the executive to whom the internal audit function reports.
   ■   persons from who replies to the report are required.
   ■   persons responsible for the activity or activities reviewed (auditees and superiors).

26-26   Issues that must be addressed and procedures that should be used by Haskin's Internal Audit Department (IAD) in the audit review of Burlington Plant's 2011 capital expenditure project include the following:

26-26 (continued)

a.

ISSUES
1. The criteria used by the Capital Budgeting Group (CBG) need to be evaluated to determine whether they are consistent with Haskin's long-term goals and objectives.
2. The internal controls in the capital budgeting process need to be evaluated to determine whether the CBG applied the criteria consistently.
3. The ROI (hurdle rate) must be tested for reasonableness to be sure the appropriate projects are selected.
4. The IAD must determine how well the project is now doing as compared to the original analysis.

b.

PROCEDURES
1. Review Haskin's long-term goals and objectives to determine the appropriateness of each evaluation criterion being employed by the CBG.
2. Review, test and evaluate the internal controls associated with the capital budgeting process. This would include a review of the capital budgeting procedures manual, if one exists, and preparing a flowchart for the capital budgeting process.
3. Review how the hurdle rate is determined now and was determined in 2010. Determine if a risk adjustment was incorporated into the decision process by such means as increasing the hurdle rate or decreasing estimated cash flows.
4. Interview and evaluate the competence of the available participants in the decision, including the originator of the CBG. Read the minutes of the CBG's meetings and review all status reports for the project from inception through its completion. Review the quantitative analysis used by the CBG to determine if data were valid, assumptions and estimates reasonable, only relevant costs were considered, and cost behavior (fixed and variable) was correctly perceived.
5. Review Haskin's internal accounting controls to assure that all acquisition and installation costs for the machines are capitalized and that operating and maintenance costs for the machines are recorded accurately and expensed. Review documents related to the acquisition of other machines and determine the actual amount of investment. Review accounting, maintenance, and production records, and other documentary evidence to determine actual operating costs and actual contribution for each machine.

a. WEAKNESSES/ INEFFICIENCIES	b. RECOMMENDATIONS
1. Quantities of materials received are not verified by the materials manager.	Besides inspecting all incoming goods to ensure that quality standards are met, the materials manager should verify quantities received by actual physical count. All material receipts do not have to be counted for a verification program to be effective. Systematically verifying one or several receipts from each vendor during a given time period can identify those receipts which are the most troublesome. Once identified, efforts can be directed to correcting the problem. The verification process is performed by comparing receiving document quantities to actual physical counts to ensure invoice totals are correct.
2. The materials manager prepares purchasing requests based on production schedules and not on requisitions received from operating departments.	Purchasing requests prepared by the materials manager are to be based on requisitions received from operating departments and not production schedules for a four-month period. Production schedules could be outdated and not reflect current sales trends. Operating departments are constantly adjusting production levels to account for changes. To improve budgetary control over expenditures, the controller's office also should review the requests in conjunction with forward planning to ensure expenditures are consistent with company sales projections. Once an analysis of inventory flows is complete the economic order quantity can be applied to determine the reorder point and to minimize inventories.
3. The majority of Lecimore's requirement for a critical raw material is supplied by a single vendor.	It is best to develop alternate sources of supply for critical materials. The obvious benefits are reduced reliance on a single vendor, and the reduced possibility of lost production because of material shortages and/or other interruptions in the operation due to a single vendor. Encouragement of competition by the effective allocation of material requirements between vendors is also another benefit that can be expected to materialize if an effective program is implemented. Other benefits such as improved vendor services and technical assistance may also result as vendors attempt to gain increased shares of the goods provided the user company.

26-27 (continued)

a. WEAKNESSES/ INEFFICIENCIES	b. RECOMMENDATIONS
4. Rush and expedite orders are made by production directly to the purchasing department without consulting the materials managers.	Rush and expedite orders should be reviewed by the materials manager to determine if any of the orders can be filled using existing inventories.
5. The purchasing department is held responsible for the cost of special orders, which can be clearly identified by requesting departments.	The direct association of special order costs with responsible departments is necessary in order to exercise proper control. Responsibility accounting obligates departments to exercise judgment and prudence over those costs they are held accountable for. Through responsibility reporting, excessive costs are highlighted so that corrective actions can be implemented.
6. Engineering changes are not discussed with other departments before the materials needed to implement the change are ordered.	A general policy outlining the authority and responsibility for implementing engineering changes must be established. The proposed changes should be reviewed thoroughly by various company departments before an order is placed. The controller's office would review the proposal in light of incremental costs or cost savings that are expected to result. The manufacturing departments would review the change from an adaptability point of view. Before placing an order, purchasing would have to receive approval from the reviewing departments. Once approval is obtained, the vendor selection process can begin.
7. Accounting is not notified by the materials manager of the receipt of partial shipments.	Besides notifying the purchasing department of the receipt of partial shipments, the materials manager should also inform the accounting department so that vendor invoices can be processed correctly. Receiving reports clearly identifying the receipt as a partial shipment is the most effective means of communicating this information. By appropriately annotating the receiving report, vendors will not be paid for materials the company has not received.

WEAKNESSES	RECOMMENDATIONS
1. An authorization document that describes the item to be acquired, indicates the benefits to be derived, and estimates its cost, is not prepared and reviewed with management.	To obtain approval for the purchase of machinery and equipment, an appropriations request should be prepared, describing the item, indicating why it is needed, and estimating its expected costs and benefits. The document also could include the item's accounting classification, expected useful life, depreciation method and rate, and name the approving company executives.
2. There is no control over authorized acquisitions. The purchase requisitions and purchase orders for fixed assets are interspersed with other requisitions and purchase orders and handled through normal purchasing procedures.	Authorized acquisitions should be processed using special procedures and purchase orders. These purchase orders should be subjected to numerical control. Copies of purchase orders should be distributed to all appropriate departments so that the acquisition can be monitored.
3. Plant engineering does not appear to be inspecting machinery and equipment upon receipt.	Purchases of machinery and equipment should be subject to normal receiving inspection routines. In the case of machinery and equipment, plant engineering is usually responsible for reviewing the receipt to make certain the correct item was delivered and that it was not damaged in transit. All new machinery and equipment would be assigned a control number and tagged at the time of receipt.
4. The lapse schedules are not reconciled periodically to general ledger control accounts to verify agreement.	At least once each year, machinery and equipment lapse schedules, which provide information on asset cost and accumulated depreciation, should be reconciled to general ledger control accounts. Furthermore, an actual physical inventory of existing fixed assets should be taken periodically and reconciled to the lapse schedules and general ledger control account to assure accuracy.
5. Machinery and equipment accounting policies, including depreciation, have not been updated to make certain that the most desirable methods are being used.	Machinery and equipment accounting procedures, including depreciation, must be updated periodically to reflect actual experience, and changes in accounting pronouncements and income tax legislation.

■ Internet Problem Solution: Institute of Internal Auditors

Internet Problem 26-1

a. Management is responsible for establishing and maintaining a system of internal controls on behalf of the organization's stakeholders and is held accountable for this responsibility. A dedicated, independent and effective internal audit activity assists both management and the oversight body (e.g. the board, audit committee) in fulfilling their responsibilities by bringing a systematic disciplined approach to assessing the effectiveness of the design and execution of the system of internal controls and risk management processes.

b. The following are the six steps to certification:
1. Decide which certification is right for you.
2. Determine your eligibility and skill level.
3. Register for the exam.
4. Prepare for the exam.
5. Take the test.
6. Receive your certificate.

c. The following certifications are available:
1. CIA (Certified Internal Auditor)
2. CCSA (Certification in Control Self-Assessment)
3. CFSA (Certified Financial Services Auditor)
4. CGAP (Certified Government Auditing Professional)

d. The four parts of the CIA Exam are:

Part 1 – The Internal Audit Activity's Role in Governance, Risk and Control
Part 2 – Conducting the Internal Audit Engagement
Part 3 – Business Analysis and Information Technology
Part 4 – Business Management Skills

Like the CPA exam, the CIA is a computerized exam, and candidates may also sit for individual sections of the exam. Like the CPA exam, the CIA exam is non-disclosed. Each section consists of 100 multiple choice questions and is 2 hours and 45 minutes in length. Candidates do not need to complete all the part of the exam within a minimum period of time, but will lose credit for any exam parts previously passed if the candidate does not take a single exam part within a two-year period from their last exam date.

(**Note**: Internet problems address current issues using Internet sources. Because Internet sites are subject to change, Internet problems and solutions may change. Current information on Internet problems is available at www.pearsonhighered.com/arens.)